Jacques Lacan

· · · · · · · ·

EUROPEAN PERSPECTIVES

EUROPEAN PERSPECTIVES

•   •   •   •   •   •

A Series in Social Thought and Cultural Criticism
Lawrence D. Kritzman,
EDITOR

European Perspectives presents English translations of books by leading European thinkers. With both classic and outstanding contemporary works, the series aims to shape the major intellectual controversies of our day and to facilitate the tasks of historical understanding.

Jacques Lacan

· · · · · · ·

Elisabeth Roudinesco

TRANSLATED BY
Barbara Bray

Columbia University Press
NEW YORK

Columbia University Press wishes to express its appreciation for assistance given by the government of France through Le Ministère de la Culture in the preparation of this translation.

Columbia University Press thanks Galith Touati, researcher extraordinaire, for her able assistance in locating bibliographical information for this English-language edition.

Columbia University Press
Publishers Since 1893
New York   Chichester, West Sussex

Jacques Lacan: Esquisse d'une vie, histoire d'un système de pensée (Jacques Lacan: Outline of a Life, History of a System of Thought) © Librairie Arthème Fayard, 1993. Translation copyright
© 1997 Columbia University Press.
Translation based on second edition of 1994

Library of Congress Cataloging-in-Publication Data
Roudinesco, Elisabeth, 1944–
[Jacques Lacan. English]
Jacques Lacan : Outline of a life, history of a system of thought / Elisabeth Roudinesco ; translated by Barbara Bray.
p.   cm. — (European perspectives)
Includes bibliographical references and index.
ISBN 0-231-10146-5 (alk. paper)
1. Lacan, Jacques, 1901–   . 2. Psychoanalysts—France—Biography. 3. Psychoanalysis—France—History. I. Title.
II. Series.
BF109.L28R6613 1997
150.19'5'092—dc20
[B]   96–30125
                                                                                  CIP

Casebound editions of Columbia University Press books are printed on permanent and durable acid-free paper.
Printed in the United States of America
c 10 9 8 7 6 5 4 3 2 1

A Olivier Bétourné, qui a voulu ce livre.

Robespierristes, antirobespierristes, nous vous crions grâce: par pitié, dites-nous, simplement, quel fut Robespierre.

—*Marc Bloch*

Contents

. . . .

Illustrations

• • • • • • •

Preface

Jacques Lacan sought to bring plague, subversion, and disorder to the moderate Freudianism of his time. It was a Freudianism that, having survived fascism, had adapted itself so well to democracy that it had almost forgotten the violence of its origins. Lacan's story is the story of a French passion, a passion out of Balzac. It is the story of the youth of Louis Lambert, the prime of Horace Bianchon, and the old age of Balthasar Claës.★ But it is also the history of a doctrine that, following on from Freud's, tried to rescue humanity from the universe of religion, dreams, and the occult, even if this meant revealing the inability of reason, knowledge, and truth to bring about such a deliverance.

The two volumes of my *Histoire de la psychanalyse en France* (History of psychoanalysis in France) covered a hundred years of Freudianism: from 1885, when Freud first encountered Charcot at the Salpêtrière hospital, up to 1985, when French-style Freudianism found itself split between internationalist legitimism on the one hand and a multiform and divided Lacanianism on the other. This third volume, which may be read independently of the other two, is set against the same background and follows the same method. It retells a story of conflicts, influences, differing generations, concepts, masters, disciples, groups, analyses, and a perpetual migration from east to west.

Wherever necessary, references to events covered in the earlier volumes are indicated in a note or in the body of the text. Sometimes, when new sources have thrown fresh light on a point or shown it from a different perspective, I have preferred to rewrite the relevant passage.

★*Translator's note:* Louis Lambert is the main character in Balzac's short story of that name, a distinguished scholar who starts life as a young prodigy. Horace Bianchot is an eminent doctor whose fictitious career is mentioned in twenty-seven of Balzac's novels. Balthasar Claës is the hero of *La Recherche de l'absolu* (*The Quest of the Absolute*), a man obsessed with his search for the philosopher's stone.

My aim in going over the same ground again is not to retell the life story of a leading creative figure in terms chiefly of the individual and subjective aspects of his teachings but rather to trace how, throughout the intellectual history of a whole era, one man worked deliberately to found a system of thought based on his belief that the modern, post–Auschwitz world had repressed, obscured, and diluted the essence of the Freudian revolution.

Acknowledgments

Many thanks to Sibylle Lacan, whose presence helped me throughout the writing of this book and who placed her own memories and personal archives at my disposal.

Thanks as well to Marc-François Lacan, whose help to me extended over ten years, through frequent discussions and a lengthy correspondence.

Many thanks too to Thibaut Lacan for his friendly presence, help, and many personal accounts.

Finally, I should also like to express my gratitude to Cyril Roger-Lacan, Fabrice Roger-Lacan, Bruno Roger, and Madeleine Lacan-Houlon for their contributions to this book.

I am also grateful to the following people for making the book possible:

Georges Bernier and François Wahl, whose personal accounts have been indispensable.

Angel de Frutos Salvador, who put at my disposal all his erudite knowledge of the various texts of Lacan's written works.

The staff at the Editions du Seuil, who since 1986 have made all their archives available to me.

Jean Bollack, for his interpretation of the Lacanian *logos*.

Olivier Corpet and François Boddaert, who gave me access to the Louis Althusser archives at the Institut mémoire de l'édition contemporain (IMEC: Institute for the Records of Contemporary Publishing).

Catherine Dolto-Tolitch and Colette Percheminier, who made the Françoise Dolto archives available to me.

Madeleine Chapsal, Olesia Sienkiewicz, Celia Bertin, Maria Antonietta Macciocchi, and Catherine Millot, for their friendly contributions.

Didier Eribon, who allowed me to see his notes, passed on the results of his researches, and told me of many sources.

Yann Moulier-Boutang, with whom I had some useful conversations.

Didier Anzieu, Annie Anzieu, and Christine Anzieu, who agreed to talk to me about the story of Marguerite.

Renée Ey and Patrick Clervoy, for giving me access to the archives of Henri Ey.

Peter Schöttler, for his researches on Lucien Febvre.

Henri Febvre, for his testimony.

Michel Surya, for his help on the subject of Georges Bataille.

Pamela Tytell, Michel Thomé, François Rouan, and Jean-Michel Vappereau, who made it possible for me to write the last part of this book.

Maître Muriel Brouquet, for her advice and support.

Dominique Auffret, who put some of Alexandre Kojève's manuscripts at my disposal.

Caterina Koltaï, for her cooperation throughout.

Céline Geoffroy, for her work on my manuscript.

Michel-Edmond Richard, for his skill as a genealogist.

Per Magnus Johansson, for his helpful comments.

Elisabeth Badinter, who read the manuscript; Claude Durand, who made me welcome at Fayard's; and Jacques Sédat, who corrected the proofs and put his library and archives at my disposal.

In writing the present book I have again made use of the archives, personal accounts, and documents that were put at my disposal for *Histoire de la psychanalyse en France*. They were made available by the following people in particular:

Jenny Aubry (d.)

Laurence Bataille (d.)

Serge Leclaire (d.), Wladimir Granoff, Jacques Derrida, Paul Ricoeur, Jean Laplanche, René Major, Jean-Bertrand Pontalis, Robert Pujol, Daniel Widlöcher, Solange Faladé, Moustapha Safouan, Sylvia Lacan (d.), Jacques-Alain Miller, Julien Rouart (d.), Kostas Axelos, Georges Canguilhem (d.), Xavier Audouard, Maud Mannoni

My thanks also to all the others who have given me assistance with the book or supplied personal material:

Julien Green, Claude Lévi-Strauss, and Louis Leprince-Ringuet, of the Académie française

Abbé Jean Milet, of the Collège Stanislas

Henry Cohen and Peter Swales, of the Library of Congress, Washington

Michael Molnar, of the Freud Museum, London

Jean-Eric Green, Florence Bellaiche, Dominique Bonnet, Silvia Elena

Tendlarz, Hélène Gratiot-Alphandéry, Jean Allouch, Sven Follin, Paul Sivadon (d.), Jacques Postel, Geneviève Congy, Claude Dumézil, Léon Poliakov, Françoise Bernardi, Dominique Desanti, Jean-Toussaint Desanti, Stella Corbin, Christian Jambet, Jeffrey Mehlman, John Forrester, Henri F. Ellenberger (d.), Michel Ellenberger, Muriel Drazien, Flavie Alvarez de Toledo, Nadia Papachristopoulos, née Pastré (d.), Françoise Choay, René Gilson, Gabriel Boillat, Jean Jamin, Frédéric François, Zanie Campan, Baber Johansen, Pierre Rey, Françoise Giroud, Robert Georgin, Raffaella di Ambra, Françoise de Tarde-Bergeret, Renaud Barbaras, Deirdre Bair, Jean Schuster, Jean-Baptiste Boulanger, Paul Roazen, Irène Diamantis, Florence Delay, Madeleine Delay, Nadine Mespoulhes, Jean-Pierre Bourgeron, Claude Cherki, Anne-Lise Stern, Houda Aumont, Patrick Aumont, Thérèse Parisot, Jean Paris, François Leguil, Pierre Vidal-Naquet, Patrick Valas, Serge Doubrovsky, Maud Mannoni, Mario Cifali, Michel Coddens, Bertrand Ogilvie, Pierre Macherey, Michel Plon, Didier Cromphout, Marie-Magdeleine Chatel, Danièle Arnoux, Guy Le Gaufey, Erik Porge, Claude Halmos, Roberto Harari, Denis Hollier, Paul Henry, Jacques Le Rider, Roland Cahen, Michel Fraenkel, Julia Borossa, Jean Lacouture, Pierre Verret, Jean-Pie Lapierre, Daniel Bordigoni, Charles Reagan, Edmonde Charles-Roux, Pierre Morel, Jean Szpirko, Michel Roussan, Thierry Garnier, Alain Vanier, Phyllis Grosskurth, Jean-Pierre Salgas, Françoise Gadet, Jacqueline Pinon, Sandra Basch, André Haynalo, Maurice de Gandillac

Jacques Lacan

• • • • • •

PART I

Father Figures

1

· · · · · · ·

Vinegar Merchants

E ver since the days of the first Capetian kings, the recipe for making vinegar had been a well-kept secret in old Orléans. Even at the end of the nineteenth century, experts still believed the gruesome myth that human excreta were used in the process. Thus as reputable a source as Domachy told how some manufacturers had had the bright idea of ordering their workers to relieve themselves into barrels of wine. Within days the liquid had turned into a fine vinegar, without a hint of the dubious catalyst that had set off the fermentation.

Of course, generations of tavern keepers, cooks, vinegar merchants, and mustard makers had done their best to counter a rumor so damaging to their craft and a tradition stretching back into the mists of time. Members of the fraternity claimed the most illustrious names as their ancestors. Hadn't Hannibal cleared a path through the Alps for his elephants by pouring vinegar over the snow? Didn't a drunken soldier use a sponge dipped in vinegar to moisten Christ's lips on Golgotha? Vinegar was as old as wine. For a long time it *was* the wine of the poor, of beggars, and of the legionaries.

For centuries vinegar makers worked in collaboration with coopers and winegrowers. The former repaired the vinegar barrels on their own premises; the latter would store the full casks in their own cellars. Such arrangements were supervised by the guilds, which protected men against masters. But these ancien-régime traditions were swept away by the Revolution and the rise of economic liberalism.

In 1824 Charles-Prosper Dessaux, who worked for a firm called Greffier-Hazon, took advantage of the rapid industrialization of the vinegar trade to set up a business of his own. Thus at the age of thirty-four he became his former employer's chief competitor. But two years later, in the interests of efficiency, the two men decided to join forces, and to seal the partnership they arranged a marriage between their heirs. Charles-Laurent Dessaux, still scarcely more than a boy, was required to wed young Marie-Thérèse Aimée Greffier-Vandais. The two firms became one, with the Dessaux family ruling the joint kingdom. Father and son got on well together. Business flourished.

The vinegar makers of the Orléans region had chosen early in the nineteenth century to adopt the Chaptal method, based on Lavoisier's description of the acetification process. And it was this decision, together with the special quality of the white Loire wines, that won their products universal fame. The celebrated Orléans technique, admired the world over, made use of the *mycoderma aceti* bacterium, which oxidized the alcohol in the wine.

Every Assumption Day from 1821 on, the guild, which now included all the Orléans manufacturers, held the annual vinegar festival. But although the ancient Loire town, with its Joan of Arc connections and its devotion to the Virgin Mary, liked to show off its attachment to the Catholic religion, that didn't prevent local families from being torn apart by political quarrels. And when the time came for Charles-Prosper to retire, he was forced to admit that his two sons would never see eye to eye. Charles-Laurent, the older brother, was a Bonapartist; Jules, the younger, was a republican. The dissension between them proved disastrous for the family business. And despite the founding father's many attempts to reconcile the pair, he couldn't prevent the dynasty from splitting into two branches. In 1850 Jules started a rival firm, leaving his elder brother to run the Dessaux fils business on his own. Charles-Laurent was delighted by Prince Louis-Napoleon's coup d'état in December 1851 and embraced with gusto the lifestyle of the Second Empire (December 1852 to September 1870). Charles-Laurent was a lazy, violent-tempered man who preferred hunting, loose living, and the pleasures of the table to managing the business. After sixteen years in charge of it had left him on the brink of ruin, he brought in his first son, Paul Dessaux, to help run things.

The ravages wrought by phylloxera on the wine trade started just as vinegar-making techniques were being transformed by the experiments of Louis Pasteur. His famous lecture on acetic fermentation, showing the oxidizing effect of the mycoderm, opened the way to research on the use of rapid heating to destroy the ferments causing the many diseases that inhibited normal acetification.

While winegrowers were painfully replanting their vineyards and vinegar makers taking advantage of Pasteur's discoveries, a dangerous source of competition burst onto the market in the form of spirit vinegar. A fierce struggle began, in which many factories that still clung to the old wine vinegar tradition went broke.

It was at this time, after the premature death of his elder brother, Paul, that Ludovic Dessaux took over the management of the family firm. Ludovic had a touch of genius, and with this and thirty years of unremitting effort he turned his father's works into a modern factory: a huge expanse of somber stone buildings at number 17 in the rue Tour-Neuve, where the barrels of precious "condiment wine" were made and stored. Ludovic, the master, lived on the premises with his family, and the same grim walls enclosed a workforce, laboring night and day, that by 1900 would number a hundred and eighty.

To get the better of his competitors, Ludovic had the bright idea of making his own spirit vinegar, thus managing both to carry on the tradition and to survive in the market. His spirit vinegar was used for pickling gherkins; his wine vinegar for consumption at the dinner table and use in the kitchen.

To improve distribution he availed himself of a new form of mass communication: advertising. A label proclaiming that the firm of Dessaux fils was founded in 1789 established the brand name in every grocery store in France; the creative chronology on the bottles ignored the fact that Charles-Prosper, founder of the present firm, was not even born until 1790. But this was just after the establishment of the Third Republic, and perhaps Ludovic wanted to remind the public that Dessaux fils had been born out of the ancient house of Greffier-Hazon.

Seeing danger looming in the growing trade union movement and the spread of socialist ideas, Ludovic Dessaux decided to take a leaf out of the progressives' book and adopt a program of preventive reforms. Mechanization was by now so far advanced it took only ten men, working round the clock, to barrel forty thousand liters of vinegar in twenty-four hours. Fifteen times as many staff were employed in maintenance, supply, and administration. To keep his workers under control and counter the influence of the "revolutionary messianism" that had been in the air since the Paris Commune of 1871, Ludovic worked out a system based on paternalism and respect for morality and religion. In 1880, in a set of house rules arranged under thirteen headings, he defined the cardinal virtues essential to the proper functioning of the firm. Godliness, cleanliness, and strict attention to duty were the watchwords. Employees were expected to put in thirteen hours a day for six days a week, to say their prayers every morning, and to refrain from talking during working hours. Wine, spirits, and tobacco were forbidden. Dress was scrutinized severely: nothing unconventional was allowed, no bright colors, no stockings with holes in.[1] At the dawn of the twentieth century the firm of Dessaux fils was still plunged deep in a dull gray world of monotony, silence, and narrow-mindedness.

Marie Julie Dessaux, Ludovic's older sister, had met Emile Lacan in 1865, when she was twenty-one. He came from Château-Thierry, where his family had for several generations been in the drapery and grocery trades. Emile liked to travel, and Dessaux fils had taken him on as a salesman. Hardworking, thrifty, and assertive, Emile soon recognized that by marrying the boss's daughter he could not only achieve prosperity but also become a member of one of the most highly regarded families in Orléans. No mean prospect for a grocer's son.

Ludovic approved of the marriage. Now he would be able to bring his three sons—Paul, Charles, and Marcel—into the business without opposition from his sister: she'd want any children of her own to be brought in too. The wedding took place on January 15, 1866, and a son, René, was born nine months later (he died at the age of twenty-eight). Marie Julie had three more children, two girls and a boy—Marie, Eugénie, and Alfred. Alfred Charles Marie Lacan, known as Alfred, was born on April 12, 1873, in his parents' home at 17, rue Porte-Saint-Jean. He was named Alfred after a maternal uncle who had died young; Charles after his maternal grandfather, himself named after the founder of the dynasty; and Marie after the mother of Jesus, also the patron saint of Orléans vinegar.

By the end of the century Ludovic had set up branches in the colonies and become a big name in the food industry. He sold pickled gherkins, mustard, brandy, and vinegar in the West Indies; he imported rum from Martinique and coffee from Guadeloupe. Emile Lacan, still traveling for the firm, had left Orléans and moved to the center of Paris, where he lived at 95, boulevard Beaumarchais in a comfortable apartment block built in 1853.

At street level, the plaque of a commissioner for oaths symbolized the respectability of the neighborhood. It was inhabited mostly by lawyers, people living on modest private incomes, and traveling salesmen like Emile himself. Further along, at the corner of the rue Saint-Claude, stood what had been the home of the ill-fated adventurer Cagliostro, alias Giuseppe Balsamo.[2]

In the 1860s this area, as far as the boulevard du Temple (long known as the "*boulevard du crime*" because of the sensationalist plays performed there), was a center of popular entertainment. Clowns cut capers on portable trestle stages, competing for attention with dwarfs, living skeletons, performing dogs, and ventriloquists. The novelist Paul de Kock had lived nearby. He was the working girls' idol and swaggered about the boulevard dressed in a blue flannel suit and a velvet skull cap, peering at passersby through his lorgnette.

But after the Franco-Prussian War and the Commune the boulevard had changed. In the name of law and order the victorious middle classes had crushed the suburban proletariat, hoping to destroy their egalitarian dreams. The open-air stages and ventriloquists were banished, and the bourgeoisie were left safe in their calculated comfort, smugly content with their industrious lives and their official art.

Emile Lacan, though despotic and difficult, was under his wife's thumb, and she was inflexibly obedient to Catholic dogma. So Alfred was sent as a boarder to the school run by the priests of Notre-Dame-des-Champs. He left there full of resentment against his parents for denying him the warmth of family life.[3]

As soon as he was old enough to work Alfred joined the flourishing firm of Dessaux and soon showed himself a perfect embodiment of its ideals. He was not much interested in culture and cared as much about his own savings as about the financial interests of the business. With his portly figure and his mustache, he looked what he was—an ordinary belle epoque tradesman living in the shadow of an all-powerful father.

In about 1898 he met Emilie Philippine Marie Baudry. Her father had been a goldbeater but now lived off the income from his investments in real estate. The Baudrys lived at 88, boulevard Beaumarchais in a building just like the Lacans.' Emilie had gone to a church school and come under the influence of Cécile Gazier, a childhood friend with Jansenist views. Charles Baudry, Emilie's father, was a pleasant if commonplace fellow; her mother, Marie-Anne Favier, was deeply religious. At the age of twenty-three, Emilie too was very austere. Slim, dark-eyed, always dressed in black, she seemed to be driven by an abstract kind of Christianity in sharp contrast to the simple provincial piety of the Dessaux family.

She and Alfred were married on June 23, 1900, in the church of Saint-Paul-Saint-Louis. Ten months later, at 2:30 in the afternoon of April 13, she gave birth to her first child. He was named Jacques Marie Emile. His father and both grandfathers registered the birth at the *mairie* (town hall) of the 3d Arrondissement. He was baptized at the church of Saint-Denis-du-Sacrement.

Emilie Baudry-Lacan became pregnant again right away and in 1902 produced another son, Raymond, who died two years later of hepatitis. By April 1903 she was expecting another child, and this time it was a girl, Madeleine Marie Emmanuelle, born at 1:30 A.M. on December 25. On the morning of the twenty-seventh her father registered the birth in the presence of two witnesses: the manageress of a shop on the boulevard Sébastopol and the baby's maternal grandfather. Emilie was now twenty-seven. It was not until 1908 that she had her fourth child, Marc-Marie (he later changed his name to Marc-François), born on December 25, ten minutes after midnight. Emilie was exhausted after this last pregnancy, developed abdominal pains, and had to have an operation. After that she couldn't have any more children.

When Jacques was born, Emilie had engaged a young governess named Pauline who was fond of all three children but soon grew especially attached to little "Marco." Although he was himself his mother's favorite, Jacques—or "Jacquot," as they called him—was jealous. At quite an early age he was already willful and domineering, constantly asking for food or money or presents on the grounds that he was the eldest. But he was always very fatherly toward Marco, as if to make up for Alfred's deficiencies.

To all appearance the three children grew up in a home united by religion. But in fact there were bitter quarrels between the two families living in the same apartment block on the boulevard Beaumarchais. Emilie didn't get on with Marie Julie, her mother-in-law, who in her opinion ordered Alfred about too much. As for her sisters-in-law, Marie and Eugénie, Emilie couldn't stand their narrow-mindedness. So Alfred fell out with his father, who retired and went back to Orléans to live. Alfred took his father's place in the business, and now, instead of traveling around France, he stayed where he was and soon became Dessaux's chief Paris agent. He was friendly and tactful and on excellent terms with the customers as well as wise in the ways of Parisian commerce.[4]

Jacques's memory of his childhood in that apparently normal and conventional family was terrifying. Brought up in an atmosphere that combined stifling religiosity with constant domestic squabbles, he too was always quarreling with his despised grandfather, of whom he painted—publicly—an extremely hostile portrait a year after his own father's death. "The meaning of 'My grandfather is my grandfather' is this: that the said frightful petit bourgeois, the horrible individual thanks to whom I learned at an early age how to perform the essential act of cursing God—this person is precisely the one officially recorded as the father of my father, since he was married to my father's mother and since my father's birth was the subject of the document in question."[5] Lacan couldn't forgive Emile for being the sort of father who gave fatherhood a bad name. As Marc-François has written, "Jacques was given the name Emile after his paternal grandfather, who played a more important part than Alfred did in the discovery of the *name-of-the-father*." And again: "Whenever Emile punished Jacques by standing him in the corner instead of correcting him in a proper paternal way, his reaction was, 'Well, if that's a father, I say a curse on fathers!' Yet his real father, Alfred, was both loving and loved."[6]

When Emile went back to Orléans, Alfred too left the boulevard Beaumarchais and moved with his family to the rue du Montparnasse. It had been decided that Jacques should go as a day boy to the Collège Stanislas, where the Catholic upper-middle and middle-middle class sent their most promising progeny. The choice shows that, some years after the separation of church and state, the Lacan-Dessaux-Baudry clan were still steeped in clericalism and hostile to secular and republican values.

For a long time Alfred remained on bad terms with his father, and until the First World War he spent his pleasantest leisure moments with his wife's family. He rented a comfortable house in Jouy-en-Josas, on the outskirts of Versailles, which they called the Villa Marco after the younger son. The family had enjoyable country gatherings there, with Emilie's brother Joseph, her sister Marie and her husband, Marcel Langlais, together with the couple's four children, Roger, Anne-Marie, Jean, and Robert. The Langlais youngsters liked to play ninepin bowls with their Uncle Alfred. "Jacquot" was thrilled when his father bought a smart car. He was already mad about speed and would often take the steering wheel and pretend to be driving or sit proudly in the passenger seat beside Gaston, Alfred's chauffeur.[7]

The Collège Stanislas's great renaissance had begun after the 1848 revolution: the street barricades and popular riots frightened the ruling classes, formerly so Voltairean and anticlerical, into sending their children to church schools. During the years that followed, the number of pupils at Stanislas rose to more than a thousand. By the end of the century the Marist fathers who ran the *collège* had added new buildings containing lecture rooms, laboratories, and a fencing school.

Impressive traditions were built up too. An academy of science and liberal arts was founded: members wore a gold-embroidered sash on ceremonial occasions. It became the custom to hold a banquet for the most successful classes on January 28, the feast of St. Charlemagne, patron saint of schools: the brightest pupils had to make a speech to their formmates on some literary or philosophical subject.

But in July 1901 the whole situation was changed by a law making it necessary for the Marists to apply for official permission to teach. Their application was refused. A great fund-raising campaign was launched immediately to circumvent this decision. Some old pupils formed a real estate company to buy the buildings, furniture, and corporate name of the *collège*. Stanislas became a privately run Catholic school with a teaching staff of lay masters and secular clergy.[8]

Marc Sangnier, founder of the paper *Le Sillon* (The furrow) and of the short-lived *Silloniste* Christian Democratic movement, joined in the effort and was elected chairman of the new board of governors. Thus one of Paris's most conservative religious establishments was saved by a spiritual son of Lamennais who in 1910 was to be condemned by the Vatican for trying to introduce the spirit of the Enlightenment into a reactionary and hidebound church.[9]

In 1903 Sangnier resigned from the post of chairman of the school board, and the abbé Pautonnier became headmaster. Pautonnier's reign, which was to last seventeen years, made an unforgettable impression on the pupils who were at Stanislas at the same time as Lacan. Though Pautonnier had a degree in mathematics and was more at home solving equations than running a school, he devoted all his energies to his young charges. He called them all by their first names, took as much care of their health as of their studies, and continued to follow their progress after they had left school. As well as providing poorer parents with assistance out of his own pocket, he also changed the school regulations so that needy liberal arts students could help finance their university studies by supervising the *collège's* older pupils. Several of the pre–First World War pupils went on to become famous. Charles de Gaulle was there from 1908 to 1909, preparing for the entrance examination for the Saint-Cyr military academy. Georges Guynemer, who was younger than de Gaulle, won a reputation at the *collège* for his pranks.[10] He went on to become an aviator and war hero before being shot down in 1917.

In 1908 Abbé Jean Calvet was put in charge of literary studies in the highest grade at Stanislas. One of his teachers at the seminary in Cahors had been Fernand Dalbus, a moral philosopher who had tried to reconcile the Anglican and Orthodox churches, and Calvet himself sounded like a cross between Bossuet and Confucius. After studying at the Sorbonne under Gustave Lanson and Emile Faguet, he had become a specialist in the French classics. During his time at the Collège Stanislas the teaching of literature tended to be clerical, rationalistic, and narrow. Seventeenth-century authors predominated, with Pascal and Bossuet in first place, followed by Racine, Malherbe, and La Fontaine. The eighteenth century, and by the same token the works of Ernest Renan, were passed over. Modern poetry was represented by Edmond Rostand and Sully Prudhomme, not by Baudelaire, who was considered "morbid," nor by Mallarmé, who wasn't even mentioned. The deputy head, the abbé Beaussart, was always warning any aspiring Rimbauds in his classes against the temptations of literature: "Be on your guard against doubt, the neurasthenia of the mind!" he told them.[11]

In philosophy, Descartes enjoyed pride of place. In fact, throughout his schooldays in that elderly fortress of Christianity, the young Lacan was exposed to a classical culture almost untouched by Enlightenment values and closed off from modern thought. Instead, everything was focused on the Christian Cartesianism reflected in the school motto: French without fear, Christian without reproach. The pupils in Lacan's year also included Louis Leprince-Ringuet, a future Academician; Jacques Morane, a future prefect; Paul de Sèze, who was to make a career in medicine; and Robert de Saint Jean, a writer and a close friend of Julien Green.

After 1915 the monotony of the Lacans' family life was broken by the war. Alfred was called up and made a sergeant in the commissariat, leaving Emilie to take over his work as agent for Dessaux.[12] Part of the Collège Stanislas was converted into a hospital for soldiers wounded at the front. It might have been the sight of these men, with their missing limbs and dazed expressions, that made Jacques want to be a doctor. At that age, though, he seemed chiefly interested in himself and his efforts to make top of the class in every subject. "Even the teachers were scared of Lacan," writes Robert de

Saint Jean. "Always coming first. Fine eyes. Manner half serious, half mock-ing. Without seeming to do so he kept a distance between himself and the other boys. At recess, when the rest of us were chasing Red Indians, he never joined in. When someone else for once got a better mark than he did in French composition, he remarked coolly to his rival, 'How could you lose? You write like Madame de Sévigné!' "[13]

He had never cared for children's games, and now that he was in his teens, arrogance was the keynote of his character. Yet in spite of what Robert de Saint Jean says, Lacan never actually made top of the class (it was always Jacques Morane who did that) nor won a first prize. He was a very bright pupil, shining especially in religious studies and Latin translation, but in other subjects he had to be satisfied with a few honorable mentions. His grades when he was in his last year ranged from nine to nineteen out of twenty (from a C to an A+ in U.S. terms). His best average was about fif-teen (an A in the United States). The comments of his teachers in his reports for the academic year 1916–1917 show him as rather eccentric, a bit con-ceited, occasionally tiresome, and in particular unable to organize his time properly and behave like the other boys. He was often off sick or playing hooky and suffered from a kind of ennui, a mixture of listlessness and will-ful melancholy.[14]

Toward his younger brother, Jacques was fatherly and protective. He acted as mentor too and used to hear Marco recite his Latin homework. "From about 1915, when he was fourteen and I was seven, he used to help me with my Latin. I can still see the letters he wrote me, in beautiful script, all about cases and moods."[15] It was around that time that Jacques discovered the works of Spinoza. He hung a diagram on the wall of his bedroom that depicted the structure of the *Ethics* with the aid of colored arrows.[16] In that world of minor tradesmen this amounted to an act of subversion, a step toward the assertion of his own desires against the wishes of a father he always believed to be set on having his elder son succeed him in the family business.

In the school year 1917–1918 Lacan had the good fortune to be taught by Jean Baruzi, an exceptional man who later became a friend. While teaching philosophy at the Collège Stanislas, Baruzi was writing a doctoral thesis on the life and works of St. John of the Cross.[17]

The writings of Baruzi—a rationalistic Catholic thinker whose work had elements in common with that of Etienne Gilson, Alexandre Koyré, and Henry Corbin, all later influences, direct or indirect, on Lacan—belong to a current of French thought that originated in 1886 with the addition of a religious sciences section (section 5) to the Ecole pratique des hautes etudes (EPHE; a graduate school for advanced research). Eighteen years after the launch of section 4, devoted to philology and history, section 5 was set up to take the place of the old faculties of theology, which since 1885 no longer existed in the university. For although church and state were now separated, it was necessary to ensure the survival of the subjects formerly taught under the heading of theology. But religions must now be the object of scientific, historical, and comparative study. This new initiative came under attack on the one hand by the Catholics, who refused to separate the study of sacred texts from questions of faith and divine revelation, and on the other hand by the anticlerical Left, for whom religion was a superstition that had no place in a university.[18] But the creators of the new section took their stand on a different ground. They were not fighting either for or against Catholicism: they held that religious phenomena should be studied in a critical spirit with the tools of pragmatic science. "As a matter of fact," Koyré wrote in 1931, "the section's staff included—and still includes—scholars both Catholic and Protestant, free thinkers, practicing Jews, and even some Christian clerics and Jewish rabbis."[19]

Jean Baruzi's work fit in with this conception of religious studies. Against a strictly lay and anticlerical tradition he maintained that "it is impossible to understand a Christian mystic without attempting to live with him in the world of grace."[20] But when he was arguing with theologians he declined to accept the dogma of grace as such.

Baruzi's teaching, together with the early discovery of Spinoza, brought about a transition in Lacan's development. Instead of the devout Catholicism practiced in his family, he encountered a scholarly, aristocratic Catholicism, one that might serve as a cultural substratum or critical instrument in the examination of things religious. Here Cécile Gazier, Emilie Baudry's childhood friend, also played an important role. Lacan admired her, and she introduced him to the writings of her father, Augustin Gazier, on the history of Jansenism.[21]

At the age of seventeen Jacques had his first sexual experience, with one of his father's customers, at a wedding at which his brother Marco was an usher.

Ever since he was a small child, Marco had always said he wanted to be a priest, though that didn't stop him from falling in love with a cousin and planning to marry her. But in his teens his choice of a monastic life put an end to any prospects of sex and marriage. "My mother was the only woman I ever admired unreservedly," he said. "She was a true Christian, unlike my father. She had nothing to do with my becoming a priest, but she was very happy about my decision, whereas my father was against it."[22]

Jacques, accompanied by Francis Goullin and Robert de Saint Jean, started going to Adrienne Monnier's bookshop, Shakespeare & Co., at 7, rue de l'Odéon. Adrienne Monnier, with her smooth round cheeks and her full, pleated skirts, organized public readings where her customers could meet writers who were already famous, such as André Gide, Jules Romains, and Paul Claudel. Lacan was also interested in dadaism and soon discovered the new outlook and early manifestations of surrealism through the review *Littérature*. He met André Breton and Philippe Soupault and listened spellbound, at Shakespeare & Co., to the first readings of James Joyce's *Ulysses*. It was at this period, when he was going through a bad attack of melancholy, that Jacques violently rejected the family and the Christian values he had been brought up in.[23]

In about 1923 he heard about Freud's theories for the first time, but it was the ideas of Charles Maurras (founder of the right-wing group Action française and later a collaborator during the Second World War) that really caught his attention. Though not anti-Semitic himself, he met Maurras several times and went to some meetings of the Action française.[24] The radicalism and elitism he heard propounded there distanced him even further from the family background he hated so implacably.

Alfred and Emilie began to worry about their son's attitude. He despised his origins, dressed like a dandy, and seemed to aspire to be another Rastignac.[25] One day Jacques met Robert de Saint Jean going past the entrance to the Parc Monceau and told him he still hadn't made up his mind about a career. "Medicine perhaps? Or why not politics?" Lacan was in fact thinking seriously about getting a job as secretary to some influential figure.[26]

Lacan's loss of faith and rejection of religion were reinforced when he started reading Nietzsche in the original German. In 1925 he wrote a brilliant eulogy of Nietzsche's thought for his brother to deliver at the St. Charlemagne banquet. The text was an open challenge to the Stanislas authorities. It maintained that English philosophy was useless and contrasted it with the great German tradition. When young Marc-Marie had finished, Beaussart stood up and damned the whole speech in one furious phrase: "Nietzsche was crazy!"[27]

In 1926, while Jacques was scandalizing his family with his taste for free thought and the doctrines of the Antichrist, Marc-Marie made the final decision to become a monk. The call came to him on May 13, as he was reading the Rule of St. Benedict. He wrote down the word *Benedictine*, and the sight of it acted on him like a revelation. Jacques was furious when he heard of his brother's decision and advised him to wait and go on with his law studies. For a year Marc-Marie did so. Then he went to Saint-Cyr for six months and did his military service as a reserve officer.

But in the autumn of 1929 Marc-Marie set out for the Abbaye de Hautecombe, a monument to a bygone age and an important center of the Benedictine order. The abbey was on Lake Bourget, made famous by Lamartine's elegiac love poem *Le Lac*. Jacques, seeing his brother off at the railroad station, watched in consternation as the train bore away, with

Marco, all his own childhood memories. As his younger brother's self-appointed keeper, he had done all he could to stop him from imprisoning himself like this. And now he blamed himself for not persuading him to be a tax inspector. On September 8, 1931, Marc-Marie took his vows, changing his second name to François in honor of St. Francis of Assisi. Four years later, on May 1, 1935, Jacques was present at his brother's ordination. After that he never went to Hautecombe again.

Meanwhile, Alfred and Emilie had left the apartment on the rue du Montparnasse and gone to live out at Boulogne-sur-Seine, where they had had a house built at 33, rue Gambetta. On January 20, 1925, Madeleine, their daughter, had married Jacques Houlon, a businessman from the other branch of the Lacan family. The couple were to live for many years in Indochina. Thus, each in his or her own way, all of Alfred's children severed their links with the family, the first through an intellectual break, the second by going to live abroad, and the third by entering the priesthood.

At the end of 1928 Madeleine fell ill with tuberculosis. She was in a sanatorium, about to have one lung collapsed, when Jacques came to see her. He angrily forbade the operation, saying she would recover naturally. He was right.[28]

2

. . . .

Faces on the Ward

*A*t the time when Lacan was embarking on a medical career, interest in Freud was increasing markedly in every area of French thought. But psychoanalysis was being introduced into France by means of two coexisting but conflicting modes. On the one hand there was the medical approach, the pioneers of which set up first, in 1925, the Evolution psychiatrique (Psychiatric Development) group and then, in 1926, the Société psychanalytique de Paris (SPP; Paris Psychoanalytical Society).[1] On the other hand there was the intellectual approach, that of the literary and philosophical avant-gardes, whose interpretations of Freud's discoveries varied greatly from one group to another. But neither of the two approaches took the lead: they intersected; they contradicted one another; but they advanced with equal vigor.

In the medical field, Freud's ideas were entering a territory divided into three zones: dynamic psychiatry, which had its origins in the philosophy of the Enlightenment but had been refashioned at the beginning of the twentieth century by the Zurich school; psychology, as developed by Pierre Janet, Charcot's former pupil and Freud's great rival; and finally the philosophy of Henri Bergson, whose ideas served as a filter for Freud's.[2] These three zones were part of a culture dominated by an ideal view of France and things French that assumed its own so-called Latin and would-be universal civilization was superior to a Germanic kultur seen as inferior, barbarous, and regionalistic. The French claim to superiority, first formulated by Taine and reinforced by the Germanophobia of the First World War, clashed head-on with Freud's teaching on sex, which seemed to some people to aim not only at pansexualism but also at pan-Germanism.[3]

By a historical paradox, this doctrine originated in France, for it could be traced back to the meeting of Freud and Charcot at the Salpêtrière in 1885, though it was subsequently developed, in stages, in Vienna. Charcot had earlier used hypnosis to demonstrate that hysteria was a functional nervous illness unconnected with the uterus. He eliminated the idea of any sexual etiology, showing that hysteria affected men as well as women. Freud later reintroduced the sexual etiology, though he transferred it from the uterus to the psyche. He subsequently formulated the theory of transference, which allowed him to dispense with hypnosis and in 1896 to invent psychoanalysis. Lastly, in 1905 he revealed the workings of infantile sexuality. It was this that made Freud's opponents suspect him of "sexual imperialism" and led to the use of the term *pansexualism*.

And so the earliest pioneers of the French psychoanalytic movement based their efforts on a kind of homegrown version of Freud that was closer to Janet's psychology than to Freud's own teaching and driven more by their own ideal of latinity than by a genuine theory of the unconscious. But such transplants never take completely, and Freud's ideas were not yet properly assimilated: for the time being, people only thought they understood and saw connections in what were really misrepresentations. Psychoanalysis might well bring healing to every kind of society, and the discovery of the unconscious might indeed have universal relevance; that didn't stop every country interpreting Freud in its own particular way.

As to the intellectual approach to Freud in France and its ideological answer to the medical one, that was in the hands of certain writers and the literary reviews. From Romain Rolland to André Breton and Pierre-Jean Jouve, from the surrealists to the *Nouvelle Revue française* (New French review), they brought a different view of Freudianism to the Parisian scene.[4] Whereas the physicians were chauvinistic and took a strictly therapeutic view of psychoanalysis, the writers accepted the idea of a wider sexuality, declined to look on Freudianism as a "Germanic culture," and maintained that psychology did not belong exclusively to doctors. Writers and artists of all kinds saw dreams as the great adventure of the age: they wanted to use the omnipotence of desire to change mankind; they invented a utopia where the unconscious was free of all restraint; and they admired the courage of the dedicated scientist who had defied bourgeois convention and risked scandal and isolation in order to listen in to the most intimate urges of humanity.

Jacques Lacan's first presentation of a patient was made to the Société neurologique on November 4, 1926, under the direction of the great neurologist Théophile Alajouanine, a friend of Edouard Pichon and a member of Action française. The case was one of fixed gaze caused by hypertonicity, together with extrapyramidal syndrome and pseudobulbar disorders of the spinal cord. It was an ordinary enough story concerning an unfortunate man of sixty-five who was taken ill while riding his bicycle and hospitalized at the Salpêtrière. He had a fixed stare and a respiratory tic, and the furrow between the nose and the chin was deeper on the left side of the face than on the right. When the patient bent his knees to sit, he remained poised for a moment above the chair before falling down onto the seat. Lacan's clinical comments were lengthy, detailed, strictly technical, and devoid of emotion: an arid bit of ordinary hospital routine.[5]

By a curious coincidence the presentation took place on the day the SPP was founded. There were ten members: Angelo Hesnard, René Laforgue, Marie Bonaparte, Eugénie Sokolnicka, René Allendy, Georges Parcheminey, Rudolph Loewenstein, Adrien Borel, Edouard Pichon, and Henri Codet; they were later joined by Charles Odier and Raymond de Saussure, both from Geneva.[6]

And so the date when Lacan's name first appeared in the history of French psychoanalysis was the same as that when the first Freudian association was created in France. But the twenty-five-year-old Lacan still had a long way to go before he became a part of that honorable institution, now the longest-lasting and most influential of its kind. It would take him eight years to become a member and four more to be made a training analyst.

Meanwhile his career followed a normal course, and he went on from neurology to psychiatry. From 1927 to 1931 he studied the clinical treatment of mental and cephalic disorders at the Hôpital Sainte-Anne, one of the top mental hospitals, and then went to the Special Infirmary of the Préfecture de Police (Paris police headquarters) where so-called dangerous individuals were brought in for emergency treatment. There followed two years at the Henri Rousselle hospital, where the most advanced psychiatric research was carried out and Lacan qualified in forensic medicine. In August 1930 he attended a two-month course at the famous Burghölzi clinic, attached to the University of Zurich, where at the beginning of the century Auguste Forel, Carl Gustav Jung, and Eugen Bleuler had arrived at a new conception of madness, based not only on a sound nosography but also on the results of listening to patients talking. In this already legendary center of dynamic psychiatry, Lacan worked under Hans Meïer, Bleuler's successor. The following year he went back to Sainte-Anne's as an intern, and in the staff room there he mixed with the men of his own generation. Henri Ey, Pierre Mâle, and Pierre Mareschal were his best friends, but he also knew Henri Frédéric Ellenberger.[7]

Ellenberger, born in South Africa in 1905 into a family of Protestant missionaries, had always wanted to be a historian. But his father made him study medicine and sent him to France: first to Strasbourg and then to Paris, where he met Lacan when they were both interns. "I kept my distance," says Ellenberger. "We saw each other in the staff room, where he joined in the general horseplay, though his jokes were a cut above the usual run. His witticisms were sharp and hurtful. He affected a sort of aristocratic arrogance. His barbs always struck home, and he didn't spare even his patients. I remember him saying of someone, 'He's very well thought of . . . by his concierge.' But Lacan was very charming in private."[8]

In the interns' canteen he and a few of his friends constituted the upper crust of the young medics. Lacan sat at Henri Ey's "little table," where everyone used the elegant jargon of phenomenology and looked down their noses at Edouard Toulouse's old-fashioned organicism. The younger generation dreamed about the October Revolution, proclaimed themselves surrealists, and fancied they were thoroughly modern. "Lacan had a precious way of speaking," says Paul Sivadon, "and he could be quite sadistic toward his chosen victims. . . . It so happened that Henri Ey made me treasurer for some of his projects. . . . Naturally, this meant collecting contributions. The only person I never got a cent out of was Lacan. . . . The patient who helped in the staff room used, for a small fee, to keep us supplied with cigarettes. Lacan often owed him money. Such trifles are evidence of his 'anal' personality. But he was a fine clinician right from the start of his career."[9]

Although the work of Freud and Breuer had transformed the nosology of psychiatry, the mental asylums of the thirties had still not emerged from the age of incarceration. Patients had to wear uniforms; their mail was opened; and personal belongings were confiscated. Women were registered under their maiden names and thus often robbed of their usual identities. Manic patients might be put in straitjackets, though that was only an ordinary humiliation. Violent cases were sometimes chained by the neck and left to sweat it out as they swooned in baths of hot water.

Senile patients were a particularly heartrending sight on their beds of seaweed filthy with excreta. For "chronics," the "choke-pear" was still in use, an iron contraption that could be inserted between the patient's teeth and screwed open to hold the jaws apart for forcible feeding. To discourage anyone who might have courted this torture for fun, hefty doses of castor oil were also poured down the funnel. Milder cases worked in the kitchens or the laundry, peeling vegetables in strange fits and starts or pushing heavy trolleys about like slaves. But when they were sent to work in the interns' quarters, they became the young men's companions and licensed buffoons.[10]

If the bourgeois conformism of Vienna at the end of the nineteenth century was reflected in Freud and Breuer's *Studies on Hysteria*,[11] the working-class alienation of the thirties was equally evident in all the cases published by the younger generation of French psychiatrists. Chronic hallucinatory psychosis, Parkinson's disease, mental automatism syndrome, hereditary syphilis: such were the sorts of sufferings the young Lacan witnessed at Sainte-Anne's. Until 1932 he wrote his case histories in collaboration with his fellow students or his teachers: with Adolphe Courtois for biological psychiatry, with Georges Heuyer for infant neuropsychiatry, and with Jean Lévy-Valensi for modern clinical method.[12]

Lacan's most interesting case in this period was the one he and his friend Maurice Trénel described to the Société neurologique on November 2, 1928: "Abasia in a War-traumatized Female Patient."[13] The subject was a woman from Brittany, a hysteric whose house had been destroyed by a shell in June 1915. Her peculiar gait and appearance, sometimes reminiscent of a dancing dervish, had made her a picturesque feature of the Paris hospital landscape. She had been trapped by one leg in the shattered floorboards when her house collapsed and had suffered superficial injuries to the scalp, nose, and back. At the Hôpital de Saint-Paul in Béthune the army doctor had told her to stand up straight, and from then on she had walked with her body thrust forward, rocking from side to side and scuffing her feet as children do. She later added another step to her bizarre choreography, crossing one foot in front of the other as she went along.

Hers was the only case of hysteria that Lacan put his name to during his psychiatric training. He remembered it clearly in 1933, when he said that this modest contribution to the "problem of hysteria" had acted as a transition to his more recent research in psychiatry.[14] So by then he believed his account of a case that "presented no neurological sign of organic origin" had allowed him to move from neurology to psychiatry. This meant he now regarded the case as one of hysteria in the Freudian sense. By 1932 he had come to understand the meaning of Freud's work, so there was an inconsistency between the way he presented the case in 1928 and the way he spoke of it in 1933. Neither of the authors of the 1928 account made any reference to hysteria: the terminology they used was exclusively that of Babinski. They employed the term *pithiatism*—a neologism formed from the Greek words for *persuasion* and *curable*—alluding to Babinski's demolition of Charcot's theories, in which he suggested that the word *pithiatic* might replace the word *hysterical*. Babinski thus, as is well known, made possible the beginnings of modern neurology,[15] though at the same time he also caused hysteria to be reclassified as a kind of simulation, curable by suggestion.

However, from 1925 onward Babinski's terminology had been falling into disuse: neurology was establishing itself as a genuine science and had less need to employ hysteria as a scapegoat. Moreover, Marie Bonaparte and Rudolph Loewenstein's 1928 translation of Freud's "Case of Dora" encouraged a truer conception of hysteria.[16] But as Trénel and Lacan had shown in their account, pithiatism was still alive and well in 1928 in the vocabulary of psychiatry. The pioneers of French psychoanalysis were no better: in 1925, in an article on Charcot's influence on Freud published in *Le Progrès médical* (Developments in medicine) to mark the centenary of Charcot's birth, Henri Codet and René Laforgue couldn't make up their minds between the three attitudes then dominating the critical approach to hysteria: Janet's psychophilosophy, Babinski's neurology, and Freud's doctrine.[17]

The surrealists were readier than the psychologists to follow Charcot, as they showed in 1928 when they paid tribute not to him but to Augustine, his famous patient. "We surrealists wish hereby to celebrate the fiftieth anniversary of hysteria, the greatest poetic discovery of the late nineteenth century. And we do so at the very moment when the concept of hysteria appears to have been completely dismantled. . . . We therefore propose a new definition of hysteria as a more or less irreducible mental state characterized by the subversion of the links between the individual and the moral world to which he thinks he for all practical purposes belongs, quite apart from any kind of delusion. . . . Hysteria is not a pathological condition and may be considered in every respect a supreme means of expression."[18]

But two more years still had to go by before Lacan incorporated the surrealist attitude into his work and then went on to effect a synthesis between psychiatry and Freud's discoveries.

3

. . . .

Psychiatry Teachers

T hree very different teachers of his prentice years left a deep impression
on Lacan. They were Georges Dumas, Henri Claude, and Gaëtan Gatian
de Clérambault.

Georges Dumas, a professor of psychopathology at the Sorbonne, was a
friend of Pierre Janet and Charles Blondel and a doughty opponent of psychoanalysis. He was always making fun of it, mocking what he called its jargon, not to mention its ideas about sex and its German connections. But
philosophy students and psychiatry interns all flocked to Sainte-Anne's to
hear his Sunday morning presentations, drawn there irresistibly by the
charm of both their content and their form. Claude Lévi-Strauss painted a
memorable portrait of him:

Dumas would make himself comfortable up on the rostrum, his sturdy, rugged figure surmounted by a head as knobbly as some great gnarled root silvered and
smoothed by immersion in the depths of the sea. . . . One didn't learn all that much
from his lectures. He never prepared them, trusting instead to the physical spell he
knew he could cast over his audience by the mobility of his mouth, twisted into a
perpetually changing smile. And especially by his voice—at the same time husky
and melodious, a real siren's voice, with strange inflections recalling not only his
native Languedoc but also, even more strikingly, certain ancient modes of the music
of spoken French. So voice and face, though appealing to two different senses, both
conjured up the same rustic but incisive style, the style of the fourteenth-century
humanists, the physicians and philosophers whose race he seemed to perpetuate in
body and mind. The second hour and sometimes the third too were devoted to the
presentation of cases, when the audience was treated to extraordinary performances
got up between the wily practitioner and patients trained to this sort of thing by
years in hospitals. They knew exactly what was expected of them and would either
produce symptoms in response to a signal or offer just enough resistance to demonstrate their trainer's skill. The spectators weren't taken in; on the contrary, they
enjoyed being dazzled by such a display of virtuosity.[1]

Henri Claude, a great rival of George Dumas, whose crude anti-Freudianism he disliked, was the undisputed monarch of Sainte-Anne's. Born in 1865, in 1905 he was made assistant at the Salpêtrière to Fulgence Raymond, himself the successor to Charcot. In 1922 the death of Ernest Dupré brought Claude a professorial chair at Sainte-Anne's, where he became the official patron of psychoanalysis as adapted to the "Latin spirit." He put René Laforgue in charge of a group consisting of Adrien Borel, Henri Codet, Angelo Hesnard, and Eugénie Sokolnicka. And so a dynamic and organicist French school grew up around Claude, a group Henri Ey would later inherit.[2]

Claude made use of Freudian theory in this new venture, though hoping all the while that it might take on a "Latin" form. "Psychoanalysis," he wrote, "is not yet suited to exploring the French mind. Some of its investigative methods offend our delicacy when it comes to private emotions, and the more far-fetched examples of its symbolism seem to me to make some of its generalizations, though applicable perhaps to other races, unacceptable in Latin clinical practice."[3]

René Laforgue had chosen to work under Claude rather than Dumas, despite Claude's jingoism. But Freud was uncompromising on this subject, and Laforgue's position became untenable. The crunch came in 1927, with the founding of the *Revue française de psychanalyse* (RFP), later to become the official organ of the SPP, itself affiliated with the International Psychoanalytical Association (IPA), founded by Freud in 1910 and bringing together all the psychoanalytic societies deriving from the Freudian movement. Originally Freud was to have been the *Revue*'s distinguished patron, but in order not to offend Professor Claude, the "protector" of psychoanalysis in France, Laforgue asked Freud to withdraw his name.

The third teacher to influence the young Lacan's career was Gaëtan Gatian de Clérambault. He was neither against psychoanalysis (he knew nothing of its findings) nor for Latinity (he wasn't interested). But he was undoubtedly the most flamboyant and paradoxical figure in the early part of the saga of Lacan and French psychoanalysis.

He was a confirmed misogynist who wouldn't admit women to his courses, and he surrounded himself with admirers from whom he required adoration and obedience. He was jealous of the influence wielded by Henri Claude, whom he dismissed as a mere neurologist. "There's a fellow who wants to make a name for himself," he would say scornfully, "out of two first names and no surname!"[4]

He was a pupil at the Collège Stanislas thirty years before Lacan and had studied law before turning to medicine. While serving with the army in Morocco he had fallen in love with the Arab style of dress and would describe in detail how skillfully eastern women draped their robes, sometimes gathering them together and sometimes letting them follow the lines of the body. He spent the First World War making wooden figurines and dressing them in draperies; he kept them for the rest of his life.[5]

When he got back to France he was appointed head of the Special Infirmary (for mental cases) of the Paris Préfecture de Police, where he ruled with panache until his suicide in 1934. A formalist and aesthete who saw madness as a kind of clairvoyance, Clérambault, at a time when Claude's group was moving in the opposite direction, built up the impressive theory of *mental automatism syndrome.* Dynamism abandoned the idea that psychosis could be constitutional, that is, have a basis in heredity. Clérambault, trying to bring coherence into the classification of mental disorders, defined them on the basis of their common element of mental automatism. In his view the origin of the syndrome remained organic, though the resulting disorders seemed to attack the patient suddenly and from outside, as in the case of automatism. In this respect Clérambault's position was structurally not unlike Freud's. But he rejected any reform in the matter of treatment. For him psychiatry necessarily involved a regime of incarceration and repression. As master of the police infirmary he was always improving his system, disregarding patients' distress and neither blaming nor pitying them: all he wanted was to wring out confessions.

Lacan adopted a different attitude toward each of these very different masters. With Henri Claude, the successful but limited bourgeois with considerable powers of patronage and a name that might prove useful, he was just a deferential pupil. He flattered Claude's narcissism by always agreeing with him, while remaining secure in his own mocking superiority. To Georges Dumas he was very respectful: he admired his clinical genius and was always trying to exercise his charm on him. With Clérambault he had a conflictual love-hate relationship.[6]

In Clérambault a passion for texture and draperies and a fascination with the clothed bodies of Arab women went with an intense interest in erotomania. On the basis of his mental automatism syndrome he distinguished between hallucinatory psychoses and passional delusions. Among the latter he placed the illusion of being loved that is called erotomania, of which the chief source is immense sexual vanity. The story was always the same, resembling that of countless ill-fated heroines of romance. The individual concerned thinks he or she is loved by the object of his or her chaste desires, usually some famous personage such as an actor, a king, or a member of the Academy. Madame X, for example, is convinced that the Prince of Wales is making advances to her, following her about, and making appointments with her that he doesn't keep. She resents his behavior, accuses him of infidelity, and goes to England to catch him in the act. When she gets back to Paris she assaults a policeman in the street and is brought to the office of the head of the Special Infirmary to be dealt with.

Clérambault described erotomania as a representation of reality that though insane was "logical." Despite his conservatism regarding theory, he agreed with Freud and the surrealists that madness was close to truth, reason to unreason, and coherence to delirium.

Clérambault's influence was evident in Lacan's first theoretical text, published in July 1931 in the *Semaine des hôpitaux de Paris* (Paris hospitals' weekly bulletin).[7] The title, "Structures of Paranoid Psychoses," was suggestive of things to come, and the very individual style clearly foreshadowed that of the 1932 thesis.

Lacan began by paying tribute to Emil Kraeplin, Paul Sérieux, and Joseph Capgras, whose work had made it possible to identify paranoia.[8] But he immediately criticized their legacy by putting forward a notion of "structure" in the phenomenological sense. This could be used to reveal a number of breaks in continuity: between normal psychology and pathology, to begin with, and then between the different kinds of delusion. Lacan then distinguished between the clinical and forensic points of view and divided paranoid psychoses into three types: those arising from a paranoid constitution; interpretation delusions; and passional delusions.

To describe the first of these types, he put forward, without criticizing them, the traditional explanations, setting out the four themes around which the paranoid constitution is organized: pathological overestimation of the self; suspiciousness; defective judgment; and social maladjustment. To these he added "Bovaryism," quoting one work by the philosopher Jules de Gaultier and another by the psychiatrist Genil-Perrin.[9]

"Bovaryism," derived from the name of the heroine of Flaubert's famous novel, had made its philosophical debut in 1902 in the work of Jules de Gaultier, a Nietzschean who used it to denote all forms of delusion related to the ego and dissatisfaction, from fantasizing about being someone else to belief in free will. Alienists, in their efforts to save criminal lunatics from the guillotine, used the term to suggest that the accused were not responsible for their crimes. In 1925 Genil-Perrin adopted the word invented by Gaultier and established a link between Bovaryism and paranoia. He put forward the idea of a gradual transition from a normal to a morbid state and described the paranoid constitution as an extreme form of pathological Bovaryism.

Just as in 1928 he had approached hysteria with the theoretical tools provided by Babinski, so in 1931 Lacan, describing the structures of paranoia, made use of a conservative doctrine with which a year later he would completely disagree. Thus he wrote of the paranoid patient as "one of the awkward squad," a schoolboy always in trouble, an autodidact admired by the ignorant, or a pathetic rebel whose desire for "pantheistic liberation" was merely a symptom of delusion. "If he's lucky," he wrote, "and fate puts him in the right place, he may become a social or cultural reformer, a 'great intellectual.' "[10]

The last part of the article contained Lacan's first written reference to the discoveries of Freud. But although he mentioned the theory of stages he immediately went on to defend the sacrosanct doctrine of constitutions. And when he spoke of the "technicians of the unconscious," he swiftly went on to show that though they might be able to explain paranoia, they couldn't cure it. At the beginning of the thirties Lacan still hadn't made any real use of Freudian theory. And at the same time that he was praising Clérambault for a theory he would soon demolish, he was also agreeing with Claude and mixing with the surrealists, who were against putting the mentally ill in asylums and regarded the language of madmen as sublime involuntary poetry.

It was an awkward situation. Clérambault, as Lacan knew very well, was a tyrant who expected undivided loyalty. He was also afraid of having his ideas stolen or copied. So when Lacan quoted Clérambault he was careful to add a footnote: "This image is borrowed from the oral teachings of our mentor, Monsieur G. de Clérambault, to whom we owe so much of both our matter and our manner that to avoid the charge of plagiarism we should really acknowledge him as the source of every expression we use."[11]

Taken aback by the ambiguity of this fulsome tribute, the head of the Special Infirmary promptly disowned his pupil. After the article was published he burst into a meeting of the Société médico-psychologique and threw his inscribed copies of Lacan's works in their author's face, accusing him of plagiarism. Henri Ellenberger recalls the incident: "He called Lacan a plagiarist, and with incredible nerve Lacan returned the compliment and told the elderly psychiatrist it was *he* who had plagiarized Lacan. It caused a great stir. Lacan had a marvelous flair for publicity."[12]

While he was praising Clérambault, Lacan was making his way forward in psychiatry under the auspices of Claude. It was with him and Pierre Migault that on May 21, 1931, he presented two cases of "simultaneous madness" to the Société médico-psychologique. According to traditional teaching, there were in such situations one inducing and one induced mania, the latter disappearing when the former was removed. But in these particular cases no induction was involved. The patients were two mother-and-daughter pairs in whom paranoid delusion was the most prominent feature. In Blanche, aged forty-four, it took a very peculiar form:

She sees herself as a four-headed monster with green eyes. What made her realize this is that her blood is scented. In high temperatures her skin goes hard and turns into metal, then she is covered with pearls and sprouts pieces of jewelry. Her genitals are quite unique: she has a pistil, like a flower. Her brain is four times as powerful as other people's brains, and her ovaries are tougher. She's the only woman in the world who doesn't need to wash. . . . The patient admits to some very strange habits. She makes broth with her menstrual blood: 'I drink some every day; it's very nourishing.' She arrived at the hospital with two hermetically sealed bottles: one contained urine and the other stools, and both were wrapped in weirdly embroidered cloths.[13]

After the cases of "simultaneous madness," Lacan turned his attention to anomalies in writing, and in November 1931, with Lévy-Valensi and Migault, he presented another case of female paranoia.[14] This one concerned Marcelle, a twenty-four-year-old primary school teacher suffering from erotomania. She believed she was Joan of Arc and wanted to restore France to its former greatness. She thought what she wrote was revolutionary. "I am renewing the language," she said. "The old forms need shaking up." Her delusion concerned one of her professional superiors, a man who had died the previous year. Clérambault had sent Marcelle to Sainte-Anne's: she was claiming compensation of twenty million francs from the state for sexual and intellectual deprivation and dissatisfaction. The following is a sample of her "inspired writing":

Paris, May 14, 1931

To the President of the Republic, Monsieur P. Doumer, at present on vacationing in gingerbread and mintstrel land
Dear M. President of the assiduous Republic,

I should like to know everything so as to give you the but mouse so of a coward and of a test cannon but it takes me much too long to guess. From the unkind things done to other people one might guess that my five Vals geese are chickwee and you are the bowler hat of the Virgin Mary and test pardon. But we must reduce everything from the Auvergne word list for unless one washes one's hands in a rock spring one will wetwee the dry bed and madelaine is without tradding the tart of all these new-shaved men so as to be the best of her prears of whooch is sweet and the cheek bright. I'd like to have said nasty things about the toalmerchantess without prejudice to plenary life and of free of charge one does some detective work. But one has to astonish people to be the accursed rascal of barbanella and of bedless one does some toalmerchantess.

The authors of the presentation didn't try to interpret any of Marcelle's writing; they simply analyzed its paranoid structure in terms of semantic, stylistic, and grammatical abnormalities. They were drawing on the surrealist experience rather than the model provided by traditional psychiatry. In their opinion the mental automatism syndrome was not constitutional in origin but the result of a process similar to that which lay behind the poetic creations of Breton, Eluard, Péret, and Desnos: i.e., it was partly automatic and partly deliberate.[15]

If we compare "Ecrits inspirés" with the text published a few months earlier in the *Semaine des hôpitaux de Paris*, we see that Lacan was siding simultaneously with two conflicting tendencies in the psychiatry of the day. On the one hand he was linking the notion of paranoid structure with a constitutionalist view of psychosis, assuming a norm and a need to repress that which departed from it. On the other hand he was subscribing to the idea that madness might be compared to an act of linguistic creation that was half "staged elsewhere" and half intentional. It was a strange set of contradictions: from Clérambault's teaching and his own reading of the French and German classics he derived the idea of structure, though this meant retaining the notion of constitutions; from the dynamic approach he took the study of the language of madness, which really implied abandoning constitutionalism.

The presenters of the Marcelle case also cited Pfersdoff and Guilhem Tuelié on schizophrenia, Head on aphasia, and Henri Delacroix on language and thought. In the first quarter of the century these authors had studied the links between psychosis and anomalies in written and spoken language.[16] In 1913 Kraepelin introduced the word *schizophasia* to denote a schizophrenic state of which the earliest symptom was disordered speech. Hence also the word *schizography*, which Lacan and his friends used for a similar situation involving "inspired" writing. But the most interesting reference is to a work by Delacroix published in 1930, because it is a valuable indication of what the young Lacan was reading at this period.[17] In support of his thinking on aphasia, Delacroix, who taught Sartre philosophy, drew on Ferdinand de Saussure's *Cours de linguistique générale* (Course in general linguistics), published in Geneva in 1915.[18] So there can no longer be any doubt about it: it was in this now forgotten writer that Lacan first came across Saussure's theory of language, of which he was to make such fruitful use two decades later.

Crazy Ladies

The Story of Marguerite

*A*t this point in his development Lacan came across a crucial article in the first number of *Surréalisme au service de la Révolution* (Surrealism in the service of the Revolution), published in July 1930. This paper—"L'Ane pourri" (The rotten donkey), by Salvador Dali[1]—made it possible for Lacan to break with the theory of constitutionalism and move on to a new understanding of language as it related to psychosis. Dali was putting forward a novel thesis on paranoia. By now surrealism's first phase was over, and André Breton's *Second Manifesto* had proclaimed the necessity of seeking out a "point of mind" from which man might resolve the contradiction between real life and dream. Experiment in hypnotically induced sleep and automatic writing was a thing of the past; a new field of operations must be found in political action. The old chimera of changing mankind must take concrete form; what was needed was a new technique for arriving at a knowledge of reality.[2]

It was at this point that Dali made surrealism a present of his famous notion of paranoia-criticism. "It is through a plainly paranoid process," he wrote, "that it has been possible to obtain a double image: i.e., the representation of an object that, without any anatomical or figurative distortion, is at the same time a representation of a completely different object, itself devoid of any deformation or abnormality that might imply some kind of arrangement."[3]

According to Dali, paranoia functioned in the same way as hallucination: that is, as a delusional interpretation of reality. It was a pseudohallucinatory phenomenon, producing double images—the image of a horse, for example, might simultaneously be the image of a woman—and the existence of the double image invalidated the classical psychiatric idea of paranoia as an "error" of judgment and "reason" gone mad. In other words, delusion is already an interpretation of reality, and paranoia a creative activity dependent on logic.

At a time when Lacan was reading Freud, Dali's point of view provided him with just the element he needed to turn his own clinical experience on paranoia into a theory.[4] He asked to meet the painter, who received him in his hotel room with a bandage on the tip of his nose. Dali expected his visitor to register some surprise, but he was disappointed. Lacan just sat and listened quietly as Dali expounded his ideas.[5]

Meanwhile he had translated for the *Revue française de psychanalyse* (*RFP*) an article by Freud entitled "Some Neurotic Mechanisms in Jealousy, Paranoia, and Homosexuality."[6] The theme of this article related to Lacan's search for a new conception of paranoia, and Lacan's version formed part of an SPP project for translating some of Freud's work.[7]

Although he didn't actually speak the language, Lacan had an excellent theoretical knowledge of German, which he had learned at the Collège Stanislas. His translation was remarkable, following the syntax of the original very closely and remaining faithful to both its form and its content. His version also showed how completely he accepted the terminology then current in the French psychoanalytic movement. Just like his contemporaries, he translated *Trieb* (drive) as *instinct* (instinct), *Trauer* (mourning) as *tristesse* (sorrow), and *Regung* (motion) as *tendance* (tendency). He also undertook to translate for the *RFP* a chapter of Otto Fenichel's book on schizophrenia.[8] But this never came to anything.

The year 1931 was a watershed for Lacan, for it was then that, starting from the basis of paranoia, he embarked on a synthesis of three areas of knowledge: clinical psychiatry, the teachings of Freud, and the second phase of surrealism. His remarkable knowledge of philosophy, and in particular of Spinoza, Jaspers, Nietzsche, Husserl, and Bergson, also contributed to the making of the great work of Lacan's youth: his medical thesis. *De la psychose paranoïaque dans ses rapports avec la personnalité* (Paranoid psychosis and its relation to personality) appeared in the winter of 1932 and made its author the leader of a school.

The story of the encounter between Lacan and the woman he was to call Aimée began at 8:00 in the evening on April 10, 1931. That evening Marguerite Pantaine, aged thirty-eight, took a kitchen knife out of her purse and tried to kill the actress Huguette Duflos when she arrived at the Théâtre Saint-Georges. The intended victim was due to play the lead in *Tout va bien* (Everything's fine), a play by Henri Jeanson that had opened three days earlier. The play, an undistinguished middle-class comedy about a sentimental lady, her poor but carefree lover, and a rich but boring financier, was designed to show that in the France of the 1930s, despite the economic crisis and the rise of the parties of the Far Right, all was for the best in the best of all possible worlds.

Huguette Duflos, confronted by her attacker at the stage door, coolly

grabbed the blade of the knife and deflected the blow, in the process sever-
ing a couple of tendons in the little finger of her right hand. Marguerite was
overpowered and taken to the police station. From there she was sent to the
Special Infirmary and then to the women's prison at Saint-Lazare, where
she fell into a delusional state that lasted nearly three weeks. On June 3,
1931, she was confined in the Sainte-Anne asylum on the recommendation
of Dr. Truelle, who diagnosed "systematic persecution mania based on interpretation delusion, with megalomaniac tendencies and a substratum of erotomania."[9]

On the day after the murder attempt, various newspapers told the sad
story of Marguerite Pantaine, a countrywoman who had come down in the
world and worked up her feelings by reading novels and trying to get her
own fiction published. "She's a native of Auvergne," said the *Journal*, "stub-
born, hard-faced, accentuating her masculine appearance by wearing a
starched collar over her sweater. . . . She has a good job in the postal order
department of the Louvre Central Post Office, where she told us she earns
eighteen thousand francs a year. She has few visitors apart from a couple of
female teachers with whom she plays music and studies for examinations.
She was certainly rather strange but didn't seem to think she was being persecuted."[10]

Edouard Toulouse, asked for his opinion by *Le Temps,* characteristically
used the old terminology of hereditary degeneration: "In my view this is a
clear case of persecution mania, and it probably manifested itself earlier by
various irregularities or oddities of behavior that must have been obvious to
those around her. It is my opinion that every criminal is to some extent
degenerate: his or her particular anomaly reveals itself in outlandish conduct
and strange words and actions that attract the attention of relatives and
neighbors. I see no reason in this case to depart from what I never cease to
maintain: it is in the best interest of such patients to come forward and
apprise us of their situations. The prevention of crime is not merely possible: it is easy."[11]

A novelist called Pierre Benoit told of the odd circumstances in which
he had encountered Marguerite: "The would-be murderess used to go regularly to my publisher's office in the hope of seeing me. One day I actually
met her. The unfortunate woman is certainly not normal. She claimed she
was targeted in several of my novels, the subjects of which, she repeatedly
maintained, were suggested to me by Madame Huguette Duflos. Perhaps
the blows aimed at that charming actress were really intended for me."[12]

Pierre Benoit, an author belonging to the conformist Right, had come
into prominence with the publication of *Koenigsmark* in 1918. He practiced
a kind of mass-production technique, with traditional plots set either against
some exotic background or in the "backward" French provinces. Every

book dealt with a similar situation, ran to the same number of pages, and had a heroine whose first name began with *a*. His *Atlantide* (Atlantis) (1919) brought the famous Platonic myth up to date and set it in the French colonies: the quest for an imaginary wilderness was seen as an illustration of the tragedy of modern man, unable to resist the temptations of the Devil as represented by Woman in every shape and form.[13] The book shows a virtuous colonial army officer falling under the influence of Antinea, a satanic oriental figure luring the West to its destruction by enticing lost travelers to her palace in the Hoggar. There, in the heart of the Sahara, she casts spells on her guests and turns them into mummies. It was against the author of such works that Marguerite Pantaine directed her accusations.

As for Huguette Duflos—her real name was Hermance Hert—she bore some physical resemblance to the Antinea of Benoit's novel. She was born in Tunis in 1891 and studied at the Paris Conservatoire. At the same time a member of the Comédie-Française and a leading actress in the silent cinema, she was a melodramatic figure: haughty, mysterious, vulnerable, and emotional. She was the victim of her own celebrity, always in the news over her sensational lawsuits: one was against the Comédie-Française; another against her husband.

All the time she was in a state of delusion, Marguerite kept repeating how much she hated the actress. She asked reporters to correct the public's condemnation of herself because it might harm her "future career as a writer."[14] She wrote to the manager of her hotel and to the Prince of Wales, complaining about the actresses and authors who were persecuting her. Then, when her delusions left her, she wept and completely reversed her attitude, saying Huguette Duflos didn't wish her any harm, nor was anyone trying to persecute her. In any case, Mme Duflos didn't bring charges, and everyone else was equally lenient toward the unfortunate postwoman.

Jacques Lacan met her for the first time on June 18, 1931. He took an immediate interest in the case and issued a two-week certificate written in the grand manner of Clérambault: "Paranoid psychosis. Recent delusions culminating in attempted homicide. Obsessions apparently resolved after the attack. Dreamlike state. Interpretations significant, extensive, and concentric and grouped around one overriding idea: threats to her son. Emotional preoccupation: her duty toward the latter. Polymorphic impulses provoked by anxiety: approaches to an author and to her future victim. Urgent need to write. Results sent to English royal family. Others of a polemic or bucolic nature. Caffeine dependency. Dietary deviations, etc."[15]

From that day on and for a whole year, Jacques Lacan and Marguerite Pantaine were inseparable. By the time the brilliant psychiatrist had completed his extraordinary study, he had appropriated the woman's fate and made it into a "case" through which he projected not only his theories on madness in women but also his own fantasies and family obsessions. He filched all Marguerite's writings, her photographs, her whole life history; and he never gave any of it back. This meant a constant distortion of their relationship, a coldness and hostility between them that nothing could remove. Lacan was interested in the woman only in order to illustrate his ideas on paranoia and write a theoretical work that would make him the founder of a new school of Freudian discourse. But she steadfastly refused to fill the role he wanted to force on her. She was an unwilling collaborator and reproached Lacan as long as she lived for using her case in support of a psychiatric method that she condemned as repressive.

The full history of this strange incident can now be told because of various documents and accounts that have been made available to me.[16]

A first Marguerite Pantaine was born in Mauriac, in the department of Cantal, on October 19, 1885. She was the daughter of Jean-Baptiste Pantaine and Jeanne Anna Donnadieu, who had been married in Chalvignac eight months earlier. Jeanne had two other daughters after Marguerite: Elise, born in September 1887 and known as Eugénie or "Nène," and Maria, born eleven months later. But in December 1890 tragedy struck the young peasant family: one Sunday, before mass, five-year-old Marguerite went too near the fire in her best organdy dress and went up in flames before her younger sister Elise's very eyes. Jeanne was pregnant again soon afterward and had a stillborn child on August 12, 1891. Eleven more months went by, and on July 4, 1892, a fifth child and second Marguerite was born: the Marguerite Pantaine who was to meet Jacques Lacan thirty-nine years later. She was given the same first name as her dead sister. "It is no accident," wrote her son, "that my mother spent her whole life trying in every way she could to escape the flames of hell. . . . That is what it means to fulfill one's fate. In her case a tragic one."[17] After the second Marguerite, Jeanne Donnadieu had three sons.

Marguerite had a country childhood that followed the rhythm of the passing seasons and recurring rural tasks and fostered in her a love of daydreaming and solitude. Her mother, Jeanne, whom people regarded as slightly crazy, was hypersensitive in her dealings with the rest of the village community. Her anxieties were easily transformed into suspicions: if the woman next door said she thought a sick animal might die, Jeanne would conclude that her neighbor meant to poison it. She often felt she was being spied on or persecuted and interpreted everything as a sign of ill will against herself. As her favorite daughter, Marguerite enjoyed special privileges, and her sisters grew jealous. With her father and brothers she was tough and difficult, resisting what she saw as tyrannical attempts at imposing authority.

Elise Pantaine, Marguerite's oldest surviving sister, got into the habit of

running the house for her ailing mother. But in 1901, when she was fourteen, Elise left the village to go to work in her uncle Guillaume's grocery
store in town. In 1906 he married her. Meanwhile Marguerite, who was
exceptionally good at her lessons, was sent away to a school where her parents hoped she might start to train as a teacher. But she missed the country
and accused the lay mistresses of neglecting their pupils. What she hankered
after was the grandeur of some religious ethic.

In 1910 she went to live with her married sister. By this time she was a
tall girl of eighteen, sturdily built, strong willed, clever, sensitive, and good-
looking. She had left school and given up the idea of teaching in order to
take a job in the post office. In town she was soon seduced by the local Don
Juan. "This affair," wrote Lacan, "which displays all the enthusiasm and
blindness typical of the innocent, was to determine the course of her affections for three years."[18] Although she was transferred to a remote village,
Marguerite went on loving her seducer and had thoughts for nothing else.
She wrote to him in secret, hiding her feelings from her colleagues. This passion lasted for three years, after which Marguerite's love turned to hatred
and the former Don Juan was demoted to the rank of cad.

Marguerite was then moved to Melun, where she remained until 1917.
Meanwhile she had fallen in love again, this time with a female post office
worker, Mademoiselle C. de N. This "practiced schemer," as Lacan called
her, belonged to a noble family that had been reduced to working for its living. Mademoiselle C. de N. had nothing but contempt for her job in the
post office and set herself up among her colleagues as an authority on fashion and manners.

Marguerite was an easy prey. Mlle C. de N. regaled her with stories that
might have come straight out of *Madame Bovary*. It was from Mlle C. de N.
that Marguerite first heard about Huguette Duflos and Sarah Bernhardt: the
former was supposed to have lived on the same landing as one of the elegant postwoman's aunts, while the latter was said to have met her mother in
a convent. Marguerite, listening to all this, came to look down her nose at
the humble world surrounding her and dream of a better universe full of
Platonic ideas, manly strength, and romance. When she decided out of the
blue to marry one of her post office colleagues, Mlle C. de N. encouraged
her in extravagant expense. This lengthy period of almost hypnotic suggestion lasted four years and came to an end only when the "practiced
schemer" was moved to another post. But the two women went on writing
to one another.

René Anzieu was the son of a baker in Sète, on the south coast of France.
Orphaned at twelve, he nonetheless rose rapidly through the ranks of the
post office and became an inspector. He liked traveling around by bicycle
and studying the geography of communications on the spot. Level-headed,

pragmatic, simple, and fond of sport, he seemed like a steady and balanced character—just the opposite of Marguerite. When she decided the moment had come to marry and that he was to be her husband, her family made objections: her lethargy, her habitual daydreaming, and her craze for reading rendered her unsuitable for marriage. But the betrothed couple disregarded all warnings, exchanged confessions about their pasts, and were married on October 30, 1917.

Despite Marguerite's attempts at housekeeping, the couple was soon at loggerheads. René hated anything that wasn't definite and down to earth and couldn't stand seeing his wife spend all her time reading books and learning foreign languages. She for her part complained that he took no interest in things that concerned her. Each invoked the other's premarital confessions and used them as a basis for retrospective jealousy. The wife's sexual frigidity did nothing to soothe the husband's aggressiveness, and soon the ill-assorted relationship was heading for the rocks. Marguerite's behavior gave cause for alarm: she took to laughing for no apparent reason, moving in fits and starts when she was walking, and compulsively washing her hands.

It was at about this time that Guillaume Pantaine died of a war wound. Elise, his widow, had had a complete hysterectomy four years earlier and could never have any children. So, not knowing what to do with herself, she sought refuge with her sister Marguerite in Melun, where she took over the housekeeping that should have been Marguerite's role vis-à-vis René. Marguerite, ousted from a position she had never managed to occupy successfully herself, grew even more estranged from her husband and lost the power to struggle against her own pathological tendencies. Although she felt humiliated by her sister's intrusion and constant criticism, she let herself be dominated by Elise in just the same way as she had submitted to Mlle C. de N. But while part of the time Marguerite admitted the contrast between Elise's strengths and her own inefficiency, there were also moments when she silently rebelled against her sister's tyranny. The results of this ambiguity were disastrous.

In July 1921 Marguerite found she was pregnant, but in her case the prospective "happy" event only brought on persecution mania, accompanied by fits of melancholy. "Her colleagues' conversation," wrote Lacan, "seemed to be directed against her. They appeared to be criticizing what she did, slandering her, and predicting misfortune. Passersby in the street whispered about her and looked down their noses. She spotted hostile references to herself in the newspapers."[19] Her confusion grew worse as her pregnancy advanced, and nightmares were added to the persecutions of the day. Sometimes she would dream of coffins. Sometimes she would get out of bed and hurl an iron at René's head. One day she slashed the tires of a fellow worker's bicycle.

In March 1922 she produced a daughter, but the child was stillborn, strangled by its own umbilical cord. She at once blamed the accident on her enemies. And because her former colleague, the "practiced schemer," telephoned to ask how she was, Marguerite immediately held her responsible for what had happened. For many days she withdrew into herself, refusing to speak and abandoning her usual religious observances.

When she became pregnant for the second time she fell into another depression, but when the child was born, in July 1923, she grew passionately devoted to it. This time it was a boy, who was named Didier. Just as Marguerite herself had come into the world after a stillborn child, itself conceived in order to replace an earlier Marguerite, so Marguerite's son succeeded a stillborn sister. "That dead sister," he wrote later, "the symbol of my parents' first failure, lingered on for a long while in all they said and thought. I was the second-born, a child to be cared for and watched over all the more intently because it must be saved from its predecessor's sad fate. I suffered the consequences of their fear that it might happen again. In order to justify my mother and father, I had to survive at all costs. But they looked on my survival as very uncertain. The slightest attack of indigestion, the faintest draft, was seen as a threat. All this put me in a very peculiar and difficult situation. I was supposed to take the place of a dead girl."[20]

For months Marguerite doted exclusively on her son. She refused to let anyone else go near him or feed him until he was fourteen months old. Sometimes she would stuff him with food so rich that he threw it up; at other times she would forget to give him his bottle. To protect him from contact with the air she wrapped him up in layer on layer of clothing. Looking back as an adult, he compared his infant self to the center of an onion. His mother started quarreling with those around her and interpreting everything they said as threats. One day she accused some motorists of driving too near the perambulator in which she was taking the child for an airing. On another occasion she forgot all about him and let him suck the grease off one of its wheels. It was then that Elise, the baby's godmother, decided to make up for her own childlessness by taking charge of Didier herself.

From then on Marguerite felt completely alienated from her surroundings. She planned to go to America, obtained a passport made out in the name of Peyrols, and handed in her notice at the post office.[21] Her idea was to seek her fortune in foreign lands and become a novelist, and she refused to give up these extravagant notions despite all Elise's and René's fulminations. So they decided to have her put into a clinic in Epinay.

From there she issued vigorous protests against her incarceration. "I can't help being really amused," she wrote, "at the way I'm always a victim, always misunderstood. Mother of God, when I think of all that's happened to me!

You know the story; almost everyone knows it, people run me down so constantly. And as I know from your books that you dislike injustice, I appeal to you to do something for me."[22]

During the time she was kept in the clinic Marguerite lost touch with reality and sank deep into megalomania. On admission she was described as delusional, with a "background of mental weakness, hallucination, and persecution mania," but after six months, at her family's request, she was released. She rested for a while, took charge of her son again, and went to see Mlle C. de N., intending thereby to make up for all the harm she had wished her. Of course Marguerite's hostess had no idea she was supposed to have persecuted her former colleague. In August 1925 Marguerite left Melun and her family. She had asked to be transferred to Paris in order to track down those she imagined were trying to destroy her son.

She soon embarked on a very weird way of life. On the one hand there was the everyday world of her post office activities, in which she more or less adapted to reality. On the other hand she led an imaginary existence made up of dreams and delusions. On the Right Bank, Marguerite worked in the central post office in the rue du Louvre; on the Left Bank she lived in the Hôtel de la Nouvelle France in the rue Saint-André-des-Arts. As soon as she left her place of work she became an intellectual, taking private lessons, haunting libraries, addicted to coffee. But despite all her efforts she failed one professional examination and in three attempts at the *baccalauréat*.

While she was leading this double life, Marguerite's delusions grew worse. One day, hearing someone mention Huguette Duflos, she remembered a conversation she had once had with Mlle C. de N. in which "I had spoken ill of her. Everyone else said she was well-bred and distinguished. . . . But I said she was a whore. That must be why she has a grudge against me."[23] Marguerite had come to believe the actress was trying to persecute her, and as the Paris papers were always talking about Huguette Duflos's quarrels with the Comédie-Française, she became angry about the amount of attention the press paid to the theatrical fraternity. She went twice to have a look at her future victim: first at the theater, where Mme Duflos was playing the grand duchess Aurore in a stage adaptation of Pierre Benoit's novel *Koenigsmark*, and then at the movies, where Duflos appeared in the film version directed by Léonce Perret. The plot told of a murder set in a Gothic palace, complete with brocade hangings, paneling and trompe-l'oeil corridors. The name of the actress was popularly linked with that of the author.

Marguerite believed two more leading figures in the Paris theater were among her persecutors. Sarah Bernhardt and Colette were both adored and successful women, living in luxury. Both also embodied an ideal—that of a freedom painfully won and maintained at some cost—to which Marguerite herself had always aspired, though she had never achieved any success, either social or intellectual. The great Sarah had died in 1923. In everyday life she, like Zola, had been a passionate defender of Dreyfus; on the stage she had been sublime as the doomed prince in Rostand's *L'Aiglon* and as the melancholy revolutionary heroine, Théroigne de Méricourt, in Hervieu's play of that name. Colette, still very much alive and at the height of her career, had published *Le Blé en herbe* (The unripe corn) in 1923, using her own name for the first time. At the age of fifty-three she was causing a great scandal by living with a pearl merchant sixteen years her junior.

Marguerite's delusions were at the mercy of her reading. She had only to open a newspaper to see "references" to her own private life. One murky affair in particular, dating from 1923, fostered all her fantasies of murder and revenge. Philippe, grandson of Alphonse Daudet (the author of *Lettres de mon moulin* and *Tartarin de Tarascon*) and son of Léon Daudet (a right-wing journalist), had shot himself in the head after unsuccessfully trying to persuade his anarchist friends to assassinate his father. But Alphonse Daudet refused to believe his grandson had committed suicide and accused the anarchists of murdering him. Marguerite, transposing this imbroglio to apply to herself, believed that the OGPU—the Russian secret police—was planning to kill her son, Didier.[24]

During her first year in Paris she did all she could to bring about a meeting between herself and Pierre Benoit, a member of the French Academy, even going so far as to lie in wait for him at a bookshop he often patronized. When she actually approached him and reproached him for exposing her private life to public view, he took her for some brazen and mysterious eccentric. However, stung by her accusations, he took her for a walk in the Bois de Boulogne, where she claimed to have recognized herself in Alberte, the heroine of his latest book.

Admittedly, Benoit's writings might have been designed to fuel the madness of this unusual reader. *Alberte* told the story of a mother who took her son-in-law as her lover, unaware of the fact that he had killed his wife. After a stormy ten years, the incestuous mother finds out about the murder and denounces both herself and her daughter's murderer. Marguerite, who saw this somber affair as a reflection of her own fate, told Lacan: "I was both that mother and that daughter."[25]

At this point one is bound to remember the story of Marie-Félicité Lefevbre, which Marie Bonaparte related and commented on in the first issue of the *RFP*.[26] Lacan later referred admiringly to the case.

In August 1923 Marie-Félicité Lefevbre shot dead her pregnant daughter-in-law. The court at Douai found her responsible for her actions and sentenced her to death. Marie Bonaparte bravely intervened in the name of psychoanalysis, maintaining that the crime had been committed in a state of delusion in which the murderess was unconsciously acting out a death wish previously entertained in relation to her own mother.

In Pierre Benoit's story, a husband who murdered his wife slept with his mother-in-law. In the case of Mme Lefevbre, a mother became a murderer out of hatred for her own mother and to prevent her son from having any offspring. Both narratives dealt with a sinister trio of characters in which the places of mother and daughter were interchangeable, where the daughter was always the victim and the son sometimes a murderous and sometimes a passive husband.

Marguerite didn't make any reference to the story of Marie-Félicité Lefebvre, though it was a frequent subject of press comment at that period. Her delusions found enough raw material in her reading of *Alberte*, her meeting with Benoit, Colette's flamboyant way of life, and Huguette Duflos's lawsuits. She referred to Benoit by the hated name of Robespierre and anathematized all journalists, artists, and poets, whom she held responsible for bolshevism and war, poverty and corruption. She saw herself as crusading against them all to restore the ideal of brotherhood among nations. She sent poems and anonymous letters to the Prince of Wales, asking for his protection. She warned him, the object of her erotomania, to beware of the plots fomented against him by revolutionaries and "printed in italics" in the newspapers, and she covered the walls of her room with press clippings about his life and travels.

Her antibolshevism didn't stop her laying siege to a communist newspaper to try to make them publish articles against Colette and expounding Marguerite's own claims and complaints. At the same time she made a complaint at her local police station against Pierre Benoit and the Librairie Flammarion. Then, in order to devote herself more completely to her literary career, she stopped spending her leaves with her family. She believed she had a mission and would waylay passersby in the street to regale them with wild stories. Some of the people she approached were none too scrupulous, and she had more than one narrow escape when she found the encounter was ending up in a hotel room.

In August 1930, eight months before the murder attempt, Marguerite wrote two novels one after the other and had them typed. The first, *Le Détracteur* (The detractor), was dedicated to the Prince of Wales and told of a rural idyll that unfolded in time with the seasons of the year. The author rhapsodized about the virtues of life lived in tune with nature, in the manner of Rousseau and using a regional vocabulary. The country was idealized; the city seen as a source of corruption and decadence. The hero, David, was a young peasant whose mother had died after drinking "murky water." He was in love with a girl called Aimée. Her portrait was peppered with references to rural lore and terminology: "Aimée worked like a real countrywoman. She could *parfiler* [refurbish] old clothes, *défroisser* [iron] a mountain of laundry after the harvest, and pick out the best cheese from the *clisse* [wicker tray]. She never killed a fowl that was too stringy and knew how to measure out *jointées* [bushels] of grain and gather bunches of leaves for animals that went off their fodder in winter. She could cook chicken so that it was easy for children to eat and make dolls for them out of beads, cardboard, and different kinds of pastry. She could cook an elegant meal for special occasions: river trout in cream sauce, chicken stuffed with chestnuts, a dish of fish stew."[27]

But during the summer a stranger and a courtesan came to the village and sowed discord in Aimée's family. The woman was "painted like an autumn rosebush, with roses too bright for her black and leafless branches." She wore shoes "not meant to be walked in" and was altogether like "a museum, a collection of models so outlandish and eccentric that the general effect was grotesque." The sinister couple's baneful influence soon spread throughout the village as a whole, until the place was full of rumors, plots, and factions. In the autumn, misfortune struck Aimée's own family. Her brothers and sisters started to waste away, her mother fell ill, and she herself was the subject of calumny. She took refuge in dreams. She watched enviously as a happy family passed along the main road: a proud husband and a wife with a child smiling up at her as it nursed at her breast. When winter came the sinister strangers went away. The novel ended with Aimée's death and her mother's despair.

The story embodied significant figures in Marguerite's madness: a lovelorn heroine with a name straight out of the novels of Pierre Benoit; a courtesan in whom we recognize the female celebrity at once admired and despised; a slanderer who hatches plots; and a family destroyed by a malevolent couple.

The second novel, *Sauf votre respect* (With all respect), was also dedicated to the Prince of Wales. It told the same story as the *Le Détracteur*, but in reverse. This time the heroine, instead of staying in the country to become the victim of invaders from the city, took up her cloak and dagger and rode off to conquer Paris and the French Academy. First she observed with the horror and dismay of an innocent the various spectacles presented by a corrupt civilization. Then she came up against the great Buccaneer, her chief persecutor, also known as "the Hard-Assed Incorruptible," who was in charge of the guillotine. "He didn't drink, and he didn't have women, but he cravenly killed thousands of them. Blood flowed from the place du Trône to the Bastille, and the carnage didn't stop until Bonaparte trained his guns on Paris."[28] After traversing the dark alleys of this urban inferno, full of communists and decapitators, the heroine attacked the Republic itself, together with writers and street performers, whom she accused of wanting to "kill

her in effigy." Against all these she took up the defense of monarchy, criticizing religion and explaining miracles as the result of suggestion. "Miracles
are not found among all Christians," she wrote. "But it is difficult to make
you understand an obvious fact already accepted by the medical profession.
You probably approach your particular idol with so much emotion it makes
you forget your sufferings and endows you with fresh strength.... No doubt
you have at some time been cured of a headache by a friend telling you an
amusing story; similarly, when the emotion involved is in proportion to a
much loftier kind of feeling, you are in the presence of a miracle."[29] At the
end of the narrative the country lass goes back home to her streams and
meadows and the bosom of an idyllic family.

On September 13, 1930, Marguerite left a manuscript at the office of the
Librairie Flammarion. She had signed it with her maiden name. Two months
later the editorial committee turned the book down. When Marguerite
heard the news she demanded to see the general secretary, but he was busy
and asked the literary editor to talk to her instead. When he did so,
Marguerite brandished the letter of rejection and wanted to know the name
of the person responsible. When the literary editor declined to tell her, she
fell upon and nearly strangled him, yelling, "You're a pack of academics and
murderers!"[30] She was thrown out but couldn't accept the fact that all her
hopes had been frustrated. During the long period of wandering that led up
to the murderous attack in April 1931, she felt a violent longing for revenge
rising within her. She asked her landlord to lend her a revolver and, when
he refused, asked for a stick with which "to frighten them" (the publishers).
One last time she sought the protection of the Prince of Wales, sending him
both her novels and letters signed with her own name.

Every day she went out to Melun to make sure her son wasn't being
attacked. In January she told her sister she was going to get a divorce. She
accused her husband of beating both herself and the child. In March she
bought a hunting knife from a shop in the place Coquillière. On April 17, a
private secretary at Buckingham Palace sent back her letters and novels with
a formal note. She received it in her cell in the women's prison. It read: "The
Private Secretary is returning the typed manuscripts which Madame A. has
been good enough to send, as it is contrary to Their Majesties' rule to accept
presents from those with whom they are not personally acquainted."[31]

5
. . . .

In Praise of Paranoia

*A*t the Hôpital Sainte-Anne Lacan spent a year doing all he could to build up a case of self-punishment paranoia, though this was closer to his own theoretical preoccupations than to Marguerite Pantaine's true situation. Marguerite, whose attempt at murder had failed, did present real signs of paranoia, and she was undoubtedly suffering simultaneously from persecution mania, megalomania, and mystical delusion. But there is nothing to show that her paranoia was as structured and organized as Lacan maintains. Even so he managed to hand down to posterity a case history that came to contain more truth than just the fate of Marguerite herself, a woman whose real name was swallowed up in the anonymity of a psychiatric ward and whose individual identity was long to remain in oblivion.

In his dealings with her, Lacan moved freely from clinical psychiatry to sociological research, and from psychological investigation to medical examination, without trying to listen to any truths other than those that confirmed his own hypotheses. He concealed the patient's real identity under the name of Aimée, a character in *Le Détracteur*, one of the novels Marguerite had tried in vain to publish. He said she worked for the railways, and he used initials when referring to people and places in her life. He also modified certain events in her story to such an extent that it is still difficult even now to distinguish between intentional distortions and genuine mistakes. He asked his friend Guillaume de Tarde, son of a well-known sociologist, to do a graphological analysis of the patient's handwriting. De Tarde's report mentioned indications of artistic leanings, culture, infantilism, anxiety, and an exaggerated tendency to insist on one's rights. But not for a moment did it mention psychosis.[1]

Lacan put forward five factors to be taken into account in defining paranoia: personality, psychogenic factors, process, discordance, and parallelism. Though he didn't actually cite Georges Politzer, he made use of his work on concrete psychology, in particular *La Critique des fondements de la psychologie* (Critique of the foundations of psychology), published in 1928.[2] But it was from Ramon Fernandez that Lacan borrowed the term *personality*,[3] which he held to be influenced by three things: *biographical development*, meaning the way subjects reacted to their own experience; *self-concept*, meaning the way they brought images of themselves into their consciousness; and *tension of social relations*, meaning their impressions of how they affected other people.[4]

With this definition Lacan introduced, as Freud had done before him, a characteristic idea that was to recur throughout his intellectual career. In 1932 he saw the subject as simply the sum of conscious and unconscious representations brought into play dialectically in relationship with other people and with society in general; in other words he was presenting the subject in terms of psychiatric phenomenology. As for personality, it had a special organization that acted as a corrective to the phenomenological aspect. Lacan called this organization *psychogeny*, referring to Henri Ey's critical work on mental automatism. Lacan deliberately used the term *psychogeny* rather than *psychogenesis* because it was further away from constitutionalism. It didn't involve any organogenesis or imply any static functioning, and it did incorporate the idea of dynamism.

Three conditions were necessary to make a symptom "psychogenic": the *causal event* had to be determined in terms of the history of the subject; the *symptom* itself had to reflect a state in the psychical history of the subject; and the *treatment* had to depend on a modification of the subject's life situation. Without rejecting organic causality altogether, Lacan emphasized that it fell outside the sphere of psychogeny. He was thus simultaneously challenging three other hypotheses: the theory, put forward by Sérieux and Capgras, according to which there was a *core* or *kernel* of conviction in insanity; Clérambault's theory on the syndrome of mental automatism; and Ernest Dupré's theory on the four cardinal signs of paranoid construction. According to Lacan, the etiology of paranoia and of psychosis in general was related to the concrete history of the subject's relations with the world, even when symptoms of organic origin were also involved.

This approach derived from the work of Eugène Minkowski, whom Lacan quoted with admiration. Minkowski, a founder member of the Evolution psychiatrique (EP; Psychiatric Evolution) group, had introduced the phenomenological ideas of Edmund Husserl and Ludwig Binswanger into postwar French psychiatry.[5] As early as 1923, when dealing with a case of melancholia, Minkowski had invoked a comprehensive theory of mental illness centered on the existential history of the subject in his relation with time, space, and other people and making use of a notion about change in these relationships that conceived of structure as dynamic rather than static.

But Lacan invoked this terminology only to reject it at once in favor of that of Karl Jaspers, from whom he borrowed the notion of *process*. The French translation of *General Psychopathology* had caused a great stir when it appeared in 1928. Paul Nizan and Jean-Paul Sartre, both students at the time at the Ecole normale supérieure (ENS) in the rue d'Ulm, had helped in the preparation of the French text.[6]

In this major work, first published in Berlin in 1913, Jaspers showed how psychiatric thought could be organized on the basis of clinical differentiation between psychoses. To this end he made a distinction between *practices of meaning* and *sciences of causation*. The former belonged to the realm of mere comprehension (*verstehen*), the latter to that of the explicable (*Erklärung*). In the case of comprehension, each state depends on the preceding state: a lover reacts by becoming jealous if he is deceived; a student is miserable when he fails his examination and happy if he passes. But in the case of the explicable there is an element of *incomprehensibility*. And in order to understand it one must resort to a logic different from that of reaction to fact. The voices heard by someone suffering from hallucinations, the persecutions imagined by a paranoid person, belong to the realm of the explicable because of a causal concatenation. Hence the idea of *process*, which implies a change in the life of the psyche and falls outside the comprehensional relation when it gives a rational account of the nonmeaning characteristic of delusion.

It is easy to imagine how helpful Lacan found such a notion in constructing a science of personality. The idea allowed him to assign more importance to a formal logic of causality than to a mere comprehension of meaning. But, as François Leguil has observed, Lacan was putting forward a "biased application" of Jaspers's work.[7] Having already absorbed the main principles of Freud's discoveries, Lacan didn't need to see the comprehensible and the explicable as distinct: he knew they were hand in glove with one another. That is why he worked out the theory of the three causes, which, while not strictly Freudian, was still very different from Jaspers. At all events, it contradicted the idea of dichotomy. I shall come back to this later.

It remains to be determined why Lacan was so zealous in invoking other men's works and claiming to base his own arguments on them, when in reality he was departing from their teachings, leaving behind mere skeletons.

The fact is that Lacan treated Jaspers just as he treated most of the authors by whom he was influenced. Every conceptual borrowing, every reference to an idea, every glance at a theory served only to make him distance himself and act simultaneously as destroyer of old values, heir to a long and venerable tradition, and solitary pioneer of new knowledge. As elusive as a phoenix, he was forever playing off classicism against modernism, subversion against ancestor worship. Then he would transform himself into an opponent of his own theories. And all this was conveyed by means of a baroque style in which a dialectic between presence and absence alternated with a logic of space and motion.

Lacan's fascination with Marguerite was also like a game of hide-and-seek. He came of a long line of drapers, vinegar merchants, and grocery salesmen, but he had refused to go into trade, dreaming instead of intellectual power and glory. With him the will to succeed was the most important signifier in a Bovary-like desire for a change of identity. Marguerite was in a way his double, less well off and closer to the soil than he was, but descended from the same broad mass of the French people, *la France profonde*. She too aspired to fame and intellectual success. And so, though in 1931 Lacan had been denouncing males who were paranoid and consigning them to the hell of insanity, a year later he was performing a turnabout because of a lonely self-educated woman whose fate might have been his if instead of pursuing a career in medicine he had lapsed into wandering and delusion. It was probably necessary that Lacan's paranoid patient be a woman for him to be able to see, in the mirror she held out to him, a reverse image of his own family universe: a normal enough universe, but one in which the extravagances of madness might exist for years disguised as ordinary love. Lacan was thinking of his brother's sequestered life as well as Aimée's criminal passion when he wrote the following lines:

Modern society leaves the individual in a cruel state of moral isolation, one especially painful in regard to occupations so indeterminate and ambiguous that they themselves may be a source of permanent internal conflict. Others besides myself have emphasized the extent to which the ranks of paranoia are swelled by those unjustly denigrated as inferior or limited—schoolmasters and schoolmistresses, governesses, women employed in minor intellectual activities, self-educated people of all kinds. . . . That's why it seems to me this type of subject should greatly benefit from being incorporated, according to his individual abilities, into some kind of religious community. Here, in addition to other advantages, he would experience a disciplined satisfaction of his own self-punishing tendencies. If this ideal solution is not available, any community would serve the purpose so long as to some extent it fulfilled the same conditions: the army, for instance; any militant political or social grouping; or some association devoted to good works, philosophy, or moral uplift. It is well known, moreover, that such kinds of social outgoing afford people with repressed homosexual tendencies a satisfaction that is all the greater because it is sublimated and so less likely to lead to any conscious revelation.[8]

Lacan's exposition of Aimée's case served both as an illustration to the first part of his thesis and as the hub around which his arguments revolved. In dealing with it, he was leaving the realm of psychiatry for that of psychoanalysis. Henceforward he would borrow clinical concepts from Freud and his disciples while looking to philosophy for the theoretical infrastructure of his work. He demonstrated first of all how the unconscious meaning of the paranoid theme was to be seen in a *délire à deux* mechanism in which the elder sister stood for the mother, and then how the onset of Marguerite's paranoia coincided with the loss of her first child; he also showed that the patient's erotomania was linked to an element of homosexuality.

On the one hand Marguerite was attracted by famous women because they represented her ego-ideal; on the other hand she fell in love with the Prince of Wales both to confirm her rejection of homosexual relationships and to obscure the drives that impelled her toward her own sex. By striking at the actress she was striking at her own ideal: "But," wrote Lacan, "the object she strikes has a purely symbolic value, and the act brings her no relief. Nonetheless, by the blow that rendered her guilty in the eyes of the law, Aimée has also struck at herself, and this brings her the satisfaction of fulfilled desire, and the delusion, having become superfluous, disappears. It seems to me that the nature of the cure reveals the nature of the disease."[9] If Aimée struck herself and thus brought about her own punishment, it was because she was transforming a paranoid demand for satisfaction into a *self-punishment* paranoia. And Lacan regarded this mechanism as a genuine prototype, so much so that he wanted to add "a new entity" to "the already copious nosology of psychiatry."[10]

Applying this approach to Marguerite's case, Lacan took up again the theory of the three causes. In his view, the *efficient* cause of Aimée's psychosis resided in the moral conflict with her sister. This determined the structure and permanence of the symptom and manifested itself in a fixation of the personality at the sibling complex stage. Added to this were the *occasional* or immediate cause, which brought about a change in the organization of the subject, and the *specific* cause, which was the concrete and reactive tendency. In Aimée's case, the latter was a drive toward self-punishment. With this theory of three causes, Lacan rejected any idea that psychosis might have a single origin. On the contrary, he reinforced the notion of multiple determination.[11]

While an illness has no single cause, it has no single essence either, since its nature is shown by the nature of its cure. In other words, madness arises out of a life, and thus out of a materialist nexus—and a materialist nexus whose materialism is a "historical materialism," at that. Thus Lacan accorded special importance to the history of the personality: in this context, paranoia emerged as a reorganization of the personality, a transformation of the ego, a *hiatus* between a prior situation and the onset of madness. As for the self-punishment paranoia, one of its distinctive features was that it was curable. And if this particular form of psychosis could be cured, why not revive the great idea that madness itself could be both cured and prevented? (This was a notion put forward just before the French Revolution by Philippe Pinel but abandoned by his successors as asylums multiplied and belief grew in the organic origins of mental illness.)

But Lacan did not move in this direction. He was hostile to the Encyclopedists and the spirit of the Enlightenment and never advocated the virtues of moral treatment. He thought madness was inscribed in the heart of man like a web made up of many threads or causes, but he didn't believe it contained a vestige of reason that might always manage to gain some ground over folly. He approached the continent of madness from the direction of the Freudian revolution and the primacy of the unconscious. And just as the Freudian revolution had solved the vexed question of the relation between freedom and alienation—man is free, but he is not master in his own house—so Lacan rejected en masse the philosophical prejudices that, as he saw it, dominated the history of medicine. He dismissed with equal vehemence both *vitalism*, which posited a "vital" principle connecting the body and the soul, and *mechanism*, which reduced life to a mere interplay between moving forces. For the true founder of psychiatric observation, Lacan looked back beyond Pinel, Aesculapius, Galen, and especially Esquirol, whom he regarded as the "wicked stepfather" of psychiatry, to Hippocrates.[12]

To inflict on all psychologists and organicists the unkindest cut of all, he didn't hesitate to leap across twenty-three centuries and proclaim himself the direct and legitimate heir to the "god" of medicine—preferably the Greek version of the divinity. But being obliged to descend from the heights of Olympus into the ordinary world below, he recommended that treatment be adapted to the nature of the illness. He thereby wisely abandoned the repressive attitude he had adopted when he was still a disciple of Clérambault and instead sang the praises of psychoanalytic therapy, prophylaxis, and tolerance. In short, in spite of himself he was joining the main current of Enlightenment alienism and dynamic psychiatry, represented in France by the school of Claude and the founders of the EP and the SPP.

But Lacan took up his position on a different epistemological terrain. Before him, the first generation of French psychiatrists and psychoanalysts had introduced the teachings of Freud into a psychiatry based on a recasting of the heredity-and-degeneration theory; it was by absorbing the new into the old that the status quo was modified. Now, for the first time in the history of the French movement, Lacan inverted the process and produced a novel confrontation between dynamism and Freudianism: a close encounter of the second kind.[13] Not only did he refuse to incorporate psychoanalysis into psychiatry; he also showed the absolute necessity of putting the Freudian unconscious first in any nosography derived from psychiatry.

Furthermore, he didn't hesitate to value German philosophical and psychiatric thinking above its French counterparts. He thus became the

spokesperson for those of his contemporaries who believed that the chauvinism of their elders, together with their insistence on a mythical "Latin"
and "classical" background, needed to be replaced by a genuinely scientific
approach. Lacan's antichauvinism, combined with his stress on the primary
importance of the Freudian unconscious, brought him close to the position
of the surrealists vis-à-vis Freud's doctrines. Lacan was thus the first of the
second generation of French psychiatrists and psychoanalysts to effect a synthesis between the two main paths by which Freud's thought had penetrated
France.

And yet even while he was inaugurating the reversal that was to turn him
into a founding father, Lacan was using a Freudian terminology that conformed to the prevailing orthodoxy: "The therapeutic problem regarding
psychosis," he wrote, "seems to me to make a *psychoanalysis of the ego* more
necessary than a psychology of the unconscious; in other words, it is likely
to find technical solutions in a better study of the subject's *resistances* and a
new analysis of their *manipulation.* We do not blame a technology that is still
in its infancy for not having found these solutions before: we have no right
to do so, given our own profound inability to suggest any other controlled
psychotherapy."[14]

If Lacan accorded such primary importance to resistances and the analysis of the ego, as against the exploration of the unconscious, it was because
at this stage he still shared an idea of Freudianism based on one particular
reading of the theory of the unconscious. Two interpretations were possible
after 1920: one aimed at reviving the idea that unconscious determination
exercised supreme power over the subject (the id being "stronger" than the
ego), while the other ascribed the most important influence to the ego. But
during the period between the two world wars the second interpretation
came to prevail within the IPA because it favored the so-called standard
techniques thought necessary in the training of psychoanalysts.[15] And it was
through this second interpretation that Lacan discovered psychoanalytic
practice, if not Freud's teaching itself.

So there was a disparity between the theoretical advance Lacan was making in knowledge of psychiatry and the terminology he was using to think
it through. It was as if at this period Lacan couldn't match his Freudian revision of the field of psychiatry with an adequate reading of Freud's work on
the unconscious. His entering into analysis with Loewenstein in June 1932
probably had something to do with this discrepancy.

Be that as it may, Lacan was very uneasy about his inability to give Aimée
the full Freudian treatment: "I should like to note, in conclusion," he wrote,
"that if I did not subject my patient to psychoanalysis, the omission, which
was not made voluntarily on my part, circumscribes both the scope and the
value of my work."[16] Lacan had begun to take an interest in Marguerite in

June 1931, a year before he began his own analysis. The fact that he felt it
necessary to mention the omission and to stress that he was not responsible
for it shows how he situated his thesis in the evolution of his own development: it is *still* a work of psychiatry as well as being *already* a psychoanalytic
text. We know now, thanks to the afterword Didier Anzieu wrote for Jean
Allouch's book on the story of Marguerite, that it was she who declined to
be analyzed by Lacan. "When he examined her in the course of a series of
interviews," writes Anzieu, "Lacan was not yet trained as a psychoanalyst and
made no attempt at psychotherapy, a kind of treatment that in any case she
would have refused: she often told my wife and myself that she found Lacan
too attractive and too much of a clown to be trusted."[17]

6

......

Reading Spinoza

On the first page of his thesis, Lacan made a point of quoting proposition 57 from book three of Spinoza's *Ethics*: "*Quilibet unius cujusque individui affectus ab affectu alterius tantum discrepat, quantum essentia unius ab essentia alterius differt.*" At the end of the thesis he returned to this quotation, giving his own translation and comments. "It's as if," writes Robert Misrahi, "the whole of Lacan's thesis were placed under the aegis of Spinoza, and as if the theory that Lacan was putting forward was inspired by the same spirit as the work of Spinoza himself."[1] And Lacan did in fact present Spinoza's philosophy as the only one capable of accounting for a science of personality, which is why he invoked the idea of *parallelism*, mentioned in book two of the *Ethics*: "The order and sequence of ideas is the same as the order and sequence of things . . . and so, whether we conceive of Nature as a manifestation of Space, or of Thought, or of anything else, we shall discover in it a single order or, in other words, a single concatenation of causes: i.e., the same things following on from one another." Was Lacan remembering the diagrams and colored arrows he pinned up on the walls of his bedroom in the apartment on the boulevard Beaumarchais?

In 1932 Spinoza's idea helped him to fight another conception of parallelism, one which had prevailed in France since Hippolyte Taine (1823–1893) published his researches on the mind (*De l'intelligence*, 1870, 2 vols.) and throughout the long saga of the heredity-and-degeneracy school. To explain the union of soul and body, Spinoza advanced the idea that parallelism can only really exist if there is not merely a correspondence between bodies and somatic processes but also a *union* between the mental and the physical, in a relationship similar to that of *translation*. This true parallelism had nothing to do with the notion of psychophysical parallelism prevailing in the field of psychiatry that posited a relationship of determination between physical phenomena and psychic facts. This latter parallelism led to a conception of personality in terms of either mental automatism (hereditarism, constitutionalism) or dualism (phenomenology). In Lacan's view, personality was not "parallel to neurotaxic processes, nor even just to the individual's somatic processes as a whole, but to a *total made up of the individual and his or her own environment*. This concept of parallelism must moreover be recognized as the only one worthy of the name, if we remember that this was its original form and that it was first given expression in the teachings of Spinoza."[2]

So, with regard to proposition 7 in book two of the *Ethics*, Lacan thought of personality as the attribute of a unique substance: the existence of an individual seen in terms of a social existence made up of a complex web of different kinds of behavior. A mental phenomenon was just one factor among others.[3] So Lacan's Spinoza-derived idea in 1932 might be described negatively as neither phenomenological, nor ontological, nor constitutionalist. This idea opened the way to forms of monism, materialism, and historical anthropology that would be greeted with all the more enthusiasm by the younger generation of psychiatrists, together with the surrealists and the communists, because it saw paranoia—and madness in general—no longer as a phenomenon of deficiency, arising out of some anomaly, but just as a difference or *discordance* in comparison with normal personality.[4]

The term *discordance*, introduced into France by the great alienist Philippe Chaslin, denoted a disharmony between symptoms that seemed independent of one another until they were brought together in a recognized case of dementia. In this category Chaslin included hebephrenia, paranoid dementia, and discordant verbal dementia.[5] The word *discordant* translated the notions of *splitting* and *dissociation* that were to be found at that time in German terminology, in Bleuler on the one hand and in Freud on the other. It was this notion that lay behind the invention of the word *schizophrenia* in 1911. *Schizein*, in Greek, means to split, rupture, or break; in German, dissociation is translated as *Spaltung*. Late-nineteenth-century research had already addressed the problem posed by the coexistence within the psyche of two groups of phenomena, or two personalities, living together but ignorant of one another: hence the ideas of dual consciousness, split personality, and a sense of strangeness.

On this basis, psychoanalytic and psychiatric concepts were constructed in parallel, sometimes giving rise to great confusion. In Bleuler's view, *Spaltung* was a disturbance in the associations governing the flow of thought: hence the term *schizophrenia* to denote the first appearance of the disturbance. The primary symptom was a direct expression of the morbid process itself, while the secondary symptom was the sick mind's reaction to the disorder. *Zerspaltung* denoted not merely a disturbance but a real disintegration of the personality. Both in Bleuler's terminology and in the French ideas of dissociation or *discordance*, psychosis originated in a deficit or lack.

Freud's position was quite different. He put forward the term *Ichspaltung* (splitting of the ego) to designate an intrapsychic division by which the subject was separated from part of his or her own representations. This discarded the ideas of deficit and duality and put in their place a "topographical" theory of the mind. From 1920 on, the concept changed under the impact of a second topography. *Ichspaltung* was to be found not only in psychosis but also in neurosis and perversion. It reflected the coexistence of two positions of the ego, one that takes account of reality and another producing a new reality just as "true" as the first.[6]

Lacan provided a key to his interpretation of Spinoza when, in a coda, he made his own translation of proposition 57 of book three of the *Ethics*, which he had used as an epigraph to his thesis. Where Spinoza had written *discrepat*, Lacan introduced the notion of *discordance*: "Any affection in any individual exhibits as much discordance with an affection in another individual as the essence of the one individual differs from the essence of the other."[7] Lacan was here departing from Charles Appuhn's 1906 translation of the passage in question, still current in 1932 though it was revised in 1934 after Carl Gebhard produced a new edition of the Latin text. Spinoza himself had used two words—*discrepat* (depart) and *differt* (differ), where Appuhn used only one. Hence Appuhn's translation, which may be translated into English as: "Any affection in each individual differs from another as much as the essence of one [affection] differs from the essence of another."[8]

Lacan corrected Appuhn in order to bring out more clearly a distinction made by Spinoza in the original. But he didn't choose the word *discordance* by chance. What he was really doing was borrowing the word from psychiatry, modifying its meaning, and then reintroducing it into a context where the idea of madness had been recast in terms of parallelism: "What I mean by this is that there is a *discordance* between the *determining conflicts*, the *intentional symptoms*, and the *impulse reactions* of a psychosis on the one hand and on the other hand the *comprehensional relations* defining the development, the conceptual structures, and the social tensions of a normal personality—a discordance the proportions of which are determined by the history of the subject's affections."[9] In other words, both the affections known as "pathological" and the affections known as "normal" are part of one same essence that defines their discordance. There isn't a "pathos" for some of them and a norm for the others. And discordance, as well as marking the contrast between a psychotic individual and a normal personality, can also be found throughout a subject, defining the relationship between his or her ordinary personality and a psychotic incident. Lacan was thus taking over the notion of discordance from Spinoza and approximating it to Freud's concept of *Ichspaltung*.

Appuhn, in his French version of the *Ethics*, had shrunk from using the word *affect* to translate the Latin *affectus* because there was no such word in

French. Nor did he wish to use an equivalent of the German *Affekt*. So he translated *affectus* by *affection*. In 1932 it didn't occur to Lacan to correct Appuhn, though he might well have followed Freud and made use of the term *affect*, which by then had already been introduced into psychoanalytic terminology to denote either an emotional effect or the subjective expression of a quantity of pulsional energy. So here again we see that Lacan hadn't yet mastered the conceptual vocabulary of psychoanalysis, even though he had already perceived the essence of Freud's discoveries themselves. It would take him twenty years to bring his theoretical revision of Freudianism as a whole and his reinterpretation of Freud's concepts into line with one another.

It should be noted in passing that it was not until 1988 that the philosopher Bernard Patraut produced a French translation of the *Ethics* that took into account both Freud's *Affekt* and Lacan's *discord*. This gives a new version of proposition 57 of book three: "Any affect of each individual exhibits as much discordance with the affect of another as the essence of the one differs from the essence of the other."[10]

The way Lacan used Spinoza's philosophy is a valuable pointer to his general approach to other people's writings. In the case of the *Ethics* he produces a commentary that, instead of merely following the concepts contained in the original, "translates" them, i.e., gives them a new meaning. Lacan had already shown a preference for a system that assimilated other elements rather than distancing itself from them. Instead of basing himself on or deciphering a model, he gave it a meaning of his own and treated that meaning as the only one possible. His view was that every text contains a truth waiting for a *single* interpretation. In adopting this attitude he was challenging any method of approaching the history of science that was based on a merely critical approach, as well as any historical interpretation of texts. He didn't believe a body of work could develop over time into the sum of all its possible interpretations. On the contrary, he thought any interpretation or explanation of a text that didn't correspond to its presumed truth should be dismissed as aberration or error. When confronted with a text he assumed the position of a layer-down of the law, the authorized translator of truth itself. The mode of knowledge he used in his textual commentaries *simulated* the mode of knowledge typical of paranoia. So it's not surprising that, in the full flush of surrealism, he contrived to rehabilitate paranoia as a "discordant" equivalent of so-called normal personality.

In his 1931 study of schizophrenia, Lacan had dealt with experiences relating to the Immaculate Conception, though he still made use of the classic notion of automatism. But in the same year his encounter with Dali began to have its effect. It soon led him to reject automatism and place the full anthropological significance of madness at the center of the human mind. Thus every so often the thesis on paranoia that he completed in the

autumn of 1932 reveals a tendency to appropriate the positions of the surrealists. But he didn't breathe a word in avowal of this major influence. He
was careful not to quote the relevant sources, never even mentioned any of
the great surrealist texts that lay behind his own, and made no reference to
Dali, Breton, or Eluard. He was anxious about his career and didn't want to
offend either his masters in psychiatry, who rejected the literary avant-garde,
or the supporters of orthodox Freudianism, of whom he was still a disciple.
But he had guessed wrong: the first people to do him honor were those
whose importance to himself he had disguised, and the first people to decry
him were those he had tried to please.

As an intern at the Hôpital Sainte-Anne, Lacan lived in a modest furnished
apartment, ugly and dark, on the ground floor of a block in the rue de la
Pompe, a stone's throw from the Bois de Boulogne. At this period he was the
lover of Marie-Thérèse Bergerot, an austere widow fifteen years his senior.
With her he discovered Plato and went on several study trips. In 1928 he
took her to see the tombs of the Saadi dynasty in Morocco and scrupulously
noted down the complicated genealogies. This was the first sign of a strong
hankering for the East that would later take him to Egypt and Japan.[11]

Some time around 1929 Lacan fell in love with Olesia Sienkiewicz, the
second wife of his friend Pierre Drieu la Rochelle, who had just left her for
the brilliant Victoria Ocampo. Olesia, born in 1904, was the daughter of a
Catholic banker of Polish origins.[12] Her grandmother had married Hetzel,
the famous publisher of Jules Verne's illustrated novels; her godmother had
been the wife of Alexandre Dumas the younger, author of *The Lady of the
Camellias*. Olesia and her two sisters had been brought up in a sensitive and
elegant environment, where she divided her time between the family apartment in the fashionable Plaine-Marceau in Paris, the château de Dumas in
Marly, just outside the capital, and a house at Bellevue, near Meudon, inherited from Hetzel.

Drieu had been smitten by Olesia's mischievous wit and androgynous
appearance; she aroused strong homosexual feelings in him.[13] She herself,
shattered by an unhappy love affair, had forsworn all physical relations with
men—until the day she succumbed to the charm of Drieu, the great seducer.

For several months Drieu was very happy in his second marriage. Olesia
helped him, listened to him for hours on end, and typed his manuscripts.[14]
He felt so guilty when the marriage broke up that he was delighted to learn
that his friend Lacan was courting Olesia. Lacan wrote him long, obscure
letters setting out the reasons for his passion. Right from the beginning of
the affair, which lasted until the autumn of 1933, Lacan shrouded himself in
a typical "double life" atmosphere of secrets and clandestinity. Though officially he was living in the rue de la Pompe, he went on putting his parents'

Boulogne-sur-Seine address on his visiting cards. But most of the time he slept in the hospital, where Olesia used to join him. At the same time he still carried on a relationship with Marie-Thérèse that only his brother really knew about.

Lacan soon swept Olesia up into a wild passion that took them from Paris to Madrid, from Corsica to the coast of Normandy. Though he hadn't yet learned to drive, he already adored cars and loved making impromptu trips with his young friend, motoring at top speed around France. Together they visited the Ile-aux-Moines in Brittany and Mont-Saint-Michel between Brittany and Normandy; then they took a plane to Ajaccio and toured Corsica.

In June 1932 Lacan asked Olesia to type his thesis. He got into the habit of hurrying up the stairs several times a week to the charming attic in the rue Garancière into which she had moved in February, bringing her the latest batch of pages he'd written out rapidly in his own dreary bachelor apartment. He finished the manuscript on October 7; Olesia completed the typescript; and Lacan handed it over to Le François, a publisher who specialized in medical books. Marie-Thérèse Bergerot made a large contribution to the cost of printing the thesis, which was dedicated to "M. T. B." To this symbolic figure in his own private romantic serial, Lacan also addressed a line in Greek: "Without whose help I would not have become what I am."

It was on a November afternoon in the Faculty of Medicine that Lacan defended his thesis and obtained his medical doctorate. The examination, which lasted an hour, ran its course without incident. Lacan faced a jury directed by Henri Claude; behind the candidate sat an audience of about eighty spectators, including both Olesia and Marie-Thérèse. They'd never met, and neither knew the other was there. Both, however, were familiar with Lacan's friends from Sainte-Anne, who had come to see how their comrade, who represented the avant-garde of the new psychiatry, would acquit himself. They had often seen Olesia come round to the interns' common room in the evening; they called her "Cold Water," an allusion to a play by Drieu la Rochelle, produced by Louis Jouvet, with Pierre Renoir and Valentine Tessier in the cast. Lacan's friends called Marie-Thérèse "the Princess." She never slept at the hospital but would sometimes send in a bottle of milk to help her protégé through a difficult morning. The examination proceeded amid whispering and anxiety, like the performance of a play where not only were women dressed as men and servants disguised as their masters but even the members of the audience seemed not to recognize one another.[15] The only participant missing was Marguerite Pantaine.

Lacan remembered the occasion with distaste. In a letter to Olesia written in August 1933 he was already complaining about the precious years he had been forced to waste studying medicine. After the war, at a conference at Bonneval, he hit out retrospectively at a member of the jury whom he accused of trying to put him down. Later still, when the thesis was out of print and unobtainable, he was reluctant to have it reissued. This growing attitude of rejection is understandable when one realizes how different Lacan's subsequent development was from what had been suggested in his thesis. Not only did he fail to produce any science of personality, but he never added any Lacanian type of self-punishment to the nosology of psychiatry, either. Lacan's career was not to be in a psychiatry based on psychoanalysis. And so far did he come to forget that his thesis was his first venture into the field of Freudianism that he dated it 1936.[16]

At the time, it was ignored by the first generation of French psychoanalysis: not a single review appeared in the *RFP*. Even Edouard Pichon made no reference to it. Lacan was furious. But he was so sure his entry into the world of psychoanalysis had been a success that he sent a copy of his thesis to Freud himself, showing that he sought recognition from the master no matter how reticent his French disciples might be. But Lacan was in for a dreadful disappointment. From Vienna, in January 1933, came the laconic reply: "Thank you for sending your thesis." The great man hadn't even deigned to open the manuscript that the young stranger had commended to him, no doubt with great ardor. As Lacan's cover letter had been headed with his official address in Boulogne-sur-Seine, followed by his real one in the rue de la Pompe, Freud not unnaturally solved the problem by putting both addresses on his answering postcard.[17]

The world of psychiatry was the first to react, in the person of Lacan's loyal comrade Henri Ey, who even before the thesis was published wrote a generous article in *L'Encéphale* (The encephalon, i.e., the brain): "It is with some hesitation," he wrote, "that I undertake to examine a work whose 'inner history,' and the effort that went into its creation, are known to me through a friendship based on a shared vision of the problems of psychiatry, though not necessarily of their solutions. But friendship will not make my analysis any less impartial. On the contrary, my knowledge of the author helps me to a better understanding of a thesis long meditated and allows me to bring out the vividness and solidity of an argument cast in a form so abstract and difficult, because so condensed and complex, that it might otherwise deter some readers."[18]

But in 1933 four well-known literary figures helped to establish Lacan as the leader of a future French school of psychoanalysis capable of breaking away from the chauvinistic and conservative ideals of the older generation. He was thus thrust on to the political stage of the intellectual Far Left, a mixture of orthodox communists, dissidents, and surrealists, all in conflict among themselves over their varying commitment to Marxism. And so this ardent admirer of Maurras and of the novels of Léon Bloy, a man hitherto uninterested in political engagement, found himself being regarded as the champion of a *materialistic* theory of mental illness.

The first comment came from Paul Nizan, in an issue of *L'Humanité*, the communist newspaper, published on February 10, 1933: "This is a thesis presented for a medical doctorate," he wrote, "and as such may seem rather unsuitable for comment here. But it is right to draw attention to a book that, against the main streams of official science and despite the precautions imposed on the author of an academic thesis, reflects the definite and conscious influence of dialectical materialism. Dr. Lacan has not yet clarified all his theoretical positions, but he does react against the various idealisms currently corrupting all research in psychology and psychiatry. Materialism will triumph over the ignorance of the learned professors and emerge as the true method of scientific progress."[19]

In May 1933 it was René Crevel's turn to praise Lacan's thesis. He did so in an article in *Surréalisme au service de la Révolution*. Crevel, who was more involved than Nizan in the battle against official psychoanalysis, was torn between his membership in the Communist party, his own homosexuality, and his friendship for both Breton and Aragon, who were now enemies. But he also wanted to get his own back on traditional treatment. He had been analyzed by René Allendy, of whom he had just published a vitriolic portrait in *Le Clavecin de Diderot* (Diderot's harpsichord), comparing him to the oafish père Ubu in Jarry's satirical farce *Ubu Roi* (1896) and describing him as a "pretty fellow with a beard and a very good opinion of himself." Crevel, regarding the old school of psychoanalysis as corrupt and steeped in bourgeois idealism, saw Lacan as the spokesperson of a new spirit: his "materialism," Crevel thought, made it possible to link together the individual and social aspects of every human being. For Crevel, materialism and concrete analysis were synonymous. But he was mainly interested in the sad fate of Aimée, about whom he wrote less coldly and clinically than Lacan himself. Crevel saw her as a rebel homosexual, a hysterical embodiment of the female proletariat: "Aimée doesn't loiter about or compromise. She makes straight for a wonderful convulsive state that is both appalled and appalling. But her impulses collide with a horribly uncomprehending mass. Her need for moral and intellectual sympathy has been thwarted at every turn. So she concluded she 'had to go to the men.'" After paying this handsome tribute to his own female double, Crevel went on to assert that Freud had made the mistake of rejecting communism, the USSR, and Marxist analysis, and this was why he had failed to revolutionize the world: "He is tired and clings to his mementos. We can forgive him for that. But where is the young psychoanalyst who is going to take over?"[20]

In June 1933, having already been hailed as the leader of a school that combined Freudianism and Marxism and as the harbinger of the coming revolution, Lacan was also saluted by Salvador Dali. In the first number of *Le Minotaure*, after going over some already familiar ideas, Dali went on to praise Lacan's thesis: "Because of it we can for the first time arrive at a complete and homogeneous idea of the subject, quite free of the mechanistic mire in which present-day psychiatry is stuck."[21] This view was shared by Jean Bernier, who wrote a well—researched article in *La Critique sociale* (Social criticism) setting Lacan's work in the context of the history of psychiatry.

Bernier was a writer, journalist, and sports lover belonging to the same intellectual generation as Breton and Aragon. He, like them, had gone through the horrors of the First World War and then set about confronting bourgeois society with a radical challenge. Together with Boris Souvarine, the first founder of the French Communist Party, he had come out in support of Trotsky at the thirteenth congress of the Soviet Communist Party in 1924. Two years later he met Colette Peignot, a woman so passionately committed to the cause of the revolution that although she had tuberculosis she went to live on a *kolkhoz*, or collective farm, among the poorest of poor peasants. From her passion for bolshevism she emerged a sick woman; from her love for Bernier she escaped through a suicide attempt: she tried to shoot herself, but the bullet just missed her heart. She had a stormy affair with Boris Pilniak in Leningrad. In Berlin she lived with Edward Trautner, master of scatology, sadist, and wife batterer.

In 1932 she met Boris Souvarine, and together they started *La Critique sociale*, the first important communist review to position itself to the left of communism, though without following any particular faction of the opposition. Colette Peignot and Boris Souvarine gathered around them a group of writers and former members of the French Communist Party that included Raymond Queneau, Jacques Baron, Michel Leiris, and Jean Piel. Georges Bataille, who had just ended his experiment with the review *Documents*, joined the group in 1931 and decided to attend Georges Dumas's presentations of patients at the Hôpital Sainte-Anne. It was against this background, where Marx and Freud were studied simultaneously, that Jean Bernier joined the team of *La Critique sociale*. He was a close friend of Drieu la Rochelle, and it was through Olesia Sienkiewicz that he met Lacan, at the time that the latter was publishing his thesis.[22]

Unlike Nizan, Dali, and Crevel, Bernier had some criticisms to offer.[23] Although he saw Lacan as a future master and agreed with most of his conclusions, he criticized him for the obscurity of his style, for not giving sufficient thought to Aimée's infantile sexuality, and for paying much too little attention to therapy. Bernier was expressing a "leftist" attitude to psychoanalysis and psychiatry, both of which he accused of neglecting the social dimension of psychosis and not properly denouncing the pathogenic effect on the individual of bourgeois society.[24]

7
. . . . . .

The Papin Sisters

The way the story of Aimée was received and commented on in French intellectual circles was to have some influence on the young Lacan's future development. Until his thesis was published, his main philosophical authority had been a form of phenomenology derived from Husserl and Jaspers. His own interpretation of Spinoza helped him construct his theory of personality. But from 1932 on he could look to a new philosophical horizon, the more so because the avant-garde had welcomed his thesis in the joint name of surrealism and communism, both of which, despite their differences, supported a "materialist" philosophy they claimed to have derived from the works of Hegel, Marx, and Freud.

Pointing to the extreme poverty of French philosophy as it was then, plunged deep in Bergsonian spiritualism, academic neo-Kantianism, or a Cartesianism diverted from its original inspiration, the materialist avant-garde liked to contrast this deplorable state of affairs with the splendor of German thought. They saw this as both Hegelian and Marxist but also enriched by the new gospel of certain great contemporaries: Husserl, of course, but also Nietszche and Heidegger, who had just (in 1926) published his famous *Sein und Zeit* (*Being and Time*).

Lacan, having thus been dubbed a materialist, accepted the mirror held up to him by the avant-garde. He abandoned his "Spinozan" theory of personality—while retaining Spinoza as his authority for a few other operations, renounced phenomenology as interpreted by psychiatry, and converted to a different Husserl and a Hegelian-Marxist materialism. But it would take him four years to come to grips, through the teaching of Kojève and Koyré, with Hegel's *Phenomenology of Mind* and Heidegger's philosophy.

Lacan's turning toward the new horizon could be seen in his first article for *Le Minotaure*, which dealt with the problem of style and the psychiatric conception of paranoid forms of experience. Although, as far as content was concerned, the article advanced the same points of view as Lacan had expressed in the Aimée case, he was now using a different terminology. In addition to a straight refutation of what its author considered a mistaken psychiatric tradition, the article showed a rebelliousness reflected in the use of a Marxist vocabulary: for the first time Lacan spoke of "theoretical revolution," "bourgeois civilization," "ideological superstructure," "needs," and "anthropology." In short, he had listened to the message transmitted by Nizan, Crevel, Dali, and Bernier.[1]

It was against this background that early in 1933 Lacan became interested in the famous crime of the Papin sisters, which staggered public, press, and intelligentsia alike, not only because of its social significance but also because it was so strange and puzzling.

On February 2, in the town of Le Mans in northwest France, Christine and Léa Papin, two maidservants of poor peasant stock, brought up in the local orphanage of the Good Shepherd, savagely murdered their employers, Madame Lancelin and her daughter, Geneviève. A power failure had prevented Christine from finishing the ironing; Mme Lancelin, who had been out, came home and scolded her, whereupon Christine attacked both her employers and called on her younger sister to join her in the carnage. They gouged their victims' eyes out and used kitchen utensils to hack up the bodies, scattering blood and brains everywhere. Then they bolted the front door, went upstairs, and huddled together in their bed to await the arrival of the police. They had taken off their bloodstained clothes and put on dressing gowns.

The crime was all the more shocking because the two young women had seemed to be model servants, well treated by their employers and content with their lot. But beneath the appearances of normality lurked some disturbing facts. The girls' father had been his elder daughter's lover; their grandfather had died an epileptic; one of their cousins had gone mad; and an uncle had hanged himself in his own barn. And some time before the murder, the maids had complained to the local authorities of being "persecuted."

Three psychiatrists called as expert witnesses examined the two young women, who had confessed to the killings. The experts pronounced them of sound mind and body and thus responsible for their actions. They were both charged with unpremeditated murder, for which one faced a death sentence and the other life imprisonment. After five months in prison, Christine suffered from fainting spells and hallucinations. She would try to gouge out her own eyes, spread her arms as though on a cross, and indulge in sexual exhibitionism. Sometimes she announced that in some future life she would be her sister's husband; at other times she said she saw her in a dream, hanging from a tree with her legs cut off. She resented being put in solitary confinement and having to wear a straitjacket. When asked why she had stripped Mlle Lancelin's clothes off, she said: "I was looking for something that would have made me stronger." Despite all this, one of the psychiatrists said she was malingering and should stand trial. But Benjamin Logre, another expert, came to the aid of the defense and, though he wasn't allowed to examine the sisters, diagnosed them as mentally abnormal and suffering from hysterical epilepsy, sexual perversion, and persecution mania.

On September 29, 1933, in the criminal court of the department of the Sarthe, a number of conflicting opinions confronted one another. According to the prosecution, the Papin sisters were bloodthirsty monsters devoid of all human feeling. For others, they were sacrificial victims on the altar of bourgeois cruelty. The surrealist writers Paul Eluard and Benjamin Péret invoked Lautréamont's demonic *Chants de Maldoror* (first published in 1868). Sartre denounced the hypocrisy of "respectable" society.

The lawyer representing the Lancelin family argued that the Papin sister *were* responsible for their actions and tried to persuade the court that the killings were "semipremeditated." A woman lawyer, Germaine Brière, cited Logre's diagnosis and maintained that the sisters were insane. As in other cases of this kind, the supporters of dynamic psychiatry were ranged against those who argued on grounds of heredity or constitution or said that the sisters were malingering. In the midst of the battle, the maids admitted they had had no grudge against their victims. This pointed to the hidden meaning of an act that they themselves didn't understand. Christine knelt down to receive the death sentence, soon afterward commuted to life imprisonment. A year later, again suffering from fits of delusion, she was sent to the mental hospital in Rennes, where she died three years later of vesanic cachexis: in a kind of paranoid self-punishment, she virtually starved herself to death for her own crimes. Léa went back to live with her mother after serving several years of her prison sentence.[2]

So here was a crime that fit in perfectly with the theory Lacan had put forward in 1932. It involved female sexuality, *délire à deux*, apparently unmotivated murder, social tension, paranoia, and self-punishment. For this reason Lacan, while paying tribute to Benjamin Logre's courage, began by dismissing the diagnosis of hysterical epilepsy. Then he set out to show that only paranoia could explain the mystery of the sisters' act. The episode of insanity seemed to arise out of a seemingly everyday incident: a power failure. But this incident might well have had an unconscious significance for the Papin sisters. Lacan suggested it stood for the silence that had long existed between the mistresses and the maids: no current could flow between the employers and their servants because they didn't speak to one another. Thus the crime triggered by the power failure was a violent acting out of a *non-*

dit: something unspoken, of whose meaning the chief actors in the drama were unaware.

If Aimée had attacked the actress who, according to Lacan, represented Aimée's own ego-ideal, the Papin sisters had murdered the Lancelin women for similar reasons. The real motive for the crime was not class hatred but the paranoid structure through which the murderer struck at the ideal of the master within herself. Lacan's analysis was the same for the unsuccessful murder attempted by Marguerite and for the successful murder carried out by the Papin sisters: his diagnosis in both cases was paranoia and self-punishment. But he was well aware that the two cases were different. The case of the maids involved neither Bovaryism nor erotomania, nor was it a matter of a woman who was unknown attacking another who was well known: it concerned an act of brutal slaughter that took place between ordinary women, who had known one another for years, in the intimacy of an ordinary home. The Le Mans crime could only end in out-and-out massacre, in a total annihilation of being. That was what made it so astonishing. It seemed to reflect the social reality of class hatred, but in fact it reflected another reality: that of paranoid alienation. While the story of Marguerite Pantaine might have come straight out of the great tradition of the French nineteenth-century novel, that of the Papin sisters seemed to hark back to Greek tragedy, while at the same time it illustrated the ferocity of a world torn by rising social, racial, and national hatreds. Aimée was a Flaubert character ending her life in a melodrama by Paul Benoit. Christine was a heroine of the house of Atreus who had strayed into the fields and woods of northern France and thence been catapulted into the modern world of class struggle and the craving to exterminate one's fellowmen.

The difference between the two stories was reflected in Lacan's way of writing about them. As a background to the Le Mans murders he sketched out a vast theater of cruelty going back to time immemorial, the time of myth, legend, and the unconscious. But another reason for the change of style was Lacan's introduction of a new philosophical dimension. Before the Aimée case he had never studied the works of Hegel. Hegel's name was not mentioned in the 1932 thesis, in which the phenomenological element was derived from psychiatry and not from any first-hand reading of Hegel, Husserl, or Heidegger.

But after October or November of 1933, when Alexandre Kojève's seminar began, Lacan, though he wasn't yet actually attending the class, began to discover "genuine" Hegelian phenomenology, either through Koyré's articles or through other sources. And the effect of this can be seen in Lacan's article on the Papin sisters, where the crime was interpreted in terms of a master-slave dialectic typical of the struggle between minds or consciousnesses. Madness itself was defined in terms of the idea of "*conscience enchaînée*" (mind or consciousness bound, as in *Prometheus Bound*): mental alienation had become alienated "consciousness."[3]

So, between the two crimes, that of Marguerite and that of Christine, Lacan had moved from a Spinozan monism according to which he saw personality as a totality including both the normal and the pathological to a Hegelian monism that led him to abandon the idea of personality in favor of the notion of self-consciousness. But Lacan's encounter with Hegelian philosophy didn't really produce its full effects until 1936—that is, until after he had begun his analysis with Loewenstein and started attending Kojève's seminar.

PART III

Man's Estate

1. In the middle of the front row, Ludovic Dessaux, with his son Paul on his right and his sons Charles and Marcel on his left. (Source: Rights reserved)

2. The Dessaux factory at the beginning of the twentieth century. (Source: Rights reserved)

I

3. The Lacan family
in around 1915:
Alfred, Emilie,
Madeleine, Jacques,
Marc-Françoisc.
(Source: Madeleine
Lacan-Houlon)

4. Jacques Lacan in
the common room at
the Hôtel-Dieu,
1928 (detail).
(Source: Pierre
Morel collection)

5. Sylvain Blondin in 1932. (Source: Sibylle Lacan)

7. Marie-Louise Lacan and his daughter
Caroline in around 1939. (Source: Cyril and
Fabrice Roger-Lacan)

6. Jacques Lacan and Marie-Louise
Blondin on their wedding day,
January 29, 1939.
(Source: Sibylle Lacan)

8. Thibaut, Sibylle, and Caroline Lacan in around 1943. (Source: Sibylle Lacan)

9. Jacques Lacan and his daughter Caroline on the day of her marriage to Bruno Roger, June 26, 1958. (Source: Cyril and Fabrice Roger-Lacan)

10. Jacques Lacan with his grandsons Fabrice and Cyril in around 1972. (Source: Cyril and Fabrice Roger-Lacan)

11. Sylvia Bataille in Jean Renoir's *A Day in the Country*, 1936. (Source: *Cahiers du cinéma* archives)

12. Laurence Bataille in 1984. (Source: Catherine Basch-Mallet; photograph by Laurent Mallet)

13. Olesia Sienkiewica, summer 1931. (Source: Olesia Sienkiewica)

14. Jacques Lacan, summer 1931. (Source: Olesia Sienkiewica)

15. Louis Althusser and Jacques Lacan, witnesses at the marriage of Jacques Nassif and Caroline Eliacheff, January 9, 1971. (Source: Caroline Eliacheff; photograph by Manuel Bidermanas)

16. IPA Congress, Amsterdam 1951. *In the middle*, Jacques Lacan with Serge Lebovici on his left. *In the front row, front left to right*: Jeanne Lampl-de-Groot, Marie Bonaparte, Ernest Jones, Anna Freud, Donald W. Winnicott. (Source: Jean-Pierre Bougeron collection)

17. Jacques Lacan and Jenny Aubry at the E F P conference in Aix-en-Province, May 23, 1971. (Source: Ginette and Emile Raimbault)

18. Marc-François Lacan, abbaye de Hautecombe, October 1991. (Source: Cyril Roger-Lacan)

19. Jacques Lacan and Salvador Dali in New.York, December 1975. (Source: Pamela Tytell; reproduction forbidden)

20. Jacques Lacan leaving his seminar, March 1980. (Source: Gamma Agency. Photograph by Maurice Rougement)

21. François Wahl at Argentière in 1966, while he was editing the *Ecrits*. (Source: Severo Sarduy)

22. Pierre Soury at the Maison des sciences de l'homme in June 1981, for the exhibition of dolls by Raymonde Archier. (Source: Michel Thomé)

8

. . . .

Private Life and Public Life

Forty years after his thesis was published, Lacan said it was the Aimée case that had led him to psychoanalysis, and that in it he was applying Freudianism "without realizing it."[1] We know now the truth was more complex than that. Lacan's view of his past was not without the frailty inherent in all human testimony. When he was writing up the story of Marguerite he was not really applying the principles of Freud's teaching "without realizing it." On the contrary, by that time he already had a sound knowledge of Freudian theory and was using it quite consciously. If, when he was on the brink of old age, it seemed to him that he hadn't consciously been a Freudian forty years before, it was because he couldn't see how his own idea of what was or was not Freudian had changed over the years. The fact that Lacan's Freudianism was different in the thirties from what it had become by the seventies doesn't mean he wasn't consciously Freudian in 1932.

There can be no doubt about it: he became a Freudian at the same period as when he first met Marguerite, and by the time he wrote up Aimée's case he had already in a general way assimilated the theories of psychoanalysis. So in the period from 1972 to 1975 Lacan was mistaken about the date when he had really accepted Freudianism as a coherent and organized whole. On the other hand he was right to say his work on the Aimée case had led him toward the *experience* of psychoanalysis. In June 1932 he started his sessions with Rudolph Loewenstein, and, as I have noted, the analysis began just as he was finishing his interviews with Marguerite, prior to embarking on the final draft of his manuscript. It is easy to understand his regret at not having made use of Freudian techniques of treatment in the Aimée case. Being in analysis himself when he was finishing his thesis, he could see with hindsight that if he had had that experience earlier it would have enhanced his understanding of his subject. In this respect, the hypothesis I put forward in my *History of Psychoanalysis in France*—that Aimée was for Lacan what

Wilhelm Fliess and Anna O. together were for Freud—is still valid, despite any new assessment one might make today of Lacan's training analysis as it took place in the context of the SPP.[2]

With Marguerite, Lacan tried out a kind of "primal analysis" in the course of which he became a Freudian both theoretically, through his interpretation of the texts, and clinically, by listening in on a case of psychosis. For this reason he would always have a special feeling not only for the woman whose case made it possible for him to reintroduce into France, and at the same time put a new spin on, Freud's teachings but also for female paranoia in general. The Marguerite experience led Lacan to undertake a training analysis with a man who—to put it mildly—would never be his master in the sense that Freud was both analyst and master to his chief disciples. Lacan would always think of Loewenstein as at best a disappointing teacher in the characteristic style of the IPA in the thirties.

Rudolph Loewenstein, born in Lodz in central Poland in 1898, when Poland was still part of the Russian empire, was a perfect representative of a famous type: the wandering Jewish psychoanalyst forever seeking a promised land and forever being hounded from east to west by anti-Semitism and pogroms. Having been forced to flee his native land, Lacan's future analyst then had to retrain as a doctor no fewer than three times: first in Zurich, where he made the acquaintance of the new psychiatry; then in Berlin, where he worked under Hanns Sachs in the most advanced coterie of modern Freudianism; and finally in Paris, where he settled in 1925 with the material help of René Laforgue and the support of Marie Bonaparte, who became his mistress and arranged for his naturalization papers to go through quickly. Before long this brilliant doctor, with his humor and charm, had attained a position of eminence in the SPP, training therapists of both the first and second generations.[3]

Although neither Loewenstein nor Lacan ever revealed anything about what happened during the analysis, we know now that it was stormy. When Lacan first started going to 127, avenue de Versailles he had a very good opinion of himself, a flair for mixing with the cream of the Paris intelligentsia, and a brilliant academic record. Moreover, he knew he was more gifted than not only his contemporaries but also his mentors in the field of psychiatry. As for the pioneers of the French psychoanalytic movement, he loftily ignored them except when they could be useful to him in his career. With the exception of Edouard Pichon, whose influence he warmly acknowledged, he had little sympathy for his elders, who admittedly were no great innovators.

And so, when "Loew" saw this magnificent charmer walk in, with his head held on one side, his protruding ears, his inimitable smile, and deceptively nonchalant air, he had misgivings: Lacan was no ordinary analysand.

He was a creative genius in his own right, and he hadn't come to Freudianism by way of official psychoanalysis. Someone like this was unlikely to submit easily to rules and constraints, even if they were necessary for the realization of his ambitions. Lacan was by temperament a free man, and his kind of freedom brooked no restriction and accepted no censure. It was as if such independence, won by previous generations' sheer hard work through a century of industrial change and upheaval, had, in this last scion of the rising middle classes, become second nature. Lacan would acknowledge no outside authority whatsoever over his person or the managing of his desires. Not having had to bow to a father's command, unable to resist his own slightest whim, by 1932 he was driven by a will to power that a thorough and fruitful reading of *Zarathustra*, backed up by his passion for Spinoza, could only make more fierce—especially in combination with a supreme disdain for common or garden stupidity.

Lacan, then, had arrived at man's estate after suffering only the typical kinds of bourgeois tribulation: the pains of perpetual dissatisfaction, of impatience driven to the limit, of not yet being master of the universe. Imaginary suffering, in short, accompanied by the more ordinary neuroses. He had never known real privation: hunger, poverty, lack of freedom, persecution. Too young to have had to waste his best years under fire at Verdun, he had watched the war from the gardens of the Collège Stanislas, his only whiff of its epic madness brought to him in glimpses of shattered limbs and eyes awaiting death. He had never been choked by the stench of blood on a battlefield; he had never had to fight against real oppression. Pampered from the cradle by generations of comfortable merchants, he had inherited only the hardships of family constraints, and they had made him anything but a hero. But this lack of heroism came with a defiant refusal to conform in any way. Lacan was a kind of antihero, not at all cut out for a normal life, destined to eccentricity and incapable of knuckling under to the countless commonplace rules of behavior—hence his excessive interest in the discourse of madness, as the only key to understanding a crazy world.

All this was very different from Rudolph Loewenstein, whose whole existence had been bound up with exile, hatred, and humiliation. Unlike Lacan, he had learned all there was to know about oppression, in the full sense of the word: first as a Jew in an empire where discriminatory restrictions on education and professional activity still applied and then as an emigrant without a homeland. Condemned to wander from country to country learning new languages as he went, he knew the price of freedom and felt no need to cheapen the word or squander what it stood for. At every stage of his long journey he had had to take a realistic view of the dangers lying ahead, to be encountered with no companion but a battered passport.

When he settled in France he thought he had reached a safe haven at last.

He saw it as a place of hope: France, the homeland of the rights of man, the cradle of an egalitarian republic, reigning over Europe by virtue of her sumptuous elegance and proud intelligence. What did the other France matter, the France of Maurras and Rivarol, of anti-Semitism and patriotic leagues? Loewenstein did not deign to notice it. And yet, fifteen years later, it was that same France which would make him an exile once again, seeking liberty in the United States, the land of the free. But could he have guessed this other France existed when in 1925 he was welcomed to Paris by a trio consisting of a republican princess, a native of Alsace raised in the culture of Germany, and a grammarian of genius who was both pro-Dreyfus and a member of Action française? So, lapped in the kindness of his friends Marie Bonaparte, René Laforgue, and Edouard Pichon, Loewenstein, for better or worse, became a French citizen. Why then did dissension and rivalry arise between him and Lacan in the first year of the analysis?

Despite all the differences between them they had one thing in common: they were both materialists. Both had accepted the sweeping Freudian doctrine on universalism, the death of God, and a proper critical attitude to religious illusion. An honorable peace could have been reached between the cradle Christian, estranged from his vinegar-making kin by his public flouting of their values, and the assimilated Jew, admirer of the revolutionary abbé Grégoire. But it was not.

Lacan hadn't hesitated in his choice of an analyst. Not only was Loewenstein, after seven years in France, the best training analyst in the SPP and the most typical representative of the alluring Freudian world Lacan so longed to join; he also shared Lacan's materialism. And when the time came for Lacan to go on to a control analysis, he would turn to another analyst of the same bent: the Swiss Protestant, Charles Odier, trained in Berlin by Karl Abraham and Franz Alexander, two eminent figures in the Freudian saga. And so Lacan, a Catholic from the Aisne and the Loire, the heart of ancient France, was initiated into analytic practice by a Jew living in permanent exile and a Protestant whose ancestors had fled France after the revocation of the Edict of Nantes in 1685. Perhaps it was a necessary step on the way to the final break with the bigotry of the boulevard Beaumarchais.

At the same time, by going to two practitioners who belonged to the pure orthodox line, Lacan became indirectly, across a generation, the pupil of three of Freud's most illustrious disciples: Hanns Sachs, his analyst's analyst, of Viennese origin and the great organizer of standardization in the IPA; Karl Abraham, the first analyst of his control analyst, a specialist in psychosis and the founder of the Psychoanalytic Society in Berlin; and Franz Alexander, his controller's second analyst, who was himself analyzed by Sachs and who was to pioneer a technique for reducing the length of treatments.

Oddly enough, Lacan never told anyone he had undergone a control analysis, and even his son-in-law and close relatives knew nothing about it until it was revealed to me in June 1982 by Germaine Guex. She was certain that Lacan had been in analysis at one time with Odier (whose mistress she was at that period), having seen him come often to the house over several months and always at the same time. But was this in 1935 or 1937? She couldn't remember the exact dates when I talked to her.[4] But everything now seems to show that Lacan went to Odier not for true analysis—he was going to Loewenstein for that—but for supervision or control, a process made more or less compulsory for candidate analysts in 1934, when a French institute was set up similar to those already functioning in societies belonging to the IPA.

The fact that later Lacan never saw fit to mention having undergone a control analysis doesn't mean he didn't do so. He probably thought it was enough that he had had one analysis for his contemporaries to know his own position as a leader was different from Freud's: he, Lacan, had been analyzed, and not on just any old couch: on a regular, orthodox one. But he knew well enough that one day, when he was dead and gone, some inquisitive historian, either through deduction or as a result of evidence from a surviving witness, would come across this buried scrap of truth. Memory always gets there in the end.

There was a yawning gap, then, between the two men who met in the apartment in the avenue de Versailles several times a week for six years, from June 1932 to December 1938. Lacan saw freedom as the long, untrammeled exercise of desire. For Loewenstein, freedom was a right that had to be fought for, a victory that had to be won over intolerance. He knew the value of freedom because he had had to go without it, and he was not prepared to sacrifice it to the dictates of desire. It was better to use it sparingly, within limits set by rules that applied to all. And for Loewenstein, a migrant who every time he moved on lost all that he thought he had gained, the rules were those established by the IPA for the "free" practice of psychoanalysis. They drew their authority from their supranational character and from the fact that they applied, from 1925 onward, to *every* society that belonged to the IPA.

Between the two wars the Freudian empire consisted largely of Jews from central Europe; it was a sort of nation in itself, in which unity and equality were maintained through the observation of generally agreed-upon rules and traditions. The rules might frequently be broken, but they still acted as a moral framework allowing the psychoanalytic community to exist, held together by a social bond and resting on an ethical foundation. Loewenstein, a pure technician of the great IPA fraternity, observed the common faith—

but without giving up his own passions. By analyzing his lover, the princess, whose son he had already treated, he was breaking the very rules he was supposed to embody. In this he was like Lacan, his most dangerous rival. But unlike Lacan he really believed that obedience to the rules helped the free practice of Freudian psychoanalysis as it moved toward the promised land of the IPA. Even though he now identified with France and many of its republican values, he was sure the SPP must do all it could to become part of the great standardizing movement of the IPA.

This sort of thing didn't interest Lacan. For him, travel and international relations were simply means of satisfying his enormous curiosity, and he saw no need whatsoever for obeying any rules. For him, the IPA was neither home nor promised land but just an institution that conferred Freudian legitimacy on its members. And without that legitimacy, no career was possible in the French psychoanalytic movement.

One can get some idea of what Loewenstein's analysis of Lacan was like from a reading of the former's two major texts on analytic practice. The first of these was a report presented to the third conference of French-speaking psychoanalysts, held in Paris on June 28, 1928, and the second is a paper read to the SPP in 1930, entitled "Tact in Psychoanalytical Technique."[5] In these texts, Loewenstein gave a fundamental account of general psychoanalytic guidelines, emphasizing the importance of the unconscious. Then he stated the individual rules underlying analytic practice: the therapist must rely on his memory rather than on notes; he should analyze resistances rather than try to find repressed material; the patient should not read books about psychoanalysis while undergoing treatment. Lastly came advice about the length and number of sessions and how to deal with delays.

Transference was seen in terms of positive and negative poles. Treatment came to an end when the positive transference could be interpreted and the patient thus freed from the analyst's hold over him. As for the "moral" rules, Loewenstein stressed that analysis should take place independently of any friendly relationship there might be between the two people concerned. It was this calculated, rational, standardized technique that he used in his analysis of Lacan, and I have already noted elsewhere how he would lose patience with Lacan's continual fluctuations between on the one hand a frenzied desire to act and know and on the other a maddening deliberation when it came to working out and elaborating ideas.[6]

Loewenstein referred only once in writing to the problem Lacan's analysis represented for him, and his comment then was negative. But he often expressed his opinion orally to the people around him: the man was unanalyzable. And Lacan *was* unanalyzable in those conditions. Personal and theoretical differences stood in the way of transference, and Loewenstein wasn't flexible enough to adapt his methods to suit such a patient. How could he have been?

Lacan once told Catherine Millot what he thought of his analysis. In his opinion Loewenstein was not intelligent enough to analyze him. Cruel but true! It was in his own Seminar, said Lacan, that he felt he was really analyzed (he never recognized the fundamental role Marguerite had played in this respect). To illustrate the situation between him and Loewenstein, Lacan told Catherine Millot of an incident that occurred at the time. One day he was driving his little car through a tunnel when a truck came at him head-on from the opposite direction. He decided to keep going, and the truck gave way. He told Loewenstein what had happened, hoping to make him see the truth about their transferential relationship. But he got no answer. And the mortal struggle, for which Lacan was acquiring a taste at Kojève's seminars, ended in open conflict. Not only was the analysand admitted to membership of the SPP against the advice of his analyst, though with the support of Pichon, but Lacan also escaped from the analysis as soon as he could, despite having promised to go on. And ultimately he became for France what Loewenstein never was: an intellectual leader.[7]

All the time he was in analysis, Lacan went on with his theoretical work, outside the sphere of official psychoanalysis. True, he took part in the SPP's internal discussions and mixed socially with his colleagues, but he was acquiring knowledge neglected at that period by the Freudian community itself. So he remained a marginal figure, whose development was followed with a mistrustful eye and the oft-expressed opinion that he was no ordinary psychoanalyst. Having constructed his thesis on the basis of Spinoza, phenomenology, surrealism, and dynamic psychiatry, he would go on to extend his philosophical examination of Freud still further. This led him to formulate his first theories about desire, the status of the subject, and the role of the imaginary order. But strangely enough, between the end of 1932 and the middle of 1936—i.e., during the first four years of his analysis—Lacan produced no important texts. It was as if this fallow period was the symptom of a great transformation, a transition from psychiatry and the discovery of Freud himself to an interpretation of Freudianism that would develop into a whole philosophical system. And those "empty" years were also a kind of "latency period" in which Lacan's eventful private life was helping to forge his personality.

At the end of August 1933 Lacan left Olesia in Paris and went off with Marie-Thérèse for two weeks' vacation. They went by train from Saint-Jean-de-Luz to Madrid, via Salamanca, Burgos, and Valladolid. Lacan wrote passionate letters to his mistress back in France. He read a lot. His old voracious curiosity had revived after all the "lousy years" spent in the ridiculous "clinical" rat race. He told Olesia she was perhaps a better friend to him than he deserved. For "friend" he wrote "*ami*," the masculine form of the word.[8]

After referring to his beloved in the masculine gender, Lacan told her in another letter what a wonderful time he was having. He said he felt like getting up to the most "quixotic" antics. He declared his hostility to Christianity and in the same breath said he'd like to go to see his "patron saint," St. James of Compostela. He described the charms of the Spanish railroads and an excursion to the monastery of San Domingo de Silos. In Valladolid he went into raptures over a piece of polychrome sculpture: it was "strident, heartrending, soul-searing." Finally, in Madrid, he went to the Prado and found that the paintings of Velázquez no longer touched him as they used to do. On the other hand he was moved to tears by Goya's intelligence, and his palette reminded Lacan of the artists who had once made him "hear the call of Venice." After this lyrical flight Lacan turned to the past and gave free reign to his feelings for Olesia. He still promised happiness to come, mingling expressions of affection with the language of passion— burning kisses, moments of ecstasy, breathless desire. He asked her to wait for him, to be beautiful for him, to forgive his constant hesitations and evasions. They would have a winter full of warmth and happiness.[9]

When he got back to Paris he returned to the analyst's couch, and elation was replaced by depression. He was in a dilemma. He didn't want to leave Marie-Thérèse, and he loved Olesia best when they were apart. He couldn't bring himself to be either off with the old love or on with the new. At the beginning of October he went to Prangins to attend a meeting of the Swiss Psychiatric Society and discuss the problem of hallucinations. It was on this occasion that he first met Carl Gustav Jung, who had come to talk about his experiences among African tribes. Lacan, together with Henri Ey, reasserted the theory that explained hallucinations in terms of psychogenesis: they are produced, he said, neither by automatism nor by "constitution" but by a disturbance of the patient's sense of the wholeness of his or her personality.[10]

On October 24, just before a session with Loewenstein, Lacan wrote Olesia a letter that contrasted strangely with those he had sent her in August. The lovers were on the verge of a breakup, and Lacan didn't try to disguise his melancholy mood. He complained that he always missed out on happiness, blamed himself for his attitude in the past, and trusted, without much hope of success, that he could make up for lost time. Over lunch at the Auberge Alsacienne in the avenue de Versailles, he remembered a bad patch he had gone through the previous year and how upset he had been. He told Olesia how unhappy he was and suggested she too might be due for a wild passion, a chance to let herself go. As ever, he wanted to make up for wasted time.[11] But dreams and longings didn't mend matters between the lovers.

Just as he was trying to exorcise his misery, Lacan was awakened from it by a new love.

Marie-Louise Blondin—Malou for short—was nearly twenty-seven. Lacan had known her for a long time: she was the sister of an old friend and fellow intern, Sylvain Blondin. Sylvain, born on July 24, 1901, came from a respectable republican family belonging to one of the higher strata of the French bourgeoisie. His roots lay in Charente on the mother's side and in Lorraine on the father's. After a brilliant school career at the Lycée Carnot, Sylvain had decided to become a doctor, like his father. When he came second in the interns' final examination in 1924, he decided to make a career in surgery. He started off in the clinic at the Hôtel-Dieu and stayed there until 1935, when he passed another examination to become a surgeon in the general hospital service.

Sylvain Blondin was extremely attractive: tall, slim, and lively. He affected bow ties and hid his fair wavy hair under a hat tilted back at an elegant angle. A keen collector, he spent his first paychecks on pictures by modern artists such as Braque, Léger, and Picasso. He performed operations with his left hand, wrote with his right, and could draw with both. He always refused to learn to drive and preferred to travel around by taxi or in a chauffeur-driven limousine.[12]

Lacan got on famously with him, and their relationship, based on mutual fascination, was a factor when Jacques fell in love with Malou. She was devoted to her brother and ready to find all the qualities she admired in him in his friend: talent, beauty, originality, and intelligence. She herself, narcissistic and unyielding, with a self-image that was grandiose but volatile, managed to detect distinction behind the mask of eccentricity. And so she chose Lacan from all the rest. She saw in him a man who measured up to her ideal of superiority, and she set out to conquer him. Sylvain, who had no sympathy for Freudian theory and thought it was in psychiatry that his friend would carve out a brilliant career, was delighted to see the sister he was so fond of in love with the friend he looked on as his own double.

Malou was strikingly beautiful, with a very slim body and narrow hips. She lacked the masculine charm with which Olesia had so bewitched Drieu: hers was a more fragile, feminine type, hinting at a melancholy languor—something between Greta Garbo and Virginia Woolf. She could just have gone on being her mother's daughter or her adored brother's sister. She might just have lived up to the ideal handed down to her, and become an enlightened bourgeois wife virtuously standing behind an ordinary decent husband, preferably a doctor, one who would be a collector in his spare time or a patron of the arts, with a comfortable apartment in a handsome stone building in the faubourg Saint-Germain. But she chose not to follow the prescribed pattern. Even when she was still quite young she stood out from her background: she had a gift for painting, a flair for style that showed in her knack for dressing up and making her own clothes, and an original sense of humor that made her see the funny side of everything. Her friends were astonished by her knowledge of traditional French songs. All these elements of a real artistic temperament prevented her from ever dwindling into an ordinary wife. But her natural nonconformity stopped short of genuine intellectual independence, and she clung to the conventional ideal of marriage still accepted by most women of her generation. She was modern in her tastes and aspirations but fettered to the old order by her conception of love and the family.

This was the woman whom Lacan fell for in the autumn of 1933, when he was still hoping to win Olesia back. And to possess the sister of the friend he admired as his own alter ego, he was ready to do anything. He knew that a woman such as Malou, with no experience of the physical side of love, was not the type one asks to be one's mistress. The question of marriage therefore came up almost at once.

At the end of 1933 Lacan let himself in for a regular marriage with all the trimmings, blessed by the Roman Catholic Church. Had he forgotten that only a few months earlier he had been writing to his mistress from Spain about his strong anti-Christian convictions? Be that as it may, Marie-Louise Blondin and Jacques Lacan were legally married at the city hall of the 17th Arrondissement in Paris on January 29, 1934, in the presence of some distinguished witnesses. On Lacan's side there was Professor Henri Claude, there at his pupil's request to stand surety in the name of orthodox French psychiatry for a man whose name would soon supplant his own. On Malou's side there was Henri Duclaux, surgeon to the Chamber of Deputies and an old family friend of the Blondins. Duclaux had been there when Malou's birth was registered in the same city hall on November 16, 1906. Duclaux came to the wedding as a sign of his fatherly affection for the bride. Claude's presence was a social and professional favor to the groom.

But if the humanist spirit of surgery and psychiatry presided over the civil ceremony, the religious ceremony was designed to meet the requirements of the Lacan family. Lacan himself was fascinated by the rituals of the church and wished to keep up Catholic appearances. And he didn't want to disappoint his mother, who would never have accepted the idea of her son being married without the blessing of the church. So Lacan asked Dom Laure, the abbot of Hautecombe, where his brother Marc-François was a monk, to perform the ceremony at the church of Saint-François-de-Sales.

Jacques and Malou went on the traditional Italian honeymoon, traveling as far south as Sicily. It was the first time Lacan had seen Rome, and he was enchanted with it. As soon as he got there he started throwing his weight around. "I am Dr. Lacan," he said to the astonished hotel porter, who had never heard of him. He went to see Bernini's studies in ecstasy; the baroque sculpture of the fountains gave him so much pleasure he had qualms of conscience: on February 10, right in the middle of his honeymoon, he felt guilty at having abandoned Olesia and sent her a telegram: "Worried about you, dear. Wire general delivery Rome. Jacques."

It is unlikely that Malou had recognized how far Jacques was from believing in her own ideal of love and fidelity. And he, impatient as always to capture the object of his desire, probably hadn't understood that a woman like her would never consent to share him. The apparently happy couple was headed for disaster. Lacan, polygamous by nature but wanting and needing a conjugal life, was as incapable of leaving a woman as he was of being faithful to her. So, determined not to pretend to be other than he was, he began to lead his own life according to the same dialectic between the true and the impossible that he was later to expound so famously in his work. As for Malou, she saw too late that the man she revered could never fulfill her aspirations. She held on to her ideal but paid for her persistence with despair.

For the time being, however, Lacan seemed to have made a success of his transition to man's estate. The newlyweds moved into a well-appointed apartment on the boulevard Malesherbes, a stone's throw from where Henri Claude lived. Malou's elegance, dress sense, and lifestyle had a visible effect on Lacan. His clothes were now more fashionable, even recherché, and he got used to living in ordered and comfortable surroundings.

There was never an outright break between him and Olesia, and no final word was spoken. They just stopped seeing each other. Olesia had been abandoned once again, but although the romance with Lacan had been real enough, she never loved him with the passion she had felt for Drieu. She considered Jacques a remarkable thinker, and she admired his intelligence, spirit, and charm, but Drieu remained the object of her obsession. She thought of him all the time, cultivating her sense of loss in order to go on enjoying the painful pleasure of disappointment. She chose to be unhappy loving a man who didn't want her rather than happy with one who intended to love her but was always putting it off. Lacan was well aware that his mistress would always be bound to another man. And as he himself had kept waiting a woman he was sure of in order to pursue another who might elude him, he could understand Olesia acting in such a way as to invite abandonment. The bohemian flavor of their secret meetings, arranged at short notice, sometimes prevented but all the more exciting when they did take place, had lent their affair an atmosphere of sophisticated comedy, like something out of Marivaux. And as time went by both Lacan and Olesia came to look back on it as bathed in the aura of excitement and ardor with which memory always surrounds a young love lost beyond recall. They met forty-three years later over dinner for two at the restaurant La Petite Cour.

But much as they might have liked to recapture time past, they had nothing to say to one another. Their affair had left a trace, however, in the memory of Victoria Ocampo. She happened to be briefly in Paris at about this time and asked some friends to arrange for her to meet Lacan. When they expressed surprise—what possible interest could she have in the great man of Freudianism?—her answer was the priceless phrase "Era el amantito de la mujer de Drieu" (He used to be Drieu's wife's boyfriend).[13]

In May 1934 Lacan took the competitive examination held to select chief doctors for mental hospitals. He nearly got himself rejected for the arrogant way he showed off his knowledge of phenomenology at the oral examination. "A tiresome young man," reported the examiners.[14] He ranked eleventh out of thirteen successful candidates, having put on a stunning performance in the test called "Examination of a Patient," which involved a twenty-minute presentation of a case without prior knowledge of the patient or his or her file. But Lacan wriggled out of taking the hospital post allotted to him. He was already practicing privately as an analyst and would acquire official status on November 20 of the same year, when he became a member of the SPP.[15] But his failure to take up a hospital career didn't mean he was losing interest in madness. Far from it. He would always return to it, and never forgot the link between his interpretation of Freud and the clinical study of psychosis, nor that between the latter and its basis in paranoia.

It was in a café on the place Blanche that Lacan first saw the man who for several years would be his first and only long-term analysand apart from hospital patients. Georges Bernier belonged to a Jewish family that originally came from Russia.[16] He was studying history but also took an interest in modern painting, avant-garde movements, and new ideas in general. He had first seen Lacan in the Café Blanche, sitting at the same table as André Breton, but came across him again in the winter of 1933 at Georges Dumas's lectures at the Sorbonne, where Bernier was then studying for a qualification in psychology.

Lacan wanted to get a degree in philosophy, but Bernier, who was thinking of going in for psychiatry, felt the need for a Freudian analysis. He went to Allendy for a few sessions but didn't think he was very bright and decided to go to Lacan instead. The analysis went on until 1939. After that they met again in Marseilles, where, in the confusion following the fall of France, both were involved in enterprises I shall deal with in due course.

The first sessions of the analysis took place in the rue de la Pompe and followed the standard pattern. Then they moved to the boulevard Malesherbes. There were three sessions a week, each lasting an hour. Every two or three weeks Lacan would suggest making a sort of synthesis. He would speak at length to explain what had been happening and to help the patient make progress. In this first analysis there were already features typical of Lacan's future style: his habit of merging with the patient, of not analyzing the transference, of exchanging books, objects, and ideas with the analysand, and of keeping friendship and the professional relationship strictly separate.

During the years of gestation that lay between the publication of Lacan's thesis and his harnessing of the great philosophical current of his age to his own purposes, he spent a good deal of time with other members of the SPP. In his dealings with men of the first generation of French psychoanalysis, he emerged as a theoretician to be reckoned with. His longest-running debate was with Loewenstein, Paul Schiff, Charles Odier, and Edouard Pichon. Relations between him and Marie Bonaparte were extremely frigid on both sides. She was the official representative of the powerful listening ear in Vienna, and reigned like a queen over the SPP. It was not surprising there should be a resounding silence between her and the architect of a new version of Freud. She didn't seem to have recognized yet the importance of this stranger in her universe. Her private journal (never published), though it relates in detail all the day-to-day problems of the psychoanalytic movement, never once mentions Lacan's name.

Not that Lacan's contributions to the discussions held at this period were particularly interesting. They showed he attended SPP meetings regularly, but until 1935 he simply repeated what he had already said about paranoia. But in 1936 he began to be interested in the *stade du miroir*, or mirror stage. Drawing on Henri Wallon, Alexandre Kojève, and Alexandre Koyré, he devised a theory of the subject that, while making use of the Freudian revolution, gave it a new twist. The development of his thought can be traced in answers he gave in 1937 and 1938 to questions from Marie Bonaparte, Loewenstein, and Daniel Lagache about the divided body, narcissism, and the death drive. The traces are clearer still in the paper of October 25, 1939, entitled "De l'impulsion au complexe" (From impulse to complex), in which Lacan summed up his theories in response to Odier's complaint that his previous speech on the subject had been too long.[17]

It should be noted that at this point Lacan's analysis with Loewenstein represented a serious problem for the members of the SPP. There had been no difficulty in 1934 about accepting Lacan as a member, but after the setting up of the Institut de psychanalyse (IP: Institute of Psychoanalysis) and the drawing-up of strict rules about admission to the status of training analyst, the situation started to deteriorate. It grew still worse in 1936, when Lacan started producing theories that seemed incomprehensible to the current psychoanalytic establishment. So, because they couldn't understand, let alone accept, his intellectual innovations, they rejected him for not obeying the rules.

Not only had Lacan's analysis with Loewenstein been going on longer that was usual at the time, but it looked set to last indefinitely, prolonged by reciprocal gestures of blackmail and defiance. Loewenstein thought Lacan should continue the analysis as part of his training, while Lacan carried on with it just as a means of acquiring the title of training analyst in the SPP. Pichon would have to step in to put an end to the drama.[18]

Fascism: The End of the Viennese Epic

hile the SPP was going through these little private tragedies, history itself was catching up with the psychoanalytic movement as a whole. In March 1938, with the arrival of the Nazis in Vienna, the departure of Freud and the last of his companions could not be far off. But the old man, who had recently undergone an operation to have part of his jaw removed and had already been harassed several times by the Gestapo, lost neither his composure nor his sense of humor. Since moving to Vienna in early childhood he had always lived in the city where his chief discoveries were made, and he wanted to remain at his post until the last possible moment.

While, with the help of Max Schur, William Bullitt, and Marie Bonaparte, Jones was making arrangements for the master to leave Vienna, he was also trying for the second time to carry out a plan he had already employed in Germany itself a few years earlier. Jones had adopted the policy of Aryanization advocated from 1933 onward by Matthias Heinrich Göring, a convinced Nazi, rabid anti-Semite, and former pupil of Emil Kraepelin; and a corollary of this policy was a move to create a psychotherapy movement containing no Jews and banishing the use of Freudian terminology. Among the members of the Deutsche Psychoanalytische Gesellschaft (DPG: German Psychoanalytic Society) were two men who distinguished themselves in the execution of this project. Felix Boehm and Carl Müller-Braunschweig were neither ideologists nor Nazis: they were just jealous of the eminent Jewish colleagues who had pioneered Freudianism in Germany. And when the National Socialists came to power, they saw their chance to further their own careers. Aware of their inferiority to their Jewish mentors, they were prepared to act as lackeys to the infamous authorities. Many Jewish members of the DPG went into exile abroad; by 1935 only nine of forty-seven remained. Boehm and Müller-Braunschweig argued that by forestalling the orders of the Nazis and expelling the last remaining Jewish members of the DPG, while pretending that they were resigning voluntarily, they were depriving the government of a pretext for banning psychoanalysis altogether.

This "rescue" operation, which Jones went along with, led to the forced resignation of the DPG's last remaining Jewish members. One single non-Jew refused to acquiesce in the shameful procedure: Bernard Kamm chose to leave of his own accord out of solidarity with those who were forced to go. Göring was able to fulfill his dream of creating an institute of psychotherapy that brought together Freudians, Jungians, and independents. Freud disapproved of all this, and when Boehm went to Vienna to try to sell him the "rescue" theory, he stood up angrily and left the room. But although Freud disapproved of these ignoble maneuverings, he had long ago relinquished control of IPA affairs, and let Jones support the project. And this was interpreted as tacit approval.[1]

Jones was to continue along the road of compromise. On March 13, 1938, Freud and his friends met in Vienna to wind up their society, which had moved into new premises only two years before. Anna was in the chair, and everyone, in that dark hour, was thinking of the great occasion in May 1936 when Thomas Mann gave his famous lecture on the future of psychoanalysis. "Sigmund Freud," he had said,

that mighty spirit in whose honour we have gathered together, founder of psychoanalysis as a general method of research and as a therapeutic technique, trod the steep path alone and independently, as physician and natural scientist, without knowing that reinforcement and encouragement lay to his hand in literature. He did not know Nietzsche, scattered throughout whose pages one finds premonitory flashes of truly Freudian insight; he did not know Novalis, whose romantic-biologic fantasies so often approach astonishingly close to analytic conceptions; he did not know Kierkegaard, whom he must have found profoundly sympathetic and encouraging for the Christian zeal which urged him to psychological extremes; and, finally he did not know Schopenhauer, the melancholy symphonist of a philosophy of the instinct, groping for change and redemption. By his unaided effort, without knowledge of any previous intuitive achievement, he had methodically to follow out the line of his own researches; the driving force of his activity was probably increased by this very freedom from special advantage.[2]

Dissolving the society, Anna asked Richard Sterba what his plans were. As the only non-Jewish member of the group he could have taken charge, as Jones wished him to, of an operation designed to "rescue" Viennese psychoanalysis. But he refused, and this was Freud's comment: "When Titus destroyed the Temple in Jerusalem, Rabbi Hochanaan ben Sakkai asked permission to set up a school at Jahné for the study of the Torah. We shall do the same. Our history and our traditions have accustomed us all to persecution." Turning to Sterba he added, "All of us but one."[3]

On June 3, 1938, Freud left Vienna on the Orient Express, never to return. He left behind his four sisters, Rosa, Mitzi, Dolfi, and Paula. All were to disappear into the darkness of the final solution, at Theresienstadt or Treblinka. At the Nuremberg trials a witness recalled seeing one of them being received by the camp's *Obersturmbannführer:* "A middle-aged woman approached Kurt Franz, showed him her *Ausweis* [identity card] and said she was Sigmund Freud's sister. She asked to be given a simple office job. Franz looked carefully at the *Ausweis* and said there seemed to be some mistake. He led her over to the railroad timetable and told her there was a train back to Vienna in two hours' time. She should leave her papers and valuables with him and go and take a shower. She went through the door into the shower room and never came back."[4]

At 9:45 on the morning of June 5, 1938, Marie Bonaparte and William Bullitt were at the Gare de l'Est to meet Freud for a twelve-hour stopover in Paris. Late that afternoon he met some French psychoanalysts in the salons of the princess's mansion in the rue Adolphe-Yvon. Lacan was not present. He said later that he had chosen to stay away because he didn't want to kowtow (*"faire de grâces"*) to Marie.[5] The truth was probably different, for in fact the gathering at Marie Bonaparte's was a private occasion, and Lacan wasn't invited. In any case, he had nothing to gain at that date from a meeting with the sage from Vienna.

In August, when all Europe was living in dread of war, the IPA congress took place in sweltering hot weather in a room in the avenue d'Iéna. Jones, opening the proceedings, paid tribute to France. Using French for this part of his address, Jones declared: "France may be considered to have provided the framework for modern psychology. It was French psychologists, impelled by a typically French intuition, who first discovered the importance for psychology in general of the results of clinical and therapeutic observation....This prepared the ground for the major discovery, that of the normal unconscious, though the discovery itself was made elsewhere. To use a farming metaphor, by the end of the last century the soil of France had been overcultivated for a hundred years and was completely exhausted. The signs of infertility were becoming clear: a fallow period was needed." For four days French and foreign psychoanalysts held forth on various subjects. Loewenstein, Pichon, Allendy, Lagache, Sophie Morgenstern, and Marie Bonaparte followed each other onto the platform. One man—Jacques Lacan—was conspicuous by his absence. In his closing speech, Jones summarized the situation, and his own presidential activities, in the countries where Freudian societies had been established. Speaking of Germany, he announced the success of his "rescue" policy. Without mentioning Göring, the nazification process, the forced Jewish resignations, or the exodus of the flower of the psychoanalytic intelligentsia, he expressed satisfaction at the "considerable autonomy" that the German Psychoanalytic Society, though it continued "to live a somewhat delicate existence," "enjoyed" in its new form as a "separate department" of the new German Institute for Psychological Research and Psychotherapy, founded in May 1936: "many candidates have been trained," said Jones, now speaking in English, "and the total membership list increased." Turning to the Austrian question, he deplored the "unhappy fate" of the Vienna Society: "How unlikely did it seem when I participated in its first meetings more than thirty-two years ago that it should be my lot to have to recommend the practical dissolution of this, the mother of all psychoanalytic societies, on March 20 of this year. . . . The President of the [Vienna] Society, Professor Freud, accepted the recommendation that the goodwill and duties of the Society be transferred to the German Psychoanalytic Society, but of the final outcome of this procedure we are still in doubt."[6]

When this depressing speech was over, those attending the congress adjourned to Saint-Cloud for a reception held in the gardens of the princess's magnificent residence. The Viennese exiles, on their way to the United States, gave one last thought before the apocalypse to this fairy-tale Europe whose splendors they would never see again. The great Yvette Guilbert, whom Freud greatly admired, sang "Dites-moi que je suis belle" (Tell me I'm beautiful) and at the age of eighty held everyone spellbound by her voice and her charm.[7]

Lacan was probably there, but only as one of the crowd.

The signing of the Munich agreement, a presage of France's collapse, had an important influence on the way Lacan, with the aid of the grammarian Edouard Pichon, escaped from his interminable analysis. Pichon, knowing he had lost his battle for a "French" psychoanalysis and anxious in those somber days not to see the spp dominated entirely by its orthodox elements, decided to modify the list of candidates for the title of training analyst: for Heinz Hartmann, who had come to Paris as a refugee when the Nazis occupied Vienna, he "exchanged" Lacan. So it took strong-arm tactics by a member of Action française to make Lacan's reluctant colleagues grant him his rightful place among them. He applied for the status of training analyst in the spp on November 15, 1938, and on December 20 it was granted.

By this move, made shortly before his death, Pichon was not only indicating a possible heir to the French tradition for which he had fought so hard; he was also righting a wrong. After Lacan's six years on Loewenstein's couch there was no reason why he should be refused membership. Loewenstein's bitter sense of humiliation at the way the analysis ended is still evident in the rancorous letter he wrote to Marie Bonaparte on February 22, 1953: "What you tell me about Lacan . . . is distressing. He has always represented a source of conflict for me; on one hand there is intellectual worth which I value highly, though I disagree violently with him. Nevertheless, the misfortune is that much as we agreed that he would continue his analysis after his election [to the society], he did not do so. One does not cheat on such an important point with impunity (this between us). I certainly hope that his hastily analyzed (that is to say incompletely analyzed) trainees will not be admitted."[8]

In another letter, dated September 12, 1967, and addressed to Jean Miel, Loewenstein let drop a few more details about Lacan's election and his own views about his analysand. "Lacan was elected in 1937–1938, and I played a decisive part at that time in overcoming colleagues' objections." And about the 1953 schism he added:

When it became clear that the training Lacan gave was unacceptable, he said he would mend his ways and obey the standard rules. But he immediately put up for membership an unusually large number of candidates analyzed by himself. So again he was forced to admit that the training he had provided was unorthodox, because he had economized on time. . . . As regards Lacan's ideas, my view is that he shows penetrating imagination in pursuit of the signifier but has no interest in the signified. With this defect, no scientific discourse, aspiring to be a branch of knowledge, can claim to be complete. And so when I read his work I can't help thinking, "Words, words, words." And yet I love and admire Mallarmé.[9]

10

. . . .

The Philosophy School:
Alexandre Koyré and Others

At the time Lacan was writing for the *Minotaure* he was exasperated with his medical studies but still interested in the philosophical topics of his day. This brought him into contact with Pierre Verret, a communist student slightly younger than himself who was looking for some private coaching to help make ends meet. Lacan, who wanted to get a certificate in logic and general philosophy from the Sorbonne, asked Verret to instruct him in the broad outlines of the subject, and for four months—from September 1933 to January 1934, when he met Georges Bernier—he had his "professor" come to the rue de la Pompe twice a week from 7:30 in the evening till midnight. Sometimes they would have a pleasant meal together, prepared in advance by the housekeeper. "They weren't ordinary lessons, organized systematically to cover a definite program," writes Verret. "Instead he would bombard me with questions out of the blue and requests for further information that often flummoxed me, novice that I was. He was interested in everything, and he was the one who really conducted the 'lesson.' If I may venture the comparison, it was more like a Platonic dialogue in which answers to questions produced more questions, with me as a pretty poor Socrates. . . . The doctor never deducted anything from my fees to cover the excellent dinner that sometimes accompanied our verbal jousts."[1]

Meanwhile, through his relations with Jean Bernier and the surrealists, as well as by the publication of his thesis, Lacan found himself in the midst of the debate about communism that was then exercising the French intelligentsia. So although he never sought any political commitment for himself, he did follow the battle over Freud and Marxism that raged in 1933 among the communists, the surrealists, and the friends of Boris Souvarine. One day at a lecture delivered at the Mutualité—a building in the Latin Quarter where public meetings are held—the speaker, a young philosopher called Jean Audard, was fiercely challenged by Georges Politzer, and the two men came to blows. Lacan wasn't present, but he read Audard's paper and thought he would like to meet him. He said to Verret, "If I can get to the meeting of the AEAR [Association des écrivains et des artistes révolutionaires: Association of Revolutionary Writers and Artists], I'd like to have a drink with you and Audard, before dinner perhaps. I'll let you know tomorrow if I can make it."[2]

Audard's text was original at the time. Instead of siding either with the anti-Freudians or with the Freudo-Marxists, he argued that psychoanalysis, being more "materialistic" than Marxism, could tone down the latter's idealism. He also pointed out that the Marxism of the Russian communists was different from the communism preached in Paris.[3]

But all this was marginal to the real subject of Lacan's preoccupations during the long gestation period between the publication of his article on the Papin sisters and the working out of his theories on the illusions of the ego. And it was his contacts with Alexandre Koyré, Henry Corbin, Alexandre Kojève, and Georges Bataille that introduced him to modern philosophy and set him reading Husserl, Nietzsche, Hegel, and Heidegger. Without this widening of his frontiers, as well as his encounter with the surrealists, Lacan might have been imprisoned forever within the confines of psychiatry and an academic understanding of Freud.

Alexandre Koyré was born in Taganrog in Russia in 1892, the son of an importer of colonial goods. Young as he still was, he took part in the political activities that followed the 1905 revolution and ended up in prison. Nevertheless by the age of seventeen he was at the university of Göttingen, studying under Husserl and Hilbert. From there he went to Paris, where he attended Bergson's and Brunschwicg's lectures at the Sorbonne. He returned to Russia and took part in the February revolution but opposed the October one. In 1919, after fighting on the Russian front in the First World War, he left Russia for France, this time for good.

In 1914 Koyré had written a paper entitled "The Idea of God in the Philosophy of St. Anselm." His supervisor at the time was François Picavet, a freethinker and specialist in medieval philosophy who passed on to his pupil his own passion for Neoplatonism[4] and a secular approach to the history of religious philosophy. This didn't stop Koyré from attending Etienne Gilson's lectures in 1921, though Gilson's position was quite different from that of Picavet. Gilson, a Christian philosopher and an immensely prolific author, had completely transformed the study of medieval philosophy with his new method of interpreting texts. Students came to hear and watch him, first at the Sorbonne and then at the Fifth Section of the EPHE (Ecole pratique des hautes études). "Gilson would read out the Latin texts," writes Corbin, "give his own translation of them, and then bring out all their underlying as well as their overt meaning in a masterly and penetrating commentary."[5] This method made it possible to place an author or a work in a historical context where philosophy and religion could coexist. So, in contradistinction to the secular tradition represented by Emile Bréhier, Gilson converted a whole generation of researchers to the idea that sacred texts could supply material for genuine philosophical thought. (As I have noted, Jean Baruzi, who taught Lacan philosophy at the Collège Stanislas, used Gilsonian methods in his lessons.)

Koyré entitled his degree thesis *The Idea of God and the Proofs of His existence in the Works of Descartes*, and after Picavet's death he was appointed a temporary lecturer in the Fifth Section of the EPHE. In 1929 he received his doctorate in philosophy for his thesis on Jakob Boehme, and two years later he became director of studies in the Fifth Section and professor of the history of religious ideas in modern Europe. So began the teaching career of a man of great magnanimity, whose less than perfect delivery was outweighed by his distinguished personality and outstanding intelligence. He became one of the greatest historians of science in this century. Following on directly from Paul Tannery, he rejected the idea that the history of science could be treated in isolation, as well as the notion that human knowledge was gradually but inevitably progressing toward first a key to the understanding of reality and ultimately to that understanding itself. In place of this approach, based on a selective chronology of the evolution of ideas, Koyré proposed a philosophical history of science that, instead of restricting itself to a chain of connections between scientific exploits, would include in its consideration of any period all that era's ideas and beliefs. He wanted the history of science to include the study of how science understands, at any given time, what is contemporary with it and what preceded it. "When I began my researches," he wrote in 1951, "I was spurred on by the belief that all human thought, especially in its highest forms, formed a connected whole. It seemed to me one couldn't keep philosophical and religious thought in separate compartments: philosophy is always involved with religion in one way or another, using it either as a springboard or as a target."[6]

Koyré's ideas on the history of science were splendidly exemplified in his studies on Galileo, begun around 1935.[7] He showed how the scientific renaissance that led to the destruction of the medieval idea of the universe arose largely out of a philosophical argument between Platonism and Aristotelianism concerning the role played by mathematics in man's understanding of the world around him. For the Platonists, who included Galileo, mathematics ruled the universe. For the Aristotelians, who represented traditional scholasticism, mathematics dealt merely in abstractions, and physics was the science of the real.

The science of Galileo rejected all finalist explanations of the universe and brought the idea of a hierarchically ordered cosmos a step closer to destruction. The notion of an infinite and autonomous universe undermined traditional proofs of the existence of God, banished man from his place at the center of creation, and forced him to seek for God within himself. Medieval man had lived in a space where the truth was "given" in the form of revealed religion. But the man of the new Galilean order, whom Descartes bade "philosophize as if no one had ever philosophized before," found himself in a space where thought reigned supreme and thought was lodged in him. The closed, finite, hierarchical world of the Middle Ages was being replaced by a limitless universe in which man stood alone, save for his reason, his uncertainty, and his dismay.[8]

The philosophical parallel to this scientific isolation is to be found in Descartes's *cogito*, subjected to the opposing poles of truth and freedom. The individual is free; he has nothing to lean on outside himself; and he has to confront a truth to which no preexisting authority has set any bounds.[9]

Such meditations on the birth of modern science and the status of the *cogito* had originated in the great philosophical shake-up brought about by Husserl, Koyré's former teacher. Knowledge of Husserl's theories had been gaining ground in France since the 1920s, and especially since February 1929, when Husserl delivered his famous lectures, "Cartesian Meditations," to the Société française de philosophie (French Philosophical Society). Starting from the *cogito*, Husserl's phenomenology asserted that nothing could be known for certain except *my* existence as a thinking being. At the *cogito* stage, being must be reduced to the *I* who is thinking, i.e., to the being of the *ego*. Hence the notion of *phenomenological reduction*, which posits the primacy of the *ego* and of thought and goes beyond ordinary experience to see existence as consciousness of the world. If the existence of the world presupposes that of the *ego*, phenomenological reduction makes *my* existence consciousness of the world. The ego then becomes *transcendental*, and consciousness becomes *intentional*, since it is directed at something. As for ontology, that is an *egology* in which, if my idea of an object is real, then the object itself is also real. Thus the ego acquires a sense of the *other* or of the *alter ego*, through a series of experiences that define transcendental intersubjectivity as the reality out of which each individual *ego* emerges.

In 1935, in *The Crisis of European Sciences and Transcendental Phenomenology* (in German, *Krisis*), Husserl showed how the quest for intersubjectivity could save the human sciences from inhumanity. In other words, by saving the *ego* from scientific formalism, transcendental phenomenology was preserving the possibility of a science of man in which the *ego* could be seen as life itself. So, in the face of the rising tide of barbarism and dictatorship that was threatening the peace of the West. Husserl's phenomenology appealed to the philosophical consciousness that Europe had inherited from antiquity and that found an echo in men and women who wanted to be free to govern their own lives. "There are only two escapes from the crisis of European existence: the downfall of Europe in its estrangement from its own rational sense of life, its fall into hostility toward the spirit and into barbarity; or the rebirth of Europe from the spirit of philosophy through a heroism of reason that overcomes naturalism once and for all. Europe's greatest danger is weariness."[10]

Between the wars Husserl's works fascinated the French intelligentsia, and this showed itself in various ways. Read in conjunction with Heidegger, and particularly in the light of his *Being and Time*, published in 1927, Husserl's writings made it possible to situate the tragic side of existence and the flaws in being within the individual, thus striking a decisive blow at the popularity of Bergsonian optimism about the possibilities of the ego. The resulting critique of the idea of progress led sometimes to a rejection of democratic values in favor of a return to the original roots of being and sometimes to a notion of *nothingness*, or *void*, a tragic symbol of the finiteness and mortal end of a human existence devoid of all transcendency. But Husserl's philosophy did offer modern reason two escape routes. One lay in refocusing Western spirituality on a philosophy of experience and the individual; in France this path would be followed by Jean-Paul Sartre and Maurice Merleau-Ponty. The other solution was to construct a philosophy based on knowledge and rationality, as did Alexandre Koyré, Jean Cavaillès, and Georges Canguilhem. Lacan would follow a middle course between the two that involved both a new exploration of the subject—i.e., of individual experience—and an attempt to define a form of human rationality based on a deeper knowledge of the Freudian unconscious.[11]

Koyré's views on the evolution of science were in tune with the work of the historians who in 1929, led by Marc Bloch and Lucien Febvre, had started the review *Annales d'histoire économique et sociale* (Annals of economic and social history). As early as 1903, in the *Revue de synthese* (Synthesis), founded by Henri Berr, François Simiand had challenged the positivist methods of Ernest Lavisse and Charles Seignobos and advocated the destruction of the three graven images of orthodox history: first, the idol of politics, which required events affecting society as a whole to be reduced to the conscious decisions and deeds of the princes of this world; next, the idol of individuality, which limited the story of all mankind to just the lives of the famous; and last, the idol of chronology, which favored a linear narrative made up of strings of facts supported by sacrosanct "documents."

It was no coincidence that *Annales*, which would give birth to a new school of history, was founded not only in the same year as the Wall Street crash but also at the time that the Husserl revolution was preparing a philosophical rethinking of the question of human existence. At the heart of both the historical and the philosophical movements lay deep doubt about the idea of progress as inherited from eighteenth-century philosophy. Not only had any descriptive history based merely on stirring battles and idealized heroes been rendered obsolete by the recent horrors of Verdun, but these new perceptions of the complexity of "real" and living history ruled out restricted or simplified theories purporting to explain past phenomena. So instead of a Manichaean representation of events, Bloch and Febvre and their friends aimed at creating a vast multiple history that would include the study of lifestyles, habitats, attitudes, feelings, collective subjectivities, and social groups. All these would combine in an epic narrative that could bring a whole era back to life in the reader's imagination. The pioneers of this new history were encouraged in their task by researches in three other fields: the teachings of Vidal de la Blache, who had freed geography from its obsession with administrative divisions and changed it into a largely visual science studied in the field; the work of Emile Durkheim, who had transformed sociology from mere fact collecting into a study of structural patterns; and developments in economic history.

The *Annales* revolution tended in the direction of a temporal and spatial deconstruction of the subject not without analogy in Husserl's philosophy and Einstein's theory of relativity. In this new type of history, man, immersed in the infinite duration of the "long term," was master of his fate no more. Torn between a social and a geographical time dimension no longer limited to his own personal experience, he was nonetheless denied any place in a universal nature, since nature was now "relative," varying from one culture and one period to another.

The cultural relativism of the "Annalists," together with their condemnation of narrative history with a patriotic or nationalistic stance, challenged the high-handed assumptions that made Western civilization see its history in terms of progress: a progress based on the colonization of "minority" cultures. The new historians didn't reject the heritage of Enlightenment philosophy, but they did apply it to different ends. Their object was not so much to reassess "reactionary," "primitive," "barbaric," or prejudice-ridden forms of social organization as to find a new way of thinking about difference and identity, sameness and otherness, reason and unreason, science and religion, error and truth, the occult and the rational. And the demand for relativism, and for an end to the idea that one civilization is superior to another, made possible a new universalism, able to create a living encyclopedia of human societies by incorporating into history the work of other sciences—psychology, sociology, and ethnology—now also expanding rapidly.[12]

Koyré's lectures on Renaissance hermetism and Paracelsus were a factor in bringing together Febvre's and Koyré's influences. In 1931 a group of

French historians of science was formed, and a year later Abel Roy founded the Institute for the History and Philosophy of Science, with offices in the rue du Four and Koyré on the management committee. And so a link was forged between the Annalists and the new scientific historians that would make it possible to trace the evolution of human thought by studying it in creative action.

Febvre's attitude to the possibility of a history of philosophy can best be seen in a review he wrote in 1937 of a book by Georges Freidmann on the current crisis concerning the idea of progress. "It struck me that it would be useful to compare the history of philosophy as written by philosophers with the way we historians proper deal with ideas when the occasion arises. And having done so I was dismayed at how often 'historians proper' are content just to describe new concepts as though they were generated spontaneously, without any reference to their different economic, political, and social backgrounds; as if they were produced by disembodied minds living unreal lives in the sphere of pure ideas."[13] Instead of showing lone eccentrics spinning atemporal systems of thought out of their own entrails, Febvre's history of ideas would deal in real people inventing new thoughts, whether consciously or unconsciously, by means of the *outillage mental* (intellectual apparatus) of their age.

The idea of *mentality*, or mental outlook, revived in the work of Lucien Lévy-Bruhl, had first been used to compare the prelogical thought systems of children and "primitive" peoples with the more abstract functioning of the modern, "Western" mind. But in the 1930s the notion acquired a structural tinge through the use of the phrase *outillage mental*. Whether in Marc Bloch's "symbolic representations," Lucien Febvre's "psychic universe," or Alexandre Koyré's "conceptual structure," the aim was always to define a model of what was thinkable at any given period, using the categories of perception, conceptualization, and expression then available for the organization of individual and collective thought.[14]

All this reflected a French approach to the structural analysis of human societies that could be seen in Lacan as early as 1938 and that a new intellectual generation would take up again twenty years later in the light of Saussurian linguistics.

"In 1925, when I was twenty," writes Jean-Paul Sartre, "there was no chair of Marxism at the university, and communist students took good care not to use any ideas from Marxism, or even to mention it, in their essays. Otherwise they would have failed all their exams. So great was the horror of anything dialectical that we'd never even heard of Hegel."[15] Sartre was describing the state of mind of a generation about to enter the 1930s and caught up in a total contradiction between what they were being taught at

the university and what they were discovering for themselves as they began
to read first Husserl and then Heidegger.

After 1870 Kantian philosophy became more or less the official ideology
for teachers under the Third Republic, and they added to it their own brand
of Cartesianism to provide secular education with a set of ethical standards
to go with its rational theory of knowledge. This, together with Bergson's
life force, seemed capable of solving all the moral problems facing modern
man and all the antinomies of the individual in his or her relation to the
world. So Hegel's philosophy came to be rejected or ignored because of its
idealism and its hostility to mathematics, not to mention its alleged atheism,
immorality, and fatalism. It was accused of dwelling on the nothingness of
being, the nothingness of becoming, and, on top of all the rest, the certainty
of the nothingness of death. It was perceived as a pathological, even an
obscurantist doctrine. To crown all, there was the classic charge of pan-
Germanism. Hegel's "Protestantism" was deemed incompatible with the
categories of "Latin thought," and his philosophy of law was read as an
apologia for the Prussian state. But now all those who were discovering the
greatness of Husserl and awakening to the new light shed by Heidegger felt
a need to go back to the origins of the modern science of consciousness and
to the works of its founder, Georg Wilhelm Friedrich Hegel.

Ever since Victor Cousin's attempt to adapt Hegelianism to the politics
of the Bourbon Restoration—stripping it, in the process, of negativity and
absolute rationality, two of its fundamental ideas—Hegel's thought had
made its way in France clandestinely or through unofficial channels.
Unorthodox academics like Lucien Herr lectured on it; self-taught enthusiasts like Proudhon studied it; poets like Mallarmé and Breton reflected it
in their work. But things suddenly took a radical new turn when Jean Wahl,
Alexandre Koyré, Eric Weil, and Alexandre Kojève initiated the three-
decade "generation of the three Hs (Hegel, Husserl, and Heidegger)."[16]

Koyré again played a leading part. He tackled Hegel for the first time in
the academic year of 1926–1927, in the course of a seminar on German
speculative mysticism. He showed that the *unhappy consciousness*, i.e., the
consciousness that was liberated but a prey to doubt and anguish, was only
a substitute for the consciousness of sin, a negative stage in the evolution of
the mind from which religion had disappeared. He called this theory "opti-
mistic personalism."[17]

In the years that followed, Koyré went on to teach the philosophies of
John Amos Comenius, John Huss, and Nicholas of Cusa. Alexandre Kojève,
who settled in Paris in 1926, began to be a regular attendant at Koyré's seminar, followed by Henry Corbin, who was specializing in oriental studies and
had become a close friend of Jean Baruzi, and by Georges Bataille. Bataille
had recently joined Boris Souvarine as a contributor to *Critique sociale* and

embarked on a polemic with Jean Bernier about Krafft-Ebing's *Psychopathia sexualis*.[18]

The centenary of Hegel's death in 1931 gave rise to an important revival and updating of his thought. The surrealists, especially André Breton, had already related it to the teachings of Freud.[19] On the other hand Bataille, in the early numbers of the review *Documents*, had been hostile and taxed Hegel with "pan-logism." For him the true revolt of man didn't mean overcoming paltry abstract contradictions in order to attain "another life"; it consisted in bursting out altogether from the constraints of reason and philosophy. So he was critical not only of Hegelianism but also of the Marxist and surrealist readings of it. Bataille himself was engaged in reviving gnostic theology, with its love of darkness and its cult of a "base" matter that had no room for reason or ideals.[20] At this point his anti-Hegelianism was based on an anti-Christian stance that would ultimately lead to an apologia for Nietzsche. But after 1930 his earlier attitude to Hegel changed, as a result of the influence of Jean Wahl, of Bataille's own reading of Husserl's *Cartesian Meditations* and Heidegger's article "What Is Metaphysics?" and of a discussion between Bataille and Raymond Queneau triggered off by an essay by Nicolaï Hartmann.[21]

On August 6, 1930, Henry Corbin, just back from Berlin, noted tersely: "Read Heidegger."[22] Corbin, the first person to introduce Iranian Islamic philosophy into France, was also the first French translator of Heidegger's *Being and Time*. His version of "What Is Metaphysics?" appeared in 1931 in the review *Bifur*, with an excellent introduction on Heidegger by Koyré:

He is the first person in the postwar period with the courage to bring the philosophy of heaven down to earth and speak to us about ourselves; to speak—as a philosopher—about very "ordinary," very "simple" things: about life and death, about being and nothingness. . . . He has posed again, with unique freshness and force, the eternal problem faced by any true philosophy, the problem of the self and of being. What am I, and what does being mean? . . . Monsieur Heidegger—and this above all is what makes him so valuable and important—has undertaken an enormous demolition job. The analyses in *Being and Time* are a kind of destructive but liberating catharsis. They take man in his natural state (being in the world). They are about his perception of things, about things themselves, about language, thought, becoming, time. They let us see the work of "One," the impersonal subject. And they guide us toward the ultimate pyre of Nothingness, where all false values, all conventions, and all lies vanish, and man stands alone in the tragic grandeur of his lonely existence: "in truth" and "unto death."[23]

This program of destruction and annihilation went against every kind of theology, even the negative kinds. For as Koyré pointed out, Heidegger's nothingness was neither God nor the absolute: it was just a void that lent a tragic dimension to the grandeur of man's finiteness.

There was a reference to this tragic dimension in an article by Bataille called "A Critique of the Basis of Hegelian Dialectic."[24] But the article links Bataille's change of attitude more closely to a Marx-inspired interpretation that gave Hegel's philosophy an anthropological slant, showing it as providing a kind of family tree of the human condition. This led Bataille to a fascination, later found in Kojève, with the struggle between master and slave and with the defense of a proletariat doomed to a negative existence. Bataille intended this anthropological gloss to enrich Hegelian dialectic with the findings of Freud's psychoanalysis and Durkheim's sociology.

To mark the Hegel centenary, Koyré produced three important articles on his works and added a new lecture to his 1932–1933 seminar on the history of religious ideas in modern Europe. The first article was a historical survey of Hegelian studies in France. The second pointed out a paradox: the difficulty many people had in reading Hegel arose from the fact that he used a living language made up of ordinary words instead of the artificial though familiar jargon of academic philosophy. The third article was a lengthy meditation on the lecture Hegel gave during the Jena period (1802–1807), between the writing of *Fragment of a System* (1801) and *Phenomenology of Mind* (1807).[25]

Koyré said that the period of the Jena lectures was a crucial stage in the evolution of Hegel's system of thought, a dialectic phase during which he realized that it was necessary to explain the world, rather than reform it, and formulated the theory that this "realization" was the dialectical force behind the quest of the mind. From this there emerged the idea of overturning all traditional notions about human understanding and creating a system in which *anxiety* would lie at the core of being: a dialectical ontology of being and nonbeing, of a mobile infinity and a motionless eternity, of annihilation and generation. But if anxiety is at the core of being, that is because the dialectic is defined in terms of human time: "it is in *us*, it is in *our life*, that the *present* of the mind exists," a present always projected into the future and triumphing over the past.

But dialectical time, though it has no end, is built upon the future. Hence, says Koyré, the contradiction in Hegel's system: if human time fails to arrive at some form of completion, no philosophy of history is possible. Yet completion would rule out the primacy of the future and of the motive force behind the dialectic of history. If there is to be a Hegelian history, it must be possible for history to have an end. "Hegel may have believed this. He may even have believed it was not only a necessary condition of the system—the owls of Athena come out only at night—but also that this necessary condition *had already been* realized, that history had actually ended, and that this was why he might be—or had been—able to complete his system."[26]

So Koyré concluded his 1933 course on Hegel with the hypothesis *of an end to History*, a view of Hegel's thought as a realization, in Jena, that the old world had collapsed and that philosophy must be reborn as "the owl of Minerva." The idea caught on. That year's seminar had been attended by the old friends Corbin, Kojève, Bataille, and Queneau. The discussions were lively and continued afterward in useful exchanges at the Café d'Harcourt on the corner of the place de la Sorbonne and the boulevard Saint-Michel. "Who will give us back our d'Harcourt?" wrote Corbin later.

I went back there after the war and found it had been turned into a religious book-shop. And now it's a men's outfitter's. Yet it was at the d'Harcourt that part of the French philosophy of the period was worked out, with the revival of Hegelian stud-ies looming large. Among the people who gathered around Koyré there were Alexandre Kojève, Raymond Queneau, myself, and philosophers like Fritz Heinemann; also many of our Jewish colleagues who had chosen exile and whose harrowing stories told us what was going on in Germany. Things got pretty heated sometimes. Kojève and Heinemann interpreted the phenomenology of mind in completely opposite ways. Comparisons were often made between Husserl's phe-nomenology and that of Heidegger.[27]

It was in this climate of philosophical revival that Corbin and Koyré founded *Recherches philosophiques* (Philosophical studies). The review first appeared in 1933, and there were six issues from then to 1937. Henri-Charles Puech was the leading figure in this venture, with the charming Alfred Spaïer acting as secretary until his premature death in 1934. Spaïer was born in Jassy in Romania in 1883 and in 1914 enlisted as a volunteer in the French army. Six years later he came top in the *agrégation* examination in philoso-phy. Now a senior lecturer at Caen and an enthusiastic admirer of Freud, Spaïer attracted to the review all the psychiatrists and psychoanalysts who were interested in phenomenology—people like Eugène Minkowski, Edouard Pichon, and Henri Ey. Jacques Lacan attended meetings of the group from the 1933–1934 session onward, after he had started attending Kojève's seminar. Contributors to the review included Georges Bataille, Georges Dumézil, Emmanuel Lévinas, Pierre Klossowski, Roger Caillois, and Jean-Paul Sartre, whose *Transcendance de l'ego: Esquisse d'une description phénoménologique* appeared in its pages in 1936.[28]

At a session of his 1960–1961 seminar devoted to Plato's *Symposium*, Lacan described one of his meetings with Kojève. Although by that time Kojève was France's leading representative at international trade negotiations, he spent such time as he could spare on his three-volume history of pagan phi-losophy. He had completed the first volume two years earlier and was work-ing on the second when Lacan came to see him about it. Kojève spoke of his discoveries concerning Plato but told Lacan he hadn't read the *Symposium* for a long time and had nothing to say about it. But he did point out, in general, that Plato's talent lay as much in the way he concealed as in the way he revealed his thought. Kojève linked this to his own approach to philosophy, according to which a text is only the history of its interpretation. And he added enigmatically: "You can never interpret the *Symposium* properly if you don't know why Aristophanes had hiccups." Lacan, reporting this to his audience, reminded them, not for the first time, that it was Kojève who had introduced him to Hegel. Then he commented dutifully on Aristophanes' hiccups.[29]

Kojève was an extraordinary man, and Lacan was only one of many who were captivated by his teachings. He was a very fluent lecturer and spoke perfect French and German, though with an accent that was half Slav and half Burgundian. At every session of his seminar he used to read out a few lines from *The Phenomenology of Mind* and then give a marvelous translation that brought out all the meaning and expressed it in absolutely modern terms. He could be flippant and amusing as well as narcissistic and mysterious. His irreverent tone, the assurance with which he seemed to go to the heart of things, and his great rhetorical skill all combined to hold his hearers spellbound. Georges Bataille was "shattered, overwhelmed, rooted to the spot." Queneau was "staggered."[30]

Born Alexandre Kojevnikov in Moscow in 1902, Kojève was the nephew of Wassily Kandinsky: his paternal grandfather had married the painter's mother. His father, Vladimir, Wassily's half-brother, died in action in Manchuria in 1905, during the Russo-Japanese War that ended with the rout of the czar's army. His mother returned to Moscow and got married again, to her late husband's best friend and comrade-in-arms, who was an excellent stepfather to the young Alexandre. The boy had a privileged upbringing amid the cosmopolitan, cultured, liberal bourgeoisie, living in the smart Arbat district of Moscow and distinguishing himself as a pupil at the Medvenikov Lyceum.

In January 1917, a few months before the revolution, Kojève recorded in his "Philosophical Journal" his thoughts on "the battle of the Arginusae Islands."[31] This was a famous episode in the Peloponnesian War between Sparta, a land power, and Athens, a maritime one. The battle took place in 406 B.C., and the Athenian generals won. But as they were sailing home they met with a dreadful storm and had to jettison the bodies of the dead warriors that, in accordance with Greek law, they were taking home to be buried. The ships were now light enough to weather the storm, but when they reached Athens the generals were tried and executed for sacrilege because they had denied burial to heroes killed in battle. As a result, the democracy fell and was replaced, until 403 B.C., by the tyranny of the Thirty. Only Socrates spoke out against the sentencing of the generals, pointing out that they had had to choose between saving the fleet by sacrificing the corpses or sinking with them onboard and losing the fleet: in either case they would have had to leave the dead unburied and so would be guilty of sacrilege. They were bound to commit a crime but at least they had chosen one evil instead of two. Kojève agreed with Socrates' conclusion but opposed the execution of the generals for a different reason: he absolved the generals of guilt because they had acted as they did not out of a desire to commit a crime but for the common good.[32]

Battles, crime, and death were not merely subjects for philosophical reflection in young Kojève's life. They were important signifiers, landmarks in his own experience. In July 1917, twelve years after his father's death in battle, Kojève saw his stepfather murdered in the family's country home by a gang of looters. A year later he himself was imprisoned in Moscow by the Bolshevik government because he and his schoolmates had been dabbling in the black market. In his cell he realized that "something essential" to the history of mankind was happening, and he became a communist. But because of his bourgeois origins he wasn't allowed to go on with his studies, so despite the fact that it meant leaving his beloved mother behind, he went off to Poland with his friend Georges Witt, providentially carrying a handful of jewelry in his pocket.

One night in 1920, working late in the library in Warsaw, he had a "revelation" similar to the one Nietzsche had in Sils-Maria. As Kojève was meditating on Eastern and Western culture, he had a vision of Buddha and Descartes confronting one another like "the irony of the *cogito*"—like *nonexistence* challenging the ontology of the ego. This was Kojève's first experience of negativity. "I think, therefore 'I' am not," was his conclusion.[33] Moving on to Germany and to Heidelberg University, he preferred Jaspers's lectures to those of Husserl, studied Sanskrit, Tibetan, and Chinese, and tried without success to read Hegel. "I read *The Phenomenology of Mind* right through four times, but though I slogged away as hard as I could I didn't understand a word."[34]

By 1926 he was living in Paris, where he made friends with his fellow countryman Alexandre Koyré in rather comical circumstances. Kojève was the lover of Cécile Shoutak, the wife of Koyré's younger brother, and Koyré's wife sent her husband round to scold him. But Koyré went home all smiles and told his wife, "Cécile's done the right thing—that chap's much better looking than my brother!"[35]

Kojève, an enthusiastic frequenter of Koyré's lectures, joined in the rediscovery of Hegel, going to the famous Café d'Harcourt with Corbin and Bataille and mixing with the *Recherches philosophiques* group. In 1933, when Koyré discovered he had to be away at the end of the year, he suggested that his friend Kojève take over his EPHE lectures on Hegel's religious philosophy. The ministry of education agreed, and Kojève spent the summer of 1933 rereading *The Phenomenology of Mind*. This preparation resulted in the

famous seminar, which was to take place at 5:30 every Monday afternoon
for six years. Afterward, some of the audience of "the two Ks" would
adjourn to the Café d'Harcourt for further discussions. From the 1934–1935
session to that of 1936–1937, Lacan was listed as "regularly present" at the
seminar.[36]

Although Kojève had neither Koyré's philosophical genius nor his skill as
a theorist, he possessed a wonderful talent for transforming philosophy into
a vivid human epic. He could change an abstract concept into an allegorical figure as colorful as any character in Gogol or Dostoyevsky and relate it
to everyday reality. As the lecturer put himself in the place of Socrates or an
Athenian general, Hegel's ideas came across as completely relevant to contemporary events. For when Kojève spoke of the mind, self-awareness,
absolute knowledge, recognition, desire, satisfaction, the unhappy consciousness, or the master-slave dialectic, he was really talking about events
that had marked his own and his audience's youth, events they now examined as men on those Monday afternoons and late into the evening. Koyré's
Socratic commentary on *The Phenomenology of Mind* was a kind of serial
story reflecting the anxieties of a generation shattered by the rise of the dictators, haunted by the prospect of war, and tempted by the new nihilism,
whether in the form of Nietzschean worship of the superman or of
Heidegger's "being-for-death," a negation of all human progress.

Koyré had shown how Hegel's use of ordinary language broke with academic tradition and had put forward his own hypothesis that the "end of
History" was necessary to make Hegelian philosophy possible. Kojève's
commentary followed Koyré on both counts.

Twice—in October 1806 and in May 1807—Hegel spoke with awe of
Napoleon's exploits. "I saw the emperor, heart and soul of the world, ride
out of the city on reconnaissance." "My book was finished at last during the
night before the battle of Jena." As he pondered these two remarks, Kojève
had a "revelation" about the underlying significance of Hegel's attitude: his
book had been written in circumstances that amounted to the end of
History. "I read *The Phenomenology of Mind* again, and when I got to chapter 6 I realized it [i.e., the end of History] was Napoleon. I started giving my
lectures without preparing them. I just read and commented, and everything
Hegel said seemed crystal clear. . . . It's all to do with the end of History. It's
very funny. Hegel said it himself. But when I explain that Hegel said it himself, said that history is over, no one will accept it: no one can stomach it. To
tell the truth, I thought at first it was nonsense myself, but then I thought
about it some more and saw it was brilliant."[37]

In December 1937 Kojève supplemented this idea in a lecture he gave at
the Collège de sociologie (College of Sociology). "That was the day Kojève
informed us that Hegel had seen right but was off by a century: The man of

the end of History was not Napoleon but Stalin." But Kojève changed his mind again after the Second World War: He had given the correct date for the end of History: it was 1806.[38]

Hegel had shown that consciousness moves to become mind, but for that to happen consciousness must cease to be concerned with certainty about itself and let the mind function as a truth without a subject. Kojève, influenced by both Marx and Heidegger, offered an anthropological interpretation of the movement in question. He saw historical man as a void-creating subject, exercising his negativity in struggle and labor and driven by a desire that by its very nature could never be satisfied, "That's where Kojève was so clever," says Pierre Macherey. "He showed us the child that Heidegger might have had by Marx, and passed it off as Hegel."[39]

This reading of Hegel, involving the end of History and an allegorical version of the master-slave relationship—which Lacan was to reformulate—led to the idea that it might be possible to do away with man himself. Having defined him in terms of dissatisfaction and negativity, Kojève dismissed both these categories and turned man into either a "Sage" or an "idle layabout." This was how History really ended: man returned to the nothingness of his animal nature and accepted the world order just as it was, princes and tyrants and all. In this context, no revolution was possible, and the philosopher-intellectual (the Sage) had to choose between two attitudes: either he became an anonymous servant of the state—which is what Kojève himself did—or like a noble romantic soul he went on dreaming of revolution that already lay in the past.

George Bataille denied there was any such dilemma and rebuked Kojève for condemning intellectuals to "pointless negativity." Against the animal passivity of the Sage he urged holy terror and Nietzschean madness, which together could once more subvert the social order. This was the idea behind the Collège de sociologie.[40]

I have spoken before of Kojève's influence on Lacan's development, especially in his escape from the negative transference situation with Loewenstein.[41] Kojève's teaching left a permanent mark on Lacan's reading of Hegel. It also provided an enduring model for Lacan's own method of teaching. He too would reign over a whole intellectual generation by means of oral teaching, seminars that in his case were centered on the works of Freud. He too would have an amanuensis to record what he said, and he too would occupy a paradoxical position, at once marginal and essential, in French academic life.

But Kojève's teaching also encouraged the nihilism Lacan had gone in for during his adolescent admiration for Maurras. In this respect Lacan would prove both more conventional and more of a terrorist than Kojève's Sage. The latter always believed in the possibility of man as a hero, even if only in the service of the existing state of things. But while belle epoque nihilism had provided the young Lacan with an escape from the gaping void of family life, and though he carried its ideas to extremes, it never inspired him with any real desire to change the social order or even to offer it any resistance when the occasion arose.

It was this complex of attitudes that produced Lacan's determined assertion of the omnipotence of the ego as against that of God, the community, or the state, even though he went on to dismantle the ego's very structure. The same complexities also led to Lacan's cultivation of pessimism, ennui, decadence, and hatred of any kind of heroism, an attitude arising out of a lucid appraisal of the decline, not to say degradation, of the role of fatherhood in the West. From the same source sprang Lacan's desire to modernize human subjectivity so that it might rival even the sweeping advances of science. Nor was it any accident that, in the field of literature, Lacan's admiration for Maurras had a parallel in his liking for the works of Léon Bloy, archprophet of verbal violence and Promethean excess who attacked the ideals of freedom and revolution and preached instead a fanatical Catholicism imported from the wilder shores of exegesis.

Bloy was a kind of mirror image of Lacan, condensing all his ambivalences. The new French interpreter of Freudianism was constantly solicited by a hyperactive ego that confronted him now with his own negativity, now with the illusion of having at last attained satisfaction. Not surprisingly, Lacan's love of excess, which included a need to identify with a paranoid mode of cognition—a link, here, with Bloy's interest in female dementia—also entailed a visceral, almost fetishist fondness for money, rare books, and works of art. This approach to philosophy via its opposites in alienation and fetishism was Lacan's version of "idle negativity." Followed, as in his case, in a spirit of mockery, it might seem dangerously close to imposture. But it also provided a framework for a genuine system of thought.

The time Lacan spent with philosophers and at Kojève's seminar first showed its effects in a 1935 contribution to *Recherches philosophiques*: a review of Eugène Minkowski's book *Le Temps vécu: Etudes phénoménologiques et psychologiques* (Lived time: Phenomenological and psychological studies).[42] While paying tribute to the author, a master of phenomenological psychiatry whose work had played an important part in his own training, Lacan tore into contemporary psychiatry as a whole. "Most of the material presented to the official learned societies," he said,

offers, to one long obliged by his profession to seek information from this dismal source, nothing but a picture of utter intellectual stagnation. . . . The futility of the content is obvious from the terminology. This is derived entirely from an academic psychology still hopelessly stuck at Victor Cousin; its scholastic abstractions have never been broken down through the techniques of association. Hence all the verbiage about images, sensations, hallucinations; about judgment, interpretation, intelligence, and the rest; and, last but not least, about affectivity, a catchword that came in very useful for a while to help advanced psychiatry avoid a number of issues.[43]

Lacan then went on to show how right Minkowski was to call attention to the usefulness of Clérambault's researches. This allowed Lacan to acknowledge his own debt to Clérambault and stake a claim to being himself the real reformer of contemporary psychiatry. He reminded his readers how he had introduced the new notion of "paranoid cognition" into the field. Finally, in a complete turnabout, he pointed out the limits of the psychiatric conception of phenomenology and proposed instead a new reading of the "real" phenomenology, that of Hegel, Husserl, and Heidegger, which had revolutionized the history of philosophy. Lacan was thus rejecting the version of phenomenology that had been useful to him up till 1932 and replacing it with a version derived from his direct contacts with the French school of historians of science and religion. This was the first time he mentioned Heidegger—evidence that he had come to him via Kojève's commentaries on *The Phenomenology of Mind*. "I allude here to a notion frequently encountered in the philosophy of Monsieur Heidegger. What little we have so far been able to take in of this philosophy, filtered to us as it is through the sieve of abstruse language and international censorship, has given us an appetite that here is left unsatisfied. In a note on page 16, Monsieur Minkowski says he was unaware of Heidegger's ideas until after his own had taken final shape. Given his dual culture (he stresses that his early works were written in German), it is a pity he has not undertaken to introduce into French philosophy the vast development that has taken place in recent years in its German counterpart."[44]

So, even though his worth had been recognized in psychiatric circles, Lacan was distancing himself from them and entering a new intellectual milieu: one that was already supplying the ideas he needed for the work of reconstruction that was to follow his years of silence. A letter he wrote to Henri Ey on May 4, 1935, shows that his relations with his best friend in psychiatry were already less relaxed than they had been. "My dear fellow," he wrote, "Of course I'd be delighted to see our old but still living concord show signs of flourishing again. It's more than time for the four of us to resume our get-togethers."[45]

On July 20, 1936, as Lacan was preparing his paper on the *mirror stage* for his first contribution to an IPA congress, in Marienbad at the beginning of August, Kojève was writing a strange note in Russian, probably intended for his friend Koyré. It ran: "Hegel and Freud: attempt at a comparative interpretation. 1. The genesis of self-awareness. The beginning is urgent as it is to be written [for] you in collaboration with Dr. Lacan and published in

Recherches philosophiques. (Only part of the 'introduction' is written, six paragraphs, which make a comparison between Hegel and Descartes.) Unfinished. (There's a sort of summary 15+1 pages.) Started 20/VII/36."[46]

The handwritten note was never sent to Koyré and remained among Kojève's papers. Today, thanks to the documents discovered by Dominique Auffret, Kojève's biographer, it is possible to understand what it means. That year, Kojève and Lacan decided to join forces in a study to be entitled *Hegel and Freud: Attempt at a Comparative Interpretation*. It was to be divided into three parts: (1) "Genesis of Self-awareness"; (2) "The Origin of Madness"; and (3) "The Essence of the Family." A chapter on "Prospects" was to be added. The article was probably meant to appear in the review *Recherches philosophiques* under the auspices of Koyré, who would either just look the text over or else add his own point of view.

Whatever the case, the project never took off. All that got consigned to paper was Kojève's attempt at the first part: an unfinished introduction covering fifteen handwritten pages—six paragraphs plus a page of notes—in which Kojève compared Descartes's *cogito* with Hegel's self-awareness and showed that philosophy is nothing but the desire to philosophize. "It is in Hegel," Kojève wrote, "that the first *I think* of Descartes becomes the *I want* . . . from which will finally come the *I want to philosophize* that in satisfying itself will reveal the true nature of the original want." And

My intention is simply to show the gist of the introduction to philosophy proper that is what Hegel's *Phenomenology of Mind* really is. And I think that gist is particularly clear in his replacing of Descartes's *I think* by *I want*. . . . But we must not forget that in Descartes's philosophical system the ego is not reduced to thought, i.e., to an adequate revelation of being through consciousness. The ego is also will, and will is the source of error; that is, it is the fact of the ego-as-will that brings about the imperfection needed for philosophy to be transformed into "philosophizing" and thus plays a role similar to that of the ego-as-desire in Hegel's system. So in order to compare the two systems we need first and foremost to compare these two similar but different concepts of the ego.[47]

At the same time as Kojève was noting the change from a philosophy of *I think* to a philosophy of *I want*, he was introducing a split between the *je* (I), site of thought and desire, and the *moi* (me, or ego), source of error. Part of Lacan's task in the joint production would certainly have been to complete the project by placing Freud in context in the same way as Kojève had placed Descartes and Hegel. The other two sections of the essay, on the origin of madness and the essence of the family, would presumably have been dealt with in a similar way, by comparisons made in relation to Freud and Hegel.

But Lacan wrote nothing, and Kojève didn't continue, though in the fifteen manuscript pages of his introduction to "Genesis of Self-awareness" there are three major concepts that would be used by Lacan in 1938: the *I* as subject of desire, *desire* as revelation of the truth of being, and the *ego* as the site of delusion and the source of error. These three concepts would be found, mingled with the themes concerning the origin of madness and the essence of the family, in all the texts about the subject that Lacan published between 1936 and 1949: in "Au-delà du principe de réalité" (Beyond the reality principle) and in "Les Complexes familiaux" (Family complexes); in "Propos sur la causalité psychique" (Remarks on psychical causality) as well as in the second version of "Stade du miroir" (The mirror stage).

So it is not without interest that the second great theoretical renovation carried out by Lacan, which led him from his already Freudian reading of psychiatry to a philosophical reading of Freud, originated in the plan for a two-handed collaboration, a partnership in which the "mentor in Hegel" to a whole generation brought the ideas of his "pupil" within the sphere of a vast phenomenological whole, centered on such "Hegelian-Freudian" questions as desire, the cogito, self-awareness, madness, the family, and the illusions of the ego.[48] One can hardly overemphasize the fact that the transferential relationship that led Lacan to become both an analyst and an intellectual authority occurred *beside* rather than *on* the couch in the avenue de Versailles. In other words, it arose from the "negativeness" of that analysis and in a completely different space: a space giving rise to a new dialectic of self-awareness that would be quite incompatible with the positivist norms of official Freudian institutions.

11

. . . .

Marienbad

*I*t was with such studies behind him that Lacan set off for his first IPA congress, just at the time when Ernest Jones, the president of the association, was completing the sellout of psychoanalysis in Germany by agreeing that Göring's institute should swallow up the DPG. Freud, too ill to come to the congress, stayed behind in Vienna: Marienbad was chosen as the venue so that Anna wouldn't be too far away in case of an emergency. But the institutional heart of Freudian legitimacy, to which Lacan was bringing his paper on "the mirror stage," was rent with fierce disputes: the bone of contention was child psychoanalysis; the adversaries were the supporters of Melanie Klein and those of Anna Freud. The Kleinian group, backed by Jones, held that child psychoanalysis should be a special domain using special techniques, such as play, modeling, drawing, and cutting out; the Anna Freud group wanted to keep child analysis within the field of pedagogy and under the control of parents, on the model of Sigmund Freud's own methods with "Little Hans."[1] So, in a setting of theoretical debate, the Freudian community engaged in internal family battles reminiscent of Shakespearean tragedy. Between the two world wars the IPA congresses resembled the auditorium of some ancient theater, where the princes of the Freudian empire gave vent to their passions before an audience made up of the affiliated societies. Edward Glover, after Jones the most powerful man in the British Psycho-Analytical Society (BPS), proved a particularly formidable figure in the Anna Freud–Melanie Klein conflict, which was to lead to the famous "Controversial Discussions" in London during the war.

Edward Glover was born in 1888 into a strict Presbyterian family. He was analyzed by Karl Abraham and became a member of the BPS on his return from Germany. His brother James was already involved with the society as a teacher and scientific secretary. In 1926, when James died, Edward asked Jones to let him take over his brother's functions. Permission was given, and

Edward went on to become chairman of the scientific committee; in 1934 he rose to the distinguished position of secretary to the IPA's training committee. His caustic personality and great attractiveness to women couldn't conceal the fact that his life was overshadowed by a great tragedy: in 1926 his daughter was born with Down's Syndrome. He would never acknowledge her abnormality and took her with him everywhere, on his travels and to the IPA congresses, where she was present during the interwar years at the arguments over the psychoanalytic treatment of children.[2]

When Melanie Klein published her book on the analysis of children, Glover was quick to point out the importance of her ideas. "I have no hesitation in saying," he wrote of her work, "that it constitutes a landmark in analytic literature worthy to rank with some of Freud's own classical contributions."[3] He was right. Melanie Klein was the first person within the Freudian movement to consider the question of child analysis. Before that, Freud, Hermine von Hug-Hellmuth, and Anna Freud hadn't believed it was possible to reach children directly in this way.[4] They either went back to a patient's childhood via the analysis of the adult, as Freud did with the Wolf Man, or they approached a child through its parents. Taboos about the alleged innocence of childhood were so strong that despite Freud's discoveries about infantile sexuality it was thought that analyzing young children without using their parents as intermediaries would worsen their condition and lead to further deterioration in their personalities. This attitude was reinforced by the belief that children were not conscious of their disorders and that their attachment to their parents would make transference impossible.[5]

Melanie Klein's masterstroke consisted of ignoring the taboos and breaking through all the theoretical and practical barriers that had previously prevented the establishment of a child psychoanalysis modeled on the treatment of adults. Like all the great innovators, she had tested her discoveries and inventions on her own family, analyzing her two sons and her daughter when they were small.[6] In this she was simply following Freud, who had been Anna's analyst when at the age of twenty-five she decided to embark on a career as practitioner and teacher. Klein's work may have been a corollary of Freud's, but it is easy to see why she was forced to analyze her own children. It was the only way of acquiring experience, as no one else had yet dared to do such a thing. Freud was the first to discover the repressed child in the adult, but it was Melanie Klein who discovered the infant who had already been repressed in the child. And while she was at it she suggested not only a theory but also a framework within which specifically child-oriented analysis could be carried out. As Hanna Segal writes:

She provided the child with an appropriate psychoanalytic setting: that is, the child had his or her sessions at strictly defined times—fifty minutes five times a week. The room was specially adapted for the child. It would contain only simple and sturdy furniture, a small table and chair for the child, a chair for the analyst, a small couch. The floor and the walls would be washable. Each child would have its own box of toys, used only for the treatment. The toys were carefully chosen. There were little houses, little men and women, preferably in two sizes, farm and wild animals, bricks, balls, maybe marbles, also play material such as scissors, string, pencils, paper, Plasticine. Besides that, the room would have water, since in some phases of the analyses of many children water plays a very important role.[7]

The first point of departure for Klein's innovations was the great revision of Freudianism that took place in the 1920s with the introduction of a new dual system of drives or instincts (of life and death) and of a second topography (id, ego, and superego instead of unconscious, preconscious, and conscious). Klein drew next on her own analysis with Ferenczi, which directed her attention toward children very early on, and on the teaching of Abraham, her second analyst, whose work on the psychoses, particularly melancholia, located their origin in early infancy. Klein's adoption of the idea of a death drive and of a topography in which the unconscious played a preponderant role, together with the study of the origins of adult psychosis, paved the way for the examination of psychosis in young children. Thus it was that in 1935 Melanie Klein's work took a new direction. And having started out from psychosis to study the importance of the first years of life in a child's psychological development, she pushed on even further in the search for origins and, using the changes that had come about in Freud's own thought, described the very first object relations as they occurred in infancy.

Her aim was to show how the mechanisms of psychosis exist in every human being at different phases of his or her development. At the beginning of an individual's life, according to Klein, the duality of drives or instincts brings about a split in the objects to which the subject relates, some being seen as *good* and some as *bad*. Whether it is a part object, as in the case of the breast, the excreta, or the penis, or a whole object, when it is concerned with a person, the object is always an *imago*—the image of a real object that the subject absorbs by introjection into his or her ego and endows with the status of a fantasy.[8]

In the first four months of life the infant's relation with its mother is mediated by the breast, experienced as a destructive object. Melanie Klein called this point in human development the *paranoid position* (not *stage*). It is followed for about eight months by a so-called depressive position, during which the split narrows. After this, the child is able to represent the mother to itself as a whole object. Anxiety, instead of being experienced as a kind of persecution, takes the form of a fantasized dread of destroying and losing the mother. According to this theory the pathological differed from the normal only as to organization. If the paranoid position was not gone through "normally," it recurred in the subject's childhood and either continued into or recurred again in adulthood, when it gave rise to states of melancholy.

Thus during the interwar period Melanie Klein had begun constructing a theory about the structure of the subject and its "imaginary order" that answered the questions all her contemporaries were asking themselves. They were of course the same questions as those preoccupying Lacan and the whole second generation of French psychiatrists and psychoanalysts. Like Klein, but following different routes, Lacan had queried the theory of constitutions, which created an artificial barrier between the normal and the pathological. Like her, by choosing to work in the field of psychosis he had placed the history of madness within the sphere of the history of the human subject in general. Like her, he was trying to solve the riddle of man's "imaginary" condition by exploring the earliest elements of object relationships. And, like her, he approached Freudian theory as an established body of work in need of a new impetus. But whereas Klein carried out her reform within the Freudian system and with the conceptual tools forged by Freud himself, Lacan drew continuously on other fields: psychiatry, surrealism, philosophy. Without these constant outside references he would probably not have reinterpreted Freud in the way he did from 1936 on, for the Freud to whom he had first had access was an academic Freud, the Freud of French Freudianism, a Freud sometimes of Pichon and sometimes of Loewenstein, but always the Freud of the ego, of resistances and defense mechanisms: the Freud of Anna Freud and of the future "American" trend of ego psychology.[9]

It was because in 1932 Lacan was still reliant on this version of Freud that his thesis favored a treatment of psychosis based on an analysis of the ego centered on resistances. It was for the same reason that he didn't react until 1937 to the progress made by Klein. Only after 1936, when he had arrived at his second reading of Freud, could he take her work on board and see that, by paths different from but parallel to his own, she was asking the same questions as he about the status of the subject, the structure of object relations, the early role of the Oedipus bond, the paranoid position of human knowledge, the site of the imaginary order, and so on.

In this connection Lacan's borrowing of the psychologist Henri Wallon's notion of a *mirror stage* was crucial.[10] Its importance may be measured by his attempts to play down Wallon's name and present himself as the sole originator of the term. An account of his different definitions of it reads like a serial story. He spoke passionately of it on about a dozen occasions, and when he published his *Ecrits* (Writings) in 1966 he emphasized again that the term had always been the pivot on which the development of his thought system turned. "I didn't wait until now to think about the fantasies leading to an apprehension of the *ego*, and if I put forward the 'mirror stage' in 1936, at a time when I was still not a training analyst [in the SPP] and was having only the first of my many experiences of an IPA congress, I think I deserved some credit." He added a note: "It was on July 31, 1936, at the Marienbad congress, that this first pivot of my contribution to psychoanalytic theory made its appearance. An ironic allusion to this incident may be found on pp. 184–185 of the present volume, with a reference to the volume of the *Encyclopédie française* that officially authenticates the date of the introduction of these theories (1938). The fact is, I neglected to hand in my text for inclusion in the proceedings of the congress."[11]

Before I piece together the stormy history of that text, which was forgotten, lost, merged with another, then in 1940 entirely recast for another IPA congress, I had best give a first definition of the notion of the *mirror stage* as it appears in Lacan's terminology between 1936 and 1938.

Kojève's seminar had led Lacan to examine the genesis of the ego in the light of a philosophical approach to self-awareness. Then, like Melanie Klein, he interpreted Freud's second topography in a way that ran counter to any ego psychology. Two options were available after Freud's 1920 revision of his theories. One was to see the ego as the product of a gradual differentiation of the id, acting as a representative of reality and responsible for controlling the drives (ego psychology); the other rejected any idea of making the ego autonomous and instead looked to find its genesis in identification. The first alternative meant trying to extract the ego from the id and making it the instrument of the individual's adaptation to external reality, while the second option moved the ego closer to the id and sought to show it structuring itself in stages by means of imagoes borrowed from "the other." Melanie Klein chose the second alternative, and so did Lacan when he took over and completely transformed Wallon's notion of the *mirror stage*.

Wallon subscribed to the Darwinian idea that the individual turned into a subject through the succeeding stages of a natural dialectic. In the context of this transformation, during which the child has to resolve its conflicts, the so-called mirror ordeal is a rite of passage that takes place between the ages of six and eight months. It allows the infant to recognize itself and to unify its ego in space. The experience thus represents a transition from the specular to the imaginary and then from the imaginary to the symbolic.[12]

Lacan transforms this experience into a stage, i.e., a position in the Kleinian sense, without any reference to a natural dialectic (psychological maturing or progress in knowledge) that allows the subject to unify its functions. This being so, the *mirror stage* no longer bears any resemblance to either a mirror or a stage (in the developmental sense), or indeed to any concrete experience. It becomes a psychological, even an ontological operation, by which a human being comes to exist as such by identifying with his *sem-*

blable—his likeness, fellow, or "neighbor"—when as an infant he sees his own image in a mirror. And so the *mirror stage* in the Lacanian sense is a matrix foreshadowing the evolution of the ego as imaginary. Lacan gave his own best definition of the *mirror stage* in 1937, commenting on a lecture by Marie Bonaparte; he also included it a year later in his own text on family complexes. "I refer," he writes, "to the narcissistic representation I attempted to describe at the international congress when I spoke of the 'mirror stage.' That representation explains the oneness of a human body; but why must this oneness be established? Precisely because man is painfully aware of the threat of fragmentation, fear of which installs itself in the first six months of biological prematuration."[13]

While Lacan was working on the first theory of the imaginary, and planning, with Kojève, a systematic comparison between Freud and Hegel, discord within the BPS was becoming more and more heated. Edward Glover, who had spoken highly of Klein's ideas, considered nonetheless that their validity depended on their usefulness in the analysis of adult psychotics. His reservation was made with a purpose: to preserve psychosis as the domain of medically qualified analysts and to prevent the inroads that Klein, who had no medical training, might make into the society via her pupils. But quite apart from this rivalry there was still the fundamental question: what specific contribution does psychoanalysis make to the treatment of psychosis? As we have seen, Lacan had been asking this question ever since he studied the Aimée case.[14]

Controversy soon turned into combat when Melitta Schmideberg, Melanie Klein's daughter, arrived in London in 1932, when her mother's ideas were beginning to gain acceptance. Melitta, after undergoing analysis with Ella Sharpe, started on a second analysis with Glover and with his help launched a general offensive against her mother's teachings. When Melitta was elected a member of the BPS in October 1933, she was awarded the clinical essay prize for the essay she had submitted in support of her candidature, on the analysis through play of a three-year-old girl. For a time Melitta was quite popular with her colleagues, but the virulence with which she expressed her views began to embarrass them, the more so because she made all kinds of shocking allegations about her mother, sometimes accusing her of "stealing" her daughter's patients, sometimes hinting that she had analyzed children who were less than three years old, which would have been considered outrageous.

Meanwhile the quarrel between the Vienna school, dominated by Anna Freud, and the English school, which had gone over to Klein, had taken a particularly lively turn. When William Gillespie returned from Vienna in 1932, after his analysis with Eduard Hitschmann, he was struck by the extent to which the various groups ostracized one another. He had never heard his

Viennese colleagues mention Klein's work, now the bible of the London analysts. Ernest Jones, wishing to placate Freud, who sided with his daughter, tried to distract Anna from her battle with her rival by inducing her to make a scapegoat of Klein's daughter. In this way he hoped to preserve the unity of the British Society by getting rid of an adversary who had become a problem, to keep the IPA united around Freud, and to avoid a direct confrontation between Vienna and London. But Anna declined to go along with Jones's plan, which in any case was soon thwarted by the rise of Nazism in Germany. In 1934 the Viennese started to leave Austria, some of them with the intention of settling in England. So, after the Anschluss and the outbreak of war, the battle became an internal concern of the British Psycho-Analytical Society.[15]

At the Marienbad congress, the symposium on the therapeutic effects of psychoanalysis gave rise to a mighty confrontation involving all the different factions. While the supporters of Anna Freud mounted a systematic attack on the Kleinians, Glover, backed by Melitta Schmideberg, publicly dissociated himself from the views of Melanie Klein, though at first the Viennese couldn't understand the ins and outs of the family feuding and went on thinking of Glover as a Kleinian.

Such was the atmosphere in which at 3:40 P.M. on August 3, 1936, at the second scientific session of the congress, Lacan rose to speak. Ten minutes later, Jones cut him short in the middle of a sentence. "I read a paper on this subject at the Marienbad conference in 1936," Lacan wrote later.

At least, I did so until exactly ten minutes into my text, when on the very stroke I was interrupted by Jones, who as president of the London psychoanalytic society was chairing the proceedings. I assume he qualified for the position by virtue of the fact that I never met one of his English colleagues who had a good word to say for him. However, the Viennese group, gathered there like a flock of birds about to migrate, did receive my paper quite warmly. I didn't send it in for inclusion in the proceedings of the congress, but its essentials are summed up in a few lines in my article on the family published in 1938 in the *Vie mentale* (Life of the mind) volume of the *Encyclopédie française*.[16]

The day after the incident with Jones, Lacan left for Berlin, though Ernst Kris, one of the founders of American ego psychology, had said to him, "That sort of thing isn't done."[17]

We now know the contents of the famous lost lecture. Lacan had read the gist of it to the SPP before he went to Marienbad, and full and painstaking notes taken on that occasion by Françoise Dolto confirm that Lacan used the same terms in the article on the family as he had done in his paper. This was divided into a number of sections: the subject and the I, the body, the expressiveness of the human form, the libido, the body image, the image of the double and the specular image, the libido of weaning, the death instinct,

the destruction of the vital object, narcissism and its link with the fundamental symbolism of human knowledge, the object rediscovered in the
Oedipus complex, twins (see appendix F).

The discussion among Loewenstein, Odier, Parcheminey, Paul Schiff,
Lagache, and Marie Bonaparte was about interpreting the second topography and the idea of adaptation. Lacan was already stoutly asserting the central tenet of his future system: "Man does not adapt himself to reality; he
adapts reality to himself. The ego creates a new adaptation to reality, and we
try to maintain cohesion with this double."[18]

It is easy to understand the rage and humiliation Lacan must have felt
when Jones cut him short. Thirty years later, when he published the *Écrits*,
he was still angry enough to record the exact time, date, and place where
someone had dared to interrupt him. After being ignored by Freud when
he sent him his thesis, he now found himself being snubbed during his first
appearance at an IPA congress. To the great disciples of the Freudian era,
fighting their Shakespearean battles at Marienbad, this young Frenchman
was a mere nobody. No one yet knew who he was, no one had read a line
of what he had written, and no one realized that a section of the Paris intelligentsia regarded him as a future master of French psychoanalysis. The new
direction Lacan had taken with his *mirror stage* was in keeping with the
Kleinian revolution, but no one, neither the Kleinians nor the Anna-
Freudians, were in a position to see this. And Lacan himself, knowing little
about the IPA's family squabbles, was not best placed to grasp the implications of his own theoretical tendencies. That much is plain from his—perfectly genuine—belief that the Vienna group gave him a favorable reception. If he really did think that, and there is no reason to doubt it, there must
have been a complete misunderstanding all round. His views were radically
opposed to theirs, and the friendly reception, if there was one, must have
been due either to a certain amount of personal sympathy or to some verbal exchanges on the common ground of familiarity with Freudian and
other texts. Lacan had read them, the Viennese contingent would have
admired his erudition, and he might have got the impression that it was his
own views that were going down so well. We know now that Anna Freud
didn't share her compatriots' approval, if such it was. Always on the lookout
for deviations from the pure Freudianism of which she considered herself
the legitimate representative, she noted that day the behavior, bearing, and
style of the young French psychiatrist who already had such a good opinion of himself. She didn't like the man and began to be suspicious of his
views.[19]

With his antiparliamentary and nihilist leanings and despite his encounter
with surrealism, Lacan never showed the slightest interest in fighting for any

revolutionary ideal of freedom. He was never a communist; he never put his name to any political pamphlet; he never seemed to believe in the idea of human freedom. Yet the spirit of Rimbaud's "JE est un autre" (I is another) ran right through his earliest writings, and the philosophical renaissance of the 1930s was an essential preliminary to his reading of Freud. But his relationship to modernity in both literature and thought was a strange one: it seemed to affect only his work, touching his way of life and personal opinions scarcely at all. His behavior and views were those of a member of the middle class who was at once conventional and eccentric, careful with his money but capable of throwing himself body and soul into his passions.

But though Lacan was apolitical, this didn't mean he took no interest in political matters. On the contrary. A corollary of his avoidance of personal commitment was an open fascination with the most extreme forms of power in action: the hypnotic power of dictators, the transferential power of teachers, the manipulative power of tyrants, the wild power of madness when madness itself was in power. In short, the man who himself aspired to be a leader enjoyed observing, and commenting on, how the masses were enslaved by their masters and how willingly they accepted their subjection.

And so when Lacan left Marienbad he went on to Berlin to attend the XIth Olympic Games, of sinister memory. Having spoken a few days earlier of the anguish of the ego when threatened by the fragmentation of the body, he was so preoccupied with the *mirror stage* theory that he applied its terminology to the world of the gladiators now parading past him. Later he made a rather obscure analysis of fascism, which he hated and saw as a threat. According to him the Nazi organization was a source of anguish to the masses it claimed to rule. And Lacan saw the cause of that anguish in Hitler's democratization of the hierarchical structure of the German army. I shall return to this subject later.[20]

The principal outcome of Lacan's visit to Marienbad and his side trip to Berlin was his article "Au-dela du principe de réalité" (Beyond the reality principle), a résumé of all the themes arising out of his reading of Wallon and of Freud's second topography, and out of the teaching of Kojève. This text is a link between the uncompleted plans made in July for a comparison between Freud and Hegel, and the long article on family complexes into which he would insert the first published version of "Le Stade du miroir."

Lacan wrote "Beyond the Reality Principle" at Noirmoutier, where he was spending the vacation with Malou, now five months pregnant. At the age of thirty-five, about to become a father for the first time, he was greeting the triumphal advent of a second generation of psychoanalysts and commending to them a nonpsychological approach to Freud. It was a doctrinal call to arms. On the beach where he liked to go swimming he might have noticed another mass phenomenon just as significant as the Olympic junketings: factory workers enjoying their first holidays with pay. But he did no such thing. Here is the curious portrait Guillaume de Tarde drew of him in his diary in June 1936: "All this time Lacan is living on the plane of eternity. As an intellectual, and therefore in a lofty position, open to ideas of every kind, supremely and indisputably impartial, a master of language, by nature incapable of banality or prejudice, he looks down on ordinary events from a great height. Human beings, outmoded, doomed, defending their class interests against inexorable reality, clearly seem to him mere puppets. They present a pitiful spectacle, like the last scene of a tragedy, half touching, half comic! He reigns majestically over their anguish."[21]

In the history of the international psychoanalytic movement it is customary to refer to the circle of disciples gathered in Vienna at the beginning of the twentieth century as "the first generation." This well-known group of pioneers—Adler, Jung, Jones, Ferenczi, Rank, Abraham, Sachs, and Eitingon—was succeeded by another generation that began to form in 1918, consisting of both those in direct contact with Freud and the people they analyzed. Already at a distance from the spirit of adventure that had inspired their elders, this second generation supplied most of the leading members of the IPA in the 1930s. Although the founding father was still alive, the IPA had moved away from him; its real center was neither a man nor a city but an organization. And the importance of that organization was enhanced when, during the Nazi regime, it came to represent Freudianism's true home and a symbol of resistance against barbarism. Later came a third generation, taught by members of the second generation in exile, and with them came the great controversies over the interpretation of Freud's works. In the international context, Lacan belongs to that third generation by virtue of his training, his distance from Freud himself, and his reexamination of a doctrine that he came on when it was no longer subject to revision by its founder.

But if we look only at the French history of psychoanalysis, the chronology of the generations is rather different. Freudian theory took off in France fifteen years later than anywhere else in Europe. In this more circumscribed context, the first generation of French psychoanalysts, to which the twelve founders of the SPP belonged, were men and women whose careers or outlooks placed them in the second generation of international Freudianism. And this was the explanation of some of the problems they had with the IPA. In the French chronology, Lacan was, as we have seen, a member of the second generation. But that was connected with what, in the international chronology, was the third generation. And he knew it.

When he got back from Marienbad, humiliated and disappointed, he produced a text in which for the first time he linked the interests of a nec-

essary "Freudian revolution" with those of a hypothetical "second generation" belonging to the 1930s.

> The new psychology admits not only psychoanalysis; the fact that we encounter it
> constantly at the growing point of other disciplines, beginning from other starting
> points, demonstrates its pioneering value in general. So it is from what might be
> called a general angle that psychoanalysis is approached by what I shall call, perhaps
> rather arbitrarily, the second analytic generation. And I try to define this angle of
> incidence in order to indicate the angle of reflection. Like all revolutions, the
> Freudian revolution takes its meaning from its circumstances, i.e., from the psy-
> chology of its time. And that psychology can only be appraised through a study of
> the documents in which it has expressed itself.[22]

Was Lacan trying to present himself as the leader of the second French
generation of psychoanalysts or as one of the brilliant second wave of international Freudians he had met at Marienbad? Both, probably; hence his
equivocal way of expressing himself. In any case, he wanted his rethinking
of Freud's teaching to be seen as symmetrical with Freud's own revision in
1920. Lacan's call for something "beyond the reality principle" looked very
like a corollary to Freud's *Beyond the Pleasure Principle*.

If the structuring of the ego is not an adaptation to reality, that is because
mental identification leads to knowledge. Hence Lacan's idea of calling the
three elements that make up Freud's second topography "postes imaginaires
de la personnalité" (imaginary stations of the personality) and then distinguishing a fourth, the *je*, or I, the site where the subject can recognize itself.
To this—Lacan's earliest formulation of his theory of the imaginary, in
which, as in Melanie Klein, the genesis of the ego is thought of as a series
of operations based on identification with imagoes—was soon added the
idea of a *symbolic identification*, defined as yet only in a manner still vague,
hesitant, and obscure.

So by the autumn of 1936 the disastrous encounter in Marienbad had
proved to be quite productive. Lacan had set down the prolegomena of a
theory of the subject that could be grafted onto Freud on the basis of
Kojève's reading of Hegel. Lacan announced a two-part sequel to his
"Beyond the Reality Principle" that would never get written: one part was
to have been about "the reality of the image"; the other about "the forms of
knowledge." Instead, at Wallon's request, he produced the article on family
complexes. But meanwhile his meeting with Georges Bataille was to lend a
more Nietzschean dimension to the new work plan.

PART IV

Family Histories

12

· · · · · · ·

Georges Bataille and Co.

Georges Bataille was one of those interwar authors who, like Michel Leiris, Raymond Queneau, René Crevel, Antonin Artaud, and a few others, were influenced by the theoretical adventure of Freudianism and also had experience of the analyst's couch, but whose interest in the theory was independent of their views on the treatment. To sympathize with the Freudian revolution was for them an intellectual act, whereas to go to an analyst merely meant one wanted to have one's malady dealt with as directly as possible. This attitude explains why someone like Michel Leiris could, in his novel-writing technique, make the most respectful use of Freud's teaching, while at the same time regarding Freudian treatment as no more than a kind of medication. "Maybe," he wrote in August 1934, "we can't expect much of psychoanalysis, but we can always take it, just as one takes an aspirin."[1]

I have already had occasion to comment on Bataille's analysis with Adrien Borel, a psychiatrist with a liking for the good things of this world who was a founding member of the SPP. A wine and food connoisseur, Borel, like Allendy, enjoyed having artists and other creative people as his patients.[2] It was on the advice of Dr. Dausse, a medical friend who had collaborated with Bataille on *La Critique sociale* and who was concerned about Bataille's sexual obsessions, that Bataille first met Borel and decided to go to him for analysis. Several of Bataille's friends thought he was "sick": he was a gambler, an alcoholic, and a frequenter of brothels. According to Leiris, he had even risked his life playing Russian roulette.[3]

At their first encounter Borel gave Bataille a photograph by Louis Carpeaux, taken in April 1905 and reproduced in George Dumas's famous *Traité de psychologie* (Treatise on psychology). It showed a Chinese man who had murdered a prince being cut into a hundred pieces. Dumas, who was present at the scene recorded by Carpeaux, had observed that the victim's reactions resembled those of mystics in a state of ecstasy. But he also pointed out that this was because the man had been given a number of opium injections to prolong the process of execution. It was indeed a terrifying sight: with his disheveled hair and an awesomely mild expression despite his mutilated body, the man was strangely reminiscent of one of Bernini's virgins, radiantly transfigured by a divine visitation. The sight of this photograph was a turning point in Bataille's life: "What burst upon me . . . was the fact that these two complete contrasts were identical—divine ecstasy and extreme horror."[4]

Borel encouraged Bataille to write, without trying to end the state of intellectual violence from which he claimed to be suffering.[5] Even so, the analysis gave Bataille a sense of liberation that made it possible for him to write *L'Histoire de l'oeil* (The story of the eye), and the text was discussed at every session—and sometimes revised too. Bataille told Madeleine Chapsal: "I was only able to write my first book after being analyzed—yes, on emerging from analysis. I think I can truly say it was only because I was liberated in this way that I was able to write it."[6]

After a treatment in which the work of transference had encouraged literary creativeness, Bataille felt better physically too. He remained on friendly terms with Borel: as long as his former analyst lived he sent him the first numbered copy of each of his books. It was as a result of the analysis that Bataille met Sylvia Maklès, his future wife. The actual encounter probably took place in Raymond Queneau's studio in the square Desnouettes near the porte de Versailles, where a number of writers used to meet. But the person really responsible for the meeting was Bianca, Sylvia's elder sister, who was married to Théodore Fraenkel, the "fourth musketeer" of French surrealism. "When I first met [Fraenkel]," wrote Aragon, "he had just come back from Russia, where he had been an assistant medical officer in the French expeditionary corps. He talked like Père Ubu. And he always remained the same as he was then, with that sudden deep laugh that put everything and everyone in their place."[7]

Henri Maklès, Bianca and Sylvia's father, was a Jew of Bulgarian extraction, a merchant and traveling salesman. But he was also something of a bohemian, interested in culture and the arts and not much of a success at business. He was often broke, and his wife, Nathalie Chohen, was beset with money problems all her life. She was friendly, pleasant, and generous, and very anxious for her four daughters—Bianca, Rose, Simone, and Sylvia—to attain the social stability she herself had never enjoyed.[8] Her son, Charles Maklès, was like his father.

Bianca was good-looking and clever and became a medical student at a time when women weren't generally expected to go in for intellectual careers. It was at the medical faculty that she met Breton, Aragon, and

Fraenkel. Fraenkel was the only one of the three to become a doctor. He was a prey to melancholia and in 1916, when serving at the front on the outskirts of Verdun, had described his own condition in clinical terms that were astonishingly precise. "In the circularity of my moods," he wrote, "depression predominates . . . and the manic depressive psychosis is only an exaggerated form of a constant phenomenon. . . . I often observe extremes of melancholia that are just dreary self-depreciation. Manic excitement takes the form of pride. Mental degeneration affects nine-tenths of the human race—me among the rest. Now I understand—though without changing my opinion—the meaning of Nordau's book."[9] In 1922 Bianca married Théodore and gave up her studies to become an actress. She became a member of Charles Dullin's Atelier, or Workshop Theater, and acted, under the name of Lucienne Morand, in Pirandello's *Cose è (se vi pare)*, translated into French as *Chacun sa vérité*.[10]

In 1931 Bianca died in tragic circumstances. While out for a walk one day near Carqueiranne on the Côte d'Azur, she fell off a cliff and was killed. Fraenkel was in Paris at the time and had to travel down to identify the body.[11] Nathalie Chohen, Bianca's mother, never recovered from the shock, especially as people around her hinted at the possibility of suicide. She came to believe that Fraenkel himself had pushed Bianca off the cliff, in a fit of madness. But Nathalie maintained that Bianca wasn't killed: she had merely lost her memory and would one day remember what had happened and return to her family and friends.[12]

Sylvia, born on November 1, 1908, had gone to the same school as her sisters in the avenue de Villiers. The Kahn sisters went there too. Sylvia had always wanted to be an actress, but her dream didn't come true until after she was married. When Bianca married Fraenkel, Sylvia went to live with them; she got on very well with her elder sister and tried to model herself on her. But Fraenkel fell in love with Sylvia and made several passes at her. So the family decided to marry her off to Georges Bataille. She liked Bataille and agreed, and the wedding ceremony took place in the town hall at Courbevoie, just outside Paris, on March 20, 1928.[13]

Bataille's friends hoped, without much conviction, that marriage to a respectable woman of stable character and with a stimulating personality might help him if not to give up then at least to moderate his dissolute ways. But it was not to be. "All the evidence seems to show," wrote Michel Surya, "that he didn't really share his life but went on going to nightclubs and brothels, taking part in (if he didn't actually organize) orgies. With his wife or without her? He made all—or almost all—the women he lived with into his accomplices. So it's not unlikely that he did the same with the woman who as far as we know was the first of the series."[14]

Three months after she was married, Sylvia, still dreaming of going on the stage, went to the Théâtre du Vieux-Colombier to see the first public showing of Jean Renoir's silent film *La Petite Marchande d'allumettes*, based on Hans Andersen's story "The Little Match Girl."[15]

Renoir had made the film in Chaplinesque style and with a great display of technical virtuosity, using panchromatic stock, dramatic lighting, and plenty of special effects. The main part was played by his own wife, Catherine Hessling, who had also been his father's last model. Sylvia was bowled over by the character of the heroine, which she could have played very movingly herself, and had no hesitation about accosting Renoir as he came out of the theater and telling him she wanted to act in films. "You'll have to wait," he said.[16]

She waited. In the first two years of her marriage she moved house three times: the Batailles had apartments first in the avenue de Ségur, then in the rue Vauvenargues, then farther out in Boulogne-sur-Seine and at Issy-les-Moulineaux. According to Bataille, Sylvia was a silent witness when in 1930, while she was pregnant, he paid his famous tribute to the corpse of his mother, Marie-Antoinette Tournadre. In his writings Bataille records the scene in three different ways: once in a single sentence that claimed to be absolutely accurate; once in fictional form, without any admission that the act in question actually took place; and lastly in a brief, very simple hand-written account entitled "Le Cadavre maternel" (The mother's corpse).

The first version reads: "I jerked myself off naked, at night, in the presence of my mother's dead body."

The second:

"She died in the course of the day. I slept at her place with Edith."
"Your wife?"
"My wife . . . I lay in the dark beside Edith, who was sleeping. . . . I crept out into the passage in my bare feet, shivering. . . . I trembled with fear and excitement in the presence of the corpse, I was carried away with excitement. . . . I was in a trance. . . . I took off my pajamas. . . . I . . . you know what I mean. . . ."[17]

Bataille must have derived the content of this thrice-recounted homage from the extensive catalog of perversions compiled by Krafft-Ebing. But the deed itself must be seen as part of Bataille's autobiographical account of episodes arising out of his parents' madness, which he'd witnessed at close quarters since he was a child. His father, Aristide Bataille, syphilitic, paralyzed and blind, was confined to a wheelchair; "he peed where he sat" and "shat in his pants." In or around 1911, in a fit of madness, he accused his doctor of "screwing" his wife. Thereupon his wife herself nearly went out of her mind, and after making a dreadful scene with Aristide, at which their son was present, she went off to hang herself in the attic. The suicide attempt failed, though in 1915 Bataille's mother had another bout of insanity: she had left Aristide in August of that year, at the time of the German advance, and couldn't bear the thought of going back to him. She did so, nonetheless. "When we knew he was dying," wrote Bataille, "my mother agreed to go back with me. But he died a few days before we got there, asking for his children. All we found in the room was a closed coffin."[18]

The spectacle of the closed coffin, hiding the dead father from his son's sight, is paralleled by the episode of the mother's corpse, "exposed" to the obscene act of the narrator who "pays tribute" to her in the presence of his wife (Edith), who is pregnant. On the one hand there is the disappearance of the body of a father who was blind when he begot his son; on the other the appearance of the body of a mother to a son abandoned just when he was confronting the ordeal of fatherhood. "My father having begot me blind (literally blind)," writes the narrator, "I can't tear out my own eyes, like Oedipus. But, like Oedipus, I have guessed the riddle: no one more so."[19]

Laurence Bataille, only child of the marriage between Georges and Sylvia, was born on June 10, 1930. At that time Georges Bataille, together with Michel Leiris, Carl Einstein, and Georges-Henri Rivière, was writing for the review *Documents*. In it Bataille fought against surrealism and crossed swords with his great rival, André Breton, proclaiming the need to take the expression of bestiality to still further extremes so as to show all revolt to be merely the negation of revolt. In other words, Bataille countered surrealism with an aggressive anti-idealism capable of producing what he called the *impossible*. You had to blaspheme, destroy, break all rules until you encountered that which is beyond all bounds.[20]

Meanwhile, Sylvia's dream of being an actress was coming true. At about this time she met Jacques Prévert in a café in the rue Fontaine where she had gone to ask André Breton to sign a book for her. She spoke to Prévert as she left, and they walked around together until the early hours of the next morning. They were dazzled with each other.[21] Sylvia soon became a member of the famous "gang" that, after Prévert's break with surrealism, became the October group.[22]

The two Prévert brothers and their merry band were keen admirers of the classic American cinema and the great comic stars of the silent movies. Like other fans they almost lived in that dream world, and they spent hours discussing Charlie Chaplin, Buster Keaton, and Mack Sennett. Jacques Prévert was a wonderful storyteller who could torpedo the meanings of words with what seemed like chance juxtapositions but were really part of a mocking logical game. Pierre, his brother, was modest, shy, and charming, like a character out of *A Midsummer Night's Dream*.[23]

Through J.-B. Brunius, Jacques Prévert met Jean-Pierre Dreyfus (later Jean-Paul Le Chanois) and Pierre Batcheff, the actor in Buñuel's film *Un*

Chien andalou (1928). They worked together on a scenario, but the project came to an end with Batcheff's suicide. Then came the meeting with Raymond Bussières from the Federation for Working-Class Theater, who with Léon Moussinac had founded the October group. The Prévert brothers became the leaders of the group, together with Louis Bonin, the director, known as Lou Tchimoukoff, and Marcel Duhamel. They were later joined by Jean Dasté, Maurice Baquet, and Joseph Kosma. The Octobrists saw themselves as fellow travelers of the flamboyant kind of communism displayed by the first generation of the Bolshevik intelligentsia. And despite the advent of Stalinism they still felt an ardent loyalty toward the USSR, home of the first proletarian revolution. And it was as heirs to this revolution that they were trying to revive popular theater. They took as their models Brecht and Piscator, agitprop, and the proletarian theater. The brand of poetic realism invented by the October group, led by the Prévert brothers, used verbal humor to show the absurdity of bourgeois conformism and was to triumph in the French cinema of Jean Renoir, Marcel Carné. and Jacques Feyder. In 1933 they presented *La Bataille de Fontenoy* (The battle of Fontenoy) in Moscow and Leningrad and won first prize in the International Olympics of Workers' Theater.[24]

At the heart of the group was Sylvia Bataille, now, at the age of twenty-four, a beautiful actress. Her dead-white complexion, slight lisp, and childlike slimness lent her a special charm. Her trim yet ambiguous figure seemed partly the work of a secessionist painter, partly that of an impressionist, with colors by Klimt and curves by Seurat. Her willfulness was matched only by her good humor. But her black eyes held a suppressed sadness, a gleam of thwarted rebellion, reflecting the position of women in the thirties. Renoir might well have been thinking of this when he cast her as the female lead in *Une Partie de campagne* (A trip to the country): Sylvia Bataille seemed to him to speak with the voice of Maupassant's unlucky Henriette Dufour.[25]

Meanwhile she had left Georges Bataille. He didn't describe their love affair in detail in his books, but he did tell the story of their breakup in *Le Bleu du ciel* (The blue of the sky), in which he called the narrator's wife Edith. "I behaved like a coward," says the narrator, "toward everyone I loved. My wife was devoted to me, and went crazy because of me while I was deceiving her."[26] The narrator also quotes from a shattering letter Edith wrote him in which she relates a dream. "We were both somewhere with a few friends," says Edith, "and someone said if you went out you'd be murdered. . . . A man came to kill you. To do so he had to switch on a flashlight that he had in his hand. I was walking beside you, and the man, who was trying to show me he was going to kill you, switched on the flashlight. And it fired a bullet that went right through me. . . . You went into the bedroom with the girl. Then the man said the time had come. He switched on the flashlight, and it fired a second bullet. It was meant for you, but I felt it hitting me and knew I was finished. I put my hand to my throat; it came away warm and sticky with blood."[27] This account of Edith's dream is all the more interesting because it anticipated reality. In 1939, eleven years after Georges and Sylvia were married, Théodore Fraenkel, who was still in love with her, waited for Bataille outside the Bibliothèque nationale (National Library), armed with a gun. He fully intended to kill his "rival," even though Sylvia, the object of his passion, had left Georges several years before. Fortunately the episode ended in roars of laughter.[28]

Laurence was scarcely four years old when her parents separated. But although she often told those around her how much she suffered as a result of the breakup, it wasn't until 1984 that she wrote an autobiographical account of it. Like the woman in Bataille's *Le Bleu du ciel*, she recounted a dream: one she had managed to interpret in 1963 in the course of her analysis with Conrad Stein. In the dream she had seen a wren trying to escape from a weasel that had torn out the bird's tail feathers, leaving a stain of blood in their place. The wren looked back and flapped its wings helplessly. "It was odd, I suppose," said the dreamer, "that I should have represented my father as a wren. But for me he never counted for much. He left when I was four years old. I used to see him occasionally, but I didn't have any feelings toward him. His death, a year before, had left me cold."[29]

The bloodstain referred to a painful memory that Laurence conjured up, making the same use of metaphor as Bataille had in his *Histoire de l'oeil*. She recalled how, as a little girl, she had pulled out an eyelash by mistake when playing with her mother's eyebrow tweezers. Looking in the mirror, she had seen her eye suddenly stained with blood. By a series of associations she deduced from her dream the way the Bataille-Maklès family was organized: the men let the women wear the trousers in order to keep the field of thought for themselves. "In my family," she said, "thought was reserved exclusively for the men. That was their privilege, the attribute of the male, and if anyone else usurped it the result would be chaos. So there was no chance for a woman to get a look in. Not for me, anyhow. And that's why I've always taken great care never to do any thinking."[30]

But though the Maklès sisters weren't allowed to think themselves, they all married intellectuals. Sylvia and Bianca, alike in beauty, talent, and artistic temperament, were also both strongly committed to the Far Left. Rose and Simone, the other two sisters, were different. Rose was always an excellent housewife and remarkable cook. She exercised a great influence over André Masson when she married him in 1934: at the time he still wasn't earning enough to live on from his painting. He had just emerged from a tumultuous love affair with Paule Vezelay, also a painter, who suffered from violent nervous attacks made worse by drinking. Masson, himself an alcoholic and prone to depression, couldn't cope with a woman who was a creative artist in her own right and refused to settle down into quiet married life.[31] But with Rose he found quiet and equilibrium and was able to work in peace.

Simone tended to be middle class and conservative. Just before the war she married Jean Piel, a civil servant and economist who later helped Bataille start the review *Critique*. So after Bianca's death, Sylvia was the only member of the family to carry the standard of revolt. When she was earning a living as an actress she gave her sisters, parents, and brother constant moral and financial support. For her, political commitment went with a spirit of devotion capable even of sacrifice, and in this respect Bataille was right when in his writings he depicted her as a victim. But Sylvia Bataille had hosts of friends and was loved not only for her beauty and charm but also for her warmth and magnanimity.

Other clans joined the Bataille-Maklès tribe: Michel Leiris and the Kahnweiler family on the one hand, Raymond Queneau and the Kahn family on the other. Leiris concealed the real origins of his wife Louise Godon, whom he married in 1926. She was known as Zette and had a background similar to that of Aragon. She was born in 1902, the daughter of Lucie Godon, whose parents brought her up as their own child, pretending that Lucie was her sister. She found out the truth when she was eighteen. Her real mother had already been married for a year to the famous art dealer Daniel-Henry Kahnweiler, who had launched most of the cubist painters and owned a huge collection of Picassos. After she married Leiris, Zette worked in her so-called brother-in-law's gallery, taking care not to reveal her true history. Only members of the clan itself knew the "secret." Meanwhile, Raymond Queneau had married Jeanine Kahn, whose sister Simone was André Breton's first wife. The Kahn sisters and the Maklès sisters had known one another since going to school together in the avenue de Villiers.[32]

Bataille availed himself of the privilege of thought in the same style as the narrator in *Le Bleu du ciel*, half killing himself with drink, lack of sleep, and sex. "I get pleasure now," he wrote, "out of being an object of horror and disgust to the only being I'm close to"—i.e., Edith-Sylvia.[33] Even after he and his wife parted he remained on terms of very close friendship with her, though he now lived with Colette Peignot, whom he called Laure.

Unlike Sylvia, Laure accepted Bataille's excesses in a spirit of sacrifice, as if they were showing her the way to her own death. She too underwent analysis with Adrien Borel, before dying of tuberculosis in 1939. "All who came near her," wrote Leiris, "know how steadfastly she valued what is noble, how fiercely she rebelled against the standards to which most people subscribe."[34] After her death Bataille published her writings and himself produced a biography in which he recorded her sexual practices with cruel accuracy. As for Souvarine, with whom, as we have seen, she founded *La Critique sociale* in 1931, he regarded her as mentally sick and tried to save her from herself; he never forgave his rival for having taken her away from him and said Bataille was "sexually unhinged." In 1934 Bataille had told Olesia Sienkiewicz, his friend and confidante, of his sufferings, thanking her for her help. "Perhaps, when it's too late, she [Colette/Laure] will become sincere and open again, as she was in the years when I first knew her. . . . Even though she left me, I'd still have liked her to be loyal to our common past, to the ideas we shared, and to the indescribable tenderness there was between us. . . . Anyone who encourages her to reject all moral values does Colette herself a grave disservice."[35] Olesia had seen the relationship between Colette Peignot and Souvarine breaking up just as her own affair with Lacan was deteriorating.

Sylvia's screen career was helped on by Pierre Braunberger, who was madly in love with her. And it was with the actors belonging to the October group that she got her first part in a Renoir film, *Le Crime de M. Lange* (Monsieur Lange's crime), made in collaboration with Prévert. *Le Crime de M. Lange*, a masterpiece inspired by "the theater of life" and the idea of communal effort, paid glowing tribute to the actors of the October group, who gave their best in it. Sylvia played the part of a girl who worked in a printing press and fell victim to the wicked seductions of Jules Berry.

Prompted by Braunberger, Renoir thought seriously about finding Sylvia an important part. He agreed with René Clair that there ought to be a special age of the cinema just as there had once been a special age for *commedia del arte*. And he believed it ought to relate to the second half of the nineteenth century. "[We should] throw off realism," he said, "and make all our movies with costumes belonging to the special age of the film—the opposite of cinema verité."[36] And for Renoir the "special age of the film" was the period depicted in his father's pictures: the period of *déjeuners sur l'herbe* (picnics in the country), boating parties, and open-air cafés by the river. From Maupassant's short story, "Une Partie de campagne" (A trip to the country), he took the characters, the settings, the locations, and the tragic final scene.

One fine summer morning Monsieur Dufour, who keeps a hardware store in Paris, decides to take his wife, his daughter Henriette, and his assistant Anatole to have lunch in the country at Père Poulain's inn on the banks of the Seine. After the meal, M. Dufour goes fishing, accompanied by the dim Anatole. Meanwhile Henriette and her mother flirt with two vacationers who are boating on the river. And so the girl has her first sexual experience: "In a sudden furious burst of resistance she turned onto her back to avoid him, but he threw the whole of his body on top of her. It took some time for his lips to find hers. . . . Then, carried away by a wave of desire, she returned his kiss and clasped him to her bosom, all her resistance vanishing as if crushed by an overwhelming weight."[37]

Years go by, and one Sunday Henriette goes back to the same part of the river with Anatole, now her husband. There she meets her former seducer in the very place where they had once made love. "I think about it every evening," she tells him, before returning to her present dreary existence. "The love scene on the island," wrote André Bazin, "is at once one of the finest and one of the most terrible moments in world cinema. And it owes its electrifying power to the heartrending emotional realism with which Sylvia Bataille endows a few gestures and a look."[38]

Georges Bataille made a brief appearance in the film, dressed as a seminarian. His fleeting presence in this tragic hymn to love was particularly significant because his wife was playing the part of a heroine at once resigned to a life of servitude and rebelling against it.

Sylvia's first big part ought to have led to a career in motion pictures, but circumstances were against it. *Une Partie de campagne*, produced by Braunberger and lasting fifty minutes, was shot on the banks of the Loing, where the landscape still resembled that along the banks of the Seine in 1880. But rain held up the proceedings, and Renoir had to make changes in the script. After a fierce quarrel with Sylvia, he finished the film without shooting all the scenes originally planned. As a result it had to wait until 1946 for its first public showing, and the film that should have made Sylvia a star in 1936 remained unknown for ten years.

In the same year the October group folded for lack of money, and the "good companions" dispersed and went their separate ways. But Sylvia was still great friends with Prévert and was given a small part in *Jenny*, Marcel Carné's first film, for which Prévert wrote the script. The following year she was included in the team that made Jacques Feyder's *Les Gens du voyage* (Traveling people), starring Françoise Rosay. But then the war put an end to all Sylvia's hopes, not only because Pétain's anti-Jewish laws forbade her to go on acting but also because she was too politically committed to want to work under such a regime. By 1946, when she could at last be seen in Renoir's movie, it was too late. Sylvia was now thirty-eight and Lacan's companion: she had chosen another life. And it was with some wistfulness that she shared with *Les Cahiers du cinéma* her memories of the making of the film: "Renoir was a great conductor," she said. "He would take his time helping an actor to identify with his part, but if the actor kept getting it wrong he would fly into a rage. Our acting wasn't always good when we worked with him, but it was always true."[39]

Just as Lacan and Kojève were preparing to embark together on a comparison between Freud and Hegel, Bataille was launching the first number of the review *Acéphale* (Acephalous, i.e., headless). The cover reproduced a strange drawing by André Masson of a headless man with all his viscera showing and a skull in place of his sex organs. After a short-lived experiment in the form of a journal called *Contre-Attaque* (Counterattack), in which Bataille, reconciled with Breton, had supported the Popular Front in its fight against the rise of fascism, he was now rejecting the "idle negativity" to which Kojève said intellectuals were doomed. History was "finished," French society was on its deathbed, and war seemed imminent. As for the moral crisis, it was so ominous and all-pervading that Bataille wanted to counter it with *acéphalité* (headlessness). He proposed abandoning the enlightenment of the civilized world in favor of the ecstatic power of worlds that had disappeared. This rebellion against an unquestioning faith in progress, which would never be able to arouse mankind to a spiritual reawakening, echoed in some respects the attitude of the symbolists in the 1880s. As early as 1891, in his novel *Là-bas* (literally, Over there), which Bataille greatly admired, Joris-Karl Huysmans had portrayed a mythical dimension, beyond subjectivity, that drew the narrator toward an initiatory journey resembling the "atheological experience" that Bataille himself was heading for in the late 1930s. So the message conveyed by Masson's decapitated man was the need to offer up the head, the seat of human thought, as a sacrifice to a radical critique of Western reason.

This being so, the review *Acéphale* was only the visible aspect of a secret society of the same name. It was a very strange club indeed: its members preached the "nonknowledge of gnosis," as against all forms of rational logic, and even practiced "ritual crimes" as evidence of their total dissent from a world hurtling toward disaster. Georges Bataille and Roger Caillois were the leading lights of this "sacred conspiracy"; Michel Leiris, still attached to the virtues of the rational and scientific mind, was more critical. The initiates promised to found a new religion inspired by Zarathustra and to remain silent about the society's activities. But there was no question of any "plot" against the state or any act of terrorism: these "conspirators" were the heroes of a nihilist rebellion that derived both its form and its content from ethnology.

Bataille, who had been a great reader of Freud ever since he came across his *Group Psychology and the Analysis of the Ego*, also took on board the theory of the death instinct, the cause of a great upheaval in the psychoanalytic movement. For Bataille, the physical death of Masson's headless man represented the death of anyone claiming to see his destiny as based on reason: "We are fiercely religious," he wrote, "and insofar as our very existence is itself a condemnation of all that is recognized now, we are bound to be just as fiercely intransigent. What we are embarking on is war."[40]

The marquis de Sade and Nietzsche were the two emblematic figures at the head of this sacrificial crusade, together with Kierkegaard, Don Juan, and Dionysos. Klossowski laid the group's cards on the table in an article called "The monster," which appeared in the first issue of the review. "Sade's characters," he wrote, "having renounced the immortality of the soul, apply by way of compensation to be admitted to total monstrosity."[41] This monstrosity, the negation of the self, proclaimed the absolute power of dream over consciousness, of dispossession over self-possession, of impossibility over possibility. Sade's version of man was the prototype of modern man without God: he had to escape from his prison, just as the *acéphale* had to escape from his head and the individual from his reason, if he was to destroy the real presence of—and then enjoy—the objects of his desire. This apologia for a monster born out of a confrontation between the Freudian *Wunsch* (wish or desire) and Hegel's and Kojève's *Begierde* (appetite)[42] was followed in January 1937, in the second number of *Acéphale*, by a tribute to Nietzsche entitled "Nietzsche and the Fascists," in which Klossowski gave an account of the current state of Nietzschean studies.[43]

At the end of the nineteenth century the works of Nietzsche had begun to be known and translated in various French literary reviews. Jules de Gaultier, as I have mentioned, linked Nietzsche's doctrine to Bovaryism on the grounds of its nihilism and antirationalism. But at the same time it circulated less directly in the writings of André Gide and Paul Valéry. Maurras, for his part, admired Nietzsche's works for their criticism of Bismarck and their antisocialist stance.[44] Breton was by no means so enthusiastic, though he did recognize how radical was Nietzsche's offensive against all the values of Western reason.[45] This was the same Nietzsche that Lacan had praised in the mid-1920s (minus the devotion to the ideas in *Zarathustra* and in particular to the superman theory).

France's attitude to Nietzsche's philosophy had been transformed after the war by Charles Andler's monumental study of the philosopher's life and works, together with his sources. Andler destroyed the Wagnerian straitjacket in which Nietzsche had hitherto been confined and revealed him as a European thinker, cosmopolitan and even universal. And so Nietzschean thinking became part of the history of philosophy, though according to an interpretation of that history colored by Hegelianism and the French approach to sociology. Andler, a Germanist and socialist, admired the Germany of Goethe and Beethoven, and although he finished his book just before the first battle of the Marne in 1918, he held back its publication until 1920.[46]

But in 1935 it was not this "enlightened" version of Nietzsche who was being idolized in Germany. After a series of similar misapplications going back forty years, Elisabeth Forster, Nietzsche's sister, made use of the ambiguity inevitably present in any great body of work to present Nietzsche's philosophy as favorable to Nazism and fascism. Convinced that Hitler was an embodiment of her brother's dreamed-of superman, Elisabeth Forster was a fanatical supporter of the Führer and with great pomp and ceremony deposited a copy of *Zarathustra*, together with *Mein Kampf* and Rosenberg's *Myth of the Twentieth Century*, in the Tannenberg monument celebrating the victory of Germany over Russia in the First World War. "I am certain," she wrote, "Fritz would be delighted to see Hitler taking on with such peerless courage the full and entire responsibility for his people."[47]

Bataille attacked this outrageous misapplication of Nietzsche's thought in the second issue of *Acéphale*, in January 1937. He reminded Nazis and fascists alike that Nietzsche had fiercely criticized the anti-Semitism of his sister and her husband and had never adopted any doctrine whatsoever concerning soil, race, or fatherland. He had constructed a body of philosophical works that called on modern man to face up to the consequences of the death of God and throw off all forms of servitude. A genuine Nietzschean superman was inspired by a will to power: he was a man with a new culture and a new metaphysics, both derived from an act of creation arising out of an act of destruction. Bataille pointed out that, setting aside the swindle perpetrated by Elisabeth Forster, Nietzsche's work was open to two possible interpretations. One, referred to as the rightist reading and inspired by German neopaganism, led straight to the annexation of Nietzsche's theory of the superman by propagandists of Aryan superiority. On the other hand a so-called left-wing interpretation regarded this same superman theory as ushering in a creative revolution through which man could free himself from the "masses," outstrip the self, and achieve existential freedom. In *Acéphale*, Bataille opted for the latter reading, and Klossowski praised Karl Jaspers's study, published in German in 1936, which interpreted Nietzsche in the light of Kierkegaard, showing that both had broken once and for all with the philosophy of objective rationality.[48]

The way Bataille defended a left-wing reading of Nietzsche was similar to the way the Recherches philosophiques (Philosophical Research) group adopted Hegelian thinking via their reading of Heidegger. In both cases the problem was how to approach human freedom and the historical commitment of the individual in a God-less world that everyone felt to be threatened with destruction through the advent of modern dictatorships. Against this background Bataille's Nietzschean revolt appeared as a kind of "holy terror": a last way of subverting the social order before history came to an end. And it was no accident that the last two issues of *Acéphale* were again devoted to Nietzsche. They contained portraits of Dionysos and Kierkegaard's Don Juan, together with a commemoration of the fiftieth anniversary of the philosopher's going mad—a celebration reminiscent of the surrealists' 1928 celebration of the fiftieth anniversary of hysteria.

Bataille shared the surrealists' idea that madness, far from being an illness, was an integral part of the human personality. His conception of the Freudian unconscious, however, was different from that of Breton.

Breton, after approaching the teachings of Vienna via dreams and Janet's automatism, examined the signs of madness in search of a form of writing, a language, an aesthetic; he saw the unconscious as a dimension that was beyond consciousness and hence able to communicate with real life in such a way as to bring about a revolutionary change in humanity. Bataille's approach was quite different. Having been attracted to Freud through mass psychology and the phenomena of collective identity, he saw madness as an extreme experience leading to the void and acephality, and the unconscious as a nonknowledge within consciousness that revealed the conflict inside the individual and the attraction he feels for abjection, ordure, and all that is vile: an instinct without any origin in biology.[49]

Bataille, after being one of the first French Nietzscheans, was then influenced by Kojève's interpretation of Hegel, after which his belief in Nietzsche was reinforced by a large dose of nihilism. But, having studied the history of religion under Koyré and been influenced by Marcel Mauss and Durkheim, Bataille also believed there was a philosophical doctrine to be found in mysticism and the sacred. This probably explains why he was fascinated by fascism, just as Breton was fascinated by occultism. Bataille maintained that the weapons brought into being by fascism should be used to turn popular fanaticism and fervor against fascism itself. Since democracy had shown itself unable to defend the world's conscience, antidemocratic methods must be pressed into service: "A Nazi can be madly in love with the Reich," he said. "And we too are capable of fanatical devotion. But what we love, although we're French, is not the French community but the community of mankind. . . . We appeal to the universal conscience that is linked to moral freedom. . . ."[50]

However, just as Breton never actually gave the occult any real theoretical approval,[51] so Bataille never supported real-life fascism in any way. When the *Contre-Attaque* group broke up in the spring of 1936, fascism was the bone of contention. Bataille had signed a pamphlet written by Jean Dautry that contained the following passage: "We are against scraps of paper, against the slavish lucubrations of the chancelleries. We think declarations drawn up around green baize tables are only binding on ordinary people against their will. Anyhow, though we're not taken in by it, we prefer the antidiplomatic brutality of Hitler: it's not so certainly fatal to peace as the slobbering frenzies of diplomats and politicians."[52]

The surrealists thereupon labeled Bataille's friends "Souvarinian superfascists," the adjective deriving from the fact that the *Contre-Attaque* group grew out of the old Democratic Communist Club.[53] But quite apart from polemics there was a genuine philosophical quarrel with Breton here. If Bataille wanted to turn the weapons of fascism back on fascism itself and if he anathematized parliamentary democracy—which in any case had abased itself before Hitler—it was because he drew his political philosophy from a so-called *heterological* or scatological view of human society.

In pathological anatomy the term *heterological* is used to denote morbid tissues composed differently from the normal tissues around them. But Bataille used the word *heterology* to mean a science of the unassimilable, of the irrecoverable, of ordure and "remains." He wanted to oppose the kind of philosophy that reduces everything to what is thinkable. "Above all," he wrote, "heterology opposes every homogeneous representation of the world—i.e., every philosophical system. . . . It aims at a complete inversion of the philosophical process that, having formerly been an instrument of annexation, now enters the service of excretion and introduces a call for the violent satisfactions implicit in social existence."[54] The heterology that Bataille placed at the center of his thinking, accusing surrealism of still being too attached to the ideal of bourgeois emancipation, advocated not mere personal rebellion but the awakening within each individual of a "doomed element" inherent in both man and society. And so Bataille, together with Roger Caillois and Michel Leiris, started the College of Sociology, which was founded in March 1937 and remained active until the war.

The College of Sociology was nothing like an ordinary college, and its founders were not sociologists. They came from various backgrounds and set up their strange and short-lived moral community with the object of first understanding and then explaining the obscure springs of social and human phenomena in the field of myth and the sacred. The college thus officialized the secret activities of *Acéphale* and supplied them with a theoretical content. Many other writers and philosophers beside Bataille and his friends were invited to give lectures, among them Kojève, Paulhan, Jean Wahl, and Jules Monnerot. The meetings took place in a room behind a bookstore in the rue Gay-Lussac, and the audience included people such as Jules Benda, Drieu la Rochelle, and Walter Benjamin, rubbing shoulders with refugees from the Frankfurt school living in exile in Paris until they emigrated to America. In a brief but vivid aside, Denis Hollier describes the strange atmosphere that prevailed in the two years preceding the collapse of French society: "The background was extremely somber during the years when Daladier was trying to crush the Popular Front, against which everyone had some grudge or other, and while Hitler, on his side of the Rhine, was pursuing a resistible rise that was already making him feel short of living space. Robert Aron has called this 'the end of the postwar [i.e., the post–World War I] period'; Raymond Queneau's name for it was 'the Sunday of life,' Jean-Paul Sartre's 'the suspended sentence.' "[55]

While the influence of Kojève's and Koyré's teachings is quite explicit in the work of Lacan, his borrowings from Bataille are never apparent. The two men had been friends since 1934, when they both took part in the revival of Hegelian philosophy in France, and so were partners in the same intellectual adventure, inspired by the same ideas and concepts, members of the same family. But around 1932 and 1933 Lacan was still very close to the surrealists, in particular to Crevel and Dali. His doctoral dissertation was greeted by them as an event, and he contributed to *Minotaure*. Moreover, his attitude to Hegel was different from Bataille's, and for him the most significant thing that happened between 1933 and 1936 was the discovery not of Heidegger but of Nietzsche. Lastly, Lacan's Freud bore no resemblance to Bataille's. Nonetheless, while Lacan the writer stood aside from Bataille's universe, he remained present as a distant but curious and fascinated spectator. The earliest meetings of the *Contre-Attaque* group were held in his apartment in the boulevard Malesherbes, as were the gatherings that gave rise to the College of Sociology. His silent presence at the secret activities of *Acéphale* is attested by all the contemporary witnesses. So Lacan was with Bataille and his "family" all the time during the period when he was undergoing analysis and passing from bachelorhood to marriage and thence to fatherhood.

But Lacan's long friendship with Bataille is rather puzzling. It included many intellectual exchanges, and we know Bataille encouraged Lacan to publish and make himself known. But we also know that Lacan's work left Bataille cold. He never referred to it in his own writings, and they contain no evidence that he was ever influenced by it. One almost wonders if he really read it: there is no proof that he did so. At all events, it left no trace on his work.

Lacan on the other hand *was* influenced by his friendship with Bataille, whether or not he made a close study of his work. And through taking part in all the activities organized by Bataille, he was able to make some fundamental additions to his own researches. Not only did Bataille's reading of Nietzsche supply Lacan with a new interpretation of the philosophy that had influenced him throughout his adolescence, but Bataille also initiated him into a new understanding of Sade, whose writings would later lead him to a formulate a non-Freudian theory of pleasure. Moreover, Lacan borrowed Bataille's ideas on the impossible and heterology, deriving from them a concept of the "real" seen first as "residue" and then as "impossible." The constant though implicit presence of Bataille in Lacan's evolving work and the total absence of Lacan's writings in the work of Bataille, together with the long, subterranean friendship between the two men themselves, who despite their family links were so unlike one another, are all evidence of a long-drawn-out transaction where what was at stake was basically a woman: Sylvia Bataille.

We left Jacques Lacan in 1936, on the beach at Noirmoutier, an island in the Vendée, wrestling with an article announcing and describing the advent of a second generation of psychoanalysis. A few months later, on January 8, 1937, Malou gave birth to a lovely little girl, called Caroline after her maternal grandmother. Lacan added a second name, Image, following a tradition by which all the Blondin family had a nickname or a diminutive. Marie-Louise was "Malou," Caroline Rousseau "Babouine" (in French, the feminine for *baboon*), Sylvain was "Petit père lapin" (Mr. Bunny); and so on.[56] But the word *image* also referred to the importance Lacan attached to the mirror stage theory: Caroline was conceived while he was writing his lecture for the Marienbad conference.

The experience of fatherhood made Lacan happy for about eighteen months. But coming after three years of married life it lessened none of the problems arising out of the misunderstanding on which the marriage was originally based. The man Malou had chosen, idealizing him utterly and certain he would father clever children,[57] failed to live up to her expectations. Not only was he a womanizer and a libertine, moody and impossible to satisfy, but he was also possessed by the idea that he was a genius who would produce great works and by an immense desire to be recognized and famous. All he thought about was himself and his work.

His hunger for fame and knowledge made him insatiably curious, assailing with question after question anyone whose learning he might hope to absorb. He looked at people so intently they often took him for some sort of diabolical being, possessed himself and trying to possess them. Yet there was nothing diabolical about him. The fascination he exercised on others came from the extreme swiftness with which his mind worked, combined with the extreme slowness of his bodily movements. Always deep in thought, he was at once tyrannical and attractive, inquisitorial and anxious, a show-off and a man haunted by the truth, and all these things militated against the conjugal fidelity to which Malou would have liked him to adhere.

As he mixed with the intelligentsia of the avant-garde and pursued ever more abstruse philosophical researches, he was confronted with a new universe and new ways of thinking that helped him with his reinterpretation of Freud. He had felt horribly abandoned by his brother's departure to Hautecombe and by his parents' failure to understand his own intellectual development, and he couldn't bear to have to abandon people who loved *him*. And just as he hadn't been able to break with Marie-Thérèse or Olesia, so now he couldn't make a definite choice between Malou and Sylvia, and left it to Malou to decide they should part.

He had met Sylvia for the first time in the second half of February 1934, after he got back from his honeymoon and she was in the last few weeks of her life with Bataille. At the time she seemed set for a successful career as an actress. Sylvia and Bataille went to dinner in the boulevard Malesherbes; she didn't take to Lacan at all and thought he and Malou made a terribly bourgeois and conventional couple. When they met again two years later at Bataille's place, Lacan set his cap at Sylvia and said the only reason he had come was to see her. She slipped away. Then, around November 1938, they met by chance in the Café de Flore and fell in love; after that they were always together. At the time Lacan had another lover[58] and was in the process of breaking off his analysis with Loewenstein.

So the liaison with Sylvia began twenty-one months after Caroline was born, and just as Malou found out she was pregnant with Thibaut. "Caroline was everyone's favorite," said Thibaut. "My mother's, my father's, and my uncle Sylvain's. She lived for two years with my parents while they still got on together, before my father's affair with Sylvia. That was what gave her a strong character. She got her self-confidence and assurance from the two years of happiness she had as a child."[59]

By falling in love with Sylvia, Lacan was moving away from a world that was no longer quite his own: the world of the great medical bourgeoisie of Paris, whose members revered wealth and success and prided themselves on being the elite of the whole country. That world had once been necessary to Lacan: through his contact with it he had been raised up from his original background. For his roots lay in the typical French petite bourgeoisie, Catholic, close to the land, provincial, and austere, devoted to Joan of Arc rather than to the elegant cosmopolitan culture beloved of the Blondin family. By choosing to mix henceforward with the avant-garde intelligentsia, Lacan was leaving a "Right Bank" lifestyle for one that was less conformist, less rigid, and more bohemian.

But in spite of everything Malou went on thinking their marriage could still be made to work. And although she didn't accept Lacan's infidelities and wished him to be quite different from what he was, she went on saying how clever he was and referring to him as a genius.[60] How could she do otherwise? She had only fallen for him because he was a model of the elite to which she was sure she herself belonged, so diligently did she and her brother cultivate the aesthetic values belonging to the cult of self-love.

While Malou's pride concealed a puritanism and moral rectitude that made her haughty and unyielding, Sylvia's bohemianism reflected a cheerful temperament that made her, apparently at least, more likely to put up with the escapades of a man whose life she had chosen to share because she loved him. But her profession as an actress never prevented her from expressing her opinions frankly. Her opposition to the established order, to injustice and inequality, was always loud and clear. And through her marriage to Bataille and later love affairs, she had acquired an experience of sex such as Malou never even dreamed existed. So, as Lacan felt recognized and at home in Sylvia's circle, in 1939 she became his special companion.

Different as the two women were, Malou and Sylvia did have something in common: they both destroyed many letters that Lacan wrote to them, in which he talked about his ideas and his opinions on people and things.[61]

Lacan and Sylvia were frequent visitors to Charles and Marie-Laure de Noailles's salon, which had become the center of artistic and fashionable life in Paris during the thirties. "In their private mansion in the place des Etats-Unis," wrote Boris Kochno, "they often entertained a host of friends, mixing members of the aristocracy and world celebrities with budding artists of revolutionary tendencies. And among all these, Balthus, dashing and Byronic . . . stood apart from the general hubbub, looking on in silence at the motley spectacle. But from his impish look and ironic smile one could guess what he was thinking."[62] In July 1939 Lacan met André Masson and, through Kahnweiler, bought a painting from him: *Le Fil d'Ariane* (Ariadne's thread).[63] He subsequently bought many others, including portraits of himself and Sylvia. Like Sylvain Blondin, Lacan was a great collector of master paintings: Picasso, Masson, Balthus, Zao-Wou-ki were his favorites. He also collected books and primitive art.

13

....

Between Lucien Febvre and Edouard Pichon

We already know the circumstances in which Lacan came to collaborate in the great task on which Lucien Febvre embarked in 1932, at the suggestion of Anatole de Monzie, the French minister of education.[1] Wallon, who was a close friend of Febvre, had been made responsible for volume 8 of the *Encyclopédie française* (French encyclopedia), which he entitled "The Life of the Mind." Wallon wrote many of the articles himself but also made use of other contributors, including two of the best representatives of the second generation of French psychoanalysis: Daniel Lagache and Jacques Lacan. Among the contributors were such figures as Pierre Janet, Charles Blondel, Georges Dumas, Eugène Minkowski, and Paul Schiff.

Thanks to a memorandum entitled "Notes for Use in Compiling the History of the *EF*," written by Lucien Febvre himself but unknown until now, it is at last possible to explain how Lacan came to write the famous text on the family that appeared in 1938 in Wallon's volume of the *Encyclopédie*.[2] Lacan's essay was so complex that Febvre took the trouble to add nine paragraphs of notes explaining to future historians the extraordinary nature of the author's thinking on the Oedipus theory.

Wallon had asked Lacan for two articles, pointing out to his colleagues that although Lacan was "difficult" to deal with, he was the only person who could do the job properly. Lacan sent the first article in quite quickly, but it took Mme Febvre three months to gouge the second out of him page by page. In September 1936 the manuscript was handed over to the *Encyclopédie* to be typed. It was then that Rose Celli first saw it. She was a novelist who had specialized in literature at the Ecole normal supérieur at Sèvres, just outside Paris, and had become one of Febvre's most valued colleagues. But try as she might she couldn't make out the meaning of some of Lacan's more obscure passages, especially those dealing with the Oedipus complex. So she made numerous corrections throughout the text to render it more comprehensible. She then handed over the corrected manuscript to Lucien Febvre, who passed it on to Wallon, asking him to give it back to Lacan for him to indicate whether "the translator had made any mistakes in her attempt at translation." Lacan was also asked to elucidate the meaning of doubtful passages. "Dr. Lacan," says Lucien Febvre, "*did a considerable amount of work on his text* and tried very earnestly to clarify it. But he made the mistake of giving his text back to the *EF* without informing either me or the editor concerned. He gave it to Mme Pischari, a chatterbox who instead of declining it and referring M. Lacan to myself or the editor concerned, took it upon herself to rush all over the office telling everybody all about it, from Nénette to the concierge's cat and the concierge herself, not forgetting the head of administration, who stoked up the scandal further. And so on. . . ."[3]

When Febvre saw the text as corrected by Lacan he realized that the author's modifications had made it much more readable. But three pages about the Oedipus complex were still unintelligible. Lacan himself couldn't find a way of improving them, and Febvre observed: "Doctor Lacan's style isn't 'bad'—it's an extremely personal system using words in special senses, such that the only solution is either to rewrite the whole thing once one has understood it—or else to ask the author to take it back yet again for revision."

While Febvre himself set to work on the final version of the article, rumors circulated more furiously than ever in the corridors of the *Encyclopédie*'s headquarters in the rue du Four. Everyone made fun of the impenetrability of Lacan's style. The "scandal" reached its height when "someone" showed Anatole de Monzie the original instead of the corrected version. Monzie was of course unaware that the text in front of him had already been changed several times: first rewritten by Rose Celli, then revised by Febvre, then modified by Lacan, then rewritten yet again by Rose, then read again by Febvre, and so on. So Monzie, thinking the article in front of him was supposed to be ready to go to the printer, flew into a rage and roared, "Get it translated into normal language!"[4] Febvre had fun castigating the stupidity of Nénette and the rest in their attempt to make editors and authors out to be idle and useless. He saw himself as Jocrisse when he championed the truth and wrote Monzie to tell him what had been going on.[5]

Febvre's memo is an interesting piece of immediate history. It shows on the one hand how as early as 1937 Lacan was valued appropriately by the most brilliant minds of his age and on the other hand the problems presented even then by his style of writing. It was obscure and illegible; he couldn't observe deadlines; he seemed to shrink from the idea of publication. It is worth noting that Lacan's impenetrability dates from 1936, when under the influence of Kojève and Koyré he started to put Freud in a philosophical context. Compared to his "Beyond the Reality Principle" and his text on the family, Lacan's doctoral thesis seems a model of lucidity. It is as if it was his early, as yet exploratory, contacts with philosophy that made him incomprehensible. But Febvre's memo also shows that Lacan was ready to accept criticism of his style: he wanted to be understood and was quite willing to revise his text if the changes were suggested by intelligent people to whom he could really talk. Lucien Febvre's own comments on Lacan's article on the family made its points with great clarity. In the midst of the storm unleashed by "Nénette," the concierge, and her cat, he recognized the talent of a man whose difficult style might well make fools and ignoramuses laugh: Febvre stood up to them and took care to leave posterity tangible evidence of his righteous wrath.

As it finally stood, Lacan's article on the family was at once remarkably clear and extremely obscure. It was clear because of the many alterations made by Rose Celli, Lucien Febvre, and Lacan himself. But it was still obscure, because it was transitional. On the one hand Lacan was setting down the results of his recasting of earlier concepts—hence the synthetic and formal nature of the text—but on the other hand he was treating new ideas that he found difficult to express lucidly. His theoretical system was still far from being completely worked out. Hence the apparent haziness and lack of form in parts of what was a very extraordinary piece of work.

First there were the subheadings that Febvre and Wallon insisted on and Lacan accepted, probably after discussing and selecting them with his two editors' help. This pair played an important part in organizing Lacan's text, supplying a theoretical line from which it is possible to derive some of the concepts and ideas that were later to serve as a framework for the whole of Lacan's thinking. They included, in no particular order, the image of the mother's breast, the weaning complex, the appetite for death, general nostalgia, mental identification, the mirror stage, the castration complex, the archaic superego, the decline of the paternal imago, delusional forms of knowledge, self-punishment neurosis, and the prevalence of the male principle. These terms were borrowed from various fields of knowledge, mingling together traces from all the disciplines that had contributed to the young Lacan's thinking.

As for the text itself, as far as psychoanalysis was concerned it was a masterly synthesis that combined the vocabulary of psychiatry (Claude, Minkowski, Clérambault), already present in Lacan's 1932 thesis, with the terminology of the French school of psychoanalysis (Pichon, Laforgue, etc.). To this was added, for the first time, a very assured reading of Melanie Klein's article "Early Stages of the Oedipus Conflict."[6] As to philosophy, it was the teaching of Wallon and Kojève combined that enabled Lacan to arrive at an interpretation of Freud that was nonbiological and phenomenological, taking as its central point the differentiation among the *ego*, the *I*, and the *other* and leading to a theory of the imaginary that had more in common with Klein than with Freud. As for Lacan's "sociological" analysis of the individual within the family, that offered an astonishing potpourri of ideas about the sacred, antibourgeois nihilism, and a sense that Western civilization was deteriorating: all themes arising out of Lacan's association with the College of Sociology. All this was supplemented by interpretations of the works of Marcel Mauss and Jakob von Uexküll.[7]

From Uexküll, a German biologist, Lacan's main borrowing was the general concept of *Umwelt*, or environment: the world as experienced by all the animal kingdom. Uexküll had revolutionized the study of anthropology at the beginning of the century by constructing a theory of behavior showing that the environment of any animal (including human beings) must be seen as the internalizing of that environment in the relevant species' lived experience. Whence the idea that an individual's link with his environment should no longer be defined as a contract between a free individual and a society but rather as a relationship of dependence between an environment and an individual, the individual himself being determined by specific actions arising from a particular way of internalizing elements from the environment.

What Lacan borrowed from Uexküll in 1932 allowed him in 1938 to move to a new view of the way a mental phenomenon was organized: it was no longer a simple psychical fact but an imago, a group of unconscious representations, the mental form of a more general process. The word *imago*, derived from Jungian terminology, served not only to bring into the unconscious the two poles representing the model of the family—father and mother/patriarchy and matriarchy—but also to explain the organization of the family in the light of Uexküll's innovations: an individual cannot be "human" except insofar as he belongs to an organic social entity. To this was added the Aristotelian principle of a human essence defined by the proportions in which at least three elements—man, woman, and slave—are combined.

In a very pertinent study published in 1987, Bertrand Ogilvie explains that Lacan "unites what is usually contrasted." He sees family organization in the organicist and naturalistic terms of the philosophers of the Counter-Revolution while at the same time appealing to a secular conception of society derived from the philosophy of the Enlightenment. Very true. And Ogilvie goes on to show that Lacan went back, through Maurras, to an attitude inherited from the positivism of Comte, according to which society is made up of families rather than individuals. It was also through Maurras that

Lacan rediscovered Aristotle as a theorist on the social identity of the individual. Ogilvie remarks on the "astonishing combination of a collective perception of the dimension of the individual that, taken together with a biological view, leads to a scientific anthropology, freed of the ideological limits of nationalism. Lacan never cites Maurras, however; his debt to him seems to consist in being deaf to psychological individualism rather than in having actually adopted any of his arguments. But in this way, unwittingly, Lacan was joining the French tradition that goes back through Comte to Bonald and his theory of the 'outer man' who exists only in the context of his social relationships."[8]

Then there was the long section on the family that displayed a mixture of darkness and light characteristic of Lacan's style: "an extremely personal system using words in special senses," as Lucien Febvre observed. But that shifting of the meaning underneath the words was a translation of thought, and as such it was as purely French as the style of Maurras, Lacan's model, yet at the same time as iconoclastic and cosmopolitan as the Enlightenment ideal that was another constant source of inspiration to him. This was the great paradox of Lacan's development. Instead of being like that of Freud himself it resembled Thomas Mann's description of him: "explorer of the depths of the soul and psychologist of instinct, one of the line of nineteenth- and twentieth-century writers who . . . opposed rationalism, intellectualism, and classicism; in short, the faith in the mind that belonged to the eighteenth and even to a certain extent to the nineteenth century. These writers stressed the nocturnal side of the nature of the soul; they saw this as the really decisive and creative factor of life; they cultivated it and threw scientific light on it."[9] Lacan, a true son of Léon Bloy and René Descartes, was also heir to the line of those who explored darkness and light: in his view, the family was at the same time the traditional crucible of a social organism and an anthropological subject that must be rigorously examined and analyzed according to scientific criteria.

The first part of the study opposed complex to instinct and defined the three structures that contribute to the development of the individual. The word *complex*, borrowed by Freud from the Zurich school, denoted a group of representations that were to a greater or lesser degree unconscious. Lacan used it in a Freudian sense, to describe a structure in which the cultural factor predominated over fixed instinct and to argue that the consciousness of the subject intervened in representation.

But whereas, in a complex, a representation was virtually conscious for the subject, in the imago it became essentially unconscious. The complex, of which the imago was a constituent part, was the concrete factor that made it possible to understand the structure of the family, somewhere between the cultural phenomenon that determines it and the imaginary links that organize it. Thus a hierarchy consisting of three levels was the model for all interpretations of individual development. In it were to be found the weaning complex, the intrusion complex, and the Oedipus complex. Three "phases," in the Kleinian sense, which foreshadowed what after the war would be the Lacanian topography of the *real*, the *imaginary*, and the *symbolic*: "The weaning complex," Lacan wrote, "fixes the nursing relationship in the psyche in the parasitic mode imposed by the needs felt by a human being in his or her earliest days; it represents the primordial form of the imago of the mother. Hence it is the basis of the most archaic and stable feelings linking the individual to the family."[10]

Thus weaning left a trace in the psyche of the biological relationship that it interrupted, at the same time as it gave its expression to an older imago: that which separated the child from the womb at birth, forcing on it a prematurity specific to the human race, from which arose a disquiet that no maternal care could cure. It was this prematurity that distinguished man from animals. Refusal to be weaned was the basis of the positive aspect of the complex, reestablishing in the form of an *imago of the mother's breast* the interrupted nursing relationship. The existence of this imago dominated the whole of human life, a kind of appeal to universal nostalgia. It explained women's permanent sense of motherhood. But when this imago was not sublimated so as to allow social relationships, it became lethal. For then the complex, instead of corresponding to the vital functions, reflected their congenital inadequacy. From this arose an "appetite for death" that could take the form of nonviolent suicide, such as anorexia, drug addiction (by mouth), or gastric neurosis: "In abandoning himself to death the subject seeks to find the imago of the mother again."[11]

The intrusion complex fixed, by means of mental identification, the subject's dyadic relationship with his fellow creatures. Whether in the domestic drama of sibling rivalry, when order of birth placed each individual in a dynastic position of possessor or usurper, or in the mirror stage, when each individual restored his own lost unity, the same narcissistic structure of the ego was built up with the *imago of the double* as its central element. When the subject recognized the other in the form of a conflictual link, he achieved socialization. But when he went back to the maternal object he was clinging to a mode of destroying the other that tended toward paranoia.

Finally, the Oedipus complex introduced a triangulation that made it possible to define the specific form of the human family. Lacan stressed that Freud had been the first to show the importance of sexuality with regard to the family, basing his theory on a dissymmetry between the sexes. But having done this, Lacan then proposed a "psychological revision" of the Oedipus question, to be arrived at by linking his own researches with those of Melanie Klein, with which he had just become acquainted.

So far as sociological relativity was concerned, "Lacan's revision" was expressed in Bergsonian terms. In *Les Deux Sources de la morale et de la religion* (The two sources of morality and religion), published in 1932, Bergson had contrasted a morality of *obligation* with a morality of *aspiration*. The first was seen as a kind of enclosure, by which the human group closed in on itself in the interests of cohesion, while the second was defined as a kind of opening, by which the group universalized itself through exemplary figures such as heroes and saints. Lacan, taking this bipolarization as a point of departure, saw the prohibition of the mother as the concrete form of primordial obligation or *closed morality*. This was contrasted with the *open* form, which Lacan related to the paternalist authority of the father. It was this, he thought, that explained "the prophetism of the Jews," which "is to be understood," he wrote,

in terms of the elite situation of the Jewish people, chosen to be the upholder of patriarchy in the midst of other groups that went in for matriarchal religions, and in terms of that people's convulsive struggle to maintain the patriarchal ideal despite the irresistible attraction exercised by those other cultures. Thus throughout the history of the patriarchal nations we see a dialectical movement in society between the demands of the individual and the universalization of ideals: evidence of this is to be found in the legal forms perpetuating the mission that ancient Rome performed both as a power and as consciousness, which was embodied in the already revolutionary extension of the privileges of a patriarchy to a vast proletariat and to all the other nations.[12]

This detour by way of Bergson drew Lacan into a lengthy excursion on modern man and morals in marriage, which ended in a pessimistic view of the future of Western society, marked by the *decline of the paternal imago*. After maintaining that the rise of "the families of eminent men" was due not to heredity but to selective transmission of the ego-ideal from father to son, Lacan sprang to the defense of the values of the traditional family, which he considered more subversive than the educational utopias of totalitarian systems. According to Lacan, only the modern, middle-class, patriarchal family could ensure social liberty: he was here proclaiming the power of long-term history as against that of revolutionary upheaval, which seemed to him futile and doomed to failure. This led him to ascribe more liberating power to an ancient institution that he had suffered from and loathed than to any violent attempts at reformation. Having started out from Maurras he now came to Freud, recalling, like Tocqueville, how much, unlikely as it might seem, tradition might favor progress. But this "Freudianization" of the family question involved a set of even more fundamental choices: of universalism against culturalism, of the socialized against the tribal family. In other words, of culture as a civilizing force versus the worship of roots, of science versus magic, of cosmopolitanism versus chauvinism, and so on. "The nineteenth-century ideologists who subjected the paternalist family to the most sub-versive criticism," he wrote, "were not those least affected by it. I am not one of those who lament an alleged weakening of family ties. Is it not significant that the more the family has incorporated the highest cultural progress, the more it has tended to be reduced to its biological pattern?"[13] Then Lacan pays a resounding tribute to Freud, the product of Jewish patriarchy, who dared to invent the Oedipus complex at the very moment when, amid the industrialization of Western societies and as a result of economic concen-tration, the paternal imago was beginning to decline. This decline, itself the result of a psychological crisis, was related to the birth of psychoanalysis, which was seen as the recognition of a socially inevitable decline in pater-nal authority. And with this observation the first *Encyclopédie* article ended.

In the second and less innovative of his two articles, Lacan gave an exhaustive account of pathological complexes, including the results of his own work on psychosis and a Freudian point of view on neurosis. Then, in a kind of echo of his first article, he described "the mother's confiscation" of family authority as "domestic tyranny." He saw this usurpation as symp-tomatic of an inevitable social progress through which, by a psychological inversion, the predominance of the "male principle" asserted itself. According to Lacan, this principle, unfortunately for fathers and for men in general, was now vested in mothers and in women in general. The violence of his mockery of the marriage bond and of the role of mothers in family life no doubt derived from his uneasiness about his own failed marriage and from childhood memories of his parents' marital difficulties. But his attitude to the family was not merely a reflection of his own experience. It was first and foremost the result of a theoretical study, reminiscent of Nietzsche, of the crisis of modernity that at the turn of the century had hit not only intel-lectual circles in Vienna, where it brought forth the researches of Freud, but also European society as a whole. The crisis was seen as arising from a new polarization of the categories of masculine and feminine, reflecting the feel-ing that Western society was being feminized and paternal authority was in decline.[14] And because of his relations with Kojève, Bataille, and the College of Sociology, Lacan approached the question of the "fin de siècle" crisis in a spirit colored by a sense that the "end of history" itself was at hand.

Edouard Pichon soon reacted to Lacan's argument, at first privately in a let-ter to Henri Ey and then publicly in an article in the *RFP* entitled "The Family As Seen by M. Lacan."[15]

Pichon's letter to Ey, dated July 21, 1938, was couched in ambiguously mixed terms:

On the one hand I have just read with attention the text Lacan has written for the *Encyclopédie*: a difficult one, like everything he writes. On the other I recall your saying you were preparing a paper on the moral value of psychoanalysis. I'd like to give you a brief idea, without for now claiming to provide a formal account, of the fellow's rather silly amorality. He talks about "the failure of moral conceptions." (And at one point he makes a fierce attack on my theory of oblativity [selfless giving], though without actually mentioning me, either from fear of my name or out of utter disdain. In either case, it's very discourteous!) This attitude of being "beyond good and evil" strikes me as patently absurd: from the social point of view, any kind of society needs standards, or in other words some moral code, whatever our fine Supermen may say; and from the point of view of individual psychology, the existence of guilt feelings is such an established fact that Lacan himself calls it a constraint characteristic of the human race. Well, then?[16]

In his reply to Lacan in the *RFP*, Pichon, who died soon afterward, inveighed against him as if bequeathing a written testimony to his own anti-Nietzschean views on ethics and the family. He began by giving Lacan a grammar lesson, accusing him of employing jargon, inventing neologisms, and misusing ordinary words. In this Pichon agreed with Febvre, though he didn't draw the same conclusions. What had really infuriated Pichon was the way Lacan, without explicit acknowledgment, appropriated ideas and concepts previously used by his elders, including Codet, Laforgue, and Pichon himself. Pichon also resented Lacan's sarcastic attacks on authors he didn't even deign to mention. But the main thrust of Pichon's diatribe concerned the difference between "culture" and "civilization."

Pichon agreed with Lacan that the family was a product of tradition rather than heredity. And, like a true disciple of Maurras, he was not displeased to find that his pupil's arguments included some of his own. But the two men disagreed entirely on the subject of culture. Lacan rejected out of hand any claim that French civilization was better than all others. In so doing he was dismissing Maurras's teaching, based on a belief in the universal superiority of France's eternal, monarchical, rational civilization over all other cultures, and in particular over German *Kultur*, seen as individual inwardness shrouded in "Teutonic" mists. It was against this background that Pichon accused Lacan of being Hegelian and a Marxist—i.e., a "German"—and of misusing the word *culture*. "The French language," wrote Pichon, "has long made a distinction between the collective phenomenon *civilization* and the personal phenomenon *culture*. Monsieur Lacan forgets this distinction: he keeps saying *culture* instead of *civilization*, a practice that in a number of passages has a very adverse effect on his clarity. One might have hoped that the gross blunders made in France during the Four Years [i.e., the 1914–1918] War about German "coultour" would at least have taught most of us to discriminate between *culture* and *civilization*. To adulterate this notion is a disservice to both the genuine culture and the true civilization of our country."[17]

In 1938 Lacan's universalism was that of modern anthropology: the anthropology of Febvre, Freud, and later of Lévi-Strauss. Lacan maintained the universal existence of human reason and human culture in the face of nature, whatever internal differences might exist between their various forms. But Pichon's universalism, derived from Maurras, was inegalitarian, based on an absolute belief in the superiority and potential universality of so-called French civilization. Hence his declaration that

French civilization, so lively and so rich, has kept its precious humanism despite all attempts to destroy it, such as the Reformation, the bloodthirsty masquerade of 1789–1799, and the democracy that sprang from the movement of the Fourth of September. Monsieur Lacan, without renouncing any of his originality, is on our side as regards this fundamental Frenchness. However steeped he may be in Hegelianism and Marxism, he does not strike me as being in the least infected by the humanitarian virus: he is not foolish enough to be *just any* man's friend, though we feel he is the friend of *every* man. The fact is that this psychoanalyst is an opti-mate or patrician, at once because of his ethnic and family background and because of his medical training in Paris. Come now, Lacan—go on stoutly blazing your own trail, but kindly leave enough little pebbles behind for us to be able to catch up with you. Too many people, having lost all contact with you, imagine you've lost your way.[18]

But Jacques-Marie Lacan, as Pichon called him throughout his article, would never return to the fold of a "Frenchness" he had abandoned long ago.

PART V

War and Peace

14

· · · · · · ·

Marseilles, Vichy, Paris

On the page of her diary dated September 23, 1939, Marie Bonaparte wrote simply: "11:45 P.M., death of Freud."[1] The circumstances of Freud's death, just after war had been declared, have often been described, and I have already had occasion to show how the French press dealt with the event.[2] Here I shall merely recall a few lines from the newspaper *L'Oeuvre*, which beneath a pretense of objectivity revealed all the chauvinistic hatred, at once anti-Semitic and anticosmopolitan, that the French Right felt for Freud's discoveries: "After the Anschluss, in March 1938," said *L'Oeuvre*, "the distinguished scientist, who was Jewish, could not fail to figure on the list of personalities proscribed by the Nazis. A certain amount of time went by before he was able to leave Vienna, where he had lived for more than fifty years, and follow Einstein on the road to exile. As is well known, Britain welcomed him with open arms."[3]

Whereas in Germany some psychoanalysts had, under Jones's influence, adopted a policy of collaboration with the Nazis, in France the situation was different. War broke out at a time when the psychoanalytic scene was already changing because of the arrival of the second generation of French practitioners, the generation of Lacan, Nacht, Lagache, and Françoise Dolto. Codet, who had been ill, died in December 1939, followed in January 1940 by Edouard Pichon. Borel was already likely to resign, and Hesnard, who was loyal to Marshal Pétain, continued his career in the French navy. Starting as chief medical officer for the navy in Algeria, he next became medical director of the Fourth Maritime Region and in 1943 was appointed inspector-general of naval medical services in Africa. It was in the fortified camp at Bizerta that he wrote his famous "philo-Semitic" text on "The Jewishness of Freud."[4]

René Allendy, who served in the army first in the *département* of La Manche and then in Brittany, eventually went to live in Montpellier in the

Unoccupied Zone, where he met with a tragicomic adventure: the medical authorities thought his name "sounded Jewish," so he had to prove that he was a "pure Aryan." In 1941 he went to Switzerland, where he met Jung and Baudoin at the ceremonies held for the rehabilitation of Paracelsus. Just before the rounding-up of Jews in the Vélodrome d'Hiver in July 1942, he died in Paris, having written an account of his fatal illness in his *Journal d'un médecin malade* (Diary of an ailing doctor).[5]

Whereas the nationalistic elements of the SPP were decimated in the early years of the war, the internationalist group was forced to break up, and most of them went into exile. Charles Odier returned to Switzerland; Raymond de Saussure, Heinz Hartmann, and René Spitz arranged to be transferred to the psychoanalytic society in New York; and in 1942, after spending many months in Marseilles, Rudolph Loewenstein too finally left for the United States.

As for Marie Bonaparte, after closing down the Institut de Psychanalyse and removing the archives, she took refuge first in her house in Brittany, where she had Loewenstein to stay, and then in her place at St. Cloud, which had meanwhile been looted by the Nazis. She then decided to go to her villa in St. Tropez, where she was joined again by Loewenstein. But, unable to practice professionally, she too went into exile, arriving in Athens in February 1941. From there she embarked with the Greek royal family for Alexandria and after that went on to South Africa, where she spread the Freudian word and planned to return to France after the siege of Stalingrad. She was in London in the autumn of 1944 and back in Paris by February 1945, fearing the SPP would again be rent by internal quarrels but determined to play a leading role once more.[6]

The two women pioneers of child psychoanalysis in France both met with tragic fates, the victims of melancholy and anti-Semitism. Eugénie Sokolnicka, isolated not only as a woman and an analyst without medical qualifications but also as a foreigner and a Jew, gassed herself in 1934. Sophie Morgenstern, already afflicted by the death of her daughter Laure, killed herself on June 14, 1940, the day the German army entered Paris.

Among that first generation of French psychiatrists and psychoanalysts, two men stood out from the rest because of their diametrically opposite attitudes to the war. Paul Schiff was the only representative of his generation to become an active member of the Resistance. René Laforgue was the only one, apart from Matthias Göring, to be a collaborator, though his efforts ended in complete failure.[7]

The very fact of abstaining from all public activity, including writing, amounted to an act of passive opposition to Nazism. In this respect, Marie Bonaparte's attitude was exemplary. Unlike Jones, she made no attempt to "rescue" psychoanalysis. By going into exile and springing at once to the aid of the Jews, she forestalled any attempt to form an "Aryan" version of the psychoanalytic society. As she had gone and the EP group under Henri Ey was also unavailable, there could be no negotiations between the occupying authorities and the leaders of the SPP, all in exile, dead, or absent.

In other words, in June 1940 the situation of French psychoanalysis did not lend itself to the creation of a nazified therapeutic society like the one in Berlin. Hence the failure of René Laforgue's attempt at collaboration: he couldn't persuade Göring to "Aryanize" a group that no longer really existed.

While the first generation was absent from the Parisian scene, the second generation had not yet acquired enough power within the SPP to make it a force to be reckoned with. Its members were in the same state of abeyance as their older colleagues; each individual had his own fate to cope with as best he could. Daniel Lagache, a professor at the university of Strasbourg who had taken refuge in Clermont-Ferrand, helped Jews and members of the Resistance, while Sacha Nacht was an active member of the Resistance network from November 1942 to September 1944.[8] John Leuba, who had already fought in World War I, served in the Paris civil defense, not so much out of opposition to the Nazis as because of his deep hatred for the "Huns," as he always called them.

A letter Leuba wrote to Jones on December 31, 1944 gave a good description of the situation of the handful of Parisian psychoanalysts of both generations who chose to carry on with their professional activities during the war, like the ordinary French people who neither favored collaboration with the enemy nor fought in the Resistance. "The only ones left in Paris at the beginning of the Occupation," he wrote,

were Mme Dolto (formerly Mlle Marette) and myself. Parcheminey and Schlumberger, then Lacan, came back later, after they were demobilized. Parcheminey, Schlumberger, and I did some very good work. (I mention Lacan just for the record, since he didn't seem to do much at Sainte-Anne—I only saw him there once or twice.) Our own work consisted mainly of treatments and training analyses. Several interns and directors of clinics asked us to analyze them. . . . There was no question of publishing anything during the Occupation. We were barely tolerated. At one point, even, we nearly came to grief because of Laforgue's inept activities: in the end his clumsy dealings with the Huns made him dangerous. . . . I may add that Mme Dolto did some excellent work with children at the Hôpital Trousseau. Mme Codet went on performing analyses.[9]

An ordinary and yet nonconformist Frenchman: such was Jacques Lacan throughout the whole of the Occupation. "He felt," says Georges Bernier, "that he had a superior mind and belonged to the intellectual elite. So he saw to it that the events that history forced him to confront should have no effect on his way of life."[10] Admittedly, in September 1939 he was mainly preoccupied by his affair with Sylvia Bataille, his marriage problems, and the health of his month-old son. As a result, all the hostility he felt toward the family as an institution, together with the deep pessimism it aroused in him, combined to color his verdict on the collapse of France.

In August 1939 Malou had given birth to a son, who was named Thibaut. She knew Jacques had been unfaithful to her for some time but seemed unaware that the famous *coup de foudre* that smote Sylvia and Jacques at the Café de Flore had occurred just when she found she was pregnant. The two lovers had been inseparable ever since, but Jacques did not tell Malou how serious the affair was. He went on fulfilling his various obligations as if nothing had happened. Thibaut, who was born with pyloric stenosis, had to have a serious operation. In a letter dated October 4, 1939, Lacan told Sylvain Blondel about his worries: the baby's vomiting, the weight loss, and then the remarkably successful operation. He described how the danger hanging over his son made him forget all other perils and marveled at the infant's will to live. He called him "the Hero." He also praised "the Baboon," Malou's mother, though he was highly critical of his own family, especially his parents: with the best of intentions they had tried to exercise their Christian influence over the infant's fate by suggesting he be given extreme unction.

Lacan then spoke of the collapse of French society and the need to change in order to survive. People had all been torn away from a way of life with which they "couldn't wholly go along" but which had nevertheless allowed everyone to preserve the best of himself. Conflicts left unresolved within, he went on, get resolved externally. But now everything he valued was temporarily exposed to the elements. Some aspects of our lives might be empty or false, he said, speaking in the first person plural, but such aspects were dear to us and it was painful to have to change them. Finally, he said he was doing little therapy but a lot of medicine, and his letter ended with a touching anecdote about his daughter Caroline. She had said to her grandmother, "My sleep won't come. I'm waiting for someone." The phrase delighted her father.[11]

He had been directed to serve as an assistant doctor in the neuropsychiatry department of the military hospital at the Val-de-Grâce, but at the same time he went on dividing his life between his two partners. By March 1940 Malou was pregnant again. She had spent a few days in the country with Jacques, hoping to revive a relationship that was heading for disaster. On May 29, when French troops were embarking at Dunkirk, Lacan, full of anxiety, wrote another letter to his brother-in-law. Malou had just gone to Rohan to stay in the family house with her friend Renée Massonaud. Lacan was worried about what might happen to her, to Caroline, to the "Thibautin," and to the expected baby. "What can I say? I entrust them to you if need be. Please remember this if things get dangerous." He described his routine at the hospital, where he saw between fifteen and twenty patients a day. From the professional point of view he felt in better shape than ever, and his output surprised even himself. He felt at home and believed he was well thought of. Then came another diatribe against the French political system, the self-constituted elites, and the mandarins of the hospital hierarchy—those "supercilious morons."[12]

At the end of spring 1940 he was posted, again as assistant physician, to the hospital run by the Franciscans in Pau. It was about this time that Malou began to see what was really happening. Lacan had been gradually drifting away from her, and now it was with Sylvia that he was meeting new friends and sharing the pleasures of a new way of life. Sylvain too had been called up, and in April he was appointed head of a surgical ambulance unit in Luxeuil. On June 14 he was ordered to Mâcon; three days later he was withdrawn to Gérardmer; and on June 20 he arrived in Saint-Dié. When the German army entered the town he remained with his patients, and at the end of August he was sent home.[13]

Meanwhile Georges Bataille had taken Denise Rollin to Drugeac, a small village in the Cantal, near Mauriac. (Bataille had met Denise Rollin in the autumn of 1939, when she was living in a handsome apartment at 3, rue de Lille. "More than any other woman I know she was silence personified," says Laurence Bataille. "To put it metaphorically, she recorded what other people said. And it was amazing what reverberations they set up in her.")[14] Bataille then went back to Paris but rejoined Denise after June 11. "It's an exodus," he wrote, "and a horrible toss-up between good and bad luck. So far I've been lucky, and I'm especially aware of it because only an hour ago I thought I was going to have to take to the road on foot."[15] Sylvia and Laurence, followed by Rose and André Masson, soon turned up in Drugeac.

On June 24, in Pau, Lacan asked to be allowed to go to Aurillac, "for reasons that, with your permission, may only be given verbally."[16] His reasons were that he wanted to go to see Sylvia in Drugeac. His request was granted. Not long afterward he was demobilized.

In the autumn of 1940, everyday life began again in a France now divided into two zones. In early September Sylvia and her mother went to Vichy, where she met Jean Renoir; he was there to collect the documents necessary for emigrating to the United States. "The only thing to do is get the hell out," he said. "There's nothing to be done here. It's going to be terrible. A whole country up for grabs—a house in exchange for a handful of beans."[17] A month later, Vichy passed the laws against the Jews. Sylvia fled with her mother to the south of France: first to Marseilles and then to Cagnes-sur-Mer, where she rented a house. As a doctor, Lacan could get sufficient gasoline and enough travel permits to cross the demarcation line once every two weeks, and for two years he was able to race back and forth between Paris and Marseilles in his 5 CV Citröen. For getting around in the

South he bought a bicycle, which he later kept as a memento of the dark days of the war.[18]

His decision not to be affected by the course of history did not prevent him from having a very lucid view of politics. Hating as he did anything that resembled fascism, Nazism, or anti-Semitism, he had no illusions about Marshal Pétain's intentions regarding the Jews. That was why, when he found out that Sylvia and her mother had been naive enough to register themselves with the French authorities as Jewish, he rushed to the police station in Cagnes to retrieve the documents in question. Too impatient to wait for them to be handed back, he climbed on a stool, grabbed the file from a shelf, and then, as soon as he got outside, tore to shreds all the papers in it.[19]

Though he was never a Pétainist, he had little sympathy for the Resistance, either. He hated oppression but was scornful of heroism. Two contradictory accounts show his tendency to say different things to different people about this period of his life. With some he denigrated his own attitude, making it out to be uncompromisingly pragmatic; with others he claimed to have thought of joining the Resistance. Catherine Millot remembers him calling certain of its intellectual members "irresponsible" and saying he himself "had had no hesitation about going to the Hotel Meurice and fraternizing with the German officers to get a permit to go and see Sylvia in the Unoccupied Zone."[20] With Daniel Bordigoni he spoke of quite a different attitude. "He was shattered by the Occupation," Bordigoni reports Lacan's having told him one day, "and couldn't make up his mind whether to withdraw and devote himself to study or to join the underground movement. He was chiefly worried about not being properly recognized in France and contemplated becoming a philosopher. It was François Tosquelles's letter to him about his thesis that put him back on the path of psychoanalysis."[21] (Tosquelles had first learned of the Aimée case when Lacan's thesis was published, but he started studying it in January 1940 at the Saint-Alban hospital, where, in a context of militant antifascism, institutional psychotherapy began. "Perhaps you are aware," wrote Tosquelles, "that many members of the 'psychic' world who were at Saint-Alban went away with homemade copies of the thesis in question, which was out of print and unobtainable in the bookshops.")[22]

There is truth in both versions, however. Lacan was undoubtedly shattered by the fall of France, but he was undoubtedly much more concerned about recognition for his work and for himself than about joining in the struggle. His hostility toward the occupying power took the form, first and foremost, of aesthetic rebellion, together with an individualistic instinct for survival and for outsmarting the system. Above all he looked out for himself and his nearest and dearest, displaying great ingenuity in the process. But his thesis, still his major work at that time, continued to be interpreted as an act of resistance to psychiatric oppression. And in its own way, through Saint-Alban, it helped to encourage the fight against the Nazis.

It was in the autumn of 1940 that Lacan and his former analysand, Georges Bernier, met again in Marseilles. The two men became very good friends and were inseparable for almost two years. To show their dislike of Pétainism, they got into the habit of going several evenings a week to sit on the terrace of the Cintra, a famous bar on the Canebière that at the time acted as a rendezvous for a number of exiled intellectuals. There Lacan and Bernier displayed a fierce Anglomania: "We felt very deeply that England was the world's last hope, and as a result English literature and English thought were the only ones that existed for us."[23] Lacan, who had been so greatly influenced by German culture and philosophy, had begun to study the English language with René Varin, a senior official at the Quai d'Orsay, the French ministry of foreign affairs. Though he couldn't actually speak English well, Lacan was an avid reader, and he acquired a copy of *For Whom the Bell Tolls* from one of the last American ships moored in the harbor.

As they sat outside the Cintra, he and Bernier started translating some of the poems of T. S. Eliot. One evening they decided they must see the King James version of the Bible, not easy to find in those circumstances. In an attempt to get hold of a copy, Lacan did the rounds of all the Protestant churches in Marseilles. The two enthusiasts had chosen the King James or "Authorized" version of the Bible advisedly. Published in 1611, it retained many of the cadences of the Old Testament's Hebrew original. As Julien Green has said "Few English-speaking people, when they read their Bible, remember that they are reading a translation. They love it as sincerely as the Jews love the Hebrew text. . . . The translation is an original text in itself. The book has been rewritten rather than translated, and the *King James Bible* reproduces the spirit of the Hebrew text itself."[24]

So here was Lacan reading the story of the people of Moses in the language of Shakespeare and in the company of a former analysand who was both Jewish and as much of an atheist as Lacan himself. Lacan's Anglophilia included even the wearing of British officers' overcoats, made over by a tailor. And it was with a similar aesthetic passion that he openly indulged in every available pleasure, as if to set at naught the general shortages. "We used to have black market dinners," says Bernier, "in a Provençal literary restaurant run by a Pétainist. Whenever we ran out of cigarettes Lacan would vanish for half an hour or so and come back with four packs of Craven A, two red and two green. He really knew his way around. For instance, one day he noticed Guerlain had some unsold stocks of baby soap, and he managed to supply himself from them throughout the war. As a doctor he had many privileges, and he always made good use of them."[25]

It was in this same restaurant that Lacan met Gaston Defferre (later socialist mayor of Marseilles and government minister), who put Bernier up for some time. The two friends also saw Roland Malraux, who was trying to help his brother escape from a camp near Sens, where he was being held prisoner. He asked the two friends for help in the form of money and civilian clothing; Lacan didn't give him anything. But a little while later André Malraux got to the Côte d'Azur, where Dorothy Bussy put her villa at his disposal.

Just off the main coast road leading from Pointe-Rouge to Les Goudes there lived an already legendary lady who resembled an eccentric character out of a children's story. Lily, born in 1891, was the daughter of Baron Double de Saint-Lambert and in 1918 had married Count Jean Pastré, by whom she had three children: Dolly, Nadia, and Pierre. The Pastrés had gone into industry and owned Noilly-Prat, the firm that made the aperitif of that name, which had large premises on the rue Paradis. When she separated from her husband, Lily Pastré had kept his beautiful house at Montredon, and there, from 1940 on, she most generously sheltered many painters, musicians, actors, and other artists obliged to emigrate or go into hiding. She was a music lover, a patron of the arts, and a nonconformist, and she drove about in her red motorcar distributing largesse. As well as helping the poor she aided those in spiritual distress: she was sympathetic to every kind of unhappiness. Because of her the Campagne Pastré, as the Montredon estate was known, became a kind of center for much of the exiled elite of Europe. Among those who came there, some briefly, some for lengthy stays, were Boris Kochno (Diaghilev's lover and a habitué of Marie-Laure de Noaille's salon), Francis Poulenc, Clara Haskil, Lanza del Vasto, Samson François, and Youra Guller, a woman pianist of Romanian origin.[26]

It was out of these encounters that the Festival of Aix-en-Provence was born. The countess herself played a major part in its founding. As soon as war broke out, her daughter Nadia had joined the surgical ambulance service in Verdun, where she met her friend Edmonde de Charles-Roux, whose family had traditional links with the Pastrés. Dolly had a more tragic fate. She was already suffering from melancholia when she married the handsome prince Murat. He left at once to join the Resistance and was killed in 1944. Dolly never got over this loss and suffered severe depression despite the fact that she had started an analysis with Lacan and been treated with drugs by Jean Delay.

Lacan began to visit the Campagne Pastré in the autumn of 1940, though at first he met with reserve there and was regarded as "enigmatic," "uncomfortable," and even "diabolical."[27] But Lacan became especially friendly with Youra Guller and often went to see André and Rose Masson, who were given a house of their own on the Montredon estate when they arrived in Marseilles at the end of 1940. Bernier spent a merry New Year's Eve with them on December 31. Sylvia was three months pregnant but had not been inactive since arriving on the Mediterranean coast. Together with other former habitués of the Café de Flore now emigrated to the Southern Zone, she worked to support her family by the manufacture and sale of preserved fruit, made from scraps of the dates and figs that were still being shipped over from Africa. The people concerned formed a small company, which was allowed to sell its "blackish objects" throughout the region and even in Paris. They were said to taste vaguely like the real thing.[28]

Toward the end of the summer Malou had gone to see Lacan and asked him to break off his affair with Sylvia. Not receiving any positive answer, she gave him a year to make up his mind to come back to her.[29] On her way home she met René Laforgue getting off the train from Paris at the Saint-Charles station in Marseilles. He was on his way to his house, Les Chaberts, at La Roquebrussanne near Toulon. When he saw how upset she was, he realized she and Lacan had parted and invited her to spend a few days at his place in the country. She accepted his invitation.[30]

When Lacan found out, in October, that Sylvia was expecting a child, he did not hesitate to pass on the good news to Malou. He was delighted at the thought of becoming a father again and wanted to share his happiness with his lawful wife, regardless of the fact that she herself was eight months pregnant and soon to give birth. She had already been very distressed by his affair with Sylvia, which she had tried in vain to bring to an end. This latest cruelty from the man she still loved was too much for her, and she sank beneath the humiliation. Lacan then said an amazing thing to her: "Je vous le rendrai au centuple" (I'll make it up to you a hundredfold). Sylvain advised Malou to divorce Lacan as soon as possible. On November 26, in a depressed mood that only revealed a state of melancholia she had so far managed to suppress, she gave birth to a daughter, who was named Sybille.[31]

It is probable that Lacan felt something for Malou's sufferings, but as Georges Bernier so aptly remarks, "he was wonderfully cool in his dealings with women."[32] So he went on shuttling to and fro between Paris and Marseilles, though he was thinking of moving house: it wasn't possible to go on living on the boulevard Malesherbes. Earlier on, at the beginning of the war and in the middle of the crisis with Malou, he had stayed for a month with André Weiss, whose wife, Colette, was a friend of the Blondins and whose sister, Jenny Weiss-Roudinesco, was to become one of the pioneers of child psychoanalysis in France. Lacan's stay at 130, rue Faubourg-Saint-Honoré left an unforgettable memory. André Weiss's children were brought up

---

Translator's note: Weiss-Roudinesco married Pierre Aubry in 1953; she was the author's mother.

according to very strict principles and not allowed to speak at the table when guests were present. But Lacan used to break this ridiculous rule and speak to them directly. "It made us feel we mattered." says Françoise Choay, "to have a grown-up take an interest in us. He made a great impression on us."[33]

It was Georges Bataille who solved the practical problem arising from the Lacans' separation. At the beginning of 1941 he told Lacan an apartment was about to become free at 5, rue de Lille, near the flat he himself shared with Denise Rollin. Lacan bought the place immediately and lived there for the rest of his life. Malou was granted her divorce on December 15, 1941. Jacques hadn't bothered to present himself for the "conciliation" provided for by the law.[34] In the eyes of the Blondin family he had simply "disappeared."[35]

In the course of his trips to Marseilles, he visited not only the Campagne Pastré but also the "network" created by Jean Ballard around the review *Les Cahiers du Sud* (The southern notebooks), The *Cahiers*, founded by Marcel Pagnol in 1914, had by 1925, under Jean Ballard, become an avant-garde publication specializing in the work of the surrealists. In 1933 it opened its columns to German writers fleeing Nazism. Klaus Mann wrote for it, as did Ernst Toller and above all Walter Benjamin, together with Pierre Klossowski, brother of the painter Balthus. After 1940 Jean Ballard did all he possibly could to keep the *Cahiers* going. The writing of every issue amounted to a daily struggle against the occupying power, and it was this battle that gave rise to the first use of the expression *poète engagé* (committed poet).[36]

And so, in Marseilles, between the Campagne Pastré and the Ballard network, Lacan went on leading a social and intellectual life that was a continuation of his prewar existence in Paris. He was also able to meet some of the surrealists who during the winter of 1940–1941 stayed in the villa Bel Air under the auspices of the Emergency Rescue Committee. These included André Breton, Hans Bellmer, Victor Brauner, and René Char. André Masson also went there regularly.

In March 1941 Georges Bernier thought seriously of emigrating to England. But in order to do so he needed two visas, one for himself and one for his wife. Remembering that he knew an official in the Ministry of Foreign Affairs he decided to go to Vichy, where the man now worked. Lacan offered to take him there in his Citröen. They drove to Vichy a first time at an alarming rate and then went again to collect the visas. When they tried to book a room at the Hôtel du Mexique they were told to come back after dinner. They were then told to wait in the foyer. On the stroke of midnight Jacques Doriot himself suddenly appeared at the top of the stairs, flanked by his bodyguards and followed by Henri du Moulin de Labarthète, head of Pétain's civilian cabinet. And Lacan and Bernier spent the night there, amid clouds of cigarette smoke, in the room where the marshal's men had held their meeting.[37]

Bernier stayed on in Marseilles until the end of the year. Then he went to the United States, leaving there for England, where he worked on war propaganda for the Psychological Warfare Board. He stayed in England until September 1944 and then returned to Paris, where in 1955 he started the review *L'Oeil*. Just as Bernier was getting his exit visas, Rose and André Masson were leaving France for the United States. André Breton had gone there a week earlier. As soon as the Massons got to New York they started doing all they could to bring Sylvia and Laurence to America. They were still hoping for their arrival on December 21, 1941. But in vain: Sylvia had decided to stay in France.[38]

On July 3 of that year, during the darkest days of the Occupation, she gave birth to a daughter named Judith Sophie, registered at the city hall in Antibes under the name of Bataille. For although Sylvia had been amicably separated from Bataille in 1934, she had remained legally married to him, while he at the time was officially the partner of Colette Peignot. After Colette died in 1938, Bataille lived with Denise Rollin. But if his marriage to Sylvia no longer had any social meaning, it was still legally valid. Lacan, for his part, was still the lawful husband of a woman with whom he no longer really lived but from whom, unlike Bataille, he had never been officially separated. Attached as he was to a traditional family ideal that he violently rejected—though he had written an apologia on it for the *Encyclopédie*—Lacan continued with Malou in a relationship based on ambiguity and things left unspoken. He had never clearly decided on any separation, and he did not initiate the break.

Sylvia, for her part, couldn't apply for any kind of legal separation while she knew she was carrying Lacan's child. If she had asked for a divorce during the winter of 1940–1941, she would have lost the protection that at the time still derived from being married to a non-Jew. Whence the complicated situation that arose in July 1941: the newborn child was biologically Lacan's daughter but could not possibly bear her father's name. He was still married to Malou and under French law was not allowed to recognize a child born to any other woman. So it was Georges Bataille who gave his name to Lacan and Sylvia's child. There was an absurd discrepancy between the legal order, which made a child bear the name of a man who was not her father, and everyday reality, in which she was the daughter of a man whose name she could not bear.

There can be no doubt that one of the origins of Lacan's theory of the name-of-the-father, a key element in his teaching, lay in this imbroglio, lived through in the midst of war and destruction.

Lacan still went on crossing France from north to south after Bernier's departure to the United States. When the big deportations began in the spring of 1942, Simone Kahn's parents were denounced to the Gestapo by their concierge. When Queneau asked Lacan to help find a place where they could hide, he got them into a clinic in Versailles. The price was exorbitant, but when Simone protested, Lacan replied sharply: "They're a couple of bourgeois—they can pay!"[39] By the beginning of 1943 the situation was getting more and more dangerous for the Jews who had taken refuge in what was formerly the Southern Zone, now occupied by the German army. Georges Bataille, who was living in Vézelay, suggested to Jacques and Sylvia that they, together with Laurence and Judith, should join him in a house he had rented for them in the cathedral square. In the end, only his daughter, Laurence, went. But when Bataille and Denise Rollin parted after he met Diana Kotchoubey, he suggested Lacan should rent the apartment at 3, rue de Lille, and this made it possible for Sylvia to go and live there with Laurence, Judith, and Nathalie Maklès.[40]

And so Lacan returned to the Left Bank of the Seine, where he had spent his youth as a pupil at the Collège Stanislas. By making the district favored by the literary intelligentsia the setting of his new life with Sylvia, Lacan was breaking with Parisian psychoanalytic tradition. Most of the pioneers of the movement had got into the habit of settling in the elegant 16th Arrondissement, and at the beginning of his career Lacan had done the same. Analysts received their patients in luxurious apartments modeled on those of the medical bourgeoisie and large enough to contain on the one hand both a consulting and a waiting room and on the other enough private space to accommodate a family and servants. The decorations often included collections of valuable objects: paintings, rare books, oriental carpets, Dresden china, and Chinese ceramics. A passion for collecting was the only one of the middle-class habits and tastes that Lacan retained. He often visited antique dealers, and he bought many pictures from painters who were Sylvia's friends: Picasso, Balthus, and of course Masson. Though Lacan didn't have André Breton's expert eye for works of art, he did have a great thirst for possession.[41]

Meanwhile the Blondins were dealt a crushing blow by the death of Sylvain's brother-in-law, Jacques Decour, whose real name was Daniel Decourdemanche. A communist and writer with a degree in German, he cofounded with Jean Paulhan the journal *Les Lettres françaises* (French literature). Decour was arrested at the same time as Georges Solomon and Georges Politzer, and on May 30, 1942, after being savagely tortured, he was shot by the Nazis. Aragon described him as a "young man with fine features, a pale complexion, and thin, mocking lips, who but for the powdered hair was just like an eighteenth-century pastel portrait by La Tour. . . . Yet we know he reacted to all the traps set by the judges, all the physical sufferings inflicted on him, by asking if they hadn't nearly finished, because he was guilty of all he was accused of. But that wasn't what the Gestapo wanted. They were waiting for names and addresses. But those thin, mocking lips did not reveal them." Sybille still remembers how, and in what grave and feeling tones, Malou, long after the war, used to read out to her three children the last letter Jacques Decour ever wrote to his family.[42]

In Lacan's new neighborhood in Paris, literary life still went on. Adrienne Monnier, in her bookshop in the rue de l'Odéon, saw the arrival of a new generation of young intellectuals. Above all they loved American music and literature, but they also admired the early books of such still relatively unknown writers as Sartre, Camus, and Malraux. In the winter of 1941–1942, in the Café de Flore, where collaborators rubbed shoulders with members of the Resistance, Simone de Beauvoir, as yet unpublished, got into the habit of arriving as soon as the doors opened so as to get a seat near the stove. She was reading *The Phenomenology of Mind* in order to help Sartre with *L'Etre et le néant* (*Being and Nothingness*).

Before 1939 those who didn't read German had known Hegel's work only through the commentaries of Kojève, Koyré, and Wahl. But in 1939 volume one of the first French translation of Hegel's *Phenomenology* was published, followed in 1941 by volume two. It was the work of Jean Hyppolite, a young philosopher who thereby opened up a new era of Hegelianism in France. By a strange quirk of historical logic, Hegel finished his *Phenomenology* just as the French army was bringing a breath of freedom to Jena, while Hyppolite finished his translation of the same work just as the Nazis were invading France to impose dictatorship and slavery.[43]

On October 25, 1942, Giacometti introduced Sartre to Leiris. Simone de Beauvoir has painted a striking portrait of Leiris in *La Force de l'âge* (*The Prime of Life*): "What with his shaven skull and formal clothes and stiff gestures I found Leiris a somewhat intimidating character, despite the calculatedly cordial smile he switched on. . . . His particular blend of masochism, extremism, and idealism had led him into heaven knows how many painful and preposterous scrapes, all of which he related with an air of mildly astounded impartiality."[44] As they started to mix with all the veterans of surrealism, Sartre and Beauvoir, who had a very grand idea of that brilliant generation of writers, felt they were meeting men already the heroes of an intellectual adventure that they themselves dreamed of taking over. Simone embarked on intimate relationships first with Zette, then with Leiris, but she never shared in the famous genealogical secret known only to the family circle linking Picasso, Masson, Bataille, and Lacan. . . .

Leiris never felt up to joining the Musée de l'Homme (Museum of mankind) resistance network led by Anatole Lewitzky and Boris Vildé, but he knew about their activities. When they were executed at Mont-Valérien on February 23, 1942 it was a terrible blow to him, and for months he was haunted by their memory. As his decision not to fight arose from the realization that he lacked physical courage, he set out on a course of moral opposition, writing only for reviews that supported the Resistance. He produced only one book: *Haut mal* (Epilepsy; literally, "Greater Evil").[45]

At the beginning of the Occupation he fell out for a while with his friend Georges Bataille, who had had the unfortunate idea of starting an "apolitical" review produced by the Young France group and financed by the Vichy government under Georges Pelorson. Pelorson suggested the editor should be Maurice Blanchot, a writer from the Maurrassian right who since 1936 had been writing anti-Semitic and antiparliamentary articles against Blum and the Popular Front in *Combat* and *L'Insurgé*.[46] The review never materialized, but Bataille did meet Blanchot and gathered several members of the Young France group around him at 3, rue de Lille. According to Michel Surya, Bataille was responsible for Blanchot's ideological turnaround during the Occupation.

Bataille did not contemplate joining in the anti-Nazi struggle, and between 1941 and 1944, under a pseudonym, he published a number of books, including *Madame Edwarda* and *L'Expérience intérieure* (Inner experience). His political attitude was different from that of Leiris, and the distinction between them had been evident ever since the days of the Collège de sociologie. Leiris believed science was a much greater liberating force than the holy and was skeptical about the far-fetched practices of the "conspirators." He thought they lacked rigor and were out of place in a Western democracy. In short, Leiris was not such a convinced nihilist as Bataille and didn't share his hostility to bourgeois parliamentarianism. Nor had he ever been at all attracted by fascism, not even in order to turn its efficiency back on itself. So the two men's attitudes to the war were bound to be different. Leiris believed in heroism and in the fight for freedom, whereas Bataille, an ultraleftist, rejected science so totally that he wanted to abolish all thinkers as representing Western reason itself. Thus Bataille saw the coming of war as an end of History, the latter embodied in the Hitler of the *Blitzkrieg* instead of in Kojève's Stalin. Hence the need to pay tribute to evil, not through any sort of collaboration but through an inner recourse to a dark kind of mysticism, in which Madame Edwarda, symbolizing an unclean, prostituted France, displayed her rags and wounds in a brothel in the rue Saint-Denis, while taking herself for God.

When they met Louise and Michel Leiris, Sartre and Beauvoir, who were thoroughly hostile to Nazism and Pétainism, were publishing articles not only in such organs of the Resistance as *Les Cahiers du Sud* and *Les Lettres françaises* but also in more dubious places, such as the review *Comoedia*, which in order to remain entirely "cultural" and "apolitical" refused to accept contributions from either Jews or the more committed antifascists. For Sartre and Beauvoir, commitment went no further than their activities in the group Socialisme et liberté (Socialism and freedom) with Maurice Merleau-Ponty and Dominique and Jean-Toussaint Desanti: i.e., distributing leaflets, holding meetings, carrying out clandestine missions, and so on. There was also an interview with Jean Cavaillès, which ended inconclusively, and a meeting with Malraux at Saint-Jean-Cap-Ferrat. All Malraux believed in then was the firepower of Russian tanks and the American air force.[47]

In June 1943, with the approval of the clandestine *Lettres françaises*, Sartre arranged for Charles Dullin to put on *The Flies*, a play he had written at the same time as *Being and Nothingness*. In it he denounced very plainly the apologetics of the Vichy regime and came out in moral support of those who committed violent deeds in the name of a certain idea of freedom—specifically, a conception that made the terrorist hero feel so responsible for his actions that he felt remorse and was tempted to denounce himself. Although the play had been censored by the Germans before it could be performed at the Théâtre Sarah-Bernhardt (renamed Théâtre de la Cité to sound more "Aryan") the collaborationist press gave it a harsh reception. "Nauseating," they called it; "Cubist and Dadaist bric-a-brac." It soon closed. But when it was revived in December 1943, Michel Leiris wrote an excellent article on it in *Les Lettres françaises*: "Orestes, once the victim of fate, has become the champion of freedom. If he kills, he does so no longer because he is impelled by obscure forces, but in full knowledge of the facts and to ensure that justice is done. And through that deliberate decision he finally exists as a man."[48] So Sartre was not, as his detractors allege, an arriviste maneuvering under the Nazi heel. And if he did not have the heroism of Cavaillès, Canguilhem, Decour, or Politzer; if he submitted to German censorship when publishing his books and having his play performed in an "Aryanized" theater, he wrote nothing during this period that did not support the fight against oppression.

It was at the dress rehearsal of *The Flies* that Sartre met Albert Camus, a few months after he had written an article for *Les Cahiers du Sud* on Camus' *L'Etranger* (*The Stranger*), published at the end of the summer of 1942. Before long Sartre, Leiris, Camus, and Beauvoir were seeing one another regularly, and Leiris introduced Sartre to Queneau. "These meetings took up a good deal of our time," wrote Beauvoir. "We listened to the BBC, and passed on the news bulletins, and discussed them. . . . We agreed to remain leagued together in perpetuity against the systems and men and ideas that we condemned. But their defeat was imminent, and our task would be to shape the future that would then unfold before us. . . . We were to provide the postwar era with its ideology."[49]

When the Allied victory seemed near, Sartre, Camus, and Merleau-Ponty thought seriously of starting a review that would blossom in a France set free from fascism. Georges Bataille was often with them, and he became closer to Sartre after the latter wrote an article on *L'Expérience intérieure* (Inner experience), in which he described the author as a "new mystic" and someone "hallucinated by the world beyond."[50] Sartre's commentary was concise, severe, and ironical, but not devoid of admiration. Sartre made Bataille out to be sick, bereaved, and inconsolable but able to survive the death of God. Because of his "*mauvaise foi*" (bad faith), Sartre consigned him to the couch not of Freud or Adler or Jung but of someone who practiced the existentialist psychoanalysis Sartre advocated in *Being and Nothingness*. Still, Sartre did recognize Bataille as a genuine heir of Pascal and Nietzsche, though he reproached him for preferring brief pantheistic ecstasies to political and historical time. In short, Sartre's Bataille was a hole-and-corner Christian whom Sartre confronted with a new humanism of freedom. "The pleasures to which M. Bataille invites us, if they can only refer back to themselves, if they cannot enter into the framework of new ventures and help to form a new humanity that will surpass itself in search of new goals, are worth no more than the pleasure of drinking a glass of spirits or sunning oneself on a beach."[51]

Sartre and Bataille drank a few glasses of spirits together during the first three months of 1944, meeting either at Leiris's or at Marcel Moré's place and talking sometimes about sin and sometimes about philosophy. "One evening they danced face to face, vying with each other in absurdity. . . . The third party was a figure made from a horse's skull and a huge mauve-and-yellow-striped dressing gown."[52]

In the spring of 1944 Lacan, now an established member of the circle around Leiris and Bataille, was invited to meet Sartre, Beauvoir, and Camus for the first time. The encounter took place on March 19 in Leiris's apartment, when a public reading was given of a play Picasso had written in January 1941. *Le Désir attrapé par la queue* (Desire caught by the tail) echoed the grand surrealist style of the twenties and revolved around the fantasies arising from the food shortages of the Occupation. Camus was master of ceremonies and banged on the floor with a stick to indicate scene changes. Leiris played the part of Gros-Pied (Big Foot), and Sartre was Bout-Rond (Round End). Beauvoir was the Cousin. Dora Maar, Picasso's partner, played Angoisse-Grasse (Fat Anguish), and Zanie Campan, a young actress married to the publisher Jean Aubier, was the Tart. The appreciative audience included Bataille, Armand Salacrou, Georges Limbour, Sylvia Bataille, Jean-Louis Barrault, Braque, and all Sartre's entourage. (Two days later Brassaï got all the main actors and members of the audience back together for a photograph.)[53] The friends kept the party going until the small hours.

Mouloudji sang *Les Petits Pavés* (The cobblestones); Sartre sang *J'ai vendu mon âme au diable* (I've sold my soul to the devil). "Paris was one big prisoner-of-war camp," Beauvoir wrote, "drinking and talking together in the dark was so furtive a pleasure it felt illicit. It was a sort of clandestine happiness." She observed Lacan at some length that evening and was impressed by his energy and flow of ideas but too overawed to do more than utter an "occasional platitude inspired by alcohol."[54] Zanie Campan, who had already seen Lacan in Louise Leiris's art gallery and greatly admired Sylvia as an actress, thought the two made a "comical" couple. "She didn't look her age and seemed more like his daughter than his partner. One sensed he had the mind of a mischievous inquisitor and a creative power that was going to bowl everyone over."[55] Picasso gave everyone involved in the performance an original copy of the play printed on handmade paper.

The next day, despite his nocturnal efforts, Leiris attended a memorial service in the Eglise Saint-Roch in honor of Max Jacob, who had been killed by the Nazis. While everyone in France was eagerly awaiting the Allied victory, many of those who had been deported to Germany were being exterminated.

After the Picasso performance the various participants threw other parties or "fiestas." Everyone was looking for a new way of living, a reason for hope, as they waited for the promised but ever-postponed Allied landing. The festivities produced their own actors, playwrights, acrobats, and spectators. One evening Dora Maar mimed a bullfight while Sartre conducted an orchestra, Limbour carved a ham, and Bataille and Queneau fought a duel with bottles. Lacan enjoyed himself with the rest, but Leiris, Bataille, and Queneau, though they had known him a long time by now and went on seeing him all their lives, did not read what he wrote, or if they did they never mentioned it in their own writings. It was the same with Kojève and Koyré, though for Lacan their teaching remained an inexhaustible source of inspiration. In all the group he began to mix with at the end of the Occupation, only Beauvoir and Merleau-Ponty were sometimes to read him with interest.

In 1948, when she was working on the book about women that was to become *The Second Sex*, Beauvoir came across Lacan's paper on the family and studied it at length. She became so interested in the psychoanalytic movement's internal quarrels about female sexuality that she telephoned Lacan to ask his advice on how she should deal with the question. He was flattered and replied that they would need to talk for five or six months in order to sort out the problem. Beauvoir already had plenty of material for her book and didn't feel like spending all that time listening to Lacan, so she suggested they might make do with four interviews. He declined.[56] As for Merleau-Ponty, his important intellectual relationship with Lacan had a family aspect too: Sylvia and Merleau-Ponty's wife, Suzanne, became friends, and Judith and Marianne Merleau-Ponty often spent their vacations together.

Even before the war, the fact that Lacan moved in intellectual circles had brought him a certain amount of notoriety and a small private clientele, which included the singer Marianne Oswald, Dolly Pastré and her nephew Jean-François, Dora Maar, and a number of others. He was also Pablo Picasso's personal doctor.[57] But up till 1947 or so he was seldom asked to do training analyses. Not only was he not yet regarded in psychoanalytic circles as an authority, but among the second generation he was outshone by Sacha Nacht, who enjoyed a certain amount of prestige because he had met Freud and whose qualifications were more in keeping with the standards of the IPA. But after 1948–1949 the situation altered in Lacan's favor as the third generation of French psychoanalysts became increasingly attracted by his teaching. After that he worked full-time as a private psychoanalyst.

In October 1944 Georges Bernier returned to Paris and went to stay at 5, rue de Lille. Sylvia and Judith were living there then. Bernier took part in some of the "fiestas." Having lived in the English-speaking world, he had become a fervent advocate of parliamentary democracy, and one day he asked Lacan and his entourage if they ever by any chance voted. The result was general stupefaction, roars of laughter, and a chorus of noes. . . .

Bernier resumed his analysis for two years. Lacan's technique hadn't altered, and the length of the sessions was still the same. "He was very good at keeping friendship and treatment separate from one another, and I regard the analysis as successful. It taught me to stop believing the moon is made of green cheese and to manage my life better. But something had changed." Bernier was struck by the mannered style of speaking and dressing that had succeeded Lacan's former dandyism and was already verging on obsession. He had first-hand experience of it in 1946. One day, when he was outside a bookshop in the rue des Saints-Pères, Bernier felt a tap on the shoulder: it was Lacan, out for a drive. Bernier got in beside his friend. Lacan was very worked up; he was hunting for a special kind of black doeskin to have made into a pair of evening shoes to go with a particularly sumptuous suit. Bunting's, the famous London shoemakers where Lacan had his shoes made to measure, had asked him to look in the leather shops in the rue de la Montagne-Sainte-Geneviève for the necessary material. "We spent a couple of hours searching," Bernier remembers, "before he found what he wanted."[58]

15

$\cdot \quad \cdot \quad \cdot \quad \cdot \quad \cdot \quad \cdot \quad \cdot$

Thoughts on Human Freedom

Jacques Lacan didn't publish a single line while the war lasted, and by the time it ended he had become another man. His life, his habits, his friends: all had changed. Yet there was a definite continuity between the ideas that preoccupied him during the College of Sociology period and those that presented themselves to him after the Liberation. At both times they were concerned with the relationship between the individual and society. Like Bataille, Lacan had needed to find out how fascism managed to harness human aspiration in the service of evil. Unlike Bataille, he could never believe that the fantastic weapons fascism made use of could be turned in the opposite direction. But from 1936 onward he was always reflecting on the nature of the inner identifications governing the organization of human groups in general. In so doing he was not only asking the same questions as Bataille; he was also entering the same territory as Freud when he dealt with group psychology.

Lacan's article on the family had already made many references to these questions, so it isn't surprising to find him still struggling in 1945 with problems concerning the essence of the social bond. But now, instead of seeing them in terms of the crucible of the family, he approached them from the point of view of Freudian group psychology. And like Freud, Lacan, when he wanted to analyze a group, chose the army as his example.

We know from his correspondence with Sylvain Blondin what Lacan thought about military psychiatry as practiced during his service in Val-de-Grâce hospital. For him it was a completely negative experience, and he couldn't find words harsh enough to castigate the "self-appointed elites" of the French psychiatric establishment, whom he blamed for making the debacle of the French army even worse than it might otherwise have been. In particular he criticized the inadequacy of their selection procedures, which led them to recommend completely unsuitable men for service as officers at the front. But though Lacan was very clear-sighted about such negligence and condemned it very severely, he never made any protest. He had been called up as an auxiliary doctor, and he simply obeyed orders. He supplied diagnoses and opinions and carried out examinations in accordance with the rules imposed by his superiors. In that position he felt quite at home and was even pleased to be appreciated by the very mandarins he criticized so severely.[1] With Lacan things were never simple. He often disparaged people whose recognition he sought and mocked at values he secretly admired.

He had been very pro-English in 1940 and became even more so when in September 1945 he spent five weeks in England visiting the Hartfield rehabilitation center for returned ex-prisoners-of-war and overseas veterans. Back in France, in the presence of some guests from London, he gave a lecture to the Evolution psychiatrique (Developments in Psychiatry) group in which he praised England's heroism during the war: "The courage of her people rests on a true relationship with reality that is often misunderstood because of her utilitarian ideology. In particular, this relationship is completely misrepresented by the word *adaptation*; even the noble term *realism* is ruled out, because of its base misuse by the same 'treacherous clerks' whose profanation of the word has long deprived mankind of the values they insulted."[2]

The reference to Julien Benda's 1927 book *La Trahison des clercs* (The treason of the clerks; i.e., the betrayal of both themselves and society by writers, artists, and thinkers who abandoned their former independence in politics) allowed Lacan once again to criticize the French intellectual elite to which he always wanted to belong. But the eulogy of English utilitarianism revealed a theory about the social bond and the relationship of the individual to truth that was going to be the mainspring of Lacan's thinking in the early postwar years. It was also to be found in his article "Logical Time and the Assertion of Anticipated Certainty" and in the paper on psychological causality that he read at the colloquium held in Bonneval in 1946.[3]

In 1939 English psychiatrists had decided to make use of slowpokes, shirkers, dullards, and delinquents by assigning them to various tasks in the rear. Without actually segregating them, they separated "misfits" from ordinary fighting men so as to spare the latter the neurotic shock of contact with disturbing elements. The "misfits" themselves improved as a result of being regarded as useful and functioning as independent subgroups. Each subgroup chose and worked toward its own goal, supervised by a therapist who supported everyone without acting either as leader or authoritarian father. Lacan, praising this utilitarian classification of the maladjusted, claimed that the ability to reshape human relationships in time of war was made possible by English psychiatry's general assimilation of Freudian ideas. The British

experiment, he added, invalidated the doctrine of constitutions that he himself had criticized as early as 1932, as well as testifying to the decline of the
paternal imago, noted by him in his article on the family. And indeed, if
organizing people in small groups implies their identification with the ego-
ideal of the therapist, it leaves no room for the strong leader, recruiting
sergeant, or rabble-rouser. Lacan was referring here to the work of John
Rickman and Wilfred Bion, which he had come across in articles in the
British medical review *The Lancet* in 1943. Rickman and Bion had carried
out a conclusive wartime experiment in the mental hospital at Northfield,
near Birmingham. Bion, born in India in 1897, had become a Kleinian after
a distinguished medical career. And it was with Rickman, who had been
analyzed first by Ferenczi and then by Melanie Klein, that he did his training analysis during the war.

With this eulogy of Freudianism's conquest of English psychiatry, Lacan
was approaching the London psychoanalytic movement via the school of
Melanie Klein, though her advocates and those of Anna Freud were still
locked in controversy. But at the same time he was suggesting a revision of
the Freudian theory of group psychology that allowed him to combine his
own conception of the family with an approach to human communities
based on the idea of the group.

When in 1921 Freud published *Massenpsychologie und Ich-Analyse* (*Group
Psychology and the Analysis of the Ego*) he distinguished between groups with
and groups without a ringleader. He took as examples two organized groups
that have survived through time: the church and the army. According to
him, both were structured around two axes: a vertical axis stemming from
the relationship between the group and the leader and a horizontal axis
involving the relationships among the individuals of which the group is
composed.[4] In the first case, the individuals identify with an object (the
leader) that replaces their own ego-ideal; in the second case, they identify, at
the level of the ego, with one another. Of course Freud thought of the possibility that the place of the leader might be filled not by a real man but by
an idea or an abstraction: God, for example. And he referred to the communist experiment to show that the "socialist bond," replacing the religious
one, might lead to the same intolerance of outsiders as in the days of the
wars of religion.

In Freud's theory of identification the vertical axis was the more important of the two, and the horizontal axis depended on it. Identification with
the father, with the leader, or with an idea came before the relationship
among members of the same group. The 1921 text represented a fundamental break with all previous sociological and psychological arguments, which
were based on the idea that suggestion or hypnosis, not identification, was
behind the fascination that existed between groups and their leaders.

During the thirties, Freud's new theory served to explain the political functioning of fascism. In France, Bataille made considerable use of it when, with Allendy, Borel, Schiff, and others, he founded the Société de psychologie collective (Group Psychology Society). "Freud suggests a conceptual framework," says Michel Plon, "that makes it possible to begin thinking about questions on the formulation of which this century's sociology, history, and political philosophy, forgetting both Machiavelli and La Boétie, are still far from being able to embark."[5] Everyone who adopted the new hypothesis thought it provided an advance explanation of fascism. They didn't understand that in 1921 Freud himself was thinking of communism as the ideology likely to take the place left empty by religion.

When Lacan began thinking about the vertical axis and shifted it in the direction of the family, he at first put forward the idea that modern Western society of the democratic type was organized around the inevitable decline of the paternal imago. And he was struck by the fact that fascism combined a caricatured rehabilitation of that imago, in the form of idolization of the symbols of leadership, and a kind of martial egalitarianism among the members of the tribe, all fanatical worshipers of an idea in the service of the death wish.

But seven years later Lacan's study trip to England showed him Freud's idea needed overhauling. If English wartime psychiatry had succeeded in integrating all the misfits, first through a method of detecting personality factors based exclusively on psychogenesis and then through the successful experiment of "leaderless groups" based on the theories of Bion, this meant Freud had paid too much attention to vertical and too little attention to horizontal identification. So it was necessary, not to reverse Freud's model, but to work out a social bond where the horizontal axis was no longer dictated by the vertical one. In other words, Lacan, on the basis of a field study, was showing implicitly that Freud had still relied to some extent on a conception of group psychology based on Le Bon, even though his whole theory of identification was constructed in opposition to the tradition that saw hypnosis or suggestion as the only factor creating the social bond between groups and their leaders.

In particular, Freud had retained the principle of a dominant vertical axis: i.e., the function of the leader in the organization of the group. Because of this, his theory of power might apply only to closed and unchanging groups and not to the ordinary functioning of politics in modern democratic societies.[6] Like all the men of his generation, Lacan noticed that Freud's theory lent itself very well to the analysis of fascism. But he also saw that it was necessary to take into account the idea of the decline of the paternal imago in order to understand on the one hand the evolution of the family in industrial societies and on the other hand the omnipotence attributed to the leader in Nazism. And the English experiment had shown him retrospectively how right he had been. During his visit he had seen that a theory of "the power of the group without a leader," based on the predominance of the horizontal axis, was better than a theory of "the power of the leader over the group," based on the superiority of the vertical axis. Bion's thesis not only made it possible to integrate delinquents into society more satisfactorily; it also helped make them freer and more efficient than a doctrine based on disciplined obedience to a warrior chief. Thus in 1945 Lacan was praising the English democratic system for having incorporated Freudian theory into its way of thinking and then having used it as a weapon against fascism.

Opting for Bion over Freud but also for Freud as revised by Bion, Lacan proposed to modify Freud's theory of identification by setting aside the old theories of suggestion and adducing a better analysis of modern democratic societies. But it is worth noting in passing that this did not lead him to commit himself to any particular political system.

Lacan's latest revision of Freudian doctrine succeeded his similar prewar overhaul in the light of Hegelian philosophy. And it was not by chance that Lacan now reaffirmed the absolute necessity of ridding psychiatry once and for all of any kind of organicism: his modification of Freud's theory of the primacy of the vertical axis went hand in hand with the acceptance of an exclusively psychogenetic conception of human personality. For if any notions of constitutionalism, race, heredity, and instinct are retained, man is made so dependent on his biological heritage that he must be seen as subject from time immemorial to an inescapable alienation linked to the origins of the world itself. This is why, at the Bonneval colloquium in 1946, Lacan was so critical of the organodynamism of his friend Henri Ey, though both men were engaged in the fight against constitutionalism. In Lacan's view, organodynamism was still too organicist an approach to mental illness to be retained within the framework of his new schema, which put forward psychological causality as the one and only origin of human madness.[7]

This attitude also led Lacan to observe for the first time that Clérambault had been his only master in the observation of patients. He thus acknowledged retrospectively his debt to the great representative of constitutionalism whose teaching he had set aside in 1932 in favor of the more dynamic doctrine of Claude. It was to the latter that Lacan owed his structural and psychogenetic conception of madness, which in Clérambault was obscured by the oft-proclaimed belief in the doctrine of constitutions.

But the revision of 1945 also made Lacan abandon what still remained of Maurras in his own thinking. He now chose democratic utilitarianism in the English manner in preference to French-style positivist familialism: the community group made up of free individuals rather than the formative crucible based on links with the land. So, at the dawn of a new era, he saw himself as the spokesperson of a unitary conception of both anthropology and a science of man. He was convinced that what was true would always be new: "You have heard me speak with pleasure of the roles played by Descartes and Hegel in the search for truth. It is fashionable nowadays to 'go beyond' the classical philosophers. I might just as aptly have started with the excellent dialogue with Parmenides. For neither Socrates nor Descartes, Marx nor Freud *can* be 'gone beyond,' insofar as they carried out their researches with the single-minded passion that aims at discovering the truth."[8]

In the same year as his visit to England, Lacan made use of a sophism to illustrate his revision of Freudian theory. A prison warden summons three convicts before him and suggests that whichever of them can pass a certain test shall be set free. "Here are five discs," he says, "three white and two black. I shall fix one of these discs on each of your backs without telling you which color I select. You are not allowed to speak or to use a mirror, but you can look at one another. The first one to guess the color of the disc he is wearing can go free, providing he can explain how he arrived at his conclusion." The prisoners agree to take the test, and the governor puts a white disc on each of their backs. After looking briefly at one another, they all leave the prison yard together. Each one, by the same argument, has realized that he was wearing a white disc.

Lacan had come across this sophism one evening in 1935 at Sylvain Blondin's apartment. It was there that he first met André Weiss, who told him about the puzzle without revealing the solution. Lacan lay awake trying to find the answer. At three in the morning he phoned Weiss, who told him the answer, though he was furious at being woken up in the small hours.[9]

There were three possible alternatives: (1) If prisoner A sees two blacks (on B and C), he deduces that he is white and leaves immediately. (2) If A sees one black and one white, he argues, "If I were C (who is white) and saw two blacks (A and B), I would leave. As C hasn't left, I deduce that I'm white, and I leave." (3) If A sees two whites, he argues, "If I were black, B and C would both see a black and a white. Each of them says to himself, 'If I am black, the other who is white (B or C) sees two blacks.' They would then deduce that they were white, and leave. But as they haven't done so, I deduce that I, A, am white." All three prisoners use this third argument simultaneously, and all give the same reasons for leaving.

Lacan had tried out the puzzle of the discs several times on his friends at the College of Sociology. At the Liberation, Christian Zervos, who had started *Les Cahiers d'art* (Art notebooks) in 1926, decided to celebrate the victory of freedom over oppression by bringing out a special retrospective number covering the period of the war. He asked Lacan, whom he had met through André Masson, for a contribution, and so it was that "Logical Time and the Assertion of Anticipated Certainty" was published. In it Lacan announced that he was writing an essay on group logic—which never saw the light of day—and started by launching an attack on Sartre's conception of freedom as he had just expressed it in *Huis clos* (variously translated as *No Exit, In Camera,* and *Vicious Circle*), first performed at the Théâtre du Vieux Colombier on May 27, 1944. "We are not one of those recent philosophers," wrote Lacan, "for whom confinement within four walls is but another expedient for attaining the ultimate in freedom."[10]

Yet the situation described in his sophism did resemble that in Sartre's play, which was originally called *Les Autres* (Others). On the one hand there was the story of three men who all succeed in freeing themselves through a correct process of reasoning, while on the other there were three characters, three "dead consciousnesses," imprisoned forever between four walls because they had all condemned themselves never to break their chains. In *Huis clos* Sartre expressed the same theory of freedom as in *Being and Nothingness* and the series of novels generally entitled *Les Chemins de la liberté* (*The Road to Freedom*): freedom is the stake being played for in a dialectical battle between the opposing forces of alienation and existential intentionality. It does not therefore possess the simple certainty of something an individual can opt for on his own responsibility. But it *is* the finest manifestation of a philosophy of consciousness, though we must realize this consciousness is the site of mental processes concealed from the individual himself by the deceptive screen of bad faith. Sartre had invented this expression to replace the Freudian notion of the unconscious, which he regarded as too biological and mechanistic.

Bad faith combines with consciousness to produce a pathology of ambivalence in which the subject is forced to unite in one act an idea and its negation, transcendence and artifice. In this context, Sartre rejected so-called empirical psychoanalysis (Freud's) in favor of existential psychoanalysis. He accused the former of repudiating dialectics and neglecting the essence of freedom in order to stress the individual's early affectivity—"the blank slate before the story"; he saw the latter as capable of abolishing the unconscious and asserting that nothing exists until the first stirrings of freedom.[11]

Lacan's objections to all this are plain. Not only is man not free to choose his own fetters—there are no first stirrings of freedom—but in order to be free he is doomed to become part of the community of men, via a process of logical thought. In other words, only belonging, in terms of the horizontal axis described by Freud, can relate the individual subject to others, and only the power of logic can lead man to truth: i.e., to acceptance of the other in a dialectic of recognition and nonrecognition. After Husserl therefore, and against Sartre, Lacan stood for a philosophy of concepts, into which he tried to incorporate a nonsubjective philosophy of the subject or, as he put it, an "existential indetermination of the 'I.' "[12] In so doing he made all human freedom dependent on a temporal event: to each individual comes a "*temps pour comprendre*" (time for comprehending) in the light of which he can make a logical decision.

Looking back on the three alternatives in the puzzle of the prisoners, it is clear that the first argument proceeds in terms of logical exclusion. The "time for comprehending" is reduced here to a simple observation: B and C are black. In the second alternative, a "time for comprehending" must come before the "*moment de conclure*" (moment of concluding): A has to put himself in C's place and make a deduction. The third alternative is more tricky, because A has to make a deduction in two stages (as have B and C). To begin with he supposes he is black and puts himself in B's place, attributing a deduction to C and vice versa. As all three prisoners argue in the same way, they all help to hasten both their conclusion and their departure. The "time for comprehending" coincides with the "moment of concluding," which merges into the "*instant du regard*" (instant of the glance). Each of the prisoners realizes he is white not through seeing the others leave but through seeing them *hesitating* to leave. Lacan uses the phrase "*assertion de certitude anticipée*" (assertion of anticipated certainty) to describe the process of anticipation that characterizes the phenomenon of "true" decision and makes this phenomenon the condition of human freedom.

By choosing, in contradistinction to Sartre's existentialism, a theory of human freedom based on a logic of truth that excluded subjective consciousness, Lacan, who hadn't been a member of the Resistance and would never try to make the actions of his private life accord with his system of thought, was unwittingly paying tribute to the heroism of Jean Cavaillès. "[Cavaillès's] mathematical philosophy," Georges Canguilhem wrote later, "was not constructed with reference to a Subject who might be briefly and precariously identified with Jean Cavaillès. It was a philosophy from which Jean Cavaillès was completely absent, and it produced a form of action that led him by the narrow paths of logic to the bourne from which no traveler returns. Jean Cavaillès embodies the logic of the Resistance lived through unto death. Let the philosophers of existence and of the individual do as well next time, if they can."[13]

Double Life

Malou had arranged for Lacan to renounce his parental authority, thinking in this way to punish him for having deserted her. But although it was she who had wanted the divorce, she decided to conceal the truth from her children. She thought she was acting "for their own good." Until several years after the war they didn't know their father was living with Sylvia, nor that he had married her. They weren't aware, either, that they had a half sister, Judith. And Lacan went along with this game of saying nothing and conforming to middle-class respectability. Malou used to say he was away on professional business and too busy with his intellectual work to spend much time at home. "She didn't want to admit the failure of her marriage," says Célia Bertin, "and after they separated she did everything she could to keep up appearances, even though it meant practicing deception. She went on unreservedly worshiping Lacan—or rather the image of him that she wanted to cherish and pass on to the children."[1]

Every Thursday Lacan went to the rue Jadin to have lunch at the modest apartment in the 16th Arrondissement where Malou had gone to live with Caroline, Thibaut, and Sibylle. He usually came and went in a hurry, stiff and apparently embarrassed at having to deal with such a situation.[2] He paid Malou a not-very-large allowance that didn't even cover the cost of the children's education. So she decided to work. She designed scarves and then did illustrations for children's books by the comtesse de Ségur. Sylvain, seeing she was having difficulties, took her on as his anesthetist;[3] he had grown very close to her since the divorce. He regretted having no children of his own and was glad to take over the paternal role that Lacan had forfeited. At the end of the war Sylvain and Denise Decoudemanche had separated, and he had started to live with Madeleine Simon, who became his wife in 1949. She was a practicing Catholic with a son, Bruno Roger, who was sixteen when his mother married Sylvain. Bruno immediately grew fond of his elegant stepfather, who adopted him as a son. Malou and Madeleine (known as Linette) became good friends, and Caroline saw more and more of young Bruno, whom she married in 1958. Sylvain was doubly happy: he was marrying a niece he regarded as his daughter to a stepson who looked on him as a father.[4]

Caroline seemed to suffer less than her brother and sister as a result of her parents' situation. She was the only one whose early childhood had been happy, and she was her mother's favorite: the two were very alike. Caroline, haughty and elegant, was as sure as Malou herself of her own beauty and intelligence and the fact that she was one of the elite. She liked wealth, houses furnished and run with good taste, and the values of economic liberalism. But she also liked strong family traditions, Catholic morals, and middle-class magnificence when it came to the major turning points in life. So her "cousin" Bruno was dazzled by her. He and she shared the same culture; they both studied at the School of Political Science—the famous Sciences Po—and went into finance. He became one of Paris's most famous financiers.

Although Lacan loved Caroline and took her on trips to Venice and Austria, although he sought her financial advice and took a close interest in her professional successes, he didn't have a real intellectual relationship with her. She didn't read what he wrote, or enter into his world, or understand his work and teaching. And this situation was reinforced after 1945: Lacan's private life was now quite inseparable from his intellectual activity. Just as he had earlier chosen Sylvia's entourage as his real family, so now he presided over a "family" of disciples capable of reading his works and understanding him as a man.

The split affected Thibaut and Sibylle more adversely than it did Caroline, not only because their early childhood had been overshadowed by their mother's distress and melancholy but also because it was more difficult for them to avoid being torn between the world of their father, which they could imagine but which was concealed from them, and the concrete reality of an everyday life all the more unsatisfactory because they sensed intuitively that it was based on pretense. As a result they both had great difficulty in finding their own identities and fitting in socially.

In 1949 they had a very bad shock. One Thursday Thibaut and Sibylle spent the afternoon—Thursday afternoon was then a school holiday—in the *Jardin d'acclimatation* (zoo). On their way home they saw a car stop at a pedestrian crossing. They immediately recognized their father, seated behind the wheel. A woman was sitting beside him, and there was a little girl in the backseat. Thibaut and Sibylle ran toward Lacan calling out "Dad! Dad!" Lacan glanced at them in surprise, then looked away as if he hadn't seen them, started up the car, and vanished into the traffic. This was the Lacan children's first "meeting" with Sylvia and Judith. When they told Malou about their misadventure she answered sharply that Lacan had obviously neither seen nor heard them. She was trying to excuse his behavior—the behavior of a father whom she wanted to go on living up to the image she had made of him. Sibylle forgot the incident, but Thibaut always remembered it vividly.[5]

Through plentiful allusions to "the other woman" in grown-up conversation, Thibaut gathered that his father was leading a double life. But it was not until 1951, when he was twelve, that he found out about Judith—found out that he had a half sister. During the summer vacation his father picked him up and drove him over to a school in England where he was to spend a month. There he got to know a boy of his own age, the son of one of Jacques and Sylvia's friends. One day in conversation the boy mentioned Judith's name. Thibaut said, "I don't know who you mean," though in fact he had understood very well who must have been meant.[6] But he didn't say anything to anybody, and Sibylle didn't find out about her father's double life until much later. When Caroline was about to get married, Jacques and Malou decided it was time for pretense to come to an end.

As far as Alfred Lacan's side of the family was concerned, no one knew anything about Jacques's new family circumstances. But in the summer of 1941 Marc-François had had an idea things were getting worse, and to find out more he went to see Malou in the Pyrénées-Orientales, where she was vacationing at the home of her friend Madeleine Guerlain. Seeing what a desperate state she was in, he realized the couple must have broken up. He was bitterly sorry his sister-in-law wasn't Christian enough to turn to the spiritual life, which he thought might have helped her emerge from her unhappiness and brought her closer to God.[7] He prayed for her and for his brother.

But he didn't give Alfred and Emilie a clear account of the change that had come about in Jacques's life. When he first met Sylvia, at a dinner party in the rue de Lille during the Occupation, he was obliged to work out for himself that she was his brother's partner: neither she nor Jacques told him they were living together. Marc-François, who loved his brother very much but thought he hadn't been sufficiently Christian in his dealings with women, observed:

Jacques wanted to own women. He'd always been possessive ever since he was a child. He didn't realize women weren't just "nothing" and that one didn't simply collect them. I deplore this aspect of him: it seems that being a genius doesn't mean you can understand a woman's otherness. Married life is an alliance that should find its model in God. It's a relationship that helps to form the individual. It makes it possible for both the male and the female concerned to live in a giving relationship and at the same time preserve their otherness. Jacques missed out on this. Dom Laure should never have married him and Malou: neither he nor she was a Christian.[8]

It had been a very long time since Lacan had shared the Christian spirituality to which Marc-François had consecrated his life. But had he really been a Christian up to the age of sixteen? It's doubtful. In any case, by the end of the Second World War his atheism was so evident he no longer needed to identify himself with the Antichrist, as he had in the past. Even so, he still valued some of the conventions of the respectable bourgeoisie. Judith was sent to a church school[9] and made her First Communion, even though her mother was not only an atheist but against all religious practices.

Emilie Baudry-Lacan, Lacan's mother, died unexpectedly on November 21, 1948. Suffering from abdominal pains, she had been admitted as a matter of urgency to the Hartmann Clinic, and Sylvain Blondin had performed a hysterectomy. Everything seemed to be going well, and Emilie wrote to Marc-François saying she was quite better. Then she died in her room from an embolism caused by a postoperative complication; the nurse doing her rounds found her lying there holding the bell switch she hadn't had time to press to summon help. Emilie's daughter, Madeleine, was the first to hear the news, and she phoned Jacques to ask him to remove their mother from the clinic as soon as possible; she thought Alfred wouldn't be able to bear the thought of his wife having died in such circumstances. Jacques did as his sister asked, and the body was taken back to the rue Gambetta just as if Emilie had gone out somewhere and been taken ill. So officially she died at home, at the age of seventy-two, in the arms of Alfred, her husband. Marc-François was especially upset by his mother's sudden death: the news reached him just as he was reading the letter in which she said she felt very well.[10] On November 25 she was buried, with the usual religious rites, in the family vault in the cemetery at Château-Thierry. "Let me add," Lacan wrote to Ferdinand Alquié, "that I had the misfortune to lose my mother a month ago."[11] He complained about having to deal with his grief-stricken father.

Emilie always remained unaware of Judith's existence, though finally she had vaguely come to know her son had "another life." But she deliberately tried to ignore it, believing Jacques's marriage had been a genuinely Christian one and that Malou was properly devout.[12] Some time after Emilie's death, however, Madeleine decided to break the silence. She told Alfred about Judith, and he immediately wanted to "see the little girl."[13] Marc-François, who had recently met his niece in the rue de Lille, approved. But when he said as much to Sylvain Blondin, Malou's brother was completely against it and made his opinion known in a furiously angry letter.[14] Madeleine paid no attention and took Judith to see her grandfather anyway. Soon afterward, Sylvia got to know Madeleine and was very helpful to her when she had a serious road accident.

Thus when Thibaut, at school in England, found out about his half sister,

Judith had just been admitted into his father's family. But he didn't know that.

After the Liberation, Sylvia and Jacques lived together in the apartment at 5, rue de Lille, while Judith, Laurence, and their maternal grandmother lived at number 3. Then, as the years went by, the two places drew apart. The apartment at number 3 became Sylvia's special territory, where dinners and parties were held, and the apartment at number 5 became Lacan's. It was there he worked, received his mistresses, and carried out his analyses, though he had lunch at number 3. In March 1948 a young Spanish girl named Gloria Gonzalès entered his employment. She had been a maidservant since she was thirteen and was used to hard work. At first she was very devoted to Sylvia, and then gradually she concentrated her loyalty on Lacan, whom she served with such enthusiasm and tact that she gradually became indispensable to both his intellectual life and his work as an analyst.

Sylvia had exquisite taste, and she took charge of the decoration and fitting out of Jacques's consulting room. She helped him buy furniture for it, including a Napoleon III *crapaud*, or "toad": the squat armchair in which he was to sit and listen to his patients for the rest of his life. In 1948 she bought him a single bed just over three feet wide that for thirty-three years was to be his famous couch, the silent witness of a long intellectual adventure. Both armchair and couch were covered with modest gray material that was replaced whenever it wore out.

In 1951 Lacan bought a charming country house at Guitrancourt, near Mantes-La-Jolie. It was called La Prévôté (The Provost's House). As well as going to Guitrancourt on Sundays to work, he also received patients and gave sumptuous parties there. He loved putting on an act for his friends, wearing disguises or fancy dress, dancing and flaunting extravagant clothes. At La Prévôté he started a collection of books that gradually became a huge library, bigger than the one in the rue de Lille. A mere list of their titles gives an idea of the immense erudition behind the passion with which he sought out first and rare editions.

A spacious outbuilding with a high bay window overlooking the garden was turned into a study, which he filled with valuable works of art. The finest item was a painting hung in the loggia that looked down on the single room: *L'Origine du monde* (The origin of the world), painted by Gustave Courbet in 1866 for Khalil Bey, a Turkish diplomat. It was a nude, offering a direct view of the private parts of a woman immediately after she had been making love. The picture had caused a scandal at the time it was painted. It amazed both the Goncourt brothers, who thought it "as beautiful as the flesh in a Correggio," and Maxime du Camp, who pronounced it filthy enough to illustrate the works of Sade. After Khalil Bey's death the picture disappeared into a series of private collections. The Second World War found it in Budapest, where it was confiscated by the Nazis. It later passed into the hands of the victorious Soviets and was then sold to other collectors.

Lacan came across it in 1955. In order to conceal what was regarded as the terrifying eroticism of undisguised sex, the canvas itself had been covered with a wooden panel depicting a landscape, By now the panel had disappeared, but Sylvia still thought the picture so scandalous it ought to be kept hidden. "The neighbors and the cleaning lady wouldn't understand," she said. So she asked André Masson to make another wooden cover. He came up with a superb panel reproducing in abstract form the erotic elements of the original. A secret mechanism made the panel slide back to reveal the Courbet, but most of the time it remained hidden.[15]

Lacan had always loved traveling and seaside vacations. He had been to Morocco, Spain, and the Côte d'Azur with Marie-Thérèse, to Brittany with Olesia, and to Italy with Malou. As soon as the war was over he followed the same pattern with Sylvia. In particular there was a trip to Egypt, where he demonstrated all his old interest in seeing and understanding everything. He also got into the habit of going away for winter sports but was hopelessly clumsy at skiing and even at putting on his boots. He fractured his leg twice, and the accident that affected his thigh left him with a slight limp. which on occasion he used very skillfully to intimate that the master was exhausted by the stupidity of his pupils. He would drag his feet and say, with a kind of exasperated sigh, "I'm dead. They're killing me. They don't understand a word I say."[16]

In the summer he often spent family holidays with Sylvia, Judith, Laurence, and the Merleau-Pontys at Le Mouleau, a little place near Arcachon. After long days spent working, he would lead the others on hikes, during which he took photographs of the sunset. He also loved the beauty of southern Italy: he stayed at the villa Cimbrone in Ravello and liked going on boating expeditions around Capri from the coast near Amalfi.

It was in the village of Le Tholonet, near Aix-en-Provence, that he married Sylvia on July 17, 1953. The wedding took place privately in the town hall in the presence of Rose and André Masson, who had a delightful house called Les Cigales (The Cicadas) on the route de Cézanne, which links the places where the painter lived and worked. Jacques wore a quiet, light-colored suit, a bow tie, and a flower in his buttonhole; Sylvia wore a simple white blouse and full skirt. She had divorced Georges Bataille on July 9, 1946.[17] At that time he was already living with Diane Kotchoubey, whom he married on January 16, 1951, two years after she had presented him with a daughter, Julie, born on December 1, 1948. So when Sylvia, aged forty-five, changed her name from Bataille to Lacan, her daughter Judith became the legal stepdaughter of the man who was really her father, and the stepsister of Malou's children, though she was really their half sister too. She went on being regarded as the full sister of Laurence, though she was in fact her half sister, and as the half sister of Julie, to whom she was in fact no blood relation at all. The situation was all the more confusing because the legal facts contrasted in every way with reality. Lacan was less of a father to the children of his first marriage than to his daughter Judith and his stepdaughter, Laurence. Laurence, as time went by, felt closer to him than to her own father, whom she admired but from whom she had been separated since she was four years old.

Lacan really adored Judith. It was a bitter grief to him that he hadn't been able to give her his name, and he loved her with a passionate and exclusive love. He was lost in admiration as he watched her grow up, and her beauty, gifts, and talents duly blossomed. She was brought up among the intelligentsia with whom he himself mixed; even in her teens, she formed part of the circle of his disciples and shared in the rapid evolution and rising influence of his thought. She went to school at the Collège Sévigné and came top of her year in the philosophy *agrégation* (the highest competitive examination for teachers). She was known as Judith Lacan, the name that should rightfully have been hers. Many of Lacan's colleagues and friends tried to make him love her more moderately; his passion for her was completely inconsistent with the oedipal doctrine he taught. But Freud himself had shown Lacan the way. Had he not shown the same exclusive love for his daughter Anna?

Judith returned her father's devotion. She could never see him except through the eyes of a filial piety that soon became hagiographical. For her he was a living god of unshakable character and flawless magnanimity, forever being betrayed by unworthy disciples but always valiantly getting the better of those rash enough to oppose him. And Lacan encouraged a worship that satisfied his deepest desires.

But such favoritism had its effects on the children of his first marriage, especially on Thibaut and Sibylle. They were unhappy at not being part of their father's life, and the only thing they could take pride in was bearing his name. Judith on the other hand, though she knew she was the favorite, suffered because she had not been made legitimate, and was afraid of being called a "bastard."[18] All this gave rise to a growing rivalry between the two families.

On April 13, 1956 Lacan gave a party at Guitrancourt to celebrate his birthday. The day before, he took Thibaut out to dinner in a restaurant and asked him if he wanted to come to the party. Thibaut was very pleased but said he had to ask his mother for permission. Lacan spoke to Malou, who objected at first, reminding him of her own unhappiness, but gave way in the end. The next day Thibaut stepped into a wonderful new world: the world of his father. Maurice Merleau-Ponty was there, and so were Claude

Lévi-Strauss and many other brilliant people. Thibaut met Sylvia and Laurence, who both gave him a warm welcome. That summer he joined his father at the Massons' place at Le Tholonet. There he met Judith for the first time and was dazzled by her charm and intelligence. Lacan hoped his son might take an interest in his world and above all in his work. Thibaut didn't want to, though: he felt out of place. So he got the impression his father was disappointed in him. But Sylvia went on inviting him. (One day, with tears in his eyes, he spoke to her about the episode near the *Jardin d'acclimatation*. She told him it had made her feel ill too.) Thibaut always got on very well with Laurence, and for several years he mixed in his father's circle, though without playing either a professional or an intellectual part in it. He studied science and eventually made a career in banking.

In 1958 Thibaut visited the Massons again. On this occasion Jacques and he went to see old Alfred Lacan, who had gone to live with a former singer in the Hôtel Nègre Coste on the Cours Mirabeau in Aix-en-Provence. Thibaut observed the gulf that separated his father from his grandfather; Jacques's behavior was that of someone merely performing a family duty.[19]

Caroline's marriage on June 26, 1958, conformed to all the traditions of the French Catholic bourgeoisie: white gown, church service, careful observance of ritual and convention. Marc-François came from Hautecombe to bless the union, which he hoped would prove genuinely Christian. Caroline was an agnostic, like her uncle Sylvain and her mother, but she felt she belonged to a Catholic culture. There was an elegant reception at Sylvain's apartment in the avenue de la Grande-Armée, where Jacques's two families met together officially for the first time.[20] The period of pretense had been succeeded by one of hidden rivalry.

Caroline's relationship with her father included both unspoken understanding and discussions about financial matters or the work that needed to be done at Guitrancourt. She spent family holidays with him, which meant she saw Sylvia and Judith too. As for her husband, Bruno Roger, he had adopted all the prejudices of his own circle on the subject of psychoanalysis: he thought it was dangerous, especially for his own family.[21] But this didn't stop him respecting Lacan the man, and Lacan, once he was rich, needed Bruno's advice on his investments.

Sybille, whose birth had been so dramatic, was an isolated figure amid the Blondin clan. She had inherited the rectitude and moral austerity of her mother, whom she adored, and was the only member of the family to rebel openly against leftist political opinions. She was interested in modern languages and studied literature at the university. Like Thibaut, but in a different fashion, she took to going to see her father, but often she went in order to plead her mother's cause, and she was clear-sighted about her father's faults and weaknesses. The emotional relationship between Lacan and

Sibylle was complicated further by the rivalry that arose when she found out about Judith. At first she was delighted to learn she had an unknown half sister. But things went sour when, on vacation first at Saint-Tropez and then in Italy, she saw and was deeply hurt by the passionate love that existed between Judith and Lacan.[22]

Laurence Bataille, who was much the oldest of the girls, probably had quite a different relationship with Lacan. His affection for her was a reasonable one, and she was adored by her mother, who always remained very close to Georges Bataille. When she was sixteen Laurence became Balthus's favorite model, and he painted some excellent portraits of her as well as helping her in her attempts to become an actress. In 1953 she played an important role in Ugo Betti's *Goat Island*, in which other parts were played by Sylvia Montfort, Alain Cuny, and Rosy Varte. Balthus had designed the sets and costumes for the play, and the plot, in which a widow bestows her daugher on her lover, had a good deal in common with the life led by him and his friends. Pierre Valse, the director, described it as follows: "Three lonely women deprived of love suddenly meet again, together with a man called Dionysus. An erotic frenzy follows, but Dionysus proves difficult and the women kill him. . . . The strangest things become normal when people live in isolation. There are no more social constraints."[23]

The following year Laurence went on tour with the same company in Algeria, and when she came back she joined the French Communist Party. Lacan thought this a preposterous idea: he regarded the French Communist Party as a kind of church. But he didn't press the matter and accepted his stepdaughter's decision. But when the communist deputies voted in favor of giving special powers to Guy Mollet's government, Laurence handed in her party card. In the spring of 1958, she and her cousin Diego Masson joined a group, led by Robert Davezies, whose object was to help the FLN (*Front de libération nationale*, i.e., Algerian Freedom Fighters). She worked at raising funds for the cause at the same time as she went on with her medical studies.

On May 10, 1960 she was arrested and sent to the Prison de la Roquette for six weeks. Lacan brought her the typescript of his seminar "The Ethics of Psychoanalysis." The text was very apt: it was a commentary on Antigone's rebellion against Creon. The lawyer Roland Dumas got Laurence's case dismissed, making the acquaintance of Lacan in the process. He later became his friend and defender; in particular he helped him initiate the procedure for recognizing Judith as his daughter. In a letter to the English psychoanalyst and pediatrician Donald W. Winnicott, written in August 1960, Lacan talked of the pride he took in his stepdaughter's political commitment. "She's given us a lot of anxiety (we're proud of it), having got herself arrested because of her political connections. She's free now, but we're still worried, as the matter isn't yet closed. We also have a nephew

[Diego Masson] who lived in my house like a son when he was a student, and now he's just been sentenced to two years in prison for opposing the war in Algeria."[24]

Laurence Bataille was a remarkable woman. She called to mind the tragic heroines in the films of D. W. Griffith, though her radical views made her more like Antigone. She was generous, sensitive, intelligent, and sympathetic to all forms of human rebellion. And she became one of the best psychoanalysts of her generation, occupying a central place in the harem of the Lacanian movement.

Meanwhile, by an extraordinary coincidence, a figure had reappeared from the past. After Lacan's mother died, at the end of 1948, the fate of Marguerite Anzieu, the woman who had launched him on his career, intersected with that of his father, Alfred.[25] After Saint-Anne, Marguerite had been sent under her maiden name to the hospital at Ville-Evrard, where she was classified as "constitutionally unbalanced" by doctors unaware that her case had been the subject of a thesis opposing the doctrine of constitutions. In 1941 she decided she wanted to return to normal life and asked for her situation to be reexamined.

A year or so later, after repeated requests, she got her way. On July 21, 1943, Dr. Chanès, who had read Lacan's thesis, agreed to give Marguerite back her freedom. Sven Follin, who was Chanès's assistant at the time, had occasion to examine her. "She was very quiet and spent her time sewing. She never spoke of the past and didn't mention that she had been the subject of the Aimée case. She still believed in the persecutions. She was one of those people described in mental hospitals as 'retired from madness.' " So that was what Marguerite had become in the eyes of psychiatry, a decade after her encounter with Lacan. When he came across the file in 1989, the psychiatrist Jacques Chazaud added a comment of his own: "I wonder what Aimée's original interpreter, who invented the theory that the Subject is symbolically rooted in the Law, would have thought of what is recorded as the real remains of his patient several years later: scraps of writing and pure nonsense. . . . Marguerite, whisked far away from the young Faust, became just an ordinary patient again."[26]

Once Marguerite was free again she became another woman, unlike either Aimée or the inmate of the hospitals at Sainte-Anne and Ville-Evrard. The people she worked for as cook-housekeeper knew nothing of her past and never noticed the slightest sign of madness in her behavior. For them Marguerite was a friend: generous, cultivated, art loving, intelligent, full of consideration for others, and an ardent Christian.[27]

In 1947 Didier Anzieu married Annie Péghaire. After thinking of becoming first an actor and then a writer, he went instead to the Ecole normale supérieure to train as a teacher and graduated with a degree in philosophy. But what he remembered about his mother made him take an interest in psychology, and in 1949 he started an analysis with Lacan, not knowing that Marguerite had been the subject of the Aimée case. It was Didier's wife who helped him find his mother again. Annie had been trained as a psychologist and analyzed by Georges Favez, and she was eager to meet the woman whose madness had been hushed up by her family. She also thought Marguerite, living alone, must be unhappy at having lost contact with her son. The meeting took place very simply. One day Annie saw a woman outside the apartment block where she lived and thought it must be Marguerite. She was right. Marguerite, without letting anyone know, had come to see her son. She soon became part of the family again.[28]

By this time, Marguerite, already working in Boulogne-sur-Seine, had been taken on as cook by Alfred Lacan, and there she met her former psychiatrist and asked him yet again to give back her manuscripts and photographs. Meanwhile Didier Anzieu's analysis proceeded (it ended in July 1953), though Lacan didn't recognize his patient as the son of the former inmate of Saint-Anne's. Anzieu learned the truth from his mother in the course of conversation. She told him not only about the thesis that had been written about her but that she hadn't read but also about what went on at Alfred Lacan's place, where she had been taken on just by chance. She'd noticed that when Jacques went to see his father, he "clowned around" in order to fill in the silences.

On hearing all this, Didier Anzieu rushed to the library to read the 1932 thesis. Lacan, questioned about not having recognized the identity of his present patient, admitted that he had in fact fitted the pieces of the story together in the course of the analysis. But he said he hadn't known Aimée's surname; she'd been admitted to Sainte-Anne under her maiden name.

We know now that in 1949 the name Anzieu couldn't really have been unknown to Lacan. But he had repressed the knowledge and didn't want to admit as much to Marguerite's son. Later on, in a letter he wrote to me after the publication of *L'Histoire de la psychanalyse en France* (The history of psychoanalysis in France), Didier Anzieu observed: "The most debatable idea, in my opinion, is your amplification and embellishment of the part the Aimée case played not only in the intellectual but also in the 'psychoanalytic' development of Lacan. She was neither his Fliess nor his Loewenstein. She was certainly a brilliant woman (too brilliant for her provincial environment), but she was also an unfortunate one, who fought a losing battle with the feeling that she had made a mess of her life. But still, your idea is your idea, and it belongs to you. It's your own interpretation of the matter as a historian."[29] To Jean Allouch he wrote: "I don't know anything about Aimée. Marguerite is the only one I knew."[30]

This testimony shows clearly that no one will ever know who the true Marguerite was. First she was a tabloid heroine and then a case reconstructed by Lacan and celebrated by an upcoming generation of psychiatrists. Lastly she became a myth, sung by the surrealists. Like Charcot's Blanche Wittmann, like Breuer and Freud's Bertha Pappenheim, and like Janet's Madeleine Lebouc, she owed her notoriety not to her own talent or identity but to an acting-out episode that precipitated her into the history of madness. When the case, the myth, and the madness all were over, her fate became the anonymous one of any mental hospital patient. She who had been observed, ransacked, fabricated, travestied, and made into a myth for the benefit of psychiatry had now just to survive and find a new identity. Her return to normal life was made even more strange than it would otherwise have been because chance threw her once again in the path of the hated Jacques Lacan.

Christine Anzieu, born in 1950, had an intense and warm relationship with her grandmother Marguerite. Like her parents, Christine knew about the past, and far from denying Marguerite's madness she saw traces of it in many of her attitudes. But she never felt she was face to face with such an organized paranoia as Lacan had described. She sensed the persecution, the passion, the mysticism, the desire to better herself, the violence, but what struck her most was an extraordinary capacity for love. And Marguerite was interested in knowledge of all kinds, ranging from physics to Hinduism and including the Breton language. She wanted to learn everything, know everything, read everything. She helped the parish priest in many good works. She had a clear view of the power play and rivalries that were rife within the bourgeois families she had known. She was very severe about the avarice and hypocrisy to be found among the Lacans.

She remembered with horror the time she had spent in hospital and blamed Lacan for never having done anything to get her out of the asylum, for never having helped her or listened to her properly. In her opinion, he had stolen her life story and turned it into a thesis. When he became famous she resented it, and feelings of persecution again rose up strongly in her. She never forgave Lacan for not having given her back her manuscripts.[31]

After Lacan's death I asked Jacques-Alain Miller to look for them. I knew how much Marguerite's son wanted to have them back, though he didn't want to ask for them himself. But I never received any answer.

An Unsatisfactory Encounter with Melanie Klein

*I*n October 1942 the opening shot was fired in the series of Controversial Discussions that for four years, in the midst of war, were to rend the British Psycho-Analytical Society. Glover put the evaluation of Melanie Klein's theories on the agenda, while Jones vanished into the country for the whole of 1943 to avoid having to choose between the supporters of Melanie Klein and the advocates of Anna Freud. Michael Balint too, now living in Manchester, also escaped the crossfire. The main discussions were mostly among the women, partly because each party was led by a woman and partly because most of the male members of the BPS were absent, having been called up to organize the famous wartime psychiatric service that Lacan so much admired.

The Controversial Discussions created a situation completely new in the history of the international psychoanalytic movement. For the first time since Freud's death there was a split that led neither to a schism nor to a dissident movement but instead to a compromise based on the need for peaceful coexistence. Both the opposing parties could justly appeal to Freud himself; neither contested the founding father's teaching as such. On the contrary, each tried to outdo the other in Freudian legitimacy. But Melanie Klein saw herself as an innovator and regarded her rival's attitudes as unenterprising and the product of mere habit. Anna Freud, for her part, saw Kleinianism as a deviation to be eliminated in the same way as those of Jung and Adler. The dispute about legitimacy was the more acute because Freud hadn't officially condemned Klein's theories when he was alive. He had clung to an appearance of neutrality, while privately agreeing with his daughter.

So the situation in 1942 was a strange one. Anna Freud, the legitimate heiress of the founding father, was being challenged because of her attachment to academic theories. Melanie Klein, who claimed no hereditary legitimacy, represented a version of Freudianism more innovative than that of her rival. So she was "more Freudian" than Anna Freud herself, in that she brought a breath of fresh theoretical air to a body of doctrine that but for her might have undergone a lethal process of sanctification.

In the BPS the Kleinians had long been the real representatives of an "English school" of psychoanalysis. But they knew very well there was no question of their expelling Freud's daughter and her supporters. Freud had chosen England as his last place of asylum, and Anna and the Viennese in general had been welcomed into the BPS as political refugees and victims of Nazism. In such circumstances, schism was impossible, and the two parties were bound, in the long term, to sign a nonaggression pact. The Kleinians tended to be recruited from among first-generation emigrants from Hungary or Berlin, whereas Anna Freud's advocates were chiefly Viennese who had been forced into exile. The first group, having left their own countries voluntarily, were better integrated into English society, while the second group found it relatively difficult to adapt. For many years, despite having acquired British nationality, they were painfully homesick for their native city. They still thought of it as decked in the charms of Freud's own day, when Freudianism itself was influenced by the great artistic upheaval that colored the end of the nineteenth century.

But in the course of all the controversies there grew up between the two opposing camps an independent group composed mostly of "native" English. In their view the current quarrels concerned individuals rather than ideas and were taking a religious turn unsuited to scientific debate and therefore harmful to the BPS as a whole. As early as 1940 James Strachey, one of the pioneers of the English school, pointed out the dangers inherent in a split in the society: "My own view is that Mrs. K. has made some highly important contributions to πα [Greek initials for *psychoanalysis*] but that it's absurd to make out (a) that they cover the whole subject or (b) that their validity is axiomatic. On the other hand I think it's equally ludicrous for Miss F. to maintain that πα is a Game Reserve belonging to the F. family and that Mrs. K.'s ideas are fatally subversive. These attitudes on both sides are of course purely religious and the very antithesis of science."[1] In the same context, Winnicott ended up violently denouncing both the tyranny of Melanie Klein and the despotism of Anna Freud. "I consider it to be of absolutely vital importance to the future of the Society," he said in 1954, "that both of yourselves shall break up the groupings in so far as they are official. No one can break them up except yourselves and you can only do this while you are alive. If it should happen that you should die, then the grouping which is officially recognised in the nomenclature will become absolutely rigid and it will be a generation or more before the Society can recover from this disaster which will be a clumping based not on science but on personalities."[2]

As for Edward Glover and Melitta Schmideberg, who before the war had played such an important part in the opening of hostilities, they both left the BPS in order to take up other interests. Melitta emigrated to the United States, where she worked with delinquents and drug abusers, and Glover pursued similar activities until in 1963 he became chairman of the scientific committee of the Institute of Criminology in London.

To begin with, the arguments were about the appraisal of Klein's theories, but soon, as Winnicott points out, debate centered on the training of analysts. Anna Freud's party saw the object of analysis as the undoing of the effects of repression and the reduction of defense mechanisms, in order to give the ego better control over the id. Transference should not be analyzed until the defenses have been reduced. This training technique corresponded to the interpretation of the second topography put forward by ego psychology, whose main contributors were linked to Anna Freud. She, Kris, Hartmann, Loewenstein, and the Viennese in general shared the same adaptative view of psychoanalysis, though it was not the view of Freud himself. As most of this group emigrated to the United States, "Anna-Freudianism" became a leading trend in the IPA.

But for the Kleinians treatment began with recognition of the primacy of the transferential bond and the necessity of analyzing it from the outset, regardless of any control the ego might have over the id. These arguments rested on a reading of the second topography that was the opposite of the Anna-Freudians's interpretation and close to the positions at which Lacan was to arrive. So Kleinianism contained no theory of adaptation, which explains why it was never able to establish itself in America. Kleinians compared treatment to a stage production in which the analyst was not a real character but instead represented the introjected objects that had constructed the superego. They believed the subject's anxiety situation was revived by the unfolding of the analysis and had to be reduced by dealing immediately with the phenomenon of transference.

These two interpretations of Freudian doctrine were so incompatible that the BPS had to establish two different systems of training. But as it was also necessary to preserve the unity of the society, internal links were created between the two opposing methods. In June 1946 the Controversial Discussions ended when the BPS was officially divided into three groups: group A taught the theories of Melanie Klein, group B taught those of Anna Freud, and the third group consisted of independents. The main committees of the society, and in particular the training committee, had to include representatives from each of the three groups. This compromise, though it avoided schism, had a paralyzing effect on the general functioning of the BPS. Hence Winnicott's denunciation of it in 1954.

In his article on the family, Lacan had already noticed the parallels between his own approach and the theories of Melanie Klein. But it was not until after the war that he had a chance to meet Melanie Klein herself.

In 1947 Henri Ey decided to start an international association to organize periodical world conferences on psychiatry. A first meeting, under the chairmanship of Jean Lhermitte, Maxime Laignel-Lavastine, Jean Delay, and Pierre Janet, was held to define the plan, to which twenty-five societies later agreed.[3] The first conference was held in Paris in the autumn of 1950, by which time Henri Ey had managed to get together representatives from about a dozen countries and forty or so societies (the original twenty-five and fifteen or so that joined subsequently): more than fifteen hundred participants in all, including the great names of the French psychoanalytic movement from the first to the third generation. To represent the American version of neo-Freudianism, Ey had asked Franz Alexander, president of the American Psychiatric Association, to open the debate. Alexander then advised the organizers to invite Anna Freud, and she agreed to come. But Ey wanted Melanie Klein to be there too, so he asked Juliette Favez-Boutonier to write to her. Klein declined the invitation by return of post, offended by the fact that Anna Freud was to be present. At this point Lacan intervened to help his old friend Ey. He got in touch with Melanie Klein and asked her to use her influence to get the people in London to vote for a discussion on "the progress of psychoanalysis." He explained that he was fighting as hard as he could to get this subject tabled for discussion but was encountering great opposition from "reactionary tendencies" in the SPP. Representing himself to her as the most progressive member of his own society, he launched into an eloquent attack on Anna Freud as being too conservative to represent the field of child psychology at the conference.[4] He managed to persuade his correspondent and wrote to Ey saying: "I'll be sending Melanie Klein to Bonneval for you in ten days' time."[5]

In May 1948, in a paper on aggression presented to the eleventh conference of French-speaking psychoanalysts, in Brussels, Lacan had repeated all the arguments contained in his previous texts on the subject and included a certain number of Klein's theories. He had put forward an interpretation of the second topography that drew a distinction between the *ego*, the imaginary site of all resistances, and the *I*, which indicated the position of the subject in reality. In borrowing Klein's idea of *paranoid position*, he turned the ego into an agent of *méconnaissance* (misrecognition or misconstruction) organized into a paranoid structure. If such a structure exists, it must be taken into account in treatment. Hence the idea that analytic technique serves to bring into play a negative transference by inducing, as against the *misrecognition* of the ego, a *directed paranoia*. Thus Lacan agreed with Melanie Klein on the need for analytic training to accord a primary importance to transference and not to make the ego the site of an appropriation of the id. But he retained an approach of his own to the question of the separation of the *I* and the *ego* and to that of directed paranoia.[6]

At the IPA congress in Zurich in the summer of 1949, Lacan returned to the same theme in a paper entitled "The Mirror Stage as Formative of the Function of the I."[7] He had chosen this subject to get his own back after the Marienbad meeting, where he hadn't been able to express himself freely. But the theories he put forward in 1949 were no longer the same as those he had favored in 1936. Lacan now linked psychoanalysis to a non-Freudian philosophy of the subject, *diametrically* opposed to any philosophy based on the cogito, in which the *I* was differentiated from the *ego*. The object of this profession of faith was not to criticize Descartes but to attack ego psychology and the Anna-Freudians: i.e., the assertion of the primacy of the ego over the id. But this did not prevent Lacan from paying tribute to Anna Freud for her description of defense mechanisms, which in his view remained accurate provided the ego was made the site of the defense system.

That sixteenth IPA congress was an event. For the first time the Americans dominated the proceedings; the Europeans were divided among themselves. The most "disgraced" and humiliated country there was Germany, represented by people who had collaborated with the Nazis. Compared with Germany, France seemed successful but misunderstood, unknown for the most part to the English and the Americans except through Marie Bonaparte, seen as the only representative of genuine Freudian legitimacy. The host country, Switzerland, was brilliantly represented by Oskar Pfister, Henri Flournoy, and Philippe Sarasin. The Americans, who advocated an adaptive neo-Freudianism, were almost all of European origin, though this didn't stop those Europeans who hadn't emigrated from seeing them as having come out best in Freudianism's great shift to the west. Their triumph was complete, and the psychiatrist Leo Bartemeier was elected president of the IPA in succession to Jones, who had held the office since 1932. To Melanie Klein, whose ideas had won over the majority in the BPS, the triumph of North America seemed like a victory for the ideas of Anna Freud. A disaster. But the Kleinians did find new support among the Latin Americans present who had gone to London for training.

The French were represented in Zurich by the legitimists of the first generation—Bonaparte and Leuba—and by the second generation, including Lagache, Nacht, and Lacan. None of them belonged to any school of thought to be found in the IPA, though each stood for a different tendency in France. Nacht embodied the authoritative, medical ideal of the SPP conservatives; Lagache the academic liberalism based on the merging of psychology and psychoanalysis; and Lacan a movement of continuity combined with revision comparable to though different from that of Melanie Klein. That year he was beginning to gather around him the most brilliant members of the third generation of French psychoanalysis. Among them were the musketeers of the future troika: Serge Leclaire, Wladimir Granoff, and François Perrier.[8]

Anna Freud didn't like Lacan, and her friendship with Marie Bonaparte could only encourage her to reject in its entirety a doctrine already thought to be "paranoid" and too obscure to be incorporated into legitimist Freudianism. As for Melanie Klein, she wasn't interested in what Lacan had to say: she found it difficult to understand, untranslatable, and of little use to her. She was very much aware, however, of the help Lacan could be to her in France, and she knew how much he was admired by the younger generation. So she was very pleased to see him there in Zurich. Lacan, for his part, was still determined to get her support in promoting the idea of the "progress of psychoanalysis." So he offered to translate the German version of her book *The Psycho-Analysis of Children*, which had been published simultaneously in Vienna and London in 1932.

When he got back to Paris, however, he handed the work over to René Diatkine, who was then undergoing analysis with him. Some time later Diatkine finished translating the first half of the book and gave it to Lacan, without keeping a copy for himself. Meanwhile Françoise Girard, who was following Lacan's teaching, had also suggested to Melanie Klein that she herself might translate the English version of the book into French. Klein declined the offer, but didn't say that Lacan was already working on the translation. Instead she suggested that Girard should translate her *Contributions to Psycho-Analysis*, published in 1948. In March 1951 Françoise Girard married Jean-Baptiste Boulanger, a psychiatrist from Montreal who had come to France to be trained and shared her enthusiasm for Klein's ideas. In August Diatkine told Klein that half the translation of *The Psycho-Analysis of Children* was finished but that it wasn't Lacan who had done it. In the autumn, during a control group, Lacan asked Françoise Boulanger whether her husband spoke English. When she said he did, Lacan suggested the couple should both translate the second half of *The Psycho-Analysis of Children*, saying he had already done the first half.

Françoise and Jean-Baptiste Boulanger set to work at once, and in December they asked Lacan to let them have the other half of the text so that they could compare the two translations and make sure the French translation of Klein's terminology was consistent throughout. Lacan looked for the manuscript in both his apartments in the rue de Lille, and then at La

Prévôté, but couldn't find it. At the end of the month Françoise Boulanger made an appointment to see Melanie Klein, and on January 27 she and her husband had lunch at Klein's house in London. They told her the hair-raising story, so typical of Lacan's way of doing business: "[He] never *revealed* or admitted officially," says Jean-Baptiste Boulanger, "that he'd lost the translation Diatkine had done from the German."[9]

Lacan lost all credibility with Melanie Klein and her supporters. Klein moved closer to Lagache and backed him up in the negotiations that began in 1953 with the object of getting the IPA to readmit the Société française de psychanalyse (SFP). The French version of her book was eventually published by PUF (Presses Universitaires de France) in 1959, in the series edited by Lagache. She was delighted and wrote him a number of letters, as well as thanking Jean-Baptiste Boulanger in the following terms: "I very much wish that I could have put the work in your hands some years ago when Madame Boulanger first offered, after the congress in Zurich, to translate it. It would have been a much better arrangement for you, and how much worry and trouble I should have saved myself! But, as you know, I could not take it away from Lacan."[10]

PART VI

Elements of a System of Thought

Theory of Treatment: Kinship Structures

On June 16, 1953, Daniel Lagache, Juliette Favez-Boutonier, Françoise Dolto, and Blanche Reverchon-Jouve resigned from the spp after a conflict that had lasted a year.[1] To begin with, the teachers belonging to the society had clashed over the founding of a new institute of psychoanalysis designed to establish training principles consistent with the standards of the ipa. The pupils entered the fray after Jenny Roudinesco, on March 15, 1953, wrote a letter to Sacha Nacht, her analyst, and to Jacques Lacan, her controller.[2] The juniors' rebellion, following on the discord among the masters themselves, opened a rift that would eventually become a split. The Freudian cause in France now had to weather the same kind of storm as had ravaged its English counterpart during the Controversial Discussions.

But the spp's position was quite unlike that of the bps. In Britain there was a clear conflict between two opposing doctrines, and the advent of a third school had forced the adversaries to conclude a treaty of peaceful coexistence. Things were quite different in France. The opposing forces—that of Nacht on the one hand and of Lagache on the other—didn't represent two contradictory readings of Freud's teaching, as the schools of Melanie Klein and Anna Freud had done on the other side of the Channel. The French battle was about the training of analysts, and it opposed the authoritarianism of the medical profession to the liberalism of the academics. Only Lacan had proposed revisions comparable in scope to those of Melanie Klein, but his position in the spp between 1949 and 1953 was not yet analogous to hers during the Controversial Discussions. He wanted to avoid a split and did all he could to prevent one. In his opinion, the liberals' rejection of the medical model and their turning instead to psychology was disastrous, and the conservatives' clinging to hidebound medical teaching no less so.

As an Anglophile with no love of revolution, Lacan always tended to prefer sound reform to insurrection. But though he was by nature a follower of Tocqueville his democratic principles were continually contradicted by his personality and the content of his teaching. And however strongly he might defend traditional institutions, his words, his image, and his manner all inspired a kind of Jacobin enthusiasm. And so, for the young French psychoanalysts of the 1950s, he became the spokesperson of a strong revolutionary trend. The conservatives, led by Nacht and Marie Bonaparte, accused him of using his influence to sow rebellion among the students. On June 16, 1953, he had no choice but to resign from the SPP and join Lagache and his friends, who had just started the SFP. And just like the others, Lacan failed to realize that in leaving the old group he was ceasing to be a member of the IPA.

For as long as the battle lasted he was challenged by his own peers not for his teaching but for his analytic practice.

For some time it had been growing increasingly evident that Lacan did not obey the technical rules that had been in force in the IPA since the twenties and thirties. According to these rules an analysis was supposed to last for at least four years and consist of four or five sessions a week, each session lasting at least fifty minutes. These requirements applied, in principle, to training analyses as well as to therapeutic ones, though in fact it was only for the former category that they were strictly insisted on. In the case of therapeutic analyses, the clinician was regarded as free to contract with the patient as to the number of sessions on which the latter wished to spend his time and money. The rule governing the length of the sessions was designed to limit the analyst's theoretically unlimited power. He was not supposed to manipulate the time he devoted to a patient through arbitrary changes, and the patient had the right to speak for a length of time agreed in advance, even if he chose not to exercise that prerogative. These standards were accepted by all the members of all the societies affiliated to the IPA; in fact, the unity that prevailed during the forties in the empire Freud had founded was due entirely to this codification, which acted with the force of a generally accepted law. So while different theories as to how treatments should be conducted were tolerated, any breach of the rules about time might always result in expulsion.

Lacan did not obey the rule prescribing a fixed length of time for each session. Though he didn't yet go in for what were later to be known as "short sessions," he did use a technique of variable ones, bringing sessions to an end arbitrarily when he himself saw fit. He reversed the rule protecting the patient's right to speak and put the all-powerful analyst in the position of interpreter in the transference relationship.

This refusal to obey the generally accepted rule was condemned by the other members of the SPP. Lacan's de facto introduction of variable-length sessions meant that he could take on any number of applicants for analysis, while his colleagues, by keeping to the rules, doomed themselves not only to having two or three times fewer pupils than he but also to seeing their influence within the society considerably reduced. Since Lacan towered over all the members of his own generation in terms of personal charisma as well as clinical and theoretical genius, he naturally attracted the most brilliant future teachers of the younger (i.e., the third) generation;[3] all of them followed his teaching, and most of them chose to be analyzed on his couch.

By temperament Lacan was incapable of limiting his own desires, and his analysis with Loewenstein had done nothing to improve matters. He had resented this inordinately long treatment as a curb on his ambition and nearly died of boredom throughout the fixed sessions. It was evident that Lacan's intelligence was crushingly superior to that of his analyst, who couldn't understand that his patient was not analyzable in terms of the standard criteria. Lacan knew he had a distinguished future in front of him, and for too long he had been misunderstood and rejected. And now, at the very moment when fame was at hand and long-awaited recognition imminent, a bunch of stuffed shirts wanted to impose a bunch of stuffed-shirt rules on him in the name of some bureaucratic setup light years away from the glorious Viennese epic he meant to revive!

Three times he expounded his views on variable-length sessions to the members of the SPP: first in December 1951, then in June 1952, and for the third time in February 1953.[4] He didn't publish these three lectures, and they remain unpublished to this day. But according to witnesses he justified his contravention of the rules by maintaining that shorter and less frequent sessions produced a sense of frustration and separation in the patient that was beneficial. The point was to turn the transference relationship into a dialectic by halting a session at certain significant words in order to reactivate unconscious desire.

But after trying to justify the technique of variability on theoretical grounds and challenging the inflexible ritual of exactly timed sessions, Lacan was obliged to change tactics and disguise what he was really doing. The SFP had been embarrassed from its inception by the fact that its members no longer belonged to the IPA. So, as they never for a moment really contemplated breaking with Freudian legitimacy, they immediately entered into negotiations designed to bring them swiftly back into the fold. But for this they needed to prove to a commission of inquiry that all the training analysts in the SFP obeyed the standard rules about the length of sessions.

In July 1953 Lacan already had a third of all the SFP's pupils on his couch, i.e., about fifteen people. At the rate of four weekly sessions each lasting fifty minutes, these fifteen training analyses would have represented fifty hours'

work a week. In addition there were controls and private patients, amount-
ing, say, to some twenty hours more. Seventy hours a week in all. This exorbitant figure couldn't be real; it was obvious that Lacan gained time by shortening his sessions. The average length was about twenty minutes; in other
words, an actual session might last from ten to forty minutes. This being so,
Lacan's practice stood firmly in the way of the SFP's ever being incorporated
into the IPA.[5] And as he was the first to want to be readmitted into Freudian
legitimacy, he couldn't, after July 1953, try to justify variable-length sessions.
Thus he never published the famous lectures delivered to the SPP on this
taboo subject, and he went on giving variable-length sessions within the
framework of the SFP, while at the same time publicly declaring that he had
"normalized" his practice.

In a long letter to Michael Balint written on August 6, 1953, he explained
that after having experimented with variable-length sessions he had abandoned that technique and reverted to obeying the rules. He referred to the
zeal with which his "opponents" tried to harm him by hinting that he gave
"short sessions" and "abbreviated analyses." He countered these alleged
accusations with the assertion that his analyses lasted between three and four
years, with the same number of sessions per week as was usual everywhere,
or at least in the SFP. He recalled that he had given some lectures to the SPP
on variable-length sessions, but he had not used that technique since January
1953. Then he said how much importance he attached to the paper he was
going to deliver on September 26 and invited Balint to Rome to hear it.
Finally he asked Balint to get him English editions of Freud's *Studies on
Hysteria*, "with the Anna O. case by Breuer alone," and *Inhibitions, Symptoms
and Anxiety* (originally published in the United States as *The Problem of
Anxiety*). To cover the costs involved, Lacan enclosed a check sent to him by
an English friend with the payee's name unspecified and then made out by
Lacan to Balint. This detail points to a curious feature of Lacan's attitude to
money: his habit of settling what he owed with checks, usually from his
patients, on which the payee's name had deliberately been left blank so that
Lacan might use them for this purpose.[6]

It was in the Massons' house at Le Tholonet, just after his marriage to Sylvia,
that Lacan started to write the five hundred pages of his "Rome
Discourse."[7] He finished it "hastily" at the end of August. Then, conscious
of the importance of his own teaching and anxious to occupy first place in
the new society founded by Lagache, he set about looking for support in
what he took to be likely places: psychiatric circles, the Communist Party,
and the Catholic Church. At the beginning of September he sent Lucien
Bonnafé a copy of his text without asking for any comment. But Bonnafé
understood what he meant: "Lacan was trying to attract the attention of the

party leadership to his teaching."[8] Lacan's approach to the church was much more explicit. At Easter 1953, in the midst of the internal conflict at the SPP, he wrote his brother a letter in which, between the lines, and not without some equivocation, he claimed that his teaching belonged to the Christian tradition. He asserted that in this second half of the twentieth century everything would depend on how men dealt with one another, and this perhaps not only on the secular plane. Psychology, he added, occupied a "supereminent" position, yet the one idea of all its practitioners was to fall away from that height and join in some great and general degradation. He himself was almost alone, he concluded, in propounding a doctrine that might at least enable the movement as a whole to preserve its roots in a great tradition, a tradition in which man could not be reduced to the status of a mere object.[9]

Lacan was not really renouncing atheism. But he knew that his way of reading Freud in the light of philosophy and from a nonbiological point of view might attract a lot of Catholics who didn't accept the "materialistic" aspect of the master's own teaching. When they read Lacan they felt on familiar ground, that of a Christian evaluation of human personality.[10] Moreover, the SFP looked more kindly than did the SPP on the aspirations of priests and other Christians who wanted to become analysts. Many of these had no medical studies behind them, and they felt more comfortable in Lagache's new more academic-minded society than in that of Nacht. Lacan was well aware of this, which was why he tried to persuade his brother of the good Christian intentions reflected in his teaching. But he went even further. In September, just before leaving for Rome, he wrote to Marc-François again, telling him about his marriage to Sylvia and restating the importance he attached to religion. Then he came to the real point: he was determined to have an audience with the pope, in order to talk to him about the future of psychoanalysis within the church. So he asked Marc-François to intercede with the relevant authorities. The letter was couched in suitably emphatic terms. Lacan stressed that the heart of his teaching lay in Rome, where according to him the importance of speech and language to the individual was demonstrated. So Lacan wanted to "do homage to our common father" in the Holy City.[11]

Marc-François was much moved by this declaration, and though he didn't know anyone in Pope Pius XII's entourage to whom he might pass on Lacan's request, he sincerely believed his brother had been reconverted to Christian doctrine. In his eyes, though Jacques was still leading a life of sin, he was saved now by his teaching, which showed at last a wonderful return to the values of Catholic spirituality. But the summit meeting never took place. Lacan even invoked the aid of the French embassy, but to no avail: the pope didn't grant him a private interview. Despite this rebuff, Lacan, together with Serge Leclaire and Maryse Choisy, did attend a public audience at Castel Gondolfo.[12]

In the autumn of 1953 Lacan was in a very odd situation. Professionally he was concealing his variable-length sessions and pretending to keep to the rules; in his private life he was concealing his second marriage and new family from the children of his first marriage; and on the ideological plane he was telling his brother he had become a Christian again while at the same time trying to forge links with the leadership of the Communist Party. And in the thick of this imbroglio he started work on a system of thought that was entirely inconsistent with all his own deviousness. For what was of supreme importance in Lacan's system was the elucidation of the individual's relation to the truth.

As we know, Lacan had already, through his reading of Henri Delacroix, discovered the importance of Ferdinand de Saussure's *Course in General Linguistics*). Later on, under the influence of Pichon, he had gone into the subject further. But his real initiation into Saussure's system and the principles of structural linguistics dates from his encounter with the works of Claude Lévi-Strauss. For Lacan, as for a whole generation of philosophers who would come into prominence in and around the fifties, the appearance in 1949 of Lévi-Strauss's *The Elementary Structures of Kinship* was a major event.[13]

Freud thought the Oedipus complex lay at the very heart of human personality and that its triangular structure was to be found in the most varied kinds of culture. In its positive form it involved a death wish directed at the rival belonging to the same sex as the subject, and sexual desire for the person belonging to the opposite sex; in its negative form it manifested itself in the subject's love for the parent of the same sex, and jealousy of the parent of the opposite sex. The triangular structure of the complex derived its effectiveness from the incest taboo. In other words, Freud saw this prohibition as the necessary condition of all culture: incest was an antisocial act that the human race had had to renounce in order to be able to exist.

To give this theory more substance, Freud, in *Totem and Taboo*, published in 1912, made use of the Darwinian fable of the primitive horde and of James G. Frazer's and Robertson Smith's work on totemism. He showed that the origin of culture was based on an act of patricide: in the mythical tribe, the jealous and violent father was slain by his sons and eaten by them in the course of a totemic meal. Then, seized with remorse, the sons refused to have sexual relations with the women thus liberated and hastened to draw up laws forbidding incest. Thus was born the first principle of a social organization that has been handed down from generation to generation.

The story of the totemic feast, which resembled some imaginary extrapolation, a product of fantasy, was challenged in the early twenties by British and American anthropologists. They had given a favorable reception to most of Freud's ideas about dreams and symbols, but they were taken aback by the weakness of an argument based on the notion that every culture had a single origin and implying that this origin was the same for every society. And they accused Freud of making use of an evolutionist theory that had already been overtaken by anthropology.

It is true that Freud had committed a double error in relying on Frazer, whose hypotheses were based on a deductive method independent of any practical work in the field. This meant not only that Freud was contradicting his own approach, based on direct observation, but also that he was venturing into the realm of pure speculation. For, like Frazer, he had never studied "primitive" societies in the field, and his claim to explain how they functioned was based merely on his knowledge of psychoanalysis.[14]

Bronislaw Malinowski was the first to enter into the controversy that eventually led to the establishment of first a functional and then a cultural form of anthropology. Born in Kraków in 1884, he was influenced by the teaching of Ernst Mach, Wilhelm Wundt, and Emile Durkheim. But he was introduced to Freud's theories by Seligman and Rivers, both of whom had accepted the new hypotheses arising out of the discovery of the unconscious. Earlier, in the autumn of 1917, Malinowski had gone to the South Pacific and shared the life of the Trobriand Islanders. There, all alone in a Conradian "heart of darkness," he took the opportunity to observe his own feelings, which included not only erotic desire for the native women but also a sense that he was confronting instinctual forces common to all humanity.[15] As a result, he came to reject Lucien Lévy-Bruhl's theories on primitive mentality and the idea of a collective consciousness, embracing instead a new humanism based on the analysis of people as they actually lived.

Four years after his return from the South Seas, Malinowski set out to overhaul Freud's teaching. Among the Trobriand Islanders he had observed a matrilineal type of social structure in which ultimately the role of the father in procreation came to be ignored: a child was conceived by the mother and the spirit of an ancestor, and the place usually occupied by the father remained empty. In consequence, law was embodied in the form of the maternal uncle, and it was he that the child saw as a rival. The incest taboo applied to a child's sister instead of to his mother. Malinowski did not deny the existence of a "nuclear complex" but maintained that it was variable, depending on the family structure typical of the society in question. He thus undermined both Freud's Oedipus theory and his hypothesis about the original patricide. The first applied only to patrilineal societies, and the second took no account of the diversity of cultures. This diversity was so great that no one original transition from nature to culture could possibly account for it.

Reaction was swift. Although Malinowski had shown himself anxious to preserve as well as to update Freud's ideas, he was soon condemned out of hand by Ernest Jones, the chief representative of Freudian legitimacy. In 1924 Jones objected that the Trobriand Islanders' refusal to recognize paternity was merely a tendentious denial of procreation by the father. The Oedipus complex remained universal, because the matrilinear system, with its avuncular complex, was merely the negative expression of an original oedipal tendency that had been repressed.

But as Jones was not an anthropologist and had never done any field-work, his assertions didn't make Freud's arguments any more credible. As for Jones's interpretations of Malinowski, they were little more than an abstract inversion of the anthropologist's own theories.

The controversy was revived in 1928, when Geza Roheim decided to test Malinowski's hypotheses and set out on an expedition—financed in part by Marie Bonaparte—to New Guinea. The inhabitants of Normanby Island lived in a society very similar to that of the Trobriand Islanders, and Roheim lived among them for some ten months. But he emerged with completely different conclusions from those of Malinowski. Not only did Roheim reveal the importance of anal eroticism, which Malinowski had preferred not to see, but he also showed that "a man who makes love to his sister and lives in a relation of rivalry to his uncle" is very similar to the oedipal man of patrilinear societies. So Roheim proclaimed there could no longer be any doubt about the existence and universality of the Oedipus complex.[16]

Thus the debate about anthropology ended in deadlock. The legitimist Freudians stood by the idea of a universal Oedipus complex, suggesting that the ban on incest derived from a feeling of horrified aversion common to the whole human race. The culturalists believed in diversity, not seeing that the incest taboo really did arise from a principle universally recognized, even if only by denial.

Once more the argument, after alternating between Vienna and London, burst forth more fully on the fertile soil of American anthropology. But nothing like that happened in France. The only member of the Parisian psychoanalytic movement who took a personal interest in these problems was Marie Bonaparte. And she helped both Malinowski and Roheim. As for the ethnologists, they didn't enter into the Freudian debate.

Until 1950 the study of so-called primitive societies was divided among three schools of thought. One of these derived from the old tradition of physical anthropology inherited from Broca. Another, typified by the researches of Marcel Mauss, linked society with symbolism. The third trend, which included Bataille, Leiris, Caillois, and Rivet, was anticolonial and interested in the revival of the idea of the sacred. It was against this background that, in postwar France, Claude Lévi-Strauss was to become the true founder of anthropology in the modern sense of the word.[17]

Lévi-Strauss began in 1949 by throwing new light on the question of the incest ban. Instead of either trying to find the genesis of culture in man's hypothetical renunciation of the practice of incest, or pointing to the vast variety of cultures, he avoided any such polarization, showing that the prohibition provided a transition from nature to culture. "The prohibition of incest is in origin neither purely cultural nor purely natural," he wrote. "Nor is it a composite mixture of elements from both nature and culture. It is the fundamental step because of which, by which, but above all in which, the transition from nature to culture is accomplished. In one sense, it belongs to nature, for it is a general condition of culture. Consequently, we should not be surprised that its formal characteristic, universality, has been taken from nature."[18]

This new expression of the nature/culture duality led to a revaluation of the study of societies. Moreover, to underline the novelty of his approach, Lévi-Strauss took over the old name *anthropology*, which had become obsolete in France, and gave it the same social and cultural content as had already been ascribed to it by British and American researchers. He included in it both *ethnography*, defined as the first phase of research in the field, and *ethnology*, described as the first phase of synthetic thought. To *anthropology* he gave a centralizing role: its point of departure lay in the analyses produced by ethnography and ethnology, from which it would draw theoretical conclusions valid for all human societies. The universalized incest taboo was paralleled by a system of marriage exchanges regulated by a structural organization independent of individual consciousness. In elementary structures, strict and narrow prohibition is accompanied by the imposition of a compulsory mate: the only marriages allowed are those that repeat the pattern of unions entered into by the spouses' ancestors. In complex structures— those of present-day Western societies—the ban is less narrow, permitting a free choice within the limits laid down by the prohibition.

The universalization of the incest taboo could not be properly studied unless it was set in the context of a coherent system of kinship and brought under ampler scientific scrutiny. Hence Lévi-Strauss's revival of the term *anthropology* to provide a model for a synthetic understanding of human institutions.[19]

Jacques Lacan met Claude Lévi-Strauss in about 1949 at a dinner party organized by Alexandre Koyré. Lacan was silent that evening, looking very intently at the others present.[20] But the two men soon became friends, largely on the basis of their shared love for works of art. When Lévi-Strauss separated from his second wife and needed to raise money, he sold a collection of Indian objects. Lacan bought half of them. "We were very close for a number of years," Lévi-Strauss says. "We used to go with the Merleau-Ponty's for lunch at Guitrancourt, where Lacan had a country house. Once, my wife and I wanted to find a hideaway in the country, and Lacan had just bought a new car he wanted to try out. The four of us took off together. It was a lot of fun. You should have seen Lacan descending upon a shabby provincial hotel, and in his most regal manner ordering them to run a bath for him! We hardly ever talked about psychoanalysis or philosophy; instead it was usually art and literature. His knowledge was vast. He used to buy paintings and works of art, and this was often the subject of our conversations."[21]

Claude Lévi-Strauss had known Merleau-Ponty since 1930, when they had both done the preliminary part of the *agrégation* course at the Lycée Janson-de-Sailly in the 16th Arrondissement. When they met again fifteen years later, in the winter of 1944–1945, they exchanged their impressions about intellectual life in Paris during the Occupation. The ethnologist, who had spent several years in the United States, asked about the future of existentialism, and the philosopher told how he intended to revive ancient metaphysics.[22] Merleau-Ponty knew Lacan already. They had both been present at several of Louise and Michel Leiris's famous "fiestas" during the war, and the links between the two had grown closer still in 1944, when Suzanne, Merleau-Ponty's wife, began to work at helping deportees settle down into normal life again. She had studied medicine and specialized in pediatrics. Lacan offered to help her take a degree in psychiatry and suggested that she take as her thesis subject neurosis as it occurred in concentration camps. To introduce her to the relevant nosology he presented her with an inscribed copy of his own thesis.[23] All these relationships resulted in a close friendship between the two couples: Suzanne and Maurice, Sylvia and Jacques.

At this time Lacan was still interested in the history of Nazism, and he had heard the story of Rudolph Hess from his friend Jean Delay, who had served as an expert witness at the Nuremberg trials. This prompted Lacan to think of writing an article on the "case" for the review *Critique*, though eventually he gave up on the idea.[24]

Lévi-Strauss met Merleau-Ponty again in 1948, after spending another three years in the United States. He successfully defended his thesis on *The Elementary Structures of Kinship* but failed twice in an attempt to be elected to the Collège de France, an ancient and eminent academic body independent of the university. Rivet appointed him assistant director of the Musée de l'Homme (Museum of Mankind), however, and then Lévi-Strauss met Michel Leiris, whose work he then read with great pleasure.

It was at a dinner at Lacan's house that Lévi-Strauss met Monique Roman, who was to become his third wife. She was a friend of Sylvia's and saw a lot of the Leirises. Before they actually married, she and Lévi-Strauss lived in the rue Notre-Dame-de-Lorette. One evening they were finishing dinner, which happened to consist of crabs, when Lacan arrived unexpectedly and to their astonishment devoured all the remains that were left on their plates.

Such eccentricities did not prevent Lacan from becoming a member of Paris's postwar intelligentsia, in which he was respected for his talent, originality, and erudition. But though he was valued, he was still not understood. And it irked him that his writings continued to be thought obscure by the very people from whom they borrowed so many ideas. "I would have needed to understand them," says Lévi-Strauss. "But I always had the impression that, to his fervent admirers, 'understand' meant something different from what it meant to me. I'd have had to read everything five or six times. Merleau-Ponty and I used to talk about it and concluded that we didn't have the time."[25]

Nor did Lévi-Strauss's interpretation of Freud owe anything to Lacan's. Lévi-Strauss had first come across Freud when he was studying philosophy in high school. Marcel Nathan, the father of one of his schoolmates, had translated some of Freud's writings in collaboration with Marie Bonaparte. One day Monsieur Nathan gave his son's young friend the *Introduction à la psychanalyse* (*Introductory Lectures on Psycho-Analysis*) to read. Later on, during his stay in the United States, Lévi-Strauss mixed in New York psychoanalytic circles. And it was in New York that he met Raymond de Saussure, when the latter became cultural counselor there.

In the articles he wrote about Freud after 1949, Lévi-Strauss compared psychological treatment with shamanistic healing techniques. In the latter, he said in substance, the sorcerer speaks and causes an abreaction—i.e., liberates the patient's repressed affects—whereas in the former it is the patient who speaks while the doctor listens. In addition to this comparison, Lévi-Strauss showed that in Western societies there was a tendency for a *psychoanalytic mythology* to grow up and act as a system of collective interpretation: "A considerable danger thus arises: The treatment (unbeknown to the therapist, naturally), far from leading to the resolution of a specific disturbance within its own context, is reduced to the reorganization of the patient's universe in terms of psychoanalytic interpretations."[26] If a cure is arrived at through a collective adoption of a founding myth, with the myth acting as a system of structural reorganization, this means the system itself has a predominantly symbolic efficacy. Hence the idea put forward by Lévi-Strauss in his *Introduction à l'oeuvre de Marcel Mauss* (Introduction to the work of Marcel Mauss) that what is called the unconscious is merely an empty space in which the symbolic function achieves autonomy: "Symbols are more real than what they symbolize; the signifier precedes and determines the signified."[27]

It is easy to imagine what a shock it was to Lacan to read Lévi-Strauss's *Elementary Structures of Kinship* and his various articles. "If I wanted to describe how I've been helped and supported by Lévi-Strauss's thinking, I'd say it resides in the stress he has laid—I hope he won't reject this rather sweeping way of putting it, it's not meant to cover the whole extent of his sociological and ethnographic researches—on what I shall call the function of the signifier (in the sense that the word has in linguistics), inasmuch as this signifier, I'd say, not only is distinguished by its own laws but also prevails over the signified on which it imposes them."[28]

Lévi-Strauss's theories not only shattered the notion of the family, offering instead the idea of kinship, but also made possible a rethinking of the oedipal universalism postulated by Freud, so that instead of being based on the feeling that there is a "natural" fear of incest, it derived from the existence of a symbolic function understood as a law governing the unconscious organization of human societies. Lacan's encounter with the thought of Lévi-Strauss meant he had at last found a theoretical solution to the problem of how to make a complete overhaul of Freudian doctrine. In the process, the unconscious was to a large extent freed of the biological cast that Freud had lent it, in a direct line from Darwinism. Instead it was seen as a language-related structure. The *Ich* (I or ego) escaped from all the psychological conceptions constructed by the neo-Freudians and was split up into an *ego* and an *I*, the first becoming the site of the illusions of the imagination and the second the vehicle of speech. Lastly, the Oedipus complex, instead of being related to a natural universal, was set in the context of a symbolic universal. As Lacan said,

There's absolutely no need for the symbolic universal to be spread over the entire surface of the world for it to be universal. Besides, as far as I know, there's nothing which entails the world unity of human beings. There's nothing which is concretely realized as universal. And yet, as soon as any symbolic system is formed, straightaway it is, *de jure*, a universal as such. . . . [Lévi-Strauss] is afraid that the autonomy of the symbolic register will give rise to a masked transcendentalism once again, for which, as regards his affinities, his personal sensibility, he feels only fear and aversion. In other words, he is afraid that after we have shown God out of one door, we will bring him back in by the other.[29]

The first stage of Lacan's construction of a system of thought, which I have called an *orthodox sublation of Freud's doctrine*,[30] began at the height of the crisis in the SPP with a talk he gave on March 4, 1953, at the Collège philosophique. Its subject was "the individual myth of the neurotic" (or "poetry and truth in neurosis"), and it was on this occasion that the expression *nom-du-père* (name-of-the-father) was used for the first time. The process continued on July 8 in a lecture entitled "The Symbolic, the Real, and the Imaginary Orders," in which, also for the first time, Lacan claimed that his aim was a *return to Freud's own writings*, a return that according to him had begun in 1951. The whole process of construction reached its climax in Rome on September 27, in "The Function and Field of Speech and Language in Psychoanalysis," which proposed a genuine structural theory of psychoanalytic treatment. Further development can be seen in the two seminars of 1953–1954 and 1954–1955, the former entitled *Freud's Papers on Technique*, the latter *The Ego in Freud's Theory and in the Technique of Psychoanalysis*. The lecture Lacan delivered in Vienna on November 7, 1955, marked the end of this first phase in the construction of his system of thought. He made its current purpose explicit in the title: "The Freudian Thing; or, The Meaning of the Return to Freud in Psychoanalysis."[31]

In "The Individual Myth of the Neurotic" Lacan compared Freud's account of the "Rat Man" case with Goethe's autobiography, *Dictung und Wahrheit* (Poetry and truth).[32] In a ponderous and obscure commentary on the two texts, he harped obsessively on a theme that had been dear to him since 1936: the mirror stage and the deterioration in the role of the father. But at the same time he carried out a structural revision of the idea of the Oedipus complex: it ought to be seen as a myth, and the triangular system needed to be replaced by a quaternary one. The first element in this new system was the *symbolic function*, which in the modern family, said Lacan, was identified with the role of the father—a role played by a father who was humiliated, pathogenic, and discordant, torn between a name (the name of the father) and a biological reality. The second component of the new system, the *narcissistic relationship*, itself divided into two poles: the ego and the subject. "What is the ego, if not something the subject experiences first as being alien to himself within himself? . . . Thus the subject is always in a relationship that precedes his own complete development, which relegates him to a level of fundamental inadequacy and bears witness within him to a flaw, a split, and, to borrow a term from Heidegger, a 'dereliction.' "[33]

Having thus defined three elements of the system—the role of the father, the ego, and the subject—Lacan introduced a fourth factor in the form of *the experience of death*, "a component of all manifestations of the human condition" but especially perceptible in the experience of the neurotic. Lacan's phrase, the *experience of death*, alluded simultaneously to Freud's *death drive*, to Hegel's and Kojève's *fight to the death*, and to Heidegger's vision of *being for death*. But it was to Freud, the man of the Enlightenment and devoted reader of Goethe, that Lacan was really paying tribute as the one who had had the genius to proclaim the ultimate tragedy of the human condition.

Three years later, in 1956, at a lecture by Lévi-Strauss on the relationship between mythology and ritual, Lacan explained how he had made use of the grid of kinship structures in 1953:

I tried almost at once, and, I make bold to say, with complete success, to apply the grid to the symptoms of obsessional neurosis, and especially to Freud's admirable analysis of the case of the "Rat Man." . . . I was even able to set out the case strictly in accordance with a formula supplied by Claude Lévi-Strauss, by which an *a* who was first associated with a *b*, while a *c* was associated with a *d*, changed partners with the *c* in the second generation, but not without there being an irreducible residue left in the form of the negativation of one of the four terms, which acts as correlative to the transformation of the group: in which may be seen what I might call the sign of a kind of impossibility as to a total resolution of the problem of the myth.[34]

In his 1953 commentary on the Rat Man, however, Lacan made use without attribution of Lévi-Strauss's description of the Crow-Omaha systems (similar to those of contemporary Western societies), according to which the offspring of a marriage between a member of clan A and a member of clan B cannot contract a similar marriage for a certain number of generations. This is an example of extended prohibition, a set of complex structures in which every marriage has to be different from those preceding it. Thus the marriages of previous generations specify *negatively* the marriages that are possible at any given time. On the other hand, in the case of narrow prohibition (elementary structures), there is a *positive* specification of permitted marriages, since previous unions must be repeated in an analogous manner. The two types of system, the elementary and the complex, can, however, be translated into one language. Inasmuch as the prohibitions of a complex system are the negative images of positive prohibitions, the two types of system are one: the structure is the same in both.[35]

All this being so, Lacan was particularly interested in two elements in the story of Ernst Lanzer, Freud's Rat Man: on the one hand a marriage choice and on the other the matter of a debt.

Heinrich Lanzer, the patient's father, having one day contracted a gambling debt, was saved from dishonor by a loan from a friend. The money was probably never repaid. "After he had left the army," wrote Freud, "he had tried to find this friend in need so as to pay him back the money, but had not managed to trace him. (The patient was uncertain whether he had ever succeeded)."[36] Before his marriage Heinrich had been in love with a woman who was poor, but it was a rich woman named Rosa whom he had married and who was to be Ernst's mother.

Five years after Heinrich's death, in 1899, the two elements—the debt and the marriage—played an important part in the organization of Ernst's obsessional neurosis. In 1905, aged twenty-seven and in love with a poor woman named Gisela, he refused to let his mother marry him off to a wealthy wife. Two years later, in the summer of 1907, having lost his pince-nez during some military maneuvers, he wired his optician in Vienna asking him to send a replacement by return post. Two days later his captain handed over his new glasses, informing him that the postal charges had to be paid over to the lieutenant who looked after the mail.

Ernst, faced with having to pay back some money, began behaving in an almost crazy manner, obsessed with the notion of repaying the debt. To make matters worse, the pince-nez episode had been preceded by another dramatic incident. In June 1907 he had heard the captain telling a story about an oriental torture in which a prisoner, forced to undress and kneel down, had a chamberpot with a rat in it strapped to his buttocks. The rat, which had been starved beforehand, was prodded with a red-hot iron rod (introduced through a special hole in the pot), and in its efforts to escape being burned entered the victim's rectum and inflicted horrible wounds on him with its teeth. After half an hour the rat died of asphyxiation, just as the victim himself expired.

This was the man, obsessed by the rat torture, who came into Freud's consulting room on October 1, 1907. He, together with "Dora," the "Wolf Man," "Little Hans" and President Schreber was to be one of the five most famous cases dealt with by Freud.

Lacan, applying the grid of complex structures to the case, claimed to show how the impossibility of contracting unions analogous to previous marriages was handed down from one generation to another in the form of a negative specification. And there is indeed a repetition of the *same signifying structure* in the lives of the father and son. But the elements of that structure are organized differently in the two cases. The father marries a rich woman; the son marries a poor one. The father does not manage to repay his debt; the son does. And in the process of repetition with several differences, the transition from one generation is brought about at the cost of a neurosis. What Lacan calls the *individual myth of the neurotic* is thus none other than a complex structure by which each individual is affected according to a primal pattern whose different elements go through various combinations and permutations from generation to generation, as in a diagram depicting a family tree.

The story is that of modern man, man in our modern civilization, marked by the ineluctable decline of the ideals of the paternalistic family. We see here how Lacan was reading Freud in the fifties. He began by interpreting Freud's theories in the light of a grid derived from Lévi-Strauss and then added hypotheses of his own that were found in neither Freud nor Lévi-Strauss. In this way Lacan, starting from complex structures, invented a quaternary structure made up of notions worked out before the war but now revived in terms of new categories.

Freud had realized there was an unconscious process by which nonanalogous elements were repeated, handed down from one generation to another through identification, and he had located this process within the oedipal organization of the family. But, when attempting to give his oedi-pal system a universal dimension, he had failed to solve the problem of the relation between this universal and the multiplicity of cultures. Hence the invention of the beautiful myth in *Totem and Taboo*, which instead of explaining the process simply illustrated the way in which every human society—and Freud himself—tries to recount its own history through a col-lective imagination.

Back in 1938, in the light of Maurras and Comte, Lacan was already explicitly criticizing the oedipal emphasis in Freudian theory. He showed that it had arisen out of a crisis in Western society stemming from a new bipolarization of the categories of masculine and feminine. Fifteen years later, after having abandoned the idea of a "family melting pot" and gone through that of "small groups," he was exploding the whole system of the Oedipus complex. Lévi-Strauss had succeeded in reducing the organization of kinship to a single principle from which he derived the infinite variety of particularisms. He thus avoided getting lost, like the culturalists, in a mass of different explanations. Lacan, acting on this reversal of perspective, gave the name of *symbolic function* to the single unconscious principle around which it was possible to organize the multiplicity of situations particular to every subject. And it will surprise no one to learn that he turned this struc-ture into a myth, and this subject into a neurotic. What he wanted to do was promote a rational and scientific interpretation of Freud's teaching and to emphasize its subversiveness.

According to Lacan, psychoanalysis can never be an agent in the adapta-tion of man to society. Having sprung from a crisis in Western society, of dis-order in the world, it is doomed to live in the world and to see disorder in the world as a disorder of consciousness. And that is why, when Lacan was enunciating the principle that every subject is determined by his belonging to a symbolic "order," he also put forward another theory, according to which the subject's recognition of this belonging is the source of an origi-nal rift and an inevitable neurosis.

This introduction of a new structural system was paralleled by the estab-lishment of a new topography consisting of three terms or orders—the *sym-bolic*, the *imaginary*, and the *real*. Lacan had borrowed the first two from Wallon. But in 1953, grouped for the first time with the *real*, they took on a different value. Lacan included in the category of the *symbolic* all the revisions he had derived from the system of Lévi-Strauss; the Freudian unconscious was reinterpreted as the site of a mediation comparable to that operated by the signifier in the realm of language. The category of the *imag-inary* included all the phenomena connected with the construction of the ego: annexation (captation), anticipation, illusion. The *order of the real* con-sisted of what Freud had called *psychical reality*: unconscious desire and its related fantasies. According to Freud this reality presents a coherence comparable with material reality and indeed takes on the value of a reality as substantial as external reality, to such a degree as to act as a substitute for it.

Lacan's conception of the *real* included not only Freud's definition of psychical reality but also an idea of morbidity, of *reste* (vestige), of *part maudite* (doomed or accursed part), borrowed without attribution from the heterological science of Bataille. From this arises a tremendous change in meaning. Where Freud saw a subjective reality based on fantasy, Lacan thought of a desiring reality excluded from all symbolization and inaccessible to all subjective thought: a black shadow or ghost beyond the reach of reason.

It was in his "Rome Discourse" that Lacan incorporated a theory on treatment into his structural system. Unlike the two previous stages in the "sublation" process, which were ordinary lectures, the discourse was a carefully composed text written in a splendid baroque style. Using the two terms from the sophism about the prisoners—the time for comprehending and the moment of concluding—Lacan indirectly justified the idea of variable-length, or "punctuated," sessions. In a treatment, he said in essence, the analyst is in the position of the prison warden. Like the Sphinx addressing Oedipus, he promises his patient freedom in return for solving a riddle: the riddle of the human condition. But the prison warden is hoist with his own petard: having promised freedom to only one prisoner, he must grant it to the other two as well. In other words, the analyst is indeed the master of the truth toward which the subject's discourse progresses, but his mastery has two limits. On the one hand he can never foresee how long any subject will take to understand, and on the other he himself is the prisoner of a symbolic order. If a man speaks because symbols have made him a man, the analyst is only a "supposed master," acting as an amanuensis. He is a *practitioner of the symbolic function*; later on Lacan would call him a *subject supposed to know*. Whatever the case, the analyst deciphers what his patient says as a commentator glosses an original text.

This is where haste comes in. In order to lead the analysand along the path of truth without allowing the idea of a fixed duration to provide him with an escape route, the analyst must do something to forestall this. In doing so he is acting like one of the prisoners in the sophism, enabling another prisoner to arrive at his own decision on the basis of what he supposes his neighbor's decision to be.

Lacan was here giving a veiled reply to the accusations of his adversaries: it is better to conclude "too soon" than to leave the patient to conclude "too late" and get bogged down in empty words. The object of *punctuation*—of ordering the patient's discourse as a scribe orders an original text—is to get the subject to produce genuine and valid speech by reducing the time for comprehending to the moment of concluding: "I would not have so much to say about it," said Lacan, "if I had not been convinced that, in experimenting with what have been called my short sessions, at a stage in my experience that is now concluded, I was able to bring to light in a certain male subject fantasies of anal pregnancy as well as the dream of its resolution by Caesarean section, in a [time frame] where I would otherwise have had to go on listening to his speculations on the art of Dostoyevsky."[37]

Observe that Lacan spoke of this technique in the past tense, as if to suggest to his audience that he was justifying it on a theoretical level but had already abandoned it in practice. But it was plain to everyone that whatever he said or seemed to say, he was carrying on as before.

19

A Resounding Tribute to Martin Heidegger

*A*fter 1945 Heidegger's works, extolled in the thirties by French philosophers who had read them in the light of questions previously raised by
Husserl, came to be regarded with suspicion. This was because Heidegger
himself had been a supporter of Nazism, particularly in 1933–1934, during
the period known as the Rectorate. In May 1945, three weeks after French
troops entered Freiburg-im-Brisgau, Heidegger's house was blacklisted for
having possibly had Nazi connections. And in July there began a long investigation that ended in January 1946 with the philosopher being forced to
retire and abstain from teaching.

Karl Jaspers played an important part in this train of events. Heidegger
himself had asked for his former friend's opinion to be taken into account.
And Jaspers, though he would have preferred to remain silent, was obliged
in December 1945 to write a report, in which he pointed out the complexity of Heidegger's stance toward Hitlerism, though he avoided the question of whether there was a relationship between Nazism and Heidegger's
philosophy. As for the accusation of anti-Semitism, he recalled two incidents. In 1931 Heidegger had caused Eduard Baumgarten, a Jewish teacher
who had applied to be his assistant, to be expelled from the university. In his
place he had brought about the appointment of Werner Brock, another
Jewish teacher, whose ideas were acceptable to him. But in 1933 Heidegger
had sent to the society of Nazi professors at Göttingen a copy of a report
containing the following passage:"Baumgarten was anything but a National
Socialist. In terms of family background and intellectual sympathies his
roots lie in the Heidelberg circle of liberal-democratic intellectuals around
Max Weber. Having failed to secure an appointment with me, he established
close contact with the Jew Fraenkel, who used to work at Göttingen
University and has now been dismissed from here."[1] Yet Heidegger protected Werner Brock from the persecution he might have faced. Jaspers con-

cluded that Heidegger was probably not an anti-Semite earlier but became one after 1933. "This does not always rule out the possibility that in some cases . . . anti-Semitism went against his conscience and his inclinations."[2] Then, while recommending that Heidegger be allowed a pension to enable him to pursue and publish his work, Jaspers also suggested he should be suspended from teaching for a few years; the situation should then be reviewed in the context of what he had published meanwhile. Jaspers ended with a perceptive portrait:

Heidegger is a significant figure, not only in terms of the content of his philosophical world-view, but also in his ability to handle the tools of speculative thought. He has a philosophical mind whose insights are undoubtedly intersting, although my own view is that he is uncommonly uncritical and a long way removed from "science" in any true sense. He sometimes comes across as a blend of the earnest nihilist and the mistagogue-cum-sorcerer. In the full flow of his discourse he occasionally succeeds in hitting the nerve of the philosophical enterprise in a most mysterious and marvellous way. In this, as far as I can see, he is perhaps unique among contemporary German philosophers. It is imperative, therefore, that he be allowed to pursue his studies and writings without restrictions.[3]

The debate about Heidegger's relations with Nazism had been opened in France even earlier, by Jean-Paul Sartre. In December 1944 he issued his famous statement: "Heidegger was a philosopher well before he was a nazi. His adherence to Hitlerism is to be explained by fear, perhaps ambition, and certainly conformism. Not pretty to look at, I agree; but enough to invalidate your neat reasoning. 'Heidegger,' you say, 'is a member of the National Socialist Party; thus his philosophy must be nazi.' That is not it: Heidegger has no character; there is the truth of the matter. Are you going to have the nerve to conclude from this that his philosophy is an apology for cowardice? Don't you know that sometimes a man does not come up to the level of his works?"[4]

A year later, on October 28, 1945, Sartre delivered his famous lecture "Existentialism is a kind of humanism," in which he gave a popular version of his philosophy of freedom, based on the theories set forth in *Being and Nothingness* (1943). He then threw open the columns of *Les Temps modernes* to the debate about Heidegger's political commitment. Many articles on this subject were published between 1946 and 1947, including pieces by Maurice de Gandillac, Frédéric de Towarnicki, Karl Löwith, Eric Weil, and Alphonse de Waelhens. In 1946 Koyré also published a long piece on Heidegger's philosophy in *Critique*. Georges Friedmann produced an article on the same subject in 1953.[5]

All these commentators asked the same question: was Heidegger's political stance due to a temporary mistake on the part of someone deceived or self-deceived, or was it the product of a philosophical attitude that, by stressing man's rediscovery of the roots of his inner conflict and his "being-for-death," had ended up finding a satisfactory doctrine of salvation in Nazi nihilism? All the postwar articles on the subject tried to answer this question. Some commentators maintained that Heidegger's support of Nazism was an "accident," something incidental that did not detract from the validity of his work. Others declared that Nazism and Heidegger's political commitment derived from one and the same source.

Friedmann rightly observed that Heidegger had never accepted racist theories based on biology. "Let us note," said he, "that in his teaching he never defended Nazi 'biologism,' and as a result he soon fell from favor. But if we examine the facts impartially we see that, far from proclaiming his resistance to the regime (a resistance that would have had a considerable moral and even political effect), his main concern, until the fall of Hitler, was to pass unnoticed."[6]

In the midst of the argument a young philosopher made a new contribution to the debate. Jean Beaufret, born in 1907 in the department of the Creuse in the Massif Central, liked to reminisce about his childhood spent wearing clogs and to say it had made him grow up as a peasant with simple tastes. He was fond of good cooking and good wine and sympathetic to the kind of French virtues that derive from the land. He was admitted into the Ecole normale supérieure in the rue d'Ulm in 1928, the same year as Simone Weil, Maurice Bardèche, Georges Pelorson, Thierry Maulnier, and Robert Brasillach. But it was in 1930, during a visit to the French Institute in Berlin, that he first came up against traditional German philosophy. Till then he had been a firm Cartesian.

Just before the war, impressed by the early writings of Sartre, Beaufret discovered the works of Husserl. When the fighting began he was called up and soon taken prisoner but managed to escape into the Unoccupied Zone by leaping from the train taking him to Germany. In 1942, by which time he had become a member of the "Pericles" Resistance network, he met Joseph Rovan, a student of German who was also an expert at forging false identity papers and a great admirer of Heidegger's philosophy. The two men became close friends and spent their evenings studying *Being and Time*: "We used to pore together over the mysteries of *Dasein*, ontics, and ontology," wrote Rovan. "My ideas about philosophy were very rudimentary, but I knew more German than Beaufret. So we advanced happily into the mysteries of a philosophy couched in a language whose poetry and rigor still enchant me. We had heard about Heidegger's rectorate and his weaknesses. The imperfections of the man irritated us, but his work held us spellbound."[7]

At the Liberation, Beaufret, increasingly impressed by a philosophy that threw so much light on individual destiny confronted with the violence of the world, wondered what had become of the author of *Being and Time*. On learning that Heidegger was still alive, Beaufret sent him a letter by an intermediary and was delighted to receive in reply one of the philosopher's books and an answer written in his own hand. This was the beginning of a real dialogue. The two men actually met in September 1946, when Beaufret went to the chalet in Todtnauberg in the Black Forest where Heidegger used to go for his vacations and to think. He had just come out of the Schloss Haus Baden, the sanatorium where he had been undergoing treatment for the psychosomatic disorders that followed his expulsion from the university.

Heidegger's attitude toward the postwar purges was that of a victim. He admitted having wrongly believed in Hitler's historic mission and in National Socialism as a possible agent of spiritual revolution, but he tried to play down his former political attitude on the grounds that he had gone into a kind of inner exile: this absolved him from having to explain the darker aspects of his support of the Nazis. At the most he privately admitted that he had been "very foolish." But he refused—as he continued to do all his life—to make the slightest reference to genocide. He expressed no remorse, no regret, no self-criticism. Instead of admitting his error, he seemed to blame it on a historical movement that had failed to live up to the metaphysical truth he had thought it contained.[8] Moreover, true to the ultraconservatism of his prewar attitude, he still showed much more hostility toward Western democracy and communism than toward Nazism. In the early fifties he was still speaking of Germany as "a metaphysical nation" caught "as in a vice between Russia and America."

This was the man whom Jean Beaufret was to hero-worship for thirty years.

When the French philosopher, with his well-attested past as a member of the Resistance, arrived on Heidegger's doorstep, the German soon saw how useful Beaufret's genuine friendship might be at a time when his own work was discredited in his native land and the subject of critical debate in France. The affection of his new disciple allowed Heidegger not merely to minimize his past political involvement but even to pretend it had never occurred. And it wasn't long before Beaufret, impressed by the master's genuine philosophical power, came to accept his version of the facts. He ended up both believing and saying that Heidegger had never sympathized with the Nazis.

But at the same time, through his dialogues with Heidegger, Beaufret introduced into France a new interpretation of the German philosopher's work.[9] In the context of Sartre's thinking, Heidegger's philosophy had been read as a kind of existential anthropology. Hence the idea that existence precedes essence and that human freedom derives from a humanism based on the humanization of *le néant* (nothingness, the void): man is king in the midst of *l'étant* (what is) and in a lonely and empty freedom.

But in 1946 Heidegger himself refuted the existentialist interpretation of his work that had been largely accepted since the war. Beaufret had asked him to intervene in the debate that was going on in France and to comment on Sartre's attitude to humanism. Heidegger was glad to enter the fray, and in his *Letter on Humanism*, which was to influence a whole new generation, he challenged the use of the word.[10] He maintained that humanism, in Sartre's sense of the term, was a new metaphysics that merely radicalized the power of reason over man. Like all metaphysics, it was based on a "forgetting of being." Heidegger proposed to save being from oblivion by making it preeminent. To bring this about and to save man from the alienation imposed on him by the forgetting of being, he advocated a wholesale return to origins. If all history is merely the history of the forgetting of being, the only way to get close to being, which nevertheless is "always veiled," is to attempt an "unveiling." Heidegger said it was necessary to go back beyond Socrates and Plato, beyond "Western reason," to the dazzling beginnings of Greek thought: in other words to the true word of the pre-Socratic philosophers, Parmenides and Heraclitus. Thus Heidegger tried to strengthen and lend substance to modern man, mired in an existence conditioned by technology and in an ideal of progress that made him believe he acted freely.

It is obvious how this new reading of Heidegger's thought allowed him to exonerate himself from his Nazi past and permitted Beaufret to take up the cudgels against the interpretations of the existentialists and the phenomenologists who followed Husserl.

The denazification process slackened off in Germany at the beginning of 1949, just before the founding of the Federal Republic. Now was the time for Heidegger to take advantage of the popularity of his philosophy in France to ask to be readmitted to the university. His supporters said how important it was to reinstate a philosopher in whose works the whole world was interested. His enemies expressed doubts about the intellectual stature of a man who was accused of being a charlatan and whose ideas were thought to threaten democracy.

In the spring of 1950, while the department of philosophy in the University of Freiburg was deliberating on his fate, Heidegger gave some outstandingly good lectures, first on Nietzsche's *Zarathustra* and then on the principle of reason. The lectures were a great success, and the following summer Heidegger made a real breakthrough at a meeting held in Munich on the subject of "The Thing." In the winter semester of 1950–1951 he was authorized to teach again, and he began to feel he had been rehabilitated. By the autumn of 1952 he thought "the ring of mistrust and hatred surrounding the master—and friend—had finally been broken." When he gave a lecture, students crowded around to listen and applaud. The past could be forgotten. In Germany, criticism gradually faded, though it didn't entirely disappear. In France, Jean Beaufret, now the official spokesperson for Heidegger's philosophy, did his best to ensure that no further attacks were made on his beloved master.[11]

It was in April 1951, just after Heidegger had been readmitted to the university, that Jean Beaufret entered into analysis with Jacques Lacan.

At that time it was unusual for a psychoanalyst to look on homosexuality as merely one among many admissible forms of sexuality. In Freudian circles homosexuality was regarded not merely as a perversion but even as a kind of social deviance. So even when a psychoanalyst agreed to treat a homosexual, his attitude was likely to be negative. A homosexual who said he wanted to become a psychoanalyst himself was either refused altogether or taken on but guided back toward the straight and narrow path of heterosexuality. But Lacan refused to conform: he accepted homosexuals as ordinary patients and didn't try to make them "normal." That was why so many of them came to him to be analyzed.

When Jean Beaufret presented himself at the rue de Lille he was in a very disturbed state. His male lover, who was also being treated by Lacan, had just left him. Beaufret had met the man a year ago at a dinner party where Lacan and Sylvia were among those present. There had been a brief liaison that had ended when the other man, in the course of his analysis with Lacan, noticed that Lacan was showing rather too much interest in Beaufret. Beaufret's lover subsequently abandoned his analyst as well as his boyfriend.[12] Thus Beaufret began his treatment in the midst of a strange transferential imbroglio. Beaufret went to Lacan because Lacan was his lover's analyst, and Lacan was especially interested in Beaufret because of Beaufret's special relationship with Heidegger.

Beaufret soon noticed Lacan's interest in Heidegger's work. He also realized it would be easy to use Lacan's desire to meet Heidegger to advance the German philosopher's interests. And he skillfully employed the transferential relationship as a trap, into which Lacan allowed himself to be lured. Not only did Beaufret keep talking about Heidegger throughout his treatment, but one day, exasperated by Lacan's frequent silences, he made a direct appeal to his narcissism by remarking, "Heidegger spoke to me about you." Lacan started. "What did he say?" he asked.[13]

The analysis ended in May 1953, and the least one can say is that it didn't cure Beaufret's blindness to Heidegger's political past. On the contrary, Beaufret seems to have emerged believing even more firmly in the innocence of his idol. As for Lacan, he managed to make good use of the "trap" his patient had set for him.

Still pursuing his recasting of Freud in the light of Lévi-Strauss, he adopted a different approach to Heidegger's writings from that he had favored before the war. To all intents and purposes he accepted Beaufret's interpretation while rejecting Sartre's philosophy of freedom. The clearest evidence of Beaufret's influence is to be seen in the "Rome Discourse," written two months after the end of the analysis.[14] Lacan, fascinated by Heidegger's style, recognized again the talent for commentary that had once so impressed him in Kojève, and borrowed from the German philosopher the notion of the "quest for truth," which seemed to him compatible with Freud's "unveiling of desire." Both theories involved a "being-there" of truth, forever being forgotten and repressed, which made it possible for desire to "reveal" itself. But above all, Lacan's new encounter with Heidegger led him back to the great tradition of German philosophy that his Anglophilia had caused him to neglect somewhat. He thus moved from a great admiration for English democracy and the theory of small groups to a diametrically opposed system of thought. Still, while rediscovering in the antidemocratic, antiprogressive, and antihumanist Heidegger of the fifties the ultra-Nietzschean vision of the world into which Bataille had initiated him before the war, Lacan never relinquished his scientific and rational ideals. Hence the astonishing mixture of darkness and light in the "Rome Discourse," just as in the 1938 essay on the family.

On the one hand Lacan's reworking of Freudian thought in the context provided by Lévi-Strauss helped him give new life to a universalist psychoanalysis based on the philosophy of the Enlightenment; on the other hand a doubt was introduced into the resulting edifice by the influence of Heidegger, who saw human existence as a bottomless pit where truth is expressed amid error, deceit, and ambiguity.

On Easter 1955 Lacan went to Freiburg with Beaufret. There, as if by chance, the conversation among the three men turned on the question of transference. "Heidegger," writes Beaufret,

seemed rather preoccupied about the question of transference as an affective relationship on the part of the patient toward the analyst, and through me he questioned Lacan about it. The following dialogue ensued:

Heidegger: "But what about transference?"

Lacan: "It's not what it's usually said to be. It begins as soon as a patient decides to go to a psychoanalyst."

I translated this into German for Heidegger's benefit. "Transference is not an episode occurring within psychoanalysis but the a priori condition of it, in the same sense as the a priori conditions of experience in Kant's philosophy."

"*Ach so!*" said Heidegger.[15]

In the course of the conversation, Lacan asked Heidegger for permission to translate an article of his called "Logos" and to publish the French version in the first issue of *La Psychanalyse* (Psychoanalysis), a journal that was supposed to express the ideas of the SFP. The number for which Lacan was responsible dealt with speech and language. Several eminent contributors had already been lined up, including Emile Benveniste, Jean Hyppolite, and Clémence Ramnoux. Lacan included his own "Rome Discourse" and his dialogue with Hyppolite. Heidegger gladly gave his permission, and Lacan set to work.[16]

Three months after the meeting in Freiburg a conference on the works of Heidegger was held in Cerisy-la-Salle, from August 27 to September 4. Among the fifty-four people present were the young Gilles Deleuze, Jean Starobinski, Gabriel Marcel, Paul Ricoeur, Kostas Axelos, and Maurice de Gandillac. Sartre and Merleau-Ponty demonstrated their hostility by staying away. Alexandre Koyré refused to meet Heidegger in any circumstances. In the middle of the conference, Lucien Goldmann read out extracts from texts Heidegger had written during the Rectorate, much to the disapproval of the other participants, who accused him of breaking the consensus.[17]

Lacan had not signed on for the conference at Cerisy, but he invited Martin Heidegger, his wife, Elfriede, Jean Beaufret, and Kostas Axelos to stay with him for a few days at La Prévôté. Sylvia, though shocked by Elfriede's anti-Semitism, went to great trouble to serve the Heideggers a German-style breakfast, including sausage, every morning. To her surprise, Heidegger didn't touch the sausage. But Lacan himself wasn't bothered about his guest's tastes in either food or politics; what he wanted was to talk to him. As he himself didn't speak German and Heidegger didn't speak French, Lacan asked Kostas Axelos to act as interpreter. Conversation could then flow freely. Later, leaving Axelos and Beaufret behind at Guitrancourt to work on a translation of "Was ist die Philosophie?", Lacan took Heidegger, Sylvia, and Elfriede on a lightning visit to Chartres Cathedral, driving his car at the same breakneck speed as he conducted his sessions. Heidegger, sitting beside the driver, didn't blanch, but his wife kept up a stream of protest in the back. Sylvia called Lacan's attention to this, but to no avail. On the way back, Heidegger was as silent as before, despite Elfriede's renewed complaints. Lacan only drove the faster.[18]

After the trip to Chartres, Lacan started on the "Logos" translation. Its title was the most important signifier in the history of Western philosophy, and its content formed part of a text called "Moira, Alethea, Logos," three commentaries on fragments from Heraclitus and Parmenides. In this work, Heidegger sought to show that pre-Socratic truth—i.e., the true or mythical origin of the being-there of man—had been obscured by two thousand years of philosophy. Heidegger also maintained that the German language, being superior to all others, was the only one capable of rediscovering the original truth of the Greek tongue and thus providing the human race with a doctrine of salvation through which it could transform the world.

It was in the second version of "Logos," published in 1954, that Heidegger clearly expressed this doctrine, in an additional paragraph that hadn't appeared in the 1951 version. In other words, far from disowning his previous speculations about the superiority of the German people, he was transposing them into this "commentary on a commentary," in which he maintained that only a belief in the superiority of the German language could cure the degradation of Western civilization and save both philosophy and humanity.[19]

Fragment 50 of Heraclitus, one of those chosen by Heidegger, said literally: "The secret is really to listen not to me but to reason, so as to be able to say together everything in one." That is, the individual must allow language to produce its effect, by listening properly, without limiting himself merely to the intention of the speaker. From this it may be concluded that discourse must invoke an authority that overrides it. As Jean Bollack points out, Heraclitus' logos does not refer to any "ontological positivity": "In no way does it denote any identity between related contraries or their 'combination' in some original totality." So the Heraclitean "one" is not a unique "one" in the sense of that which unites; on the contrary, it is "one" in the sense of that which separates or distinguishes itself.

On the basis of this fragment, Heidegger invented a Heraclitus made to measure to his own taste. By bracketing him with Parmenides he made him into a representative of an ontology in which the referent was no longer the structure of language but instead the being-there of an original presence. With this ontologization of Heraclitus' thought went a blurring of division in favor of a unitary conception of being. Moreover, by playing on the aural similarity between the Greek words *logos* and *legein* and the German verbs *legen* and *lesen*, he linked "reading," "lying," "meditating," "placing," and "meditation" so as to show that the logos is "stretching out" and "repose" and also "the harvesting of being and thought from the nonhidden"; this process was to be understood as corresponding to unveiling. Thus Heidegger's Heraclitus heralded the true word of being, to be harvested by the individual in meditation and the embracing of excess.

Two things seem to have persuaded Lacan to translate Heidegger's commentary on Fragment 50: on the one hand Heraclitus' own conception of language and on the other the fascination of Heidegger's style. Heraclitus is a master who claims to speak on no other master's authority: there's no point in having listened to anyone else's teaching if that teaching hasn't enabled one to arrive at any meaning. But Heraclitus is also the philosopher who speaks of a logos (or language) that forces the subject to efface himself before a truth that he expresses but which is beyond him. *Let the logos or the signifier act*: such is Heraclitus' message as reproduced by Lacan in his "Rome Discourse." What is being discussed is a spoken word that speaks in man's stead and to which we must listen in order to reconstruct its meaning. And, needless to say, Lacan puts himself forward too as a master without a master, one who has broken with all academic establishments and is the only person capable of listening to the true word of Freud.

Lacan was adopting a Heraclitean notion of language, but he never alluded directly to Heraclitus' own text. Instead, he referred the reader to the German translations used by Heidegger and translated them himself into French. So in fact he was "using" Heidegger's text to introduce his own preoccupations. This involved two kinds of nuance. On the one hand he followed Heidegger as far as obscurantism and primitivism were concerned, sometimes even out-Heroding Herod, as, for example, when he translated "lesson" as "reading." Sometimes, on the other hand, instead of indulging in etymological variations, he chose to prune the German text of its "Black Forest" populist bad taste. "In short," says Jean Bollack, "Lacan's translating method is very free and high-handed. He wrenches the text in the direction of science, art, and language and accords more importance to hearing than to speech. He adds a touch of Mallarmé."[20]

For example, where Heidegger played on the fact that the verbs *legen* (German) and *legein* (Greek) sounded alike, Lacan played on the similarity, in French, of the words *léguer* (to bequeath), *legs* (legacy), and *lais* (poetic lays). This Mallarméan transposition was clearly one way of nullifying Heidegger's claim that the German language was philosophically superior. He also denegativized the text: wherever Heidegger used the term *Unverbogenheit* (nonobscurity, unconcealment) to denote that which perceives being in Heraclitus, Lacan translated it as *dévoilement* (unveiling), giving more importance to the act of exposure itself than to the idea of a quest carried out via "*nonoccultation*" (de- or uneclipsing).[21]

But above all he committed sacrilege. Instead of translating the 1954 version—which he knew perfectly well, because he quoted it several times in his notes—he used the 1951 text. In other words, without offering any explanation, he took the liberty of removing the last section of Heidegger's final text: i.e., the famous "commentary on the commentary," in which the philosopher enunciated his view that a return to the West's great beginnings could save modern man from the domination of science and technology.[22]

It was probably by mistake that Lacan translated the 1951 instead of the 1954 version. But given that, in the actual work of translating, he keeps referring to the second version in order to correct the first, we are obliged to interpret the "amputation" of the coda literally. It seems to show that Lacan preferred Heidegger the commentator on Heraclitus to Heidegger the preacher of salvation and German superiority. In other words, he gave prominence to the side of Heidegger's work that dealt with his conception of language, retaining, as far as style was concerned, only his technique as a commentator and stressing, as a method for discovering the truth about desire, not ontology but structure, an unveiling rather than a quest via *nonoccultation*. It is easy to see why Beaufret and the dogmatic supporters of Heidegger remained silent about this translation: it went against their own work of turning Heidegger's language into a kind of etymological code. And so thoroughly was Lacan's version ostracized that it wasn't mentioned either in André Préau's later version or in commentaries on the logos by Heidegger's French disciples.

This insidious murder-by-translation of a text indicates the general tenor of Lacan's activities in the ten years after the war. Between 1951 and 1956, he did produce an anti-Sartrean interpretation of Heidegger, largely inspired by his own transferential relationship with Beaufret. But as early as the "Rome Discourse" and despite many ambiguities, he was departing from the main themes of Heidegger's philosophy, in particular from any apocalyptic vision of science and any ontology of quest, origin, or presence. Later, in his commentary on Plato's *Symposium*, he was to move even further away from Heidegger's idea that the evolution of the modern world had obscured the origin of being.[23]

If Lacan was able to use Heidegger's work in this way, that was because in postwar France it lent itself to such a process. Sartre was right when he said: "If we encounter our own thought in someone else's, what does it matter what Heidegger himself is like?" Very true. Heidegger's thought exercised an almost hypnotic fascination on a whole generation because it wasn't a system, because it placed itself from the outset in a complex situation "between two languages," in a confusion of truth and untruth, an inextricable tangle of existence and appearance, running the twofold risk of being impossible to transmit (because of its manifold variations) and impossible to translate (because everyone could find in it the echo of his or her own words). It was because of this paradoxical position that Heidegger's philosophy played such a crucial initiatory and pedagogical role in French thought in the second half of the twentieth century. And Lacan, together with Sartre and later with Foucault and Derrida, was one of those who made Heidegger's writing readable. Unlike Beaufret and the German philosopher's most dogmatic followers, they rejected close fidelity to Heidegger's text in order to bring out more clearly the essence of his teaching, which concerned the ability to find in the other that which is in oneself.

Thus Lacan, like a whole generation of his contemporaries, made a detour through Heidegger in order to discover, and to help, himself. This is borne out by the introduction to the first issue of *La Psychanalyse*, which contained the "authorized" translation of "Logos." "As for the presence here of M. Heidegger," he wrote, "for those who know where the most lofty meditation in the world is to be found, it is enough in itself to guarantee that at least there is one way of reading Freud that does not exhibit so cheap a philosophy as is rehearsed by a certain official supporter of phenomenology."[24] But this resounding tribute to "M. Heidegger" was more like a ruse. Not content with censoring the text of someone whose "lofty meditation" he was eulogizing, Lacan also used his name against that of Sartre: the "official supporter." He did so in order to boost his own strategy for taking over the French psychoanalytic movement, a strategy based on a nonphenomenological interpretation of Freud's work.

But while there were frequent references in the "Rome Discourse" to Heidegger's problematic of unveiling truth and "letting the word act," it had disappeared four years later when Lacan gave a lecture at the Sorbonne called "The Agency of the Letter in the Unconscious or Reason since Freud."[25] Here he put forward a theory of the signifier no longer based on interpretations of Saussure or Lévi-Strauss but deduced logically from Roman Jakobson's work on metaphor and metonymy. In this system, in which the unconscious was formalized on the model of linguistic structure and a claim was made for Freud to be admitted into the realm of science, Lacan abandoned ontology altogether. In other words, the way he made use of Heidegger's work varied in accordance with his two successive interpretations of structural linguistics. In the first, reflected in the "Rome Discourse," when he hadn't yet worked out his theory of the signifier, he retained Heidegger's thought on origin and unveiling. But in the second, in "The Agency of the Letter," he differentiated himself from it by a determined effort to locate Freud's discoveries within the field of science, thanks to a reference to reason and to the Cartesian cogito.

And it was just when he was departing the furthest from Heidegger's work that he paid emphatic tribute to the man himself. "When I speak of Heidegger," he wrote in 1957, "or rather when I translate him, I do my best to let his own words retain their supreme significance."[26] A curious way of mixing truth and untruth in order to dismiss the person by whom you claim to be inspired! Heidegger is allowed to retain the "supreme significance" of his words, but this is something far removed from the science of the signifier to which Lacan himself aspires. As for the business of translating "Logos," that operation served to illustrate Lacan's teaching rather than to convey Heidegger's text.

But the fact that Lacan wasn't a real disciple of Heidegger didn't prevent him from wanting passionately to be recognized by him, though Heidegger didn't understand Lacan's work at all.[27] As a result, while each in his own way was pondering the question of speech and language, a weird relationship grew up between the two men, based on silences, misunderstandings, and cross-purposes, Lacan was silent about the incomplete translation of "Logos"; Heidegger was silent about the censorship involved therein; there were confusions, at Beaufret's expense, about transference; silence or absence of speech reigned in the unsuccessful dialogue at Guitrancourt and on the way to and from Chartres; there was more silence, on the part of other translators of Heidegger, about Lacan's version of "Logos"; there was silence on the part of Lacan about Heidegger's Nazi past. And two other important phases of this erratic relationship produced silences of their own.

In 1959, at a dinner at which Lacan and his daughter Judith were present—together with Maurice de Gandillac, Jean Beaufret, and Dina Dreyfus, Lévi-Strauss's second wife—a lively argument arose about Heidegger's past. Dina Dreyfus refused even to recognize his philosophy, while Beaufret argued that it had nothing to do with Nazism. Lacan said nothing, merely stroking Judith's hair and trying to change the subject. Yet in 1958, when *Les Temps modernes* had published an article by Jean Wahl in which Lacan thought he was being attacked, he hadn't hesitated to write to Wahl explaining as clearly as he could that he had always been on the side of the victims during the "Nazi ordeal" and that he wouldn't for a moment let it be doubted because of any "grudges against Heidegger."[28]

Seven years later Lacan sent Heidegger an inscribed copy of his *Ecrits*. In a letter to the psychiatrist Medard Boss, Heidegger wrote: "You too have no doubt received Lacan's large tome (*Ecrits*). Personally, I haven't so far been able to get anything at all out of this obviously outlandish text. I'm told that in Paris the book is creating as much of a stir as Sartre's *L'Etre et le néant* once did." A few months later he added: "I enclose a letter from Lacan. It seems to me the psychiatrist needs a psychiatrist."[29] So that was what Heidegger thought about Lacan. . . .

Finally, hearing that Heidegger was ill, Lacan, accompanied by Catherine Millot, went to Freiburg and told the German philosopher about his theory of knots. Lacan held forth at length; Heidegger was silent.[30]

20
· · · · · · ·

Intersecting Fates: Jacques Lacan and Françoise Dolto

*A*fter Lacan, Françoise Dolto was the second most important figure in the history of Freudian psychoanalysis in France, and the recent publication of her correspondence with her close relatives makes it possible to paint a more accurate picture of her life than I was able to provide in my *Histoire de la psychanalyse en France.*[1] Françoise Marette was born in November 1908 into a family of soldiers and polytechnicians of the conservative Right, very religious people who shared the ideas of Charles Maurras. So she was raised in accordance with the educational principles of the great Parisian middle class who got their ideas from a daily perusal of *L'Action française.* From earliest childhood Françoise Marette was given works of piety to read and taught a lot of foolish nonsense about sex. For a long time she believed babies came in boxes sent down to earth by the Sacred Heart of Jesus, that physical love was repulsive, and that women were doomed to pass from virginity to motherhood without ever tasting intellectual or any other kind of freedom.

A letter from a maternal great-uncle, an officer in the colonial army in Tonkin, shows the kind of education that was thought suitable for little girls of her social class in 1921: "I'm glad you are enjoying yourself and doing a lot of cycling. But while I agree it's a good thing that women should go in for sport, I disagree with the present fashion of their doing so with the sole object of becoming cross-country champions. I fear that in the process they may neglect more important matters and fail to cultivate the moral and intellectual qualities that should be their true prerogative and impart the virtues proper to a model wife and mother."[2]

In September 1922 her mother, Suzanne Marette, née Demmier, expressed exactly the same views, chiding Françoise severely after learning that she had had a "conversation" about "sexual matters" with a male cousin. "Such things only arouse unwholesome curiosity and should be acknowledged in the confessional. . . . It is neither nice nor proper, and I want my daughter to be clean and proper, a real young lady who can be proud of her unblemished soul, and even jealous of it in the sense that she will allow no one to sully it. When I was in the convent and my schoolmates came to me with that kind of question, I used to box their ears and tell them they were disgusting, etc."[3]

Such were the maxims that governed a childhood further overshadowed by the horror of the Verdun trenches. And although young Françoise was mischievous and lively, her native rebelliousness did not, even in adolescence, take the form of open revolt. In any case, relations within the family, among parents, children, servants, and governesses, were so warm that no one would ever have suspected they reflected anything but perfect Christian love. In reality, though, the show of affection and charity concealed all kinds of hatred. Germanophobia, racism, and anti-Semitism were the earliest spiritual nourishment of one who was to become the founder of child psychoanalysis in France.[4]

The simultaneous existence of these two contradictory realities—charitable appearances on the one hand and various kinds of hatred on the other—meant that in the Demmler-Marette family the conscious quest for an ideal supreme good concealed a pathological organization of their emotional relationships. And it was in the confusion between those two realities, between explicit standards and unconscious pathology, between repressed hatred and professions of love, and all against a background of militant patriotism, that the young Françoise's personality was formed. Between 1908 and 1920, as her letters and autobiography show, two men and three women were the main actors in a great neurotic drama that nearly set her on the path to profound melancholia.[5]

First there was the father, Henry Marette, an artillery captain who specialized in the making of shells and explosives. Then there was the maternal uncle, Pierre Demmler, captain in the Sixty-second Batallion of the *chasseurs alpins*, or mountain infantry, who was fatally wounded in the Vosges on July 6, 1916. The main female characters involved included Suzanne, Françoise's mother, nurse and housewife; "Mademoiselle," the governess, kind but narrow-minded; and Jacqueline, Françoise's elder sister, the mother's favorite and the object of Françoise's jealousy. Jacqueline was good-looking and intelligent; she possessed every virtue and was always being held up as an example. She died on September 30, 1920, suddenly struck down by bone cancer.

From the beginning of the war, when she was scarcely seven years old, Françoise saw herself as her uncle Pierre's fiancée, and they exchanged letters as if they were really sweethearts. Instead of keeping his distance, Pierre, egged on by Henry and Suzanne, encouraged Françoise and even promised to marry her when the war was over. Whereupon she began to follow the fighting, urging her father on with his work: "You must work harder at making shells," she wrote in September 1915, "to kill the lousy krauts who hurt the poor French, who suffer because of the wicked krauts, who are cruel and kill babies only one or two years old."[6]

At St. Clothilde's, the school she started to attend that same year, anti-German propaganda was at its height: for homework, the pupils were asked to write an essay entitled "A Bayonet Charge." Françoise reveled in it: "You kill three or more soldiers, you stick the bayonet into a kraut's body, you pull it out in disgust, but you're pleased too and stick it in again."[7] As well as being encouraged to express open hatred of the Germans, Françoise was more subtly influenced toward racism in general. The family always spoke of the Germans as France's hereditary enemy, guilty of the most extreme barbarity. The position of Negroes was rather more ambiguous. On the one hand a black man might be seen as a well-behaved colonial soldier—a Senegalese infantryman, for example—neatly got up in his legendary uniform and happy to act as cannon fodder in France's crusade against the Teutonic foe. But at the same time he had something diabolical about him, a kind of primitive, animal sexuality that was a danger to civilized human beings. All this gave rise to a state of confused apprehension, in which poor Françoise found herself involved at the same time as she tried to wage her war against the Hun.

Uncle Pierre, on hearing that his "little fiancée" had been kissed by a Senegalese infantryman—he was a casualty being nursed by Suzanne, and Françoise reminded him of his own young daughter—treated his niece to a jealous scene. He told her to keep away from seductive black men: "Of course they are very good-looking, but not as good-looking as the *chasseurs alpins*." Mademoiselle, for her part, scolded Françoise and made haste to give the contaminated cheek a thorough wash. Henry Marette, to comfort his daughter, who was being made to think a kiss from a black man was some kind of sexual and bacterial contagion, sent her a postcard depicting four handsome black children in the style of the famous Banania cocoa advertisement: "Here are some nice little friends for you," he wrote. Françoise was filled with terror and guilt. When she passed a "Negro family" in the street she wouldn't even glance at them, much as she longed to. She was so scared of looking at what she really wanted to see that her mother tried to calm her down by sending her a picture of a Negro dressed as a Senegalese infantryman. "Are you frightened?" she wrote on it.[8]

So Françoise, caught up in a discourse where hatred was expressed in words that seemed to be those of love, played a half-deliberately, half-involuntarily submissive part in a lethal comedy forced on her by the adult world. When her uncle died she acted as if she really was a war widow, and throughout her adolescence she was unable to get over the loss of that first

love. How could she have, in a family where after the armistice the commemoration of war heroes, far from lessening the anti-German hatred rife
in the days of the trenches, simply changed it into a new thirst for revenge?
Pierre Marette, Françoise's elder brother, was a fierce embodiment of this
spirit. A product of the military academy at St. Cyr, an ultranationalist and
antirepublican, he took over the role of the dead uncle whose name he bore
and whom he dreamed of avenging in another war. His hatred of the
Germans was accompanied by a fervent anti-Semitism that intensified at the
same rate as his activities in the *Action française*. He had a classical career as
an officer in the colonial army, dividing his time among garrison life, leave,
and the "pacification" of the natives.

The death of Jacqueline, the elder sister, helped to prolong Françoise's
feelings of bereavement, sorrow, and guilt. Suzanne Marette, their mother,
never recovered from Jacqueline's death, despite the birth of her last child, a
son, in September 1922: brain fever, accompanied by attacks of delirium, was
followed by depression, which revealed a chronic melancholia hitherto concealed by the round of domestic tasks and marital duties. After such an
upbringing, spent in the company of a mother who, though loving and
devoted, was nonetheless an unresisting victim of the ideals of her class,
Françoise entered her twentieth year in a state of severe neurosis. Obsessed
by being slightly overweight, haunted by a much disliked self-image, she was
incapable of dealing with any kind of sexual life, of taking up any real profession, or of constructing an identity for herself. "I am twenty years old, and
I look twelve," she wrote. "I'm afraid I may be unable to struggle any more
. . . and if that should happen I'd rather die there and then."[9]

For exceptional women of that generation longing to cast off the family
straitjacket that still forced an outdated model of femininity on them even
in the early 1930s, there were several ways of escape. They might become
active in politics or go in for feminism or religion; or they could rebel indi-
vidually and gain independence by acquiring a profession. Françoise
Marette chose the last of these alternatives when, several years after her
younger brother Philippe, she began to study medicine. Her object was to
cure herself of her education and avoid becoming merely a wife and
mother, repeating the mistakes of her parents. She wanted to be a "doctor
in education," and this brought her into contact with the pioneering stage
of French Freudianism in the person of René Laforgue. Her analysis started
in February 1934 and lasted three years.[10] It brought about an almost miraculous change in Françoise's life, a kind of revolution in consciousness. But it
was a revolution carried out via the unconscious that transformed her into
virtually another woman: one aware of herself and no longer alienated, able
to feel she was a woman sexually instead of having a morbid and infantile
self-image.

The nature of this transformation can be seen in a letter she wrote to her father on June 15, 1938. Henry Marette had been complaining about how Françoise had changed, not understanding that she now rejected his ideals. So she explained to him very firmly the meaning of the change, making use of what she had learned from reading Freud, from her experience of analysis, and from her contacts with psychoanalytic circles in general. Instead of going over pointless grievances, she gave a clinical account of her mother's melancholic unhappiness, with which she herself had identified for several years.[11] Thus Françoise Marette was awakened from her neurosis through the acquisition of clinical knowledge, and freed from the prejudices of her class through access to a new culture.

It is interesting to compare Jacques Lacan's family background with that of Françoise Dolto. He came from the commercial middle classes, which were Catholic, chauvinistic, and conformist. They were still attached to their old peasant roots, and the acquisition of a fair amount of money and material possessions was their ideal of social success. As we know, Albert Lacan, who cared nothing for art, culture, and knowledge, regarded trade and commerce as the most respectable fields of activity. As for Emilie, his wife, Christian spirituality was the only kind of intellectual endeavor she could lay claim to. The mystical element in her character partly explains her younger son's decision to become a monk. She adored him from the moment he was born, and he always regarded her as a saint.

The case of his brother Jacques was quite different. In him the desire to belong to an intellectual aristocracy was allied to a strong desire to rise up the social ladder. He therefore had to identify himself with values quite opposed to those of his origins. By making a definitive break with his family he became one of the upper middle classes and nobody's son. He frequented the most distinguished salons in Paris and was as manifestly an aesthete, nihilist, and cosmopolitan as his parents were chauvinists and conformists.

Françoise Marette on the other hand belonged to a social class that saw itself as responsible for handing down the intellectual and moral traditions of patriotic, nationalist, and antirepublican France. And because she was raised in accordance with a set of educational principles that implied first and foremost a belief in a system of thought, her break with her family could be expressed in conflict and verbal exchanges; it could be spoken, admitted, explained, debated. This was quite different from the intellectual void, the absence of words, the impossibility of communication that marked Lacan's relations with his parents. Quite different therefore, and more radical, was Lacan's break with his family, where the son was unable to challenge his father because the latter was intellectually incapable of understanding the younger man's aims. They didn't speak the same language; they had ceased to belong to the same world.

Françoise rejected only the most pathological aspects of her "*Action française*"-type education: the prejudices about sex, the humiliation of women, the excessive authority of parents over their children. But as her analysis with Laforgue was not so much an intellectual initiation into a new culture as an emotional awakening caused by an introduction to clinical knowledge, she still, on the plane of thought, retained the values handed down to her by her background. Evidence of this may be seen in an episode to which she refers in a letter she wrote in June 1938. Her brother had accused her of "being kept by the Jews," a reference to Freudianism as a "Jewish business" not at all unexpected in a supporter of *Action française*.[12] Françoise, instead of rebuking him for anti-Semitism, simply objected to the accusation itself and told her father it wasn't true.

Instead of calling into question the bases of the Maurrassian philosophy that had affected her personality for so many years, she preferred to avoid the issue through a kind of amnesia and a refusal to intellectualize.[13] This was what made her adoption of Freudian thought so much like a religious conversion. What in Lacan's case was a rational adventure leading to a theoretical reworking of Freud's teaching, belonged, in Dolto's life, to the order of mystical revelation. Her analysis with Laforgue and her introduction into psychoanalytic circles invested her with the grace of a new initiate: it altered even her physical image. From 1935 on she attended many SPP lectures, diligently taking notes. At the same time, during the courses she followed as part of her medical studies at Maison-Blanche, at Vaugirard under Heuyer, at the Necker hospital for sick children, and at Bretonneau, she gradually witnessed the awakening of what was to be her own special genius: a wonderful ability to listen to children, to speak their language, and to talk to them as an equal. In this she resembled the Gypsy fortune-tellers Sandor Ferenczi used to enjoy meeting in the suburbs of Budapest at the beginning of the century, when psychoanalytic practice still retained some of the simplicity of its origins.

Françoise's gift for listening to children emerged when she met Edouard Pichon, who was to become her second mentor. Just as Laforgue, himself imbued with religious spirituality, had avoided challenging his patient's Catholic beliefs, trying rather to broaden them into a more ecumenical Christianity, so Pichon refrained from urging her to reject or analyze the Maurrassian mode of thinking that she had inherited. And as a result of the attitudes of these two masters, Françoise became part of the chauvinistic wing of the SPP, a position that later involved her in some serious problems with the IPA. Did she realize this? Certainly not:[14] her conversion to Freud deintellectualized or, as she liked to say, "depolluted" her. In other words, it freed her from the constraints of reason, admitting her to a kind of primitive, natural thinking preceding ratiocination.

An affectionate friendship grew up between her and Pichon, giving rise to both cordial exchanges and critical advice. Because of him she chose "psychoanalysis and pediatrics," a topic dear to his heart, as the subject of her medical thesis; in it she supported his campaign for the introduction of Freud's teaching into hospital medicine and training.[15] His "little Marette" was more of an ideal pupil to Pichon than Lacan had been: he saw her as someone who would genuinely continue his own mission as the ideologist of Freudianism in France. He corrected the manuscript of her thesis with a combination of firmness and tact, making brilliant comments on her style, syntax, grammar, and ideas and encouraging her to add historical references. In particular he suggested she should quote Eugénie Sokolnicka, Anna Freud, Melanie Klein, and himself.[16]

The thesis, defended on July 11, 1939, and published at the end of the year, was very strange. The first section contained a simplistic account of the main elements of Freud's teaching and referred to no authority but the master himself. Yet in fact Dolto drew heavily on the entire tradition of the French school, and especially on the terminology introduced by Laforgue and Pichon. For example, she used the word *aimance* as if she herself had introduced it.[17] There had been other similar instances, hence Pichon's corrections.

Dolto always said her master in the field of child psychology was Sophie Morgenstern: "She taught me how to make children talk confidentially, without being afraid that what they say will be passed on to the grownups."[18] And it was true: Morgenstern, whom she met when she was working with Heuyer, did indeed play this role. Dolto also maintained that she hadn't read any Melanie Klein when she wrote her thesis. This too was probably true, but even so she did have a general idea of the argument that divided the English school from the Viennese school. Even if the single reference she made in this connection was to the case of Little Hans, she must have been aware of the debate, if only through articles on the subject in the *RFP*, not to mention from Pichon's own teaching.

In an interview she gave in April 1986 she tells how she met Melanie Klein at Marie Bonaparte's house in or around 1936: "She carried out a kind of test on the children who were there in the princess's garden, and I could see she believed a child of eight months had to go through an anaclitic phase and that there had to be either a good or a bad mother. All this struck me as artificial. A mother is neither good nor bad: she is a mother for the oral or for the anal, take her or leave her. . . . But I did feel that Melanie Klein had astonishing charisma. . . . She was very interested in child psychology, but it seemed to me all her ideas were too theoretical and cut-and-dried, whereas every child introduces something new."[19] But there is no avoiding the conclusion that if the two did meet, the encounter did not take place in 1936. Melanie Klein and Marie Bonaparte weren't on visiting terms between the two wars. In 1934 the princess read Klein's book on infant psychology, and in October 1935 she attended a lecture on Klein's work at the BPS. But she came away "bored stiff" and of the opinion that Klein's errors "infested" the English society. Her diary contains no mention of any meeting that might confirm Dolto's assertion.[20] It wasn't until after 1945, that, despite her friendship with Anna Freud, Marie Bonaparte began to take an interest in Klein's theories, especially in the notebooks she kept as a little girl.[21] So it looks as if the meeting to which Dolto refers took place between 1946 and 1953.

And so, when she wrote her thesis, Dolto had no opinion on the subject of Melanie Klein's practice. Her knowledge of the then-current debate about child psychoanalysis and feminine sexuality was very vague, and the theoretical account she gave of it in the first part of her thesis was meager and simplistic. But the second part was very different: there, following Sophie Morgenstern, she invented a method of child analysis that laid the foundations of her own original contribution.

Dolto's biographer, Claude Halmos, has suggested in a lecture the position she should be accorded in the history of child psychoanalysis.[22] He sees this position as "culturalist," following on the work of Melanie Klein, who was the first to discover a specifically childish universe. According to Halmos, Dolto, in choosing to be on the side of the "race of children," created a "culture" of childhood. This hypothesis throws further light on Françoise's transition to psychoanalysis itself. The method she invented rejected play technique and the interpretation of drawings and instead required the therapist to appropriate the language of childhood. The psychoanalyst was to employ the same words as the child and to show him the meaning of his own thoughts in terms of reality. This method is demonstrated in the sixteen cases put forward in Dolto's thesis. They give the impression of having been written to be read by children: one feels closer to Charles Perrault's stories than to Freud's almost novelistic narratives. The people in them belong to the popular fairy-tale tradition of Snow White, Tom Thumb, ogres and ogresses. The glossary contains definitions such as "*enuresis*: wetting the bed"; "*encopresis*: messing your pants."

Such was the clinical genius of this extraordinary woman. In an old-world manner and with the aid of a traditional vocabulary she invented a new kind of speech, one that allowed her to interpret the language of childhood as might an ethnologist who chooses not only to observe the rites of his favorite tribe but also to share in its joys and sorrows. Because of her desire to be a spokesperson for children, her position was that of a shaman rather than of an ordinary psychoanalyst. And that was the only revenge she took on her social origins. Born into the middle classes, she never aspired to rise higher. On the contrary, she always sought to maintain an old-fashioned relationship with the common people. But her vital need for an emotional bond, which took the form of a love of childhood, never made her seek to dominate. She used her powers of suggestion not to rule over a race of slaves but to serve the cause of the oppressed. In her private history, the oppressed were first of all children in general—or rather the dream inhabitants of an imaginary childhood of which she herself had been deprived by a benighted upbringing—and then, within that world of infancy, the most oppressed of all its citizens: children who were poor, deprived because of their social origins, their mental inadequacies, or their physical shortcomings. She concentrated her attention on all children who suffered, whether they were neurotic or psychotic, paralyzed or disabled, blind or deaf or mentally defective. And, as we know now, she performed miracles. Miracles akin to that of her own conversion to Freud.

The paths of Jacques Lacan and Françoise Marette first crossed at the SPP in 1936. We know from the voluminous notes she took how impressed she was by his June 16 lecture on "the mirror stage." (Lacan's text has been lost, and Dolto's notes are now all that survives of it.) After that they saw each other regularly, but they didn't really meet until about 1938, when she read his article on the family. During the war they went their separate ways. While he was making a new life for himself and confronting the problems of fatherhood and separation from Malou, she finally met the man in her life, Boris Dolto, a Russian émigré doctor born in the Crimea. She married him on February 7, 1942, and a year later gave birth to her first child.[23] Like Lacan, she neither collaborated with the Germans nor took part in the Resistance; she went on working at the Hôpital Trousseau throughout the Occupation.

After the war, Jacques and Françoise became the best of friends and got into the habit—very rare as far as Lacan was concerned—of addressing one another by the familiar *tu*. He addressed both his wives and his mistresses by the formal *vous*, at least in public, and used the second person singular only with men of his own generation and former hospital contemporaries such as Nacht, Lagache, Ey, Mâle, and so on. So Françoise enjoyed a form of address that Lacan usually restricted to members of a purely masculine fraternity. She was one of the few women in his circle with whom the question of a physical relationship never arose. He didn't attempt either to seduce or to flirt with her. She, like Jenny Aubry, was just a genuine friend.[24] Both women believed they could be followers of Lacan without having to express their loyalty in the form of flattery or adulation. Because each was successful in her own right, both could have a relationship with him based on equality and intellectual independence. And Françoise had genius: in France she was even more popular than Lacan and would have been no less so even if she had never become one of his disciples. As for Jenny Aubry, Lacan was very much impressed by her degrees and other qualifications, her influence in various organizations, and her social origins. He would often tell Françoise Dolto, "You don't need to understand what I say because without theorizing about it you say the same thing." He was always reminding the other, to her great annoyance,[25] that she was the sister of the suffragette Louise Weiss. He took a snobbish pleasure in name-dropping, just as he liked meeting important people and anyone who was in the limelight—models, actors, journalists, politicians, philosophers, writers, and so on.

In 1949 Françoise presented two cases of neurosis to the SPP. The patients were two little girls, Bernadette and Nicole. Bernadette kept shouting unintelligibly; Nicole didn't speak, though she wasn't deaf. Bernadette, trying to destroy herself, treated living creatures as things and plants and vegetables as people; Nicole remained both dumb and motionless. Françoise had the bright idea of asking Bernadette's mother to make something the child might use as a scapegoat on which to vent her destructive tendencies and thus get rid of them. Thus was the "flower doll" born—a stem covered with green cloth, standing for the body and limbs, with an artificial daisy for a face. Bernadette projected her lethal drives on to the object and started to talk. And thanks to the doll, Nicole too emerged from her former silence. The experiment showed that a symbol could act as a mediator in the process of restoring speech. It also showed that Françoise Dolto had by now assimilated the Kleinian idea of a "bad object" and had also added play technique to her practice. Lacan was enthusiastic when he heard her account. The "flower doll," he said, fit in with his own researches on the mirror stage and the fragmented body. He promised he would one day supply Françoise's clinical discoveries with a theoretical commentary.[26]

At the time of the first split in the SPP, in 1953, Dolto and Lacan were both on the same side, though they didn't share the same point of view. Françoise was in favor of the break and thought it inevitable, whereas Jacques did all he could to prevent it. At the Rome congress she spoke after he did, thus playing for the first time the part that she was to perform for thirty years and that added further prestige to the movement led by Lacan. She compared Lagache and Lacan to two big dragons and herself to a little one. Then she launched into a long diatribe in which, while registering her agreement with Lacan's theories on language, she criticized his idea of "instinctive maturing." The fact was that she accepted Lacan's hypothesis ascribing a linguistic structure to the unconscious, but she was still attached to the biological factors that Lacan had downplayed during his reworking of Freud's teaching. Nor did she ever change her mind on this score. Lacan was so impressed by what she had said that he rushed over and embraced her, saying a heavenly voice had just made itself heard through her. "What did I say?" she asked. "I was so strung up by having to speak at all, I didn't think of what I was saying!" "My goodness, Françoise, you little dragon," replied Lacan, "you didn't need to think! You made us a present of your words perfectly well without thinking!"[27]

So what *did* she say? She had dwelt at length on the physical relationship of a child to its mother and stressed that the main role of the psychoanalyst in dealing with a neurotic adult was to understand him "over and above the language he has borrowed from the world of adults and give him back the language belonging to the age of his real development."[28] It was this passage that interested Lacan so much. Françoise Dolto once told me she had often pondered about what Lacan's early childhood was like.[29] She wondered why he never spoke of his parents or family origins; why he was so awkward in everyday life, so anxious about his image, and so obsessed with his outward appearance. Why did he feel such a need to disguise himself, to go to masked balls and wear such extravagant clothes? Dolto sensed that this ludic behavior served to conceal a kind of emptiness. It struck her that Lacan was like a narcissistic and wayward child from whose early childhood some essential element had been missing. So she approached him as she did the children in her consulting room. She spoke to him as to a child, not to infantilize him but to give back, to the overly infantile adult he had become, the real childhood of which he had been deprived.

This unusual mode of communication can be seen in the letters they exchanged with one another between 1956 and 1978. He urges her to attend important SFP meetings, "secretly" invites her opinion about his teaching, or asks her for information to use in his seminars. From 1960 on, she got into the habit of wishing him a happy New Year with a small present—candy or some little toy or gadget. When he thanks her he tells her how fond he is of her and that she is one of the few people who "completely *are*." In his writings the idea of plenitude is often associated with strength. Lacan thought Dolto was "sturdy" but didn't hesitate to advise her to diet. In February 1961, when he is staying at the Hôtel Mont-d'Arbois in Megève, he tells her about his misadventures. After a week of brilliant performances and sunshine, during which all his friends have been singing his praises, he has sprained his ankle. The ways of fate are unfathomable, he says, asking his friend to be as silent about the incident as if it were a state secret. The following year his tone is even more affectionate, and he tells her how very dear she is to him. Year after year he declares that she is the only person whose presents really give him pleasure, the only one who knows how to spoil him.[30]

A strong clinical relationship had also grown up between them. Lacan got into the habit of telephoning Dolto in the middle of the night to arrange for her to see analysands he couldn't deal with himself, whether they came to him for therapy, control, or training. One day he sent her a very wealthy patient whose analysis was "stuck," pointing out that she could ask for a handsome fee. She did the opposite and lowered her price:"In view of what you do I'll charge you less," she told the man. His analysis got off to a fresh start.[31]

21

. . . .

The Symposium and the Storm

*F*or Lacan and Dolto the ten years the SFP lasted were a decade that saw the blossoming of their thought and their teaching. In an association in crisis, which saw the emergence of the third generation of French psychoanalysis, each of them gradually reached a dominant position with regard to their respective rivals, Daniel Lagache and Juliette Favez-Boutonier.[1] I have already spoken of the many reasons that led to this brilliant success. Two were paramount: Dolto and Lacan were both geniuses, while their counterparts in the second generation (SFP and SPP) were merely gifted, so naturally it was Dolto and Lacan who attracted the most candidates for training (though they didn't both necessarily attract the same individuals or attract them in the same way). Another reason for the success of this flamboyant couple was that they were then the only SFP members of their generation whose interpretation of Freud was completely uninfluenced by the French tradition of academic psychology.

Lacan, who had no academic training in philosophy, decided as early as 1933 to establish a special relationship with the best contemporary thinkers. His often-difficult personal contacts with Koyré, Kojève, Corbin, Heidegger, Lévi-Strauss, Hyppolite, Ricoeur, and later Althusser and Derrida show that in his opinion any serious continuation of Freud's mission had to involve philosophical inquiry. But he never abandoned the field of clinical psychiatry and encouraged all his pupils to study medicine. He thus arrived at a perfect synthesis between the two main approaches indispensable to the introduction of Freudianism anywhere: the medical approach, whereby the world of madness is reached through clinical knowledge, and the intellectual approach (literary or philosophical), the only one that can provide a body of teaching with a theoretical basis.

Lagache adopted a diametrically opposite approach. A philosopher by training, he spent his whole life working not for a philosophical reshaping of Freudian doctrine but rather for its incorporation into the general field of academic psychology, all the various branches of which would ultimately be united. Lagache was always the representative of psychoanalysis among its adversaries the psychologists, as well as being psychology's missionary to a Freudian movement that rejected any such inheritance. The result was a resounding failure. From the theoretical point of view the psychological approach, however strong it may be in terms of institutions, is still a sideshow as far as the establishment of Freudianism is concerned.

The career of Juliette Favez-Boutonier followed a similar course. She too represented the values of a tradition inherited from Janet, and she tried to introduce psychoanalysis into university studies under the aegis of psychology. Dolto's position in the SFP vis-à-vis her was much the same as Lacan's vis-à-vis Lagache, but it was in the context of pediatrics, not psychiatry, that Favez-Boutonier established herself as a teacher, helped by Jenny Aubry, who often employed her in the various clinics she ran after the war.

While Dolto was emerging as one of the two most important founders of French Freudianism, she too was rejected by the IPA leadership because of the methods she used in her training analyses. At the conference held in London in the summer of 1953, the Central Executive, headed by Heinz Hartmann, refused to affiliate the people who had resigned from the SPP. Applications for admission from the new society were to be examined by a committee, which as usual changed into a board of inquiry. Winnicott was in the chair; the other members were Phyllis Greenacre, an American close to Ernst Kris; Willi Hoffer, an Englishman of Viennese origin and a friend of Anna Freud; and Jeanne Lampl de Groot, a Dutchwoman trained by Freud and a close friend of Anna Freud and Marie Bonaparte. This group was given the job of interrogating the "ringleaders" of the rebellion. They were all familiar with the problems presented by the training of analysts, and two of them—Winnicott and Hoffer—had been closely involved in the Controversial Discussions. Winnicott went to see Dolto: of all the members of the committee, he was in the best position to evaluate her work on child analysis. He concluded that it was very acceptable and said it should be continued within the context of the SFP. But he disapproved of her teaching; he said she lacked method and produced "uncontrolled transference" from both patients and training analysands. She was advised to avoid too much contact with the young, so as not to "influence" them unduly.[2]

The committee's verdict was thus as negative on Dolto's practice as on Lacan's. He was criticized above all for his short sessions. But there were other objections too: he exercised too much attraction on his pupils, he was no good at analyzing transference, and it was thought his influence inside the SFP itself might be excessive and unhealthy.

Neither Lacan nor Dolto was a "technician" of training analysis in the sense in which Melanie Klein and Anna Freud used the term: They didn't follow any "standard" or rule. They didn't impose restrictions on the part they themselves played in transference, countertransference, and resistance. They didn't interpret what their patients said at certain precise points in their analysis; they didn't measure time with a stopwatch; they didn't always keep to the rule of four or five compulsory sessions per week. Dolto had been trained by Laforgue, whose practice had been strongly condemned by the IPA, and she hadn't acquainted herself with the rules now in force. As for Lacan, although he had been analyzed by a technician who conformed entirely to IPA requirements, he had come to loathe the rules his analyst imposed on him. And it was this neglect of "technique" that displeased the members of the committee.

Yet Dolto and Lacan's methods with their pupils weren't at all alike. Dolto kept strictly to the rule prescribing fifty-minute sessions, not out of obedience to the IPA but because she felt it was necessary. But not many people came to her for training analysis, and she didn't commit any of the sins indulged in by such leading lights of the Freudian movement as Marie Bonaparte, Ernest Jones, Edward Glover, Melanie Klein, Jacques Lacan, and many others: she didn't analyze her own children, she avoided taking on members of the same family as patients, and needless to say she never entered into any sexual relationship whatever with a patient (as a matter of fact, she was always completely faithful to her husband). It's true that she was surrounded by admirers, but she didn't encourage idolatry. Being neither perverse nor psychotic, neither a bohemian nor an introvert nor a homosexual, she embodied, in theory, all the virtues of "normality" required of anyone who wanted to be accepted as a member of the IPA.[3] And yet she wasn't accepted.

At the congress held in Copenhagen in July 1959, the Central Executive ordered that another committee be set up to examine the French candidates. Soon it too became a board of inquiry, and it arrived in Paris on May 15, 1961, three weeks after the generals' putsch in Algiers. After setting up its headquarters at the Hôtel Westminster, the committee began to interrogate the members of the SFP, who were divided into "seniors" (the second generation) and "juniors" (the third generation).[4]

This committee was very different from the preceding one. It didn't include any famous members of the Freudian movement (such as Winnicott and Lampl de Groot, who had been on the earlier board). It did include two English Kleinians, Paula Heimann and Pierre Turquet, who were more likely to be favorable to admission than their Anna-Freudian colleagues. The latter, who were friends of Marie Bonaparte, wanted only the SPP to be regarded as legitimate. So their position was different from that of the

American friends of Anna Freud, especially Heinz Hartmann and Rudolph Loewenstein, who always stood up for the sfp, with or without Lacan.

Pierre Turquet, who was of French origin, had undergone a training analysis with Paula Heimann and spent the war reforming English psychiatry. He knew Lacan personally, and Lacan admired him, as he had been able to inform him when he gave a lecture to the bps in 1946. Paula Heimann was a Jew from Berlin who had emigrated to London when the Nazis came to power. She had been analyzed by Melanie Klein and became one of her best disciples, attracting attention at the Zurich conference with a paper on countertransference. But in 1953 a fearsome conflict arose between the two women. Paula, feeling she had become Melanie's "slave," demonstrated that she was really a rebellious rival. She was ruthlessly rejected and left Klein's group a couple of years later. At the time when she was made a member of the 1959 committee, she was regarded as a brilliant clinician and an expert on negative transference. As a disciple disappointed by her own teacher, she had experienced for herself the difficulties she would face when she examined Lacan's pupils.[5]

The two other members of the committee were less colorful. Ilse Hellman, Viennese by origin and close to Anna Freud, was always very hostile to the subversives, especially Lacan. She understood neither what he was doing nor how important it was. Not only did she believe that psychoanalysis was merely a therapy; she also denied that Freud's work required any philosophical interpretation.[6] Pieter Jan van der Leeuw, a specialist in training and a future president of the ipa, shared Ilse Hellman's convictions.

Between May 1961 and December 1963 a long series of negotiations took place, punctuated by decisions taken at two ipa congresses, in Edinburgh in the summer of 1961 and in Stockholm in the summer of 1963. In this passionate debate, the main participants were Wladimir Granoff and Serge Leclaire for the sfp and Pierre Turquet for the committee. The negotiations pitted a French conception of Freudianism, influenced by the continuing work of Lacan, against an Anglo-American interpretation of psychoanalysis. The representatives of the second school of thought were at once eager to admit an obviously lively foreign movement and anxious to control a doctrine that struck them as dangerous and difficult. The negotiations ended in disaster: Lacan and most of the sfp's pupils were excluded from the legitimacy of the ipa.

The two French negotiators, Leclaire and Granoff—good friends who acted with great mutual understanding and sensitivity—knew Lacan wouldn't give up his variable-length sessions. And they knew he was incapable of reducing the number of his analysands. They were quite right. Lacan would hold forth with great subtlety on the subject of castration and often described to his patients and pupils the dangers of believing in the omnipotence of the ego, but it never occurred to him to apply this wisdom to himself.

As ardent internationalists, Leclaire and Granoff both believed that any break between Lacan and the IPA would be a calamity at once for Freudianism in France, for Lacan, and for the IPA. But the two had different ways of operating. Leclaire was first and foremost a prince's adviser, and as such he saw loyalty as the prime virtue. He was acting in the service of a master, not slavishly or in a spirit of adulation, but because the master was the spokesperson of an innovative Freudianism that he had supported ever since 1950, when he became the first French "Lacanian." Leclaire had been analyzed by Lacan and thought the disciples who had followed him on the master's couch would be able to argue so persuasively in favor of Lacan's teaching that the IPA investigators would accept the unacceptable in the shape of the variable-length sessions. But he was wrong.

Granoff too worked to gain IPA recognition for the French form of Freudianism that was "Lacanianism." Unlike Leclaire, however, Granoff didn't see himself as the counselor of a prince but rather as an elder brother to all the men of his generation. So his guiding principle was solidarity with the group rather than loyalty to the master. Nevertheless Granoff, with his policy of bracketing leader and group together, failed just as completely as Leclaire.

Pierre Turquet thought it necessary for Lacan and the SFP to be incorporated into the IPA and sincerely believed the French master would eventually agree to treat fewer analysands so as to arrive at a compromise with the Central Executive. He was encouraged in this view by the attitudes of Leclaire and Granoff: their one idea was to get Lacan readmitted into the IPA, and they let Turquet think, without deliberately trying to deceive him, that Lacan would make the necessary concessions. But during the two long series of interrogations that Turquet conducted—one in May and June of 1961 and the other in January 1963—he perceived that Lacan was not abandoning his former practices. On the contrary: he went on increasing the number of his analysands and swearing to the committee that his sessions lasted the normal amount of time.

In view of all this, Turquet wrote two reports advising against admission. As a result of the first report the Central Executive drew up a list of recommendations consisting of twenty points, which were put forward at the Edinburgh congress on August 2, 1961. Article 13 stipulated that Lacan should not take on any more training analyses or controls. The second report, two years later, led the Executive to exclude Lacan not from the IPA but from the SFP's own list of teachers. This decision, known as the Stockholm "Directive," was taken at the IPA congress in August 1963.[7]

Evidence from Lacan's pupils provided Turquet with the facts about the transferential aspect of his analyses. There were three different situations. First came a group made up partly of former analysands and partly of disciples who hadn't been analyzed by Lacan, though they had sometimes undergone a control with him. Most of these people praised Lacan's practice and teaching, without being especially devoted to him personally. Then came the mass of pupils currently undergoing analysis. They could be divided into two categories: those in the first group, the more brilliant but fewer in number, were, like Lacan's former pupils, already either members of the SFP, entitled to conduct training analyses, or training analysts beginning their professional practices.[8] They wanted the IPA to recognize Lacan's teaching but distanced themselves from him as an analyst when they spoke to the committee about their own analyses with him. These members were thus acting, in relation to the committee, the part that Lacan would allot to the *passeurs* in the procedure known as *la passe* (the pass) that was introduced into the Ecole freudienne de Paris (EFP) in 1969.[9] In the present case, they brought about a *passage* by which the analysis ended not in a mere separation but in a split. The second and less brilliant category of current analysands formed the grass roots of the SFP and consisted for the most part of trainees (*stagiaires*) and guests. By and large, their testimony took the form of hagiographical professions of faith in the limitless powers of the master.

From these lengthy interrogations, out of which it emerged that three-quarters of the members of the SFP wanted Lacan to be incorporated into the IPA as a teacher, Pierre Turquet concluded that, on the contrary, Lacan should be forbidden to put his teaching into practice. Why? Because according to the criteria of the IPA Lacan's methods were unacceptable. He made promises he didn't keep; he exercised personal attraction over his patients, who were sometimes too servile toward him, sometimes too rebellious. In other words, Lacan was a "charismatic leader," not an educational technician. All this was quite true, but Pierre Turquet and Paula Heimann knew very well that such transgressions were equally rife in the BPS, in the entourage of Melanie Klein, yet the Kleinian school was still an essential element of the IPA. However, it should be remembered that Klein and the members of her group had worked out a doctrine on analytic technique that was acceptable to the IPA, whereas Lacan hadn't really done so at this period. Yet he had expressed his views on the matter in four long articles written between 1955 and 1960.

In 1955 Henri Ey had commissioned from him, for the *Encyclopédie médico-chirurgicale* (Medico-surgical encyclopedia), an article to accompany another by Maurice Bouvet presenting the point of view of the SPP. Bouvet wrote a piece in neo-Freudian style on a standard analysis, and Lacan undertook to provide a text entitled "Variations on the Standard Treatment."[10] Taking up again his thesis on the role of the analyst as "being-for-death" (*être-pour-la-mort*), he unfolded a theory of analysis similar to the one he propounded in the "Rome Discourse." But he rebuked Bouvet and his opponents in the SPP and attacked what he henceforth called "American psychoanalysis." By this phrase he meant not the historical reality of American Freudianism but what he described as a "delinquent" conception of Freudian psychoanalysis: a doctrine centered on the ego, not the id, and based on the view that the individual should be adapted to society.[11] He brought in a number of theories deriving from the Viennese school—including both Anna-Freudianism and ego psychology. This led him to attack the idea of defense mechanisms, which he had formerly praised, and the notion of an "autonomous ego." He contrasted this not only with the Hungarian tradition of Ferenczi and Balint, with which he had something in common, but also with his own recasting of Freudianism, centered on a search for the truth of the subject and the unveiling of the unconscious desire behind the illusions of the ego. But Lacan's article, thought to be too difficult, was withdrawn from the *Encyclopédie* in 1960, much to the fury of its author, who wrote a more virulent version for inclusion in his *Ecrits* in 1966.

The second of the four articles, entitled "The Situation of Psychoanalysis and the Psychoanalyst's Training in 1956," was published in a special number of *Etudes philosophiques* (Philosophical studies) celebrating the centenary of Freud's birth.[12] Lacan painted an acid and apocalyptic picture of what he saw as IPA bureaucracy in the mid-1950s. He divided the association up into four allegorical classes. First came the "Self-Important," the upper hierarchy of the Freudian establishment: professors, presidents, secretaries, vice presidents, and active members. Lacan accused them of knowing only the ancient form of democracy: a society of masters served by slaves. Their sole object, he said, was to reproduce ad infinitum a single type of psychoanalytic civil servant: a modern educator who identified with his own strong and independent social ego. At the bottom of the hierarchy were the "Small Fry," the affiliated members, trainees, or slaves of the "Self-Important" brigade. In between came the "Necessary Ones," appointed by the masters to train the slaves, and the "Beatitudes," the "Self-Important" class's spokespeople, whose job it was to sit on committees and guide, judge, or reject the candidates who applied for training analyses.

Lacan's description of the content of the IPA's teaching was no less severe. He called it "material for fiction," making an exception only for its medical aspect, though even this was superfluous: most candidates would be just as well served in this respect in the medical departments of universities. As for the training analysis, Lacan thought it helped reduce candidates to a kind of illiteracy that he called "deintellectualization." He maintained, moreover, that as far as training was concerned the IPA put quantity ("a hundred mediocre analysts") before quality; it preferred a mass-produced group to a circle of the elite. This preference produced a body of robotlike professionals, "with an inner- and even backward-directed look that shows they are preoccupied with the disintegrating embryo of their own resistances."[13] He ended with a reference to Poe's story, "The Facts in the Case of M. Valdemar," comparing the IPA to a mesmerized and hibernating corpse.

In July 1958, at a symposium organized at Royaumont by the SFP, Lacan made another attack on so-called American psychoanalysis in a long lecture entitled "The Direction of the Treatment and the Principles of Its Power."[14] He described Anna Freud's technique as "*postiche* work" (a *postiche*, in French, is a hairpiece) and, on the basis of a case Ernst Kris had published, also made fun of Kris's method of interpretation. The case in question concerned a man with a strong compulsion toward plagiarism. Melitta Schmideberg, the patient's first analyst, had interpreted the compulsion as the recurrence of a neurotic symptom originating in childhood delinquency: the man used to steal books and candy when he was a little boy. When Kris took over the case he noticed the man always paused when he saw the name of his favorite dish—fresh brains—on a restaurant menu. From this Kris deduced the meaning of the symptom: the patient tried to be a plagiarist in order to avoid becoming an actual thief.

Lacan challenged this interpretation, which according to him was typical of treatments centered on the analysis of defenses. He suggested another explanation: it was not the defense against the idea of stealing that made the patient take himself for a thief but the fact that he might have an idea of his own. In other words, the wish for fresh brains is an acting-out that means the patient is stealing "nothing." He is suffering not from an obsession but from mental anorexia; far from "not eating," he is eating "nothing," i.e., he is eating something. Lacan took advantage of this criticism of Kris to take over for his own purposes the idea of plagiarism, which as we know had been on his mind ever since the affair of the "mirror stage."

Having borrowed the model of the experiment from Wallon, Lacan skirted around his borrowing by presenting himself not as the initiator of the mirror experiment but as the inventor of the mirror concept. Year after year, without quoting Wallon, he reminded his audience that the invention in question dated from the congress at Marienbad, where the chief representative of the IPA had had the audacity to interrupt him, so that he went off without remembering to leave his precious text behind for publication. And now here he was accusing his own opponents of stealing from *him* and in the process referring to Kris, who had been a witness to the Marienbad affair: "In the United States, where Kris has ended up, publication means position, and teaching like mine would need to take precautions every week against the pillage it would be bound to be subjected to. In France, my ideas penetrate by a process of infiltration into a group that obeys orders prohibiting my teaching."[15]

Thus Lacan could believe in the "theft of ideas"[16] at the very moment he demonstrated that this type of theft only existed in the sick brain of a neurotic compelled to plagiarize because of a desire to steal "nothing." He ended his lecture by again eulogizing Ferenczi and the Hungarian school and then setting out in five points the essence of how to manage a truly Freudian analysis.

When such an analysis is not really authentic, he said in substance, it tends to decline in the direction of consciousness and thus into the wielding of power. An analysis, in order to be effective, must not, at the stage of transference, depart from the law governing the recognition of unconscious desire.[17] For desire to be recognized, three conditions must be fulfilled: (1) The analyst must bring into play first and foremost his own being rather than obedience to any technique. (2) He must refuse to yield to the analysand's demands; this is the only way to set limits on the narcissistic omnipotence of the ego. (3) He must accord paramount importance to what is said; this is the only way give the patient real freedom—i.e., the consciousness of unhappiness that the exercise of freedom necessarily implies.

Lacan was building up a magnificent theory of treatment that in fact reproduced the original Freudian practice. But it went against all the standards in force in the IPA, as Lacan well knew: he made his awareness quite clear when he added a severe criticism of legitimist bureaucracy. Moreover, rather than illustrating the way he actually conducted his own analyses, Lacan's theory depicted the ideal he would set before the young community to whom he saw himself acting as a spiritual guide.

In 1960 the movement Freud had founded resembled a multinational company made up of various corporate bodies. The therapists these bodies produced, while honest and competent, were completely adapted to the conformism prevailing in the democratic societies where psychoanalysis had taken root. *Mass psychoanalysis* is the term I have applied to this way of organizing Freudian orthodoxy, so characteristic of the third, internationalist generation created by the second circle of Freud's disciples. However, because psychoanalysis had been established in France relatively late, because there had been no real masters among the founders of the SPP, and because the contingent of Jewish refugees who had enriched the situation in London and the United States had had no parallel in German-occupied France, Lacan's request for affiliation seemed out of step with history. As an original founding father at a time when the IPA no longer produced anything but decent technicians, he was bound to see himself as the architect of a new orthodoxy, the representative of a new elite, confronting a movement in the process of converting to mass production. In 1960 Lacan was *orthodox* in that he advocated a return to direct descent from the original doctrine, as against any attempt at going beyond it, and he was *elitist* because he dreamed of gathering around him a *school of the chosen* similar to the first Viennese circle, a school inspired by a mystique appropriate to the cause.

This was the underlying meaning of the theory of treatment with which Lacan challenged the IPA's emphasis on technique. As for his elitist ideal, he illustrated it for a whole year in his 1960–1961 seminar. It was on the subject of transference, which it dealt with through a dazzling commentary on Plato's *Symposium* (known as *The Banquet* in French), one of the finest texts in the whole history of philosophy.[18] In Plato's dialogue, Socrates converses with six other characters, each of whom expresses a different conception of love. One of those present is the poet Agathon, a pupil of Gorgias, whose triumph the party is celebrating; another is Alcibiades, a politician of great beauty whom Socrates has rejected as a lover, devoting himself instead to love of the Supreme Good and the desire for immortality—in other words, to philosophy. No woman is present at the banquet, where, against a background of pederasty, every possible form of physical and intellectual love is discussed. Yet it is to the words of a woman called Diotima, a personage generally supposed to be fictitious, that Socrates refers in order to expound his own philosophical notion of love. Diotima is thus the eighth character in the dialogue on the question of *agalma*, which Plato defines as the paradigm of an object representing the Idea of the Good.[19]

Ever since antiquity, commentators on the *Symposium* have emphasized how Plato used the art of dialogue to express, via his characters, theories of love all relating to a desire that is consciously named, either by those present or by the author himself. Now, for the first time, Lacan in his commentary interpreted the unconscious desire of each of the characters. He thus cast Socrates in the role of a *psychoanalyst*, revealing to his disciples a truth that escapes their own consciousness. In this context, *agalma* was defined as the *object of desire*, i.e., a *manque à être* (lack of being, or, in Lacan's own words, "want to be"). Lacan later summarized this proposition in an inspired formula: "Love is giving what one doesn't have to somebody who doesn't want it."[20] Socrates, transformed into a Freudian psychoanalyst, does not choose temperance out of love for philosophy but because it can convey to Alcibiades that the true object of his desire is not him, Socrates, but Agathon. Such is the love involved in transference: it is made of the same material as ordinary love, but it is artificial because it is unconsciously directed toward an object that really reflects another object. Alcibiades thinks he desires Socrates, but he really desires Agathon.

If in 1960 Lacan cast Socrates as a psychoanalyst, it was because in his view Freudian discourse had become the only modern equivalent of the

Socratic stage in philosophy, when the members of an elite gathered around a master against the background of a golden age, a Republic of letters. But at the same time, Lacan's brilliant commentary on the *Symposium* neatly disposed of the very essence of Socratic choice as defined by Plato. It also made it possible to fix Lacan's new position with regard to philosophy. Up until the time when the unconscious was theoretically defined in terms of structure, as happened in two stages—with Lévi-Strauss in 1951 and then with Jakobson in 1957—Lacan had made use of the discourse of philosophy to carry out his renovation of Freudianism. But in 1954–1955, in his dialogue with Jean Hyppolite over Freud's *Verneinung* (negation), there was the beginning of a change, a direct result of the advent of structuralism.[21] From this point on, instead of using the discourse of philosophy to nourish Freudianism, Lacan tended to criticize or even "liquidate" it, showing how the very existence of the unconscious left philosophy in a blind alley. He began to set himself up as an antiphilosopher offering a philosophical interpretation of Freud while at the same time putting philosophy to death. This was the bone of contention at the famous meeting at Bonneval in the autumn of 1960, where the advocates of a phenomenological Freudianism opposed the supporters of structure. Lacan won a great victory, even though his friend Merleau-Ponty, on whose support he had counted, disagreed entirely with what he regarded as a totalitarian idea of the unconscious, seen as entirely governed by the laws of language.[22]

Lacan's use of the Socratic model represented a challenge. As is well known, homosexuality was a dark continent to the Freudian establishment, which ruled out the very idea of admitting a homosexual candidate to a training analysis. And here was Lacan choosing the most open, in this respect, of Plato's dialogues to illustrate the subject of transference. He was also identifying himself with a master whom the respectable citizens of a democracy made their scapegoat: a man condemned to drink hemlock for his arrogant and ironic rejection of compromise; one accused of corrupting youth. Moreover Lacan linked the name of his master with that of Diotima, a mythical woman, making the parallel quite clear: it is as if I were to invoke Françoise Dolto, he said.

It is interesting to compare that idyllic description of a Socratic school of psychoanalysis with the dreadful picture Lacan painted in a letter he wrote to Granoff from Rome on July 24, 1961, just before the Edinburgh congress. He described the leaders of the IPA as "unsweepawayable muck" and Marie Bonaparte as "a corpse out of Ionesco." He accused her of perfidy for her turnaround in 1953 and of treachery for her translations of Freud. He compared Hartmann to a "crab craving for consequence," called Jones "a vengeful little Welshman," and said Anna was "tense, timid, and harassed." He concluded by anathematizing all the men belonging to this empire as "cowards scooting like rabbits" from an armada of mothers: Klein, Lampl de Groot, Anna, the princess. Was this really the best analysis could do?[23]

Marie Bonaparte was equally fierce about her opponents. In a letter she wrote to Anna Freud in June 1961 she called Françoise Dolto half crazy, Blanche Reverchon an idiot, Loewenstein "weak." She absolutely refused to compromise: "I'll never have anything in common with these people again. I hate compromise just as your father did." In another letter, to the Executive Council of the IPA, she said Lacan saw his patients just "for a few short minutes."[24]

So why did Lacan, during all his years with the SFP, want to be part of an empire inhabited by people he thought so dreary? The answer is quite simple: At that time no one in France who claimed to be part of the history of Freudianism could even contemplate the idea of a break with the IPA. The two generations that had already come to maturity by 1960 felt they were at last on the verge of real internationalism. They were almost ashamed of the previous generation's chauvinism and wanted to wipe it out by joining the "mainstream."

So much was "belonging" taken for granted that the protesters of 1953 failed to realize that in resigning from the SPP they were ceasing to be members of the IPA. And however violently Lacan criticized the workings of the IPA, that didn't stop him from wanting to be part of it at any price. With his return to an "orthodox" attitude toward the Freudian text, he felt he embodied a doctrinal legitimacy beyond all challenge. And he dreamed of universalizing this new legitimacy by having his teaching recognized by the Americans and the British. This explains his support for the affiliation strategy followed by his two lieutenants.

After the 1963 split Lacan gave Turquet the ridiculous nickname of "Turkey" and maintained to his more credulous disciples that he himself had never gone out of his way to obtain IPA recognition. He even accused Leclaire and Granoff of having "negotiated" him: i.e., acted on his behalf without his knowledge.[25] Nothing could have been further from the truth. As is shown by the letters Lacan wrote at the time, he was the fourth player in the game, and his part was an active one until the Stockholm congress. Leclaire kept him informed of every important development. Sometimes Lacan preferred to stand aside, saying he needed time to work on his theories; at other times he would collaborate with his two lieutenants as they planned their tactics.

Just as he was haunted by the idea of plagiarism, so also he now began to believe his closest disciples were trying to persecute him. After the Edinburgh meeting, furious at having failed to escape the "Recommendations," he accused Leclaire of betraying him. Then he calmed down, thinking he had his pupils sufficiently under control to be able to confront the committee's questioning again. But he was wrong. He either did not or would not understand how and why the famous minority group of his best disciples was drifting away from him. Yet the meaning of the break ought to have been clear to him from his own theory about the emergence of desire in the process of transference and the patient's accession thereby to true freedom. But Lacan failed to follow his own logic. When Jean Laplanche terminated his analysis on November 1, 1963, telling Lacan he would still be his loyal disciple despite their differences, Lacan flew into a rage and accused him of taking advantage of him. Similarly, when Daniel Widlöcher made a clumsy attempt to make him accept his exclusion from the IPA, Lacan was extremely angry: "What do you want to do?" he said.

Ostracize me? Stop me from doing any more training analyses? You're completely crazy, my friend, to leave me just when I'm about to be famous. And have you looked to see who it is you're leaving *with*? You're not well-off, yet you're joining up with other young men who have plenty of money: the sybarites of psychoanalysis. But I'm not surprised at your attitude, all of you. Nearly all of you are doctors, and there's nothing to be done with doctors. What's more you're not Jews, and there's nothing to be done with non-Jews. You all have problems with your fathers, and that's why you join together against me. But in the future, let me tell you, I shan't fight against Lagache and the two Favezes but against all you who've profited by my teaching and then betrayed me. And when you get hit you can be sure who dealt the blow. And now we have nothing more to say to one another.[26]

But while he couldn't bear to be left, neither could Lacan bear to leave to their fate the pupils so dependent on him as to be incapable of thinking for themselves. When the committee criticized this dependence, fearing with some justification that it would recur in the future, he defended "his own" as fiercely as a mother wolf protecting her cubs. He would never tolerate any criticism of them unless it came from him. This was how he came to encourage among them an excessive personal attachment to him. He saw himself as their father, but his love for them was more like that of the omnipotent mothers whose power he denounced so vehemently.[27]

The questioning to which the members of the SFP were subjected changed Lacan's relationship with his pupils. Some of them used the dialogue with the committee as an opportunity to escape from the tutelage of a master by whose genius they felt crushed; others actually became even more dependent as a result of the interrogation. As for Pierre Turquet, he couldn't understand the policy Leclaire and Granoff were advocating. He didn't want to take the risk of affiliating someone whose practice was unacceptable, and refused to believe the process of integration might itself modify that practice through the de facto control over Lacan that it would entail. Caught up as he was in the IPA machine, Turquet overlooked Lacan's genuine clinical virtues: his extraordinary skill at diagnosis, for example; his exceptional ear for madness; the incredible lucidity with which he could detect hypocrisy or complacency—all indispensable qualities in a psycho-analyst.

Despite all these talents, Lacan misjudged the Central Executive's intentions concerning him. At the end of June 1963, when the game was already lost, he decided to go to Stockholm, certain he could convince the IPA of the soundness of both his teaching and his technique. Leclaire, who realized the folly of such a course, magnanimously warned him; a noble warning: "You think you owe it to your dignity, but you're heading for disaster. But I'm loyal, and I know how much I owe you. So I'll go with you." Lacan disregarded the warning and replied: "I don't intend to arrive in Stockholm looking as if you'd got me invited. . . . I'd rather you just joined in the fight." Then he wrote a long letter in English to Paula Heimann, challenging the conclusions in the Turquet report and accusing Lagache of stealing his ideas. Lacan gave this letter to Leclaire, who promptly put it away in his archives; he knew Lagache and Paula Heimann were friends. But he did let her know that Lacan intended to go to Stockholm to take part in a seminar.[28]

The Swedish expedition ended in catastrophe. In early July, at the preparatory meeting in London, Lacan tried to expound his doctrine to the assembled IPA dignitaries. Speaking in English, he attempted to explain the division of the subject and the site of the object. But he couldn't think of the English word for his notion of "*reste*," remainder or residue, and appealed to the audience to help him out. No one condescended to reply. At that point, with great dignity, he left the room and rejoined Solange Faladé, the friend and pupil who had kindly agreed to see him through this difficult ordeal. A month later, in Stockholm, he received the news of his banishment. On August 2 the Central Executive announced that the Edinburgh "Recommendations" were to be strictly applied and that Lacan's exclusion was to take effect by October 31, 1963, at the latest.

That day, accompanied by Dolto, Perrier, Leclaire, and his daughter Judith, Lacan visited the famous castle at Gripsholm, where in 1935 the German writer Kurt Tucholsky had committed suicide.[29]

The application of the Stockholm "Directive" meant the exclusion from the IPA of a doctrine that, far from being dissident, as were the teachings of Jung and Adler, proclaimed, as Klein did, complete adherence to Freudian orthodoxy. In this respect the 1963 split was unique. For the first time in the whole history of the psychoanalytic movement, a school of strict Freudian obedience found itself to all intents and purposes excluded from Freudian legitimacy. This novel proscription would force Lacan, whether he liked it or not, to found a movement that, though it was called Freudian, would ultimately not be able to avoid becoming Lacanian. I shall return to this later.

The "Recommendations" required that Dolto should be banished from the list of SFP training analysts at the same time as Lacan. Article 12 also laid down that René Laforgue and Angelo Hesnard should be excluded in the same way. I have already had occasion to explain the reasons behind the banishing of these two elderly founding fathers of the SPP. Laforgue was seen as an eccentric guru, and although at that time there was no tangible proof of his having collaborated with Matthias Heinrich Göring, he was regarded as a former pro-Nazi. As for Hesnard, he was the only member of his generation who had never been analyzed. As he had also been one of the chief representatives of the chauvinistic faction, there was no reason why the IPA should readmit him, especially as he was rightly suspected of anti-Semitism.[30] Thus article 12 of the "Recommendations" quietly eliminated the remains of a French psychoanalytic past that was regarded as something to be ashamed of. But what was to be done with Laforgue's and Hesnard's pupils?

As early as 1947, as we know, it had been suggested that they pursue their careers on other, more "suitable" couches. So the ranks of the SPP had undergone a kind of peaceful purge. But some of Laforgue's analysands, thinking their training already sufficient, had rejected the idea of a second phase of analysis. Françoise Dolto was in this situation—her analysis had been complemented by several group controls—so even at the time of the first inquiry she was regarded as too "Laforguian," and this reflected discredit on her practice. Juliette Favez-Boutonier's case, which was similar to Françoise Dolto's, was soon settled. She had only a few training analysands and devoted most of her time to her academic activities. So her practice didn't present the inquirers with any real problem. Dolto, on the other hand, who did few training analyses but whose consultations were followed by numerous students, upset everybody, including both the normalizers of the IPA and such mandarins of the SFP as Serge Lebovici and René Diatkine, who wanted child psychoanalysis in France to be run by the psychiatric institutions.

On September 21, 1962, a few months after the death of René Laforgue, Marie Bonaparte had died suddenly of leukemia, leaving Hesnard the last surviving representative in France of the founding generation of the SPP. At the Stockholm congress the Central Executive's "Directive" made no further mention of Dolto's banishment, and the names of Hesnard and Laforgue had disappeared from the list of those forbidden to carry out training analyses. But the "Recommendations" issued in Edinburgh two years earlier still applied, and both Hesnard and Dolto had no choice but to accompany Lacan into exile. This is how, in September 1981, Françoise Dolto remembered the man whose destiny she had followed for so long: "When I first started taking young psychoanalysts who wanted to go in for child analysis, it was among those who had been analyzed by Lacan that I found those best able to understand children and stand the shock involved. I mean it was only among them that I encountered colleagues ready to recognize a child, even a very young one, as a subject with a desire to express, not just an object of study for an academic psychopedagogue or a normalizing psychopediatrician. It was this that made me realize Lacan was a real psychoanalyst, unlike so many others who knew a lot about teaching and took pride in being called analysts but looked on it all as just a profession."[31]

In proscribing the two outstanding figures of French Freudianism, the IPA leadership were to all intents and purposes deciding to admit to their ranks only respectable practitioners of psychoanalysis for the privileged. For the sake of standardization and out of a horror of excess, they were depriving themselves of the creativity without which there can be no theoretical innovation. After June 1964 the only bodies that would be incorporated into the IPA were the old SPP and the new Association psychanalytique de France (APF). This organization was made up of thirty or so former members of the by-then-dissolved SFP, among them Lagache, the two Favezes, Granoff, Anzieu, and a number of Lacan's pupils (Laplanche, Pontalis, Pujol, Smirnoff, Lavie, Widlöcher, and so on). The Freudian France thus legitimized was a body without head or limbs. In losing Dolto and Lacan it had lost its thinking brain, as well as three-quarters of the coming generation (the fourth), whose members much preferred to follow the teaching of two transcendent masters rather than submit to a set of rules that they saw as growing more and more conservative.

The 1963–1964 break was as disastrous for the IPA as it was for the development of Lacanianism, because it made the idea of a "French exception" credible again. For the fourth generation of French psychoanalysts, raised in the lecture rooms of Lacanianism, and for the considerable part of the third generation that had remained faithful to Lacan, the Freudian empire was henceforward associated with an imperialist machine fit only for slavishly reproducing the adaptive ideas of "the American way of life": an Uncle Sam bloated with Coca-Cola. For their part, the chief dignitaries of the IPA, whether English or American, regarded those they now called the "Lacanians" as out-and-out sectarians or mystical theologians, better at fomenting intellectual rebellion than curing ordinary neuroses. As for Lacan, his permanent banishment meant he would never be able to make the Anglo-American world recognize his continuation of Freudianism as legitimate. At most it would be admitted as a dissident or deviant faction: the very opposite of what it purported to be. In other words, the man who claimed to stand for scientific rationality and a universal Freudianism was condemned to the usual fate of a prophet in his own country, proclaiming his message within parochial limits that he never ceased to challenge.

22

. . . .

Structure and the Name-of-the-Father

Madeleine Chapsal was a young journalist working for *L'Express,* her husband Jean-Jacques Servan-Schreiber's new weekly, when she met Jacques Lacan for the first time. He was wearing a shaggy ginger wig. He was introduced to her by "Jibé" Pontalis and asked her to dance. It was at one of the "egghead" parties given by *Les Temps modernes*, at which the guests usually wore fancy dress.

Lacan, now over fifty, had settled deliberately into the character of a flamboyant and eccentric master. Giving his weekly lecture in the amphitheater at the Hôpital Sainte-Anne, he spoke in fits and starts, with now and then a sigh or a roar. He always brought with him a few sheets of paper covered with notes and sketches; these served to maintain the suspense created by his intermittent delivery. Sometimes he muttered, like Oedipus at Colonus trying by ominous silence to suspend the course of time; sometimes he raised his voice like Hamlet facing death, as if to contradict the slowness of impending thought. At once somber and tumultuous, he could bring forth from broken speech or imperfect memory the rigorous logic of an unconscious whose ebb and flow he seemed to echo. His seminars used to produce a collective catharsis; everyone present felt that Lacan was speaking to him alone. Between 1953 and 1963 the amphitheater at Sainte-Anne acted as a kind of research laboratory for everyone who attended the lectures—philosophers, psychoanalysts, and writers. The atmosphere resembled that of a Socratic symposium, and though the sustained excitement disappeared later, traces of it could still be seen in stimulating exchanges between the master and members of the audience.

Madeleine Chapsal didn't go to Sainte-Anne, but she and "Jibé" spent several weekends at Guitrancourt, where Sylvia gave her useful advice and introduced her to Tristan Tzara and Georges Bataille.

Madeleine Chapsal had been fascinated by Freud ever since she had studied philosophy at the university. She was now entering high-class literary journalism via a series of lengthy interviews with contemporary writers and thinkers. Some, like Sartre, Malraux, Beauvoir, and Céline, were already famous; others were as yet known only to a few, and Chapsal gave these their first opportunity to speak to a wide public.[1] She liked the "singular," "rule-breaking" intellectuals who were trying to structure the world through language. She hadn't yet thought of becoming a novelist; her object was still to act rather as interpreter to others. She and Lacan soon struck up a friendship that both of them valued. It involved gifts of flowers, the borrowing and lending of rare books, and a correspondence that mingled poetry and prose, the formal "vous" and the more intimate "tu," a game of hide-and-seek and the art of gallantry. She delighted in his penchant for disguise, his auburn wigs, his love of social life and gossip, the way he enjoyed theatrical situations.[2]

Born into circles concerned with fashion, she was familiar with the secret rites of that ephemeral world: her mother, Marcelle Chaumont, and her godmother, the great Madeleine Vionnet, were both devoted to it body and soul. Throughout a childhood spent largely in the salons of the avenue Montaigne, Madeleine Chapsal had been close to the "spirit of haute couture," observing and admiring the workrooms where seamstresses toiled day after day to produce fabulous gowns for princesses, stars, and wealthy middle-class wives.[3]

Lacan had fallen in love with this "spirit." He shared with women and with his master Clérambault a passion for fabrics not far removed from fetishism; he was fascinated by Madeleine's manners, elegance, and exquisite taste. In February 1956, not knowing what to wear at a ball being given by Marie-Laure de Noailles, he asked Madeleine to suggest some ideas and above all not to tell anyone else about them: in this as in other fields he dreaded plagiarism. On another occasion he told his young friend that his motto was "People betray me and get away with it", an inversion of *Nemo me impune lacessit*, the device of the Order of the Thistle, the Scottish order of knighthood. He returned to this theme later when he defined a hero as someone who is betrayed with impunity. He went to the ball as Minerva's bird, the owl: a tribute to philosophy.

Although he put structure before events in his critique of historiography and proceeded by allusion instead of identifying his sources and borrowings, Lacan had an insatiable curiosity about one particular strand of historical narrative: gossip, rumor, and anecdote. He delighted in listening to confidences of the agony-aunt variety. "Whenever I went to see him," says Madeleine Chapsal, "I tried to remember the latest tittle-tattle; I knew it was the greatest treat I could give him. . . . He was more inquisitive than a concierge lurking in her *loge*. . . . But on the whole he never revealed anything about himself."[4] His keen interest in private conversations wouldn't have disgraced Proust's ferocious Mme Verdurin, and he liked going to places frequented by newspaper chiefs. His observation of these men, whose profession it was to maintain the illusion that language could be transparent, was probably a help to him when he challenged, in his teaching, what he secretly most admired about them: the power of the media, the effort to achieve clear communication. He often took Madeleine to eat ortolans in the Berkeley Restaurant in the avenue Matignon, sitting not far from the favorite table of Pierre Lazareff, the press magnate.

While quite aware of Lacan's desire to attract her, Madeleine realized he was courting her not as a woman but as a journalist to whom he might eventually offer his services. "At that time Lacan hadn't published any books. It irked him that he wasn't yet recognized, and through me he had his eye on *L'Express*."[5] That was why, while she went along with him in toying with ambiguity and pretending theirs might be something other than a platonic relationship, she never actually granted him her favors. Nonetheless his approach to her did suggest an expert attempt at conquest. "What does it matter how many lovers you have," he said in one letter, "if none of them gives you the universe?"[6]

In the spring of 1957 she suggested she should interview him for *L'Express*, on condition that the result turned out to be intelligible to the general reader. "Just as he knew how to make an entrance in public, so he was very skillful at preparing his entry into the popular press. He listened to all my questions about Freud and psychoanalysis so amiably, with such eagerness to do the right thing and be understood, that I was quite touched. Some of my questions were deliberately very elementary because I too wanted the interview to get into the paper, but he, a virtuoso of classical exposition, answered with remarkable clarity. Lacan could be as clear when he wanted to as he was obscure and baroque in his usual teaching."[7] The interview appeared in the issue of May 31, 1957. The title, "Keys to Psychoanalysis," was announced on the cover, and the front page carried a photograph of the master and a quotation from St. John's Gospel: "In the beginning was the Word."[8]

In the interview Lacan achieved the extraordinary feat of giving readers of *L'Express* a lucid explanation both of Freud's discoveries and also of what was, in his own—necessarily Lacanian—view, the only correct way of interpreting them. Freud, as we know, had applied a metaphor to history, showing that all scientific investigation inflicted humiliation upon human narcissism. He distinguished three main examples among many. The first humiliation was cosmological and occurred when the Copernican revolution destroyed the illusion that the earth was the center of the universe. The second, biological in nature, occurred when Darwinism shattered man's claim to be other than animal. The third blow was psychological and arose from the Freudian idea of the unconscious, which contradicted the belief that the ego was master in its own house.[9]

Lacan, adapting this metaphor of decentering to his own purposes, claimed that Freudian doctrine as a whole belonged to the sphere of science, logic, and rationality. Against obscurantists who accused Freud of being irrational, Lacan maintained that he not only rationalized that which had previously resisted rationalization but also showed "a reason reasoning as such, in action." Lacan went on to recall the subversive character of Freud's discovery. Then, instead of citing Christopher Columbus and Hannibal, the two great historical figures with whom Freud had identified himself, he compared him to Champollion, the Frenchman credited with first deciphering Egyptian hieroglyphics. He thus gave Freud's achievement an interpretation that, while true to its original, was still not quite the one that Freud himself intended. Freud never claimed so radically that his work could be theoretically regarded as a surge of rebellion capable of overthrowing the social order. At most he said it had aspects that were shocking and unacceptable. Nor had he claimed that the unconscious could be, in the strict sense of the term, a kind of writing, made up of signs deriving their meaning solely from the system to which they belonged. These two hypotheses—the subversive nature of psychoanalytic doctrine and the likening of the unconscious to a system of signs—formed no part of Freud's scientific conceptions. But the fact that they did not actually contradict Freud's own utterances enabled Lacan to attribute them to him. "Read *The Interpretation of Dreams*," he said. "Read *Jokes and Their Relation to the Unconscious*. Open either of them at any page, and you'll find what I say expressed quite clearly."[10]

In bringing up to date the hypothesis that Freud's work was subversive, Lacan placed himself in the direct line of the "Hannibalian" view of psychoanalysis that I have outlined elsewhere.[11] But while Freud identified with Hannibal in order to link his discovery with the principle of resistance, Lacan went much further: he wanted to make that discovery the paradigm of all possible forms of human rebellion. In this respect he was following in the tradition of "*l'exception française*": France as odd man out. France, as everyone knows, is the only country in the world where it was forcefully asserted that Freud had brought about a revolution in the full sense of the word, a revolution that was at once theoretical, political, and ideological. The origin of France's status as an exception went back in the first place to the revolution of 1789, which gave scientific and legal legitimacy to the authority of reason over madness and which also introduced asylums; and, subsequently, to the Dreyfus affair, which endowed the intellectual class with a *conscience de soi* (self-awareness). The intellectuals, by presenting themselves as an avant-garde, were then able to take over and exploit innovative ideas. To all this may be added the birth of modern literature via Baudelaire, Rimbaud, and Lautréamont, and a new kind of writing that suggested humanity could be changed on the basis of Rimbaud's "*JE est un autre*" (I is another).

Without the 1789 revolution there would have been no long-lasting body of psychiatric knowledge capable of incorporating first German nosography and then Freud's discovery; without Dreyfus there would have been no intellectual avant-garde conscious of itself and able to annex new ideas; and without literary modernity Freud's discovery would never have encountered the idea that psychoanalysis might be the expression of both the subversion of the subject ("*JE est un autre*") and a radical challenge to the social order.[12]

In order to reinforce the hypothesis about the subversiveness of Freudianism that he had inherited through his familiarity with the surrealists, Bataille, and the works of Nietzsche, Lacan had tried to trace it back to Freud himself. But how was he to prove this assertion, when evidence was nowhere to be found? Lacan had solved this difficult problem by going to see Carl Gustav Jung, in 1954.

The most famous dissident in all the Freudian saga was then seventy-nine years old. He sat in his splendid house on the shores of Lake Zurich like some elderly oriental sage, dispensing treatment, advice, and erudition to the many visitors who came to see him from every quarter of the globe. Lacan, knowing how difficult it would be to approach Jung, had asked his old friend Roland Cahen to intercede on his behalf. Cahen was a psychiatrist and German scholar who had made Jung's acquaintance in 1936, become his disciple, and undertaken the first French translation of his works.[13] At the Hôpital Sainte-Anne, after the war, Cahen had been in frequent contact with Nacht, Lacan, Ey, and Lagache, trying in vain to get them to take account of Jungian teaching in their work. When Lacan asked him for a letter of recommendation to Jung, Cahen thought the meeting might lead to a comparison of the two doctrines. "You know, old boy," he said, "what with your signifieds and our archetypes, we're really first cousins." Lacan flatly rejected this idea. "Never," he answered. "But I want to go and see Jung because I'm sure he can remember things about Freud, and I want to publish them."[14]

At that time Jung hadn't yet started writing his memoirs, his correspondence with Freud had not appeared, and no one had started researching his life. For anyone who wanted to understand the history of the origins and beginnings of psychoanalysis, Freudian hagiography was still the only available source. But Jung always seemed negative and disloyal with regard to the sacrosanct figure of the Viennese master, who was otherwise always presented as a hero *sans peur et sans reproche*.[15] So it was a very good idea on Lacan's part to get Jung to testify about his relations with Freud. The meeting took place, but to Roland Cahen's distress he couldn't find out anything about it. Lacan never told him what happened, and Jung's own memory of the interview was very fleeting.

But if Lacan wouldn't tell his friend anything, it was because he was saving it up for others. On November 7, 1955, in a lecture on the Freudian "thing" delivered in German in Vienna, he spoke for the first time about his visit to Küsnacht: "Thus Freud's words to Jung—I have it from Jung's own mouth—when, on an invitation from Clark University, they arrived in New York harbor and caught their first glimpse of the famous statue illuminating the universe, 'They don't realize we're bringing them the plague,' are attributed to him as confirmation of a hubris whose antiphrasis and gloom do not extinguish their troubled brightness."[16]

Lacan, commenting on the remark, said Freud was mistaken: he thought psychoanalysis would revolutionize America, but in fact the roles were reversed, and it was America that devoured Freud's teaching by removing its spirit of subversion. Freud's alleged comment got an unpredictably wide hearing. But while no one in France doubts that Freudianism really is subversive, and still less does anyone dare to think Freud probably never uttered the phrase in question when he went to the United States in 1909 with Jung and Ferenczi, nonetheless a study of the relevant texts, letters, and archives shows that Lacan was the only person to whom Jung vouchsafed this interesting secret. In his *Memoirs*, Jung speaks of the journey but makes no reference to the plague. Neither Freud nor Ferenczi ever uses the word. As for the historians of Freudianism, from Ernest Jones to Max Schur, and including Henri Ellenberger, Vincent Brome, Clarence Oberndorf, Paul Roazen, Nathan G. Hale, and Peter Gay, they simply have Freud saying: "They'll be surprised when they find out what we have to tell them."[17]

Fortified by a secret entrusted to him alone, Lacan constructed a truer-than-life fiction designed to impose, as against so-called American psychoanalysis, his own reformulation of the Viennese doctrine, henceforward bearing the stamp of subversion. And if the "Freudian plague" story became so well established in France that now even non-Lacanians attribute it to Freud himself, that is because it was in the direct line of the "*exception française*" that Lacan once despised but of which he became both the heir and the reformer.

In the city where the founding father had lived, Lacan didn't hesitate to conjure up the memory of a *Mitteleuropa* first engulfed by Nazism and then wiped out of history by American imperialism. And, as before in Marienbad in 1936, he tried to enlist the support of Vienna against London, then of

Europe against the New World, calling to witness Count Alfred von Winterstein, president of the Wiener Psychoanalytische Vereinigung (WPV: Vienna Psychoanalytic Society), who attended the lecture. Von Winterstein, an aristocrat and the last surviving member of the heroic era, had, with August Aichhorn, kept the mangled remains of psychoanalysis going in Vienna during the Nazi period, rejecting the "rescue" policy advocated by Jones.[18] Lacan knew this, and that was why he hoped to be listened to when he contrasted the subversive virtue of Freud's "plague" not only with the "Black Death" but also with the various adaptational theories. But Lacan's plan didn't work: despite the split in 1947 that had caused Count Igor Caruso to leave the WPV, the society had been completely incorporated into the IPA, as Lacan was to find out when he met Wilhelm Solms on the Turquet committee.

So, in the autumn of 1955, Lacan pronounced his grand anathemas in a city that had forgotten the subversive violence of Freudianism's beginnings.

In the second installment of his *Express* interview with Madeleine Chapsal, Lacan maintained, still with the American model in mind, that it was equally wrong to believe in adaptational psychoanalysis and to think that analysis could be a way of freeing oneself from all constraint. Then, referring to a famous phrase of Freud's, he declared that the ego should never be made to take the place of the unconscious or id. He was here alluding again to his Vienna lecture and to a discussion that had taken place at the SFP on November 6, 1956.

On that occasion Hesnard had commented on the sentence, "Wo Es war, soll Ich werden," which Freud had written in 1932 at the end of the chapter entitled "The Dissection of the Psychical Personality" in his *New Introductory Lectures on Psycho-Analysis.*[19] The sentence in question defined the new task that psychoanalysis imposed on civilization, a task as important for mankind as "the draining of the Zuider Zee." In 1936 Anne Bermann, a colleague of Marie Bonaparte, had translated it as "The ego must dislodge the id." The unconscious was to be adapted to the modalities of conscious thought. Lacan, of course, challenged this translation and used the couple *je/ça* (I/id), put forward by Pichon, to render the famous dictum in French as "Là où ça était (c'était), le je doit être (dois-je advenir)" (roughly: Where it was, the I must be [I must come to be]). The German verb *war* was thus restored literally, in the imperfect tense, so that the second Freudian topography might be interpreted in a nonpsychological way: the task of psychoanalysis is not to dislodge the id in favor of the ego but on the contrary to make it possible to put every element in its respective place. The *ego* is not the whole of the *Ich*, which can be subdivided into an imaginary *moi*, or ego, and an enunciating *je*, or I.[20]

Lacan had already suggested this division before the war. But as a result of new thinking, initiated in 1949, on the subject of the *cogito*, it came to be included in a wider application, which took place in two stages, of the consequences of structural linguistics. In France, Merleau-Ponty was the first to declare, in his inaugural lecture at the Collège de France, that a philosophy could be derived from Saussure's *Course in General Linguistics*: "The theory of signs, as developed in linguistics, perhaps implies a conception of historical meaning which gets beyond the opposition of *things* versus *consciousness*.... In such cases, there is a rationality in the contingent, a lived logic, a self-constitution of which we have definite need in trying to understand the union of contingency and meaning in history, and Saussure, the modern linguist, could have sketched a new philosophy of history."[21]

Lacan had got the message. He had first linked together the subject, language, and speech in his "Rome Discourse," on the basis of Heidegger's philosophy and the elementary structures of kinship. Thereafter he set out, using a logical method and abandoning all ontology, to formulate a theory concerning the relationship between subject and signifier. The work was carried out gradually, over a period of time, and in a baroque and convoluted style. Lacan never traveled in a straight line. Not only did he conceal his sources, as if to strip what he said of any historical appendages; he also attributed to Freud concepts that were really his own. What is more, he altered course between one seminar and another, as if imitating the zigzag gait of the paranoid hero of Buñuel's film *El*, of which Lacan was very fond (he said it illustrated the logical rigidity of psychosis).[22] He dealt with the subject and the signifier alternately, the former being treated in the evenly numbered seminars, the latter in seminars I, III, V, VII, etc. This procedure also conformed to the central theme of Lacan's system of thought, concerning the primacy of the signifier. But all this makes it difficult to trace the sequence and identify the stages of the conceptual reformulation contained in his teaching.

It was through his second reading of Saussure, following the researches of Roman Jakobson, that Lacan—together with Roland Barthes, Michel Foucault, Louis Althusser, and others—was to become the architect of a school of thought that is based on a break with phenomenology and has been called an "antihumanist," "structuralist," and "scientific" conception of psychoanalysis. To this "structuralism" Lacan added an element of subversion that, through his theory of object *a* (*a* for *autre*) and the "paranoid ego of civilization," reflected the Nietzscheanism of his youth. But despite this Nietzscheanism, Lacan, instead of adopting the philosophy of the Enlightenment as such, followed the scientific tradition that opposed obscurantism with atheistic rationalism. This privileging of science explains why

Lacan, despite a friendship for the man himself that lasted as long as Heidegger lived, never accepted Heidegger's philosophy.

As for Lacan's structuralism, it rested on the idea that man's true freedom stemmed from the subject's consciousness of not being free at all, because of unconscious determination. In his view this Freudian form of a divided consciousness of self, which according to him originated in Cartesian doubt, was more subversive than a belief—such as Sartre's, for instance—in the possibility of a philosophy of freedom.

Lacan's second interpretation of Saussure began on June 23, 1954; then, for the first time, instead of merely referring to ideas of language, speech, or linguistics, Lacan commented on Saussure's theory of signs.[23] On May 30, 1955, he backed up this approach by adducing Edgar Allan Poe's short story *The Purloined Letter*. On May 25 he had propounded the theory of the relationship between object *a* and the *Autre* (Other). Then, on June 8, he announced his theory of the function of the father as *symbolic father*, thus transforming the *name-of-the-father* from a simple notion into a genuine concept. He returned to the same set of themes in the seminar on *identification* (1961–1962), where in a diatribe against Bertrand Russell he identified the proper name with a *trait unaire*, or unary trait, denoting the *one* of the signifier.[24]

In a parallel move, on May 2, 1956, Lacan made his first reference to Roman Jakobson's theories on metaphor and metonymy, of which he made fruitful use a year later, on May 9, 1957—at the time of the *Express* interview—in a lecture delivered to liberal arts students at the Sorbonne: "The Agency of the Letter in the Unconscious or Reason since Freud."[25] Lastly, during a colloquium on "Dialectics" organized at Royaumont by Jean Wahl, which ran from September 19 to September 23, 1960, Lacan put forward for the first time the famous formula defining the signifier (in the Lacanian sense of the term) and making the subject an element in a structure (or symbolic chain): "A signifier is that which represents the subject for another signifier."[26] From there he was to move on in 1961 to the idea of a *topological* structure of the subject.

Meanwhile, also at Royaumont, where the International Days of the SFP were held from July 10 through July 13, Lacan had contrasted his resolutely structuralist notion of the *structure of the subject* with the personalist ideology proposed by Lagache in his paper on the structure of the personality. Lacan was doing battle against the French form of psychologized psychoanalysis of which the American form was ego psychology.[27]

Poe's story is well known. It is set in Restoration France, where Auguste Dupin, a young gentleman from an illustrious family, living in reduced circumstances, is consulted by the prefect of police about a compromising letter that Minister D— had stolen from the queen and hidden in a place that no one can discover. In fact the letter is quite visible, stuck in a compartment of a card rack suspended from the mantelpiece in the minister's office. The police were unable to see it because they were trapped in their own psychology. Instead of looking at the evidence in front of their eyes they made up intricate theories as to where the letter might be concealed. Dupin, having concluded that the minister had resorted to "the sagacious expedient of not attempting to conceal it at all," calls on the minister and under cover of a pair of "green spectacles" takes a good look round the room and spots the letter. Then, leaving a snuffbox as if by accident as a pretext to return, he goes away, prepares a replica of the letter, and comes back the next morning to substitute it for the real document. The minister, unaware of his loss, continues toward his downfall, thinking he still has the queen in his power, while she knows he has not, since it was in the possession of the letter and not the use of it that his ascendancy over her resided.

To explain his method to the narrator, Dupin remarks that many a schoolboy is a better, because a simpler and more appropriate, reasoner than the prefect of police. "I know one about eight years of age whose success at guessing in the game of 'even and odd' attracted universal admiration. This game is simple, and is played with marbles. One player holds in his hand a number of these toys, and demands of another whether that number is even or odd. If the guess is right, the guesser wins one; if wrong, he loses one. The boy to whom I allude won all the marbles of the school. Of course he had some principle of guessing; and this lay in mere observation and admeasurement of the astuteness of his opponents."[28]

At the May 1955 session of his seminar, Lacan asked his followers to play "even and odd" in order to comment more adequately on the story, which resembled that of the prisoners, although in this case the central element was no longer a subject or individual forced to make a decision so as to gain his freedom, but a letter involving a subject or individual in the process of establishing fact. In both cases, however, the ideas of looking and playing are of primary importance. A month later Lacan began the actual writing of his text on *The Purloined Letter*, finishing it in August in San Casciano, the village where Machiavelli was born. In this key article, which Lacan was to use eleven years later as an introduction to the *Ecrits*, he no longer spoke only of the primacy of the symbolical function in Freud's view of the unconscious; he also constructed what amounted to a "political" logic of the signifier: a letter always arrives at its destination because the *letter*—i.e., the *signifier*, as inscribed in the unconscious—determines, as *fortuna* did for Machiavelli, the subject's fate in its various orientations. Such then was "The Agency of the Letter in the Unconscious," the organization of which Lacan was to explain first in May 1957 and then in September 1960.

Ferdinand Saussure divided the *signe linguistique* (linguistic sign) into two parts. He called the acoustic image of a concept the *signifiant* (signifier), and the concept itself the *signifié* (signified). The linguistic sign was thus defined as the relationship between a signified and a signifier within a system of values. As for the *value* of a sign, it resulted negatively from the simultaneous presence of all the other signs in the language. The *signification* (signification or meaning), which is not the same as the value, is deduced from the link between signified and signifier. In order to interpret Freud's second topography in the light of structural linguistics, Lacan was breaking down the problematics of the sign. Whereas Saussure placed the signified over the signifier, dividing the two by a bar of "meaning," Lacan inverted this arrangement, placing the signified *under* the signifier, to which he ascribes the primary role. Then, adapting the idea of value to his own purposes, he asserted that every meaning is related to another meaning. From this he arrived at the notion that the signifier must be isolated from the signified, like a *letter* (or *word symbol*) that is devoid of meaning but determines the unconscious destiny of the subject. As for the subject, which is not the same thing as the ego, Lacan initially defined it as the *subject of the unconscious*: a subject divided in accordance with the Freudian law of *Spaltung* and split in accordance with the psychiatric theory of *discordance*.[29]

In this context the subject does not exist as a plenitude: on the contrary, the subject is *represented* by the signifier, or in other words by the letter indicating the rooting of the unconscious in language. But the subject is also represented by a chain of signifiers in which the plane of the enunciated (or the stated) is different from the plane of enunciation (or stating). Thus the subject is represented *by* a signifier to another signifier within a structural whole.

In this way Lacan replaced the Cartesian "I think" by a Freudian "it speaks." Whence the term *subject of the unconscious*, an expression quite alien to the doctrine that emanated from Vienna. What Lacan was doing, in fact, was showing that Freud did not really abolish the subject but rather annexed it as part of the reaction to Cartesianism that gave rise, after Galileo, to modern science. While Freud, with his theory of narcissistic wounds, saw himself as the heir of Copernicus and Darwin, Lacan, through the teachings of Koyré, was more in the line of Galileo. That being so, he drew the appropriate conclusions both from Cartesian doubt (which made the subject the author of his own thought) and from Kantian ethics (which made the subject the cornerstone of a moral ideology suited to industrial societies) and produced a theory of the *modern ego* defined as the "paranoid subject of civilization." In his view the Freudian experiment was the converse of the philosophy of the cogito. But by invoking Descartes at the same time as Freud and talking of a subject established by science, Lacan reintroduced the idea of doubt into the unconscious: a divided subject, an "I don't know who I am."

All that remained was to translate the Freudian concept of *Ichspaltung* (splitting of the I) and show that the human subject is twice divided, with one agency separating the imaginary ego from the subject of the unconscious and another establishing itself within the subject of the unconscious itself and representing its original division. Lacan used the word *refente* (from *fendre*, to split or crack) to denote this second division, which can never be mended, because the subject is always represented, for another subject, by a signifier. Beside the *refente* he places *fading*, a term borrowed (inaccurately) from English to denote the subject's appearance in and disappearance from the chain: a binary dissolve, as in a film.

But Lacan's "Cartesian" operation needed more assistance than Saussure alone could supply, so he turned to the work of Roman Jakobson. A few months before Lacan delivered his lecture on "The Agency of the Letter," he came across Jakobson and Morris Hall's *The Fundamentals of Language*, published in The Hague. The book contained an article entitled "Two Aspects of Language and Two Types of Aphasic Disturbances" that would help Lacan give a structural form to his theory about language and the unconscious. Jakobson pointed out a bipolar structure in language in accordance with which a speaker unknowingly performs two kinds of activity: one, related to *similarity*, concerns the *selection* of paradigms or units of language, while the other, related to *contiguity*, concerns the syntagmatic *combination* of these units. In the process of selection, a speaker makes a choice or prefers one word rather than another: for example, he may use the word "cap" instead of "hat" or "beret." In the combination process, he places in relation to one another two words that form a continuity: to describe the way someone is dressed, he may link together the words "blouse" and "skirt."

On this basis, Jakobson showed that language troubles resulting from aphasia deprive the individual concerned sometimes of his power to select and sometimes of his power to combine. Then he summoned classical rhetoric to the aid of linguistics in order to demonstrate that the selective activity of language corresponded to metaphor, while combination resembled metonymy. Troubles relating to the first kind of linguistic activity prevent the subject from using metaphor; troubles relating to the second kind forbid metonymy. Jakobson concludes by observing that both processes are to be found in the functioning of dreams, as described by Freud. He classified symbolism as belonging to metaphor, while *condensation* (*Verdichtung*) and *displacement* (*Verschiebung*) came under the heading of metonymic activities.[30]

Lacan, making use of this demonstration, put forward a new version of

Freud's concept of the dreamwork. If dreams in general consist of a process of transposition between *latent content* and *manifest content*, this may be seen, in the light of Saussure's researches, as a shifting of the signified beneath the signifier. So there are two aspects of the impact of the signifier on the signified: one is a kind of condensation and involves the *superimposition* of signifiers (as in portmanteau words and composite characters), and the other involves a *change* or *transfer* of meaning (the part for the whole, or contiguity) and denotes a displacement. Unlike Jakobson, Lacan associated the Freudian idea of condensation with metaphor and displacement with metonymy. According to him, a symptom related to metaphor when it substituted a somatic signifier for another, repressed, signifier; in metonymy, unconscious desire appeared as an ever-unsatisfied *desire for desire*.

"Is the place I occupy as subject of the signifier concentric or excentric in relation to the place I occupy as subject of the signified?" Excentric, Lacan answers, in accordance with his distortion of the cogito: "I think where I am not, therefore I am where I do not think." So Lacan's topography involved ascribing to the unconscious the structure of a language in which the I was defined as what Jakobson called a *shifter*: a grammatical unit of which the meaning is referenced to the message. A shifter thus denoted the subject of the enunciation without signifying it. Lacan depicted it in a negative signifier—for example, in the negative expletive *ne* as defined by Pichon in his famous article on negation.[31] Lacan was later to use various other formulae to describe his structural version of the unconscious: "The unconscious is structured like a language"; then "Language is the condition for the unconscious"; and finally "The unconscious is the condition of linguistics."[32]

Meanwhile, Lacan produced three formulae to describe the impact of the signifier on the signified. The general formula described the signifying function starting from the bar of resistance to meaning. The formula relating to metonymy reflected the process by which signifiers are connected with one another; in this process the elision of the signified referred to the object of desire, which is always missing from the chain. The formula that covered metaphor pointed to the substitution of one signifier for another, through which the subject was represented. Lacan uses the term *point de capiton*—button tie (an upholsterer's stitch)—to denote the point in the chain at which a signifier and a signified are knotted together to give birth to a meaning.[33] The phrase lent a more theoretical content to the idea of *punctuation* that Lacan used in the "Rome Discourse" to describe the need for an internal interruption in the course of a session.

Once again Lacan was attributing his own approach to Freud, going so far as to say the latter saw the unconscious as a chain of signifiers: "This formula . . . is mine," he said, "only in the sense that it conforms as closely to

Freud's text as to the experience that it opened up," and so on.[34] He saw himself as the latter-day organizer of a meeting between Freud and Saussure that had never taken place in reality. He was later to say, as a joke:"I was the one who invented the unconscious."

This extraordinary intellectual operation, by means of which Lacan endowed psychoanalytic doctrine with a Cartesian theory of the subject and a "post-Saussurian" conception of the unconscious, arose not only out of Lacan's reading of Jakobson but also out of his meeting with the great linguist: after Kojève and Koyré, the third representative of the exiled Russian intelligentsia to play an essential part in Lacan's development.

Roman Jakobson, born in Moscow in 1896, gave evidence very early on of an exceptional gift for languages. He learned to read when he was four years old, and by the time he was seven could speak French and German as well as Russian. By the end of his life he had mastered all the Romance, Slavic, and Germanic languages. Only his friend Evgeni Polivanov, with his knowledge of Asian languages, had managed to surpass him. Roman's parents were very close to the family of Yuri Kagan, a Moscow lawyer who specialized in literary, artistic, and theatrical contracts, and Kagan's two daughters, Lili and Elsa, were Roman's childhood friends. They called him "Romka" and liked his red hair. He fell in love with Elsa.

By 1910, the year of Tolstoy's death, Jakobson was an admirer of the symbolist poets and theorists, and he greeted the earliest futurist manifestos with enthusiasm. In March 1912 Lili married Ossip Brik and went to live in St. Petersburg, where Roman visited her six months later. "Brik was a brilliant man—I am sure of it. . . . He didn't aim at producing a body of written work. What he wanted to do was discover things. . . . What he liked best was to have some young man to whom he could entrust the actual labor. Many works appeared under other people's names that were in fact inspired by Brik."[35] During this trip Jakobson made the acquaintance of Velimir Khlebnikov, whom he regarded as the greatest poet of the century. Over a drink in a famous tavern patronized by intellectuals, the two men exchanged ideas on the "suprarational" language that the futurists had invented, based on combining imaginary words with real suffixes.

In Moscow, in the spring of 1914, Jakobson also met Vladimir Maïakovski; he became one of his closest friends. Maïakovski was a frequent visitor to Brik's literary salon, which brought together poets and other writers interested in studying poetic language. He fell passionately in love with Lili and became her lover. In March 1915 Roman Jakobson was one of the founders of the Moscow Language Club, which soon began to meet in an apartment underneath that of Maïakovsky, who used to come there and read his poems. The club arose out of the coming together of three different trends of thought: the researches of the Russian school of linguistics, whose most innovative representative, after Baudoin de Courtenay, was Prince Nicolas Troubetzkoy; Husserlian phenomenology; and the futurist avant-garde.[36] A year later the members of the club were initiated into Saussurian linguistics by one of the last pupils of the Genevan master, Sergei Karcevski, who passed on to them orally the principles of the new doctrine.

A few months before the October Revolution, Jakobson founded OPOIAZ in Petrograd. This was a society for the study of poetic language, and as well as officializing the activities of Brik's group it also served as a melting pot for what came to be called the school of Russian Formalism. It brought together such celebrated men as the linguist Evgeni Polivanov, the poet Boris Eikhenbaum, and the language theorist Viktor Chlovski, as well as Boris Pasternak, Ossip Mandelstam, and Maïakovski. The aim of the OPOIAZ was to arrive at a system of poetics exclusive of all external considerations—such as the author's "psyche," social values, the history of ideas—and concentrating entirely on the literary work itself. Thus, between them, the Moscow Club and the formalist group in Petrograd juxtaposed the study of language for its own sake and the study of literature as an autonomous form of expression. For both groups, poetry represented the quintessence of language: a language putting the emphasis on language itself.[37]

The activities of both groups came to an end after the revolution, and their members turned to other commitments. Some went into exile; others remained in Russia; still others—such as Polivanov, who was shot in the Caucasus in 1938—eventually became victims of Stalin's purges. In 1923 the LEF, or Left Front of Art, was formed, with Maïakovski and Brik at its center and the aim of moving from futurism to communism by sweeping away old attitudes and abandoning the Russian culture of the past.[38] When Elsa Kagan left Russia in 1918 to marry André Triolet, a French officer who took her with him to Paris, Jakobson wrote her a poem: "Let it be said between you and me/That with all my heart I love you/If you go to Tahiti/My pain will be extreme." He met her later in Paris, with Louis Aragon.

It was in 1920, when he arrived in Prague, that Jakobson read the *Course in General Linguistics* for the first time. He was struck by the importance Saussure accorded to the question of *oppositions*. Like the cubist painters, Picasso and Braque, he laid stress not on things themselves but on the relations between them: "The same topological attitude that preoccupied us in linguistics was at the same time appearing in the arts and sciences. . . . The word *opposition* inevitably suggested the idea of a latent logical operation."[39] In Vienna he once more met Troubetzkoy, who had fled from the revolution and was working on his principles of phonology. Together, in October 1926, they founded the Prague Linguistics Club. Two years later, at a linguistics conference in The Hague, they used the expression "structural and functional linguistics" for the first time. What had to be done now was to move from formalism to structuralism: i.e., to continue the Saussurian revolution by studying as a *system* not merely the formal structure of language but language as a whole, in all its various structural functions. This was the tenor of the nine theses put forward by the Prague Club in 1929.[40] Phonology occupied a central position in all this. It replaced the old phonetics, which described sounds physically, with a science of *phonemes*, the smallest separate units of language capable of conveying meaning. Just as Saussure made a distinction between language and speech and defined signs in terms of value, so Troubetzkoy saw each phoneme as having special characteristics distinguishing it from other phonemes. The study of phonemes made it possible to arrive at a universal structural principle common to all languages. From this arose the hypotheses put forward by Jakobson in Stockholm in 1941 on the broadest phonological distinctions present in languages in general. These are the first distinctions a child learns, and the last ones a person suffering from aphasia loses. The more subtle distinctions, on the other hand, appear late in a child's linguistic development and are the first to go in cases of aphasia.

To escape from Nazism and the war, Jakobson emigrated to New York, where he mixed with the psychoanalysts in exile, including Raymond de Saussure, with whom he discussed his father's work. As may be seen from a letter he wrote to Charles Bally in 1916, Raymond had already thought of inaugurating a new field of investigation relating to both psychoanalysis and linguistics. He did not follow this up, however, and may well have learned from Jakobson of the universal significance of his father's *Course*.[41] As for Jakobson himself, it was in New York that he first realized how much psychoanalysis "could give to linguistics" and vice versa.[42]

Alexandre Koyré, who had also taken refuge in New York, introduced Jakobson to Claude Lévi-Strauss, who at that time thought of himself as a "*naïf*" structuralist: "Jakobson revealed to me the existence of a body of doctrine that had already been formed within a discipline, linguistics, with which I was unacquainted. For me it was a revelation. . . . He was a thinker of an intellectual power that dominated all around him."[43] We know the part Jakobson subsequently played in the writing of *The Elementary Structures of Kinship*. The brotherly friendship between the two thinkers never failed, and although Jakobson became an American citizen he made regular visits to Paris, where as well as seeing Lévi-Strauss he met his much-loved Elsa Triolet and sometimes Lili Brik, when she visited from Moscow.

As the years went by, Louis Aragon introduced Jakobson to communist writers who, though loathing Stalinism, dreamed of reviving the legendary exploits of the formalist, futurist, and surrealist avant-gardes. Though Jakobson had never been an active revolutionary, these people saw him as the incarnation of the language of the revolution, because, with Maïakovski, Khlebnikov, Brik, and Polivanov, he had both witnessed and taken part in the greatest revolution of the century: the linguistic revolution. Thus France, the country of the 1789 revolution, became his second homeland, just as French had been his second language. On his earlier visits Jakobson stayed with Lévi-Strauss, but after the latter introduced him to Jacques Lacan in 1950, he stayed at 3, rue de Lille. He later had "a room of his own" at Sylvia's.

Jakobson attended Lacan's lectures on several occasions and met his colleagues and friends. He twice arranged for Lacan to be invited to lecture in the United States. Finally, in 1967, he agreed to take part in a debate within the framework of Lacan's seminar on "the logic of fantasy."[44] He replied very charmingly to Jenny Aubry's questions about linguistic problems in children, to Luce Irigaray about shifters, and to Jean Oury on the idea of context in institutional relationships. In an interview with Robert Georgin, a brilliant Belgian academic and editor of the *Cahiers Cistre*, he said that his conversations with Lacan had "influenced" the work of both men. "Our work together related chiefly to the problem of metaphor and metonymy, i.e., the two contrasting poles of semantics and its expression, which provided one of the main subjects of our discussions."[45]

This was more of a profession of faith than a theoretical reality. For Jakobson was not "influenced" by Lacan's work. Moreover, while he often expressed his liking for and sympathy with the man whose guest he so often was, he never took account of Lacan's ideas in his own researches. And when Robert Georgin wanted to get together a collective volume on Lacan's work and asked Jakobson to contribute, Jakobson politely got out of it. Lacan was hurt.[46]

The idea that language might be a production of the unconscious was widespread among the neogrammarians and structuralists. But their conception of the unconscious was not the same as Freud's. Thus Jakobson, in the direct line of Husserl's teaching, preferred to use the term *subliminal* to designate an intuitive knowledge lying in the depths of consciousness and acting without its being aware of the fact. Jakobson's antipsychological attitude involved ideas about the subjective aim and intentionality of consciousness that were not the same as Lacan's after the war.

At the beginning of this century Ferdinand de Saussure, with Théodore Flournoy, had encountered the question of the relationships between language and the unconscious in the famous episode of the Martian glossolalia invented by Hélène Smith. Saussure had come up against the same problem later when he thought he had found in Saturnian Latin poetry traces of a secret activity on the part of the poet, to which he had given the name *anagrams*.[47] But on widening his research to cover Greek epic and lyric poetry and then Latin poetry in general, he began to wonder whether the existence of anagrams, i.e., a text beneath the text, was due to chance or the author's intention. Unable to find an answer to this question, Saussure abandoned that line of research.

Because he started out from a Freudian conception of the unconscious, Lacan was the first thinker in this century to establish a useful connection between the discoveries made in Vienna and the structural revolution inaugurated in Geneva. But in order to do so he had to break with all the ideas involved in theories of intentionality and reinsert a (divided) subject into the heart of Freudian doctrine. While Lévi-Strauss was introduced to Saussure's work by Jakobson, it was through Henri Delacroix and Pichon that Lacan came to read Saussure's *Course in General Linguistics* and through *The Elementary Structures of Kinship* that he came to universalize a symbolic function seen as a transition from nature to culture. Lastly, the Prague version of structuralism worked out by Jakobson and Troubetzkoy allowed Lacan to arrive at a logic of the signifier (then of the unary trait) that included a theory of the subject. This alone would earn him a place among the great theoreticians of the twentieth century.

Lacan admired Jakobson enormously. During the ten years of his struggles with the IPA, when he was feeling more and more shut out by the Freudian diaspora, he rediscovered in this cosmopolitan scholar from old Russia all the freshness of the intellectual adventure that had led him in his youth on to the path of the Freudian revolution. He began to think of turning to the east, from which psychoanalysis had been banished: this was a logical consequence of his virulent critique of so-called American psychoanalysis. In 1953 he entrusted his precious "Rome Discourse" to the communist Lucien Bonnafé; nine years later he wanted at all costs to visit the Soviet Union. He was aware that since Stalin's death the fiery condemnations of Freudianism typical of the *Jdanovchtchina* period were no longer fashionable.[48] Soviet psychologists had begun to criticize the Pavlovian ideology of the fifties that had not only supplanted the allegedly spiritualistic doctrine of Freud but also wiped out all trace of psychoanalytic teaching in general.

The idea of going to the Soviet Union occurred to Lacan as a result of an event that overwhelmed everybody: the achievement of the Soviet astronaut Yuri Gagarin on April 12, 1962. Lacan, convinced that scientific revolutions always produce subversions in thought, contacted his old friend Hélène Gratiot-Alphandéry, a pupil of Wallon and a member of the French Communist Party. "I absolutely must go to the USSR," he told her. "I have lots of things to tell them. Everything must be looked at again. Now that man can travel in space, there will be a new psychology in Russia."[49]

Hélène had known Lacan since 1930, and her daughter was a friend of

Judith (both young women had been active campaigners for Algerian independence). Lacan also spoke of his project to René Zazzo: "He wanted to go to the USSR. Not as a tourist—as a guest. Not for just a few days—for several months. He wanted to tell the Soviets what psychoanalysis really was; he wanted to organize a seminar. Could I help? But I didn't think it would work. I told him as much, but promised to talk to Leontiev about it when he next came to Paris."[50] Alexis Leontiev, born in 1903, was vice president of the USSR Academy of Pedagogical Sciences and head of the psychology department of Moscow University. He was a convinced Marxist and an opponent of Pavlov, and he and his friend Alexandre Luria were struggling to rehabilitate the theories of their master, Lev Semenovitch Vytgotski.[51] To further this end Leontiev had asked his French colleagues, René Zazzo and Paul Fraisse, to arrange for some of Vytgotski's works to be translated into French. On the face of it he had nothing against Lacan and agreed to meet him.

Hélène was asked to organize a dinner party. But while Sylvia chatted away to Madame Zazzo, Leontiev and Lacan sat in silence. In an attempt to start up a conversation, Zazzo mentioned Gagarin's space flight and referred to Soviet research on the "psychophysiology of cosmonauts." Leontiev, under the impression that Zazzo was casting doubt on Gagarin's exploit, angrily adduced proofs. To which Lacan replied without hesitation, "There's no such thing as a cosmonaut simply because there's no such thing as a cosmos. The cosmos is an intellectual attitude." As a worthy pupil of his friend Alexandre Koyré, he was just pointing out that in the context of Galilean physics the universe could not be explained in terms of a harmonious system. The word *cosmos* did indeed belong to pre-Copernican terminology. Zazzo did his best to clear up the misunderstanding, but Leontiev was still offended. "Does your friend always talk like that?" he asked. And Lacan never received his invitation.

Later on, when his daughter Sybille was staying in Moscow, he was eager to join her. But once again he acted clumsily. Though he knew how to move through ordinary society with the utmost elegance, he was capable of behaving badly when he had to deal with men of science and with academics in general, from whom he expected recognition. For instance, when he first invited the philosopher and gourmet Jean Hyppolite to lunch in a restaurant, he asked the waiter to bring "un quart bordeaux" (a small carafe of house red). Worse still, when Judith was taking the oral examination for her teacher's degree in philosophy, he invited some of the students from his seminar to go and watch. When the examination was over and Judith was placed first out of all the candidates, Lacan went and ceremoniously shook hands with, and thanked, Georges Canguilhem, the president of the jury. Canguilhem, a scientific historian, former member of the Resistance and a great servant of secular education with a legendary reputation for strictness and integrity, never forgave Lacan.[52]

Despite the fact that he had once wanted to meet the pope, Lacan had a horror of anything resembling religious conformity. Similarly, while he wanted to persuade the Marxists to take an interest in his teaching, he had no sympathy with communism. As to the past, he regarded Mazarin as the greatest politician France had ever produced. In the present, social democracy was the system he favored, though he made no public declarations to that effect. He always retained something of both the antiparliamentary views of his youth and his admiration for British democracy—two diametrically opposite positions—but the only kind of politics he was really interested in was that which advanced his own teachings. In these, however, he was always referring to the history of political philosophy, ranging from Plato to Hegel and including Aristotle, St. Augustine, and Machiavelli. Jean Lacouture, who met Lacan at Harvard when he himself was working on a thesis on the personalization of power, was amazed at the interest Lacan took in the subject. "But what else have I ever studied," said Lacan, "but the motives and methods of power?"[53]

In 1954, through Madeleine Chapsal, he made the acquaintance of Françoise Giroud, another member of the group that started Jean-Jacques Servan-Schreiber's *L'Express*. The two became good friends. One day, at Claude Lévi-Strauss's request, Françoise Giroud arranged a dinner with Pierre Mendès France as one of the guests (at the end of the evening, François Mauriac and Servan-Schreiber appeared, probably having been working at *L'Express*). Mendès France knew Lévi-Strauss already; the ethnologist had gone to the flea market with the politician once when the latter was looking for some family papers.[54] Throughout the evening Lacan and Lévi-Strauss were silent, though their wives kept up a normal conversation. "Lacan was fascinated by Mendès France," says Françoise Giroud. "They only met that once. What interested Lacan was Mendès France's prestige and his charismatic appeal to the young." Mendès later told his hostess how puzzled he was by Lacan's and Lévi-Strauss's silence.[55]

It was at this time that Lacan formed a real friendship with Roland Dumas, later a minister in François Mitterrand's socialist government. Dumas defended Laurence Bataille when she had problems with the law and advised Lacan when, after Georges Bataille's death in July 1962, it was decided that the necessary steps should be taken for him to legitimize Judith as his daughter. The procedure took effect on the very day Lacan started as professor at the Ecole normale supérieure and delivered his inaugural lecture on excommunication. Thus by a curious chance he became the legal father of his daughter at the same time as, having been forced to leave the IPA, he began a course of lectures in which he would apply the description

"Freudian" to a school that in fact promulgated a doctrine bearing his own name. One member of his new audience there in the Salle Dussane on January 15 was Lacan's future son-in-law, Jacques-Alain Miller, not yet twenty years old. He was a brilliant philosopher at the Ecole normale supérieure and married Judith at Guitrancourt on November 12, 1966. So she used her father's name legally for scarcely two years, after which she was known as Judith Miller.[56]

As well as Roland Dumas, Lacan numbered Gaston Defferre among his friends. He had met him in Marseilles through Georges Bernier; Sylvia had put him up for a while in the rue de Lille at the end of the war. "Gaston Defferre," writes his wife, the novelist Edmonde Charles-Roux, "was personally very close to Lacan. They spent summer vacations together in Italy. Gaston Defferre tried to teach Lacan water skiing, but without success. Much might be said about this strange friendship, which grew stronger and took on new dimensions during the Algerian 'events.' "[57]

Between the time that Jacques Lacan first formulated his structure of the subject at Royaumont and the beginning, at Bonneval, of the controversy that set him against Jean Laplanche on the one hand and Merleau-Ponty on the other, Alfred Lacan, Jacques's father, died. He was eighty years old and died painlessly of a cerebral hemorrhage on October 15, 1960. Four days later the corpse was taken from Boulogne-sur-Seine to Château-Thierry and buried in the family vault there, beside Emilie Baudry and most of the other deceased members of the paternal side of the family, with the exception of Emile Lacan and his wife, Marie Julie Dessaux. Lacan, driving as fast as he could to his father's funeral, went through a red light, was stopped by a gendarme, and nearly arrived late. At the cemetery, Malou's children just wore armbands with their everyday clothes, while Judith, wearing a mourning veil over her face, was elegantly dressed in black, as was Jacques himself.[58] Once again, Alfred's son was doing his duty.

He made no reference to his father's death in that year's seminar, part of which dealt with the subject of parricide in Claudel's Coûfontaine trilogy. But seven months later he wept at Merleau-Ponty's funeral. And he made an emotional reference to Merleau-Ponty's death in the lecture he delivered on May 10, 1961: "It is a heavy blow to me.... Because of his death we shall never have time to bring our theories and observations closer together.... It was always his desire—against my own wishes, I may say—that I should occupy this chair."[59]

It is certain that Merleau-Ponty would never have agreed with Lacan about his theory of language. But two days before he died he had spent a delightful day at Guitrancourt picking lilies-of-the-valley for May Day. He had just been invited to the United States and had thoughts of visiting Mauritius. "In the last image I have of him," writes Madeleine Chapsal, "he's standing on the open platform at the back of a no. 63 bus. In his buttonhole he was wearing a sprig of lily-of-the valley that Lacan had given him, and he was waving me goodbye."[60]

Although, in the interview he gave *L'Express* in May 1957, Lacan referred to his commentary on the Rat Man, he didn't mention his interpretation of the case of President Daniel Paul Schreber, the subject of his 1955–1956 seminar.[61] But in the course of that consideration of psychoses in general and paranoia in particular, he introduced a major new concept, *forclusion* (foreclosure), which was part of his second structural overhaul. The term made its first appearance in the seminar of July 4, 1956, the last of that academic year.[62]

I have already had occasion to analyze at length the conditions under which the word entered first the history of psychoanalysis in general and then the language of Lacan himself. It all began in 1895 with Hippolyte Bernheim's introduction of the idea of negative hallucination to denote the failure of a subject under hypnosis to perceive an object present in his perceptual field. Freud adopted the term but stopped using it after 1917 because in 1914 he had put forward a new classification for psychoses, neuroses, and perversions within the framework of his castration theory. It was then that he gave the name *Verneinung* (negation) to a verbal mechanism whereby the repressed is recognized negatively by the subject but not accepted. "It is not my mother, it is not that person," meaning in each case that it is. In 1934 the term was translated into French as *négation*.

Freud also used the term *Verleugnung* (disavowal) to denote a subject's refusal to recognize the reality of a negative perception: for example, a woman's lack of a penis. *Verneinung* referred to a neurotic mechanism, while *Verleugnung* referred to a mechanism characteristic of perversion.

In parallel fashion, in France, Pichon put forward the term *scotomisation* (scotomization) to denote an unconscious mechanism or blindness by which a subject makes certain unpleasant facts disappear from his memory or consciousness. It was this expression that triggered off an argument between Laforgue and Freud in 1925. Laforgue suggested using the word *scotomisation* to translate both *Verleugnung* (disavowal) and another repressive mechanism characteristic of psychosis in general and schizophrenia in particular. Freud rejected this suggestion, proposing instead both *Verleugnung* and *Verdrängung* (repression). The situation described by Laforgue suggested the idea of a nullification of perception, i.e., the notion of a positive psychologistic phenomenon of switching off, whereas in Freud's suggestion perception was kept within the framework of negativity: the process involved not a switching-off of perception in relation to an unrecognized reality but rather the actualization of a perception that consisted in a disavowal. The argument showed that both sides lacked a term to denote a rejection mechanism specific to psychosis. Laforgue was approaching a solution by means of a denegativization, and Freud was evading the problem by placing the mechanism concerned between disavowal and repression.[63]

That was the position in 1928, when Pichon published, in Pierre Janet's review, his famous article on "The Psychological Significance of Negation in French." Pichon, starting from language rather than clinical practice, borrowed the legal term *forclusif* to indicate that the second element of negation in French applies to facts that the speaker no longer sees as forming part of reality. These facts are in a sense *forclos* (foreclosed). Pichon and his uncle Damourette illustrated their argument with a comic example concerning two members of the Action française. In an article on Esterhazy's death in the newspaper *Le Journal* of May 18, 1923, a journalist wrote: "'The Dreyfus affair,' he [Esterhazy] said, 'is now a closed book.' He must have been sorry he ever opened it." Damourette and Pichon pointed out that the verb *se repentir* (be sorry, or regret) implied that a fact that had actually existed was to all intents and purposes *excluded* from the past. They were thus, as Pichon observed, bringing *scotomisation* and the *forclusif* together: "The French language expresses the desire for *scotomisation* through the *forclusif*, thus translating the normal phenomenon of which *scotomisation*, described in terms of mental pathology by M. Laforgue and one of us, is a pathological exaggeration." The two authors were not here taking into account the mechanism of *Verneinung*.[64]

So it was not until February 3, 1954, that the discussion was revived in different terms and on another terrain: that of phenomenology. The correspondence between Freud and Laforgue had not yet been published, and Lacan did not "replace" scotomization by foreclosure. In his debate with Jean Hyppolite, who approached the question via the *Verneinung* mechanism, for which he proposed the name *dénégation* (negation), Lacan reviewed the problem on the basis of Merleau-Ponty's work *The Phenomenology of Perception*, in particular the passages on hallucination as a "phenomenon linked to the disintegration of reality" that is integrated into the intentionality of the subject.

In a passage of his analysis of the "Wolf Man," Freud explained how his patient's recognition and nonrecognition of castration arose out of an attitude of *rejection* or repudiation (*Verwerfung*) that made him see sexuality in terms of the purely infantile hypothesis of anal intercourse. By way of illustration he referred to a visual hallucination that Sergei Pankejeff had experienced in childhood. He had *seen* his little finger cut by his pocket knife and then observed that there was no wound. Regarding the *rejection of a reality presented as not existing*, Freud pointed out that this was not a repression, because "*eine Verdrängung is etwas anderes als eine Verwerfung*" (a repression is not the same as a rejection). Reading this text in 1954 in the course of his dialogue with Hyppolite, Lacan translated *Verwerfung* as *retranchement* (one connotation of which is "cutting off"). Two years later he took up Freud's distinction between neurosis and psychosis, applying to it Laforgue and Pichon's terminology, according to which, in psychosis, reality is never *truly scotomized*. Finally, after commenting at length on Schreber's paranoia, he suggested that *Verwerfung* should be translated as *forclusion* (foreclosure): for him, this was a mechanism specific to psychosis in general, defined on the basis of paranoia, which consisted in the primal relegation of a fundamental signifier to a position outside the symbolic universe of the subject. He distinguished foreclosure from repression by pointing out that in the former the foreclosed signifier, or the signifiers that represent it, are not integrated into the subject's unconscious but may return in reality when they invade the subject's speech or perception in the form of a hallucination or delusion.

What a strange road this concept had traveled! Invented by a grammarian who defined it, with reference to the Dreyfus affair, as a normal vernacular translation of the pathological process of scotomization, it reappeared in 1956 within the framework of Lacan's second structural overhaul, when he used it to translate a mechanism discovered by Freud not in Schreber's paranoia but in Pankejeff's infantile neurosis. Lacan retained the terrain of language on which Pichon had placed the term, but he used linguistics to introduce into it the trajectory of the signifier. To celebrate his victory over Laforgue, he attributed to Freud the discovery of a process (foreclosure) and the invention of a concept (*Verwerfung*) that Freud had not originated at all.[65]

The elaboration of the concept of foreclosure was also connected with the working out of the theory of the *name-of-the-father*, which Lacan had used since 1953 but first formulated as a concept on June 27, 1956. To this was added the definitive placing of two more terms, the Other (with a capital *o*; in French, *Autre*) and object *a*. Lacan had introduced the first of these on May 25, 1955; he had used the second since 1936 but now placed it in a binary context: A/a. From the unconscious as "discourse of the other," as defined in Rome, Lacan passed in his second stage to an unconscious as "discourse of the Other." As for object *a*, the space of the imaginary ego, it came to stand for something left over, between the real and the nonsymbolizable: the object as lack of and the object as cause of desire.[66] In order to make the ego fall into the position of something wasted or lost, Lacan resorted to the heterology beloved of Georges Bataille, which ensured that Lacan's structure would not smuggle God back in the guise of the transcendence so dreaded by Lévi-Strauss.

But before he could invent the binary opposition A/a, Lacan had first to differentiate a *moi-idéal* (ideal ego, *Ideal-Ich*) from an *idéal du moi* (ego-ideal, *Ich-Ideal*).[67] As we know, this distinction did not exist in Freud's topographical system, in which the *Ideal-Ich* was an intrapsychic formation denoting the subject's ideal of narcissistic omnipotence, based on the model of infantile narcissism. In 1932 Hermann Nunberg, following Freud, had introduced a split into this concept, making the *Ideal-Ich* genetically prior to the *surmoi* (superego). According to Nunberg, the subject in the course of his development leaves behind his narcissistic ideal, though he longs to return to it, for example in psychosis.[68] It was while reading Nunberg's articles that Lagache, almost at the same time as Lacan, came to adopt this distinction, which he expressed in the form of a theory at the 1958 Royaumont colloquium on personality.

Meanwhile, in March 1954, it was on the basis of the debate between Freud and Jung on narcissism that Lacan, without citing Nunberg, made his own distinction between the ideal ego and the ego-ideal. He defined the first as a narcissistic formation belonging to the order of the imaginary and originating in the mirror stage, and the second as a symbolic function capable of organizing all the subject's relations with others.[69] Thus the introduction of the duality A/a followed the establishment of the distinction between ideal ego and ego-ideal. Lacan reintroduced into this system Lévi-Strauss's division by which the universal incest taboo is seen as a transition from nature to culture. This division made it possible to see a contrast between the symbolic function of the father, representative of culture, and the imaginary position of the mother, dependent on the order of nature and doomed to merge with the child as phallic object of a missing penis.

This is the origin of Lacan's idea of the Oedipal phase understood as a transition from nature to culture. If human society is dominated by the primacy of language (the Other, the signifier), this means that the paternal pole occupies a similar place in the historical structuring of every subject. In his first phase Lacan defined this position as a *function of the father*, next as a *function of the symbolic father*, and then as *a paternal metaphor*; in his second phase, he designated the function itself as a concept: the name-of-the-father. The working-out of this concept was in its turn dependent on the establishment of a theory of the signifier and accompanied by the theoretical formulation of the notion of foreclosure, as Lacan clearly pointed out on June 20, 1956, a week before using the term as a concept for the first time: "The function of *being a father*," he said, "is absolutely unthinkable . . . without the category of the signifier."[70] This being so, the Oedipal transition from nature to culture occurs as follows: as the incarnation of the signifier, because he gives the child his name, the father acts on the child as the one who deprives him of his mother, thus giving rise to his ego-ideal.

This anthropological translation of Freud's work has parallels in Lacan's veiled accounts of his own family history. Thanks to the enlightening reminiscences of his brother Marc-François, we now know that the concept of the name-of-the-father had its origin in the place occupied in the clan by Emile Lacan, Jacques's grandfather. All his life Jacques hated "the horrible individual thanks to whom he learned at an early age how to perform the essential act of cursing God." He blamed his grandfather, whose name was on his own birth certificate, for having so tyrannized over Alfred, his father, that he was incapable of being a real father. Raised by the formidable Emile, Alfred, though an affectionate, well-disposed, and even devoted parent, could take no interest in the intellectual brilliance of his elder son, whom he regarded as volatile and irresponsible.

It was of the unsatisfactory position of Alfred, his father, that Lacan was thinking when in 1938 he referred to the inevitable decline of the paternal imago in Western society. He was thinking of it again when between 1953 and 1963 he invented a structural system based on a revaluation of the symbolic function of the father. Starting from the deterioration of the father's situation that had afflicted his own childhood, he summoned the concept of the name-of-the-father from the horror that the figure of Emile—the father-of-the-father—still inspired in him. And to his memory of Alfred's humiliation was added his own experience of fatherhood. Feeling guilty at not having been able to give his daughter his name, he formulated the idea that a mere spoken word, the uttering of a name, could allow a father to legitimize his offspring: " 'So,' I said to myself, addressing myself by my name, private or public, 'so that's why, after all, Jacques Lacan, your daughter isn't dumb; that's why your daughter is your daughter; because if we were dumb, she wouldn't be your daughter.' "[71]

Daniel Paul Schreber, born in July 1842, came from a distinguished family of lawyers, doctors, scholars, and teachers belonging to the German Protestant bourgeoisie. His father, Dr. Daniel Gottlob Moritz Schreber, was famous for his strict educational theories based on hygiene, orthopedics, gymnastics, and heliotherapy. He wanted to correct the wrongs perpetrated by human nature, arrest the general decline of society, and produce the perfect being of modern times: a strong soul in a healthy body. His educational handbooks recommended forcing children into correct postures with the aid of barbaric instruments. Anxious to elevate the German soul, he also advocated working-class housing estates with gardens, a notion supported first by the social democrats, then denounced as reformist, and finally taken over by the national socialists. In 1861, three years after a ladder had fallen on his head and just before Bismarck came to power, Schreber died of a perforated ulcer. He was fifty-three years old and had just finished his last book:

The Family Friend as Teacher and Guide for the Fathers and Mothers of the German People.

It was in 1884 that his son Daniel Paul Schreber, an eminent lawyer and president of the appellate court in Saxony, presented himself at the elections as a conservative candidate, representing the moral order advocated by Bismarck. He was beaten by a social democrat who was popular in the region, and it was at this point that Schreber's first mental troubles occurred. He was treated by the neurologist Paul Flechsig and spent two lengthy periods in the hospital. In 1893 he became president of the appellate court in Dresden, but seven years later he was banned from office, and his property placed under supervision. This led him to write his *Memoirs of My Nervous Illness,* published in 1903. The book recounted his delusions and hallucinations, and thanks to it he was released from the asylum and had his property restored, not because he had proved he was not mad but because he had demonstrated to the court that his madness was not a valid legal reason for locking him up. Even so, in April 1910 he died in the Leipzig asylum, to which he had been admitted four years earlier. At the end of 1910, Freud, who did not know whether Schreber was still alive, began to write down his remarks on the case, basing them on the 1903 autobiography.[72] This text omitted half a chapter about the narrator's family, which the publishers considered unsuitable for inclusion.

Schreber's *Memoirs* exhibited the extraordinary mental system of a God-persecuted man. Having, as he thought, lived without a stomach or bladder and having sometimes "eaten his own larynx," he had come to believe that the end of the world was nigh and that he was the sole survivor among all the patients and nurses, whom he described as "fleeting-improvised-men." God spoke to him in a "language of nerves," or "fundamental language," and told him to change into a woman and produce a new race amid the debris of decaying humanity. Man is made up of body and nerves, Schreber said, and the human soul is contained in the nerves. God consists of nerves alone. There are intimate, sensual relations between God and heaven. The "vestibules of heaven" are the nerves of men, purified after death and incorporated into God, who acts on man through "rays." Schreber, though constantly being regenerated by these "rays," which made him immortal, was persecuted by birds on which "miracles" had been performed; they were composed of fragments of the "vestibules of heaven" and unleashed on him after being filled with poisons taken from corpses. The birds also passed on to him "magic vestiges of former human souls." As Schreber waited to be transformed into a woman and impregnated by God, he stood out both against His persecutions, shrieking at the sun, and against the wicked plots hatched by Dr. Flechsig, the "soul-murderer" who had sexually abused him and then left his mangled body to putrefy.

Like all the scientists of his time, anxious to discover the genesis of the so-called mental diseases, Freud was amazed by Schreber's language and by the extraordinary story of this crazy narrator whose ravings were partly inspired by the words of the great mystics. Freud's fascination was linked to the interest he took at that period in the origin of religions, a problem to which he later gave an answer in *Totem and Taboo*. But the study of this case also enabled him to produce a sound and coherent symptomatology of paranoia with which to confront Eugen Bleuler, who wanted to include it in his new definition of schizophrenia. In the debate between the school of Vienna and the school of Zurich, of which I have spoken before[73] and which was to lead to the break with Jung, Freud wanted to give a psychoanalytic base to the organization of psychosis, of which for him the paradigm was paranoia.

In the traditional manner he included in the category of paranoia delusions of grandeur, persecution mania, and delusions stemming from erotomania and jealousy, but he also added the defense against homosexuality and the idea that the delusional idea a madman has of himself might be as true as the rational idea constructed by the doctor to explain the patient's madness, although only the latter has any theoretical status. However, when writing his study of Leonardo da Vinci a year earlier, Freud had worked out an approach to homosexuality that would help him in his analysis of the Schreber case, and it was on the occasion of his break with Alfred Adler the same year that it occurred to him to link paranoid knowledge to a homosexual cathexis and theoretical knowledge to a rejection of that cathexis. The break between the two men had revived the pain Freud had suffered at the time of his parting from Wilhelm Fliess. Hence the two famous observations, one addressed to Sandor Ferenczi in a letter written in October 1910 and the other addressed to Jung in February 1908: "This need has been extinguished in me since Fliess's case, with the overcoming of which you just saw me occupied. A piece of homosexual investment has been withdrawn and utilized for the enlargement of my own ego. I have succeeded where the paranoiac fails"; and "My one time friend Fliess developed a dreadful case of paranoia after throwing off his affection for me, which was undoubtedly considerable. I owe this idea [i.e., of a homosexual element in paranoia] to him, i.e., to his behaviour."[74]

Freud had inquired into the educational theories of Schreber's father and noted several examples of his tyrannical nature. He also showed that Daniel Paul's *Memoirs* were fiercely satirical about Daniel Gottlob's value as a doctor, accusing him of treating only corpses. But Freud did not connect the father's views on education to the son's paranoia, even though he had already observed the analogy between paranoid delusions and rigid systems that aimed at transforming human nature. In the context of his new theory

on psychosis, he saw, first, Schreber's shrieks against God as an expression of
rebellion against the father; then, repressed homosexuality as the source of
delusion; and, finally, the changing of love into hatred as the essential mechanism of paranoia. Thus the onset of hallucination appeared to be not so
much the beginning of an illness as an attempt at a cure, through which
Daniel Paul, who hadn't had a son to console him for the loss of his father
(and brother), tried to reconcile himself with the image of a father transfigured into God. Freud considered both cure and transfiguration as the result
of a father complex that was on the whole positive. In other words, he
thought old Dr. Gottlob had been as much a decent fellow as a domestic
tyrant.

In the autumn of 1955, when Lacan embarked on a yearlong commentary on President Schreber's *Memoirs*, his position with regard to paranoia
was very different from that of Freud in 1911. In his thesis in 1932 and in his
article on the Papin sisters, Lacan had been interested in the homosexual
element in female paranoia. But in his second structural phase the problem
presented itself differently. Starting from the concept of *paranoid knowledge*,
he reminded his pupils of the 1920s and the impact that the publication of
the Aimée case had had on the history of French psychiatry. He cited his
own mentors—Clérambault, Sérieux, and Capgras—and criticized the doctrine of constitutions. He had looked carefully into the studies on Schreber
then current, and referred to Ida Macalpine and Richard Hunter, two of
Glover's pupils, who dissented from the BPS and had just translated and written a preface to *The Memoirs of My Nervous Illness*. The two authors—
mother and son—noted Freud's failure to draw inferences from Schreber
senior's educational theories and suggested a Kleinian interpretation of
Daniel Paul's paranoia. According to them, a profound regression to a primitive stage of undifferentiated libido had reactivated infantile fantasies of
procreation.[75]

Lacan, while paying tribute to Freud, moved the problem to a different
ground. Instead of regarding paranoia as a defense against homosexuality, he
made it structurally dependent on the paternal function. For this reason he
suggested a realistic reading of the elder Schreber's writings in order to bring
out the connection between the father's educational theories and the son's
madness. But not content with putting forward a paternal position rather
than a homosexual element as a prime factor, he also transformed Freud's
idea of an analogy between delusional and rational knowledge. Instead of
linking the first to homosexual cathexis and the second to rejection of this
cathexis, he made use of an idea about the genealogy of madness that he had
held since 1932: that not everyone can go mad. In other words, he restated
the hypothesis that a madman is someone who has such a correct view of

madness that he sees it not as a fact but as a truth that man carries inside him as a limit on his freedom.

Within the context of the topography of 1953, Lacan, as he carried out his second structural revision, reconsidered both Freud's and his own conception of paranoia, later extending the overhaul to cover psychosis in general. He shared Freud's belief that paranoia was the paradigm of psychosis. During the year 1955–1956 Lacan's revision led to his working-out of the two concepts foreclosure and name-of-the-father, the genesis of which was dictated by the gradual elaboration of his new theory of the signifier, which in turn arose out of his reading of Jakobson, from the study of whom he was able to define Schreber's paranoia as a *foreclosure of the name-of-the-father*. This gives the following sequence: the name of D. G. M. Schreber—i.e., the function of primal signifier embodied by the *father* through educational theories aimed at reforming human nature—had been rejected (foreclosed) from the son's symbolic universe and returned in the delusional real of the narrator's discourse. With this sophisticated abstract formula, Lacan brilliantly solved the problem that all the other commentators on the *Memoirs of My Nervous Illness*, including Freud, had puzzled over before him. All of them had noticed the link between the father's educational creed and the son's delusions, but Lacan was the first to build a theory on it and to define its functioning in the autobiographical ravings of a crazy narrator. The younger Schreber's pen described a universe full of instruments of torture strangely resembling the apparatuses recommended in the books bearing the name of D. G. M. Schreber—the "name-of-the-father" excluded from or censored out of both the *Memoirs* and the memory of the son.

Lacan, aware of having made an important contribution to the conceptual edifice of the history of Freudianism and fearing as ever that his oral teaching might be plagiarized or misunderstood, wrote a synthetic account of his 1955–1956 seminar. It was published in the fourth number of the review *La Psychanalyse*, which was devoted to psychoses. He called his text "On a Question Preliminary to Any Possible Treatment of Psychosis" and gave its date of composition as December 1957–January 1958. He also initiated many other French studies on the Schreber family and published the first French translation of the *Memoirs of a Neuropath* in his series Le Champ freudien (The Freudian Field).[76]

While Freud had formulated his theory on paranoia in the course of a debate with Bleuler and Jung and as he was reliving his break with Fliess, Lacan's doctrinal revision drew on his own intimidating experience of fathers and fatherhood. How can one fail to see, in his passionate negative interest in the educational theories of old Dr. Schreber, a reminiscence of the horror Lacan had felt in his childhood at the sight of the relations between his father and grandfather on the one hand and between his mother and the other women of the family on the other? It is impossible to exaggerate how closely Lacan's masterly interpretation of the Schreber saga depends on a dialectic between a tyrannical father and a father who was humiliated, a dialectic that Lacan had already borrowed from Hegel. And from all this arose the two baroque conceptions of Lacan's structuralist period: foreclosure and the name-of-the-father.

PART VII

. . . . . .

The Power and the Glory

23

. . . .

Dialogue with Louis Althusser

*I*n the winter of 1963, with the gradual disintegration of the SFP, French Freudianism began to take on a new aspect. Instead of being the culture of an elite it was turning into a mass ideology, and at the same time, instead of being largely centered in Paris, it was reaching out to the provinces. Thus the general trend toward popularization, which in the case of the IPA had produced a kind of establishment neo-Freudianism, was now affecting the French psychoanalytic movement and moving it toward more modern forms.

As this process was taking place and the spread of Lacanianism was marking the definitive acceptance of Freudianism in France, institutions and groups took over from the small elites of earlier days. While the exploits of the third generation of French analysts were still linked to those of the two previous generations and could be seen as part of a logical and coherent network of transferential relationships, the activities of the fourth and fifth generations broke free of this pattern and left both its logic and its coherence behind. In the great expansion of the sixties, which the barricades of 1968 helped to amplify, individuals and theories counted for less than institutional trends. Such developments were bound to emphasize Lacan's already paradoxical situation. After having been the brilliant Socrates, vanquished but triumphant, of a literary Republic, he was now the leader of a new army of partisans who tended to be less learned, less cultured, and less adorned with degrees than the chief founders of the SFP had been. In short, after the 1963 split, Lacan's "social base" changed.

True, he took many representatives of the third generation with him: among them were Maud and Octave Mannoni, Serge Leclaire, François Perrier, Moustapha Safouan, Jenny Aubry, Piera Aulagnier, Solange Faladé, and Jean Clavreul. But with the next generation he lost in quality what he gained in quantity. Instead of disciples of a critical spirit debating with him at philosophical banquets, he was now surrounded, with notable exceptions, by a crowd of admirers seeking not so much knowledge itself as a mixture of certainties, formulas, and practical results. For ten years he had been able to dispense a magisterial teaching based on dialogue with his pupils and enriched by contact with the best contemporary thinkers; now, at the age of sixty-three, he was forced to exercise a completely different kind of power, that of the leader of a school.

After struggling for a long time to ensure that the preparation of training analysts should go on including a classical clinical training and an elitist study of philosophy, Lacan was now obliged to offer his teaching to a new audience—an audience of psychologists. The *massification*, or relative popularization, of the French psychoanalytic movement, which created a definite break between the third generation and those that followed, was one of the consequences of the democratization of university recruitment. The growth in student numbers between 1955 and 1965 was accompanied by a great increase in the number of academic departments teaching psychology-related subjects. The technocrats were gradually taking over from the intellectuals.

Until about 1960 there were three ways of obtaining access to psychoanalytic training: via medical studies, followed by specialization in psychiatry or neurology; via liberal arts or philosophy studies, followed (optionally) by a degree in psychopathology; or via all of these. But as a result of democratization, the study of psychology became a separate and independent discipline, and the old variety of approaches disappeared. From 1965 on, all the Freudian groups, whatever their tendency, were increasingly made up of former psychology students. Such was the last and fiercest phase of Freud's great battle for *Laienanalyse*: the triumph of psychology over medicine.[1]

The replacement of intellectuals by technocrats was reflected in the educational choices made earlier in their careers by new candidates for training analysis. More and more chose the psychological approach, the one that accorded best with the technical ideal to which the new middle-class university students aspired. The degrees obtained by this means gave access to various therapeutic institutions, including community and day clinics and health centers providing teaching and training as well as medical and psychological services. The "noble" subjects of philosophy, liberal arts, and psychiatry were regarded as out-of-date, and forsaken in favor of a single discipline, psychology, which claimed to cover all subjects through its own various "branches." The increasing lack, in the fourth generation of Freudians, of the old kind of culture led in turn to sectarianism and a cult of personality in the entourage of the most important teachers, including Lacan. In passing from the status of intellectual master to that of leader of a school, Lacan was caught up in a process as inevitable as it was uncontrollable, one in which he would allow himself to be worshiped like a god and his teaching to be treated like holy writ. In the end his following would disintegrate into a number of messianic groups.

The invasion of the university by psychology as an independent subject was denounced in December 1956 by Georges Canguilhem. In an article called "What Is Psychology?" that was to become famous, he described the subject as philosophy without rigor because it claimed to be objective but was merely eclectic; as ethics without morals, because it applied no critical judgment to experience; and as medicine without discipline, because its hypotheses about nervous diseases were unintelligible. The article ended as follows: "When you exit the Sorbonne onto the rue Saint-Jacques, you can go either up or down. If you go up you get to the Panthéon, the resting place of certain great men. If you go down you are sure to arrive at police headquarters."[2] Psychology had to choose between climbing up toward the Panthéon, where as yet no psychologist had ever been buried, and sliding down toward mere technology.

In May 1961 Michel Foucault defended his thesis, entitled *Madness and Civilization: A History of Insanity in the Age of Reason*. In front of a jury that included Daniel Lagache, he pulled to pieces the ideals on which the work of the historians of psychology was based: "This book has not tried to write the history of madmen as compared with rational men, nor the history of reason as contrasted with madness. What it has tried to do is present the history of the ever-changing proportions in which they are distributed." Invoking the authority of Nietzsche and Bataille, he denied that it was only the introduction of psychopathological concepts that made it possible to explain human madness. In his view those concepts were based on a retrospective illusion of a madness that was supposed to have existed in nature. But madness was a product of culture, not nature. And the relation between it and medical science was but one of the historical forms of the relationship between madness and reason. Georges Canguilhem, who had agreed to be the *rapporteur*, or presenter, of Foucault's thesis, recognized that it was a fundamental revision of the psychiatric approach to madness. "Therefore," he said, "what M. Foucault is calling into question is the significance of the beginnings of positivist psychiatry before the Freudian revolution. And incidentally he gives a new view of the significance of the advent of positivist psychology."[3]

Lacan, who was well aware of the danger involved in the advance of psychology on the front of French Freudianism, welcomed Foucault's antipsychological stance. Although Lacan was not a Foucauldian, believing as he did that the Cartesian basis of modern philosophy did not exclude madness, he greeted the publication of Foucault's thesis as a major event. Unlike most of the psychiatrists of his own generation, especially Henri Ey, he had accepted

the idea that madness had a logic of its own and must be envisaged other-
wise than through a one-sided discourse by reason on the subject of folly.
So he took a close interest in the Sartrian arguments of British and
American opponents of psychiatry.

In the winter of 1963, conscious of having lost part of his audience, he
turned once again to philosophy, this time in pursuit of the campaign against
psychology. So far his acquaintance with philosophers and other thinkers
had not produced the appreciation he had expected. Neither Koyré nor
Merleau-Ponty, Bataille nor Lévi-Strauss, Jakobson nor Heidegger had taken
the trouble to read his work properly and point out its importance. Only
Jean Hyppolite and Alphonse de Waelhens had been bold enough to enter
into a real dialogue. But this situation was in the process of changing with
the advent of a new generation of philosophers brought up on structuralism, among them Michel Foucault, Louis Althusser, Gilles Deleuze, and
Jacques Derrida. Unlike the earlier thinkers, however, these new philosophers did not become Lacan's friends; they were less intimate with his family and had little sympathy with the idolatry he increasingly sought. On the
other hand they were excellent interpreters of Lacan's work, and their critical comments helped to bring it the recognition for which its author had
been waiting so long.

There is no one school of thought in French structuralism. Lévi-Strauss,
Lacan, Benveniste, Dumézil, and Vernant were among the first to make use
of its methods, but while their successors—Foucault, Derrida, and
Althusser—also used them, they did so in an entirely different way. The history of French structuralism may be divided into two phases: in the first, linguistics acted as a guide in the fields of psychoanalysis, ethnology, and
ancient history; in the second, a number of very different subjects of
research all used Saussurian structuralism as their base. Within this second
field of activity, Lacan's teaching was seen as a *scientific* reappraisal of Freud.
"The turning point came," said Foucault, "when Lévi-Strauss, in the case of
societies, and Lacan, in the case of the unconscious, showed us that 'meaning' was probably no more than a superficial impression, a shimmer, a foam,
and that what was really affecting us deep down inside, what existed before
us, and what was supporting us in time and space, was system."[4]

In July 1963 Lacan was attracted by an article that Louis Althusser had just
published in the *Revue de l'enseignement philosophique* (Review of philosophical teaching) under the title "Philosophy and the Human Sciences."
Althusser wrote that "Marx based his theory on a rejection of the myth of
Homo oeconomicus. Freud based his theory on a rejection of the myth of
Homo psychologicus. Lacan has seen and understood Freud's liberating break
with the past. He has comprehended it in the full sense of the word, taking

its rigor literally and forcing it to yield up its own consequences without fear or favor. Like everyone else he may sometimes err in a matter of detail or even in his choice of philosophical reference, but we are in his debt for *what is essential*."[5]

At that time the two men had never met, but they had a long history in common, made up partly of coincidences and partly of secrets revealed on the psychoanalyst's couch.

After the Liberation, Georges Gusdorf, who was teaching philosophy at the Ecole normale supérieure in the rue d'Ulm, arranged for his students' course to include a series of lectures on psychopathology. Lacan was one of the people invited to lecture, and in November 1945 he gave a talk on the origin of madness. Althusser loathed it: he disliked Lacan's convoluted style and rejected his idea of a cogito that included madness.[6]

Ever since 1938 Althusser had suffered from attacks of melancholia that recurred every February and lasted several days. The first time he was hospitalized was in a prisoner-of-war camp, during his four years of captivity. When Lacan gave his lecture at the ENS, Althusser, after a long period of increasing disillusion, was in the process of converting from the radical Catholicism of his youth to a communism whose Stalinist aspect he was soon to discover. Although he was already a serious reader of Freud, it hadn't occurred to him that the melancholy that paralyzed him every so often, to be followed by a period of intense excitement, could be anything but a mental disease of organic origin. He therefore tried to combat it with drugs and sophisticated technological treatments.

When Althusser was thirty, his story and the history of psychoanalysis and psychiatry intersected in the mirror of his own madness. After 1948 he had to face more than twenty times the sort of confinement his pupil Michel Foucault was to describe so well. Throughout his life Althusser's relations with Freudianism were extremely ambivalent, and he always kept his position as a psychoanalytic or psychiatric patient quite separate from his position as a thinker. He was the horrified but voluntary victim of chemotherapy, yet at the same time he advocated a theory of madness that condemned the kind of treatment to which he himself had submitted.

In 1946, when visiting Georges Lesèvre, he met Hélène Rytman, a Jewish woman of Russian origin who was eight years his senior and thought by her friends to be "slightly touched." She had been a comrade of Jean Beaufret in the Resistance and a member of the Pericles network. She had also belonged to the Communist Party but had been expelled for reasons that weren't altogether clear. She was accused of "Trotskyite deviation" and "crimes" and was said to have taken part in the summary execution of former collaborators in the Lyons region.

In the interwar years Hélène had mixed with the October group, where she had probably come across Sylvia Bataille. She later acted as assistant to Jean Renoir when he was shooting *La Marseillaise*, and it was in Nice during the Occupation that she met Jacques Lacan, probably through Jean Ballard and the *Cahiers du Sud* group. She quarreled with Lacan when he reproached her for not doing enough to help Sylvia to find a house on the Côte d'Azur. Nonetheless, during a conversation one day on the Promenade des Anglais he proposed that she become a psychoanalyst: he admired her subtlety as a listener and her power to understand other people. But she rejected the suggestion.[7]

"Althusser, with his love of the absolute, is basically a mystic," says Jean Guitton. "That's why he was attracted by the woman who became his wife: she was an absolute mystic too. She came to see me. She was like Mother Teresa. He said to me, 'Maître, I'd like to introduce you to the woman I love.' We had dinner together. And I could see from the first time we met that it was she who ruled him, she who was his soul; that it was she who had replaced me as his Maître; that he lived in her and for her; and that she was going to steer him toward communism."[8] Although Althusser didn't need Hélène's "influence" to make him move toward communism, it is certain that the love she inspired in him arose out of the same elements as did his forty-year relationship with the Communist Party, the mental asylum, and psychoanalysis: the same self-accusation, the same repulsion, the same self-destruction, the same exaltation, and the same desire for fusion. In some ways Althusser's fate was like that of certain great Islamic and Christian mystics, some of whom tried to find freedom by abolishing law and setting up a "subjectless" spiritual community, while others challenged the principle of individuality, the primacy of consciousness, and the myth of progress.[9]

In this context, Althusser's experience of melancholia may be seen as containing the beginnings of an initiatory pattern that propelled him from radical Catholicism to scientific Marxism, from chemical straitjacket to oedipal transference, and then into a hell of perpetual lamentation. Nothing could overcome this tragic circular madness that took the form of an impossible desire for revolution and ended in a kind of ritual murder. Instead of fading out gently, the madness seemed to get ever more impenetrable as, for Althusser as for the generation he had taught, all hope disappeared of renovating communism and turning Marxism into a creative philosophy.

The madness of this one individual was forged through three generations, in a middle-class Catholic family that had settled in Algeria after France was defeated at Sedan. At the beginning of the twentieth century a girl called Lucienne Berger was in love with a youth man called Louis Althusser, his mother's youngest child and favorite, marked out for every kind of intellectual success. His elder brother, Charles, more boorish and less loved, was engaged to Lucienne's sister, Juliette. Louis, called up when the

1914 war broke out, was shot down and killed on a reconnaissance flight over Verdun. Both families then decided to obey the ancient Biblical law of levirate, still much observed in Mediterranean countries, by one interpretation of which, when a man died, an unmarried elder brother was obliged to marry the widow. So Charles Althusser, who was still a bachelor, married Lucienne Berger, and when a son was born of this union the child was named Louis after his dead uncle. The "madness" of such a marriage resided less in its obedience to an internalized tradition than in its excessiveness—for Louis hadn't actually been married to Lucienne. Curiously enough, Louis Althusser's genealogical background was very similar to that of Antonin Artaud: there was the same confusion about origins, the same Mediterranean background, the same denial of secret fantasies, the same initiatory journey through mysticism and monotheism. "I didn't have a father," wrote Louis Althusser, "and continued indefinitely to play the role of the 'father of the father' to give myself the illusion I did have one, or rather to assume the role in relation to myself. . . . Philosophically speaking, I had to become my own father. But that was only possible if I conferred on myself the essential role of the father: that of dominating and being the *master* in all situations."[10]

Althusser's first contact with psychiatry was a disaster. "The 'drama' began to gather pace a few days later when Hélène kissed me while sitting beside me on the bed. . . . I had never kissed a woman (though I was thirty!), and certainly never been kissed by one. Desire welled up within me and we made love on the bed. It was new, thrilling, exhilarating, and violent. When she left, I was plunged into a profound state of anguish from which I could not escape."[11] Pierre Mâle diagnosed dementia praecox and had Althusser taken to the Esquirol wing at the Hôpital Sainte-Anne, where Hélène, who was used to the wiles of clandestinity, managed to elude all surveillance and get in to visit him. She also asked Julian de Ajuriaguerra to take on his case. He demolished Pierre Mâle's erroneous diagnosis and spoke for the first time of "manic-depressive psychosis." This was a term taken from Kraepelin's modern terminology, though psychiatrists had adopted it to denote a melancholy supposed since antiquity to be characteristic of geniuses and creative artists and thinkers.[12] Althusser, like Artaud before him, was then given electroshock treatment, which was commonly used in hospitals at that time.

After a further attack in February 1950, Althusser embarked on a narco-analysis (in which the patient is in a state of partial, drug-induced narcosis) with the psychiatrist Laurent Stévenin, who was already treating Althusser's friend Jacques Martin. Later, Althusser wrote, "In our eyes he had a great deal of prestige (he ended up treating the whole family, my mother, my sister, and many other close friends) . . . since he told us he was personally acquainted with certain soviet doctors, though this remained something of a mystery. They sent him phials of 'Bogomolev's serum' which were supposed to work wonders 'in almost all cases.' "[13] This serum is reminiscent of the "little jars" dispensed by a certain Dr. Omo, a strange guru from Marseilles with whom Lucienne Althusser had become besotted before, when she became a vegetarian.

In July 1963 Lacan got in touch with Louis Althusser, hoping to be invited to the ENS. He knew about Althusser's madness through Nicole Bernheim-Alphandéry, who for several years was analyzed by Lacan and was also a close friend of Althusser. Lacan could remember his own 1945 lecture at the ENS very clearly and had heard in his own consulting room of Althusser's negative reactions to it. So in the first letter he wrote to Althusser, during the night of November 20–21, 1963, after having delivered his farewell seminar at Sainte-Anne on "the names-of-the-father," Lacan's tone was a mixture of coldness and anxiety. "Our relationship is an old one, Althusser," he said. He mentioned the negative comments that had been "reported" to him and then told Althusser that he had brought his seminar to an end. "I had to, but it hurts me." Finally he mentioned the students gravitating around Althusser at the ENS, asked him to "say something" to them, and then invited Althusser to come and see him.[14]

A strange dialogue by correspondence then ensued. Althusser sent Lacan long didactic screeds, explaining the meaning of his own work and the part played in it by the return to Freud in the fifties. Lacan sent Althusser terse messages mainly concerned with practical matters, such as the date and time of his future seminar, thanks for various favors, and so on. When he received Althusser's article "Marxist Dialectic," he merely said it was fascinating and contained the same questions he had asked himself.[15] It was obvious he wasn't at all interested in Althusser's philosophy and had no faith in his plan for renovating Marxism. Only one thing mattered to him in all this, and that was the student body at the ENS. He knew they'd been awakened to his ideas by Althusser and hoped they might prove to be potential disciples, familiar enough with philosophy to be able not only to understand his work but also to give a new impetus to his thought and his movement. Althusser's letters on the other hand were full of praise for Lacan. He explained how, in his own "obscure researches on Marx, which have been going on for fifteen years," he had made use of a theory of the decentered subject derived from the return to Freud. Then he suggested a grand alliance: "I know I am prophesying, but perhaps, largely because of you, we are entering upon an age where at last a man may be a prophet in his own country. . . . We have the right as well as the means to do so now, now that it *is* our own country at last."[16]

Lacan had been in a state of dreadful agitation ever since the middle of

September. Sometimes he would threaten to kill himself with an overdose of tranquilizers; sometimes he would fly into rages and anathematize those who had betrayed him. When Althusser first rang the bell at 5, rue de Lille, at 8:30 in the evening on December 3, he found Lacan fulminating against his banishment. They went and had dinner together in a restaurant on the boulevard Saint-Germain and then walked the streets, talking, into the early hours.[17]

They both dreamed of converting the youth of France, one to a new version of Marxism, the other to a structural Freudianism. But whereas Lacan had already built up a coherent system of thought, Althusser had published little: just a remarkable book on Montesquieu and several articles. These foreshadowed a reading of Marx based on concepts borrowed from the history of science in its traditional French form, in particular from Gaston Bachelard and Georges Canguilhem. So Althusser was hoping for an "alliance": he thought he could convert Lacan, not to communism, but to a philosophy that would go beyond the idea of structure. In his view Lacan was still too much influenced by Lévi-Strauss.[18]

Lacan knew nothing about Althusser's game of being the "father-of-the-father" and no doubt would have been taken aback to hear of the adolescent fantasy his new interlocutor was to speak about in his autobiography. "I dreamed of being called Jacques—my godson's name. . . . Perhaps it's a bit much to toy with the phonemes of the signifier—but the *J* of Jacques was a jet (that of the sperm!) the deep *a* (Jacques) was the same as in Charles, my father's first name, the *ques* was all too obviously the *queue* [prick, etc.], and the Jacques as a whole like the Jacquerie, the peasant revolt whose existence I learned of from my father."[19] Lacan and Althusser shared a religious background that probably had something to do with their shared conception of the decentered subject and of structure as *absent causality*. Was it not necessary, if one wanted to save one's soul, to tear oneself away from oneself and merge into a history stripped of all historicity, or into the *one* in the signifying chain? Similarly, they both had a mirror relationship with the ideas of "symbolic father" and "founding text."

Althusser, who came close to Sartre in his idea about the absence of the superego, regarded himself as bearing the name of a dead man: his uncle Louis. From this he derived the idea that real theoreticians, and in particular the three *penseurs maudits* (outcast philosophers) of the late nineteenth century—Nietzsche, Marx, and Freud—had been forced to be their own fathers. Lacan, who tried to be nobody's son and had derived some of his most important concepts from the curse he addressed to his grandfather, had traveled in the opposite direction from Althusser. Hence his constantly renewed attachment to Lévi-Strauss's idea of symbolic function. While Althusser believed that only by escaping from all filial symbolism could one achieve a founding act, Lacan showed that, on the contrary, while such an escape might indeed produce logical discourse, such discourse would be invaded by psychosis.

On the night of December 3 the roles to be played by the two men were allocated not only in terms of their respective theories but also in accordance with the demands each was making on the other. Althusser was looking for an alliance; Lacan sought a refuge. Althusser acted the *father-of-the-father*, ready to hear every kind of confession; Lacan was an angry plaintiff, furious at having lost his legitimacy through the treachery of his friends. The next day, in a long letter that remained unanswered, Althusser gave his diagnosis of the "Lacan case": "You say," he wrote, in substance,

> that you think about the analyst's desire. And you say you've observed that what you say transforms the attitude of your students and your patients and changes their approach to psychoanalytic reality. . . . You bring everyone a great net full of fish and then point to the sea. They can understand that the latter is their element, but they also realize that one can't catch the sea in the net. Their theoretical ignorance is such that it is pointless to try to get them to go beyond their own experience. One can't move from practice to concept without a breach. And it's from outside, not from within, that the breach has come. Now you're outside, and they're still inside, whereas they made you responsible for their external relations because you were inside.[20]

This was a good summary of Lacan's situation, and it didn't fall on deaf ears. He had been removed from the list of training analysts by the application, on October 13, of the Stockholm "Directive," but he hadn't been "excluded" from the IPA because the status of the SFP was only that of a "Study Group," and its members were not really members of the IPA. Nor, in itself, did removal from the training list entail a de facto exclusion from the IPA. Moreover, though Lacan was deprived of his training status after October 13, he was still a member of the SFP. So the problem really was a question of inside or out. If Lacan accepted his downgrading and remained in the SFP, the group would become part of the IPA. But if he refused, a break was inevitable. In the first case (in), he would become a member of the IPA through the affiliation of the SFP, forbidden to train but not forbidden to teach. In the second case (out), he would lose all IPA legitimacy but become a free teacher.[21]

At Althusser's suggestion, Fernand Braudel gave Lacan a lectureship at the Ecole pratique des hautes études, and he was allowed to give his seminar in the Dussane lecture room at the ENS. At Christmas he spent a long time preparing his first lecture, due to be delivered on January 15, 1964. Called "Excommunication," it was a long commentary on Spinoza's *herem*. The dialogue with Althusser had borne fruit: Lacan, partly influenced by the philosopher's remarks, presented his break with the IPA in terms of a transition from within to without.[22] In order to underline the importance of what he always referred to thenceforward as his own "excommunication," Lacan invited a number of people to come hear the lecture. His guests included not only those of his disciples who had remained loyal but also such well-known Paris celebrities as, among others, Robert Flacelière, the director of the ENS, Henri Ey, and Claude Lévi-Strauss.

Meanwhile Lacan had been to Rome to attend a colloquium on casuistry organized by Enrico Castelli, director of the Rome Institute of Philosophy. Lacan spoke impromptu, without any notes, about the drives and the analyst's desire.[23] He was staying at the Hassler hotel, where he had arrived in a state of great agitation, and it was in these circumstances that an obscure misunderstanding took place with Paul Ricoeur, of which I have spoken earlier. The whole thing ended very strangely. Lacan invited Ricoeur to dinner in Trastevere, and when the meal was over said: "You pay, Ricoeur—I took you to dinner at a gay restaurant after Bonneval, remember." But the next day he apologized to Simone Ricoeur for having behaved badly.[24] That was putting it mildly. Nonetheless, that same evening he said to Maurice de Gandillac, "I haven't had time to get any Italian lire—will you take me to dinner? We absolutely must find a place I know where they have sheep cheese." Having wandered around for a while, the two men had dinner in a very good trattoria. Gandillac paid the bill, and Lacan said, "You must be my guest tomorrow." But by the next day he had gone.[25]

At the same time as he was seeking an alliance with Lacan and helping him break with the IPA, Althusser advised his own pupils to study Lacan's work. Already, in the academic year 1962–1963, Althusser had organized a series of talks on "the origins of structuralist thought," in which he himself spoke about Lévi-Strauss, Foucault, and Montesquieu, Jacques-Alain Miller dealt with the archaeology of knowledge in Descartes, and Pierre Macherey with the origins of language. Jacques Rancière, Etienne Balibar, and Jean-Claude Milner also took part in the series, and it was expected that Michel Tort would speak about Lacan. Miller and Milner were studying under Roland Barthes at the EPHE, where André Green had gone to talk about Lacan's work.[26]

The lecture in which, late in 1963, Althusser introduced his students to Freud and Lacan, was in complete contrast to his later theories. The man who was to fight against both subjectivism and historicism now launched into an amazing account of the French psychoanalytic movement, going back to its beginnings. He recalled the names of Dalbiez, Hesnard, Wallon, Sartre, Henri Ey, and Politzer. He explained the ideological reasons for the French resistance to psychoanalysis and accurately pinpointed the movement's internal schisms. Lastly he spoke of the work of Melanie Klein,

Françoise Dolto, Franz Alexander, and René Spitz. Incidentally, while claiming to eschew any recourse to history or biography, he told the story of his own encounter with Freudian thought.

His approach to Lacan was equally historical. He recalled the story of the "mirror stage," the notion of a "reality" in madness, the unacknowledged borrowings from Wallon, the hostility to so-called American psychoanalysis. He concluded with the need for an alliance: "Lacan," he said, "wages an implacable war against humanism, scientism, and personalism. His theories are therefore essential to us. They make it possible to think of Freud in philosophical terms and to emerge from Politzer's blind alleys." This eulogy of Lacan's method was accompanied by a description both lucid and merciless of the master's style and his disciples' extravagance. "You need to have heard him speaking . . . to understand the splendidly wicked wit with which, having experienced surrealism, he realizes himself as an individual. . . . If you go to his seminar you'll see all sorts of people prostrating themselves before a discourse that to them is quite unintelligible. These are the methods of intellectual terrorism."[27] As in his letters, Althusser was trying to show that Lacan was surrounded by students incapable of understanding the philosophical value of his work. This was a situation that needed to be remedied.

Althusser used this talk as the basis of a very good article on Freud and Lacan in which he developed arguments that were to make his own and Lacan's work, taken together, the symbolical starting point of a new understanding of the part played by structuralism in French intellectual history. Althusser began by denouncing on the one hand the revisionism of the American school, which had facilitated the exploitation of psychoanalysis, and on the other hand the supporters of the Russian Andreï Jdanov, who had been victims of the ideology they fought against, confusing it with Freudianism. Then, after showing that Lacan was the first thinker to put forward an epistemological elucidation of Freud, he went on to pay a splendid tribute to the Spinoza-like solitude of Lacan as a man: "Whence the contained passion," he wrote, "the impassioned contention of Lacan's language, which can live and survive only in a state of alert and prepossession: the language of a man already besieged and condemned by the crushing strength of threatened structures and guilds to anticipate their blows, to feign at least returning them before they have been received . . . having to teach the theory of the unconscious to doctors, analysts or analysands, Lacan gives them, in the rhetoric of his speech, the mimed equivalent of the language of the unconscious, which is, as all know, in its ultimate essence, 'Witz,' pun, metaphor."[28]

Althusser sent Lacan a typed copy of the famous article before it was published in *La Nouvelle Critique* (The new criticism). All he got by way of answer was a few complimentary lines on the aptness and penetration of the thought and on Althusser's reflections on the theory of the subject.[29] By then Lacan had got what he wanted. And although he usually tried to analyze everyone who was interested in his own teachings, he took no part in Althusser's treatment and never offered him professional help.

But it was through Althusser that Lacan met a young man who would not only transform his family life but also modify the gist of his teaching. Jacques-Alain Miller, born on February 14, 1944,[30] was just finishing his philosophy degree when Althusser suggested he should read Lacan. He went at once to the PUF bookshop, bought every issue they had of *La Psychanalyse*, and then shut himself up in his room to puzzle them out. He emerged dazzled: "I had just come upon something extraordinary."[31] An immediate convert, the nineteen-year-old was further impressed by Lacan's seminar on "Excommunication." On January 21, at the ENS, Miller presented his first paper on the master's work. Two more were to follow.[32]

Whereas Louis Althusser, Michel Tort, and Etienne Balibar tried to explain the genesis of Freud's ideas and then show how Lacan had developed them in the light of structural linguistics and the campaign against psychology, Jacques-Alain Miller provided his readers with an open sesame into Lacan's teachings, an exposé written as a single whole, devoid of contradiction or inconsistency and without any historical element. The Lacan interpreted by Miller in January 1964 was a Lacan in the present tense, stripped of his Kojèvian, surrealist, and Wallonian past. All that remained by way of a link back to Freud was a list of names: Jakobson, Benveniste, Saussure. The return to Freud seemed to have fallen from the sky like manna, through a simple logical operation. Admittedly, Miller wasn't the only one to interpret Lacan in that way. Amid the structuralist explosion of 1953 to 1968, most of the French intelligentsia read Lacan in terms of the structuralist texts he himself had written between 1950 and 1962. Thus all they knew was the Lacan of the "Rome Discourse," the agency of the letter, foreclosure, and so on. But Miller went furthest in the strictly "structuralist' representation of the master.

Yet Miller's interpretation shut the work in on itself, regarding it as no longer Freudian but already Lacanian. Lacan's gradually evolved concepts, detached from their history and stripped of the ambivalence that had been their strength, were now classified, labeled, tidied up, sanitized, and above all cleansed of their polysemic complexity. In a way they were all ready to be put into a school textbook. The *signifier*, for example, was now always accompanied by its "primacy," its "phallus," its "loss," or by "another signifier," or its *"manque à être,"* etc. The topography of real, symbolic, and imaginary was changed into a "logo," a rubber-stamped and topologized S.I.R. And so on.

Lacan, astonished by the young orator's extraordinary ability to conjure a logical order out of the great disorder of his own thought, paid him a public tribute and announced that he would answer his questions.[33] In a letter to Althusser he merely said: "Not bad, that young man of yours."[34]

During the academic year 1964–1965, Miller took part in a group study of Marx's *Capital*, from which emerged the notion of a *lecture symptomale* (symptomal reading or interpretation). This was based partly on Bachelard's notion of *coupure epistemologique* (epistemological break) and partly on Lacan's own revisions of Freud. The aim was to bring out what was untranslatable and unthought in Marx's work and to separate the texts of his youth, still showing traces of Hegel and the category of the subject, from the texts of his so-called maturity, which suggested a move toward science.[35] A rather comic conflict arose in the group when Miller accused Rancière of having "stolen" his concept of "metonymic causality." The young man went into fits of rage, pinned his accusation up on the notice board, and demanded that the culprit make amends.[36] This was the first symptom of what would later become Miller's extraordinary identification with the legendary personality of his father-in-law, himself obsessed by the fear of plagiarism.

At first, as we shall see, Miller's theoretical reduction had a beneficial effect on the dissemination of Lacan's teaching. It made it possible to show a broad public that a body of work hitherto regarded as hermetic and ambiguous was really quite coherent and rigorous. In 1963 Lacan was at a temporary halt. He had already worked out the main part of his doctrine. So he was bound to appreciate the admiration of Althusser's pupil, the more so as Miller had all the virtues of a suitable successor. He was pragmatic, a man of action, and knew from the start how to suggest practical solutions and concrete ideas to a master who felt betrayed by his earlier disciples. Miller, who came from a family of Jews who had originally emigrated from Poland, had been raised in accordance with an educational ideal that set great store by personal success and social integration. His father, Jean Miller, was known in Parisian medical circles for his method of collecting pictures. "Why pay such a lot of money for a painting," he often said to Sylvia, "when you can get others almost exactly the same for practically nothing?"[37] The son was very clever and a brilliant student. He wasn't much interested in literature and liberal arts and was a utilitarian in both philosophy, as was shown in the hyperlogical approach of his simplification of Lacan, and politics, in which his choices were always angled toward efficiency. He was thus the exact opposite of Lacan, whose wish to become a successful bourgeois made him pursue scholarship and erudition in their most complex and subtle forms. But, at the time of the split between Lacan's school and the IPA, the old master's Socratic teaching had about it an air of traditional craftsmanship rather than pure technology, and his young disciple seemed like a harbinger of the future.

Miller's desire to go to the masses, which was eventually to lead him to Maoism, was exactly in the spirit of the time and corresponded to the superseding of the intellectuals by the technocrats who were to invade the university after 1968. "I was very struck, in the period following 1968," says Hervé Le Bras, "by the wave of rationalism that drove crowds of students to lectures on logic, for example. Such behavior reflected an acknowledgment of or obedience to the force of reason that one cannot avoid connecting with the rising interest in technology and technocracy."[38]

In January 1965 Lucien Sebag, an ethnologist who had studied under Lévi-Strauss, committed suicide by shooting himself in the face. He was thirty-two years old. He left a letter on the table addressed to Judith Lacan, together with the telephone number of a woman friend who had taken him in during a period of depression. He had been under analysis with Lacan for several years, and Lacan admired his intellectual gifts and expected him to lend a new impetus to his own teachings. Sebag belonged to a generation older than that of most of Althusser's students at the ENS. He had come across psychoanalysis in the texts published in *Les Temps modernes* and had just published a book on Marxism and structuralism.[39] Lacan, despite all his efforts, hadn't been able to prevent the suicide, and he told many people how much it distressed him. One of his confidants was Althusser:

One morning, very early, someone rang my bell at the Ecole. It was Lacan. He was in a dreadful state and almost unrecognisable. I hardly dare recount what had happened. He had come to tell me of the suicide of Lucien Sebag, who was undergoing analysis with him, "before I learnt about it through the rumours which were incriminating him, Lacan, personally." Lacan had had to give up the analysis, as he had fallen in love with Sebag's daughter Judith. He told me he had "gone round Paris" explaining the situation to all those he could contact in order to put a stop to the "accusations of murder and negligence on his part." He was absolutely panic-stricken and explained how he had been unable to continue Sebag's analysis once he had fallen in love with Judith: "It was impossible for technical reasons." He told me he had, none the less, gone on seeing Sebag every day and had even seen him the previous evening. He had assured him he would visit him at any hour of the day or night if he asked him to and that he had an extremely fast Mercedes.[40]

In the autumn of that year, after another attack of melancholia arising out of the publication of *Pour Marx* (*For Marx*), Althusser started an analysis with René Diatkine, not knowing Diatkine had been analyzed by Lacan. Althusser was afraid of committing suicide, though he never actually did so, and he didn't think Lacan, as a practitioner, made use of all the pharmacological and psychiatric resources available to prevent self-slaughter. Althusser was wrong on this point. For while there was a higher rate of suicide among Lacan's patients than among those of some of his colleagues, this was mainly because he was ready to take on suicidal types whom other analysts refused.

In this sense he was no more of a "murderer" than his accusers, who often hadn't the courage to confront the problem such patients presented.

As soon as he started his analysis with Diatkine and found out that his therapist had been trained by Lacan, Althusser began to write Diatkine long letters full of the highest praise for his analyst's analyst, thus once again acting the part of the "father of the father" and trying to have the last word. "Why do you allow yourself to belittle Lacan's work? It's a mistake or rather a sin that you shouldn't commit, and yet you do. You answer by talking about Lacan's character, but that's not the point. The point is his work and, over and above even that, that of which his work is the only existing proof. The point is the right of theory to exist in the field of analysis. Paris was worth a mass. And, between ourselves, Lacan's 'character,' his 'style,' and his eccentricities, together with all their consequences, including personal injuries— *all these are well worth the theory.*"[41]

"I hereby found . . .": Kant with Sade

To launch his appeal of June 21, 1964, and found his school, Lacan resorted to a trick. He wrote out a text and recorded it on tape, whereupon a rumor spread, in and outside the SFP, that a chosen few had been invited to a mysterious meeting in François Perrier's apartment. On the appointed day about eighty people arrived in the avenue de l'Observatoire. Everyone knew Lacan had decided to make a final break, and everyone expected him to do so with a flourish.

Then Jean Clavreul announced that the master had recorded an announcement. He asked for silence and switched on the tape recorder, from which a voice emerged proclaiming in effect the foundation of the Ecole freudienne de Paris (Freudian school of Paris):

I hereby found—as alone as I have always been in my relation to the psychoanalytic cause—the Ecole française de psychanalyse [French School of Psychoanalysis], whose direction, concerning which nothing at present prevents me from answering for, I shall undertake during the next four years to assure.

That title, in my understanding, represents the organism in which a labor is to be accomplished—a labor which, in the field opened up by Freud, restores the cutting edge of his discovery—a labor which returns the original praxis he instituted under the name of psychoanalysis to the duty incumbent upon it in our world—a labor which, through assiduous criticism, denounces the deviations and compromises that blunt its progress while degrading its use.

This working objective is inseparable from a training to be dispensed within that movement of reconquest, which is to say that therein those whom I myself have trained will be fully empowered and that invitation is extended to all those who can contribute to substantiating the ordeal of that training.[1]

Scarcely had the tape stopped running than there was a stir at the back of the room: Lacan had just made his entry among the dumbfounded listeners.

Afraid of conspiracies, as ever, he had drawn up the founding document in the deepest secrecy, even refusing to divulge the new organization's name. According to Anne-Lise Stern, Lacan had revealed the contents of the text to a select group of his closest friends. He had then asked Perrier to read it out in public on June 21, but as Perrier refused, it was decided the message should be recorded.

Lacan had always wanted to be physically present at the most important events in the history of Freudianism. Yet now, to found his own school, he let a recording, one of the modern devices he hated most, speak for him. It is hard not to see this "broadcast" call for a Freudian resistance as a grandiose gesture reminiscent of de Gaulle. Just as the disembodied voice started to fade away, the master appeared in the flesh to explain the meaning of some new expressions aired on the tape: *psychanalyse pure, science affine, plus un, cartel, analyste de l'école* (AE: analyst of the school), *analyste membre de l'école* (AME: analyst member of the school), and so on. Lacan was confronting the dignitaries of the IPA who had forced the break on him and presenting himself as the man of the moment, the only one capable of restoring Freud's thought in all its dignity and truth. The founding document was superbly written and dazzlingly right. But Lacan wasn't alone. He was carrying along with him a good hundred members of the old SFP (members, trainees, and guests), and these would be joined by about thirty newcomers.

Thus when the EFP was founded it was not a new association as far as its membership was concerned: only a third of its members had had no earlier connection with the SFP. As well as the group of philosophers from the ENS, the newcomers included some priests, some Protestant ministers, some other philosophers, and many psychologists. Here are the names of those who were to play a part in its later history: Michel de Certeau, François Roustang, Cornélius Castoriadis, Félix Guattari, Yves Bertherat, Luce Irigaray, and Michèle Montrelay.

In fact, the EFP would continue in the ways of the society it was succeeding. Thus Lacan awarded the status of AE and AME not in accordance with a new set of rules but just as he himself decided and in terms of a pre-existing hierarchy. All former members of the SFP became AEs, together with many former training analysts (Bernard This, Octave and Maud Mannoni, Xavier Audouard, Piera Aulagnier, Jean Clavreul, Guy Rosolato) and several trainees (Paul Duquenne, René Bargues, Lucien Israël, Louis Beirnaert, Jacques Schotte, and Jean-Paul Valabrega). The same held for the AMEs: in general, SFP titles were all renewed. Among the AMEs appointed by Lacan were some pillars of the fourth generation who would play an important part in subsequent developments. Among these were Charles Melman, Rosine Lefort, Claude Dumézil, Claude Conté, and Christian Simatos.[2]

Lacan worked all summer at drawing up the statutes of his school and appended both an "additional note" covering the different kinds of membership and a "preamble" analyzing the meaning of the word "school."[3] He and Serge Leclaire also wrote a fourth text, not included in the EFP yearbook, giving the main lines of the new school's teaching. This text was circulated in the EFP on September 19, 1964, four days before the statutes were officially deposited: "It is necessary to state," said Lacan, "how much rectification is required in this community if psychoanalysis is to preserve its essential character, which resides in an absolute object. That object is the reality of desire, and it has to be given scientific status. This can be achieved only by a discipline strong enough to eliminate the prejudices tending against it. A discipline exists only in the subjects trained by itself. The way a psychoanalyst sees his field is different from the way a psychologist sees his."[4]

It was at this time that Lacan had a car accident on the highway, coming back from Guitrancourt. It was only a minor mishap, with no serious consequences, yet it was carefully concealed. Lacan didn't want his disciples to think anything could happen to him just as he was founding his school.[5]

The proposal put forward on September 19 was an accurate summary of what Lacan had in mind: to make the reality of desire the object of psychoanalysis and at the same time to give psychoanalysis a scientific status that would distinguish it from psychology. So, just as he was starting a group that would come to include more and more psychologists, Lacan reasserted the fundamental difference between the two fields. But his philosophical position was changing too.

On June 24, 1964, he devoted the last session of his annual seminar to a consideration of belief, science, and illusion. He referred to Auschwitz not as "genocide" but as a "holocaust," in order to convey that it was not possible to think of this modern tragedy in terms of Marx or Hegel: in his view, it was the supreme example of a sacrifice to the *Dark God* (assimilated to the Other). He cited Spinoza as the only philosopher capable of apprehending the eternal sense of sacrifice contained in *amor intellectualis*. Lacan thus recognized Spinoza's achievement in moving from slavery to freedom via intellectual love and in being able to resist feeling at all attracted by sacrifice. Lacan was according a very special place in the history of philosophy to a thinker whose name and work had always played an important part in his own development.

Between 1932 and 1946 Spinoza's work had helped Lacan to arrive at a new approach to madness: a madman is someone who has such an appropriate idea of madness that he sees it not as a fact but rather as a truth man carries within him as a limit on his freedom. In his 1959–1960 seminar on "the ethics of psychoanalysis," Lacan had invoked the ethics of Aristotle when speaking of those of Spinoza and pointed out the absence of ontology in the works of Freud. In order to compensate for this "lack" and construct a Freudian ethic, he suggested looking at the tragedy of modern man, living in the malaise of civilization. He based the proposed ethic on the existence of desire in the Freudian and Hegelian sense of the word; what he was saying, in substance, was that the only thing one can be guilty of, in the context of psychoanalysis, is "giving up on one's desire." In other words, the Freudian ethic is a Spinozan ethic, tending to see the truth of being in the deployment of desire.[6]

Thus, six months after his "excommunication" and three days after issuing his founding document, Lacan returned to Spinoza, in connection with Auschwitz and the *Dark God*. But after putting Spinoza on a pedestal he turned to Kant to demonstrate how philosophy had been "overtaken" by psychoanalysis. "[Spinoza's] position," he said, "is not tenable for us. Experience shows us that Kant is more true, and I have proved that his theory of consciousness, when he writes of practical reason, is sustained only by giving a specification of the moral law which, looked at more closely, is simply desire in its pure state, that very desire that culminates in the sacrifice, strictly speaking, of everything that is the object of love in one's human tenderness—I would say, not only in the rejection of the pathological object, but also in its sacrifice and murder. That is why I wrote 'Kant with Sade.' "[7]

"Kant with Sade" was the title of an article Lacan wrote in September 1962. It was intended to serve as an introduction to the third volume of Sade's complete works, published by the Cercle du Livre précieux (Rare Book Club). The volume in question contained *Justine; or, The Misfortunes of Virtue*, and *Philosophy in the Bedroom*. There were also commentaries by Angelo Hesnard, Maurice Heine, and Pierre Klossowski. But Jean Paulhan, the editor, considered Lacan's article unreadable, so instead of actually forming part of the Sade volume it was published as a review of it in the April 1963 issue of *Critique*. Lacan made no mention of the humiliating rejection; he just observed how difficult it was to bring out complete editions of Sade, Kant, and Freud in France.[8]

The text itself, excellent though indeed difficult, was colored throughout by Lacan's recent reading of Foucault's *Madness and Civilization*. But it was also largely influenced by the work of Max Horkheimer and Theodor Adorno. A celebrated book written in the United States in 1944 by these two theoreticians of the school of Frankfurt had already linked Kant and Sade together in the course of a long digression on the limits of reason and progressive ideals.[9] In 1962 Lacan didn't quote from this book, but he did explicitly borrow Foucault's system of divisions (e.g., reason/madness) and his notion of an "anthropological circle." Hence the idea of juxtaposing Kant and Sade in the same way as Foucault contrasted Pinel, the founder of moral treatment, and Sade, the great promoter of a "void of unreason" and a "supreme abolition of oneself." Lacan maintained that Sade's works were the first step in a process of subversion for which Kant had provided the crucial turning point. Thus *Philosophy in the Bedroom*, published in 1795 and including the satirical tract, "Français, encore un effort" (One more effort, Frenchmen), revealed a truth already contained in the *Critique of Practical Reason*, published in 1788.[10] Between the two publication dates came a major event, the French Revolution, which via the Declaration of the Rights of Man had made possible the advent of a subject of law. Kant adopted the Jacobin view on this and didn't shrink from the paradoxical idea that law comes about and is revealed via nonlaw. He therefore condemned revolutionary violence as a suspension of law, while at the same time accepting it as a necessary condition for creating a legal order.[11]

In Lacan's 1962 interpretation, *evil* in Sade's sense was presented as an equivalent of Kant's *good*. Both authors said the individual should obey the law. But, according to Lacan, whereas Sade introduced the *Other* in the person of the tormentor and revealed the object of desire (object *a*), Kant made the object disappear by proposing a theory whereby the subject became autonomous through law. Sade stressed the necessity of *jouissance* (pleasure, orgasm, coming), and desire remained subject to law as a voluntary instrument of human freedom: "Thou shalt come." In Kant on the other hand the destruction of desire was reflected in the moral law: "Thou shalt free thyself from pathology." And so, according to Lacan, Kant's morality derived not from a theory of freedom but from a theory of desire in which the object was repressed. This repression was subsequently "illuminated" by Sade. So there was a symmetry between Sade's imperative dictating jouissance and Kant's categorical imperative.

Did Lacan, at this date, know about Hannah Arendt's 1961 newspaper reports on the trial of Adolf Eichmann? It's hard to say.[12] At any rate, via Adorno and Foucault he came close to Arendt's position. She showed that Eichmann was telling the truth when he claimed to be a Kantian, because for him the wickedness of an order was nothing in comparison to the imperative force of the order itself. Thus Eichmann had obeyed the "*aberrant*" (deviant, absurd) order of genocide without incurring guilt. Lacan was saying the same thing when he equated Sade's jouissance and Kant's imperative.[13]

In June 1964 Lacan brought the problem up to date by quoting himself. He maintained that the ethics of psychoanalysis remains Spinozan when it proposes a truth of being that is based on the manifestations of desire— "Don't give up on your desire"—but becomes Kantian when it deals with the psychoanalytic experience through which the individual is subjected to the symbolic order. When Lacan found himself obliged to take on three functions that Freud considered "impossible" to reconcile—governing, psychoanalyzing, and educating—Lacan annexed the Kantian imperative to resolve the inconsistency involved in his founding a Freudian school: the contradiction between a necessary deployment of desire and the equally necessary limitation imposed on this desire by the law.

It will be recalled that just after the war Lacan had opposed Sartre's theory of freedom and shown that in order to be free the human subject must through logical reasoning make himself part of humanity as a whole. "Kant with Sade" elaborated that position: to a logical conception of belonging (1945) modeled on Bion were added a Spinozan ethics of desire (1960) inspired by the tragedy of Antigone, and also a doctrine of the subjection of the individual to the law (1962) derived from Kant taken together with Sade. From all this there followed a series of propositions. "If we consider the rights of man from the point of view of philosophy, the truth we see emerging about them is what everyone now knows. The rights of man boil down to the freedom to desire. Much good that does us, but it does allow us to recognize our recently acquired freedom to act on impulse and to confirm that this is indeed the only freedom for which a man dies."[14] And "It's the freedom to desire that is a new factor, not the freedom to start a revolution. It's always for a desire that a man fights and dies, though it's the revolution that requires that his fight should be for the freedom of desire."[15]

This then was Lacan's new theory on human freedom: man is only free through his desire for freedom (Spinoza), which gives him the freedom to die (Antigone) but also forces him to submit to a society in which good and evil are organized in terms of one and the same imperative (Bion/Kant/Sade). Thus did Lacan—a theorist of truth in his teaching but a sophist and dissimulator in his life, an admirer of Mazarin in politics, and one who hadn't chosen to die, as Cavaillès did, for a desire for freedom—come to pay tribute to the regicides of the year II, confronted with the great enigma of a much-desired freedom that was immediately transformed into servitude.[16] When he asserted that Saint-Just might have lived and been a triumphant Thermidorian if he had remained just a free-thinking author, Lacan was commenting, without saying so, on the famous passage in Saint-Just's *Fragments d'institutions républicaines* (Fragments on republican institutions): "The revolution has gone cold; all its principles have grown weak; all that is left are red caps worn on the head of intrigue. The practice of terror has desensitized murder as strong drink desensitizes the palate."[17]

But Lacan laid particular stress on Sade because in his view Sade's work was the "first step" toward another subversion: the one inaugurated by Freud. By carrying the reversal of civilized values to the furthest extreme of savagery, Sade foreshadowed man's entry into the *Oberland* of the death drive, an area that Freud saw as being at the heart of culture's malaise. And

Lacan related that savagery to the *entre-deux-morts* (between-two-deaths) situation so characteristic of ancient tragedy.[18] In Lacan's view, the excesses of
Sade could be related to the excessive behavior of Antigone, seen as a modern figure of tragedy: they made it possible to conceive of Auschwitz, the
event that in all its horror came to typify the twentieth century.

Let us note again that in June 1964 Lacan described this event as a *holocaust*. In using this term he seemed to be agreeing with the various arguments put forward by theologians, both Jewish and non-Jewish, who saw the
genocide in question either as a punishment inflicted on the Jews for having sought redemption through human effort or as a catastrophe flying in
the face of history and heralding the final death of God. But in fact this was
not Lacan's position. He used the word *holocaust* simply in order to show
how Spinoza's theory of desire, through its detachment from the Jewish religious tradition, made it possible not to succumb to the fascination exercised
by "the idea of holocaust." In other words, he invoked Spinoza in order to
reject any theologization, whether religious or atheistic, of the question of
genocide: it was to be seen neither as a sacrificial degradation of man struggling against a monstrous slavery nor as a senseless event that abolished the
divine order. Instead of meditating on the Talmud in neo-Heideggerian
terms, Lacan preferred to universalize Auschwitz and make it the tragedy of
the century, involving the whole human race.[19]

By linking the foundation of his school to Auschwitz, Lacan was symbolically depriving the IPA of its right to represent the history of the
Freudian diaspora. As a non-Jew identifying with Spinoza, he was conveying to the dignitaries of the legitimist empire, locked into the adaptive ideal
of so-called American psychoanalysis, that they were no longer entitled to
hand down the message of Jewish dissidence, rebellion, and challenge to the
established order that Freud had bequeathed to them but that after
Auschwitz had to be radically rethought. Lacan would return to this problem in October 1967 in his suggestion concerning the "pass."

All the founding texts of the EFP, written between June and September
1964—"I Hereby Found," "Additional Note," "Foreword," and "Note on
Some Elements of Doctrine"—reflect the theory on freedom that Lacan
derived from the sophism about the prisoners and brought to its ultimate
expression in "Kant with Sade." But at the same time all these pieces were
influenced by Lacan's desire to take the opposite view from that of the IPA.
He was in fact opening the way to a new internationalization of Freud. He
used the word *school* for what the legitimists called an "association" or "society" and described as "Freudian" what was usually said to be "psychoanalytic." He was, in the basic sense of the word, *founding* a republic of the mind,
designed to produce a great laboratory of creative thought.

Such a thing had never been attempted before. Ever since 1910 the internationalization of Freudianism had taken the form of bureaucratic expansion. As is well known, the IPA was made up of a number of smaller societies whose members did not all have equal rights. Each society admitted any doctrinal tendency deriving from Freudianism but forbade the breaking of any of the technical rules. This attitude had led to the disintellectualization of Freudianism, its practitioners, and its doctrinal values. Thanks, though, to the stolidity of its bureaucracy, the system had stood firm.

But this kind of organization was completely overturned by the principles put forward by Lacan for his school. No technical rules were imposed on the members of the EFP, who were allowed to choose a training analyst and a controller freely, without having to consult a "list" or a committee. Similarly, there was no hard-and-fast rule about the length of sessions. Every analyst could use his time as he saw fit; there were no more timed sessions lasting forty-five minutes, and the frequency of the sessions did not have to be decided in advance. To the might of an empire manufacturing sound technicians, Lacan opposed the utopian excess of a desiring consciousness. So the members of his school found themselves freed from the servitude of technical rules but subjected to another form of slavery: the study of Freud's doctrine as if it were holy writ, a sacred text that only Lacan's interpretation could bring to life again. A legitimist system that accommodated many trends but never underwent any democratic reform was succeeded by a school of orthodoxy where there was no doctrinal plurality though both the institution and the training it dispensed were truly democratized. The strangest aspect of all this was that, for the sixteen years of its brief existence, the EFP, within which there coexisted egalitarian democracy, monarchical power, and an orthodox system of thought, was much more open to all the main currents of modern philosophy than were the SPP and the APF, its two rivals inside the IPA.

The monarchical structure of the EFP did not preclude the development of different trends and doctrinal divergencies. All kinds of experiments carried out in medical and psychiatric institutions found a favorable echo in the Lacanian "family," within which groups were allowed to form freely and exercise their own critical spirit. Among the experiments the most important were those of Jenny Aubry at the Necker hospital for sick children, of Françoise Dolto at the Trousseau hospital, of Jean Oury in the La Borde clinic at Cour-Cheverny, of Maud Mannoni in the Experimental Center at Bonneuil, and of Claude Jeangirard in the clinic at Chailles. Several new reviews came into being, some independent and some directly linked to the school; these included *Les Cahiers pour l'analyse* (Analytic notebooks), run by Althusser's pupils, *"normaliens"* from the Ecole normale supérieure; *L'Inconscient* (The unconscious), which took over from *La Psychanalyse* and brought together psychoanalysts from the SPP and former members of the SFP; *L'Ordinaire du psychanalyste* (The psychoanalyst's everyday fare), a lively meeting place for libertarian members of the fifth generation; *Scilicet* (To wit, I.e., or You may know), the review of the EFP itself, edited by Lacan; *Ornicar?*, edited by Miller, which succeeded *Les Cahiers pour l'analyse*; and lastly *Le Coq héron* (The male heron), the only one of these reviews that still survives, which published texts by analysts from several groups outside the EFP. There was also *Les Lettres de l'école freudienne* (Letters of the Freudian school), a day-to-day record of the school's activities: conferences, discussions, speeches, etc. The twenty-seven volumes of this huge domestic bulletin sheds invaluable light on the daily life of the institution Lacan created.[20]

But the EFP, a republic made up of elites and directed by a master who gave all his disciples equal rights but never renounced a jot of his own power, was a very fragile edifice. For one thing, its structure was unsuited to the advent of mass psychoanalysis; for another, its work concentrated on desire, transference, and love, and all these came to be focused on the person of Lacan himself. And so the institution itself resembled what its master's practice gradually became: a short session later reduced to its simplest terms and then reduced again. At once the school of a mass ideology and of resistance to mass ideology, it had a life as brief and doomed as a tragedy. In relation to the general history of Freudianism, it was the school of dream, of utopia, of revolution, of desire. In it were revealed the hopes, the conflicts, and the suffering of a generation that had learned its Freudianism through libertarian rebellion and opposition to the established order. Anticolonialism, anti-imperialism, the renovation of Marxism, and the post–Sartrean model of intellectual commitment: such were the fields of thought and activity that led the fourth and fifth generations toward Lacan, his school, and his words.

In just a few years the EFP enormously outgrew its own strength; it sank beneath the weight of its success among the younger generation in France. The move toward uncontrollable expansion began between September 1966, when the new school was founded, and January 1967. By then the school had acquired 80 new recruits, which brought its membership to over 200. And after May 1968 and the terrible schism that saw the departure of Aulagnier, Perrier, Valabrega, and others, growth accelerated still more. In 1971 the school had 267 members; in 1975, 401; in 1977, 544; and by December 1979, just before its dissolution, it had reached the record figure of 609 members. In the sixteen years of its existence it had gradually acquired 468 new members. No other Freudian society had ever expanded so swiftly; and I have already shown how this expansion benefited the French groups that belonged to the IPA. In 1985 the SPP and the APF, with 468 members, ranked fourth in the world, after the United States, Brazil, and Argentina, in terms of the number of therapists they represented, though

they came first in the number of analysts per square kilometer.[21] It would
be impossible to exaggerate the extent to which Lacanianism, the most outstanding example of the "French exception" in the history of international
Freudianism, helped the expansionist interests of the legitimist Freudians.

I have already observed that the crisis that began to affect the EFP in
December 1966 coincided with the beginning of the great expansion.[22]
Now a very interesting letter, unknown to me before and written by Perrier
to Lacan in January 1965, suggests that, seven months after their school was
founded, those involved were already aware of the institutional danger
threatening them. "You are in the process of destroying what you claim to
found," wrote Perrier,

whether it be a school or a treaty of trust with your friends. *I* can't identify *for* you
the cause and methods of this sabotage....You think you're putting societies of analysts and their "structure" on trial, but in fact you're only bringing out the fact that
your own relationship to any collegiate body is that of a loner, one who excludes
himself voluntarily and rejects all groups. The brazen conspiracy of the IPA-ites
against you and the SFP (i.e., *your* society) doesn't give you the right to forget the
IPA's evident success up till 1960 or the usefulness of its research and training even
if they are based on common statutes. Your accusations fail to distinguish between
structures and institutions. The only structure mentioned in your founding document is complex, efficient, unique, and fruitful, consisting as it does of you plus the
couch plus the seminar. But you've left out a fourth and fundamental element: the
reference to adversity. . . . Another problem is that in writing the June document
you institutionalized the structure all by yourself, thus depriving it of necessary
additions and traditional checks and balances.

The difficulty you have in relating to any independent group, especially if it consists of true friends, always brings you back to the special relationship, the two-man
understanding dependent on complicity toward any third person. And so you always
divide but never rule. The difficulty you have in accepting that you're recognized
and famous beyond dispute leads you to keep on making commando raids in an old
war, for territory virtually won....What we expect of you is serene authority based
on a theory already largely worked out, not reckless skirmishes that might be the
work of ex-guerrillas turned desperadoes.[23]

It was a wonderful letter. Although Perrier didn't offer any suggestions for
remedying the crisis, he did paint a very true portrait of Lacan himself. And
no doubt Lacan recognized the accuracy of his criticism. Yet his reply was
couched in the terms he always used now in this kind of situation. He spoke
of "treachery," said he would be careful to keep Perrier's confidence "secret,"
yet told him he would show the letter to three other people—Leclaire,
Clavreul, and Aulagnier. Then he complained of his "loneliness" and his "bad
luck" and castigated those who had abandoned him: "I neither divide nor
hope to rule," he said. He ended with the words: "Either you'll be with me,
all of you. Or else, remain together—all of you, I hope, but without me."[24]

The Ecrits: *Portrait of an Editor*

*I*n his contribution to the colloquium "Lacan with the Philosophers" in June 1990, Jacques Derrida recalled the circumstances of his meeting with Lacan at the symposium on structuralism organized in October 1966 by René Girard and Eugenio Donato at Johns Hopkins University in Baltimore.[1] "In Baltimore . . . he talked to me about how he thought he would be read, particularly by me, after he was dead. . . . The other anxiety [he told me about] concerned the presentation of the *Ecrits*, which weren't yet out but were due to be published soon. Lacan was worried, and a little displeased, it seemed to me, with the people at Seuil, who had advised him to include everything in one big volume of more than nine hundred pages: but the binding might not be strong enough and fall to pieces:'You watch,' he said, gesturing with his hands, 'it won't hold.' "[2]

That was the sort of anxiety that afflicted Lacan whenever the terrible question of publication arose. "*Poubellication*," he was to call it later, a pun on "*poubelle*" (trash can), perhaps referring to the residue or waste that might in his view be the object of his dearest desire. "*Stécriture*" was the word he used later for his seminar, a telescoping of the words for stenography and writing, his way of expressing contempt for the transition from the spoken to the written word. Here as elsewhere he was extremely ambiguous. The more Lacan feared plagiarism the more he tried to keep his wonderful ideas secret. But really his constant wish was for them to be recognized all over the world with as much commotion as possible. Despite his genius he was full of the fear inspired in him by his own image, haunted by the dread of not being liked, and positively terrified at the thought that his work might be interpreted otherwise than as he intended. So he would only agree to have his spoken words committed to paper in order for them to circulate in the restricted circle of Freudian institutions and reviews.

Just as he couldn't enter Sylvia's apartment without glancing at himself in the mirror, fearful of seeing the inevitable signs of aging,[3] so he kept his cupboards full of unwieldy files containing his seminars and otherwise unavailable offprints of his articles, as if he could never bear to part with them. He would look at them and sigh, "What am I going to do with it all?" and sometimes hand them out as rewards, accompanied by subtle dedications or equivocal confidences.

And so in 1963 Lacan's works were not available "normally" outside the circles of the initiated. His 1932 thesis, never reprinted, had sunk into oblivion. If by any chance a copy ever turned up in a specialist bookshop, Lacan made haste to buy it. "In 1967," writes Jean Allouch, "wanting to get hold of a copy of Lacan's thesis, I went to the Le François bookshop, but they were unable to supply me with one. When I questioned the bookseller, he told me that at one point, he couldn't remember exactly when, the author had swept into the shop and bought up all the copies that were still unsold."[4] The great theorist of persecution, the bibliophile who had a fear of books, must have had something in him of both Alceste and Dorian Gray.

This situation would probably have lasted longer if Lacan hadn't encountered a very unusual editor in the form of François Wahl. His father was a director of the big department store the Galeries Lafayette. His mother's medical studies had led her to spend some time in the psychiatric department at Sainte-Anne, and that was how Wahl came to hear of Freud's discoveries from Sophie Morgenstern and Françoise Minkowska, who sometimes came to dinner at his house. "I learned to read," he said, "in a textbook like Porot's."[5]

As a Jew who had been a victim of anti-Semitic persecution, Wahl felt himself exonerated from guilt when, in the midst of the exodus that followed the fall of France, he discovered he was a homosexual. In Lyons, where his father had been put in charge of the Galeries Lafayette branches in the Unoccupied Zone, he was present at the birth of the resistance movements and took part in their struggle at the same time as he distinguished himself in the first year of his philosophy studies. Early in 1943, thanks to a Benedictine friend who had arranged for him to type some Latin texts by St. Augustine, he was given shelter in a monastery. But his father, denounced by an accountant, was arrested on September 8 and subsequently deported to Auschwitz: he was an assimilated Jew who had fought in the First World War, and he never imagined such a thing could happen to him. François, under the protection of Cardinal Gerlier, went into the junior seminary in Montbrison, where he became a sort of monitor and coach under the name of Bonfils. In June 1944 he rejoined the Resistance and was in Paris at the Liberation.

In Versailles, where his mother worked for the OSE (Oeuvre de secours aux enfants: Help the children), caring for the children of deportees, he met

Elie Wiesel, and in helping him work toward his *baccalauréat*, or high school diploma, he discovered Judaism and began to think the Jews needed a country of their own. Through Robert Misrahi he joined a Paris cell of the Stern Gang, and until 1948 he worked for the creation of the state of Israel. At the Sorbonne, where he continued his philosophy studies, he went to see Lagache and said he wanted to become an analyst. Lagache did all he could to dissuade him but nevertheless gave him a letter of recommendation to Lebovici. Wahl found Lagache "unsympathetic," however, and didn't keep his appointment with Lebovici. Then, through a friend, he heard of Lacan, and went to hear him lecture on the "fin du moi" (a pun on *moi*, the ego, and *mois*, meaning "month"; *la fin* means "end," and French people often talk of "les fins de mois difficiles," referring to the difficulty of making ends meet). "Lacan," Wahl says, "had just lost his mother, and he was very lugubrious and depressed. He talked about a woman patient at Sainte-Anne who had had falls after her father died because she felt she wasn't supported any more."[6]

In March 1954, as the friend of a skeptical young man who was one of Lacan's patients, François Wahl went to tea with the "Great Witch-Doctor." "We talked about the Stoics, and Lacan said to me, 'You're being analyzed already.'"[7] The analysis began at the rate of three sessions of from five to ten minutes a week. On Sundays the two young men went out to Guitrancourt by motor scooter, and the sessions lasted an hour. François Wahl's analysis lasted from 1954 to 1961: "Lacan didn't speak; he just listened. I sorted out, simultaneously, my relationship with Plato and the problems of my private life."[8]

In May 1957 François-Régis Bastide, of the publishing house Les Editions du Seuil, gave Wahl a job as editor of their fiction list. His love for Italy led him to discover Carlo Emilia Gadda and Giuseppe di Lampedusa and to make friends with Italo Calvino and Umberto Eco. In 1956, through Michel Butor, he had got to know Roland Barthes. His analysis with Lacan ended in the spring of 1961. Wahl was then living with the Cuban writer Severo Sarduy. "I went on going to the seminar that Lacan had asked me to attend in 1959, but it was time to stop. I said so to Lacan, and he replied, 'It's obvious you've had an experience that seems to solve the problems.' I stopped seeing him after that, but he phoned me regularly at Seuil to ask for books, and he always told the girl on the switchboard that it was 'extremely urgent.'"[9]

Wahl, who had not only been a patient of Lacan but had also attended his seminars and had intellectual discussions with him, was the ideal person to overcome the master's phobias and persuade him to publish his voluminous writings. But Wahl was on the same footing with Lacan as that which the master had always imposed on his entourage. In order to win Lacan's trust and avoid being accused of treachery or plagiarism, he had either to remain completely uninvolved in all his activities or else become entirely identified with them, as in the couch-seminar-transference cycle. Lacan always respected those who criticized him from outside his circle, but fiercely resented those who, having once approached or entered it, tried to break free.

Wahl's homosexuality was another advantage. Although Lacan was a great ladies' man, he had a special affection for men who loved men. It was not by chance that he used Plato's *Symposium* as a starting point for his comments on transferential love. Wahl had occasion to observe Lacan's empathy one day when he was telling him about a car accident in which he had been involved in Tangiers in 1968. "It was a miracle. Everything else was smashed to pieces, but we emerged unscathed. While it was happening, Severo had held my hand in an especially tender and protective way, and when I told Lacan about it he started to weep. 'Heaven knows I don't believe in being sentimental about love,' he said, 'but that story really moves me.' "[10]

So in 1963 Wahl was the right man at the right time for Lacan, as Althusser was, and as Leclaire had been during the negotiations with the IPA: a *passeur*, or facilitator. It should also be said that Wahl was very good at helping "his" authors by asking them useful questions and rewriting their texts when necessary. Everyone who had dealings with him remembers how he would edit other people's work with a passion and intransigence that often aroused jealousy. His enemies, often those whose manuscripts he had rejected, accused him of being too dogmatic. They may have been right, but it should be remembered that his attitude was the result of a philosophical choice based on a love of logic and a critical view of historicism. Far from acting as a censor or standardizer, Wahl was motivated by the same principles whether his so-called dogmatism was being exercised positively or negatively. He never published a book of whose form and content he didn't approve; he never exaggerated anyone's talent for commercial reasons; and he never allowed his philosophical rigor to relax. Sometimes he would deliberately refuse to publish some important book; often he defended unknown authors whose talents were apparent only to him. In his view the Socratic ethic of truth was preferable to empty pragmatism. He was a great editor.

Umberto Eco's testimony shows how strict Wahl was about rewriting and about truth itself. Speaking of his book *The Open Opus*, he says:

I was not so much revising as rewriting it, because, pressed on the one hand by Wahl's criticisms and on the other by the experiments I was carrying out with the semiological groups being formed in Paris (Barthes in particular), as well as being absorbed in reading Troubetzkoy and the Russian formalists, I was gradually overhauling the whole book. It was amid this atmosphere of intense mental and intellectual activity that Wahl, with equal intensity, talked to me about Lacan, whose teaching he was following, and of his own efforts to persuade him to publish his collected writings. . . . When my own book *The Missing Structure* came out, François Wahl, with the frankness that always allowed our relationship to remain friendly despite many differences of opinion, wrote me in more or less the following terms (I quote from memory): "I shall not publish your last book myself, and I wouldn't really approve of its appearing in France at all. I already disapprove of its being published in Italy." I had been guilty of *lèse*-Lacanianism.[11]

Eco's criticism didn't prevent Lacan from being on friendly terms with him or even from trying to charm him. At a dinner party he said something to Eco that changed his life. "Eat your *Dasein*," he had exclaimed (literally, "Eat your being-there," a play on the resemblance between the German word and the French *dessert*, the same word as in English). "With his animal flair for devouring souls, he had understood that in speaking of other things I was really speaking of myself, and he, also speaking of other things, said what he did in order that his meaning might strike home."[12] As for Eco, he admitted that his criticism was aimed at the Lacanians rather than at Lacan himself.[13]

Wahl, who edited several different series, really ran the human sciences section at Seuil until 1989 and so contributed to the rise of French structuralism in the sixties. He published Roland Barthes, Paul Ricoeur, Gérard Genette, and the writers connected with the review *Tel quel*. In his difficult relations with Lacan he had the constant support of Paul Flamand, the founder of Seuil. Flamand had adopted an attitude diametrically opposite to Wahl's. "As a publisher and managing director," he said, "I always refused to say which books I liked. I spent an hour every week with each of my literary editors in order to understand what I was publishing."[14]

Flamand recognized that there was a special relationship between Lacan and Wahl—"something filial and paternal"—and left Wahl to it. Flamand's relationship with Lacan was purely professional; it was with Françoise Dolto, with whom he had long been friends, that his role was almost the same as Wahl's with Lacan. "She was afraid to publish, but I managed to persuade her. I admired her greatly. In the end, she published too much."[15] And so, via the friendship of these two very different men, and at a time when they had had to leave the IPA and were establishing the Ecole freudienne de Paris, Lacan and Dolto both found themselves dealing with the same publisher. Thus Seuil was to become the special mouthpiece of the French branch of Freudianism known as Lacanianism.

It was in June 1963 that Wahl suggested to Lacan that he should "publish." The idea began to germinate, but not until a year had gone by and Lacan had broken with the IPA did it begin to produce any result. On April 3, 1964,

Lacan signed a contract with Seuil to start a new series called Le Champ freudien (The Freudian field). Article 2 of the contract stipulated that the books in the series would be suggested to the publisher by Lacan and that no manuscript could be selected for inclusion in the series without his approval. The fee for the series editor (Lacan) was fixed at 2 percent of the list price of each copy sold. In the case of foreign publication, Lacan had the right to examine the translation. A month later, on May 20, Lacan signed another contract, subsequently canceled because he never honored it, in which he himself offered to write a book entitled *Mise en question du psychanalyste* (The psychoanalyst in question). At that date the idea was not to issue a collection of already published texts; what was suggested was an entirely new book. But it never saw the light of day. However, beginning a series was a first step toward publication. Lacan, taken on by Seuil as an editor rather than an author, was in a privileged position: he was free to choose the manuscripts he wanted to publish, which could include his own. The first title was, in fact, Maud Mannoni's *L'Enfant arriéré et sa mère* (The retarded child and its mother), which appeared in 1964.

Another two years went by before Lacan agreed to include a collection of his own *Ecrits* (writings) in his series. Wahl managed to persuade him after the publication in 1965 of Paul Ricoeur's book *De l'interpretation* (Interpretation) in the series L'Ordre philosophique (The philosophic order), for which, as for Le Champ freudien, Wahl had overall responsibility. As is well known, the publication of Ricoeur's book made Lacan furious: the whole text was on the subject of Freud and his disciples but made no reference to the teachings of Lacan, whose seminar Ricoeur had attended for five years.[16]

Lacan, unable to assemble his texts himself, asked his closest followers to do it for him. But as the école was already going through a crisis, no one was willing to take on the task. Finally, urged on by Wahl, he asked Sylvia and his assistant, Gloria Gonzalès, to look for his articles. They couldn't find his 1936 lecture "The Mirror Stage." Nor could Lacan. He looked through all his cupboards, but in vain. So, as both he and Wahl regarded the idea of the mirror stage as the basis of his teaching, he suggested including in the collection his 1938 article in the *Encyclopédie française*, a résumé of what he had said at Marienbad. But Wahl refused: he didn't think the text was "Lacanian." The writing was "too Freudian" to be true to Lacan's usual style. Wahl wanted the magnum opus to be exhaustive and completely intelligible. In the winter of 1965 he himself began to read the texts as they had appeared in various reviews. In March 1966, when the work grew more intensive, an extraordinary theoretical tussle began between the author and the editor that would end in the birth of the *Ecrits*.

Wahl was confronted with four kinds of text: articles already published and so in printed form; original and therefore previous typescripts of the same; other typescripts of these texts with Lacan's corrections; and typescripts that had never been printed. All these texts were now corrected, some—such as "Logical Time," "The Freudian Thing," "Variations on the Standard Treatment," "Position of the Unconscious," and "Kant with Sade"—much more than others. Wahl had to "invent" a punctuation for almost all the texts. When he came across phrases that he couldn't understand, he would question Lacan about them over lunch at Calvet's restaurant in the boulevard Saint-Germain. In the summer Wahl went to the Hôtel des Roches-Rouges at Argentière to edit the final version of the text, taking with him a thousand pages of manuscript and a suitcase full of books. Every day he sent Lacan a portion of text together with queries, and by return post he received his altered text back again, with notes at the foot of each page containing Lacan's answers to his questions. "I would see his modified text arriving," said Wahl, "but I never knew by what mental process he had got there."[17]

The mailman at Argentière had never seen packages go back and forth at such a rate. Sometimes Lacan would include a reference book. Sometimes a problem would be sorted out over the telephone. Lacan worked hard: for the first—and last—time he was obliged to reread a text that brought together the main results of a life devoted to learned research. Most of the changes were made between March and August 1966. Back in Paris in September, Wahl found on his desk the typescript of an unpublished lecture of 1958: "The Signification of the Phallus." Lacan had found it at the last minute, just before the text of the whole collection was due to be sent to the printer. The paper on which it was typed was worn and shriveled, and Lacan had written in numerous corrections in ink. Wahl was exhausted and harassed, but happy. He had managed to wrest Lacan from the grip of his own spoken word and made him produce some true writing.

Almost all the textual changes were inspired by Wahl, but he never altered a syllable without the author's permission. Only the punctuation reflected his own contribution. There had been some wrestling matches. Sometimes Wahl wanted to reorganize Lacan's mannerist swarms of subordinate clauses. But Lacan wouldn't yield: it was *his* style, *his* syntax, *his* creation. It was he who chose the title, wanting to make a distinction between the written work and the spoken work, the latter still continuing in the seminar. It was he who wanted to add an "*ouverture*" (overture, or opening) and a biographical note in which he gave a subjective account of his entry into the saga of Freudianism. It was he, finally, who insisted on starting the book with the "Seminar on 'The Purloined Letter.'" Wahl didn't agree about this, and while not asking Lacan to move the text, he did request that he add a note at the end of it, explaining its position in the book. So Lacan wrote a

"Presentation of the Order" and then "The Parenthesis on Parentheses," a logical reformulation of the paper itself.

In the biographical note, "Concerning My Antecedents," he referred to the surrealists' reaction to his thesis, claimed Clérambault as his only mentor in psychiatry (forgetting he had sided with Claude against him), mentioned neither Kojève nor Wallon, and presented himself as the inventor of the idea of the *mirror stage*. He dated his entry into Freudianism not from the writing of his thesis, but from the Marienbad congress—i.e., from his first appearance on the IPA stage, the occasion of the famous scene. The *Ecrits* were thus presented in a kind of future perfect style against a trompe-l'oeil background in the manner of Francesco Borromini. Not only did Lacan interpret the history of his earlier texts in the light of his present doctrine; he also claimed the benefit of hindsight. A book, he was saying in substance, should be read in terms of its later evolution. He was asking the 1966 reader to interpret the prewar Lacan in the light of the structuralist Lacan of "The Agency of the Letter" and to interpret the structuralist Lacan in the light of the Lacan of 1965.

This being so, the best introduction to a reading of the *Ecrits* was not so much the "Seminar on 'The Purloined Letter' " as its two appendices (the "Presentation" and the "Parenthesis"), which led on to a text called "Science and Truth." This was a transcribed version of the inaugural session of the 1965–1966 seminar *The Object of Psychoanalysis,* that had already been published in the first issue of *Les Cahiers pour l'analyse.* In this text Lacan had carried out what I have called a *logical revision* of his structural theory of the subject and the signifier, based in part on the work of his old friend Alexandre Koyré. He took from him the idea that modern science—which had produced the cogito—had brought about a dramatic devaluation of being. And from Kurt Gödel he had borrowed the second incompleteness theorem: the notion that truth cannot be fully formulated. Lacan observed that this was part of the general failure of science, which was always in search of something to make its incompleteness whole. He inferred that the experience of Cartesian doubt divided the subject or individual between knowledge and truth. In his view, the subject (divided, split, foreclosed, etc.) was a correlative of science, and this correlative was called the *subject of science.* While classical structuralism had made it possible to decenter this subject, as Freud had done, it was also, by pandering to the ideal of the human sciences, in danger of unwittingly reconstructing a humanism of the complete subject, the more so as it neglected the position of the unconscious. As a result, only entry into a logic could save psychoanalysis from remaining one of the human sciences. But according to Lacan this logic was a logic of incompleteness, the science of a fallen subject, the science of a correlative not made whole. In short, it was the science of the *subject of science,* able to listen to the *paranoid subject* abandoned by the Cartesian division and to lend an ear to the "excentric" or decentered subject of modern scientific civilization.[18]

Lacan was here playing off a logic of symbolic function against the power of logic proper. He wanted, in the name of an ideal of universalist scientificity, to combat any attempt on the part of psychology to make psychoanalysis a human science. So he charged psychoanalysis with the task of taking as its object the subject of science, itself a product of the signifier. If this were done, psychoanalysis could refute magic on the one hand and religion on the other: the former because it included the subject in the natural order of the world and the latter because it obliged him to relate the cause of his desire to God.[19]

The lecture on "Science and Truth" was an explicit reply to a paper that Jacques-Alain Miller had read at a session of Lacan's seminar the previous year,[20] which had also been reproduced in the first number of *Les Cahiers pour l'analyse*, under the title "Suture: Elements of a Logic of the Signifier."[21] Making use of Gottlob Frege's *Foundations of Arithmetic*,[22] which he and his friend Yves Duroux had just read, Miller compared the zero theory of Frege and his successors with Lacan's theory of the signifier, and gave the name of "suture" to the relationship between the subject and the chain. Then he added that the subject was there in the place of the zero as "representing a lack." While observing that the notion of *suture* did not appear in Lacan's teaching, Miller maintained that Lacan, like Frege, excluded consciousness from any definition of the subject.

Just as he did in his 1963 paper, Miller was radicalizing and simplifying Lacan. Where Lacan produced ambiguity, Miller produced clarification, singleness, closure instead of openness. Lacan recognized that the young man who was to become his son-in-law was introducing into his teaching a logical emphasis that was alien to it. That was why, without actually citing the paper on suture, he alluded to it in "Science and Truth" by taking up a completely contrasting position. Instead of calling the relationship between the subject and the chain a "suture" and favoring its closure rather than its opening, he reworked the term and said that science fails to suture or produce a complete formalization of the subject.

Lacan's logical revision of his own positions in 1965 had been inspired by the work of Althusser's pupils at the ENS, and in particular by Miller's comments. But although Miller's contribution was useful to Lacan, its tenor was quite opposite to his own. Lacan's logic of the subject was based on opening, ambiguity, ambivalence, and the idea of an impossible mastery; Miller's interpretation of that logic was the harbinger of all the dogmas that were to come.

In October 1966, after his great work had been sent to the printer, Lacan called up Wahl in the middle of the night to say: "We absolutely must have an index!" Wahl, exhausted after months of work, refused to start up again, and it was to Miller, a few weeks before his marriage to Judith, that Lacan entrusted the task.[23] In drawing up the index the young man committed an extraordinary slip: he left out the name of Georges Bataille, though of course he was mentioned in the text.[24] On the other hand, Miller did provide the book with an "Index of Major Concepts" and an "Annotated Table of Graphics."[25] These two additions were very well done but emphasized the future perfect aspect of the *Ecrits*. Instead of listing the concepts in the chronological order of their first appearance and then describing their evolution, Miller set out each concept in its structural relationship to the whole. He worked back from the most recent state of the relevant theory, dividing the work as a whole into five orders. He pointed out that certain texts were too complex to fit into his breakdown, and said the way the book was organized represented his own interpretation of Lacanianism itself.[26]

The magnum opus of autumn 1966 bore the marks of its lengthy gestation, via Lacan's rewriting, Wahl's editing, and Miller's simplifying commentary. On November 15 the book was delivered to all the bookshops. On November 30 Lacan signed a contract with Seuil for the publication of the *Ecrits*. In article 12 of that document Lacan gave the publisher first option on five further books.

On the very day the book appeared, Lacan received the acclamation he had coveted for so long and done so much to deserve. Five thousand copies were sold in less than two weeks, even before the reviews appeared in the press. More than fifty thousand copies would be sold of the standard edition, and paperback sales would beat all records for such a difficult work: the first volume (it was split in two for the softcover edition) sold more than a hundred and twenty thousand copies; the second more than fifty-five thousand. Some of the reviews were very enthusiastic; other very critical. Among the most interesting were those by Emmanuel Berl, François Châtelet, Lucien Sève, Catherine Clément, Bernard Pingaud, Louis Beirnaert, and André Jacob. Among the most ridiculous were those by Jacques Brosse, Jean-François Revel, and André Robinet.[27] In *La Quinzaine littéraire* (The literary fortnightly), Didier Anzieu launched a violent attack on his former analyst, calling him a heretic and predicting his downfall.[28] Charles Melman provided a dogmatic reply.

So Wahl had won the great battle for the publication of Lacan's written work. Henceforward Lacan would be recognized, celebrated, attacked, hated, and admired as an important thinker, not just as a leading psychoanalyst.

Lacan soon strengthened his links with Seuil. In March 1968, as part of the Champ freudien series, he started the review *Scilicet* to publish his own texts and those of the members of his school who agreed to appear anonymously.[29] But this venture ended in disaster. And every further publication involved pain and anger and difficulty. But through it all, Wahl and Flamand behaved impeccably toward their wayward author.

The first conflict arose in connection with the paperback edition of an anthology called *Ecrits I*, which was supposed to contain five texts from the standard edition of 1966.[30] On January 9, 1970, Bruno Flamand, Paul's son, who was in charge of the series Points, sent Lacan the proofs of the anthology. Three days later Lacan sent the package back with a note: "I don't think I've kept you waiting."[31] Bruno Flamand then sent the whole thing off to the printer, but a month later he noticed that the fifth article, "The Agency of the Letter," was missing. He wrote to Lacan, taking on himself the entire responsibility for the omission, which he attributed partly to the urgency of getting the book out in the Points series, and partly to the speed with which a number of tasks had to be done at the same time. In order to repair the mistake he suggested bringing out *Ecrits II* very quickly, with "The Agency of the Letter" at the top of the list of contents.[32]

Not only did Lacan reject this solution; he also flew into a dreadful rage. He told Wahl what he had decided during a long phone call, making three points: "Kindly let Seuil know that if the paperback is not redone and complete copies sent to the bookshops to replace the incomplete ones, (1) I shall forbid them ever to bring out volume 2; (2) I shall never give Seuil anything else; and (3) when I say something like this I never go back on it." Then he sent Bruno Flamand a letter demanding compensation: in order to make up for the "absurd negligence" revealed by the state of the small book as published, he suggested it should be withdrawn and every purchaser be given a corrected and complete volume instead. François Wahl gave Paul Flamand an account of his conversations with Lacan and added his own conclusion: "Speaking for myself, I'd give in without hesitation."[33] And Seuil did give in. The book was entirely reset, and the defective copies withdrawn from circulation.

Publication of the thesis presented a different problem. Wahl had been thinking for a long time of reissuing it, but Lacan strongly disagreed. When the *Ecrits* appeared, Sylvia campaigned to make him changed his mind. "You can't imagine," she told Wahl, "how important it was to my generation."[34] Lacan himself frequently referred to this product of his youth, sometimes mentioning Aimée and sometimes François Tosquelles, who had helped to circulate the thesis at the hospital at Saint-Alban, in the Lozère, during the war. Occasionally Lacan would talk of plots and plagiarisms in connection with the thesis. One day he said he had been "picked out" after the war because of it. Another time he accused Anzieu of having stolen his ideas: "I was absolutely revolted by the way it was taken over in a book that came out under the title *Self-Analysis*: it was my text, but added to in such a fashion that no one could make out what had happened."[35]

In 1972 the historian of psychiatry Jacques Postel suggested republishing the thesis for the series Rhadamanthus which he edited for the publishing house Privat. Lacan refused: "You will easily understand that I myself have something to do with the fact that it hasn't been reprinted."[36] But he went to the trouble of explaining his refusal and said he couldn't publish anything except with Seuil (this was true). But in 1974, at the request of Catherine Clément, who had for some time been interested in female paranoia, he agreed to republish the passage in the thesis that dealt with the attack on Huguette Duflos and the anamnesis involved. The occasion was the issuing of a number of the review *L'Arc* (The bow) in honor of Lacan that was made up exclusively of contributions by women.[37] Finally, a few months later, he signed a contract with Seuil for the republication of his thesis, which appeared in May 1975. Article 12 of the contract, concerning options, was canceled: Lacan had already given Seuil three seminars he had cowritten with Jacques-Alain Miller and the text of a television interview, entitled *Television*.[38] So the thesis was the sixth of Lacan's own works to appear as part of the series he edited, under the aegis of François Wahl. I shall come back to this.

While Wahl was certainly a marvelous collaborator in Lacan's transition from the oral to the written, he also contributed to the process Lacan had embarked on of revising and sometimes telescoping the history of his own theoretical development. Thus, in his two-page introduction to the new edition of Lacan's 1932 thesis, Wahl asserted that it was neither Freudian nor Lacanian but still psychiatric, because it was written at a time when people still believed psychosis had primarily organic origins; moreover, Aimée's writings were analyzed according to a linguistic method.[39] There was not a word about the real advance in psychiatry and psychoanalysis that Lacan had made in 1932. It should be recalled that Lacan was already a Freudian then, though not in the same way as in 1936; that his thesis expressed an anticonstitutionalism that was shared by all his generation; and that his analysis of the texts involved was inspired not by linguistics but by surrealism.

This presentation of a Lacan who was "already something" but not yet "something else," the son of no one, the solitary inventor of a self-generated system of thought arrived at via a pre-Freudian state followed by a fully blown Lacanian one, corresponded to the image that Lacan himself liked to convey. But it was also the product of a view of history derived from a structuralism distorted in transmission by the media. As such it was adopted and amplified by almost all those who wrote about Lacan's work between 1966 and 1975. With few exceptions, all the articles then devoted to Lacan or the republication of his thesis reproduced a pious myth: Lacan was always depicted as coming from the great Parisian intellectual bourgeoisie, the inventor of the mirror stage, the creator of a new conception of paranoia influenced by both Heidegger and Saussure, and having just one mentor in psychiatry: Georges (*sic*) de Clérambault.[40]

In other words, the dehistoricization that now lay at the heart of Lacanian teaching had led to the fabrication of an imaginary character made up of rumors and fictions.

26

• • • • • • •

Revolution: Jean-Paul Sartre and Jacques Lacan, Alternate Contemporaries

*I*n 1981, in an unpublished interview with Didier Eribon, Michel Foucault pointed out how Sartre and Lacan could be called "alternate contemporaries" (using the adjective to suggest recurrent opposites, as in "alternate rhyme" or "alternating current"). Foucault noticed that in the thirties both Sartre and Lacan had been part of an antichauvinist movement that had made possible a new approach to German philosophy. In another interview belonging to the same period and published in the Italian newspaper *Il Corriere della sera*, Foucault went into more detail. He told how important his discovery of the works of Lacan and Lévi-Strauss had been to him in the fifties: "This was what was new: we were finding out that philosophy and the human sciences were still living according to a very traditional notion of the human subject and that it was not enough to say sometimes, with the first, that the individual was fundamentally free and sometimes, with the second, that he was determined by social conditions. We were discovering the necessity of trying to liberate all that hides behind the apparently simple use of the pronoun 'I.' The subject: something complex and fragile, of which it is so difficult to speak, but without which we cannot speak." Foucault added that Lacan's hermeticism or abstruseness was due to his wish that "the obscurity of his writings should correspond to the complexity of the subject, and that the work of understanding the subject should be seen as work to be carried out on oneself." As for Lacan's alleged "terrorism," Foucault pointed out that "the influence someone exerts can never be a power he imposes." In other words, Lacan terrorized only those who were afraid.[1]

Alternate contemporaries: that really was the historical, theoretical and political situation of the two masters of freedom who since 1943 had constantly encountered, confronted, and opposed one another without ever actually meeting. At the time the *Ecrits* were published, Sartre was being widely accused of misunderstanding both Freud and psychoanalysis. The superb

Freud Scenario written at the request of John Huston had not yet been published,[2] and no one was able to see how familiar Sartre was with the scientific and theoretical content of Freud's work. As far as Sartre's relationship to psychoanalysis was concerned, the structuralist generation of the sixties had looked no further than the phenomenologist positions in *Being and Nothingness* and the incisive assertions in *Les Mots* (*Words*), to which was added his sympathy for the negative British attitude to psychiatry, seen as support for a kind of crude anti-Freudianism. Moreover, Sartre, like almost all the thinkers of his generation, had not read Lacan. His Freud was a "Sartrean" Freud, unmodified by Lacan's reinterpretation.

Lacan, on the other hand, was a great reader of Sartre. We must not forget that his own theory of the subject and his doctrine on freedom had been constructed *in opposition to* Sartre's arguments. It was the publication by Seuil of Lacan's magnum opus, as well as a change in the intellectual climate, that led Sartre to enter the lists against the unseen adversary who now threatened to become the spokesperson of a school of thought capable of rivaling the now rather elderly existentialism.

Bernard Pingaud introduced the debate in an issue of *L'Arc* compiled as a tribute to Sartre, pointing out that philosophy, which fifteen years before had been triumphant, now tended to give way before the human sciences. This meant, according to Pingaud, that the succession was open: "When we want to get rid of a great man we bury him in flowers. But what are we to do when he refuses to be buried? . . . Instead of paying Sartre useless homage, it seemed to us more worthwhile to try to place him in relation to the new current of thought that has grown up partly in opposition to him."[3]

As for Sartre himself, he rejected the human sciences' claim to replace philosophy and ditch history. He accused Lacan, Foucault, and Althusser of trying to erect a last "bourgeois" barrier against Marxism, though he didn't consign to the "structuralist bin" such genuine scholars as Lévi-Strauss, Benveniste, and Saussure. He forgot Dumézil but admitted that Lacan was true to Freud.[4]

It was an opportunity too good to miss for the press to contrast the two "charismatic leaders." In an interview with Gilles Lapouge in the *Figaro littéraire* (Figaro literary supplement), Lacan declared that it was absurd to say he and Sartre were symmetrical opposites. "I find it hard to believe," he said, "that the idea is to make Sartre more topical again. Sartre is still the most popular representative of French philosophy. But there is a difference between saying that and saying that whatever is not Sartrean must still be defined principally in those terms. . . . People try to make me out to be a kind of successor to Sartre. Allow me to point out that this reflects a curious idea of what I'm interested in. Sartre has performed a definite function that may well be much admired, but it has nothing to do with my own researches. Sartre is younger than I am, and I have followed his rise with great sympathy and interest. But I don't see myself as in any way related to him."[5]

A weighty denial! But much as Lacan might reject the comparison, asserting that his own work had nothing to do with Sartre's and that his own popularity would never rival that of the existentialist philosopher, nonetheless he, Lacan, had become the theorist of a new model of subjective rebellion that would force him, when the barricades went up in May 1968, to confront the problem of revolution. So he, like Sartre, would be caught up in the French flirtation with Maoism, in the dialectic of alternation so neatly identified by Michel Foucault.

After his encounter with the pupils at the ENS, Lacan for the first time put his signature to a couple of manifestos: one, on April 19, 1967, demanding the liberation of Régis Debray, a young French intellectual and friend of Che Guevara, just sentenced to thirty years' imprisonment for subversion in Bolivia; and the other, on May 9, 1968, in support of the protesting students.[6] He had never before committed himself in this way, though he was often asked to do so. Direct engagement in politics had always been an important question in his private life, partly because Sylvia always belonged to the Far Left and partly because Laurence Bataille had been a genuine activist during the Algerian war.

By changing his platform and supporting the work of *Les Cahiers pour l'analyse*, Lacan moved to a more extreme confrontation with this problem. In his school, crisis ridden though it was, he ruled over a "family" of disciples who had been his best traveling companions since 1950. In the ENS he was surrounded by a theoretical and logical avant-garde that differed from the other family in both its thought and its aspirations. The members of the old guard cultivated traditional clinical values and advocated a classical Lacanianism still linked to the serious study of Freud. The younger generation saw itself as much more radical. Not only did its members rather look down on their elders, whom they considered uncultured, bourgeois, and incapable of any theoretical progress, but they were also beginning to talk about a "pure" Lacanianism ideologically freed from its Freudian origins.

Despite many attempts, especially by Serge Leclaire, to maintain links between the majority of clinicians in the EFP and the active minority in the ENS, the gulf between them remained unbridgeable and only grew wider as the years went by. Leclaire, aware of this deadlock, preferred to turn to the university, and in 1969 he started the Experimental Center at Vincennes–Paris VIII, the first department of psychoanalysis as such in France: the first, that is, to free itself from the aegis of psychology. Leclaire's intention was to try out a new way of handing down the legacy of Freud and at the same time to escape the crisis that was afflicting all previously existing psychoanalytic institutions. As is well known, Lacan refused at first to support this venture, but in 1974, with the help of Jacques-Alain Miller, he took it under his own wing.[7]

In May 1968 Lacan was not as famous as Sartre, nor had he such a wide international influence. Moreover, his doctrine advocated skepticism with regard to any kind of subjective commitment that took no account of the dependence of the subject on the signifier. But both Sartre and Lacan, though from completely different directions, were to be canvassed by that section of the younger generation of French intellectuals that in the autumn of 1968 gathered around the banner of the Gauche prolétarienne (GP: Proletarian Left). And just as Lacan was torn away from his former family of disciples by his encounter with the students at the ENS, so Sartre was to break with his "family" at the *Temps modernes* through his "collaboration" with the philosopher Benny Lévy, the former leader of the GP who was to become Sartre's secretary when the older man went blind in 1973.

Both Sartre's and Lacan's changes of direction took place against the wider background of the Cultural Revolution that began in China in 1966. For the first time since October 1917 there was hope that revolution itself might be revolutionized and that communism might be criticized by communism. Mao Tse-tung was a leader who had been a founding father, a rebel, and a ruler, and now, on the eve of his death, he was organizing a mass rising of his country's youth against the officials of his own party, with the object and ideal of regenerating the people and the nation. Here was something to fire the imagination of a whole generation of philosophers, inheritors of the great anticolonial struggles, who had long dreamed that it might be possible to glorify revolutionary consciousness. Such was the context in which the sayings of the Great Helmsman would strike this intellectual elite as an expression of philosophical truth.

As soon as it came into being the GP counted among its numbers militants from various sectors of the French political Left. Within the group, the students from the ENS had split into two branches: the Lacanians of *Les Cahiers pour l'analyse*, with Jean-Claude Milner, Judith and Jacques-Alain Miller on the one hand, and on the other the Althusserians of the *Cahiers marxistes-leninistes* (Marxist-Leninist notebooks), including, among others, Robert Linhart. Benny Lévy, who had adopted the name Pierre Victor, had come to the GP by a rather different path. A Sephardic Jew of Egyptian origin, he was stateless, facing all the administrative difficulties this entailed. At the age of fifteen he had found in Sartre's works both a way of assimilating the French language and a means of constructing an identity for himself. He was extremely dogmatic, and seemed mesmerized by the mystique of tribal-type leadership and by obedience to a law of which he saw himself as the earthly embodiment. The founding group of the GP also included Christian Jambet and Guy Lardreau, two younger philosophers influenced by Althusser and Lacan.[8]

To begin with, Lacan observed the protests with amusement. In May 1968, on learning that the psychiatry students had invited representatives of the various psychoanalytic groups to the Faculty of Medicine, he asked Irène Diamantis, a young analyst belonging to his own school and to the team led by Jenny Aubry, to send the organizers of the confrontation to see him. He wanted to be invited to the encounter himself, without having to ask. Two of those involved went to the rue de Lille. Lacan listened to one of them for a few minutes and then turned him out, after fulminating against the word *dialogue* and the ignorance of medical students who didn't know anything about Freud. Referring to the presence in the Faculty of Medicine of his rivals from other schools, he cried, "Be satisfied with those colossi!" Then he called up Irène and reproached her for sending such lightweight people to see him.[9] He wanted to meet a leader. His wish was soon granted.

It was Anne-Lise Stern who, through Michèle Bargues, organized a meeting between Lacan and his entourage on the one hand and Daniel Cohn-Bendit on the other. Michèle Bargues belonged to the Movement of March 22, a protest group started by Cohn-Bendit and others at the University of Paris at Nanterre, and both her parents were former pupils of Lacan and members of the EFP. Cohn-Bendit and his friends tried to explain the aims of their own movement, while the analysts really just wanted to listen to some protesters. So the two parties hadn't much to say to one another, and Leclaire was the only person who asked a useful question. "What will you do," he asked, "with your veterans? Will you set up a national school for administrators of the revolution?" Cohn-Bendit, surprised, said that soldiers differed according to the wars they fought in: the Spanish Republicans weren't comparable with the *poilus* of Verdun. After this exchange, the psychoanalysts gave the students some money. The students then went and had dinner at La Coupole, where they met their benefactors doing the same.

That evening Lacan made no comment, but the next day he interrupted his seminar on "the psychoanalytic act" in obedience to the strike notice issued by SNESUP, the union of university teachers. He praised Cohn-Bendit and attacked his own disciples. "I half-kill myself telling psychoanalysts they ought to expect something from the insurrection. And some of them reply: 'And pray what does the insurrection expect from us?' Then the insurrection answers: 'What we expect from you is help in throwing cobblestones when the occasion arises.'" Then Lacan said that cobblestones and tear-gas canisters performed the function of object *a*, the object of desire.[10]

In August, at a meeting in Carrara, Daniel Cohn-Bendit told Irène Diamantis he had only just realized the significance of Leclaire's question.[11]

Françoise Giroud wrote about the seminar of May 15 in an article in *L'Express* entitled "When the Other was God." She quoted something Lacan had said to one of his interlocutors: "There is no such thing as dialogue. Dialogue is deception." She then went on to comment: "The deception that according to him is contained in the idea of 'dialogue' resides in the fact that there is never any real exchange between two individuals. There may sometimes be an exchange of objective information, a reciprocal communication of facts, or an arrival at a shared decision. . . . But in all other cases dialogue is only the juxtaposition of monologues."[12] Similarly, Lacan would soon declare "There is no such thing as a sexual relationship" in order to show that a sexual relationship is not a relationship. He would also say "Woman doesn't exist" in order to point out that there is no such thing as a feminine nature.[13]

Françoise Giroud's article brought out an important aspect of the way Lacan's thought evolved between 1968 and 1975: i.e., he showed a growing tendency to value formula above reasoning, slogan above proof, and neologism above argument. After 1970 the habit grew so pronounced as to change Lacan's utterance into a kind of miraculous grab bag for the use of messianic sects. So the final dissolution of Lacan's work into a mass of formulas was to be the last stage in a process that began with his encounter with the logicalist elite of the ENS, who wanted to dehistoricize his discourse in order to maintain its theoretical purity. The results were paradoxical: the logicalist reinterpretation, which saw itself as "elitist," ended up fabricating simplistic formulas that were easily accessible to the masses, the more so because the slogans resembled the media idea of those same new codes of communication that the "elitists" themselves claimed to reject.

In the spring of 1969 Jacques-Alain Miller, who was teaching in Besançon, became a member of the GP, one of whose aims was to "destroy the university." Yet he went on teaching and kept his job at Paris VIII, in the department of psychoanalysis founded by Leclaire.[14] "I remember the great change of direction," says François Wahl.

One evening in 1968 in an amphitheater in the Sorbonne. Jacques-Alain Miller and Jean-Claude Milner had faces like thunder. They felt they had been completely taken in. Miller called everything about Lacan into question. But later he came back from Besançon a convert, all worked up and enthusiastic and asking Paul Flamand for books for the workers. When the Gauche prolétarienne went underground, Lacan was anxious and upset. But he agreed to serve as a 'mailbox' or go-between. And one evening when I was having dinner with him he had a phone call from someone asking him to pass on a message to Miller, which he did as quickly as he could. But he never approved of Maoism. He thought the Maoists were mistaken, but he took his son-in-law's and his daughter's commitment very seriously and never made fun of them.[15]

In fact, the Maoist commitment of the Lacanian group connected to *Les Cahiers pour l'analyse* was a disaster for Lacan. At the ENS he had surrounded himself with a young guard, and now here he was, deserted by the very "pack" on which, since he had met Althusser, he had founded all his hopes.[16] Not only was he left all alone to confront the crisis in his school, but he found it insufferable that he, a "man of culture" in terms of Chinese language and thought, should see the maxims of a proletarian helmsman preferred to his own teachings. That is why, when Alain Geismar approached him for money to help the GP, he answered, in substance: "The revolution, *c'est moi* [I am the revolution]. I don't see why I should subsidize you. You are making *my* revolution impossible and taking away my disciples."[17] Nevertheless, he couldn't remain entirely unaffected by the great effervescence of Maoism à la française, and his work was influenced by it in a number of ways.

In October 1967, in an attempt to resolve the crisis in the EFP, Lacan had proposed the introduction of a new kind of access to the position of training analyst. He gave the name *"passe"* (pass) to a rite of passage by which an ordinary member of the school who had undergone analysis could acquire the title of AE, until then reserved for those who had been given full status automatically in 1964. (A *passeur*, in French, is a ferryman, and hence also someone who guides another across difficult territory to safety, as with Jews, escaped prisoners, and other fugitives during the war.) The procedure was as follows: the candidate for the pass, who was called the *passant*, had to give evidence about his analysis to two other analysts—the *passeurs*—who had to transmit the content of this evidence to a jury. The jury, presided over ex officio by Lacan, was made up of members of the EFP who were already AEs, elected by the Assemblée générale (AG: General meeting). The October proposal made a distinction between the idea of grade and that of hierarchy and defined the end of an analysis in terms of a dialectic of *désêtre* (debeing: the position of the analyst) and *destitution subjective* (subjective destitution: the position of the analysand). Lacan gave the name of *chute du sujet supposé savoir* (falling away of the subject supposed to know) to the liquidation of the transference, by which the analyst found himself in the position of a *reste* (residue) after having been invested with a *savoir supposé* (supposed knowledge), or omnipotence. Lacan put forward a formula that was to cause a lot of ink to flow among his adversaries in the IPA: "The psychoanalyst is authorized only by himself."[18] He meant not that anybody could become an analyst but that the *"passage"* could only occur through a subjective test linked to transference. In other words, he was seeking to lend orthodoxy to a kind of "mystique of *passage*" that was independent of all lists and committees and any form of bureaucratic selection.

Undoubtedly this procedure was suggested to Lacan by his dramatic experience at the hands of the famous Turquet committee. But it also owed a great deal to his own subjectivity. Marie-Pierre de Cossé-Brisac tells of a kind of guessing game that she witnessed in or around 1950. She was friendly at that time with the team at the *Temps modernes*, and one day someone asked Lacan to play *le jeu du passeur* (the ferryman game). "He agreed willingly, with a side glance and a smile, his hands nimble and sensitive. For a while our minds full of politics calmed down as he amused himself with our questions and answers and our dive into the psychological and symbolic universe we claimed to despise. He came back again several times to those evening gatherings and stood as before by the fireplace. And every time we became children again, in spite of ourselves. He was a magician. And I can still hear the words ringing in my head now: 'Jacques, Jacques, play *passeurs* with us.' "[19]

As we know, Lacan always needed a "*passeur*" in every task he undertook, whether intellectual or physical. And the impact of the Cultural Revolution and the revolt of the French students also influenced the genesis of the pass procedure, as well as the way it was applied. Its object was to restore the idea of a "pure psychoanalysis"; to "regenerate" the methods by which someone became a training analyst. For Lacan, it was a matter of bringing about a spiritual and institutional revolution within the EFP, in which the grass roots and the leader would force the mandarins to abandon their routine practices. But in 1967 Lacan recognized that the time had not yet come to impose the abolition of the old order upon the members of his school. Most of his former comrades in arms were hostile. And although an opinion poll told him the majority of the school were on his side, he preferred to put off the project rather than cause a split. It was a wise decision. But after the events of May 1968 he put it to the vote and won the overwhelming support of the grass roots of the EFP against the older members, thus provoking the departure early in 1969 of Valabrega, Aulagnier, and Perrier. This, the third schism in the history of the French psychoanalytic movement, led to the creation of a fourth group: the Organisation psychanalytique de langue française (OPLF: the French-speaking Psychoanalytic Organization). Given the nature of the procedure and the way it was applied, Lacan was right when he said "his" pass procedure had foreshadowed the barricades.[20]

Three other events in 1969 reflected Lacan's involvement in the history of the student revolution: Michel Foucault's lecture to the French Philosophical Society on February 22; the expulsion of the Seminar from the Salle Dussane on June 26; and the "Impromptu de Vincennes" on December 3.

In the course of a lecture on the subject of the author, Foucault, in the direct line of Canguilhem's teaching, spoke of the distinction between the author in the literary sense of the term and the author as a founder of discourse. By the latter he meant those who, like Freud and Marx, had inaugurated in their own name an infinite possibility of discourse:"They opened up the space," said he, "for something other than themselves that nonetheless belongs to what they themselves founded."[21] Foucault then made a further distinction between the initiators of a discourse and the founders of a science. He defined the initiation of a discourse as something apart from its subsequent avatars. But in the founding of a science on the other hand the science is linked to the work of the founder as to a set of basic coordinates: "When we reexamine a text by Galileo it may well change our knowledge of the history of mechanics, but it can never change mechanics itself. On the other hand, a reexamination of Freud's texts changes psychoanalysis itself, just as a reexamination of Marx's texts changes Marxism."[22]

Without mentioning Lacan by name, Foucault was making a stunning commentary on the notion of a *return to*. In order for there to be a return, he said, there had first to be a contributory and essential forgetting. Consequently, a return to a text is not a "historical addition to the discourse" but a positive work of transformation of the discourse itself. It was probably not by chance that Foucault failed to mention Lacan and his work on that occasion, though he did speak at length on the theme of the proper name and the return to Freud. His silence pointed to the blind spot in Lacan's discourse: his inability to see Freud's own discourse as something different from its later avatars. Admittedly Lacan knew he was a Freudian, and he also knew Freud was not a Lacanian, as he himself was to say on several occasions. And yet, obsessed by the problem of plagiarism, he constantly saw himself as the "author" (in the full sense of the word) of concepts that in fact he had borrowed from sources of all kinds. He therefore, using the device of the future perfect, invented an imaginary history of the genesis of his own ideas, which involved ascribing to Freud a terminology that was not his, and sometimes saying that all the founders of a discourse, from Plato to Heidegger, and including Machiavelli, were "Lacanians" *avant la lettre*. Lacan was really claiming to find in the discourse of his predecessors a *déjà-là* (already there) of his own utterances, which was tantamount to denying the difference between their discourse and his own. For the same reasons and by the same process, he described as "deviations" almost all non–Lacanian interpretations of Freud, instead of understanding that the history of Freudianism had to be seen as a history of the interpretations and reinterpretations of the original doctrine.

Lacan was at Foucault's lecture that evening and was very worried by what he heard. He said his invitation had arrived late—time out of joint yet again!—and proceeded to praise himself, under the impression that he was acknowledging a tribute Foucault had just paid to his own return to Freud: "The return to Freud is something I took up as a kind of flag on a certain battlefield, and so I can only thank you: you have done exactly what I had hoped. All you say about the meaning of the '*retour à*' in relation particularly to Freud strikes me, at least insofar as I have been able to contribute to the matter, as perfectly apt."[23]

When Foucault spoke of the relativity of the notion of author, he was replying not only to Sartre but also to his own opponents: those who had accused him of dissolving subject in structure through his prophecy of the death of man. His theory on discourse made it possible to adopt an intermediary position between those who maintained that the subject was fundamentally free and those who argued for the primacy of determination. Foucault was paying tribute to Lacan's work by declining to make an apologia for Lacan the man.

In the discussion that followed Lucien Goldmann reverted to a much more academic objection: it is men who make history, he said, not structures. He backed this up by referring to a famous sentence written on a blackboard at the Sorbonne in May 1968: "Structures don't go out onto the streets."[24] If Lacan had found difficulty in answering Foucault, he was inspired when it came to replying to Goldmann: "I don't consider it at all correct to have written that structures don't go out onto the streets, for if there's one thing the events of May prove, it's precisely that they do." The fact that the sentence was written down only proved, he added, that "an act always misunderstands itself."[25]

Lacan was here taking sides with Foucault. But above all he was giving a correct interpretation of the meaning of the celebrated sentence. For at the Sorbonne, in the academic year 1967–1968, "structures" had been the subject of a great debate among the students of liberal arts and linguistics. Many of them had later gone out onto the streets "in the name of" or "because of" structures: they demanded to be taught about the work of Jakobson, Barthes, and the Russian formalists instead of old academic nonsense. So the sentence written on the blackboard by an anonymous student reflected the struggle that had raged, before May, between the advocates and opponents of structures: what he or she wrote was a negative reaction to a fact with which he or she disagreed.[26] And this fact was that belief in the classical arguments of structuralism didn't imply a systematic refusal of the idea of human freedom. Lacan's answer to Goldmann was a clear expression of the truth of the incident.

Lacan's teaching at the ENS after 1964, which was based on "structures," was soon to become a source of embarrassment to the representatives of the established order. In March 1969 he received a letter from Robert Flacelière, the director of the ENS, telling him that the Salle Dussane would not be available to him for his seminar the following year. No serious reason was given for the expulsion, but it was common knowledge that Flacelière had complained of hearing too much talk about "phalluses" at the school, and had been annoyed to see the sidewalk in the rue d'Ulm blocked by smart automobiles at Wednesday lunchtimes. Lacan waited until June 26 to make the letter public by reading it out at his seminar. His own comments contained various puns on Flacelière's name: "Flatulencière" was one example.

But in reality Lacan was furiously angry at being treated like a black sheep again and finding himself rejected by the powerful institution where he had succeeded, against some odds, in making his voice heard. Flacelière had wanted to expel Lacan the previous year, but Althusser and Derrida had dissuaded him. As soon as Lacan had finished reading out the letter, those present at the seminar decided to occupy the director's office. Among the first on the scene were Jean-Jacques Lebel, Antoinette Fouque, Philippe Sollers, Julia Kristeva, along with many others. The press took the matter up, and numerous intellectuals signed a petition in support of Lacan. When François Wahl asked Claude Lévi-Strauss to sign, Lévi-Strauss refused, saying that when you were invited into someone else's drawing room you didn't cause a scene. But Pierre Daix went to the rue de Lille to assure Lacan that Aragon and the *Lettres françaises* were right behind him.

But he felt very alone. He was convinced there was a "plot" against him and hinted to Sollers that Derrida and Althusser hadn't done anything to stop Flacelière from carrying out his decision. One day he had lunch at *L'Express* with Sollers, Antonella Guareldi (a young Italian philosopher), and Françoise Giroud, who wrote an article about the expulsion and recorded the opinion of Gilles Deleuze. "Dr. Lacan," said Deleuze, "is one of the masters of contemporary thought. It would be extremely regrettable and disturbing if he were deprived of an official place to teach in."[27]

In December Lacan went to the university of Paris VIII–Vincennes. He wanted both to "get his revenge" for the expulsion and to undermine Leclaire's university experiment. The amphitheater was not bursting at the seams, but it was full of anonymous hecklers who shouted about how disgusted they were with the authorities, cops, and psychoanalysts. They pressed Lacan to perform a "self-criticism." Lacan remained unruffled, and when one man jumped up onto the dais and started undressing he told him to carry on. Then he reminded his audience that he had shown great sympathy for the movement of May 1968, and recalled his surrealist past. Finally he summed up what had been his political position: "As revolutionaries, what you long for is a master, You'll get one. . . . I'm only a liberal, like everyone else, insofar as I'm antiprogressive. Except for the fact that I'm caught up in a movement that ought to be called progressive, because it's progressive to contemplate the founding of psychoanalytic discourse, since that completes the circle that might enable you to identify exactly what it is you're rebelling against."[28]

When he arrived at Vincennes for this "impromptu" performance, Lacan was in the process, following Foucault's lecture and after having read *The Archaeology of Knowledge*, of working out a theory of discourse that once again would offer a reply to Sartre's conception of freedom and at the same time challenge his attitude to the GP.

Lacan, as we have seen, refused to support the GP, though he did act as a "mailbox" for members of his family. Sartre on the other hand had agreed to divert part of his attention from the writing of his book on Flaubert to become official protector of the publications of gauchist and Maoist groups after the spring of 1970, when they were disbanded and had to go underground. Although he didn't share the views of the GP activists, Sartre kept up a curious friendship with some of them that certainly prevented them from going over to terrorism. Lacan, in his own way, paralleled this, though his position was fundamentally different from Sartre's. His role was more that of a "stern father,"[29] both in his seminar, where he spoke of the inability of any revolution to free the subject from his servitude, and in his consulting room, where he took on for analysis a number of activists whom he prevented from embarking on armed struggle.[30]

The "stern father" role was well illustrated in a couple of incidents that are worth recounting; both involved attempted gauchist attacks. At the end of January 1969, Pierre Goldman, who had just returned from Latin America, contemplated carrying out a holdup in the rue de Lille. He studied the layout of the premises and drew up a plan. "The interesting thing to me about this planned robbery was that it would take place at the office of a brilliant psychoanalyst." Goldman planned to force the analysands to recite poetry by Antonin Artaud and to question Lacan himself with exquisite courtesy, explaining that the gun he was brandishing was not a phallic symbol and that the terror he could see on the master's face was not fear of castration. He duly went to Lacan's apartment, together with a black man armed with a knife. "As we were mounting the stairs, we met Lacan, together with his secretary. I saw him descend majestically. My assistant indicated to me that we had to challenge him at once. . . . But when I saw this thinker with his white hair, I was startled, struck, impressed: never could I point a gun at him. I said so to my assistant and we left."[31]

A year later, when Pierre Goldman had been arrested and charged with murder after a holdup in a pharmacy, two men turned up at Lacan's apartment intending to succeed where Goldman had failed. One of them was undergoing analysis with a former patient of Lacan's. They both threatened the master with a gun and demanded money. But Lacan refused to pay up, indicating that at his age he might die at any moment, and anyway he didn't want to go on living. To bring the scene to an end Moustapha Safouan, who happened to be present, gave the intruders a check for a thousand francs and promised not to alert the bank or the police. The two men left, and Lacan, who had made no promises, immediately called the police. The next day Safouan wanted to leave the thieves enough time to cash the check, so he didn't go to the bank until lunchtime. But there he found himself face to face with one of the previous day's attackers. The man was then arrested.[32]

Lacan knew that the young guard among his pupils at *Les Cahiers pour l'analyse* were leaving one master for another. To them, Mao Tse-tung was a founding father all the more fascinating because, like Lacan, he was a rebel as well as a leader. He had brought about a revolution within the revolution and taught that thought divorced from practice was reactionary: he therefore reduced his own thoughts to a book of precepts. Against this background, the proletariat, for the Maoist Lacanians, was an emblem of the class struggle through which the whole of thought could be dissolved into the whole of action. And that was the aim of the GP: to destroy the whole of thought—and in particular the university—through the whole of action, which included the abolition of law, anonymity, a secret society, and a Kojèvian mythology of the end of History.[33]

In his debate with the logicalism of the *Cahiers*, Lacan had always maintained, in opposition to Miller, that thought was a *pas-tout* (not-whole).[34] But this "not whole" was only possible, in his view, because of the opening, rift, or flaw introduced into science by the Freudian revolution: the divided subject, the fallen object, loss, lack, etc. So when he thought desire for revolution might reflect merely desire for a master, Lacan saw it as his duty to contrast the Maoist revolution—denounced as totalitarian—with the Freudian revolution, in his opinion the only possible alternative to a thought of the whole, and an action to match, that aimed at destroying the whole of thought.

After several attempts, Lacan got the use of an amphitheater in the Faculty of Law, opposite the Panthéon, in which to continue his seminar within the framework of the ENS. It was a huge lecture hall, and the crowd that flocked there from the very first session, on November 26, 1969, had nothing in common with the small audience of disciples at Sainte-Anne or even the somewhat larger attendance at the ENS. From now on, the seminar, like the EFP itself, would suffer from overexpansion, a victim of its own success.

For nine years, from 1969 to 1978, anyone who wanted to hear the master, two Wednesdays a month between noon and 2 P.M., had to turn up well in advance to get a seat in the amphitheater. Lacan, looking very majestic with his mane of white hair, would often arrive in a checked purple suit and a gray astrakhan overcoat; he always wore a light-colored shirt with a mandarin collar. Gloria Gonzalès almost always came with him, as discreet as she was now indispensable: she arranged his appointments, greeted his patients, looked after his correspondence and his manuscripts, and to a large extent supervised his bank account, assisted in all these tasks by Abdoulaye Yérodia, whom she had married in 1967. Yérodia was born in the Congo on January 3, 1933, and had known Lacan since 1963. A philosopher by training, he worked at UNESCO. After he and Gloria were married he got into the habit of driving her to the rue de Lille and also of acting as Lacan's chauffeur. In the place du Panthéon, at Lacan's seminar, he had became a familiar member of the master's entourage. He would reserve seats in the front row for special guests and drive the speaker home at the end of the session. From 1970 on, Gloria and Abdoulaye were entirely absorbed into the Lacan household. When Judith and Jacques-Alain Miller returned to Lacanianism, even before the disbanding of the GP, the two couples become linked together by bonds of indestructible loyalty. They shared a common political background, based on similar experience of the ultragauchist underground.

I have already spoken of the famous seminar of 1969–1970, entitled *L'Envers de la psychanalyse* (The reverse side of psychoanalysis), in which Lacan commented at length on Ludwig Wittgenstein's *Tractatus Logico-Philosophicus*, published in 1921.[35] This, the second phase of the *logical reinterpretation* on which Lacan embarked in 1965, after his encounter with the ENS, might well be called the *mathematical reinterpretation*.

The *Tractatus* explores the limits of logic and logicism. For the Wittgenstein of the *Tractatus*, language is correctly used only when it is employed to express the facts of the world. This being so, philosophy is a language game that makes it possible to "cure" someone of philosophy through a new way of using it. Wittgenstein's aphorisms suggest an answer to the question, What can be expressed? The answer may be summarized as "That which may be said may be said clearly. What we cannot speak about we must consign to silence." That which cannot be said is thus defined as a *reste*, or residue, and Wittgenstein includes in this residue the ethical and aesthetic meaning described as belonging to the category of the ineffable or inexpressible. Two realms are incompatible: on the one hand what is said and on the other what is shown. Given this incompatibility, philosophy comes to recognize an obligation to be silent, together with a kind of not-whole that eludes the whole of formalization.

It is easy to see why this incompatibility between what is said and what is shown should have interested Lacan, in view of the point he had reached in his own researches. But instead of concluding that it was necessary to maintain the two incompatibles, he wanted to see the realm of the ineffable as including the not-whole. When psychoanalysis is reduced to a therapy, he was saying in substance, it tends toward magic and the nonteachable; it becomes a religious practice. But when it evolves toward dogma, it becomes either a religion, or church, or a branch of academic knowledge. In order to avoid the ineffable without descending into dogma, psychoanalytic discourse must be able to be taught. Lacan's command that discourses must be "formalized" was thus an ultimate attempt to save psychoanalysis from its origins in the occult and mesmerism (the ineffable), and also to differentiate it from academic knowledge in a society where that knowledge tended, according to Lacan, to take the place of the church.

Making use of the notion of *quaternary group* and the teaching of his friend Georges-Th. Guilbaud, whom he had known since 1950, Lacan therefore constructed a mathematical object that he called the *quadripode*. First came the quadripode of the *master's discourse*, which was really a reformulation of the Kojèvian dialectic of 1936. The S_1, or *primordial signifier,* was in the position of agent, while the S_2, or *unconscious knowledge*, was in the position of "work." As for $, a *barred or inexpressible subject*, it was in the position of truth, while *object a*—rift, loss, or lack—occupied the place of *plus-de-jouir* (surplus jouissance). Two successive reversals of the four terms allowed Lacan to define the *hysteric's discourse* and then *psychoanalytic discourse,* each of the terms occupying the position that had been held by another in the preceding discourse. *University discourse* was deduced from the master's discourse by a pivoting in the opposite direction, unconscious knowledge then finding itself in the position of agent, *a* in the position of work, S_1 in the position of truth, and $ in the position of surplus jouissance. Lacan's moral: university discourse produces subjects it addresses as "units of value" (the French term for course credits). It claims to master truth through technique, and sees knowledge as a multidisciplinary distribution; thus it acts in order to arrive at knowledge itself, not to arrive at a master capable of producing knowledge. This last assertion enabled Lacan to include the Soviet system in university discourse and to place Maoism in the master's discourse, incidentally demonstrating that the desire for revolution within revolution would lead to the creation of a master.

This new theory of discourse only echoed the question that had haunted Lacan ever since his discussions with Bataille and at the College of Sociology, and since his answer to Sartre's *Huis clos* in 1945: How do the masses come to love their tyrants? Why is "liberation" impossible without law? In other words, in confrontation with Sartre and in the direct line of Foucault's teaching, Lacan was still putting the question about the essence of human freedom from the point of view of Freudianism: how can a subject claim to be free when he is determined by the existence of an unconscious that prevents him from being free in word or deed but never prevents him from engaging in a struggle for freedom? And so on.

Instead of answering, he launched into a long meditation on the nature of revolution, a continuation of his commentary in "Kant with Sade." He said revolution always ended up producing a master even more ferocious than the one it had got rid of. As for the events of May, he pointed out that the student protest had led to the abolition of the ancient university function of master or teacher and its replacement by a tyrannical system based on the idea of communication and the pedagogical relationship. He couldn't have spoken a truer word: it is clear today that the revolution of the barricades was one of the key stages in the university's replacement of intellectuals by technocrats.

Lacan's attitude to the idea of revolution was thus apparently the opposite of Sartre's. While the theorist of the unconscious drew back from rebellion, preferring political skepticism and Freudian pessimism, the philosopher of being and nothingness committed himself to a struggle that led to the negation of self, a consequence he just avoided by writing the book on Flaubert.

But if the first of the two men believed in freedom only under the constraint of law, while the second saw it only as a transgression, what they had in common—and also shared with Foucault—was that they never advocated resignation to any order. So they both found themselves on the side of the rebels—and of revolution in general—and they both went along with them, one in a way that was fraternal and sympathetic, the other in a manner that was paternal and authoritarian.

The seminar on "the reverse side of psychoanalysis" also contained a great lesson in lucidity. Between the lines it paints a wonderful self-portrait of Lacan in the seventies, the "reverse" of the one presented in the commentary on Plato's *Symposium*. In 1960 Lacan had been a master surrounded by disciples. By 1970 he had become a tyrant adored by the crowd, challenged by rebels, served by courtiers, and soon to be defended by the small circle of his new family bodyguard. It is easy to see why he should then have started to ponder on the future of a university that was increasingly being reduced to a psychopedagogical function, and on how Freudianism was to be handed down in a society where the masses were taking the place of the elites. After having been Socrates, Lacan saw himself as King Ubu, as if he had a presentiment, at the height of his glory, of how, in the twilight, his own thought would implode.

An interview with the philosopher Gilles Deleuze, conducted by Didier Eribon, shows how exasperated Lacan was with the situation. A few months after the publication of *Anti-Oedipus*, he summoned Deleuze, its author, to his apartment, which was full of his analysands, and told him how "hopeless" all his disciples were except Miller. Then he said, "What I absolutely need is someone like you." Deleuze was amused and remembered that Binswanger used to tell a similar story about Freud speaking ill of Jones, Abraham, etc.

348 THE POWER AND THE GLORY

Binswanger had concluded that he himself would suffer the same fate when Freud talked about him to his disciples.[36] Deleuze was right: at the same period, Lacan was grumbling about him to Maria Antonietta Macciocchi: he was convinced *Anti-Oedipus* was based on his seminars, which already, according to him, contained the idea of a "desiring machine."[37] He was still worrying about plagiarism.

PART VIII

In Search of the Absolute

27

Oriental Yearnings and a Series of Bereavements

Jacques Lacan had always been attracted by the Far East, and as we know he had learned Chinese at the School of Oriental Languages in Paris during the Occupation. In 1969, when he was working out his theory of discourse on the basis of Wittgenstein's distinction between saying and showing, he immersed himself again in an enthusiastic study of the language and philosophy of China. It was another way of responding to his pupils from *Les Cahiers pour l'analyse* and their engagement with Maoism. As always, he needed a "*passeur*" to make him work. So he suggested that he and the sinologist François Cheng should have a series of meetings:

In theory we were supposed to meet once a week, but in fact if some important problem turned up he would drop everything and ask me to come over right away. . . . Or else he would telephone, sometimes at peculiar hours, such as midnight or seven in the morning. . . . He often made use of a sort of personal telegram that still existed in those days, called the *pneumatique*, which as well as arriving very quickly had the advantage of being written by the sender, so that he could write out any Chinese words that were bothering him. . . . It seems to me that when he reached a certain time of life, Dr. Lacan was no longer anything but thought. When I was working with him I often used to wonder if there was ever a single second in the day when he wasn't thinking about some serious theoretical problem.[1]

In his descent into the heart of Chinese thought, Lacan was trying first of all to solve a mystery that had been haunting him since the publication of the *Ecrits*: how to write, i.e., to "formalize," the famous topography of the real, the symbolic, and the imaginary, which he was henceforth to refer to as the R.S.I. The text by Lao-tzu on which he was working with Cheng was "The original Tao engenders the One/The One engenders the Two/The Two engenders the Three, The Three produces the Ten-thousand beings/The Ten-thousand beings lean on the Yin/And embrace the Yang/Harmony is born of the breath of the Median-Void."[2]

Lacan's interpretation of Lao-tzu's philosophy was rather like his reading of Heidegger's commentary on Heraclitus' *logos*. Once again it was a question of showing that the one was the source of the many, over and above physical existences. While the Tao is thought of as a supreme void—i.e., as an ineffable without a name—nonetheless it produces a primal breath: the one. And this one engenders the two, embodied in the two vital breaths of the yin (passive force) and the yang (active force). Between the two and the ten thousand beings is the three, or median-void, which itself proceeds from an original void that alone can act as a link between the yin and the yang. Lacan was to make use of the notion of the median-void for his new definition of the real, within the framework of his theory of knots.

In 1973 François Cheng stopped working with Lacan in order to write a book. Lacan felt rather desperate and said to Cheng, "But what's going to become of me?" When the two men met again some years later, Lacan tapped his friend on the shoulder and said: "From what I know of you, you must have experienced several breaks in your life because of your exile: a break with your past, a break with your culture. But you've been able, haven't you, to turn these breaks into an active median-void and to link together your present and your past, the West and the East. In the end you'll be—you are already, I know—in your time."[3]

As he was emerging from four years of intensive work on classical texts, Lacan nearly confronted the "real" China, the Red China of the communist East. He had always been interested in the idea of such a journey, but the possibility of actually undertaking it occurred to him when he read Maria Antonietta Macciocchi's book *China*, which had been a great success with the French intelligentsia. When she met Lacan she noticed at once that he was neither a misogynist nor a feminist but was as fascinated by women "doomed to sacrifice" as by the madwomen of the Salpêtrière. She also observed that the numerous small pleats in his shirts were ironed almost religiously, as if the shirts were priestly vestments. She saw that he was particularly intrigued by her friendship with Louis Althusser. "Why hasn't he asked me to analyze him?" he asked her. She didn't know what to say and began asking him questions about his family background.

"My people came from Paris," he said, "as far back as my grandparents, and I can trace my family tree back to Philippe le Bel. I did think my parents were lower middle class, but then I noticed my mother had an 'at home,' a special day when she received visitors. Strange, isn't it? One of my ancestors worshiped Napoleon and turned himself into a coachman so that he could mount guard beside his coach during the Hundred Days. He always walked beside his carriage."[4]

After recounting the family legend of Laurent, a forebear on his father's side who was supposed to have saved the emperor's life, Lacan told Maria Antonietta of his Oriental yearnings. We may suppose the reference to Napoleon had been no accident.[5]

"Would you like to go to China with me, my dear? You're not interested? You're a bit doubtful? Bring your husband, and you'll have nothing to worry about!"[6]

The young woman said she was trying to "puzzle out the craze for China" that had seized the Paris intelligentsia; she wondered if it was "sincere." Lacan laughed, made some caustic but lucid comments about a few celebrities, and then explained Marx's role in the situation: "It's because of him that capitalism has been able to arrive at an accurate analysis of its own structures. In a way, he enabled capitalism to take on its own identity. And he unified it worldwide. They have rebuilt the same structure in the USSR and in Eastern Europe, and nothing has changed. That's why people are so keen on China, my dear."[7]

Maria Antonietta was invited to the seminar, and when she arrived to hear about the "knots" Lacan blew her a little kiss from the rostrum. At the end he made his usual complaint about the audience: "You've seen them. What do they come for? What do they think? Their eyes are so blank. And all those tape recorders are like guns trained on me! They don't understand; I'm absolutely convinced they don't understand anything. They come just so as to be able to say they're writing a book on Lacan, a biography of Lacan." This was Lacan's negative expression of his longing to have all kinds of books written about him.[8]

Then he said he would like to meet some Chinese. A dinner was arranged at *La Calèche* with Maria Antonietta and two young men from the Chinese embassy dressed in blue and wearing official badges. The campaign against Confucius was raging in China at that time, so Lacan launched into rhapsodies about Confucianism and said it was one of the world's greatest philosophies. He quoted classical texts to his guests, who were taken aback but in favor of his going to China.

One morning a delegation from the Chinese embassy arrived in the rue de Lille in an official car complete with a little flag. The delegation brought Lacan a passport for him and his official mistress, accompanied by a tribute from the Great Helmsman. In exchange Lacan handed over an inscribed copy of the *Ecrits* for the Institute of Sciences in Peking. The trip was supposed to take the form of a delegation including Roland Barthes, François Wahl, Philippe Sollers, Julia Kristeva, and Marcellin Pleynet. Sollers, who had gone over to Maoism after a brief dalliance with the French Communist Party, thought that by taking Lacan to China he would "break the objective alliance between Lacanianism and revisionism." He was taking an active part in the campaign against Confucius from his office in the rue Jacob, the headquarters of the review *Tel quel.*[9]

Three days after the delegation's visit, Lacan telephoned Maria Antonietta: "My dear, I would have been delighted to go just with *you*, but as things stand it will be like a sort of procession. Perhaps with Sollers—yes, he's more famous than I am—but . . ." So he pulled out of the trip. *Tel quel* issued an announcement:

> He was supposed to come with us to China. Unfortunately, as he says himself when making his apologies, he wouldn't have had enough time to brush up his knowledge of the language. Personally, we'd have liked to see Lacan talking off the cuff with the Chinese people. It would have been an interesting experience. Admittedly, he had begun to be uneasy about the anti-Confucius campaign and the fact that Confucius is being presented as the ideologue of slavery in China. But as to the criticism of the "will of heaven," "innate knowledge," and "a moderate approach to ritual"—can criticism of these things shock an established psychoanalyst? Well, maybe.[10]

In addition to being well up in the Chinese language, Lacan was also fascinated by Japan, where in 1963 he had been very impressed by the great Buddhist sculptures in the temples at Kyoto and Nara.

Alexandre Kojève had made the journey four years earlier, and it was in the Far East that he met with the "end of History." He had then gone back to a nihilism that Bataille himself would not have disowned, contrasting Western consumer society with a way of life based on cultural refinement. Japan enchanted him with its tea ceremony, the silent rituals of its courtesy, the timeless symbolism of its theater. He had discovered there a kind of Proustian "time recovered," in which the art of loving, dying, and experiencing pleasure attained the highest form of postmodern nihilism. "All Japanese," Kojève said, "live according to values that are completely formalized, i.e., entirely devoid of all 'human'—in the sense of 'historical'—content."[11]

Lacan found Kojève's idealized vision of Japan highly attractive: his own Oriental yearnings were related to a "search for the absolute" that made him want to provide a completely formalized representation of the social bond and construct a notion of human freedom based on the primacy of structure and the "group." In 1971 he went back to Japan on a study tour and to give a seminar, just as a translation of the *Ecrits* into Japanese was in preparation. When he got back to France he decided he must define the "Japanese phenomenon." By this he meant a particular mode of jouissance that he attributed to the "Japanese subject" on the basis of the calligraphic element in Japanese writing. He used a simple horizontal line to illustrate the purity of that calligraphy, unattainable, according to him, by any Western subject. He called this function of the letter the *littoral* and placed it between knowledge and jouissance. In other words, the reference to the "Japanese phenomenon" provided Lacan with a reply to Jacques Derrida in the matter of the letter, in that it made formalization—or the calligraphy of science—and literature into superior activities from which jouissance was not excluded but rather retained in the position of "residue" or "object *a*."[12]

But Lacan, as he spoke of the median-void and the Japanese phenomenon, was really talking about his own jouissance. Like his friend Kojève, but in a different manner, he had been seized with a desire for the end of History, a reflection of a Faustian longing to carry abstract knowledge as far as possible. So he was not content to dream of the *temps retrouvé* of the unchanging East; he tried to make his dream come true. In Japan he had met Maurice Kruk, who was living at the Franco-Japanese Center in Tokyo and teaching architecture at Kyoto University. When Lacan got back to France he asked Kruk to build him an *anare*-type rest house on a piece of land he had just bought at La Prévôté. He meant to study the tea ceremony there, and with this in mind he had already acquired some rare and ancient pieces, including a Mo-no-yama bowl carefully chosen for him by his favorite antique dealer.[13]

Over the years the house at Guitrancourt had become a veritable museum. Lacan was a great collector and had gathered together there all sorts of objets d'art, including paintings and rare books of every kind. "I imagine," says Maurice Kruk, "that he had them there under his own roof simply to meditate on them at leisure. From the way he would occasionally explain how he prized some of the revelations he owed to them, through their powers of suggestion and the reactions they allowed him to trigger off in others, it's always seemed to me that everything he owned gave him constant food for thought and that the presence of those works and his everyday contact with them were part of his way of life. Their value for him resided either in their links with family or friends or in the stimulating mysteries and enigmas they contained."[14]

Among the many marvels in this great Ali Baba's cave were a library of 5,147 volumes; paintings by Masson, Renoir, Balthus, Derain, Monet, and Giacometti; drawings by Picasso; Greco-Roman and Alexandrian statuettes; ivory sculptures; erotic terra-cottas; painted vases; Nasca pottery, Pueblo Indian kachina dolls; and an original edition of Diderot's *Encyclopédie*.[15] La Prévôté was looked after by a couple of caretakers of Spanish origin, Jésus and Alicia Cordobès, who, like Gloria and Abdoulaye, formed part of the Lacan household.

Between the time when Lacan immersed himself in Chinese and his final setting-out on the path of the *mathemes* and the *knots*, two tragic events occurred that were not without influence on his ultimate destiny. In December 1969 Thibaut, who had married for the second time, had his first child, a son, who was named Pierre. Jacques was wild with delight: at last a boy had been born who might bear his name. But his joy didn't last long: the infant died when he was three days old.[16]

Another dreadful bereavement followed not long after. On May 30, 1973, Caroline was killed in a road accident in the south of France. As she was crossing the main road in the dark to go into the Tétou restaurant on the beach at Golfe-Juan, she was struck by a speeding Japanese driver who was himself thrown out of his vehicle by the impact.[17] Bruno Roger, Caroline's husband, went down at once and brought the coffin back to Paris in a private plane.

Lacan was in Albania at the time with Catherine Millot, whose father was ambassador in Tirana. He was vacationing there for a few days after a trip to Budapest, where he had talked at length to Imre Hermann about Ferenczi, with Jean-Jacques Gorog acting as interpreter.[18] As soon as he heard the news of the accident he rushed back to Paris, where he attended Caroline's funeral at the church of Saint-Philippe-du-Roule. His first family was there: Marc-François, Malou, Thibaut, Sibylle, and Sylvain Blondin. "My mother never got over Caroline's death," Sibylle says. "She aged ten years overnight. Standing by the coffin, my father took my mother by the hand and wept. I had seen him cry only once before: at Merleau-Ponty's funeral."[19] Lacan's reply to a letter of condolence from Paul Flamand was, "Yes, my friend, it was my elder daughter, and I am deeply, deeply grieved."[20]

Bruno Roger had decided not to tell his two sons, Cyril and Fabrice, then aged nine and seven, of the circumstances of their mother's death, and they didn't go to the funeral. Lacan protested, saying, "It's not right to deprive children of their mother's death."[21] But he respected his son-in-law's decision and didn't say anything. He had grown very close to Caroline since 1960: she often went to Guitrancourt and looked after some of the business to do with his property.

When he was thirteen, Cyril asked his grandfather to take him on for analysis. Lacan refused but agreed to see him for three sessions. As for Fabrice, he can remember Lacan's first visit after Caroline's death: "We lived in the rue de Lisbonne then. He rang at the door once and then ten times. He was impatient, silent, enigmatic. He was very downcast and said something to us about Mother's death. It was painful for him to see us. It was only later that we found out Judith existed."[22]

Malou gave Caroline's two sons the maternal affection they needed. It was later on, when they met their great-uncle Marc-François that they gradually became Christians. They were both brilliant students at the ENS. Cyril got his degree in social sciences and went on to the ENA (Ecole nationale d'administration, a college for training senior civil servants); he later became an official in the Conseil d'Etat (State Council, a legal body). In 1983, after a long series of administrative procedures, both Caroline's sons obtained the right to use the surname Roger-Lacan. "It was because we wanted to be able to use our mother's maiden name rather than because we wanted to use that of our grandfather."[23] Nevertheless, because the change was made, they are the only males belonging to the generation of Lacan's grandchildren who bear his name. Thibaut had two daughters, Ariane and Iris, and Sibylle has no heir. Judith's children, Luc and Eve, bear the name of Miller.

28

∙ ∙ ∙ ∙ ∙ ∙ ∙

Mathemes and Borromean Knots

"*I*'m behind with all the things I ought to take further before I die, and I find it hard to go forward."[1] This sentence, uttered in 1966 at the Baltimore symposium, was a striking summing-up of the problematic of being and time that was one of the major themes of Lacan's life. Handicapped since childhood by his slowness, his inhibitions, and his anxieties, Lacan had never stopped theorizing about the *pas-tout*, even when he flaunted a great eagerness to master time, read all books, visit every important cultural site, possess every object, and collect all women. His legendary impatience and implacable determination always to get what he wanted manifested themselves in ordinary life in ways that only grew more noticeable with age. Not only did he go on reducing the length of his sessions, sleeping less than five hours a night, and driving his car in complete disregard of the most elementary rules of caution, but he was also increasingly haunted by the fantasy of the *"peau de chagrin"*—a magic piece of leather with power to grant its owner's wishes but carrying the disadvantage that every wish granted makes the leather shrink and shortens the owner's life. Dreading the signs of the old age that he knew would ultimately put an end to his intellectual activities and personal attractiveness, he was increasingly haunted by a fear of self-destruction that led him to reexamine the great myths on which he had based his interpretation of Freud: castration, residue, sex, jouissance, the letter, death, mysticism, and the trinity.

By publishing the major part of his written work at the age of sixty-five, Lacan had given an ontological weight not only to a mere collection of articles but also to a "writing," in the literal sense of a personal inscription. And for him this inscription had taken on the aspect of a *founding event*. Urged on by Wahl, he had, as we have seen, constructed his *Ecrits* as a kind of memorial or architectural monument, all the more distant from his real life story because its subjective rehistoricization often manipulated chronology.

As the years went by, the object thus constructed as a founding event had taken on the status of a sacred text, untouchable as holy writ. It had become a "littoral," an inscription that could give rise to a new elaboration of doctrine. As a result, the "author" of this production, like his disciples, felt it incumbent upon him to comment on his own original text, to become the spokesperson of his own discourse. And so around 1970 Lacan began to quote himself, to refer to himself in the third person, to toy with allographs and neologisms that he had fabricated in the past, to overinterpret his own positions, and to imitate his own old verbal mannerisms. The resulting monologue was worthy of a character out of Samuel Beckett.

But he was a genuine scholar and couldn't be satisfied with mere narcissistic repetition of himself. So, in the two years of life that remained to him, he was also motivated by a great Mallarméan longing to reach the essence of things. Once more he organized around himself a marvelous theoretical laboratory, in which again he assembled the transferential conditions his researches had always required. This mustering of forces took place at three levels: the school, the seminar, and the couch. And it adopted two modes of formalization: the *matheme* and the *Borromean knot*; that is to say, on the one hand a linguistic model based on a symbolic logic, and on the other a structural model based on topology and bringing about a fundamental shift from symbolic to real.

His elaboration of the matheme allowed Lacan to recenter his consideration of the question of science, as exemplified in the transmission of psychoanalytic knowledge. It led him to change his attitude toward the university and to support a takeover of the department founded by Leclaire at Paris VIII–Vincennes. It also caused him to launch a new clinical approach to psychosis and designate his legitimate heirs: his own family, as against the "family" of his disciples.

But his entry into the world of knots led him to the destruction of what the matheme claimed to build. Lacan, thinking he was going to be able to reach the fundamental core of thought, devoted himself so passionately to the geometry of knots, braids, tori, and bits of string that he himself finally dissolved into the silent stupor of a Nietzschean aphasia. Like Balthazar Claës, the hero of Balzac's *In Search of the Absolute* who was destroyed by his obsession with alchemy, Lacan sought the secret of the absolute. He carried out this search in the heart of a community of irredentist mathematicians, committing himself so deeply that he revived in his own life the Faustian myth of a pact with the devil, out of which, via romanticism, the discovery of the unconscious had been born.[2]

The fact that such an intellectual quest could be undertaken in Paris, at a time when technological rationalism was in the ascendant and the ideals of the Revolution were gradually losing their power, is one of the strangest phenomena in the history of modern thought.

Lacan arranged his teaching for the year 1970 in two series of talks. The first series, entitled ". . . Or Worse," was delivered in the law school; the second, "The Psychoanalyst's Knowledge," at the Hôpital Sainte-Anne. In theory the subjects treated in the two series were supposed to differ. In the seminar proper, which took place on the law school's premises in the place du Panthéon, Lacan accorded an increasingly important place to the real, i.e., the "worse," the impossible. At Sainte-Anne he concentrated on knowledge. But in fact the two series converged, and their themes overlapped. But it was not by chance that the two key notions of Lacan's last reinterpretation were worked out and expounded in two different places. The first notion, the matheme, was connected with the history of madness, and so was "invented" on the spot, in the mental hospital. The second, the knot, was a veritable challenge to science, so it was appropriate that it should be set forth against a traditional academic background.[3]

The word *matheme* occurred for the first time in the lecture Lacan delivered on November 4, 1971. The word was derived from Claude Lévi-Strauss's *mythème* and the Greek word for "knowledge," *mathema*; it didn't belong to the world of mathematics. Lacan started off from Cantor's mania: if this form of madness, he said in substance, is not caused by objective persecution, it is linked to mathematical incomprehension itself, i.e., the resistance aroused by knowledge that appears incomprehensible. Lacan then compared his own teaching to that of the mathematician Cantor: was the incomprehension such teaching encountered really a symptom? This incidentally raised the question, was it possible to transmit knowledge that "seems impossible to be taught"?

It was in answer to this question that Lacan, after reading Wittgenstein's *Tractatus*, invented the term *matheme*. Between 1972 and 1973 he gave several definitions of it, passing from the use of the singular to the use of the plural and back again. He linked the famous *quadripodes*, from the seminar on "the reverse side of psychoanalysis" (S. XVII, 1969–1970) to the matheme, which he showed to be the writing of that which is not said but can be transmitted. In other words, Lacan here opposed Wittgenstein: he refused to accept the division between the incompatibles, and instead tried to wrest knowledge from the ineffable and give it a wholly transmissible form. This form was the matheme. But the matheme was *not* the site of a complete formalization, because it always implied a *residue* that it could not capture. Defined in this way, *matheme* in the singular included mathemes in the plural, i.e., all the formulas in the Lacanian algebra that made teaching possible. If the different discourses were no longer incompatible with one another, it became possible to teach psychoanalysis in the university: to teach it as a matheme, without reducing it to academic discourse. Hence Lacan's turnabout: after having once violently criticized the university, he imposed his own teaching there, thanks to Jacques-Alain Miller, whom he made his spokesperson at Paris VIII–Vincennes in November 1974 (I have gone into that story elsewhere).[4]

In the session where he introduced the *matheme*, Lacan also amused himself by inventing the word *lalangue*, a pun based on the name of André Lalande, author of a famous philosophical dictionary.[5] He used the new word to denote the articulating of the desire for language (*langue* = language, tongue); it could also mean a "knowledge that unknowingly knows itself" and so escapes mathematical expression. Thus Lacan was again contrasting the idea of complete transmission—the matheme—with its opposite: the impossibility of exhaustiveness, the not-whole, the residue.

Just as, in the winter of 1965, Jacques-Alain Miller's interpretation of the idea of *suture* had tended to normalize Lacan's teaching, so now Miller's use of the *matheme* was of a pragmatic kind. After leaving the *Gauche prolétarienne*, he occupied an important place in Lacan's family. As far as publishing was concerned, he established his legitimacy in 1972, when he offered to transcribe Lacan's seminar in terms of the matheme, by which he meant according to a method of transmitting the spoken, in its entirety and with all its fluctuations, by means of the written. The following year a new stage was reached, when Miller acted as unseen interlocutor in a film on Lacan made by Benoît Jacquot and shown on television in March 1974. In it the master himself spoke exactly as he did in his seminars, without making any concessions. Before the film was transmitted, the text was published by Seuil under the title *Television*. No special arrangements had been made in advance concerning Miller, but Paul Flamand did write to Lacan raising the question: "Did I do the wrong thing?"[6]

Ten months later, Miller, already coauthor of his father-in-law's seminars, joined the staff of Seuil in his own right, as editor of a series called Connexions du champ freudien (Connections of the Freudian field). This was to be included in Lacan's own series The Freudian Field, but Miller was given editorial independence, "with Lacan's approval." Miller was paid a salary, and it was on the strength of his promotion that he suggested a "new alliance" with Seuil.[7]

The first book to appear in the new series was *Les pousse-au-jouir du maréchal Pétain*, by Gérard Miller, Jacques-Alain's brother.[8] It was a study of writings, myths, and sayings about Pétain, with an amazing preface by Roland Barthes in which he compared the author to Michelet and the greatest creative artists of the twentieth century: "Miller thus transposes into the form of an essay an eminently progressive kind of discourse, formerly used by Diderot, Brecht, and Eisenstein: it consists of apprehending and *reproducing*, against a clear background, a social *gestus* previously lurking half-hidden in the false nature of Pétainist phraseology."[9] Thanks both to this preface and its own real virtues, the book was greeted as an important event.

Just as it was appearing and consolidating further the Miller family presence at Seuil, Jacques-Alain was using the matheme to bring about a systematic reorganization of the psychoanalysis department that Leclaire had founded at Vincennes in 1969. "If there is a matheme of psychoanalysis, something of what experience teaches is really transmissible *in its entirety* .... Nonetheless, the matheme is still problematic. It isn't in any handbook .... So the theory of the matheme implies that only real commitment to an original work of elaboration in and based on the Freudian field *will henceforth make anyone eligible for a post in the department*."[10]

Finally, it was with the use of a matheme that was still restricted—and thus unlike Lacan's—that Miller wrote his own "Rome Discourse," delivered on October 31, 1974, at the EFP congress, to a packed audience of eight hundred at the Santa Cecilia conservatory.[11] Though only thirty years old, Miller spoke with great assurance, knowing he was now Lacan's heir apparent. He harangued Lacan's former comrades-in-arms, whom he accused of regarding psychoanalysis as a "guaranteed income," and presented himself—he had not been analyzed—as the victim of an outmoded oligarchy. He placed Lacan himself at all four corners of the quadripodes, as master, analyst, academic, and hysteric, apotheosized in accordance with a very rigid conception of power. Miller's Lacan bore no resemblance to the Lacan of everyday life. This Lacan, disguised as a kind of Great Helmsman whose duty it was to go to the people and save them from the wicked barons who made use of his knowledge to enrich themselves, had lost his sense of humor, his genius, and his surrealist style, and been transformed into a lifeless cardboard hero.

Though Lacan, who was in Rome for the congress, was not at all pleased with the image his son-in-law conveyed of him,[12] he gave Miller his unreserved support. He was exhausted and disappointed with his followers, themselves tired out by the rigors of the pass. Moreover, Miller's pragmatism appealed to him, and he was attracted by the young man's efficiency, dynamism, and determination to conquer the world. In just a few years the brilliant young *normalien* had gathered around him a large section of the younger generation of Lacanians, influenced as they were by the mass culture of the 1968 barricades and ready to be ruled by logical slogans. He had started the review *Ornicar?*, consolidated his power in the university with a clinical section where the matheme was still the instrument of a new dogma, and finally, after an analysis with Charles Melman, embarked on a career as a psychoanalyst. On the eve of the disbanding of the EFP, having made an alliance with some members of the old guard, he controlled all the power centers in the Lacanian community.

As early as 1950 Lacan had referred to mathematics in the course of his teaching. His meeting with the mathematician Georges-Th. Guilbaud is of crucial importance in understanding his increasing use of the images of topology. The two men, who were very alike physically, were great friends for thirty years. In 1951 Lacan, Benveniste, Guilbaud, and Lévi-Strauss began to meet to work on structures and establish links between the social sciences and mathematics. Each of those concerned used the teaching and topology of the others, and as well as taking part in the collective project, Lacan worked every day at mathematical exercises. Sometimes, if he came up against a problem while he was traveling, he would telephone Guilbaud so that they could solve it together. Guilbaud never attended the seminars, and his relations with Lacan remained completely personal. But in private they indulged together in their shared passion, forever tying knots in bits of string, inflating children's swimming belts, braiding and cutting things out. So Lacan was already interested in this sort of thing when he taught his students to transcribe his doctrine into topological figures.[13]

Thus the *Möbius strip*, a single continuous surface with neither obverse nor reverse, stood for the subject of the unconscious, while the *torus*, or inner tube, stood for a hole or gap, i.e., the "median-void" of Chinese philosophy: a constitutive yet nonexistent space. To these images Lacan added the *cross-cap*, which made it possible to close the Möbius strip, and the *Klein bottle*, which symbolized a hollow surface. But for twenty-five years Lacan had used all these images merely as illustrations, without developing them into theoretical form. It was his reading of Wittgenstein and his working-out of the notions of *matheme* and *lalangue* that led him, in 1971, to seek a new terminology that would make it possible to relate the psychoanalytic to other kinds of discourse. In order to do this, it was necessary to be able to pass from *saying* to *showing*; in other words, to induce every member of the audience—as well as himself—to carry out operations relating no longer to discourse but to "monstration."

A new change of direction took place at the February 9, 1972, session of the ". . . Or Worse" seminar, when Lacan spoke for the first time of the *Borromean knot*. At a dinner party, he had been told by a young woman mathematician named Valérie Marchande[14] about the arms of the Milanese dynasty, the Borromeos: these consisted of three circles arranged in the shape of a clover leaf or trefoil and standing for a triple alliance. St. Charles Borromeo, one of the family's most illustrious representatives, was a hero of the Counter-Reformation. A nephew of Pope Pius IV and himself a cardinal, he introduced a stricter discipline into clerical life in the sixteenth century. He distinguished himself by his charitable works during the plague of 1576, and by the time he died Protestantism had been partly driven out of the north of Italy. The famous Borromean Islands on Lake Maggiore were conquered a century later by a Count Borromeo, who gave them their name and turned them into one of Italy's most baroque landscapes.[15]

Lacan's discovery of the Borromean knot[16] was accompanied by a decisive encounter with several young mathematicians belonging to the same generation as Miller and the pupils at the ENS. They too had had ultraleft political leanings in the past. Pierre Soury was undoubtedly the most fascinating character among them. This is how those who loved him describe him today: "If we compare him with his contemporaries and with the scholars and philosophers who preceded him, it is easy to see that Pierre Soury will have a place in history and will before long be considered one of the giants of Western culture. His scientific and philosophical work as a whole has the same immediate importance as that of Wittgenstein. . . . For the time being, Soury is known only to the thousand or so people who attended Lacan's seminar between 1975 and 1980: Lacan mentioned him thirty times or more and asked him to speak on his behalf on two or three occasions."[17]

Pierre Soury was born in Nîmes on August 28, 1942, into a family of Protestant craftsmen. He was admitted to the Ecole polytechnique in 1961 and obtained a degree in science two years later, Though a physicist by training, he was introduced to mathematics by his classmate Christian Léger. When he was expelled from the Polytechnique in 1967 as a conscientious objector, he went before a board of psychiatrists and then underwent analysis with Jean Clavreul. By the time he had entered the Centre national de la recherche scientifique (CNRS: National Center for Scientific Research), he was already attending Lacan's seminar, while living in a mixed community that shared one room day and night and kept all their money together in a hat.

In 1968, at a general meeting of the Movement of March 22, he met Michel Thomé, a philosophy student and the son of a naval officer. Thomé had already studied the works of Freud and Lacan at the Collège de La Flèche, under a remarkable teacher named François Regnault. After the May events, Soury was arrested for breaking windows: "Technocracy is weak," he wrote later in a leaflet. "To avoid a fight they say the accused is irresponsible (madness, psychiatrists). In other words, they themselves take refuge in irresponsibility. At my trial, the department store La Samaritaine was prosecuting for broken windows and claimed damages of one franc. . . . I was set free as a madman, 'because I had refused to undergo a psychiatric examination and shouted at the judges.' "[18]

In 1971, after another attempt at life in a mixed community, Thomé and Soury decided to rent an apartment in the rue du Dahomey in the 11th Arrondissement. At first there was a third tenant, a guitarist, but soon only Thomé and Soury were left. It was then that the great adventure of the Borromean knots began. "We were social suicides; what we had in common was a fundamental rejection of society."[19] But their rejection, instead of expressing itself in terms of political commitment, was reflected in a determination to hold together the three components of a knot representing the minimal form of the social link. "Life in small groups," wrote Soury, "makes for stability in individuals. It's like marriage. . . . A small group is born and dies, but you don't enter or leave it. The ideal small group is a Borromean one, based on a comparison between small groups and the Borromean chains."[20]

Soury, haunted by the ideal of the small group, had always dreamed of starting a children's International, and out of loyalty to that utopia he refused to grow up. On holidays he used to bring his friends garlands of flowers, champagne, modeling clay, and magic candles: "I feel like a grandfather," he used to say, walking around with a bag slung over his shoulder, full of string and exercise books and whatever kind of fruit was in season.[21] At the heart of the two friends' Borromean knot was the mystery of female sexuality and hysteria. And the name of the woman who embodied that mystery and triggered off all discussions was Judith.

To translate reflection into action, Thomé introduced Soury to the women of the Psychoanalysis and Politics group, which under the leadership of Antoinette Fouque was working out a theory of femininity based on the notion of *supplement*. I have already followed their itinerary elsewhere;[22] it will be sufficient here to recall its main stages. Against Simone de Beauvoir's statement that "You aren't born a woman; you become one," Antoinette Fouque had since 1968 taken over the idea of femininity as a "supplement," a notion mooted by Perrier, Granoff, and Lacan at the conference on female sexuality in Amsterdam in 1960. But she had moved the question onto the terrain of a supposed "homosexuated sex" in women, defined as a *libido sexué*, or sexuated libido. "You don't become a woman," she said. "You *are* one." Being a woman consisted of going beyond the phallic or "feminist" stage and reaching a genital stage where you attained "homosexuation." Fouque's theory was still structural: it was based on the Lacanian notion of "supplement" and the Derridean idea of "difference." Thus Beauvoir was corrected through Freud, Freud through Lacan, and Lacan through a "postphallicist" advance in the form of a "homosexuated symbolism," as against the "*langue*," or language, of the masculine world.

Soury, meeting the women of this group, was taken aback by the realization that as a man he was branded as a rapist. This was the situation when

Thomé, pondering the question of the relationship between knots and women, and having entered into analysis, came to the conclusion that Soury and Lacan ought to meet. Dissatisfied with his analysis, Thomé wrote to Lacan in the rue de Lille, hoping Lacan might take him on as a patient. The result was a thunderbolt. On December 18, 1973, Lacan, just back from his seminar, sent him an answer on a scrap of paper. He thanked Thomé for sending him Castaneda's book *The Devil's Grass and the Puff of Smoke*, said he would like to get to know him better, and complained of seeing nothing but bores.[23] Thomé went to the rue de Lille and said to Lacan: "The knots drive people mad." "Yes," was the reply.[24]

At the time this meeting took place, Soury was already working under Bernard Jaulin at the Ecole des hautes études en sciences sociales (EHESS). At the beginning of the academic year 1973–1974 he began giving a seminar for Didactique des disciplines (University Teaching Methods), a study and research group at the University of Paris VII–Jussieu. For the next four years this seminar attracted a score or so of people, including various experts on knots: Françoise Gonon, Jean-Claude Terrasson, Pierre Achard, and Jean-Michel Vappereau. These were later joined by some psychoanalysts from the EFP who were later connected with the review *Littoral*: Eric Porge, Jean Allouch, Philippe Julien, and Mayette Viltard.

Soury's teaching, both in private and in public, aimed at constructing a mathematical mold that would facilitate the study of Lacan's logical and topological preoccupations: "What was our point of departure? There was the transition from knot to braid in the special case of the Borromean knot. Then there was the definition of a *casse-tête* [literally "head breaker": headache, brainteaser]. . . . A *casse-tête* is a simple and unforeseen problem with a solution that's not easily repeatable, conscious, transmissible, or veri-fiable."[25] Between the rue du Dahomey, the rue de Lille, and the grand amphitheater in the place du Panthéon a twilight relationship was to grow up among all the players in the topological game, a partnership that was the driving force behind a Faustian quest. With its help Lacan was able, in six years, to transform completely both his teaching and his practice of psycho-analysis: the topological objects he produced with his "little group" were later used before the wider audience of his seminar.

All this process of change was based on the "monstration" of the torus, of the turning-inside-out of the torus, of the torus with a hole in it, of the tetra-hedron, of triple tori, and of chains of knots and braids. As "monstration" took over from discourse, Lacan came to use proportionally fewer and fewer words: he would draw rather than write, and then, when he could no longer either draw or speak, he played with rings like a child. The solving of the great *casse-tête* took the form of a long correspondence between Lacan and the inhabitants of the planet Borromeo: first with Soury and Thomé alone, and then with Christian Léger, who joined them in 1977. There were fifty letters from Lacan, a hundred and fifty from his colleagues: a veritable epic made up of suffering and melancholy, in which everyone involved exhausted themselves in the attempt to solve the riddle of the unconscious by means of telegrams, *pneumatiques*, and ordinary letters. Often, after spending hours drawing surfaces, twisting the inner tubes that they had delivered in large quantities, or filling baskets with bits of string and cutouts of colored paper, the others would get a message from Lacan asking them for the solution of a problem. Neither they nor he could find it, and the search went on. "I'm going crazy," he would say. "Do please phone or come and see me."[26]

Sometimes, when he felt lonely, Lacan would go over to the 11th Arrondissement and then return home feeling better. He would congratulate his two accomplices on their discoveries and later on, either in private or at the seminar, urge them on to further efforts. His letters were full of figures, calculations, and drawings. They often contained only one line: "How are you getting on?"[27] When they all got together for a discussion, it turned on the possibility of making a knot consisting of four clover leaves, or trefoils, and the transition from the knot to the braid.[28]

Soon another mathematician joined them on the planet of the knots. Jean-Michel Vappereau was a pupil of Jean-Toussaint Desanti and had been a Trotskyite in May 1968. He then went to work in the ethnology laboratory run by Robert Jaulin, Bernard Jaulin's brother. Vappereau, who was looking for a new rationality, discovered the work of Lacan at the same time as that of Deleuze, Derrida, and Saussure. He met Lacan in 1970. Lacan, having read Desanti's *Mathematical idealities*,[29] asked its author to write him a text on intuitionism. Desanti provided fifteen pages on the subject, and Lacan asked him for the address of someone who was knowledgeable about topology. Desanti suggested Vappereau.[30]

When the young man received Lacan's phone call he was going through a depressive episode attributable partly to the aftermath of May 1968 and partly to the death of his grandfather. Roland Dumas, who was a close friend, had already advised Vappereau to see Lacan, telling him about how he himself had been with Lacan on the barricades in the spring of '68.

On the occasion of their first appointment, Lacan came out into the waiting room to have a look at Vappereau and ask him some trick questions, such as "What is an Archimedean body?" Soon the two men got into the habit of meeting in the rue de Lille once a month. Lacan asked questions about intuitionism and one day gave the young man a letter several pages long by René Thom, on catastrophes. "The mathematicians," he said, "don't understand what I say, but that's no reason for not reading them." The discussions between Lacan and Vappereau were dealing with conic sections, when one day in July 1972 Vappereau was assailed by auditory hallucinations. He asked Lacan to take him on for analysis. "He was just cleaning his spectacles. They broke. He told me to come back in September."

During the summer Vappereau left his papers with Roland Dumas and went to live in a squat at Sèvres with his brother and sister and brother-in-law. He lived there for three years in a sort of commune on the Anglo-American model, while at the same time keeping up a strange relationship with Lacan that consisted partly of an analysis with excessively short sessions and partly of exchanges about mathematics. He looked after one of the mentally disturbed people whom the antipsychiatrists used to send to the squat and whom Lacan finally took on. All the time the relationship with Vappereau lasted, Lacan repaid the young man for his contributions by giving him books: the *Écrits* and *Scilicet*, for example. During the winter of 1973 Vappereau reported an idea he had had about restricted topology, and Lacan told him he had hit on something. In the spring Vappereau drew the story of his family on a Möbius strip, explaining that "the hole in the strip kept getting smaller." Lacan exclaimed: "How is it you can understand what I say so well?" One day he saw his analysand at six o'clock in the morning and had a boiled egg and some hot coffee brought in for him. Another day he left him in the library all the afternoon to think about a book. Vappereau rightly had the impression that he was being given a child analysis: "Lacan took us to the heart of the pain of existing. If he hadn't been there I would either have died or gone mad. We are all mentally ill, but we are not all obliged to be mad. A madman is a person who blames the world for the troubles of his own soul."[31]

In 1975 Vappereau met Clavreul and asked to be allowed to go through the pass and become an analyst. Clavreul sent him to Lacan, who said, "Go ahead." He then went back to Clavreul, who said, "Lacan told me you weren't being analyzed by him." Vappereau, very surprised, returned to Lacan, who told him, "It must all be done over again." The analysis continued, and Vappereau now paid for his sessions, duly became a psychoanalyst, and then went and studied under Pierre Soury at Jussieu.[32] He didn't become part of the little group in the rue du Dahomey but began to expound his own topological researches in public, meanwhile still continuing to see Lacan.

In this experimentation with limits, the work on knots abolished the frontiers between analytic practice and theory, turning psychoanalysis itself into a kind of Borromean space in which the transferential relationship took on literal form and enabled those concerned to rediscover their childhood: the childhood of play, of nursing, of emptiness, of lack, of *béance*, and of the *not-whole*.[33]

Topological research did not serve only as a kind of quest for the Holy Grail that summoned up the signifiers of childhood and the ghosts of madness; it also led to a recasting of the doctrine on sexuality. Lacan wanted to set down for posterity the major advance he had made in this field in 1960. Moreover, he wanted to answer the arguments of the feminist movements, who had never stopped criticizing Freud for phallocentrism. In March 1972, just after he introduced the Borromean knot, he began to construct a matheme of sexual identity by including in the logical square of Apuleius what he called the *formulas of sexuation*.[34]

Lacan put forward four propositions. In the first, which was called the *universal affirmative*, he translated the statement "All men have a phallus" by the formula: "For every x, the property Φ applies to x." In the second, the *universal negative*, he translated the statement "No woman has a phallus" by the formula: "For every x, the property Φ does not apply to x." Observing that these two formulas served to define male identity on the one hand and female identity on the other as being in a relation of complementarity, Lacan indicated that there was an impasse: there can be no complementarity in a field where difference always reigns.

He therefore put forward two corrective propositions. The third of the group, the *negative particular*, gave a new translation of the Freudian fable of the primal horde: men are a universal group made up of all men subject to castration. Only one man is excepted: the father of the horde, i.e., the symbolic father. Lacan invented an allograph, the *hommoinzin* (*au moins un*, "at least one"), to denote this father, whose function it was to introduce the fantasy of an absolute jouissance that might provide the basis, for all other men, of a prohibition: the taboo on incest, that inaccessible jouissance.

The fourth proposition, the *doubly negative particular*, translated the statement, "There is no x that is an exception to the phallic function." Lacan was here referring to the principle of a fundamental dissymmetry in the unconscious between male and female sexual identity. For women, he said, there are no limits on jouissance. As a result, Woman in the sense of a universal or a "feminine nature" doesn't exist. Hence the formula "Woman doesn't exist," or "Woman is not-whole." As for feminine jouissance, it is defined as a jouissance that is "supplementary." Lacan expressed the lack of complementarity between the two modes of sexual identity in the formula, "There's no such thing as a sexual relationship."[35]

These 1973 formulations were in fact merely the expression in the form of equations of arguments that Lacan had put forward thirty years earlier and reworked during the intervening decades. Once again he was rehabilitating the paternal function "degraded by industrial society" and showing how overwhelming was female power in relation to the frailty of the phallus.

Once again Lacan was opposing the classical feminist arguments representing women as victims of male oppression. But instead of denying that oppression—which he did not challenge—he pointed out that it could, from the point of view of the unconscious, turn into its own opposite, since the relation between the sexes was governed by the principle of fundamental dissymmetry. Admittedly, Lacan, like Freud and unlike Jones, preserved the idea of an original phallicism and a single libido, but he modified it with his theory of a "supplement," derived from Bataille, the surrealists, and his close acquaintance with female madness.[36]

Thus at the end of his life he still felt the same hatred toward mothers and the same fascination for women who were mad or mystical. It was as if his own family history continued to invade his teaching, despite his attempts to provide that teaching with a basis and formalization that would free it of all affective content.

In the Lacanian family saga, the domination of mothers was always presented as destroying or debasing the function of the father. As for women's sex, since his meeting with Bataille and his reading of *Madame Edwarda*, Lacan regarded it as a site of horror, a gaping hole, a "thing" of extreme orality of which the essence was unknowable: a real, a heterology. In an astounding commentary in March 1955, he had interpreted Freud's famous dream about "Irma's injection" from this point of view, associating Irma's "open mouth" with a gaping sex organ from which a terrifying Medusa's head emerged. And then, in 1970, in Seminar XVII, as if to encapsulate in one formulation all the horror that mothers inspired in him and all the fascination he felt for the mystery of an orality seen in terms of animal metaphors, he had said: "A great crocodile in whose mouth you are—that is the mother. And you don't know what may suddenly make her clamp her jaws shut. That is the mother's desire." Lastly, his most violent outburst on the subject is to be found in his commentary on Lytton Strachey's biography of Queen Victoria: "By what fatality did a certain Albert of Saxe-Coburg fall into the clutches of the queen? He had no special liking for women. But when someone meets with what I might call a toothed vagina the size of Queen Victoria. . . . A woman who is a queen. A more efficient kind of toothed vagina it's not possible to find." He gave further vent to his fantasies by enumerating the toothed vaginas of other devouring queens: Semiramis, Elizabeth I, and so on. And all in the same style as that he had used just before the Edinburgh congress, on the subject of the "females" who ran the IPA.[37]

The discovery of the planet Borromeo had led Lacan to recover some of the major signifiers of his childhood and adolescence. So it is not surprising that his work on knots gave him the idea of linking his own search for the absolute with that of James Joyce, the most innovative literary venture of the century. Lacan had never seriously studied Joyce's writings, but, as we know, he had met Joyce himself at a crucial period in his life, when he was finally rejecting Catholicism and revolting against the paternal figures he accused of having made his childhood a nightmare: Emile, the authoritarian grandfather dominated by his wife, and Alfred, the father, crushed by his own father and like him under the thumb of a devout wife. All these characters, fashioned by the imagination of a young man in search of an identity, had ended up taking their places in Lacan's discourse as the negative heroes of a family saga.

These figures were still present fifty years later when the old master plunged with extreme jouissance into the reading of *Ulysses*, *Stephen Hero*, and *Finnegans Wake*.[38] It was a young academic, Jacques Aubert, who encouraged Lacan to follow this path early in 1975. Aubert, an intelligent reader of the *Ecrits*, had used Lacan's concepts in his own study of English literature. Before long he suggested that Lacan should take part in the fifth international symposium on Joyce, which was to be held in Paris in June. Lacan agreed. "We operated by a system of exchanges," says Aubert. "It would occur to me that he might be interested in something, a certain phrase perhaps, and I would make a note of it. He on his side used to ask me questions or consult me about whole passages."[39]

As well as working with Aubert, Lacan read a lot of books on Joyce, both biographies and critical studies. He also consulted the work of contributors to the reviews *Tel quel* and *Change*: Philippe Sollers, Jean-Pierre Faye, and Jean Paris.[40] "One night he turned up at Faye's place at one o'clock in the morning," says Jean Paris. "He wanted to use a portmanteau word I had made up."[41]

On June 16, 1975, in the grand amphitheater at the Sorbonne, Lacan, speaking after Maria Jolas, gave a very short talk entitled "Joyce the Symptom."[42] He started by recalling his meeting with the author and didn't hesitate to identify with him, his wanderings, his exile, his hatred of the family and religion: "Coming as I did from a rather squalid background, [the Collège] Stanislas, to give it a name—and so being like Joyce the child of priests, don't you know, but of priests less serious than his, who were Jesuits, and heaven knows he managed to make something of that—in short, coming from that squalid background, it so happens that when I was seventeen, thanks to the fact that I used to go to Adrienne Monnier's bookshop, I actually met Joyce. Also, when I was twenty, I was present at the first reading of the published translation of *Ulysses*." Then he added: "We think we say what we want to say, but it's really what others, especially our families, have wanted that speaks through us. . . . I apologize for talking about myself. But I think I do so only in homage to James Joyce."[43]

After taking part in the colloquium, Lacan devoted all his 1975–1976 seminar to Joyce's life and works. The title he gave the seminar was "Le Sinthome," a term based on the word *symptôme*. "If you refer to Bloch and Warburg's etymological dictionary, which is very sound, you'll find that *symptôme* was original written *sinthome*. . . . Joyce the sinthome sounds like an allusion to sanctity."[44] (In French it sounds like "saint homme," i.e., holy man.) So Lacan had invented a Joycean portmanteau word to suggest the idea of redemption through literature. The word evoked several other terms that according to Lacan could be regarded as "signifiers" in the Joycean universe: these included *home*, as in Home Rule, the slogan calling for Irish independence of Britain; and *St. Thomas*. So *sinthome* could also be written *sinthome rule* or *sinthomasaquinus*. The use of the latter word referred to the fact that Joyce had borrowed from St. Thomas a theory of creation derived from *claritas*, the third element of the beautiful, according to which an object reveals its essence as it becomes itself. It is the character Stephen Dedalus who voices this theory of creation, referred to as *epiphany*, or apparition, in Joyce's early writings. An *epiphany* is defined as "a sudden spiritual manifestation that may be translated into everyday words or acts or by some memorable phrase produced by the mind itself."[45]

For Lacan, an epiphany was a *sinthome* and could also be expressed as a "splendor of being." Joyce was thus designated by his symptom, recast as sinthome. In other words, his name merged with the theory of epiphany that he had adopted and that saw creation as taking place in a region of mystical ecstasy outside of time. This notion brought Lacan back to the major themes of all his research in the seventies: the quest for a logic freed of the constraints of time and history; the desire to attain a more and more impossible "reality"; and lastly a fascinated preoccupation with the question of jouissance, linked to the "Japanese phenomenon," mystical exaltation, "literality," and perversion (written *père-version*, i.e., father-version).

And so, as his whole research effort was taking on the form of one vast Borromean geometry, Lacan incorporated the sinthome into his new system of knots. To begin with he tried, unsuccessfully, to construct a tetrahedric link, i.e., to "make a fourfold Borromean knot." Then he challenged his mathematical friends to solve the problem, which they did. Thomé was the first to produce a drawing that included four clover leaves or trefoils. "My feeling," said Lacan, "was one of enthusiasm pure and simple, and I think I showed them something of it when I saw them a few months later. But as to how they had found it, they couldn't explain that to me."[46]

However, when adding this fourth ring, the sinthome, to the formerly threefold knot, Lacan was still trying to introduce his own doctrine and family history into Joyce's work. He pointed out that the *sinthome* or *père-version* was a "version toward the father." He was interpreting *Ulysses* as pure autobiography. He saw the relationship between its two heroes, Leopold Bloom and Stephen Dedalus, as evidence that Joyce remained rooted in his father even while he rejected him. From this he deduced that Joyce's father was mad, that the name-of-the-father was foreclosed from Joyce's discourse, and that it was to compensate for this lack that Joyce was so eager to "make a name for himself," to leave a name that would go down to posterity, to "force the academics to write about him for three centuries." "Is not Joyce's desire to be an artist in whom everyone would be interested . . . precisely a compensation for the fact that his father had never been a real father to him?"[47]

Pursuing the application of the foreclosure theory further, Lacan suggested that the schizophrenia of Lucia, Joyce's daughter, should be interpreted in terms of inadequacy on the part of her father. Joyce had in fact, said Lacan, regarded his daughter as telepathic and had defended her against the doctors. Lacan saw this belief in telepathy, the idea of a language originating in another world, as a symptom of the Joycean conception of art that was to result in *Finnegans Wake* and the reconstruction of a language fundamentally based on the dissolution of language.

By interpreting *Ulysses* as if it were an autobiographical novel, Lacan, the son of Alfred, was identifying with Joyce in order to speak of his own drama, obsessed as he always had been by the determination to make a name for himself. But when he spoke of Lucia Joyce's schizophrenia, he was referring also to the tragedy of a father haunted by the guilt of being unable to give his daughter his name. So Lacan's confrontation with the world of Joyce not only plunged him once again into a phantasmic contemplation of his own life story; it also accentuated the breakdown of his discourse, already begun through his preoccupation with knots. For while the characters in Joyce's work and life served to illustrate the eternal theme of the impossibility of fatherhood, the actual writing techniques employed in *Finnegans Wake* also suggested a linguistic metamorphosis.

As we know, Joyce took seventeen years over his great last work, provisionally called *Work in Progress*. In it he made use of nineteen different languages, including Old Icelandic, Tibetan, Greek, and Sanskrit, and exploded ordinary words into multiple meanings in accordance with the Freudian process of condensation. In arriving at his puns and other forms of wordplay, Joyce called on the researches of physicists and mathematicians as well on his own knowledge of linguistics. "Just as the primitive simplicity of atoms was broken down into protons, electrons, and neutrons," writes Jean Paris, "so words break down into logical, phonetic, semantic, and etymological elements. . . . Some, with only one electron, lend themselves to punning, as when Joyce wrote *redshields* for *Rothschild*, or turned *goat* into *Gott* (God)."[48]

The fascination Lacan felt for *Finnegans Wake* was all the greater because of the virtuosity with which he himself had so long played with words. And as his own topological research drew him into a Faustian quest similar to Joyce's, he began to speak and write in the style of *Finnegans Wake*. It was as if, having sought the secret of human madness in Joyce's last work, Lacan himself toppled over into the language of psychosis, thus linking up again, at the approach of death, with the *Ecrits inspirées* (Inspired writings) that had marked his entry into the history of psychoanalysis in the early thirties. "I myself began by writing *Ecrits inspirées*, so I shouldn't be too surprised when I look at Joyce. . . . Was Joyce mad? What were his works inspired by?"[49]

Lacan's spoken word had always imitated the language of the unconscious, but from 1975 on he was so influenced by Joyce that he almost drowned his own teaching in puns, allographs, portmanteau words, and neologisms that were often reminiscent of the basic signifiers in his life and teaching. For example: the *cra-chose* (cra-thing), referring at once to the Freudian *chose*, or phenomenon, and the method Freud invented of chatting (in which one might get so carried away as to *cracher*, or spit); *jaclaque*, which meant having enough (*avoir sa claque*; *claque* can also be a box on the ear) of Jacques Lacan; folisophy; affreud; etc., etc.

In 1978, when the proceedings of the Joyce colloquium were to be published, he sent in the following text:

Joyce the Symptom to be understood as *Jésus la caille* (Jesus the quail): it's his name. Could people expect anything else omme [of me, though in French it sounds like *emoi*, emotion]?: I name [which in French sounds like *jeune homme*, young man]. If that sounds like "young man," that's a consequence I'd say just one thing about. We're men [*sommes hommmes*, phonetically "somzoms"].

LOM [i.e., *l'homme*=man]: in French that says what it means. You only need to write it phonetically: faunetically he's *eaubscène* [=obscene]. Write it "eaub-," with the *eau* as in *beau* [beautiful], to recall that the beautiful is not otherwise.

After this the text, though still to a large extent intelligible, becomes to all intents and purposes untranslatable: "Hissecroibeau à écrire comme l'hessecabeau sans lequel hihannappat qui soit ding! d'nom dhom. LOM se lomellise à qui mieux mieux. Mouille, lui dit-on, faut le faire; car sans mouiller pas d'hessecabeau."[50]

Madness, the name-of-the-father, the real, the knot, delusion, symptom— these were the subjects Lacan dealt with during his third visit to the United States in the late autumn of 1975.

Nine years earlier, in February 1966, he had crossed the Atlantic for the first time and visited New York City, Detroit, Chicago, and Boston to give six lectures on desire and demand. Roman Jakobson had organized the three-week visit and had personally arranged for Lacan to be invited by the leading American universities. Lacan went on later to Mexico and in

October of the same year took part in a symposium on structuralism in Baltimore.[51]

Remembering how the Anglo-Americans had rejected him at the time of the 1963 split, Lacan was not sorry to get his own back during his third visit to the United States, when he saw that his teaching was beginning to be known in a few universities that specialized in French literature and feminism. But he continued to be exasperated by Paul Ricoeur's success and Derrida's celebrity in the West.

In France, by 1975, Lacan's own success and notoriety were immense. The EFP was flourishing and extremely influential despite the crisis over the pass. Books and articles were being published at a great rate. People flocked to the seminars. And, under the influence of Jacques-Alain Miller, Lacanianism was beginning to gain ground at the University of Paris VIII–Vincennes. But in the United States, celebrity and recognition lagged. Lacanianism was making some headway in the universities, but legitimate Freudianism remained unmoved. In other words, in the English-speaking countries, as in most of northern Europe, Lacan's work was regarded as belonging to the history of French philosophy and never as a clinical doctrine. Psychoanalytic circles in the Anglo-American sphere of influence were impermeable to any psychoanalytic movement that had anything to do with Lacan.[52]

After 1973 just one young New York academic was analyzed by Lacan in Paris, so for several years Stuart Schneiderman was regarded as the only Lacanian psychoanalyst on the American continent. His only knowledge of the history of France or of Lacan himself came to him in the form of legend or rumor. This, for example, is how in 1983 he related the doings of the master during the Occupation:

Where was Lacan during the war? The question has often been posed, and the answer, as far as I can tell, is that Lacan escaped from occupied France in the dead of night in a boat that took him and his wife across the Loire. For most of the occupation he was in St. Laurent-du-Var, near Antibes. Lacan's wife, Sylvia Bataille, was Jewish and, according to Catherine Clément in *Vie et légendes de Jacques Lacan*, she was denounced to the Gestapo at the beginning of the occupation. As Clément tells the story, Lacan marched into the headquarters of the Gestapo and demanded the dossier that had been compiled on his wife. Eventually he walked out with it in his hand, though Clément does not say exactly how he accomplished this, whether through bribery or force of personality. If it is true that we can tell a good deal about the character of a man by how he acts in situations of crisis, then we should recognize Lacan as a man whose personal ethical conduct was unimpeachable.[53]

The book shows how adversely the fourth and fifth generations of French psychoanalysts were affected by the process of dehistoricization triggered off by the publication of the *Ecrits* in 1966 but already hinted at in Lacan's earlier teaching and writings.

Pamela Tytell had met Lacan in July 1973 at Reid Hall on the rue de Chevreuse in the 6th Arrondissement, where Columbia University had organized a summer seminar on psychoanalysis and literature. Among the guests were Gilles Deleuze, Félix Guattari, Denis Hollier, and Catherine Clément. Lacan had just lost his elder daughter, and everyone respected his bereavement when he came to speak. But after the lecture, in a bar, Pamela Tytell, who had read the *Ecrits* and was familiar with the French psychoanalytic situation, asked some very pertinent questions. She later went back to Columbia to work on her doctorate. And she and Paul Newman, who taught French literature at Sarah Lawrence College, were given the job of looking after Lacan when he landed in New York in 1975 to give his lectures. He was accompanied by Thérèse Parisot, representing the EFP.

The first lecture took place at Yale University on November 24. Lacan talked about himself, the Aimée case, and the importance of psychosis in his researches: "Psychosis is an attempt at rigor," he said, "and in this sense I would say I'm a psychotic, for the sole reason that I've always tried to be rigorous."[54] In the subsequent debate, at which Shoshana Felman and Sherry Turkle were present, he emphasized that all historical research ought to be based on written documents: "Without written documents, you know you're in a dream. What the historian must have is a text: a text or a scrap of paper. At all events, there must be somewhere, in an archive, something that certifies in writing, and the absence of which makes history impossible.... What cannot be certified in writing cannot be regarded as history."[55] For a man who had spent his life teaching orally, dehistoricizing his own history, and speaking by allusion and anecdote, this was no small challenge to make to historians, especially in a century when new techniques of recording and communication had made oral archives reliable and invaluable.

In New York, Lacan stayed at the St. Regis Hotel. "It was the morning of Thanksgiving," writes Newman, "a special day in the American calendar, going back to the first Puritan settlers—a day of thanks and reconciliation, of family reunions, and in New York a day of silence. He had just got up in the St. Regis Hotel and sat in the lounge without speaking, settling down in his chair with a suitably crumpled cigar. After a lengthy silence, a thought transformed itself into a weary and puzzled sentence: 'America wipes me out.' "[56]

Convinced that he was world famous, he wanted to be allowed to make a private visit to the Metropolitan Opera House. "Tell them I'm Lacan," he bade his three bemused companions. Pamela Tytell solved the problem with very "Lacanian" humor: she phoned the director of the Metropolitan and told him Jean-Paul Sartre wanted to visit incognito. The director was flattered and delighted to have such an eminent visitor and agreed at once. As if warning him about one of the great man's eccentricities, Pamela advised him not to address the philosopher by name. Despite her efforts, someone did ask after Simone de Beauvoir, but the deception wasn't discovered: Lacan's English wasn't good enough to see through it, and Pamela, acting as translator, did all she could to keep up the pretense. It was a memorable day, and Lacan was delighted with his welcome: "We acted as permanent intermediaries. All communications between New York and him went through us, and we were on duty from eight o'clock in the morning."[57]

Lacan, still obsessed by the planet Borromeo, drew knots on paper napkins every time he and his minders went to a restaurant. One afternoon, realizing he had forgotten to bring along his favorite rings, made by Judith, he asked for some replacements right away. Pamela went to Macy's department store and bought some luminous plastic curtain rings in various colors. She also got some flexible telephone cord. Then she went back to the hotel, exhausted by her errand but proud of her purchases. To her amazement, Lacan flew into a rage, threw the package on the floor, and stormed out of the room. The next day he had forgotten his outburst and declared himself pleased with his new toys: the latest rings were just as good as Judith's.

One scene was often repeated. Lacan would say, "I'm going to think," take leave of his hosts, and get down to his Borromean exercises. He would arrange all the rings in the desired order, with each marker in its place, and then start to draw in absolute silence. At Columbia, and wherever he went afterward, he drew his knots on the blackboard before he began to speak.

He was delighted one evening to meet the writer Serge Doubrovsky and his partner, and they all had dinner in a skyscraper. Lacan talked about his mentor Clérambault.[58]

One morning Pamela saw Salvador Dali in the foyer of the St. Regis, where a room was reserved for him all year round. He was in New York to open a retrospective exhibit of his work and wore a splendid mink cape everywhere he went. The two men hadn't met for nearly forty years and fell into one another's arms. Dali invited Lacan and his friends to lunch at the Bruxelles restaurant. Gala, Dali's wife, was there too, and the maître d' was asked not to admit anyone else. Then came a fabulous dialogue.

"I make knots," said the psychiatrist.

"Yes, of course," said the painter. "The Borromean Islands."

Lacan grabbed a napkin. Dali snatched it away from him.

"Let me," said Dali. "You have to draw them in a certain order, otherwise it doesn't work; you can't separate them. I learned all about it in Italy. If you go to Charles Borromeo's tomb you'll see what I mean."

Then, remembering the famous meeting about critical paranoia, he asked:

"Why didn't you say anything that time we met and I had a bandage on my nose?"

"Because I knew there wasn't anything wrong with you."

"Fantastic! You're the only one who didn't say anything!"

They went for a stroll through Manhattan. Everyone turned to look at Dali, whose photograph was in all the magazines. Whenever anyone made a sign of recognition, Lacan bowed his head to acknowledge his admirers. When Dali bought some New York papers to read the articles about his exhibit, Lacan asked him to be sure to remind him to look in the papers the next day for the reports on his own lectures.[59]

In Boston, at the Massachusetts Institute of Technology, Lacan met Roman Jakobson again and spoke before an audience of mathematicians, linguists, and philosophers, among them Willard Quine and Noam Chomsky. Lacan had acquired Chomsky's books before he left Paris, at a bookshop called La Répétition in the rue Saint-André-des-Arts, where he was well known. He had chatted there with great charm and courtesy about his forthcoming trip "to America" and the fact that he would probably meet the author of *Cartesian Linguistics*. He was at once excited and anxious about the coming visit and said he was hoping he would be able to tell Chomsky about his own conception of language. After an hour, he left with a big package of books under his arm, quite forgetting to pay for them. The cashier hadn't dared say anything; anyway he was sure he'd receive a check the next day. He didn't.[60]

Be that as it may, none of the scientists at MIT was worried about the mathematical criticism Lacan was exposing himself to with his knots or about the possible search for "foundations." But not one of them understood Lacan's use of topology. The sociologist Sherry Turkle, who was just back from making a close study of the French psychoanalytic situation in Paris, witnessed the failure of communication between the two worlds. What Lacan said on the subject of inner and outer sounded quite crazy to his audience. "The only thing that seems to me to testify to it is that which we produce as excrement. The characteristic of a human being is that—and this is very much in contrast with other animals—he doesn't know what to do with his shit. He is encumbered by his shit. Why is he so encumbered while these things are so discreet in nature? Of course it is true that we are always coming across cat shit, but a cat counts as a civilized animal. But if you take elephants, it is striking how little [space] their leavings take up in nature, whereas when you think of it, elephant turds could be enormous. The discretion of the elephant is a curious thing. Civilization means shit, *cloaca maxima*."[61]

To make matters worse, Lacan scandalized everyone with his answer to a question by Chomsky on thought. "We think we think with our brains; personally, I think with my feet. That's the only way I really come into contact with anything solid. I do occasionally think with my forehead, when I bang into something. But I've seen enough electroencephalograms to know there's not the slightest trace of a thought in the brain."[62] When he heard this, Chomsky thought the lecturer must be a madman. And afterward, despite the explanations of his friend Mitsou Ronat, who did her best for several years to point out that Lacan was speaking metaphorically, Chomsky remained convinced that Lacan was so contemptuous of his American audience that he had tried to kid the MIT scientists that the seat of the human brain was in the bones or the toes. The affair gave rise to a rumor, and the rumor became a legend: Lacan had tried to convert America to another obscurantist "plague" by suggesting that the source of man's intelligence was in his feet.[63]

Lacan had made Pamela Tytell and Paul Newman go with him and Thérèse Parisot to Boston. After taking him to the airport, they made the journey themselves by Greyhound bus. The next day he was waiting for them at his hotel in front of an ample breakfast. They didn't go to the MIT lecture but met Lacan and the MIT professors afterward at the Ritz restaurant, where, as in all elegant venues in New England, gentlemen were required to wear a tie. When Lacan arrived he presented himself to his hosts dressed in a sumptuous silk shirt with a stand-up collar and a long cloak that he laid over the back of his chair. When the maître d' offered him a tie he was furious, overturned his chair, shouted obscenities, and stalked out, followed by his friends and the horrified stares of Boston's society ladies. Out in the street he called curses down on Puritan America. But a few hours later he had completely forgotten the incident, as if it had been "foreclosed" from his memory.[64]

That then was the plague Lacan took to America. Summoning up the surrealist and nihilist ways of his youth, he challenged the New World with puns, wordplay, and rages, as if, on the brink of the senility lying in wait for him, he wanted to act out as flamboyantly as possible the famous phrase reported by Jung, though Freud probably never uttered it.

Eventually he went back to Paris and the knots, the sinthome, the rue du Dahomey, and the search for the absolute. For three years the exchange of letters went on among the inhabitants of the planet Borromeo.[65]

During those years another man, not a mathematician this time, placed at Lacan's disposal his talent, youth, enthusiasm, and intelligence. François Rouan, born in Montpellier in 1943, had decided when he was fifteen to be a painter. Before he was a year old, he and his mother had been taken hostage by the pro-German French militia and shut up in a school where the pupils were subjected to torture. "He was present when it happened," writes Denis Hollier, "but he didn't see it. He belongs to the generation who were born during the war but didn't see it, those for whom it was a child-hood memory they were too young to register properly."[66]

The idea that the "desire to see" might be confronted with unnameable objects was to a certain extent reflected in the "plaiting" or "braiding" technique Rouan used in his earliest pictures. In fact, he was following in the direct line of Matisse, Mondrian, and the American minimalists, and showing what paintings usually concealed: the material nature of the medium and support. First one canvas and then another were steeped in dye, and then both were cut up and woven together. This provided the support on which the picture itself was painted: "I'd been inhibited about working," says Rouan. "At first the braiding was only a way of escaping from the inhibitions that afflicted me when I was faced with a blank canvas. I needed to paint, but I had nothing *to* paint."[67]

When he met Lacan, on Easter 1972, François Rouan had been living for a year as a boarder at the Villa Medici in Rome, an offshoot of the French Academy of Fine Arts, then directed by Balthus (artists who win the French Grand Prix de Rome are entitled to three years' residence there). Rouan had distanced himself from Maoism as early as February 1968 and left Paris with the intention of learning to paint by studying Renaissance and baroque Italian art. He was working on a series of pictures called *The Exits from Rome*, or *Gates*, which still used the braiding technique. He was later to abandon this for a painted simulation of braiding. The change was due to a new interest in Poussin, Lorenzetti, and the landscapes, gardens, and architecture of the Roman pictorial tradition.[68]

The two men met at the house of the painter and engraver Brigitte Courme, a friend of Balthus. She was fond of Lacan and used to say "If the devil existed, he'd be like him." Rouan was having problems with photographers, who couldn't reproduce his *Gates* satisfactorily. Lacan spent a whole afternoon in the painter's studio, intrigued by the technique Lacan called "painting on strips": "kinds of little squares, repetitions, surfaces, and underneaths; appearance and disappearance."[69]

Lacan took a series of drawings away with him and sent the young man his first two seminars, published by Seuil. In *Encore* Rouan discovered not only the Borromean knots, which he had never heard of before, but also a phrase that struck home with great force. Lacan described the baroque as "the regulating of the soul by corporal radioscopy" and spoke of the suffering of the martyrs with whose images the Roman churches were crammed. "That was what our painting was about," he said, "until the slate was wiped clean when people began to seriously concern themselves with little squares."[70] The two men got into the habit of meeting, and the relationship was delightful. One evening Rouan had dinner with Lacan and the correspondent of a conservative paper who had arranged a great treat for the master: by means of a key smuggled out of a convent, Lacan was to watch from a place of concealment as the nuns took part in a ceremonial washing of feet.

Some time later, passing through Paris, the young painter had his first appointment in the rue de Lille. Lacan wanted to buy all his drawings, but then a strange misunderstanding arose.

"How are things going, my friend?"

"Very well, thanks."

"Look here," said Lacan, "I didn't send you round there for you to have nothing to say!"

"Round where?"

"Where? To the Seuil editorial board, of course! I did get you the job, after all!"

Then Lacan admitted he must have made a mistake: the "other" person was Rouan's double, he said. They then got down to discussing the price of the drawings. Rouan suggested a suitable sum and offered to throw in one drawing as a present. Lacan wanted to think it over. Like everyone else, he said, he had money problems. The next morning he woke the young painter at dawn with a phone call: "My friend, I'm in the same position as everyone else—I'll have to part with two of your drawings."

Two days later, at the same hour, he rang again: "My friend! It's absolutely impossible for me to part with your drawings!" He then offered to buy them at half their value: exactly the same price Rouan would have received if he had sold them to a dealer.[71]

As their meetings went on, Rouan felt as if he were undergoing an analysis. At every meeting Lacan made him promise to bring "something," and if Rouan turned up empty-handed he looked vexed. "He always left something outstanding. Every time I sold him something he used to ask if I would mind if he didn't pay me all at once." One day he told Rouan, "I'm very famous, you know." Then he started thinking Rouan's painting techniques were similar to his own Borromean practices and the "joined strips" he and Soury were so involved with. No matter how much Rouan tried to explain that he didn't paint on strips at all—he braided canvases and then painted on them—Lacan harped on his Borromean obsession. He was sure the painter knew some secret that he couldn't or wouldn't reveal.

In the course of 1977, Rouan witnessed two odd incidents. On one occasion he and Lacan were going to Sylvia's apartment to lunch, and as they went up the stairs Lacan said proudly, "We're going to see my wife. As you know, she's Sylvia *Bataille*." As soon as he had sat down he asked the maid to bring him some pencils and paper. Sylvia, weary of seeing knots day after day, said, "Do please stop it! It was like that all day Sunday!" and left the room. Another time, Rouan called for Lacan to go out to dinner. "I'm on a diet," he said, inviting Rouan to La Calèche, where he was a regular customer. When they got to the restaurant he ordered his usual menu. This turned out to be a bottle of Pommard and a huge white china tureen full of a dark gray soup. It was a truffle delicacy, made specially for Lacan, who imbibed it with great gusto.[72]

As in the case of Joyce, but now in the work in progress of a painter, Lacan was seeking an echo of his own quest. As for his relations with the artist himself, he constructed that as if it were a transferential bond of a fusional type. It was not until much later that Rouan himself understood the effects on him of this encounter. The close contact between the old master and the young artist, made up of shared pleasures and reciprocal initiation, had enabled Rouan to detach himself from modish preoccupations and understand the meaning of Lacan's topology: i.e., the properties of a space that remain unchanged when the space itself is distorted.

Lacan had manifested a wish to write "something" about Rouan's work, which so fascinated him. So when Marcelle Latour, curator of the Cantini Museum in Marseilles, asked Rouan to suggest someone to write a preface for the catalog of an exhibit she was planning, he gave her Lacan's name. "My dear fellow! I'd love to. I absolutely must do it."

Rouan thought he was joking, but he soon found out from Gloria that Lacan was working on the preface at night. But he was already visibly ill and couldn't finish. Finally, in June 1978 he sent the fruits of his labors to Marcelle Latour. She was horrified: "It's not a text—it's just drawings," she told Rouan over the telephone. "I can't publish that—I'd be a laughingstock." Rouan made her include the master's "gift" in the catalog nonetheless, but she made it into an afterword and had the whole thing printed in mauve ink on poor-quality paper.

Rouan was shattered, and when he went to Guitrancourt with Brigitte Courme he didn't dare show Lacan the offending object. But he was forgetting the master's ways: Lacan insisted on "seeing." At dinner, where Roland Dumas happened to be another guest, Lacan flew into a rage and threatened Marcelle Latour with retribution from his friend Gaston Defferre, the mayor of Marseilles. Rouan tried to calm him down by saying how ignorant people were in the provinces, but Lacan was determined to sue. Nothing came of it, however. "He was as downcast as a little boy. He was expecting his toy, and he was disappointed."[73]

That was the last published text of Lacan's of which the manuscript survives: six pages of words and drawings jumbled together, the handwriting shaky and already dimmed by the shadow of death.[74]

In March 1977 Juliette Labin, a young analyst belonging to the EFP, committed suicide in a mountain chalet by swallowing a carefully prepared lethal dose of medical drugs. One of the fifth generation of French psychoanalysts, she had been analyst to many of those who had been on the barricades in 1968. She had always felt persecuted by institutions, but for all the rest of her generation she was a symbol of the best that Lacanianism could produce: the possibility of really being able to listen in on the unconscious. Tired of official dogmatism, she had "offered" herself as a candidate for the pass in order to challenge the jury, but after a long delay they had rejected her candidacy. Her suicide triggered off the worst institutional crisis the EFP had ever known and led eventually to its dissolution. I have already told that story.[75]

The crisis had made Lacan more silent than ever as to the fate of his earlier comrades. But he was the only member of the jury, apart from Serge Leclaire, who saw the truth about Juliette Labin's suicide. "I have said a psychoanalyst's authority comes only from himself. That's indisputable, but it entails a risk. I would add, however, that he's not obliged to run the risk involved in the pass. He undertakes that voluntarily."[76]

It was at this point that Christian Léger, who had been in analysis with Juliette Labin, rejoined Thomé and Soury in the rue du Dahomey. The business of everyone living together had presented difficulties. In December 1976 Soury had started keeping a folder containing correspondence concerning the apartment and the views of the "Dahometans," i.e., the inmates, or people "passing through." "I've overdone the part of head of a household," he wrote. "Head of an empty household, too, like my grandfather and like every paterfamilias. But it's difficult living alone, and it's a communal attempt at survival that really interests me."[77]

Soury was curious about all kinds of therapy. That year he and Thomé went to Vienna to visit a commune run by a guru named Otto Mühl who called himself an "actionist" and advocated extreme kinds of experiment. The members of the commune at Friedrichshof cut their own hair, went naked, killed animals, shouted and waved their arms about, and daubed one another's bodies with paint. When Soury told Lacan about it, he couldn't understand what it was all about. But the work on the knots continued right up to the disbanding of the school.

As Lacan sank deeper and deeper into silence, the Borromean community gradually broke up, like the school into which it had never really been incorporated. After January 5, 1980, Soury decided to apply to become a member of the new Cause freudienne (Freudian Cause), and at the same time he asked Lacan to take him on for analysis. "I'm not interested in anything but your discourse and the practice of psychoanalysis," he wrote. And: "In the last few months I've come to the rue de Lille several times, but Mme Gloria told me it wasn't possible to see you for the moment."[78]

But no answer came to Soury's long questioning, and while Lacan himself went on braiding until the silence and the twilight both came to an end, Soury solved the problem in a Borromean manner. "I'm going to have a try at suicide," he wrote to his friends. "I enclose five thousand francs for Michel to run the apartment. Either I don't pull it off, and I take the money back, or else I do pull it off, and this five thousand francs and the five thousand I'm giving Christian will help you with any problems concerning the apartment."[79]

He concocted some kind of cyanide and poured it into three small flasks. Then on July 2, 1981, he went by train to the wood called Fausses-Reposes at Versailles. (The name of the wood sounds rather like "False Rests" in French and could also mean something like "unsuccessful layings-down," of, for instance, a burden.) After walking into the middle of the forest, he stopped where three paths met and drank the contents of all three bottles. He died instantly. He was thirty-nine.

Later on, Michel Thomé gathered together the letters and working papers of Lacan's last great friend: a *passeur* of clover leaves with an angelic smile.

Psychoanalysis Reduced to Zero

*I*n the years 1977–1978 both Lacan and his school entered into a long twilight. Juliette Labin's suicide led to an institutional crisis in the EFP that
broke out in January 1978 at the conference in Deauville.[1] The introduction
of a clinical section at Paris VIII–Vincennes, together with the process of
dogmatization fostered by Miller's increasing influence at the heart of
Lacanianism, made the crisis the harbinger of a real debacle. The collapse was
all the more resounding because in the same year the Confrontation movement led by René Major and Dominique Geahchan acquired additional
strength by gathering together the dissidents who were dissatisfied with the
various psychoanalytic institutions to which they had previously belonged.[2]

In December 1976, four years after the publication of *Anti-Oedipus*,[3] in
which Deleuze and Guattari had launched a skillful critique of conformism
in psychoanalysis, François Roustang took up the cudgels on quite a different level. His *So Sad a Fate* was an iconoclastic mockery of the idolatry characteristic of Freudianism and Lacanianism.[4] But instead of forming part of
the internal criticism of the history of structuralism, as *Anti-Oedipus* had
done, Roustang's book attacked Lacan's whole system of thought as totalitarian, a kind of mental gulag. At the same time it claimed to rehabilitate a
form of humanism based on a general critique of structural determinism.

This criticism owed nothing to Sartre. It aimed at reducing Freudian theory to mere transferential discourse, and regarded doctrine as a weapon of
madness that drove others mad as well. Roustang denounced the "theoretical
antihumanism" of Lacan, Foucault, and Althusser and advocated a new moral
order valuing the individual above society, professionalism above intellectual
adventure, and humanity above a theory suspected of dictatorial ambitions.

In April 1977 Cornélius Castoriadis, a former member of the EFP who was
close to the Fourth Group, published a favorable review of *So Sad a Fate* in
the review *Topique* (Topography). "The ideologies that have infested the Paris

scene for the past fifteen years or so—and of which 'psychoanalysis' à la Lacan has been an essential ingredient—have entered into a phase of decomposition." In a lengthy and violent onslaught, he drew up a completely negative assessment of the structuralist period, accusing indiscriminately Foucault, Barthes, Lacan, and Althusser of "having carried out diversionary tactics on behalf of the Communist Party"—in other words, of having used the idea of the signifier to conceal the monstrosities of Stalinism and Maoism. He also attacked Deleuze and Guattari, whom he described as "excellent but improbable professors of philosophy who suddenly spoke as prophets for the schizophrenia of orthodox Marxists of the old regime, recklessly trying to spray their own libidinal surplus over the whole world." And so on.[5]

Behind this formidable settling of scores lay Alexander Solzhenitsyn's three-volume *Gulag Archipelago*, which appeared between 1974 and 1975 and served as a background for an agonizing reappraisal of Marxism and socialism in general. While he was at it, Castoriadis put forward a somewhat simplistic notion of the history of psychoanalysis: according to him, it was at one and the same time a cause and a product of the disintegration of the Western world. Lacan had produced a similar theory in 1938, though in a form that was much more complex and impressive. Castoriadis gave him credit for having undermined the "cretinism" of the "pseudoexperts" of Freudianism by his appeal to other disciplines, but maintained that Lacan had gradually come to prevent anyone else from thinking because of the way he tried to make all thought dependent on himself. The full force of the diatribe was concentrated on the length of analytic sessions: "This practice has been notorious for many years," said Castoriadis, "and has been connived at, by omission, by the great majority of non-Lacanian analysts. . . . Roustang is silent about the scandal of sessions systematically reduced to just a few minutes—for a long while the special prerogative of the master, but for some time now the practice of Lacanians in general. One looks in vain—and with good reason—for any 'theoretical' justification of the practice, though everyone is well aware what is meant by the deceptive phrase 'variable length.' "[6]

In 1977 Lacan had indeed reduced the length of the session to a few minutes, and this did indeed cause a scandal. But Castoriadis was wrong when he suggested that *all* Lacanians—i.e., all the members of the EFP—imitated the master. On the contrary, at this period only a few of Lacan's disciples had adopted the principle of gradually reducing the length of the session to less than ten minutes. Some chose twenty minutes as a limit. But the great majority stuck to sessions lasting at least half an hour, three or four times a week, for ordinary analyses, where the patient lay on the analyst's couch; patients they talked to face to face were seen once a week for three-quarters of an hour. IPA analysts, on the other hand, still held strictly to sessions of forty-five or fifty minutes, and some Lacanians did the same. Castoriadis was also wrong when he said Lacan's practice was connived at by his own school and by non-Lacanians alike. On the contrary, it was quite open—so much so that its flagrancy was one of the main causes of the crisis in the EFP.

After breaking with the IPA, Lacan was free from any institutional constraint. So he went on almost as before, making use of all kinds of analytic techniques and ignoring the traditional rules. Not only was he ready to analyze several members of the same family, but he was on friendly terms with his patients, though this did not prevent him from drawing a strict line between the realm of affect and the realm of the couch. Nor did he shrink from analyzing his mistresses or from choosing them from among his training analysands or ordinary patients. But he did observe certain rules. For example, he never defied the ban on misusing the analyst's couch for sexual purposes; he never threatened or brought force to bear on anyone; he never tried to exchange a sexual favor for any worldly recognition or advancement; and he never insisted on being paid. He was a charmer, not a dictator; he ruled through words and voluntary devotion, never through manipulation, fraud, or corruption. He never, for example, used his transferential power to exploit anyone who was handicapped or mentally ill. . . . As for women, he did analyze some with whom he had had or was having a physical relationship, and he did court some who were his patients, but it was always done elsewhere, never where the analysis itself took place.

His insatiable curiosity led him to explore every possible permutation and combination of the transferential bond. He was always studying the fundamental meaning of the unconscious, whether in training or in therapeutic analysis, in his seminar or in the pass, in controls or in the presentation of patients. After he became the leader of a school he exercised a kind of spiritual monarchy over his "subjects," based on a mixture of freedom and Socratic love. Between 1964 and 1979 his sessions grew appreciably shorter and shorter. He never refused anyone and set no limit to the adoration anyone chose to lavish on him. He behaved at once like a willful child and a devoted mother, though this was contrary to his theory; that denounced the omnipotence of the ego in general, though he himself asserted the supremacy of his own. While some veterans of the third generation underwent a kind of endless control by him, in the form of either an interminable or a supplementary analysis, masses of the younger generation also flocked to him, so strongly did Lacanianism respond to their own aspirations. He therefore got into the habit of not making fixed appointments, and the apartment in the rue de Lille became a kind of refuge where everyone could stroll about among the books, art magazines, and various collections.

There are numerous and very varying accounts of what Lacan's practice

was like in the last fifteen years of his life.[7] The first was François Weyergans's
Le Pitre (The clown), which appeared in 1973. It was the young author's first
novel, a long account of an analysis with Lacan and the only one published
in his lifetime. But it is fiction, and pretty far removed from reality. The doctor in the story is called the "Grand Vizier" and has features in common with
the marquis de Sade, Cagliostro, and the miserly father in Balzac's *Eugénie
Grandet*. The narrator was fascinated by his analyst's love of objects and his
ability to spirit the money out of his, the narrator's, pocket. The Grand Vizier
sent him to a brothel to be cured of impotence by a gorgeous "creature."

The second account was that of Stuart Schneiderman, published
by Harvard University Press in 1983 as *Death of an Intellectual Hero*.
Schneiderman's book gaily mingled fantasy with rumor, hagiography with
anecdotes from private life, to present Americans with a picture of Lacan as
a Zen master. But for the first time the facts about the short sessions were
explained without any fictional frills: "There was something of the horror
of death in the short sessions, in these psychoanalytic sessions whose time
could not be known in advance. . . . The combined pressure of the shortness
of the sessions and the unpredictability of their stops creates a situation that
greatly enhances one's tendencies to free-associate. When things come to
mind they are spoken almost immediately, with spontaneity, for there is no
time to mull them over, to find the nicest formulation."[8]

Later there were very brief accounts, which I collected together in 1986
in the second volume of my *Histoire de la psychanalyse en France*.

In 1989 Pierre Rey wrote a long description entitled *Une Saison chez
Lacan* (A season with Lacan, echoing Rimbaud's "Une Saison en enfer" ["A
Season in Hell"]). This was the first book devoted to the complete history
of an analysis with Lacan. The writing is lively, simple, and elegant, and the
style that of the best kind of journalism, devoid of gossip or sensationalism
and free of both misinterpretation and hagiography. Pierre Rey had worked
as a journalist, first on *Paris-Presse* and then on *Paris-Jour*, before becoming
editor of the weekly *Marie-Claire*. He had gone to Lacan on the advice of a
friend who was an analyst, a suicidal type known as "Fatty." The treatment
began at the end of 1969 and lasted until 1978; it took place face to face and
cost a fortune.[9] "My values were completely confused. The confusion
became really extreme when I got so bored with official receptions that I
turned to gambling. I would leave the dinner table earlier and earlier to go
and sit down at trente et quarante. It wasn't long before I'd stay there for
twelve hours at a time, three o'clock in the afternoon to three o'clock in the
morning, my own heart beating in time with the pulse of the casinos, thirty
lives and thirty deaths every thirty minutes, interspersed with purgatories
while the croupiers shuffled the cards between games."[10]

But after three months the patient was getting better. His phobias had vanished. Yet the analysis went ahead at breakneck speed, always circling around the subjects of suicide, sex, time, money, and works of art. One day Rey met one of Lacan's mistresses who was continuing her analysis in the rue de Lille. "She had the exaggerated beauty of a highly finished doll. She was dressed with studied elegance, made up more heavily than a whore, and gave off an aura of sexual magnetism. . . ." Rey took her to a hotel and spent the night with her. The next day he told Lacan about it, and Lacan made a jealous scene. Another time Rey brought an album of his own original drawings to the session: it was called *The Children of Phallo* and consisted of sixty-nine variations on the theme of "phallology." Rey had only the one copy. Lacan looked at the drawings and asked to be allowed to keep them for a few days. "Three weeks later, as he never referred to them, I tried to get them back. He said again how much he liked them and asked me greed-ily, trying to get round me in fact, whether by any chance—he would appre-ciate it very much—I wouldn't make him a present of them? I would will-ingly have given him my own lifeblood. But not my drawings. . . . He asked Gloria to photocopy them for him."[11]

One amazing scene shows the risks Lacan ran in taking on exceptionally difficult cases, especially in agreeing to analyze suicidal patients. One evening Pierre Rey saw a woman home from Lacan's and asked her why she had been there. She calmly told him she had jumped out of an eighth-floor window with her child in her arms. But her "burden," she explained, "had taken the shock instead of her," so she had survived. She spent hours in Lacan's library between sessions.

Jacques Lacan, 5 rue de Lille, a book published by Jean-Guy Godin a year after Pierre Rey's appeared, was the first to give an account of Lacan's treat-ment of an analyst who was undergoing both analysis and control. The style is rather ponderous, but the book provides valuable information about Lacan's technique, about the way things were organized in the rue de Lille, about the gradual reduction in the length of the sessions, and above all about Lacan's extraordinary greed for money. "To those who were there for the first time and were worried about what it would cost them . . . he would murmur, 'Just give me a little something, my friend!' . . . 'Just leave me a lit-tle something . . . ,' in the faint, quavering voice of a Neapolitan beggar." Godin also pointed out that he and some of his colleagues had self-inter-ested motives in wanting to be analyzed by the famous doctor: "The fact is that, for all of us, Lacan was a kind of company in which we all had shares; and what is more, then, at the beginning of the seventies, his shares were always going up in value. But he didn't really belong to us, even if we were under the illusion that we were paying for a part of him, that we had bought a little piece of him; for the present our shares implied only duties. As for the dividends, they would come—if they came at all—later, much later."[12]

In the same year Françoise Giroud devoted a chapter of her *Leçons parti-culières* (Private lessons) to an account of her analysis with Lacan. It lasted four years, from 1963 to 1967, and involved four hundred sessions, each last-ing about twenty minutes (at that time Lacan hadn't yet started to go in for ultrashort sessions). He had encountered Françoise Giroud at *L'Express* at the same time as he had met Madeleine Chapsal. "I had made a well-orga-nized but unsuccessful suicide attempt," she writes. "And analysts are usually chary of suicidal types. A dead patient always has an unfortunate effect. But Lacan accepted them." After the suicide episode, which followed her breakup with Jean-Jacques Servan-Schreiber, Françoise Giroud had taken refuge in the south of France. Visiting her there, Lacan took her to a perfor-mance of Mozart's *Don Giovanni* at the Aix-en-Provence festival, and on the way home she asked him to take her on for an analysis. He soon saw that she might try to take her own life again, and this indeed happened. "When I started the analysis, my private life was a wasteland. When it ended, I was able to construct a strong and harmonious relationship with a man again, on a completely new plane."[13] Lacan conducted this successful and more or less classical analysis at the same time as he was treating Françoise Giroud's son (who died in an off-piste ski accident in 1971). In 1968 he also had Françoise's daughter, Caroline Eliacheff, as a patient, and she, after studying medicine, became a psychoanalyst.[14]

The apartment at 5, rue de Lille was on the far side of the courtyard, on the mezzanine floor. It served as both a consulting room, or office, and a place of residence. Lacan had a comfortably fitted-up bedroom there, as well as four additional rooms in which to receive his patients and other visitors. The waiting room, close to the front door, was furnished soberly: extras included a painted steel jardiniere, a pedestal table with a mahogany veneer, and a black lacquered wooden stand for magazines, mostly copies of *L'Oeil* sup-plied by Georges Bernier.

This first room opened into an intermediary space leading into the con-sulting room or office on one side and the library on the other, the latter sometimes called the "oubliettes." The "no-man's-land" of the intermediary room, where Lacan sometimes prepared his seminars, contained a lot of books and a glass-fronted cabinet displaying various objects: a stone sculp-ture representing a "knot," some terra-cottas, African wood carvings, Egyptian bas-reliefs, Oriental bronzes, and so on. A painting by André Masson, *Les Baigneuses à la cascade* (Women bathing by a waterfall), hung above the fireplace. On the marble mantelpiece stood a marvelous funerary statuette from Madagascar.

The door on the right led into the library, which was used as a second waiting room. Its sixteen shelves held four hundred rare books. It contained a small mahogany desk, two wing chairs upholstered in raspberry red, and a pair of armchairs. Looking down on it all was another painting by Masson, *Le Joueur de dominos* (The Domino player). The consulting room or office was to the left of the library, and it too was reached through the free passageway of the middle room.

So the apartment in the rue de Lille seemed to illustrate Lacan's own doctrine. The rooms were arranged like the quadripods, the patients moved through them according to a ritual rather like the pass, and the spatial hierarchy recalled the labyrinth of initiation. Here every patient found a refuge appropriate to the seriousness of his state. Some might go into the "oubliettes" to be alone, stay there for several hours, and then rejoin the rest of the company if they felt like it. Others might apportion their time as they pleased. At peak hours a session lasted a few minutes; in slack periods it lasted around ten.

Lacan often received patients just after he had got out of bed, wearing an elegant dressing gown and black bedroom slippers. After dispatching a few sessions at great speed he would disappear to shave, dress, and put on some scent. Sometimes he would ask Gloria to cut his nails, whimpering like a child at each snip of the scissors. He usually saw his tailor, his pedicurist, and his barber while conducting his analyses. At lunchtime he left number 5 to have lunch with Sylvia in her apartment at number 3.

By this organization of time and space, Lacan had ended up abolishing the frontiers between his private and professional lives. And despite his prodigious memory, he came, with the passing years, to forget who was in analysis with him and who undergoing a control, who came to bring him knots or mathemes, and who simply wanted to meet him. Gloria had to keep a card index.

Between six and eight in the evening, Paquita took over from Gloria. Paquita was a young Spanish woman, phlegmatic and slightly deaf; the strange atmosphere in the rue de Lille didn't bother her. Lacan called her a "poor idiot" and got into the habit of yelling out her name. She put up with his extravagant demands with astonishing indifference. Sometimes he would tell her to go and make some tea, and, just as she was in the middle of doing so, call her back because he had changed his mind and wanted something else. She would come back, then go off to do the new errand, quite willing to come back again and again if called, until she dropped.

All this being so, Lacan's analyses no longer took place solely in his consulting room. They might go on anywhere. At first in different rooms in the apartment, then at the seminars, and finally at the café Les Deux Magots (The Two Chinamen), where the analysands would gather to discuss the content, or lack of content, of their sessions, and sometimes to produce fantastic interpretations of the master's words and deeds. When Lacan went deaf, some of his pupils refused to admit that the great and idolized ear could have failed: "He's not deaf," they said. "He's just pretending not to hear." Similarly, when the first signs of cardiovascular troubles appeared in 1978, Lacan's "blanks," his silences, his sudden rages and thumpings with his fist were sometimes regarded as subtle "interpretations" (in the technical sense of an analyst's attempt to convey to a patient the latent meaning of what the latter has said or done), sometimes seen as signs of fatigue stemming from old age. The mere presence of the master, together with nostalgic invocations of what had made his true greatness, were enough to weld together a fragile group overshadowed by the presage of death.[15]

The most striking testimony I have found relating to this period is that of Houda Aumont.

In 1974, when I decided to undergo an analysis, I was twenty-five and a student. As an Algerian immigrant, I had been an activist in a group in Geneva that was close to the Gauche prolétarienne, but I had been very disappointed. We had worked very hard for a year organizing a big demonstration in support of Portuguese immigrant workers with temporary jobs and no rights, but on the day, although we had appealed to the masses, only one of them turned up. I had come to left-wing politics through my experiences as a transient, and it wasn't until I settled in Paris that I took up my studies again. I started to read the Little Red Book in an "antimacho" spirit, and that's how I got into feminism. I'd lived in France before until I was fifteen and then gone to live in Algeria with my mother. But I didn't speak Arabic, and I felt threatened by the oppressive education doled out to Algerian women: typical Muslim exploitation that entirely prevented women from having any social life. Well, after my spell as a leftist I found myself back in Paris in 1972, in the group Analysis and Politics. But under the cover of women's emancipation, I discovered I was imprisoned once again—in a community of women, most of whom were homosexual, which I wasn't. At that time I couldn't make contact with other people, and that female community wasn't going to help me: like them I saw "men everywhere."

But for a time I labored under the illusion that, in the group, I was undergoing a kind of group analysis. We talked about male chauvinism, masculinity, and pederasty, but hardly at all about femininity; we thought that was a trap set by men. We spent our time analyzing ourselves and performing our "autocritiques" under Antoinette Fouque, our high priestess. We had meetings every day, and they sometimes lasted until the early hours of the morning: the idea was to encourage spontaneous speaking. Those meetings were sheer torture, but I have happy memories of women-only parties where the atmosphere was very warm and there was a sort of release.

I was sure then that I ought to start an analysis with a woman. So I went to the Ecole freudienne de Paris and took down the addresses of some women analysts, and, while I was at it, that of Lacan himself. Of course I didn't think of approaching him, but I did decide to go and see Radmila Zygouris, who lived in the rue de

Lille. But she didn't have room for me and sent me to another woman, who made a projective interpretation of me, so I let it drop. Then I made an appointment with Lacan to try to find out what had happened. I hadn't met him, but I did know who he was. The first interview lasted a good hour, and Lacan said very clearly that my case interested him. At first I went every two weeks. He asked me how much I could afford to pay, and the price per session remained very modest right to the end: a hundred francs during the first years and a hundred and fifty francs during the last two years. I used to go at four in the afternoon, and he always pointed it out if I was late. He was always very punctual himself and asked me questions in a language I could understand. He repeated my own words and expressions, without any jargon.

One day, when I was trying to show what a good pupil I was and talking about empty speech and full speech, he asked me what I meant and told me there was no point in my bothering with all that. For years I felt "bewitched," but Lacan never acted the guru and didn't go in for any magical practices. But he had a fantastic ear for listening to people, a human approach that was very tactful and sensitive: I always felt he understood my suffering and wasn't looking down on me.

What had brought me to Lacan was the business of my father. He was living in Lille, and the same day as I made an appointment with Radmila Zygouris I went to see him and booked a room in a hotel in Lille. My father was a very silent man, a worker. During the war of independence he'd been close to Messali Hadj's PPA [Partie populaire d'Algérie], a rival to the FLN [Front de libération nationale—Algerian Freedom Fighters]. As a matter of fact he deserted his family to campaign with the PPA. While I was in analysis I found out, with my brother's help, that my father had killed a man: an FLN activist who had denounced one of Messali Hadj's supporters to the French police. My father was ordered to kill him, and afterward he was arrested and sent to prison. I had known nothing about all this, as my parents had been divorced and I had lived with my mother. My mother never told us anything. When my father came out of prison he was disabled; he had caught some lung disease.

Lacan not only taught me how to be reconciled with my father; he also rescued me from militant feminism. He was critical of unofficial, uncontrolled, so-called group psychoanalysis. In my analysis with him I encountered a possible father—pleasant, courteous, glad to see me, and encouraging me to be active in the real world: for example, to see my father more often. In 1974 I started getting mixed up too soon with the doings of the EFP and with the people around Lacan. Meeting me one day at a cocktail party, he got me off this track by saying it might interfere with my analysis; psychoanalysis was a serious matter, and one ought to take one's time over it. After 1975 I followed his seminar and the activities of the school. I met Laurence Bataille, and we became friends. At that time some of Lacan's analysands, including me, used to meet in a café or on the sidewalk to continue or review the sessions. The atmosphere was extraordinary (especially in the last years): everyone felt free to comment on what Lacan had said and make their own interpretations. What was private to one soon became public property.

As far as my own analysis was concerned, it was in the autumn of 1978 that things went wrong. In October I suddenly heard my father had just died of cholera. I was still shattered when I arrived for my session, and I just said, "My father's dead." Lacan remained silent and impassive. Of course, it might have been an "interpretation," but it seemed to me he wasn't listening, that he didn't even understand what I was saying, that he wasn't there. That day I didn't wait for the end of the session; I just got up and left. Then the sessions went on as if nothing had happened. My confidence was shaken, but I kept up the fiction of the analysis. Then there were sessions when Lacan would stop me as soon as I started to speak: "I ought to tell you that . . ." But he would end the session there, saying, "That's exactly it . . ." I started to get depressed and cry after every session. Of course I wanted to understand what his "that" meant. I was sure he wanted to interpret my relationship to castration and mourning. By way of consolation I started eating Debauve et Gallais chocolates. I put on twenty pounds in nine months!

Then I understood what was happening to me. I could no longer see Lacan as the great analyst he had been before. I still kept up the fiction of the analysis, I still went to my sessions, but without saying anything and in a general atmosphere of craziness. Lacan let patients come every day and then threw some of them out again. Sometimes he got into terrible furies and even punched people. Sometimes they were only "sham rages." Then he got so that he couldn't bear me not to say anything. I would be lying down, and he would come over, his face stiff with anger, and pull my hair. "Say something!" he would order. I would be shocked and feel I had to defend myself against such behavior. Then the same evening he would telephone to apologize and insist that I go over and carry on with my sessions. Another time he ushered me into his office, and another patient was already lying there on the couch. When I drew his attention to this he got into a panic and started shaking. He was completely at sea. I took him quietly to his study, helped by Gloria, who always showed remarkable poise in such circumstances.

When I told my own little circle of psychoanalysts about the hair-pulling episode, they explained that it was an "interpretation." The most ingenious suggestion was: "Lacan pulled your 'tifs' [French slang for "hair"], and Sétif is the place where you were born!" We were all really obsessed with signifiers. We ate and drank Lacan; he was with us all the time. If we went to the country [la campagne], we couldn't help calling it "Lacan-pagne"!

I ended my analysis a few months before Lacan died. I could tell he was very tired, and I wanted to show respect for his age. His death affected me very much, and I really grieved for him. A few years later I had to have another period of analysis, and it wasn't until then that I was able to address the question of the end of the analysis. Then I too made myself really listen to the analysis, and I changed my practice, avoiding all imitation: for example, I abandoned short sessions.[16]

And here is the testimony of Claude Halmos, who underwent a control with Lacan between September 1974 and July 1979.

I didn't attend the seminar, but I did go to see Lacan in the autumn of 1974 to discuss starting a control. He was the only possible controller for me, a kind of father.

I was working at the time as a psychoanalyst at a child psychiatry clinic in the provinces. He made me repeat my name several times over the phone before he gave me an appointment.

In those days I used to go about carrying a large bag with other bags inside it. As he ushered me in, Lacan said, "Do you really need all that?" Then he asked who my analyst was and why I wanted to be one myself. For me, wanting to be an analyst had something to do with the fact that my father would never let me learn my mother tongue, Hungarian. When I heard other people speaking it, I couldn't understand it. I was in search of a meaning. The session lasted three-quarters of an hour. Lacan named a fee, and I thought he said three hundred francs. Then he said, "I don't want to be too heavy a burden." It was very expensive, but I said I would manage it somehow.

I went once a week, at lunchtime. I don't remember how long the sessions lasted, but they were quite long: between about twenty minutes and half an hour. I talked about a few cases, but soon Lacan said, "Is that all you have to bring me for a control?" I understood then that I wasn't supposed to bring mere raw material; I was expected to think over beforehand my notes on the previous session. A series of sessions went by, and his only remark was, "My dear young lady, you're fantastic!" It was driving me crazy. I told him I came there to learn, and I really couldn't believe I was fantastic. "That's the problem!" he replied. But by talking about the case of a little boy who had various problems and whose family name was a girl's first name, I managed to get on the right wavelength and come up with some Lacanian talk about the signifier.

Lacan brought me down to earth at once by wanting to know if I had asked the mother whether she had wanted to have the little boy. He generally avoided giving hard and fast explanations and laying down the law about the "best way" to do things. He tried to find out what made me tick and made me become an analyst through discovering, so to speak, my own "style." He made the other person accept his or her own individuality, but at the same time he was very strict about principles. You were allowed to say or do anything so long as you kept a symbolic distance between yourself and the patient: for example, you weren't supposed to talk to a patient about yourself during the treatment.

In 1976 I was looking after a child of eight who was psychotic and had made several attempts to throw himself out of the window. He couldn't read and had been suspended from school because he used adult obscenities. He had had his first epileptic fit at the age of four, beside his paternal grandfather's grave, and subsequently went into several serious comas, all unexplained. A diagnosis of encephalitis had been suggested, with a very gloomy prognosis. You might say the medical profession had already condemned him to death. His delusions took the form of an invented twin brother to whom he had given a name and whom he represented by standing on his head. Lacan pointed out that this was a borderline case between medicine and psychoanalysis. "Twenty years ago such cases weren't accepted for analysis," he said. "But now it's our duty to take them." The child's mother was delusional, and his maternal grandmother was in and out of mental hospitals, as was a maternal uncle. The father was sexually abnormal and brought out the madness in the rest of the family. He said to me from the outset, "Surely you don't think *you're* going to be able to save him?"

"It's true it's a challenge," Lacan told me, "but it's one of those we have to take up." Although, because of the child's condition, it wasn't possible to be sure about it, the boy's comments during the sessions on his own drawings and on the plasticine shapes he made did suggest to me that he had been and perhaps still was the victim of sexual abuse by some male member of his family—his father or his uncle—with the connivance of his mother. I had difficulty convincing my colleagues and the law of this: I had no proof, and they thought I was imagining things. But some years later the boy's younger sister, who was *not* delusional, arrived at her child minder's place one day with torn panties and said her parents had been "playing with her."

Lacan believed me. He listened to what I said and didn't even ask to see the drawings and plasticine models. Then he encouraged me to appeal to the law to get the child taken away from its family. Throughout the analysis he helped me to act in the everyday world to protect the child and at the same time take him through a traditional analysis. The treatment consisted first of all in turning the world the right way up for the boy and then in helping him to reconstruct himself. He soon asked me to give him his bottle. Lacan told me to agree. "Do it—after all, he's only a baby." So gradually the child was able to get rid of his "twin," who according to him was well whereas he was ill. The dissociation was so successful that one day I had a brief attack of amnesia during a session and forget to tell the boy he was going to have a medical examination. I told Lacan. He just said, "Perhaps he's schizophrenic." The epileptic fits ceased overnight when the child was sent to a home where his parents weren't allowed to see him. The attacks started again whenever the parents managed to force their way in. After the analysis had been going on for two-and-a-half years, the child had some neurological troubles, and while these were being investigated it was found that he had a benign but recurring tumor on the spinal cord, which up till then had been developing unsuspected. He had an operation. I went with him, and Lacan stood by me all that time and called me up every day.

After the operation the child began saying he didn't want to come to the sessions any more. In fact, in the course of the transference, he had put me in the place of a mother capable of giving him life, and he was trying me out to see if that mother could live without him. But I didn't understand and didn't know what to say to him. Lacan didn't tell me what to do. He just said, "You'll think of what you ought to say to him. Then phone and tell me what it is you've said." By saying that he was telling me what I ought to say to the child: that he was capable of managing on his own. So that's what I told him. He decided to go on with the analysis, and gradually he emerged from his madness.

At the end of 1978 I noticed Lacan was less "present" during the control. I wasn't capable of understanding his real condition, so I immediately started thinking his silence and the shortening of the sessions were "interpretations": a way of telling me my practice wasn't right. I thought it was all my fault. But my analyst gave me an interpretation that helped me: "There's Lacan," he said, "and there's the Lacan of your transference. They're not the same thing." I decided to break off the control. Then I got a note from Lacan with something crossed out and in very shaky writing. He asked me to come back and promised to be careful. But I didn't go back. After 1981 I did a control with Françoise Dolto, and I talked again about the boy, who was thirteen years old by then. They had found he had an inoperable brain tumor. I stayed with him till the end. During my last visit, when he was dying, the father, who was at his bedside, turned to me and said, "This time he won't answer you."[17]

As he sank further and further into the infinite "monstration" of the planet Borromeo, Lacan carried out a fantastic work of demolition on the length of the session. For the first time in the history of psychoanalysis, a thinker of genius, with an extraordinary clinical talent, reduced to ashes the great technical principle on which rested the whole edifice of transference built up by Freud. And Lacan did this in order to issue a challenge to science. In the course of a few years, with some of his patients, he transformed the short session into a *nonsession*. This transition to a psychoanalysis reduced to zero went together with the Faustian temptation of the matheme and the knots. Not only did Lacan remain silent and display his knots and braids more and more, but he also lost his power to hear what his analysands were really saying. Instead of listening, in them and in himself, to the reality of what was said, he now tried to hear the basic language of psychosis, like the one Schreber describes in his *Memoirs*: the language of the *matheme*, which can reduce to nothing the uncertainty of all ordinary speech. The *nonsession* was a symptom of this quest: unlike the short session, it didn't allow the patient either to speak—he had no time—or not to speak: he had no time to waste on silence.[18]

Very few of Lacan's analysands from 1977 to 1981 were conscious that short sessions had become nonsessions: it was as if the destruction of time, thus acted out, could not be perceived by its own agents and witnesses. Even today, most of those who took part in this descent into hell keep up the fiction of a minimal duration.

As the years went by, Lacan became increasingly keen on money, though he could be extravagant as well as tight-fisted. Gold itself so attracted him that he collected ingots. When he died he had four bank accounts.

Between 1979 and 1980 he saw an average of ten patients an hour on an average of about twenty working days a month: i.e., the equivalent of eight hours of analysis a day for ten months of the year. So he earned about four million francs a year from psychoanalysis, given that the fee for an analytic session varied between one hundred and five hundred francs, and the fee for a control session between three and five hundred. He owned two other apartments besides those in the rue de Lille: one, in the rue de Chazelles, was occupied by Marie-Louise Blondin (Malou); one of Alfred Lacan's former housekeepers lived in the other. La Prévôté had been turned into a company.[19]

So, unlike Balthazar Claës, Lacan was a very rich man when he died: rich in gold, cash, and other financial assets and in real estate, books, objets d'art, and paintings.

Tomb for a Pharaoh

*I*n the autumn of 1978 Lacan set out with Pierre Soury to drive to Guitrancourt. On the outskirts of Paris, the Mercedes swerved and went off the road. Lacan wasn't hurt, but to those around him he seemed to have changed afterward, to have started to go downhill. He tired more easily; his silences lasted longer. The subject of his twenty-sixth seminar was "topology and time." But at the opening session, on November 21, he found himself unable to speak. His audience was as silent and taken aback as he. They just sat, somehow equal to the tragedy of the scene, and looked on as the weary old man, incapable of summoning up the voice that had held generations of psychoanalysts and intellectuals spellbound for a quarter of a century, slowly drew his knots and braids on the blackboard and then got confused and stopped. He turned to the public, referred briefly to his mistake, and then left the room. "It doesn't matter," someone was heard to murmur. "We love you just the same."[1]

Despite the silence that enveloped every session of the seminar, no one wanted to accept the fact that the old master might be ill. After December 1979, when it was decided that the EFP should be disbanded,[2] people began to mention, not that he was ill—anyhow, they didn't know what was the matter with him, and there had been no exact diagnosis—but that he was old and tired. He was deliberately silent, said some, in order to listen better: his mind was as lucid, his ear as magnificent as ever. They tried to overlook the terrible suffering that was ravaging him and that showed itself in sudden facial contractions of laughter or tears.

Jenny Aubry, one of Clovis Vincent's pupils now training as a neurologist, had long been a friend of both Jacques and Sylvia. Her hospital work had always shown she had a keen talent for clinical observation, and she recognized, in the spring of 1979, that Lacan's silence was due to something other than the fatigue of old age. During a lunch when for a moment he ceased to recognize her and then showed his dismay with strangely stiff facial expressions, it occurred to her that this local paralysis might be caused by slight vascular disturbances of the brain.[3] She was right: she had detected— though not named—the preliminary signs of a very slow pathology that didn't become visible until about July 1980. Lacan never completely lost his lucidity, however; he was merely subject to "blanks," fits of rage, automatic gestures, and a kind of aphasia not easily explained by age, fatigue, or any kind of psychological depression.

Only a few people noticed Lacan's earliest "blanks," and the members of his entourage denied they existed. So Pamela Tytell is an especially valuable witness. At the end of 1978 she went to see Lacan to show him the manuscript of her book. He listened to her and then got into a muddle with his papers. His fly was open, and his dress in general careless and neglected— unthinkable in a man usually so fastidious in his personal habits. Then he suddenly stared at the wall and said, "Butterfly." Pamela told two of her women friends, who knew Lacan well, of her dismay. One refused to believe her but called Miller up and told him about the incident. He counseled silence.[4]

In November 1979, after an interview with Sylvia, Jenny Aubry made an appointment for Lacan to have a checkup on January 18 at the neurology department of a big Paris hospital.[5] A flood of calumny was then unleashed on the rash individual who had dared to say the emperor had no clothes. Everywhere pamphlets circulated accusing "Madame A." of having said "Lacan was out of his mind" or that "he was to have an operation for a brain tumor on January 21."[6]

On January 8, 1980, the members of the Ecole freudienne de Paris received through the mail the famous "Letter of Dissolution," dated January 5 and announcing that Lacan wished to put an end to his school. It was widely discussed in the press, with everyone eager to comment on certain passages: "I speak without the slightest hope. . . . I *père-sévère* [literally, "stern father," but a homophone for "persevere"]. . . . The stability of religion stems from the fact that meaning is always religious."[7] And so on. But on the same day that they received the letter—January 8—the advocates of dissolution felt a qualm of doubt: on that day, Lacan, who for a whole year had scarcely spoken at his seminar, slowly and in a monotone read out the whole letter, though now and then he had difficulty deciphering the words. Then he added something that was absent from the letter mailed to the EFP members and reproduced in the press: "This is what I signed with my name, Jacques Lacan, at Guitrancourt, on January 5, 1980. So there. Is there anything more to be said?"[8] This addition provides some useful information.

Between January 8 and June 10 there were five more sessions of the seminar. The same scene was repeated every time. Lacan spoke, which delighted an audience that had got used to seeing him silent, but he didn't speak as he used to do: instead, he read out typed texts, which were usually reproduced right away in the newspaper *Le Monde* and then in the review *Ornicar?* The same thing happened during the talks given on March 18, 1980, at the Hotel PLM–Saint-Jacques, when Louis Althusser compared Lacan to a "superb and pitiable Harlequin," and on July 12 in Caracas, where the "Lacan-Americans" were called upon to regroup in a new "*cause freudienne*" (Freudian cause).[9] As for the letters and articles, signed by Lacan or not, that accompanied first the dissolution of the EFP and then the founding of the Cause freudienne, followed by the establishment of the Ecole de la Cause freudienne (ECF: School of the Freudian cause), there was nothing either to prove or disprove that Lacan had really written them. For this reason the breaking-up of the Lacanian movement into a number of different trends, which lasted from January 1980 to March 1981 and was accelerated by Lacan's death, turned on the question of who was the author of the texts read out by Lacan at his last seminar and who had written the texts sent to the press and the members of the EFP, whether or not they bore Lacan's signature.

In 1986 I tried to suggest the beginning of an answer to this delicate question by publishing the contradictory testimony of Solange Faladé and Jacques-Alain Miller, the two main organizers of the disbanding of the EFP. Solange Faladé maintained that the decision to disband the school had been taken by Lacan without enthusiasm at Miller's residence on December 30: "It was necessary to act fast so as to produce something with him before it was too late. Lacan couldn't write anymore. It was decided that Miller should draft the letter and Lacan should edit it. He vetoed the passages he didn't like. I didn't go back to Guitrancourt, but during the first weekend of the year Miller called me up and said the letter was typed out and ready to send."

On the other hand, Jacques-Alain Miller maintained that Lacan had written the letter himself. "It was on January 6, at Guitrancourt, that he gave me the text of the letter of dissolution, to be sent out the following day. During the morning of the Tuesday [January 8] I dropped in at the rue de Lille. People were calling in from all over the place. Serge Leclaire phoned to say, 'All my love.' Lacan made a few more corrections to his letter before he went to give his seminar."[10]

Faladé and Miller agreed on two points that no one would now contest: (1) Lacan was perfectly lucid when, after some discussion, he decided to wind up his school. (2) He made some corrections to his letter. As for the rest, Solange Faladé's evidence confirms what Lacan said on January 8— "This is what I signed"—though this declaration was never published. Moreover, the original text of the letter has never been divulged, which is regrettable in the case of so controversial a document.[11]

When preparing his seminars and lectures, Lacan always provided himself with either a text or at least some handwritten notes. He followed the same procedure with official documents concerning his school. As for letters, with a few exceptions they were written in his own handwriting. Given all this, how are we to explain that Lacan left no handwritten trace of texts of such fundamental and symbolic significance as those of that period? Let us not forget the importance he attached to the *written* sources of history. Solange Faladé was probably not mistaken when she said Lacan was no longer capable of writing in December 1979. We know how difficult he found it even in June 1978 to write six pages for the catalog of François Rouan's exhibit. Moreover, all the handwritten letters I have been able to consult for the period from 1980 to 1981 bear the same witness: most of them consist of no more than a few lines, in writing that grows more and more shaky as the months go by.

By the beginning of 1980 Lacan had gone to live with his daughter and son-in-law in their newly rented apartment in the rue d'Assas, of which Lacan himself was a cotenant, having, with Jacques-Alain Miller, signed a six-year lease.[12] He spent his evenings and nights there and went back—always escorted—to the rue de Lille to see his patients, who were gradually and quietly melting away. It was horribly painful for everyone: to Lacan these departures were like unbearable acts of desertion, and he did all he could to keep his analysands around him; they, for their part, were filled with guilt at the thought of leaving him.

By the force of circumstance, and also because of the power of legality, the family, as embodied by the Millers, backed up by Gloria Gonzalès, Abdoulaye Yérodia, and, for a while, Laurence Bataille, became Lacan's only refuge. At this period Miller was already beginning to take on analysands, and so to impose himself not only as the leader of a school but also as a practitioner vis-à-vis the new generation of analysts eager to break with the master's old comrades. As coauthor of works by Lacan still to be published, cotenant of the place where he lived, lawful husband of his favorite daughter, and father of her children, Miller was in the best possible position to oversee the drawing up of the statutes of the new school, the Cause freudienne, the founding of which had been announced in February. It was at this point that the last crisis occurred, a crisis that was to lead to a break between the legal and psychoanalytic families.

At a reception given at the Maison de l'Amérique latine (Latin-American Center) to mark the official dissolution of the EFP, which had been approved by a majority vote in September 1980, it became obvious that Lacan was no longer up to managing his group. As early as September 20 the people close to him knew he had cancer of the colon. He had diagnosed it himself, after a doctor who carried out a rectal screening hadn't found anything: "He's an idiot," Lacan said. "I know what's the matter with me."[13] But at his age, and given that the disease was still at an early stage, his illness was not life threatening. The tumor was local and not invasive, and if it had been removed right away Lacan would have been cured. But Lacan stubbornly refused to have the operation. He had always had a phobia about surgery, and about physical illness in general, and couldn't bear any intrusion on his person.

When news of the cancer got out it accelerated the fall of the Cause freudienne. A "real," identified illness allowed people to open their eyes to the "other" illness, never named or diagnosed and only perceived through spasmodic symptoms visible in the face and then immediately transformed into rumor. At the gathering at the Maison de l'Amérique latine there was a sort of collective recognition of what had hitherto been repressed. When the official dissolution of the EFP was announced, writes Claude Dorgeuille, "Lacan, smiling vaguely, showed no sign of satisfaction. . . . He seemed far away, shaking the hands offered to him quite mechanically and seeming not always to recognize those who approached him. A short meeting of the business committee, the last, was held on the first floor and produced a communiqué announcing that the EFP was no more. Lacan left without having said a word."[14]

Octave Mannoni had the same impression: "He gazed at me for a long while as if trying to recognize me but remained silent. I was upset by this and spilled a glass of champagne. He didn't notice. Gloria was watching over him as if he were an animal."[15] And Maude Mannoni observes: "His people had brought him as a sort of fetish to celebrate the dissolution of his own school. He sat at a table on his own, with Gloria mothering him. He didn't recognize anyone. His eyes were blank; his hand just lay idle. For a year after that, his entourage dragged him around to lots of meetings so that his presence might legitimize what was being done in his name. What we were witnessing was the indecent exhibition of a very sick man. . . . Lacan had become completely silent, but the impact of his legend was such that suggestible people heard him speak through his silence."[16]

On October 10 Lacan went to Sainte-Anne for his last presentation of patients. For several years these presentations had been organized by Marcel Czermak, a member of the EFP and since 1972 Georges Daumézon's assistant at the Henri-Rousselle hospital. Czermak had noticed in June 1978 that Lacan was starting to have difficulty examining the patients properly. By the end of the year, several psychiatrist colleagues at Sainte-Anne had noticed a decline in Lacan's performance, which they attributed to cerebral disorders. One of these was Professor Louis Mérienne, a neurosurgeon.[17]

Now, in the autumn at the beginning of the academic year 1980–1981, Czermak observed with grief and dismay that Lacan was showing symptoms of further decline: hypersalivation, facial asymmetry, shuffling gait, irritability, and difficulties of orientation in time and space. Miller requested that the presentation scheduled for October 10 should take place in private instead of in the amphitheater. When the patient was brought in, Lacan listened to him for a few seconds, stood up, said two or three words, and left the room. After this there were no more presentations.[18]

Jean Clavreul had noticed the same symptoms as early as the summer of 1978: "Increasing difficulty in taking initiatives and almost complete inability to face up to conflictual situations. . . . These indisputable signs of illness should be compared with his performance during the 1979–1980 seminar and at the Caracas conference. These seminars were read instead of spoken, as they always had been before."[19]

A different view was taken by Jean-Louis Gault, a member of the present ECF, who in 1992 related how he had perceived Lacan's problems while he was in analysis with him between 1976 and 1980.

It seemed to me quite grotesque when people said he hadn't written his last seminars: they were on exactly the same lines as what he had always argued and as what one had been able to guess of his desire. Even if it had been proved to me that someone else was delivering his seminar, it wouldn't have changed my opinion. For me it went beyond the empirical observation (i.e., that it was he who was delivering his seminar), which might always have been called in question. I might have been accused of being deceived by my own senses. But what convinced me was the logic of what Lacan did, and his desire, which didn't depend merely on his physical presence or strength. He might well have had physical weaknesses, but that was irrelevant compared with his desire and his relationship to psychoanalysis.[20]

On November 13, 1980, Lacan dictated and signed a will, which had been typed out in due form, in the presence of a lawyer and of two witnesses—a doctor and Gloria Gonzalès. He named his daughter Judith as his sole legatee; if she predeceased him, her children were to inherit. Jacques-Alain Miller was appointed executor for Lacan's published and unpublished work; no further instructions were added about this last.[21]

A month later the breach between Miller and the majority of Lacan's long-term colleagues was confirmed, partly over the question of whether the EFP premises should be leased to the new Cause freudienne, partly over the drawing-up of that organization's statutes. It was Charles Melman, Miller's analyst and hitherto his ally throughout this period, who went on the attack and accused Miller of making use of "apocryphal texts":

The present situation makes it necessary for a "veteran" to take the liberty of saying how matters really stand. Even in its cradle the Cause freudienne exhibits a malformation that may very well carry it off or at least turn it into a monster. Why? Because everything in it is decided and recorded in the name of Lacan, whereas it must be pointed out that his only contribution to the measures being taken is a signature that is now merely automatic. That is a fact, sad but true. It is also difficult to perceive, so much has it been obscured by his pupils' hope of seeing Lacan finally set up a new organization to which they might honorably have belonged. However, we must force ourselves to face up to it: the Cause freudienne is being set up without Lacan, even if we still have the good fortune to have him among us. The deficiency attributable to age and fatigue leaves the way open to those who have his signature and even his voice at their disposal and who may thus make him endorse or even utter apocryphal texts that are pressed into service for a not-at-all-Freudian cause. It is rather astonishing that, in recent months, exegetes of Lacan's writings have failed to notice the somewhat forced mannerism of the texts put out in his name and the cruel absence of any new ideas, apart from one or two gleaned from old drafts.[22]

So it had taken twelve months and a chain of events arising out of the dissolution for Lacan's closest entourage to give official recognition to the disorders of which Jenny Aubry had long since perceived the symptoms, thus earning herself only a campaign of slander.

Miller saw all these attacks as attempts to "bury" the master.

Lacan has long set before his friends a superb image of power and vital turgescence. How people used to congratulate themselves then, how they *"plus-de-jouissaient"* (more-than-came), if I may so express it, at having at their head a most extraordinary man, analyzing crowds of people from morning till night yet also a writer and scholar, learned but luxurious, irresistible, intransigent, in short a man without peer, a man who, as I have seen for myself, lived three seconds in one, as Baudelaire says. And now he is old, very old. . . . And many of those who used to revere him—why not give them the credit for it?—would now rather have him dead and already buried, while he's still, as the poet says, "two steps from vilest earth."[23]

But by the beginning of 1981 it was no longer possible to fly in the face of the evidence. And although he accused his opponents of saying dreadful things, Miller was obliged to admit that the ECF, whose statutes had been registered at the Préfecture de Paris on January 17, had not been founded by Lacan.[24] Miller preferred to use the word *adoption* and declared that Lacan had wanted the new Lacano-Millerian group to be "his pupils' school," not "his."[25]

But the use of the word *adoption* posed a problem, because Miller had gradually placed himself in the difficult situation of speaking and writing like Lacan, of being his voice and ear, and of embodying Lacanian legitimacy. But it is one thing to be appointed the legal executor of somebody's work and quite another to claim, in the name of the law, to embody a whole doctrinal legitimacy. Through inability to distinguish between the two, and by trying to settle political and theoretical conflicts through lawsuits and other legal means, Miller ended up leading the ECF into a dogmatic blind alley. When it was founded, the organization carried ninety members of the EFP along with it, all joining together in the enthusiasm of a reconquest as yet unclouded by accusations about its beginnings. Ten years later, after suffering resignation upon resignation, it was still haunted by doubt about its origins. Certain questions kept recurring: Could this school claim privileged status as against other Lacanian groups? Could it boast of having been recognized by the master in a way the others could not? Was it or was it not the legitimate child of the father? Had it or had it not the right to lay claim to the name-of-the-father?

One of the best texts written at the time about the transition from the dissolution of the EFP to the founding of the ECF was that of Pierre Legendre, entitled "Managing Psychoanalysis." In it he showed that the transformation of Lacan into the father of a family, legitimized by the law, led not only to the shipwreck of his work but also to a hatred of his person, disguised as love.[26] I shall return to this.

On the eve of his death, the silent founder had returned to the basic signifiers of his life and teaching without giving any answer to those who questioned him. He dwelt like a sphinx in the mountains of the planet Borromeo, occasionally emerging from silence to speak truth in the form of riddles.

On August 12, 1981, Lacan was alone at Guitrancourt. Judith and Jacques-Alain were vacationing in Corsica, Sylvia was on the Ile de Ré, and Gloria was in Spain with her bedridden mother. Abdoulaye Yérodia was on a trip to Dakar. Thibaut, alone in his Paris apartment, received a phone call late in the evening and recognized the faint and anxious voice of his father.

"Why are you calling?"

"I just felt like it."

"Where are you?"

"Guitrancourt."

"Would you like me to come out there?"

But Lacan only asked his son to come and see him in ten days' time. That was their last real conversation. A last unkept appointment.

On the twenty-first, Lacan had violent abdominal pains from an intestinal obstruction and was unable to pass water. An operation was unavoidable. Gloria, who had been back from Spain since the fifteenth, immediately phoned the doctor, who quickly brought Lacan back to Paris and hospitalized him under his own name at the Hartmann Clinic, where Lacan's mother had died thirty-three years before. Judith, Jacques-Alain, Sylvia, and Abdoulaye all returned to Paris. Thibaut was instructed not to keep his appointment at Guitrancourt: Gloria told him "all was well" and that his father was the in hospital just for "tests." When he got angry and insisted on knowing more, she told him the truth but said Lacan "didn't want to say it." Thibaut went to the clinic every day to see his father.[27]

The tumor was still not invasive, and the vascular symptoms had not developed further. Two surgical solutions were possible: either an operation in two phases, involving the temporary use of an artificial anus, or a single operation using a new technique of mechanical suturing. The first alternative was the more reliable, but it was more difficult for the patient; the second was more risky but involved no disability, not even a brief one. Both the surgeon and Miller were in favor of the second solution, which was adopted. Before the operation Lacan grumbled about his injections and was very irritable with the nurses. Then for a few days he seemed to be getting on extremely well. But suddenly the mechanical suture burst, causing peritonitis and then septicemia. The pain was dreadful, and like Max Schur at Freud's bedside, the doctor decided to administer whatever drugs were necessary to bring about an easy death. At the last moment, Lacan looked daggers at him. He died on September 9 at 11:45 P.M. He had time to say just a few words: "I'm obstinate. . . . I'm dying."[28]

The body was transferred during the night to the rue d'Assas, and the death registered at 9 A.M. on September 10 at the *mairie* of the 6th Arrondissement. The certificate said Lacan had died "at his home in the rue d'Assas."[29] Marc-François, notified by Thibaut, came at once from the abbey at Hautecombe, accompanied by his sister Madeleine. He was grieved at not having been able to help his brother in his last moments. Sibylle, who was in Venice, was informed too late to be at her father's deathbed.[30]

The funeral parlor sent a specialist trained at the French Institute of Thanatopraxis to prepare the body for burial, with the usual arranging of the face and body to best advantage. Lacan was dressed in a blue-and-purple-checked jacket and a bow tie.

Dead under a false name, his place of death wrongly given as not even his real home address but somewhere where he was merely a cotenant: such was the ultimate fate of that great theorist of truth.[31]

The following day the news of his death was announced on radio and television. The wildest rumors circulated among Lacanians who hadn't seen the body. Some thought Lacan's "enemies" had infiltrated the radio and TV studios in order to make people think he was dead. On the radio station Europe 1 the presenter thought it witty to suggest that bad news never comes singly: "Lacan is dead," he announced, "and clouds are gathering in the west." That evening on television some extracts from the Louvain lecture presented the image of a guru. Only the written press and *France Culture* (the cultural program of the radio section of the national network) put together adequate obituaries, and only the daily *Libération* was bold enough to intersperse serious texts with slogans in "Lacanian style": for example, "*Tout fou Lacan*" (a pun that means "Lacan quite mad" and sounds rather like "tout fout le camp," i.e., "Everything's down the drain").[32]

The apartment in the rue d'Assas was closed to all those who had been Lacan's friends and disciples. A few ECF activists were allowed to come in a delegation to pay their respects. The date of the funeral was not announced, and the place wasn't known until afterward, when it appeared in the evening paper *Le Monde*. On Friday the eleventh, the fiftieth anniversary of his taking orders, Marc-François celebrated mass in the church Saint-François-de-Sales, in the presence of Thibaut and of Caroline's children. Sibylle wasn't there, and neither was the body. Lacan was an atheist, even if, out of bravado, he had once dreamed of a great Catholic funeral. Marc-François asked the congregation to pray for his brother, recalling that all his work was steeped in Catholic culture, although "the church and the gospel" were not essential to it.[33]

On Saturday about thirty people accompanied the funeral procession along the little country road to the cemetery at Guitrancourt. Among those who had been close to Lacan were Sylvia's friends: Michel and Louise Leiris and Suzanne Merleau-Ponty. His individual entourage was represented only by a delegation from the ECF. There were no old comrades, no personal friends, no famous personalities. Marc-François didn't attend this secular farewell, which brought together the divided members of Lacan's two families. Thibaut delivered a brief eulogy; Judith said that the person they had buried was her father. On the stone marking his grave, which lay above the village, facing the hill, were inscribed in gold letters the simple words "Jacques Lacan, 13 April 1901–9 September 1981."

One day, talking to his friend Maria Antonietta Macciocchi, Lacan had confided, with some emotion: "The Italians are so intelligent, my dear! If I could choose where to die, I would like to end my days in Rome. I know every corner of Rome, every fountain, every church. . . . And if it couldn't be Rome, I would be happy with Venice or Florence: Italy is the sign I was born under."[34]

After Lacan's death the various Lacanian schools engaged in furious battles that are not over even today. As far as family matters went, Marie-Louise Blondin's children and grandchildren, the only ones who bore Lacan's name, considered themselves unfairly treated in Lacan's will, which gave the Miller family the greater part of his fortune and absolute powers of decision over the publication of his past and posthumous works. For ten years the two branches of the family also indulged in legal battles over what was to become of certain works of art and sums of money. There was even the beginning of a criminal investigation, but the case was dismissed for lack of evidence.

In the United States, Lacan's death rated only a few lines in the *New York Times*. Lacanianism, the French form of Freudianism, had definitely won its battle to establish the discovery of the unconscious on French soil. Moreover, the work of this extraordinary master was the only corpus in the world that provided Freudianism with a genuine philosophical framework. But the Lacanian movement hadn't conquered the great bastions of legitimist Freudianism that still prevailed in the New World.

PART IX

Legacies

*When the past no longer throws light on the future, the mind
has to find its way in the dark.*

—Alexis de Tocqueville

History of the Seminar

*A*fter the *Ecrits* had appeared in print and the Champ freudien series had
been launched, Lacan was faced with the question of publishing his
Seminar, which caused him the same problems of retention and inhibition
as had his other texts.

I have already recounted part of the eventful history of how the Seminar
came to be transcribed.[1] New documents now allow me to be more precise. First let us recall the main outline of the story.

As early as 1953 Lacan asked a stenotypist to transcribe his Seminar. The
resulting texts were handed over to Wladimir Granoff, who was in charge
of the library of the SFP, and then made available to the members of the society. Three years later, and from then on until 1959, Jean-Bertrand Pontalis,
with Lacan's approval, made excellent summaries of *The Object Relation*,
Unconscious Formations, and *Desire and Its Interpretation*.[2]

In around 1960, Solange Faladé offered Lacan the services of her own
secretary to make a better stenotyped version. She also had the idea of using
a tape recorder, and this was done in 1962. Moreover many of Lacan's disciples took notes, and these are now an excellent source of information. Lacan
often gave away versions of his Seminar as presents, and frequently he had
corrected these. A cult began to grow up around the master's words. After
the EFP was started, Lacan, fearing "thieves of ideas," no longer deposited
papers anywhere, but did allow the many shorthand copies made by his
audience to circulate freely. In 1963 a team from the La Borde clinic, under
Jean Oury and Ginette Michaud, helped distribute hundreds of copies of
the seminars based on recordings. When the library of the EFP was set up, the
team deposited the stencils there, and Nicole Sels, the librarian, arranged
them into an archive with the help of Gérôme Taillandier.

Lacan both encouraged and mistrusted the dissemination of his seminars,
an ambiguity that was part of his attitude to all his work. In the same way as

he had needed a *"passeur"* to help him publish his *Ecrits*, so he waited for someone to take the initiative and oversee the transcription of his spoken words. And the only person who could perform this task was François Wahl, still Lacan's editor at Seuil.

In 1970 the work was officially entrusted to Jacques Nassif, a philosopher from the ENS and a pupil of Althusser who was preparing a postgraduate thesis under Paul Ricoeur.[3] The EFP undertook to pay Nassif a salary in the form of an advance on royalties payable by Seuil. Nassif offered to transcribe two seminars a year[4] and started on *D'Un Autre à l'autre* (From an Other to another, a play on the phrase *"de l'un à l'autre,"* meaning "from one to the other"). But the project never went any further.[5]

In 1972 Jacques-Alain Miller, attracted by the success of Deleuze and Guattari's *Anti-Oedipus*, the text of which was derived from both oral and written sources, took up the challenge and embarked on Seminar XI, the one that had marked Lacan's entry into the ENS. Miller went to Italy and in a month produced a version based on a shorthand text. Lacan gave it his approval, and Seuil drew up a draft contract that named Lacan as the only author; the work was to appear in a series entitled *The Seminar*.[6]

Lacan read the contract and at once asked Paul Flamand to modify it. He wanted the general title of the series to be clearer and suggested *The Seminar of Jacques Lacan*, followed by the title and number of each volume. He also pointed out that Miller's role was underestimated and asked for a more precise discussion about the arrangements as a whole, so as to "indicate the share of the royalties to be assigned to the person on whom the future of the project depends."[7] A final contract was signed by all the parties concerned; it stipulated that Miller was to be regarded as coauthor of *The Seminar* for the "established" texts for which he was responsible, and that he was to receive remuneration for his work. It was also agreed that the work as a whole should appear in the series Le Champ freudien. Lacan thus got an additional percentage as editor of the series.[8]

The title *The Seminar* and the idea of dividing the whole into numbered volumes came from Miller.[9] And the order in which they were to appear reflected a very "Millerian" idea of the history of Lacanianism. The first seminar published, in February 1973, was the eleventh on the list—the seminar of 1963–1964—which coincided with Lacan's break with the IPA, his arrival at the ENS, and his meeting with his future coauthor. This choice of 1963–1964, the period that saw the beginning of a Millerian interpretation of Lacan's work, thus served as a retroactive pivot, separating the work into two periods: "before Miller" and "after Miller." A dual time scheme arose, by which two volumes were to appear simultaneously every year, one from the "pre-Miller" period (1953–1963) and one from the later phase. The earlier period was to be represented in chronological order—Book I to Book XI, starting with Book I—but for the later period the order would be reversed, with Lacan's latest seminar being the first to be transcribed and so on back toward the divide.[10]

But this plan proved impossible to follow. First of all Miller soon gave up the idea of producing two seminars a year. And then he stopped obeying his own rules. After Book XI appeared, in 1973, two other volumes came out in 1975: Book I (1953–1954) and Book XX (1972–1973). Three years went by before there appeared, in 1978, Book II (1954–1955). Then another three years elapsed before Book III (1955–1956). Between 1974 and 1977 Miller got into the habit of transcribing fragments of the most recent seminars in his review *Ornicar?* (Books XXII, XXIII, and XXIV). And after Lacan's death, nothing remained of the arrangements made at the outset, and the seminars were then transcribed in no particular order or periodicity: Book VII (1959–1960) appeared in 1986, and Book VIII (1960–1961) in 1991, at the same time as Book XVII (1969–1970).

Although Miller borrowed the word *establishment* from the literary tradition to describe the production of the seminar texts, the term also recalls the history of Maoism in France. After May 1968 the word *établissement* (establishment) was applied to an activist's decision to go and work at a factory bench or "*établi.*" But this was also the name of the table where, in car factories, an older worker fixed up car doors before they went on to be fitted to the bodies.[11]

In establishing *The Seminar*, Miller made an excellent transcription of the various stenographic versions. He removed ambiguities, edited out redundancies, and invented a punctuation. The main virtue of this work was that it made available a discourse inaccessible in its previous versions. Its main disadvantage was that it flattened out the baroque and continuously gestating style of Lacan's prose. The result was a text of which Miller was the author and Lacan the guarantee. So *The Seminar* was neither altogether by Lacan nor altogether by Miller. The text as established reflected the content of a doctrine that, while it remained Lacanian, was increasingly influenced by Miller's own interpretation.

Whereas François Wahl, through his work as editor, had managed to make the *Ecrits* into a epoch-making event of long-term significance, Jacques-Alain Miller's establishment of the Seminar had quite a different outcome. There was never any controversy over the publication of the *Ecrits*, though certainly there was much criticism, and it is probably time to improve this edition of Lacan's magnum opus with additional notes and variants. Even if such a revision were carried out, however, it would be done as a continuation of Wahl's original work. It would never occur to anyone to challenge the authenticity of the text as it has existed for a quarter of a century: everyone knows for certain that Lacan is its true and only author, even though

Wahl left his mark. And when researchers compare variants in the texts, they do so without finding it necessary to discredit the definitive version. No one has ever dreamed of fabricating a pirated edition of the *Ecrits* that claims to be more "authentic" than Wahl's and offers so-called original versions of Lacan's lectures.

Wahl's relationship to the *Ecrits* was that of a free man freely exercising his own judgment. He simply left Lacan to be sole author of a work that made him the founder of a system of thought finally codified in writing.

The case of *The Seminar* is quite different. When Miller threw Lacan the challenge of a possible transcription, he was already the representative of a Millerian interpretation of the master's work. He was not an editor, like Wahl, but an individual with ideological and familial vested interests, and soon the contractual status of coauthor as well. Instead of bringing the text into written existence for its own sake and leaving himself out of it, he took possession—both legally and theoretically—of a body of work.

This desire for ascendancy was less evident in Miller's transcription methods, which consisted of simplifying an admittedly appalling shorthand text, than in the editorial choices involved in publication. Miller, hostile to all forms of academic discourse though himself a pure product of it, decided to do without the learned apparatus that is in fact indispensable in this kind of publishing. In accordance with both his political commitment and his pragmatism, he aimed *The Seminar* at the "masses," i.e., the new post–May '68 generation of psychoanalysts, whose spokesperson he had, by inheritance, become. So the Seminar began to be published without any supplementary material to help the reader understand the multiple meanings and cope with the infinite variations encountered in the texts: no notes, no index, no critical apparatus, no bibliography. And to suggest that legibility was something that could be taken for granted, Miller made little attempt to correct Lacan's own mistakes. For example, he let the master attribute quotations from Balzac or La Rochefoucauld to Musset or Hugo, make incorrect use of Greek concepts, and get names and ideas wrong. Moreover, unlike Wahl, he didn't insist that Lacan should read and revise the text properly. It was as if he were deliberately trying to convert a system of scholarly thought into an instrument for communicating Lacanian discourse.

Undoubtedly Lacan did give support to the whole enterprise, which took place at the same time as his great journey on the planet Borromeo. When *Seminar XI* came out he flew into a rage, not at the way his work had been presented (with mistakes and without critical apparatus) but against François Wahl and Paul Flamand, whom he held responsible for overlooking misprints in the text and especially in certain diagrams that at the time he regarded as of central importance. He called the book "really exceptional garbage"[12] and by way of compensation demanded that a manuscript-in-waiting by Pierre Legendre, *L'Amour du censeur* (Love of the censor), be brought out immediately in Lacan's own series. Paul Flamand complied, reminding Lacan that he had never intended to reject the manuscript anyway.[13]

So Lacan wholly supported his son-in-law's work. But he didn't share his ideas about the meaning of *establishment*. In his afterword to *Seminar XI* he used the word *transcription* and pointed out that Miller's work was not actual writing, that Miller was the person who produced the book but not the one who created the text, and that the transcript reproduced, without loss of any kind, an oral discourse. In other words, Lacan was likening the transcript to a matheme: a complete translation capable of adequately reproducing at its own level the ineffability of the spoken word.[14]

Miller, in his brief explanatory note, adopted a different position. It was his view on the one hand that he himself "counted for nothing" as author, and on the other that his transcription completely superseded the original shorthand versions. "I have tried at once to count for nothing and to derive, from the spoken work of Jacques Lacan, an authoritative transcription that will stand in the future for an original that doesn't exist." Then he added: "The texts belonging to every year of the Seminar will be established in accordance with the same principles."[15]

The two attitudes were completely contradictory. Lacan maintained that Miller was sole author of a transcript that did not supersede the original but instead completely reconstructed it. Miller, meanwhile, claimed to count for nothing in a transcript of which he said Lacan was the author, yet at the same time he put it forward as henceforward the only version with binding legal and theoretical force as a fundamental text. In short, Lacan gave a correct definition, in scientific terms, of Miller's transcription, whereas Miller posed as a layer-down of the law, henceforth invested with the powers of an executor over the legacy of Lacan's work, even though at that time he had not been so appointed in any will. Moreover he linked the idea of theoretical foundation to the exercising of a right.

But as time went by, Lacan's and Miller's positions merged so closely that the contradictions faded. Nowadays many people believe that Lacan's afterword to *Seminar XI* contains his instructions as to how his oral works were to be edited, whereas in fact these guidelines are to be found in Miller's note. Through the influence of rumor, legend, power, and misreading, the words of the son-in-law are attributed to the father-in-law.

Miller started to wield his power as a legislator with the publication of *Seminar XI*. This allowed him to assure his position simultaneously at the University of Paris VIII, the EFP, and Seuil, where, after having started another collection within the Champ freudien, he gradually came to occupy the place previously held by Wahl vis-à-vis Lacan. Up till 1981 the publisher's editor and the transcriber remained on terms of friendly collaboration. Wahl read the proofs of the seminars, corrected mistakes, and gave his opinion. He never interfered with the methods employed and never asked for any changes in the editorial presentation. Having once decided on loyal acceptance of Lacan's own choice, he gave Miller constant support. "When Miller was put in charge of the *Seminar*," he says, "I didn't feel I had the right to interfere. I left it to him. But I don't feel responsible for the seminars, though I am for the *Ecrits*. I corrected four seminars and corrected the fifth (*The Psychoses*, Book III) a little, but not the sixth (*Ethics*, Book VII), on which I didn't do anything."[16] The first five seminars, published between 1973 and 1981 (XI, XX, I, II, III) do in fact show traces of Wahl's work as editor: *technically*, they are less faulty than the others.

Other people's legal and theoretical grip on Lacan's work was reflected, after 1978, by a decision to prosecute the disseminators of the shorthand versions, which had been circulating for twenty-five years without encountering any problems with the law. These versions were sold both in bookshops and at EFP conferences. Certain undistinguished versions did make money for a few unscrupulous operators. This produced a bizarre confusion between two different kinds of problem. On the one hand there was the law of March 11, 1957, protecting literary and artistic property. On the other hand there were the demands of scientific truth and reason, and in accordance with these it had to be recognized that original shorthand versions existed that constituted genuine evidence as to what Lacan's oral work really was. There were also some tape recordings.

All this being so, Miller could make use of existing legislation to reinforce his theoretical position and go on asserting that *only* his version of the Seminar possessed the force of law against originals regarded as nonexistent. The law supported his position de facto and disadvantaged the opponents of his method, who thought it necessary for the sake of posterity to disseminate what remained of Lacan's original speech, even if only to permit comparison of the different versions. But since, unlike Lacan himself, Miller saw legal and theoretical considerations as one, he solved the theoretical problem involved in publishing *The Seminar* by legal methods: at his request, Seuil began to prosecute those responsible for pirate editions.[17] At the end of 1977 Lacan signed a typed document addressed to Paul Flamand, asking for the confiscation of a slim volume called *Travaux et interventions* (Works and speeches) that contained several of his unpublished lectures.[18] Two years later, and one month after the dissolution of the EFP, François Wahl drew up, and gave Lacan to sign, another letter, suggesting systematic action against all pirate editions.[19] Similarly, when *Seminar III* came to be published, a change was made in the division of royalties between the signatories to the contract.[20]

On July 7, 1980, a typed letter bearing Lacan's signature was sent to
François Wahl. It required that *all* the seminars to come should be published
in continuity with the preceding ones. "Obviously, it wasn't just a spontaneous letter," writes François Wahl. "It was a concession, and a very restric-
tive one, in response to Seuil's anxiety, expressed through me, about his not
having signed any agreement for a right of continuance. . . . The style is
undoubtedly that which Lacan used in this kind of correspondence."[21] In
other words the letter gave no instructions as to the way in which Lacan
might have wanted his Seminar to be published; it was intended merely to
extend the existing contract. The will signed in November contained no
instructions, either.

When he made Miller his executor, Lacan left him completely free as far
as publication was concerned. No indication was given as to the way the
work was to be presented: with or without an index, with or without critical apparatus, with or without corrections. Moreover, by making Judith his
sole legatee, Lacan restricted the share his other heirs would receive after his
death of the royalties arising from the contracts.[22] The upshot was that the
contractual change of October 1980 and the signature of the will a month
later gave the heirs born of Lacan's second marriage legal, financial, and theoretical control of his work.

Between 1973 and 1981 four seminars were published without a word of
protest from anyone in Lacan's entourage. Miller's transcription was not only
approved but actually extolled by those who later became his fiercest opponents: in this as in other matters, no trend hostile to Miller's interpretation
of Lacan's work was able to establish itself in the EFP during the master's lifetime. The controversies started just after his death, with the publication of
Seminar III, The Psychoses. This text was slightly more faulty than the others,
and as most members of the Lacanian community believed Lacan hadn't
been the author of the texts attributed to him since January 1980, Miller was
wrongly accused of using the transcript to "falsify" the Seminar in question
by means of "censorings" and "hijackings." The polemics became so heated
that no serious scientific debate on the subject was possible until 1985.

As early as 1980 even Miller's supporters decided the seminars couldn't
really be read without a critical apparatus. So throughout the period when
the EFP was being disbanded some of them got together in a coalition and
began to work on an index of names and concepts for two seminars: *The
Psychoses (S. III)* and *Encore (S. XX).* Their work was published in Toulouse
in the review *Pas tant* (Not so much, but with a play on *patent,* which sounds
the same and also means "obvious"), with a lengthy commentary by Michel
Lapeyre. "The index should reflect and record the progress of *The Seminar*
as a whole. . . . It should contribute to an *index raisonné* [annotated index] of
all the major concepts, a kind of glossary. Thus the immediate aim of the

index is to establish such a glossary for each of the volumes: this would ensure a proper orientation or vectorization for the reading of *The Seminar* as a whole. . . . The index is a research tool and so is linked to a research method it both reflects and encourages."[23] But if such an index was thought to be indispensable by Miller's supporters, who said they agreed with his method of establishing the text, why did they publish it in a review rather than incorporate it into the volumes published by Seuil, where it would have been most appropriate and most useful?

Fortified in his position by his legitimacy but attacked on all sides as a usurper, Miller was for several years regarded by his supporters as a kind of martyr—all the more so as the most virulent attacks came from the entourage of his former analyst. But instead of trying to weld together the various factions of a bereaved community, who felt they were being deprived of their intellectual heritage merely through the power of the law, Miller went into battle. As noted earlier, it was at his instigation that Seuil embarked on the systematic prosecution of those responsible for pirate editions.

Given that he was by then responsible for all of Lacan's work, Miller, after 1981, could have decided to take the articles that François Wahl hadn't included in the *Ecrits* and publish them in one or two volumes, adding all the lectures scattered in various reviews and very hard to get hold of. But instead of buckling down to this task he left the uncollected work in the same state as it had been before Lacan's death. He did republish several articles, but instead of grouping them together in one easily handled volume he printed them in different numbers of *Ornicar?*. This added yet further to the difficulties of those who hoped to work on Lacan's texts. The corpus as a whole remained scattered, dispersed, and difficult to find, and pirate editions began to proliferate.

In 1984, when Miller reissued, in the form of a slim volume, the great and beautiful 1938 text on the family, he followed the same editorial criteria as for *The Seminar*: there was no critical apparatus, and neither notes nor index were provided. Miller left out the lengthy bibliography listing the works Lacan had consulted in writing the article.[24] Admittedly he was right to omit the subtitles, most of which had been added by the editors of the *Encyclopédie*; but why did he drop the bibliography in this case, when it had been retained for the reissue of the thesis on paranoia?

In view of all this, Miller's editorial methods met with more and more opposition, in relation both to his transcription of the oral texts and to his management of the written work.

In 1983 the people involved in the review *Littoral* formed an association with the object of transcribing Lacan's seminars. The association published a bulletin, *Stécriture*, that reproduced several sessions of the eighth seminar

(*Transference*). (The word "*stécricture*" is a play on "*St.*," an abbreviation for "saint," which as an adjective means "holy," and "*écriture*" [writing]. The whole coinage also sounds rather like both "scripture" and "stricture." And so on.) The resulting transcript was an improved version of the shorthand text: all mistakes were corrected, including Lacan's own. Academic standards were observed: notes and critical apparatus were provided, and variants shown. The work broke completely with Miller's method, especially with the usual presentation of *The Seminar*. But although this transcript was very respectful of the master's word, its style was rather heavy and hagiographical. And the commentary was overdone. Even so it was more dependable from a scientific point of view than Miller's version.

But its authors had broken the law by selling the bulletin to cover their expenses. So Seuil and Lacan's executor prosecuted, and at the end of 1985 a judgment was handed down in their favor. The defending lawyer's arguments had not been very skillful: they denied forgery and claimed that the text was the original work of the group *Stécriture*, not a mere transcription of Lacan's Seminar!

Miller exulted in his victory, and told the press he was now the sole interpreter of Lacan's word: "For my part . . . I must say I had from the outset the reputation of being the one who understood Lacan. . . . I observe that people don't really catch on to a seminar until I have established it. I merely observe the fact. Until this work, which consists partly of editing but mostly of logicization, has been done, a seminar isn't understood, apart from a grain gleaned here or there. . . . Counting for nothing means putting myself in a position where I can write 'I' and that 'I' is Lacan's, an 'I' that continues the author and prolongs him beyond his death."[25]

Philippe Sollers gave evidence in *Stécriture*'s favor at the hearing. Laurence Bataille also supported her brother-in-law's opponents, though she didn't actually attack Miller. In November 1982 she had resigned resoundingly from the ECF to show her disapproval of the way Miller was using circulars signed by Lacan as texts binding on a school that Lacan hadn't founded. "The use after 1980 of texts signed by Lacan may have served a certain purpose for a while. The practice is continued by their publication in the yearbook. But are those being trained in the school really unable to stand without such help? If so, then they would be incapable of becoming proper analysts—Lacanian analysts, that is. This is an inconsistency I can no longer condone. I wouldn't be able to continue as an analyst if I went on accepting it. And that is why I'm resigning from the Ecole de la cause freudienne."[26] Laurence Bataille died suddenly of cancer of the liver six months after the *Stécriture* affair.

François Wahl played an important part in the case, but he took Miller's part, writing a long letter pointing out that Lacan had always approved completely and unfailingly of his son-in-law's work.[27] This was his last act of loyalty toward the great thinker whose publisher and editor he had been. In 1981, wanting to preserve some theoretical coherence in the now-disintegrating Lacanian movement, he had agreed, out of friendship for Contardo Calligaris, that Seuil should publish the first issue of the review *Le Discours psychanalytique* (Psychoanalytic discourse), with the condition that it should not contain any attack on Miller, the legitimate heir. But Charles Melman, editor of the review, wrote an unsigned editorial in which the following lines appeared: "Lacan's thought will be exposed to polishing up and disquisition. This process of embalming, which turns Lacan's utterances into merchandise, celebrates a reconciliation between the museum builders and the hollow homage of the media."[28]

Even before he knew the contents of the review, Miller insisted that Seuil should withdraw its name from it. Wahl gave in with dignity: he had understood that it was impossible to introduce any theoretical order into this field of ruins.[29] From that day on, the man who had been in charge of all the works published in the Champ freudien series saw the editorial edifice he had built up over the years gradually crumble away. After Lacan's death the other authors left. And in Seuil's offices in the rue Jacob, Miller was the sole editor of his father-in-law's posthumous work. Wahl was obliged to withdraw, which he did, again with dignity. The break was silent, elegant, and final. After 1985 Wahl no longer corrected either the manuscript or the proofs of *The Seminar*. He just made an occasional comment.

But although Miller had won his legal battle, the prosecution of *Stécriture* had revealed publicly that the lawful heir was not the only one with knowledge of Lacan's texts.

In a 1984 interview with François Ansermet, reprinted after the hearing, Miller declared again, as he had in 1973, that the original text didn't exist. But he went further: he maintained that Lacan had said the same thing. The master himself, he added, had decided that all the seminars should be established on the initial 1973 model, that is, by the same method and with the same editorial presentation. "Lacan never regarded the shorthand version as an original text. . . . It was decided between us that all the seminars should be done in that way."[30] In saying this, Miller was attributing his own opinion to Lacan. (We have already seen how Lacan's own words in his afterword to *Seminar XI* failed to agree with what Miller said in his note. The contradiction is evident again in this interview.)

The interview also served, from 1985 on, to popularize the idea that Lacan had left precise instructions about how his Seminar was to be edited and published after his death. But this was not the case: only his general approval of his son-in-law's work had the force of law; there were no explicit written arrangements. The distinction is very important.

But in the real world, Miller went on confusing legal rights and scientific debate. Entrenched in the solitary splendor of legitimism, he was also cut off from the past and present history of a plural Lacanianism quite different from his own. As a result, he became more and more isolated from all the connoisseurs of Lacan's work who might have enlightened him. For the SFP period, when the seminars were not recorded, he couldn't consult existing sources—including notes taken by members of the audience—that might have improved his transcript. So he was usually restricted to the shorthand version alone, and this, even when corrected, was always very defective.

When Miller published *Seminar VII* (*The Ethics of Psychoanalysis*) in the autumn of 1986, no one attacked him. His adversaries, stunned by the legal defeat of *Stécriture*, preferred to remain silent for the moment. But this seminar was more defective than the preceding ones. Miller had probably foreseen the danger, for he had sought assistance from several people: Judith Miller had helped with the Greek references; he had turned to Franz Kaltenbeck for the German quotations. Three academics had done some research, and several friends had corrected the proofs. François Wahl was thanked for having read over the manuscript, but he felt ill at ease and made only a few remarks.[31] Miller again declared that Lacan had wanted the publication of his Seminar to proceed according to the "principles" set out in 1973.[32]

He sent a copy of the book to Pierre Vidal-Naquet, with a dedication reading "To Monsieur Pierre Vidal-Naquet, who may wish to read the three lectures on 'Antigone,' this book, which would certainly have been sent to him by Jacques Lacan." Vidal-Naquet at once began to read the magnificent chapter on Antigone, and was taken aback to find at least two mistakes on every page. Not a single Greek term was correct, several quotations were wrong, there were many misprints, and none of Lacan's own serious mistakes had been spotted.

Anxious to improve the text for any new edition, the great Hellenist took up his pen and sent Jacques-Alain Miller a letter eight pages long pointing out the mistakes and adding characteristic comments of his own. He received no answer. A little while later, having occasion to see Judith about another matter, he reminded her of what had happened. She told him, in surprise, that the letter had never arrived and asked him to send another. He did so. He never got any reply.[33] Perhaps Derrida was right when he said, with reference to Edgar Allan Poe, that some letters never do arrive at their destination. However that may be, two important letters about Lacan's Antigone have never shown up from that day to this.

And yet Miller had announced, in a notice issued in 1981, that he hoped people would point out any errors. And before *Seminar VII* came out, his call had been heard. In October 1985 Gabriel Bergounioux, an expert in semantics, wrote him a letter about *Seminar II*, drawing his attention to seven misprints and a punctuation mistake. Bergounioux didn't correct Lacan's own errors, but he did suggest nine major changes (*paradis* instead of *paradigme*, *saut* [jump] instead of *sceau* [seal], etc.) and nine minor ones (*inspection* instead of *introspection*, etc.). Miller encouraged Bergounioux to carry on with his work and invited him to his seminar. Bergounioux then sent in new suggestions for changes in *Seminar III* and *Seminar VII*. For *Seminar III* there were sixteen major and twenty-one minor mistakes, as well as seventy-nine misprints—a considerable increase on the corrections suggested for *Seminar II*. In the case of *Seminar VII*, Bergounioux made the same comments as Vidal-Naquet about the use of Greek expressions. He pointed out twenty-five major errors, forty-three minor ones, and seventy-two misprints.[34]

In the autumn of 1985 an argument broke out between Jacques-Alain Miller and John Forrester, the translator into English of Lacan's first two seminars. Forrester, a brilliant academic and a specialist in the history of Freudianism, had done a remarkably good job. Not only had he corrected practically all Lacan's mistakes, but he had also supplemented the text with notes, an index, and a critical apparatus that together enabled the reader to understand all Lacan's references, allusions, subtleties of language, and so on. He had also supplied information especially designed to help English readers. Forrester's contract for the book was with Cambridge University Press, and his work conformed to the academic standards of the Anglo-American world, which did not, as we know, give Lacan's work a very easy reception.

Miller was angry with Forrester when he saw his edition, and made him remove his notes and comments and his references to Lacan's mistakes. Only the index and some specific notes were allowed to remain. In effect, Miller let Forrester's explanations of Freudian references stand, but rejected all his personal comments. He objected to such phrases as "Lacan is wrong here" or "The French text is faulty," and maintained that since printing errors had already been corrected in the translation as well as in all foreign editions, there was no point in calling attention to them in notes.[35] It should be pointed out that Miller was referring to printing errors only; in general, Lacan's own mistakes were not corrected.

In 1990 François Wahl retired, resigning from all his activities at Seuil. He was not replaced. His editorial and intellectual legacy was handed over to someone who as it happened was a friend of Judith Miller. She took on the onerous task of looking after the whole of Seuil's psychoanalytic output, together with the publication of the posthumous works of both Lacan and Barthes; she thus became Miller's editor too.

After the death of Françoise Dolto in the summer of 1988, her daughter, Catherine Dolto-Tolitch, had intended to stay on with Seuil. But after various conflicts she took her mother's correspondence and unpublished works to another publisher, Hatier. This was a great loss to Seuil: Françoise Dolto, whose work had been handled in her lifetime by Paul Flamand, had, together with Lacan, been the glory of their psychoanalytic list. After 1981 the Champ freudien series no longer had any formal existence, and Moustapha Safouan and Serge Leclaire were the only survivors among Wahl's former authors who didn't belong to the Millerian school. Then Claude Cherki, Seuil's new managing director, decided to hand over responsibility for a new version of what had been Lacan's psychoanalytic series to Judith and Jacques-Alain Miller: the definite article was dropped from the name, and the old Le champ freudien became Champ freudien. In the spring of 1991 four titles were published under the new masthead: *Le Pays de l'Autre* (The land of the Other), by Serge Leclaire; *Psychanalyse 6 heures 1/4* (Psychoanalysis at a quarter past six), by Dominique and Gérard Miller; and two seminars—*Transference* (*VIII*) and *L'Envers de la psychanalyse* (The reverse side of psychoanalysis) (*XVII*).

Miller was being somewhat provocative in publishing *Seminar VIII* six years after *Stécriture*. Everyone thought he would change his own method and incorporate corrections from the banned transcript, which was based on an almost error-free shorthand version, into the transcript he was basing on a more defective version. Not so. *Seminar VIII* was established in the same way as the previous seminars. But this time all the mistakes were spotted very quickly, because anyone could compare the *Stécriture* version with the one just published by Seuil. Controversy soon reached ample proportions in the press and on the air. As early as January, before the two books were actually out, a petition signed by intellectuals, psychoanalysts, and almost every non-Millerian member of the Lacanian community demanded that "all existing versions of the Seminar be deposited in the Bibliothèque nationale so that they may be freely consulted." The petition also called for a complete inventory of Lacan's working notes.[36]

Jacques-Alain Miller refused to take part in the scientific debates that were suggested to him, and regarded his opponents as enemies. Two people came to his defense: Catherine Clément and Claude Cherki. The former declared, in an article in *Le Magazine littéraire*, that a "witch hunt" had been mounted against Lacan's heir: "Petitions like those organized by a political party, accusations based on assumptions rather than facts, demands for registration at the Bibliothèque nationale in the face of Lacan's own last wishes, criticisms of Miller's edition (on the grounds that it lacks the 'scientific apparatus' that Lacan didn't want at any price)—the controversy has been fabricated, and it's aimed at just two people: Lacan's son-in-law, guilty of getting married, and his wife, Judith, no doubt even more guilty for having been engendered by the master whose dead blood people now thirst after. Later, no doubt, the history of the psychoanalytic movement will assess the challenge to his family in the light of the hatred behind it."[37] Rumor had run its full course; it was now possible to assert, without quoting any source or adducing any proof, that Lacan had "dictated his last wishes" and forbidden any "scientific apparatus." Where were these wishes to be found? Where had they been uttered, recorded, preserved? The author of the article didn't say.

Claude Cherki was more cautious but just as severe when he described me as "ignorant" and "partial" after I had called the defective Seminar "unusable." "The publication of the new volumes," wrote Cherki, "corresponds entirely with Lacan's wishes: in particular, there is no index, critical apparatus, or bibliography attached to a text that is a transcription of words spoken—and thus permanently topical—and not a written, academic work." In support of this statement about Lacan's "wishes," Cherki quoted a sentence from Miller's 1973 note: "The texts belonging to every year of the Seminar will be established in accordance with the same principles."[38] Once again the words of the son-in-law were being used to ascribe to the father-in-law instructions that he had never issued.

In September 1991, under the title "Transference and All Its Errata," the *Stécriture* team published a list of the mistakes contained in *Seminar VIII*. The list included omissions, mistakes stemming from similarity of sound (*saints*—saints—instead of *seins*—breasts), mistakes arising from mishearing (*restitue* restore instead of *substitue*—substitute), mistakes in rendering foreign words, wrong readings of the shorthand (*hâterologie* instead of *hâte en logique*), wrong references, and Lacan's own mistakes: in all, 587 errors.[39] The case was so overwhelming that Miller had to admit at least a quarter of the errors. And for the first time he was obliged to revise the *Seminar* for reprints and for the various foreign translations.

In conclusion, here is an excerpt from Cherki's responses during an interview I had with him in September 1992, where yet again it is said that Lacan indicated in his afterword to *Seminar XI* that his oral work was to be transcribed by Jacques-Alain Miller without any critical apparatus:

When I took up my post as managing director of Seuil in 1989, I asked Jacques-Alain Miller to start working again on the transcription of the seminars. He had stopped working on them because there had been a change in his relationships with the people in charge of psychoanalysis at Seuil. He and I knew one another slightly; I had mixed with his generation of ENS students. We work well together, and I support him. Jacques Lacan, in his lifetime, assumed the responsibility of giving his oral works to Jacques-Alain Miller—whom he appointed his executor—to transcribe. In the afterword to *Seminaire XI*, published in 1973, during his lifetime, he indicated what he wanted for the future: the Seminar as a whole was to be transcribed according to the same model and in the same way, i.e., by Jacques-Alain Miller and without critical apparatus. We respect that decision. No one today has the same moral authority as François Wahl had vis-à-vis Lacan. When Lacan was still alive, François Wahl could permit himself to suggest corrections. But today we are in a completely different situation. Jacques-Alain Miller is coauthor of the seminars. He does what seems to him desirable for Lacan's work. It was Lacan, in his lifetime, who gave him the right to do this. All posthumous works are difficult to manage, especially when they are oral. I think that, in the case of Lacan, it is better to publish his work, even if a few errors may creep into it, than not to publish anything at all.

As for *Seminar VIII*, on transference, this is what happened: Jacques-Alain Miller came of his own accord to talk to me about the criticisms that had been made of his transcription. Many of them he didn't agree with, but he admitted there were some mistakes that ought to be corrected for any future reprint. It was at his request that I decided not to make any translation rights available until the text in question was reprinted. The only exception was the case of the Brazilian publisher, who had already started work on a translation based on the proofs. I might add that I never received the document dealing with the errata. I got all kinds of petitions, but not that document. It is not for me to express an opinion about any possible errors. They didn't exist for me until Jacques-Alain Miller came and asked me to have them corrected. He is the legal administrator of Lacan's work; we are only the publishers. No one has ever prevented other transcriptions from existing or from being deposited as archives in, for example, the Bibliothèque nationale.[40]

François Wahl had been Jacques Lacan's editor and publisher; Paul Flamand had been Françoise Dolto's. Claude Cherki is obliged to admit, whether he likes it or not, that in order to keep the "name-of-the-father" in its catalog, Seuil is now the publisher of a mere legal representative: Jacques-Alain Miller.

32
• • • • • • •

Freudian France: The State of Play

Note: The information reported in this chapter was accurate as of 1993.

In 1985 Freudian France was divided among twenty associations. The Société psychanalytique de Paris (SPP, 1926) was the oldest, and it, together with the Association psychanalytique de France (AFP, 1964), represented the French component of Freudian legitimism. Between them they had 478 psychoanalysts recognized by the IPA and the same number of pupils. Two other societies stood for a moderate Freudianism, distanced from both Lacanianism and the IPA: the Organisation psychanalytique de langue française, also known as the Quatrième Groupe (OPLF, 1969), and the Collège de psychanalystes (1980): the former had 30 members, the latter 120. Both were linked to the history of Lacanianism: the OPLF because it arose out of a split with the EFP, the Collège because it was founded after the EFP was dissolved.

Thirteen other groups also emerged after the dissolution. The Ecole de la Cause freudienne (ECF, 1980), with 273 members, represented Lacanian legitimism (of the Millerian school). The twelve other associations embodied the values of a more moderate Lacanianism, less dogmatic and continually spreading. They were, in order of their creation: the Association freudienne (AF, 1982), with 123 members; the Centre de formation et de recherches psychanalytiques (CFRP, 1982), with 390 members; the Cercle freudien (1982), with 50 members; the Cartels constituants de l'analyse freudienne (CCAF, 1983), with 212 members; the Ecole freudienne (1983), with 50 members; The Fédération des ateliers de psychanalyse (1983), with 117 members; the Convention psychanalytique (CP, 1983), with 212 members; the Coût freudien (1983); the Groupe régional de psychanalyse (GRP, 1983, Marseilles); Errata (1983), with 15 members; the Ecole lacanienne de psychanalyse (ELP, 1985), with 45 members; and Psychanalyse actuelle (1985).

In addition to these associations there were two historical societies: the Société internationale d'histoire de la psychiatrie et de la psychanalyse

(SIHPP, 1983), with 165 members, and the Association internationale d'histoire de la psychanalyse (AIHP, 1985), with 60 members. Lastly, there was a teaching school: the Ecole propédeutique à la connaissance de l'inconscient (EPCI, 1985).[1]

The number of groups deriving from the former EFP grew swiftly between 1985 and 1993: fourteen more associations came into being in eight years. Six of these are new creations, two are the result of splits, and six aim at bringing together existing groups to operate on a European or international scale. So there are, at the time of this writing, thirty-four Freudian associations, not counting those that come into existence every day in Paris and the provinces, which I have been unable to list.

The six new associations are as follows, in order of foundation: the Bibliothèque de recherche freudienne et lacanienne (Strasbourg, 1986); the Séminaires psychanalytiques de Paris (1986), with 230 members; the Champ psychanalytique et social (CPS, 1989); the Association pour une instance des psychanalystes (APUI, January 21, 1990); the Echanges internationaux de recherches psychanalytiques (Aix-en-Provence, March 1990); and the Trait du cas (April 1991). These six groups were all started by former members or allies (of the EFP): Juan-David Nasio founded the Séminaires, Serge Leclaire the APUI, and Lucien Kokh the CPS.

The group called Dimensions freudiennes, founded on October 12, 1991, emerged from the split in the ECF. Analyse freudienne, founded on February 24, 1992, is the result of a sort of implosion of the CCAF.

The six European- or internationally oriented groupings are very different from one another. The Inter-Association de psychanalyse was created in January 1991 by members of the fourth and fifth generation of French psychoanalysts who wanted to "harness the differences arising out of our belonging to various institutions."[2] It now links together eleven associations: the CFRP, with 528 members; the CCAF, with 168 members; the AF, with 258 members; the CP, with 184 members; the Seminaires; the CPS; Errata; the Cercle freudien, the Coût freudien; and Psychanalyse actuelle—in other words, almost all the institutions deriving from the former EFP, with the exception of the ELP and the ECF.

The Fondation européenne de psychanalyse, founded in April 1991, emanated from the AF, which itself has become the Association freudienne internationale. The FEP aims at both reducing the institutional power of the Interassociatif—if the latter succeeds in its federative aims—and combating Millerian internationalism.

Today Lacanian legitimism, represented by the "Miller family" (in both the literal and the figurative senses), while not as strong as Freudian legitimism, is organized to resemble a bureaucratic fortress. Until 1989 the Champ freudien, directed by Judith Miller, still linked together the various

Lacanian groups in different parts of the world. While the CF was continued, another, specifically international association was added to it. For one of the characteristics of Millerian organization is its extraordinary ability to multiply the number of associations, groups, networks, and schools, and to keep them together or make them dissolve by virtue of decisions taken at the center.

Thus, while the CF still went on, Miller decided, in the autumn of 1990, to create in Barcelona the Ecole européenne de psychanalyse (EEP, September 22–23, 1990), where in theory various groups belonging to the CF were to meet. Spain was a favored terrain, and even today it is still the only country in the world where Lacanian legitimism enjoys a large majority: 80 percent of the groups there are linked to Miller and his organizations. Everywhere else, and especially in Latin America, the Lacanian movement is plural and federative, and legitimism, though powerful, tends to be in a minority. The creation of the EEP followed the founding of the Escuela del Campo freudiano (Caracas, 1985). On January 3, 1992, a third school was started in Buenos Aires in Argentina: the Escuela de la orientacíon lacaniana (EOLCF). Argentina already had three large associations linked to the IPA and 69 small Lacanian groups; only two agreed to join the EOLCF.

At the beginning of 1992 the Venezuelan ECF, the French ECF, the EEP, and the EOLCF formed a heterogeneous group: three of them were national in character, and though the fourth was supposed to be European it was mostly limited to Spain. To unify this group and add further features—for example, a Brazilian school of psychoanalysis (in preparation)—Miller was obliged to carry further the internationalization of his movement. In February 1992 he created an Association mondiale de psychanalyse (AMP, February 1, 1992), giving the name Pacte de Paris to the document that founded, for the second time in the history of Freudianism, an expansionist international. Spanish is the dominant language in the AMP, as English still is in the IPA. The signing of the pact, which united the AMP with the other four schools, was accompanied by an out-and-out declaration of war. "It is no longer a matter," said François Leguil, president of the ECF, "of 'balancing' the IPA. The institutionalizing of our expansion, the new AMP and our allies, all bear witness to our intention to start opposing the IPA and ultimately abolish it. There is no other alternative: wherever the Internationale, born of the Anna Freud gang, prevails, psychoanalysis shows the white flag and asks the state either to discipline the competition or organize the market so as to save its own skin."[3]

In 1981 Serge Leclaire had refused to found a school; he wanted to give the younger generation a chance. But ten years later he made a great comeback on the French psychoanalytic scene, provoking as usual great controversy. His initiative was new in that it aimed at unity. French Freudianism was in crisis, and Leclaire's APUI sought to provide a refuge for the practitioners of psychoanalysis for the masses: Lacan's orphans or IPA dissidents, deprived of legitimacy, deintellectualized, scattered by a historical movement in which the so-called human sciences seemed to be disintegrating before an organicist offensive linked to advances in pharmacology and genetics. "For thirty years or so," said Leclaire,

the French psychoanalytic movement . . . has been the best and liveliest in the world. This is still true, especially if we compare it with the United States. But I have a feeling that it's all becoming ossified, stiffening into a kind of war of religion, into theoretical debates that no longer contribute anything new. And it's not a good thing that the French analytical movement should enter the year 1992 in such a state of weakness. . . . The present danger is that analysis may become diluted, drowned. . . . Most of the analysts in France are not well known. They don't belong to institutions. They are a generation of people aged between thirty-five and forty, not at all interested in the quarrel of the veterans. And they need a space, a group. And there lies the strength of our initiative. It doesn't bear the mark of any established apparatus.[4]

Leclaire's project was on the right track. He aimed at gathering together all the Freudians in France, from the IPA to the ECF. He had put his finger on the dispersion that was adversely affecting the Lacanian movement and French Freudianism as a whole, though the institutions of the latter were much more stable. But the enterprise was made ambivalent by the use, in the title of its founding document, of the word *ordinal*. This evoked the notion of order in general and the Order of Physicians in particular, thus suggesting the possibility of a law-giving institution that might replace freedom of association. So Leclaire was attacked from all sides.

His idea, however, was taken over by his opponents, in particular by the organizers of the Inter-Associatif. They too had noted the crisis and wanted to counter it with an attempt at reunification. But instead of gathering individuals together, the Inter-Associatif federated institutions. The beginnings were difficult. But at the colloquium that brought together the former members of the EFP in the main amphitheater of the Sorbonne for the first time after ten years of separation, there was an atmosphere of happiness, celebration, and conviviality. The daily newspaper *Libération* reported the meeting under the headline: "The sons of Lacan are reunited" (*ré-unis*, with a hyphen—a pun on *réunis* without a hyphen, meaning simply "met together"). Patrick Guyomard, who had earlier been critical of Leclaire, didn't hesitate to declare: "His initiative triggered things off. To begin with, everyone was against the founding of an order. . . . But his analysis of the situation was accurate."[5]

Still, the increase in the number of groups doesn't reflect a real growth in the number of psychoanalysts but rather a development that has been characteristic of the Lacanian movement from the beginning. Though it wished to be orthodox, it was doomed to dissidence, and its whole history has been punctuated by recurrent schisms. The pattern is reminiscent of a short session, with its breaks, its subversion, and its revolutions. Unlike the IPA, with its long sessions and its construct of time as a kind of eternal return, Lacanianism has always been and still is the history of a perpetual acting-out, the momentary adventure, a kind of surrealist time. In this "acting of history" there's a trace of the famous French exception, mentioned earlier. France, in fact, is the only country in the world where for over a hundred years everything has combined to favor a massive introduction of psychoanalysis into all sectors of cultural life, via both intellectual and medical channels. Lacanianism reflects the "French exception" in that it was consciously created as an act of subversion, a transgression, inheriting an ideal of protest against the established order that derived partly from the French Revolution and partly from the Dreyfus affair.

The French exception found its main expression through surrealism, through the great Husserlian gesture of phenomenology, and through structuralism. But socially and politically it was only possible in a Europe influenced first by the victory of fascism in Germany, which drove the avant-garde of Freudian thought into exile, and later by the division decided at Yalta, which froze any possibility of development in psychoanalysis in Eastern Europe.

This history ends now with the collapse of the communist system, the fall of the Berlin Wall, and the awakening of national conflicts in central Europe, the crucible where Freudianism was forged. It was central Europe that gave Western psychoanalysis its form, its bearings, its geography. For sixty years, as far as Russia was concerned, and for fifty in the satellite countries, Freudianism had no legal existence: no movement, no doctrine, no institutions. This is no longer the case in 1993, where the introduction of free government, however embryonic or frail, is bound to reactivate Freudian thought. But in what form?

Psychoanalysis, which is based first and foremost on the golden rule requiring a period of time on the analyst's couch, can be practiced freely only when its own liberty is guaranteed by the existence of a free or lawful state—one that sets limits to its power over its citizens and respects those limits. The existence of such a state explains why psychoanalysis has developed in the United States, in those European countries that have best resisted fascism, and in the Latin American countries that have freed themselves from dictatorship. It has not established itself in the parts of the world that have been ruled by communism or Nazism or wherever there is no free and lawful state.

Because its existence is guaranteed by such a state, psychoanalysis is free to construct its own training models, its own rules, groups, sects, associations, and parties, just as analysts themselves, like members of political parties or other groups of citizens, are free to tear one another to pieces.

This collective freedom, having invented its own rules, applies them to itself through the two great training models that now prevail throughout the world psychoanalytic movement: the IPA and the AMP. Both are legitimist; i.e., both legally and by family inheritance, they are the guardians of an official image of the movement, its doctrine, and its practice. For a long while it was Anna Freud who embodied legitimism in the IPA. Today the force of her heritage has faded. In the Lacanian international, it is a family that dominates the scene, with Jacques-Alain Miller as political leader and executor to a body of work, with Judith Miller as heiress to a legacy and manager of communications, and with Gérard Miller, Jacques-Alain Miller's brother, as treasurer to the institutions.

The IPA model admits all kinds of doctrinal divergence but forbids any breaking of the technical rules. The Millerian model, on the other hand, tolerates no doctrinal divergence but imposes no technical rules with regard to the training of analysts. Experience shows that a psychoanalytic empire ensures its own strength better by insisting on obedience to technical rules than by dragooning its members in the matter of doctrine. This is because the first demand is more compatible than the second with the democratic liberties essential to the practice of psychoanalysis. Doctrinal dragooning always ends in narrowness, technical constraint, sclerosis. That being so, it is unlikely that Millerian internationalism will ever be as powerful as the IPA.

Lacanianism, born of subversion and a wish to transgress, is essentially doomed to fragility and dispersion. That is why Lacanian legitimism (Millerian) is in a minority in almost all the countries where it has been introduced since Lacan's death. By trying to impose an extremely centralized structure, a near-deification of Lacan himself, and a rigid theoretical line, it has contradicted the essence of the original movement, which was plural, Promethean, baroque, and unsuited to unanimity.

Its apparent institutional strength only masks its internal weakness and the difficulty it has in admitting contradiction. In order to exist on a world scale, Millerian Lacanianism has to confront externally the opposition it refuses to countenance within itself. This is why it is always fighting against the IPA, which it still sees as the absolute other, the devil, the "gang" that dared to exclude the true god from the pantheon. Thirty years after the event, Stockholm is still a nightmare to the family of the master, as if history stopped at the gates of Gripsholm castle.

So the great battle of the future will be the fight for Eastern Europe, which has already been colonized by both models. And since Lacanian legitimism is at present in a minority, there must be a third force within the

French form of Freudian renewal. And that third force is plural Lacanianism, which is largely in the majority in France, with its nineteen flourishing associations. It also exists in Argentina, Brazil, and even in Italy, where many groups have managed to establish themselves despite the disastrous policy of Lacan himself, who supported Armando Verdiglione.[6] The Italian societies include Cosa freudiana, the Centro lacaniano Napoli, and the Associazione freudiana de Torino.[7]

In France it will soon be twenty years since psychoanalysis ceased to be the prerogative of an elite, as it had been in the 1950s, when only brilliant doctors and philosophers had access to Freudian culture. By the same token, it has withdrawn from the terrain that made its implantation possible in the first place: on the one hand the terrain of psychiatry, which lent it the luster of a humanist tradition derived from Enlightenment philosophy and the study of madness, and on the other hand the intellectual terrain, from which it drew its subversive and theoretical aspects. But although psychoanalysis has lost its elitism by moving away from these two grounds and toward mass practice, it has also fallen back on a professionalism that uses the deliberately incomprehensible vocabulary of technocrats. This seems to be the way the history of the French exception is ending.

Psychoanalytic societies are to a large extent affected by the same problems that confront society as a whole. Having stopped seeing themselves as an avant-garde and lost the right to regard themselves as an elite, their members share both the ideals and shortcomings of the circles in which they live and work: desire for individual success, love of conformity, lack of critical judgment, narcissistic anguish, willing subservience to those higher up the social scale. As for the psychoanalytic groups as such, each one, whatever its tendency, is now a kind of protective cocoon. The vocabulary changes from group to group, but the jargon is always the same: it imitates an elitism that is irrevocably dead but not yet buried and forgotten.[8]

The end of the French exception manifests itself in the field of contemporary Lacanianism by a curious cleavage. As far as philosophical discourse and academic learning are concerned, Lacan's work has become an *object of thought*, detached from any clinical implications or institutional consequences. It has been *secularized* at the same time as it has been incorporated into French intellectual history, together with the work of Barthes, Foucault, and Lévi-Strauss. The best example of this secularized reading of Lacan occurred in May 1990 at an international conference organized by René Major at the Collège international de philosophie. The theme of the conference was "Lacan with the philosophers,"[9] and it was attended by psychoanalysts of all persuasions, philosophers, historians, logicians, and experts on antiquity. Alain Badiou read a paper on Lacan's use of Plato; Philippe Lacoue-Labarthe and Nicole Loraux spoke about Antigone; René Major dealt with the Derridean trend in psychoanalysis; Jacques Derrida gave a talk on his relationship with Lacan; Jean-Claude Milner raised the question of the status of science. Bertrand Ogilvie took part in the colloquium, together with Pierre Macherey, Etienne Balibar, and Mikkel Borch-Jacobsen: i.e., more or less all the heirs of Althusser, Foucault, Canguilhem, and Derrida. The gathering showed the extent to which Lacan's work still divided his various readers. At the heart of the debate, in the course of which Lacan's use of Heidegger was called into question, lay the general problem of the philosophical status of Lacan's theories. In this philosophical context arguments raged around the interpretation of Lacan's work just as fiercely as they did in psychoanalytic circles.[10]

Regarding the secularization of Lacan's work by philosophers and academics, it is worth noting that two great books have appeared in the last decade: *Les Noms indistincts* (Indistinct names), by Jean-Claude Milner, and *La Grande Résurrection d'Alamût* (The great resurrection at Alamût), by Christian Jambet.[11] Both authors are former members of the GP; the former has become a specialist in linguistics, and the latter an expert in Shia Islam, in the line of Henry Corbin, whose pupil he once was. Both books are superbly written and make excellent use of the "last Lacan," the Lacan of RSI (real-symbolic-imaginary), to speak of the melancholy of our age, the end of revolution, suicide, madness, and the loss of identity among those once known as the structuralist generation. The most extreme forms of freedom are also examined, against a background of twelfth-century Iran. And if the planet Borromeo is present in both books, it is there not in the form of strip cartoons or slogans, but as a quest for the same absolute that haunted the last days of the master in the rue de Lille.

In the psychoanalytic movement itself, on the other hand, Lacan's work is treated as if it were holy writ. As a transferential space par excellence, it acts as a founding discourse in which every group may seek guidance as to how to organize itself. This contrast between two ways of approaching Lacan's thought didn't exist in so pronounced a form while he was still alive, partly because he himself always tried to be extraterritorial, and partly because the popularization of the movement was then much less advanced.

The ECF, isolated in its fortress, produces mainly apologetic texts outside any learned or scientific tradition. The "establishment" method applied to the Seminar is followed in most Millerian publications: no notes, references, or critical apparatus. Anonymity and the group have taken over from individuals, whose object is to merge with the masses. François Leguil likes to describe himself as a "neighborhood psychoanalyst," hating elitism and all kinds of petty authoritarianism.[12]

As a result, the two chief books on Lacan produced by the legitimist school are collections of militant articles published under the aegis of the ruling family: Gérard Miller edited the first; Judith Miller wrote the second, an album of handsome photographs, with captions firmly in the tradition of *The Lives of the Saints*.[13] In his *Lacan*, published in 1986, Gérard Miller writes a lengthy apologia for Jacques-Alain Miller: "He is not one of the coauthors of this book. He is more. For over ten years his lectures and his weekly seminar at the University of Paris VIII have paved the way for a sound and rational reading of Jacques Lacan's work. All those involved in writing this book are following or have followed his teaching and have been influenced by his comments on the *Ecrits* and the seminars, the text of which he was asked to establish by Lacan himself."[14] The book ends with bibliographical references in which *The Seminar* has a page to itself, as if it were Lacan's most important work, thanks to Miller's establishing of the text. The *Ecrits* are quoted in a secondary position and dealt with in three lines; François Wahl's name is not mentioned. The book itself is an elementary account of Lacan's main theorems.

Connaissez-vous Lacan? (Do you know Lacan?), published in 1992, contains a number of texts commemorating the tenth anniversary of Lacan's death. He is presented as a Great Helmsman, an "implacable obstetrician of being," who "saved Freud from the disaster of oblivion and betrayal."[15]

The generalized practice of isolation and self-sufficiency has separated the members of the ECF from the history of Lacanianism proper. It is a Lacan done over by Miller, who is now the object of reference. The son-in-law gives a regular lunchtime seminar in which he comments on and imitates the seminars of his father-in-law. This mass is attended by a sympathetic congregation of four hundred people, half of whom are Spanish-speaking, half French-speaking. These orphans of the Lacan saga, identifying with the living replica of the dead father, feel they are assisting at the resurrection, from some intemporal void, of a word thought to be lost forever but suddenly reactivated in a kind of conjured catharsis. Unlike other Lacanians, ECF militants hardly ever go outside their own institutions, even if they recognize that plural Lacanianism exists. It wouldn't occur to them to go to former members of the EFP, or to analysts belonging to other groups, for controls or supplementary "*tranches*" of analysis. So they analyze one another, as between "brothers" of the same generation, like the pioneers. That's why they are so intent on promoting clinical teaching.

This is probably a way, which has parallels in other Lacanian groups, of dealing with the fact that Lacan, unlike Freud and the leading lights of the Anglo-American movement, never published a case (with the exception of his thesis, and in that instance, as we know, he didn't actually "treat" his patient). Just as he proposed his theory as a return to Freud's meaning, so he developed his clinical teaching by means of commentaries on important cases in the history of Freudianism. His heirs are thus faced with the problem of trying to derive a Lacanian clinical doctrine from a commentary on a commentary.

Most of the leaders of the ECF were analyzed by Lacan between 1970 and 1980. So they went through the dizzying experience of the gradually shrinking session. And as that experience cannot be acknowledged, except in terms of hagiography, they repeat with their own analysands the practice they encountered in the master's lair in the rue de Lille. So far none of them has dared actually to do away altogether with timed sessions, but a quarter of an hour has become the norm at the ECF. Some members no longer make fixed appointments, and some have reduced the length of the session to only five minutes. A good many Latin Americans are analyzed in this manner: once a year they fly to Paris for a month, during which they have three or four fifteen-minute sessions a day. This keeps the empire safely centralized.

The institution itself is organized like a centralized state, with networks and cells. Ten research sections correspond to a division of labor and power between the ECF itself and the psychoanalysis department at Paris VIII. The section for clinical and advanced studies, directed by Gérard Miller, is the model for all the others. The Instance de réflexion sur les mathèmes analytiques (IRMA) aims at rationalizing Lacan's teaching and at "total transmission, or the possible matheme"; its work is coordinated by Jacques-Alain Miller. The Céréda is a network aimed at promoting an international Lacanian clinical doctrine of child psychoanalysis. The action committee includes Rosine Lefort, Jacques-Alain Miller, and Judith Miller. GREPS is a group for psychosomatic research; Jacques-Alain Miller is one of its advisers. GRETA—another acronym—deals with drug addiction and alcoholism. The Groupe de recherche en topologie clinique (GRTC) goes in for Borromean knots. The seminars produced by the CF guarantee the delivery of a faithful transcription of ECF doctrine all over the world. The Groupe de recherche et d'application des concepts psychanalytiques à la psychose (Group for research in and the application of psychoanalytic concepts to psychosis) deals with psychiatry in France and abroad. The Collège freudien organizes ongoing training, which is directed by Dominique Miller (with Serge Cottet). Lastly, the network Scilicet II collates CF publications worldwide,[16] with *Ornicar?* at the center—though its appearance has been interrupted. Since 1992 there has also been an Association cause freudienne (ACF), whose job it is to promote Millerian psychoanalysis in the French provinces, of course in relation to the ECF.[17]

The bureaucratic complexity of the Millerian international is thus in complete contradiction to the simplicity and transparency that Lacan had in mind in 1964. And this proliferation of networks, cells, and groups is due to the fact that the ECF is still obsessed, ten years after its foundation, with the question of its original legitimacy. The doubt hanging over the authenticity of texts founding a school adopted by a Lacan who could scarcely speak remains, since Laurence Bataille's resignation, an essential factor in the short history of Millerian neo-Lacanianism. And the major crisis in the winter of 1989, which resulted in the expulsion of Gérard Pommier and Catherine Millot's resignation, unfolded against the background of this suspicion.

In September 1989 Pommier published a book entitled *La Névrose infantile de la psychanalyse* (The infantile neurosis of psychoanalysis). It contained the following passage:

Although his approach has been rejected by most psychoanalysts, J.-A. Miller, Lacan's son-in-law, nonetheless assumes a tone of legitimacy, whether it be in the media, toward the authorities, or in the university. . . . In Jean Clavreul's recent book *Le Désir et la loi* [Desire and the law], we read that "the letter of dissolution dated January 5, 1980, and all of the seminar read publicly by Lacan during the months that followed, were written by J.-A. Miller." Such a thing in itself is not illegal, and there are precedents for it. So why has J.-A. Miller always denied it? Why not admit that Lacan asked him for help, unless it's because that period and those texts have enabled him to ensure his own legitimacy?[18]

The attack wasn't very courteous, especially on the part of someone who had supported Miller in his enterprises. At the ECF's annual "open days," Gérard Miller withdrew the offending work from the sales display, upon which Pommier sent the bookstalls flying. But behind the incident lay a fundamental problem, as Jacques-Alain Miller well knew. So he went on the offensive and carried out a cultural revolution in the best traditions of his Maoist past. Launching an operation known as Acier l'ouvert, he explained that the crisis in the school "went to its very foundations. . . . The incidents that have accelerated it are of little importance in comparison with its logic. In the light of the present situation, it is clear that the crisis was inevitable. I mean it was there from the outset in the school's genetic program and handed down from school number 1 to school number 2."

A kind of autobiographical narrative followed, in which Miller demanded that he should be answered and questioned without fear or favor. "For ten years I have used the pronoun *one* instead of *I,* done my best to disappear behind the collective signature of the school's various agencies, and tried to give their texts the assured and impersonal tone that reflected the general will. Much good it did me. It's 'Jacques-Alain Miller by name' that they want. They harass him, they track him down, they flush him out with pikes and guns and flamethrowers. Well, all right: you win. Here I am. From now on I say 'I' in the school. Now see if you're any better off." Miller went on to talk about the past and the EFP, which he described as a "hydra." "Is it you who are making me abandon my reserve? No, it's She. The Beast. The Hydra of Lefpe. I've tried to tackle her often, ever since I was twenty. I thought I had beaten her, I thought all her heads had been cut off and the beast herself was no more. And now I suddenly see her rise up again in front of me in the very middle of the school, large as life, with all her legs and all her heads still there, slavering, grimacing, shrieking, and trying to snare me in an ignominious Nessus' shirt."[19]

For several months the ECF was swept by a tide of insurrection, but its system remained unchanged. A large group of practitioners, among them some former members of the EFP who had been loyal to Miller out of respect for Lacan's choice, left the ship and started a new group called Dimensions freudiennes. The break came over the question of the pass.

The blow of Catherine Millot's departure was all the greater because it echoed that of Laurence Bataille. Millot was beautiful, intelligent, talented, and respected. She had been adopted by the Miller family when she entered into analysis with Lacan in 1971 after studying philosophy at the Sorbonne. She became a member of the EFP, then a teacher at Paris VIII, and so formed part of the legitimist harem for a couple of decades. When Lacan died, out of loyalty to his decisions she joined the ECF, where she underwent a control with Michel Silvestre and a second "*tranche*" with Brigitte Lemérer.[20] This is what she wrote by way of farewell to those she felt close to in a school afflicted from the start by "a fundamental doubt":

To give pride of place to founding texts and writings on whose authenticity a doubt had been cast was to turn those texts and writings into the object of an act of faith. Everyone, by belonging to the ECF was supposed to guarantee that authenticity. . . . It was also to make those texts the object of a collective hypnosis: mesmerized by the question of whether they were false or genuine or genuinely false, people failed to see the object of the exercise. It was really a sleight of hand, installing a collective superego that guaranteed everyone's willing subjection to the supposed last wishes of Lacan, of whom the agencies of the school were to be the interpreters, and whose "moral heir" becomes when necessary his mouthpiece.[21]

But although he has made an oversimplified and reductive interpretation of Lacan's work, Miller has not led the movement of which he is the leader to break with the fundamental position that lay behind that work. In other words, the Miller school still claims to be Freudian. It preserves the idea that Lacan is connected to the history of Freudianism by his return to Freud's own texts. But how long will this last, if confusion persists between Lacan's own concepts and Miller's reading of them? Either it is possible to dissociate Freud's original thinking from Lacan's interpretation of it, in which case one can separate Lacan's teaching from that of his son-in-law, or else one merges the two teachings together and risks the delusion that Freud was a Lacanian *avant la lettre*.

That is the major theoretical problem posed by the "fundamental doubt" hanging over the origins of the ECF and the publication of the seminars. All French Lacanians are threatened by it, since Lacan himself never expressed in theoretical form the status he attributed to his reading of Freud. I have shown many times how he used to attribute to Freud innovations that were really his own.

A careful reading of all the texts now devoted to the Lacanian concept of *foreclosure* reveals, the presence of such a danger. At best, the commentators perceive that foreclosure does not exist as a concept in Freud's work. They then point to *Verwerfung* as a Freudian notion of rejection that was subsequently conceptualized by Lacan. But sometimes they make no mention of the borrowing from Pichon and the debate about scotomization, and sometimes they do the opposite and credit Pichon with having made an "already Lacanian" interpretation of the Freudian unconscious. At worst, the commentators "hallucinate" the presence of a concept of foreclosure in Freud, which they call *Verwerfung*, and then point out that Lacan translated it as *foreclosure*, extending its application to the understanding of psychoses. In such cases, the Pichon connection is passed over in silence.[22] In these circumstances we shall see more and more readers asking bookshops for Freud's "famous" texts on foreclosure. "This request has become increasingly frequent since Lacan died," says Thierry Garnier.[23]

Of course, among Freudians who are not Lacanians or who are anti-Lacanians or "de-Lacanianized," there will be no such confusion. But there is also a different danger: that of entirely underestimating Lacan's interpretation and thinking it possible to go back to a primeval, "Germanic" Freud, freed from the "carapace" of Frenchness imposed first by Pichon and then by Lacan. This was the reason behind the project for a translation of Freud's complete works to be carried out by a team under Jean Laplanche and André Bourguignon, which provoked an avalanche of controversy in 1988.[24]

The ELP is today the group most threatened by a breaking of the pact of continuity. And yet the most original researches on Lacan's work have been produced by its members, including Erik Porge, Philippe Julien, Guy Le Gaufey, Danièle Arnoux, Jean Allouch, and several of the people who write for the review *Littoral*. But as the ELP was the first to approach a rupture by calling itself "Lacanian" instead of "Freudian," it is in great danger, should a certain tendency come to prevail in it, of abolishing the historic continuity between Freud's work and Lacan's, and using Lacan's theories as a kind of hallucinatory and mystical hermeneutics.

The CFRP, at the heart of the French psychoanalytic movement of the

1990s, has become the association most representative of a plural Lacanianism open to all the components of Freudianism, including the IPA. This means it is constantly growing and so in danger of overexpansion. Two reasons, unforeseeable in 1985, lie behind this spectacular success: collegiality and the abandoning of the pass. By renouncing the latter, which, valid though it might have been, did lead to folly, the CFRP accepted the idea of a Lacanianism that was moderate in the matter of training—a mixture of the IPA and the former EFP—though of course running the risk of eclecticism. As for collegiality, it has helped the fourth and fifth generations to occupy positions of real power without always having to squabble with their elders, as was the case in the other groups led by Lacan's comrades, members of the third generation. In this connection, Maud Mannoni, who is still a member of the IPA through her affiliation with the Belgian society, plays a unifying role similar to that of Serge Leclaire. The fact that a woman has brought about the conditions necessary for a conflictual return of the Freudian heritage within a Lacanian heritage that is itself conflictual may have something to do with the stir the matter has caused.

One question remains: where are the present-day practitioners of the unconscious who never write books and reject with equal vigor jargon, bureaucracy, and indoctrination? It is difficult to say. And yet they do exist, and they do work. Sometimes, out of loyalty, they stay in their respective groups, though avoiding standardization; sometimes they withdraw from associations and go into internal exile, remembering Freud himself was in the first instance a dissident Jew and a permanent prey to doubt.

Still others circulate freely among all the groups in search of a difference. Hence the emergence—a new phenomenon in France—of a kind of "culturalism" that may study other listening techniques or ponder the history of psychoanalysis—a field, incidentally, that is simmering with excitement— and find through confronting the past an answer to questions being asked in the present. These practitioners have studied clinical practice and theory with Freud, Winnicott, Melanie Klein, Dolto, Lacan, and Ferenczi. They have worked in caring institutions with emigrants, the insane, marginals, children, AIDS sufferers, and, in their own consulting rooms, victims of ordinary neurosis and depression. They are of all ages and persuasions, and they are the future of psychoanalysis, its honor and its passion.

One thing is certain, at all events. They no longer believe, as people once did, that one technique is necessarily better than another. And while they claim to be rigorously Freudian, they try to modify their way of listening to the unconscious in the light of the changes that have come about in the last ten years, not only in the psychoanalytic movement but also in the speech of their analysands. For patients have changed, their troubles now all the more visible and their appeals for help all the louder because they are daily confronted with powerful ideals of social success, liberal consensus, fanaticism, the occult, and scientism. And they want something other than a scanning, a matheme, or a stopwatch. They too have lost the bearings that enabled the previous generation to choose one technique, one theory, or one school. These practitioners, and their analysands, will probably give yet another new impetus to Freud's discoveries.

May this book be seen as a tribute to their silent history.

APPENDIX A

• • • • • •

Members of the International Psychoanalytical Association (1993)

Regional Associations

American Psychoanalytic Association
Affiliate Societies of the American Psychoanalytic Association
Approved Training Institutes of the American Psychoanalytic Association

Component Societies

Argentine Psychoanalytic Association
Australian Psychoanalytical Society
Belgian Psychoanalytical Society
Brazilian Psychoanalytical Society of Rio de Janeiro
Brazilian Psychoanalytical Society of São Paulo
British Psychoanalytic Society
Buenos Aires Psychoanalytical Association
Canadian Psychoanalytic Society
Chilean Psychoanalytic Association
Colombian Psychoanalytic Society
Danish Psychoanalytic Society
Dutch Psychoanalytic Society
Finnish Psychoanalytic Society
French Psychoanalytic Association
German Psychoanalytic Association
Hungarian Psychoanalytic Society
Indian Psychoanalytic Society
Israel Psychoanalytic Society
Italian Psychoanalytic Society
Japan Psychoanalytic Society
Madrid Psychoanalytical Association
Mendoza Psychoanalytic Society
Mexican Psychoanalytic Association
Norwegian Psychoanalytical Society
Paris Psychoanalytical Society
Peru Psychoanalytic Society

Porto Alegre Psychoanalytic Society
Portuguese Psychoanalytical Society
Rio de Janeiro Psychoanalytic Society
Spanish Psychoanalytical Society
Swedish Psychoanalytical Society
Swiss Psychoanalytical Society
Uruguayan Psychoanalytic Association
Venezuelan Psychoanalytic Association
Viennese Psychoanalytical Society

Provisional Societies

Caracas Psychoanalytic (Provisional) Society
Cordoba Psychoanalytic (Provisional) Society
Institute for Psychoanalytic Training and Research (IPTAR) (Provisional Society)
Los Angeles Institute and Society for Psychoanalytic Studies (LAISPS) (Provisional Society)
Monterey Psychoanalytic (Provisional) Society
New York Freudian (Provisional) Society
Psychoanalytic Center, California (PCC) (Provisional Society)

Study Groups

Hellenic Psychoanalytical Study Group
Pelotas Psychoanalytic Study Group
Recife Psychoanalytic Study Group

Europe

Austria	Viennese Psychoanalytical Society
Belgium	Belgian Psychoanalytical Society
Denmark	Danish Psychoanalytical Society
Finland	Finnish Psychoanalytical Society
France	French Psychoanalytical Association
	Paris Psychoanalytical Society
Germany	German Psychoanalytical Association
Greece	Hellenic Psychoanalytical Study Group
Hungary	Hungarian Psychoanalytical Society
Italy	Italian Psychoanalytical Society
The Netherlands	Dutch Psychoanalytical Society
Norway	Norwegian Psychoanalytical Society
Portugal	Portuguese Psychoanalytical Society
Spain	Spanish Psychoanalytical Society
	Madrid Psychoanalytical Association
Sweden	Swedish Psychoanalytical Society
Switzerland	Swiss Psychoanalytical Society
United Kingdom	British Psychoanalytical Society

Latin America

Argentina	Argentine Psychoanalytic Association
	Buenos Aires Psychoanalytical Association

	Cordoba Psychoanalytic (Provisional) Society
	Mendoza Psychoanalytic Society
Brazil	Brazilian Psychoanalytical Society of Rio de Janeiro
	Brazilian Psychoanalytical Society of São Paulo
	Rio de Janeiro Psychoanalytic Society
	Pelotas Psychoanalytic Study Group
	Porto Alegre Psychoanalytic Society
	Recife Psychoanalytic Study Group
Chile	Chilean Psychoanalytic Association
Colombia	Colombian Psychoanalytic Society
Peru	Peru Psychoanalytic Society
Uruguay	Uruguayan Psychoanalytic Association
Venezuela	Caracas Psychoanalytic (Provisional) Society
	Venezuelan Psychoanalytic Association

North America

Canada	Canadian Psychoanalytic Society
Mexico	Mexican Psychoanalytic Association
	Monterey Psychoanalytic (Provisional) Society
USA	American Psychoanalytic Association
	Affiliate Societies of the American Psychoanalytic Association
	Approved Training Institutes of the American Psychoanalytic Association
	Institute for Psychoanalytic Training and Research (IPTAR) (Provisional Society)
	Los Angeles Institute and Society for Psychoanalytic Studies (LAISPS) (Provisional Society)
	New York Freudian (Provisional Society)
	Psychoanalytic Center, California (PCC) (Provisional Society)

Middle and Far East

India	Indian Psychoanalytical Society
Israel	Israel Psychoanalytic Society
Japan	Japan Psychoanalytic Society

Australia

Australia	Australian Psychoanalytical Society

A P P E N D I X   B

• • • • • • •

IPA: *World Distribution**

This list reproduces, without updates or corrections, the similar table provided in the second Fayard edition of the French original, published in 1993.

Country	Institution	Number of Members	
		1985	*1992*
USA	Institute for Psychoanalytic Training and Research	★	78
	Los Angeles Institute for Psychoanalytic Studies	★	42
	The N.Y. Freudian Society	★	168
	Psychoanalytic Center of California	★	20
	American Psychoanalytic Association (5 affiliated societies; 4 study groups; 27 institutes)	2,100	2,639
	TOTAL	2,100	2,947
Canada	Canadian Psychoanalytic Society (Société canadienne de psychanalyse; 6 branches: CPS, Montreal, Toronto, Ottawa, Alberta, Ontario)	270	342
Argentina	Asociacion Psicoanalitica Argentina	420	693
	Asociacion Psicoanalitica de Buenos Aires	160	273
	Asociacion Psicoanalitica de Mendoza	12	27
	TOTAL	592	1005
Brazil	Sociedade Brasileira de Psicoanalise do Rio de Janeiro	150	128
	Sociedade Psicoanalitica do Rio de Janeiro	140	150
	Sociedade Brasileira de Psicanalise de São Paulo	200	251
	Sociedade Psicanalitica de Porto Alegre	30	42
	TOTAL	520	626
Chili	Asociacion Psicoanalitica chilena	30	36
Colombia	Sociedad Colombiana de Psicoanalisis	45	61
Uruguay	Asociacion Psicoanalitica del Uruguay	46	82
Venezuela	Asociacion Venezolana de Psicoanalisis	64	41

	Sociedad Psicoanalitica de Caracas★		
Belgium	Belgische Vereniging voor Psychoanalyse (Société belge de psychanalyse)	50	49
Great Britain	British Psychoanalytical Society	378	418
Denmark	Dansk Psykoanalytisk Selskat	26	30
The Netherlands	Nederlandse Vereniging voor Psychoanalyse	164	195
Finland	Suomen Psykoanalyyttinen Yhdistys Finlands Psykoanalytiska Förening	84	138
Mexico	Asociacion Psiconalitica Mexicana Asociacion Regiomontana de Psicanalisis	124	90 / 28
France	Association psychanalytique de France (APF)	50	51+ 100 students
	Société psychanalytique de Paris, Institut de psychanalyse (SPP)	418	419
West Germany	Deutsche Psychoanalytische Vereinigung (12 institutes)	390	651
Italy	Società Psicoanalitica Italiana (8 branches: Rome (2), Milan, Bologna, Florence, Palermo, Naples, Venice; 3 instituts)	300	428
Spain	Asociacion Psicoanalitica de Madrid	30	50
	Sociedad Española de Psicoanalisis (Barcelona)	23	53
	TOTAL	53	105
Norway	Norsk Psykoanalytisk Forening	38	44
Sweden	Svenska Psykoanalytiska Föreningen	114	138
Portugal	Sociedade Portuguesa de Psicanalise	23	31
Switzerland	Schweizerische Gesellschaft für Psychoanalyse (Société suisse de psychanalyse)	120	123
Austria	Wiener Psychoanalytische Vereinigung	25	54
India	Indian Psychoanalytical Society	36	30
Israel	Hahevra Hapsychoanalitite Be-Israel	70	74
Japan	Nippon Seishin-Bunseki Kyokai	22	31
Australia	Australian Psychoanalytical Society	35	55
Hungary	Ideiglenes Magyar Pzichoanalitikus Tarsasag	23	31
Peru	Sociedad Peruana de Psicoanalisis		24
Study Groups	Grupo de Estudios psicoanalitico de Pelotas		8
	Grupo de Estudios psicoanalitico de Recife		19
	Hellenic Psychoanalytical		10
	TOTAL	8435	

★Temporary societies

• • • • • •

IPA *Congresses (1908–1993)*

	Year	Place	President
1st	1908	Salzburg, Austria	Informal Meeting
2d	1910	Nuremberg, Germany	Carl G. Jung
3d	1911	Weimar, Germany	Carl G. Jung
4th	1913	Munich, Germany	Carl G. Jung

1914–1918: WORLD WAR I

5th	1918	Budapest, Hungary	Karl Abraham
6th	1920	The Hague, Holland	Ernest Jones (provisory)
7th	1922	Berlin, Germany	Ernest Jones
8th	1924	Salzburg, Austria	Ernest Jones
9th	1925	Bad Homburg, Germany	Karl Abraham
10th	1927	Innsbruck, Austria	Max Eitingon
11th	1929	Oxford, England	Max Eitingon
12th	1932	Wiesbaden, Germany	Max Eitingon
13th	1934	Lucerne, Switzerland	Ernest Jones
14th	1936	Marienbad, Czechoslovakia	Ernest Jones
15th	1938	Paris, France	Ernest Jones

1939–1945: WORLD WAR II

16th	1949	Zurich, Switzerland	Ernest Jones
17th	1951	Amsterdam, Holland	Leo Bartemeier
18th	1953	London, England	Heinz Hartmann
19th	1955	Geneva, Switzerland	Heinz Hartmann
20th	1957	Paris, France	Heinz Hartmann
21st	1959	Copenhagen, Denmark	William H. Gillespie
22d	1961	Edinburgh, Scotland	William H. Gillespie
23d	1963	Stockholm, Sweden	Maxwell Gitelson
24th	1965	Amsterdam, Holland	William H. Gillespie and Phyllis Greenacre

25th	1967	Copenhagen, Denmark	P. J. van der Leeuw
26th	1969	Rome, Italy	P. J. van der Leeuw
27th	1971	Vienna, Austria	Leo Rangell
28th	1973	Paris, France	Leo Rangell
29th	1975	London, England	Serge Lebovici
30th	1977	Jerusalem, Israel	Serge Lebovici
31st	1979	New York, USA	Edward D. Joseph
32d	1981	Helsinki, Finland	Edward D. Joseph
33d	1983	Madrid, Spain	Adam Limentani
34th	1985	Hamburg, West Germany	Adam Limentani
35th	1987	Montreal, Canada	Robert S. Wallerstein
36th	1989	Rome, Italy	Robert S. Wallerstein
37th	1991	Buenos Aires, Argentina	Joseph Sandler

The 38th in 1993 will be held in Amsterdam, Holland, and the 39th, in 1995, in San Francisco, USA.

APPENDIX D

• • • • • • •

Societies and Groups Not Belonging to the IPA★

★This list reproduces, without updates or corrections, the similar table provided in the second edition of the Fayard original, published in 1993.

France and Beyond	Number of Members 1985	1992
Organisation psychanalytique de langue française (OPLF; aka Quatrième Groupe; 1969)	25	
Collége de psychanalystes (1980)	122	153
Champ freudien (CF)		
Ecole de la cause freudienne (ECF; 1981; member AMP)	France 246	Belgium 41
	other countries 27	other countries 18
TOTAL:	273	315
Association freudienne (AF; 1982) (turned "international" in 1993)	123	258
Centre de formation et de recherches psychanalytiques (CFRP; 1982)	390	273 members 255 others
TOTAL:		528
Cercle freudien (1982)	5 founders	78
Cartels constituants de l'analyse freudienne (CCAF; 1983)	212	168
Ecole freudienne (1983)	50	
Fédération des ateliers de psychanalyse (1983)	54 + 63	
Convention psychanalytique (1983; Besançon)	212	184
Le Coût freudien (1983)		
Groupe régional de psychanalyse (GRP; 1983; Marseille)		
Errata (1983)	15	15
Société internationale d'histoire de la psychiatrie et de la psychanalyse (SIHPP; 1983)	165	263

Bibliothèque de recherche freudienne
et lacanienne (1985; Strasbourg)   15
Ecole lacanienne de psychanalyse (1985; Caracas-
Venezuela; member AMP)   45   120
Ecole propédeutique à la connaissance de l'inconscient
(EPCI; 1985)
Association internationale d'histoire de la psychanalyse
(AIHP; 1985)   60466 + 23 associations
La Psychanalyse actuelle (1985)
Séminaires psychanalytiques de Paris (SEPP; 1986)   230
Champ psychanalytique et social (1989)
Association pour une instance des psychanalystes
(APUI; January 22, 1990)   120
Echanges internationaux de recherches psychanalytiques
(March 1990; Aix-en-Provence)
Ecole européenne de psychanalyse (EEP; September 22/23,
1990; Paris-Barcelona; member AMP)
L'Inter-Associatif de psychanalyse (January 1991)   federation of 10
                                                                         associations

Fondation européenne pour la psychanalyse (April 1991)
Le Trait du cas (April 1991)
Dimensions freudiennes (October 12, 1991–May 7, 1994;
scission de l'ECF)
Escuela de la Orientacion lacaniana del Campo freudiano
(January 3, 1992; Buenos Aires, Argentina; member AMP
Association mondiale de psychanalyse (February 1, 1992;
Paris Pact, among AMP, ECF [Venezuela], EEF [Spain], ECF [France], EOLCF [Argentina])
Analyse freudienne (scission des CCAF; February 24, 1992)
Ecole de psychanalyse Sigmund Freud (May 8, 1994)
Esparu analytique (October 16, 1994)
Société de psychanalyse freudian (December 28, 1994)
France and beyond   TOTAL
35 associations + 2 IPA   34

Planned: Ecole brésilienne (member AMP) and Association russe (member IPA)

A P P E N D I X   E

• • • • • • •

Principal Reviews Established After 1985*

Ecole de la cause freudienne

Palea (Strasbourg)
L'Impromptu psychanalytique de Picardie (1987)
Pas tant (Toulouse)

Convention psychanalytique

Le Feuillet (Strasbourg, 1986)
Huit intérieur (Aix-en-Provence)
Césure (1991)

Association freudienne internationale

Le Trimestre psychanalytique (Grenoble, 1987)
L'Eclat du jour (1987)

Ecole lacanienne de psychanalyse

L'Unebévue (1992)

Errata

Les Carnets de psychanalyse (1991)

Association internationale d'histoire de la psychanalyse

Revue internationale d'histoire de la psychanalyse (5 numbers, 1988–1992)
Le Curieux (Strasbourg, 1985)
Trames (Nice, 1986)
Cahiers pour la recherche freudienne (Université de Paris X–Nanterre, 1986)
Apertura (Strasbourg, 1987)
L'Agenda de la psychanalyse (2 numbers, 1987–1988)
Io (1992)

*This list reproduces, without updates or corrections, the similar table provided in the second edition of the Fayard original, published in 1993.

Bibliography for Jacques Lacan's Article on the Family for the Encyclopédie française (1938)

Objects of Psychical Activity

The Family

Sociological Definition
Bonald. *Démonstration philosophique du principe constitutif de la société*. Le Clerc, 1830.
———. *Essai analytique sur les lois naturelles de l'ordre social*. Le Clerc, 1840.
Buytendijk, F. *Psychologie des animaux*. Trans. Bredo. Payot, 1928.
Comte, A. *Système de politique positive*. vols. 2 and 4. 1854.
Durkheim, E. "La famille conjugale." *Revue philosophique*, 1921.
Engels, F. *L'origine de la famille, de la propriété privée et de l'Etat*. Trans. Bracke. Costes, 1931.
Espinas, A. *Des sociétés animales*. 2d ed. 1878.
Fauconnet, P. "Les institutions juridiques et morales: La famille." Lecture at the Sorbonne, 1932.
Frazer, J. G. *Les origines de la famille et du clan*.
Fustel de Coulanges. *La cité antique*. Hachette, 1864.
Le Play. *La réforme sociale en France*. Vol. 3, *La famille*. Tours: Mame, 1878.
Lowie, R. *Traité de sociologie primitive*. Trans. Metraux. Payot, 1935.
Picard. *Les phénomènes sociaux chez les animaux*. Colin, 1933.
Rivers, A. "La mère." In Hastings, *Encyclopédie de religion et de morale*.
Westermarck, ed. *Histoire du mariage*. Trans. Varigny. Guillaumin, 1895.
Zuckerman, S. *La vie sexuelle et sociale des singes*. Trans. Petitjean. Gallimard, 1937.

Family Complexes: Weaning and Intrusion
Baudoin, C. *L'âme enfantine et la psychanalyse*. Neuchâtel: Delachaux, 1931.
Baudoin, C., Baar, Danzinger, Falf, Gedeon, and Hortner. *Kind und Familie*. Jena: Fischer, 1937.
Buhler, C. *Kindheit und Jugend: Genese des Bewusstseins*. Leipzig: Hirsel, 1931.
Buytendijk, F. J. J. "Les différences essentielles des fonctions psychiques de l'homme et des animaux." *Cahiers de philosophie de la nature*, vol. 4. Vrin, 1930.
Freud, S. "Au-delà du principe du plaisir." In *Essais de psychanalyse*. Trans. Jankélévitch. Payot, 1927.
Guillaume. *La psychologie de la forme*. Flammarion, 1937.
Isaacs, S. "Psychologie sociale des jeunes enfants." *Journal de psychologie*, 1931.

The entries in this bibliography match those in the original French version; for the convenience of the reader, however, the layout has been standardized, and the headings have been translated into English.

Kellogg, W. N., and L. A. Kellogg. *The Ape and the Child*. London: Wittlesey House; New York: McGraw-Hill, 1933.

Lacan, J. "Le stade du miroir." Congrès international de Marienbad, 1936.

Luquet, G. H. *Le dessin enfantin*. Alcan, 1935.

Preyer, W. *L'âme de l'enfant*. Trans. Varigny. Alcan, 1837.

Rank, O. H. *Don Juan: Une etude sur le double*. Trans. S. Lautman. Denoël, 1932.

——. *Le traumatisme de la naissance*. Trans. Jankélévitch. Payot, 1928.

Ruyer, R. *La conscience et le verbe*. Alcan, 1937.

The Oedipal Complex

Bachofen. "Das mutterrecht." Preface of *Le droit de la mère*. 1861. Groupe français d'études féministes, 1903.

Declareuil. *Rome et l'organisation du droit*. Bibliothèque de synthèse historique, vol. 19.

Durkheim, E. "Introduction à la sociologie de la famille." In *Annales de la Faculté des lettres de Bordeaux*. Leroux, 1888.

——. "La prohibition de l'inceste et ses origines." *Année sociale*. 1897.

Ferenczi, S. "Die Anpassung der Familie an das Kind." *Zeitschrift für Psychoanalytische Padagogik*, 1928.

Freud, S. *Totem et tabou*. Trans. Jankélévitch. Payot, 1925.

——. "Psychologie collective et analyse du moi." In *Essais de psychanalyse*. Trans. Jankélévitch. Paris: Payot, 1927.

Klein, L. "Les premiers stades du conflit oedipien." *Revue française de psychanalyse*, 1930–1931.

——. *Die Psychoanalyse des Kindes*. Vienna: Internat. Psychoanalytischer Verlag, 1932.

Lefebvre, C. *La famille en France dans le droit et dans les moeurs*. Giard, 1920.

Malinowski, B. *La sexualité et sa répression dans les sociétés primitives*. Trans. Jankélévitch. Payot, 1932.

——. *La vie sexuelle des sauvages du nord-ouest de la Mélanésie*. Trans. Jankélévitch. Payot, 1930.

Morganstern, S. "La psychanalyse infantile." *Hygiène mentale*, 1928.

Lord Raglan. *Le tabou de l'inceste*. Trans. Rambert. Payot, 1935.

Richard. *La femme dans l'histoire*. Doin, 1909.

Russell, B. *Le mariage et la morale*. Gallimard, 1930.

Sombart, W. *Le bourgeois*. Payot, 1926.

Studien über Autoritat und Familie. With summaries in French. Alcan, 1936.

Family Pathology: Psychoses

Ceillier, A. "Les influences, syndromes et psychoses d'influence." *L'Encéphale*, 1924.

Clérambault, G. de. "Les délires passionals, érotomanie, revendication, jalousie." *Bulletin social de médecine mentale*, 1921.

Guiraud, P. "Les meurtres immotivés." *Evolution psychiatrique*, 1931.

Kretschmer, E. *Die sensitive Beziehunghwahn*. Berlin: Springer, 1927.

Lacan, J. *De la psychose paranoïaque dans ses rapports avec la personnalité*. Le François, 1932.

——. "Motifs du crime paranoïaque." *Le Minotaure*, 1933.

Laforgue, R. "Schizophrénie et schizonoïa." *Revue française de psychanalyse*, 1927.

Legrand du Saulle. *Le délire des persécutions*. Paris: Plon, 1871.

Lowenstein, R. "Un cas de jalousie pathologique." *Revue française de psychanalyse*, 1932.

Meyer, A. "The Treatment of Paranoic and Paranoid States." In White and Jelliffe, *Modern Treatment of Nervous and Mental Diseases*. London, 1913.

Minkowski, E. "Jalousie pathologique sur fond d'automatisme mental." *Annales médico-psychologiques*, 1920.

Schiff, P. "Les paranoïas et la psychanalyse." *Revue française de psychanalyse*, 1935.

Sérieux and J. Capgras. *Les folies raisonnantes: Le délire d'interprétation*. Alcan, 1909.

———. "Les interprétateurs filiaux." *L'Encéphale*, 1910.

Neuroses

Freud, S. *Hemmung, Sympton und Angst*, esp. "La Psychanalyse," the introduction. Neurosenlehre, 1926.

———. *Cinq psychanalyses.* Trans. M. Bonaparte et R. Loewenstein. Denoël, 1936.

Hesnard, G., and R. Laforgue. "Les processus d'autopunition en psychologie des névroses et des psychoses." *Revue française de psychanalyse*, 1936.

Laforgue, R. "La névrose familiale." Conférence des psychanalystes de langue française.

Leuba, J. "La famille névrotique et les névroses familiales." *Revue française de psychanalyse*, 1936.

Odier, C. "La névrose obsessionnelle." *Revue française de psychanalyse*, 1927.

Pichon, E. "Sur les traitements psychothérapiques courts d'inspiration freudienne chez les enfants." *Revue française de psychanalyse*, 1928.

———. *Le développement psychique de l'enfant et de l'adolescent.* Masson, 1936.

Pichon, E., and R. Laforgue. "La névrose et le rêve: La notion de schizonoïa." In *Le rêve et la psychanalyse*. Maloine, 1926.

Pfister, O. "Die Behandlung schwereziehbarer und abnormer Kinder." *Schriften zur Seelenkunde und Erziehungskunst*, 1921.

———. "Die Liebe des Kindes und ihre Fehlentweicklungen." *Schriften zur Seelenkunde und Erziehungskunst*, 1922.

Jacques Lacan's Report Card

•   •   •   •   •   •   •

Jacques Lacan's Report Card

Lacan *Jacques* **Année Scolaire 19̶16̶ 19̶17̶**

NOTES DES PROFESSEURS ET DES SURVEILLANTS	COMMUNICATIONS FAITES AUX PARENTS
1ᵉʳ Trimestre	**1ᵉʳ Trimestre**
Maladif bon élève — Huyberechts Gênant ne peut faire comme les autres — Nouvel T. 13 - L. 14 - O. 14 - T 14. Très bon élève qui doit malheureusement limiter son effort — Calvet -16 - Très bon — Antoine -13-13- Bon élève, absent une classe sur deux — Rebull 14 L'application laisse un peu à désirer — Jolivald #16-9.15 - Très bon élève, travailleur, intelligent, paraît souvent fatigué obligé de s'excuser pour une leçon qu'il n'a pas eu le temps de préparer. Distribue-t-il bien ses heures de travail?	Jacques est un très bon élève malheureusement trop souvent absent. Ses efforts sont limités par sa santé et ne sait pas assez bien les distribuer. Peut-être un peu de vanité en est-il la cause?
2ᵉ Trimestre Durandin -	**2ᵉ Trimestre**
16. Appliqué et sérieux (Van den Driesch) 16.15. Bon élève (Gineste) 13. 14. 14. 14. Très bon élève ; un peu fantaisiste ; les progrès seraient plus sensibles s'il donnait tout son effort. (Calvet) 11.13. Travail régulier, résultats passables (Rebull) 15.15. Très bon élève, donne cette fâcheuse impression d'être ensuché, recollé de travail ou retenu par l'état de sa santé. (Durandin) 16. Très bon (Antoine) 12. Trop souvent absent pour faire des progrès (Jolivald) 15. Très bon élève (Beaussart)	La conduite de Jacques est toujours très bonne. Il est très bon élève, mais un peu fantaisiste. En sciences, les résultats sont très bons en physique, passables en math.
3ᵉ Trimestre	**3ᵉ Trimestre**

Facsimile of Lacan's Corrections to "Discours de clôture des journées sur les psychoses de l'enfant"

APPENDIX I

• • • • • • •

Genealogy

Jacques Lacan and His Close Family

Jacques-Marie Emile Lacan, born April 3, 1901, in Paris (3d Arrondissement); died September 9, 1981 in Paris (6th Arrondissement), buried at Guitrancourt (Yvelines).
Intern in psychiatric hospitals.
Married January 29, 1934, in Paris (17th Arrondissement) to Marie-Louise Blondin, born November 16, 1906, in Paris (17th Arrondissement); died September 23, 1983, in Paris (9th Arrondissement). Daughter of Paule-Marie Blondin, doctor, and Caroline Berthe Rousseau. Sister of Sylvain Blondin, born July 25, 1901, in Paris (17th Arrondissement); died January 8, 1975, in Neuilly-sur-Seine (Hauts-de-Seine). Married Denise Decourdemanche, June 25, 1928, divorced July 3, 1946; Madeleine Simon, July 16, 1949.
The marriage of Jacques Lacan and Marie-Louise Blondin was legally dissolved on December 15, 1941, by the civil tribunal of the department of the Seine. There were three children of this marriage:
Caroline Marie Image, born January 8, 1937; died in Antibes, May 30, 1973. Married June 26, 1958, in Paris (17th Arrondissement) to Bruno Roger, son of Max Roger and Madeleine Simon
Thibaut Lacan, born August 27, 1939. Married (his second marriage) Marie-Claude Béroud.
Sibylle, born November 26, 1940.
Remarried July 17, 1953, in Tholonet (Bouches-du-Rhône) to Sylvia Maklès, born November 1, 1908; died December 12, 1993, in Paris. Daughter of Henri Maklès and Nathalie Chohen. Divorced wife (August 9, 1946) of Georges Bataille, born September 10, 1897, in Billom (Puy-de-Dôme), died July 8, 1962, in Paris (6th Arrondissement), buried in Vézelay. Two children: Laurence, fathered by Bataille born June 10, 1930; died May 8, 1986, in Paris (14th Arrondissement). Judith, recognized as Lacan's daughter in 1964, born July 1941. Married in 1966 to Jacques-Alain Miller, born in Châteauroux (Indre), February 14, 1944.

His Siblings

Magdeleine-Marie Emmanuelle, born December 25, 1903, in Paris (3d Arrondissement). Married January 20, 1925, in Paris (6th Arrondissement), to Jacques Houlon.
Marc-Marie (later Marc-François), born December 25, 1908, in Paris (3d Arrondissement).

Facsimile of Lacan's Corrections to
"Discours de clôture des journées
sur les psychoses de l'enfant"

• • • • • • •

Genealogy

Jacques Lacan and His Close Family

Jacques-Marie Emile Lacan, born April 3, 1901, in Paris (3d Arrondissement); died September 9, 1981 in Paris (6th Arrondissement), buried at Guitrancourt (Yvelines).
Intern in psychiatric hospitals.
Married January 29, 1934, in Paris (17th Arrondissement) to Marie-Louise Blondin, born November 16, 1906, in Paris (17th Arrondissement); died September 23, 1983, in Paris (9th Arrondissement). Daughter of Paule-Marie Blondin, doctor, and Caroline Berthe Rousseau. Sister of Sylvain Blondin, born July 25, 1901, in Paris (17th Arrondissement); died January 8, 1975, in Neuilly-sur-Seine (Hauts-de-Seine). Married Denise Decourdemanche, June 25, 1928, divorced July 3, 1946; Madeleine Simon, July 16, 1949.
The marriage of Jacques Lacan and Marie-Louise Blondin was legally dissolved on December 15, 1941, by the civil tribunal of the department of the Seine. There were three children of this marriage:
Caroline Marie Image, born January 8, 1937; died in Antibes, May 30, 1973. Married June 26, 1958, in Paris (17th Arrondissement) to Bruno Roger, son of Max Roger and Madeleine Simon
Thibaut Lacan, born August 27, 1939. Married (his second marriage) Marie-Claude Béroud.
Sibylle, born November 26, 1940.
Remarried July 17, 1953, in Tholonet (Bouches-du-Rhône) to Sylvia Maklès, born November 1, 1908; died December 12, 1993, in Paris. Daughter of Henri Maklès and Nathalie Chohen. Divorced wife (August 9, 1946) of Georges Bataille, born September 10, 1897, in Billom (Puy-de-Dôme), died July 8, 1962, in Paris (6th Arrondissement), buried in Vézelay. Two children: Laurence, fathered by Bataille born June 10, 1930; died May 8, 1986, in Paris (14th Arrondissement). Judith, recognized as Lacan's daughter in 1964, born July 1941. Married in 1966 to Jacques-Alain Miller, born in Châteauroux (Indre), February 14, 1944.

His Siblings

Magdeleine-Marie Emmanuelle, born December 25, 1903, in Paris (3d Arrondissement). Married January 20, 1925, in Paris (6th Arrondissement), to Jacques Houlon.
Marc-Marie (later Marc-François), born December 25, 1908, in Paris (3d Arrondissement).

His Parents

Married June 23, 1900, in Paris (3d Arrondissement):

Alfred Charles Marie Paul Lacan, born April 12, 1873, in Orléans (Loiret); died October 15, 1960, in Boulogne-sur-Seine (Seine); buried in Château-Thierry (Aisne); described as "traveling salesman" and "commercial representative." In 1900 living at 95, boulevard Beaumarchais in Paris (3d Arrondissement), and in 1934 at 33, rue Gambetta in Boulogne-Billancourt.

Emilie Philippine Marie Baudry, born August 20, 1976, in Paris (3d Arrondissement); died November 21, 1948, in Boulogne-Billancourt. Daughter of Charles Baudry, born 1837, and of Marie-Anne Favier, born 1848.

His Paternal Grandparents

Married June 15, 1866, in Orléans:

Edmé Emile Lacan, born August 18, 1839, in Château-Thierry (Aisne); died 1915, in Paris. Described as a "merchant" at the time of his marriage, when he was living in Paris (3d Arrondissement), at 74, boulevard de Sébastopol.

Marie Julie Léonide Dessaux, born September 15, 1844, in Orléans; living with her parents at 2, rue des Africains, Orléans, at the time of her marriage.

Bride's witnesses: Pierre Eugène Greffier, maternal uncle, director of civil affairs in the Ministry of Justice, officer of the Legion of Honor, forty-six years old, resident in Paris; Sylvain Jules Dessaux, paternal uncle, clerk, forty-six years old, resident in Orléans.

His Maternal Grandparents

Married:

Charles Henry Baudry, born 1837, in Paris. Living on boulevard Saint-Denis, in Paris. In 1908 he was living in retirement in Paris (3d Arrondissement), at 88, boulevard Beaumarchais. A goldbeater by profession. See *Larousse du dix-neuvième siècle* (Paris, 1867), 2:377. Before the Revolution, the goldbeaters of Paris were a guild/corporation under the jurisdiction of the Cour des monnaies (the Mint).

Marie-Anne Favier, born 1848, sister of Joseph Favier, born 1843. As well as Emilie, Marie-Anne Favier and Charles Baudry had another daughter, Marie, who married Marcel Langlais. Their children were Roger, Antoine, Anne-Marie, and Jean.

His Paternal Great-Grandparents

Married:

Henri Louis Marie Lacan, born September 14, 1812, in Château-Thierry (Aisne); died April 15, 1896, in Château-Thierry; buried there. Merchant grocer in Château-Thierry, where he later retired. The *Almanach-Bottin* for 1840 lists "Grocery Lacan-Gilbert. Linen-Rouen goods" ["Rouennerie": cotton and woolen fabrics with patterns woven in from predyed threads] under the heading "Château-Thierry." Owned property in the rue de la Madeleine.

Laetitia Clémence Aimée Gilbert, born January 3, 1815 (in the reign of Louis XVIII). Buried in Château-Thierry.

Married October 7, 1835, in Orléans:

Charles-Laurent Dessaux, born September 20, 1814, in Orléans; died January 5, 1894, in Orléans; buried in the Dessaux chapel in the cemetery there. Vinegar manufacturer in Orléans. The factory, first in the rue des Trois-Marie, moved to two houses at the top of the rue de la Tour-Neuve and a building in the rue des Africains.

Marie-Thérèse Aimée Greffier, born June 8, 1814, in Orléans; died November 17, 1886, in Orléans; buried in Dessaux chapel in the cemetery there. Residing in 1835 at 17, rue de la Tour-Neuve in Orléans. Daughter of Pierre Greffier, merchant, and Marie-Catherine Vandais. Elder sister of Pierre Eugène Greffier, born 1819, in Orléans; died 1895, in Paris. At first a lawyer in Orléans, then a judge. Local legal distinctions, then senior member of the Council of State (1869) and member of the Court of Appeal (1870). Retired in 1894 as honorary president of the Court of Appeal. Commander of the Legion of Honor. "Learned jurisconsult." Published several books on law.

Bridegroom's witnesses: Louis Raymond Bompard, maternal uncle, master *grenetier* (grain chandler), aged thirty-two, resident of Orléans, at 6, rue de la Hallebarde; and Sylvain Bataille, cousin, dealer in refined oil, aged forty, resident in Orléans, at 11, rue Carroyerie.

Bride's witnesses: André Sylvestre Poignard, maternal great-uncle, former master goldsmith, rue Croix-Parc-Dieu, Orléans; and Noël Gabriel Masson, cousin, merchant, aged forty-nine, resident in Orléans, at 120, quai du Châtelet.

His Maternal Great-Grandparents

Unknown

His Paternal Great-Great-Grandparents

Married:

Antoine-Henry Lacan, born July 8, 1787, in La Fère-en-Tardenois (Aisne); died December 27, 1872 in Château-Thierry, at his house in the rue Neuve. Son of Laurent Lacan and Thérèse Pierrot. Merchant grocer in Château-Thierry. Listed on page 374 of the *Almanach-Bottin* for 1828, under the heading "Château-Thierry," as "Grocers and linen merchants: Lacan-Bachelet." Chevalier of the Legion of Honor. Described as "property-owner." Witnesses to his death: Henri Louis Marie Lacan, son, and Louis Pasquier, son-in-law, of independent means, aged sixty-nine and living in Soissons.

Louise Edmée Bachelet, born January 22, 1788, in Château-Thierry; died November 10, 1872, in Château-Thierry. Daughter of Edmé Nicolas Francois Bachelet and Marie-Marguerite Ozanne. Witnesses to her death: Henri Louis Marie Lacan, son, and Louis Pasquier, son-in-law (see above).

Married Léon Gilbert.

Clémentine Sarazin.

Married (first):

Charles Prosper Alexandre Dessaux, born about 1790, in Orléans; died February 13, 1861, in Orléans, at 60, rue de la Charpenterie, buried in the cemetery in Orléans. Son of Guillaume Philippe Dessaux, merchant draper, and Marie Françoise Griveau. Worked in the Greffier-Hazon vinegar factory, rue des Trois-Marie. Started his own vinegar factory in 1824. In 1826 went into partnership with Greffier-Vandais. After he became a widower he married Marie-Magdeleine Elisabeth Tessire. Witnesses to his death: Alfred Martin Jamet, son-in-law, merchant, aged fifty. Resident in Orléans, at 2, rue des Africains; and Louis Raymond Bompant, brother-in-law, property owner, aged fifty-seven, living at 31, rue d'Illiers, Orléans.

Pauline Eulalie Virard

Married:

Pierre Greffier, merchant in Orléans.

Marie-Catherine Vandais.

Abbreviations

Institutions and Reviews

AAAP	American Association for the Advancement of Psychoanalysis
AAGP	Allgemeine Arztliche Gesellschaft für Psychotherapie
ACF	Association cause freudienne
AE	analyste de l'école (EFP)
AF	Association freudienne
AIHP	Association internationale d'histoire de la psychanalyse
AME	analyste membre de l'école (EFP)
AMP	Association mondiale de psychanalyse
AP	analyste praticien (EFP)
APA	American Psychoanalytic Association
APF	Association psychanalytique de France
APUI	Association pour une instance des psychanalystes
BPS	British Psycho-Analytical Society
CCAF	Cartels constituants de l'analyse freudienne
CERF	Centre d'études et de recherches freudiennes
CERM	Centre d'études et de recherches marxistes
CF	Champ freudien
CFRP	Centre de formation et de recherches
CHU	Centre hospitalo-universitaire
CMPP	Centre médico-psycho-pédagogique
CNRS	Centre national de la recherche scientifique
CP	Convention psychanalytique
CPS	Champ psychanalytique et social
DPG	Deutsche Psychoanalytische Gesellschaft
DPV	Deutsche Psychoanalytische Vereinigung
DSM-III	*Diagnostic and Statistical Manual of Mental Disturbances* (third ed.)
ECF	Ecole de la cause freudienne
EEP	Ecole européenne de psychanalyse
EF	Ecole freudienne
EFP	Ecole freudienne de Paris
ELP	Ecole lacanienne de psychanalyse

EMP	Externat médico-pédagogique
ENS	Ecole normale supérieure
EOLCF	Escuela de la orientacíon lacaniana
EP	Evolution psychiatrique (group)
EP	Evolution psychiatrique (journal)
EPCI	Ecole propédeutique à la connaissance de l'inconscient
EPHE	Ecole pratique des hautes études
ESI	Editions sociales internationales
FAP	Fédération des ateliers de psychanalyse
FEP	Fondation européenne de psychanalyse
GEP	groupe d'études de la psychanalyse (study group)
GP	Gauche prolétarienne
GRP	Groupe régional de psychanalyse
GRTC	Groupe de recherche en topologie clinique
IJP	*International Journal of Psychoanalysis*
IMP	Internat médico-pédagogique
IP	Institut de psychanalyse
IPA	International Psychoanalytical Association
IRMA	Instance de réflexion sur les mathèmes analytiques
ME	membre de l'école (EFP)
MLF	Mouvement de libération des femmes
NC	*La Nouvelle Critique*
NRF	*Nouvelle Revue française*
NRP	*Nouvelle Revue de psychanalyse*
OPLF	Organisation psychanalytique de langue française (Quatrième Groupe)
PCF	Parti communiste français
RFP	*Revue française de psychanalyse*
RHLF	*Revue d'histoire littéraire de la France*
RIHP	*Revue internationale d'histoire de la psychanalyse*
SASDLR	*Le Surréalisme au service de la Révolution*
SBP	Société belge de psychanalyse
SFP	Société française de psychanalyse
SHC	Sciences humaines cliniques
SIHPP	Société internationale d'histoire de la psychiatrie et de la psychanalyse
SPP	Société psychanalytique de Paris
TM	*Les Temps modernes*
TQ	*Tel quel*
UEC	Union des étudiants communistes
UER	Unité d'enseignement de recherche
UJCML	Union des jeunesses communistes marxistes-léninistes
UV	Unité de valeur
WPA	World Psychiatric Association
WPV	Wiener Psychoanalytische Vereinigung

People

E.R.	Elisabeth Roudinesco
F.D.	Françoise Dolto
J.L.	Jacques Lacan
S.L.	Serge Leclaire
W.G.	Wladimir Granoff

Chief Archives

E.R.	Elisabeth Roudinesco
F.D.	Françoise Dolto
IMEC	Institut Mémoire de l'édition contemporaine
J.A.	Jenny Aubry
J.-A.M.	Jacques-Alain Miller
J.-L.D.	Jean-Luc Donnet
J.S.	Jacques Sédat
L.A.	Louis Althusser
M.-F.L.	Marc-François Lacan
H.E.	Henri Ey
R.M.	René Major
S.L.	Serge Leclaire
S.La.	Sibylle Lacan
W.G.	Wladimir Granoff
X.A.	Xavier Audouard

Bibliographical and Editorial References

HPF	Elisabeth Roudinesco, Histoire de la psychanalyse en France: La Bataille de cent ans, 2 vols. Paris: Seuil, 1986. All references to this work are to the 1994 Fayard edition, which has the same pagination.
JL & Co.	Jacques Lacan & Co.: A History of Psychoanalysis in France, 1925–1985, trans., Jeffrey Mehlman (Chicago: University of Chicago Press, 1990; London: Free Association Books, 1990). This is a translation of vol. 2 of HPF.
SE	Sigmund Freud, Standard Edition of the Complete Psychological Works, trans. under the general editorship of James Strachey, 24 vols. (London: Hogarth Press, in association with the Institute of Psycho-Analysis, 1953–1974).

By Jacques Lacan

E	Ecrits (Paris: Seuil, 1966).
EAS	Ecrits: A Selection, trans. Alan Sheridan (New York: Norton, 1977)
F "La famille"	(The family), article in vol. 8 of Encyclopédie française (Paris: Larousse, 1938); reprinted as Les complexes familiaux dans la formation de l'individu (Paris: Navarin, 1984)
S	the Seminar (generally followed by a Roman numeral identifying the seminar in question); italics signify that the seminar has been published
DPP	De la psychose paranoïaque dans ses rapports avec la personnalité (J.L.'s thesis) (Paris: Le François, 1932; rpt., Paris: Seuil, 1975)

Notes

Unless otherwise specified, all translations from the French are Barbara Bray's.

PART I: FATHER FIGURES

1. Vinegar Merchants

1. Claire Bellon and Georges Costes, *La Vinaigrerie Dessaux* (Orléans: Commission régionale de l'inventaire centre, 1984); *Journal de la Sologne et de ses environs* 47 (January 1985): 36; *Orléans* (bulletin issued by the city hall, March 4, 1990), pp. 52–55; Michelle Perrot, "Workers on Strike," in *Histories: French Construction of Past*, ed. Jacques Revel and Lynn Hunt, vol. 1 of *Postwar French Thought*, series ed. Ramona Naddaf, trans. Arthur Goldhommes and others (New York: New Press, 1995), pp. 413–422.

2. The Italian Cagliostro (Giuseppe Balsamo, 1743–1795) has always been confused with the Austrian Franz Anton Mesmer (1734–1815), proponent of "animal magnetism" (see Mesmer, *Maxims on Animal Magnetism*, trans. Jerome Eden [Mount Vernon, N.Y.: Eden, 1958]). Before the French Revolution both men belonged to Masonic lodges and mixed with cranks, but Mesmer was a genuine physician and scientist, the founder of early dynamic psychiatry. See *HPF* 1:51–84.

3. Conversation with Marc-François Lacan in October 1990.

4. Separate conversations with Marc-François Lacan, December 1, 1991, and with Henri Dessaux, April 30, 1990.

5. J.L., S. IX, session of December 6, 1961, transcribed by Michel Roussan.

6. Letter from Marc-François Lacan to E.R., December 3, 1986. See part 6, chap. 22, below.

7. Conversations with Marc-François Lacan, October 5, 1990, and December 21, 1991.

8. M.-G. Chateau and Jean Millet, *Collège Stanislas*, a historical notice published by the collège, November 1979.

9. Madeleine Barthelemy-Madaule, *Marc Sangnier (1873–1950)* (Paris: Seuil, 1973).

10. Jean Calvet, *Visage d'un demi-siècle* (The face of half a century) (Paris: Grasset, 1959).

11. Robert de Saint Jean, *Passé pas mort* (The past not dead) (Paris: Grasset, 1983), p. 47.

12. Conversation with Marc-François Lacan, October 5, 1990.

13. Saint Jean, *Passé pas mort*, p. 47.

14. Archives of the Collège Stanislas; conversation with Louis Leprince-Ringuet, January 17, 1990.

15. Letter from Marc-François Lacan to E.R., October 3, 1986.

16. See *HPF* 2 (*JL & Co.*), part 1, chap. 4.

17. Jean Baruzi, *Exposé de titres pour la chaire d'histoire des religions au Collège de France; Saint Jean de la Croix et le problème de l'expérience mystique* (Paris: Alcan, 1931).

18. Alexandre Koyré, *L'Ecole pratique des hautes études* (1931), and *De la mystique à la science*, in *Cours, conférences, documents, 1922–1962* (Lectures, papers, and documents, 1922–1962), ed. Pietro Redondi (Paris: EHESS, 1986), pp. 6–15.

19. Koyré, *L'Ecole pratique*, p. 14.

20. Baruzi, preface, *Saint Jean de la Croix*, p. iv.

21. Augustin Gazier, *Histoire du jansénisme* (listed in catalog of J.L.'s library at Guitrancourt, S.La.); conversation with Marc-François Lacan.

22. Conversation with Marc-François Lacan, October 5, 1990.

23. Conversation with Georges Bernier, based on an account by Lise Deharme, October 2, 1991.

24. See *HPF* 2:119 (*JL & Co.*, p. 104).

25. Another Balzac character: a young provincial, corrupted by ambition, who uses his personal charm to gain wealth and position in Paris (Cf. footnote in *Preface*, p.xv).

26. Saint Jean, *Passé pas mort*, p. 47.

27. Conversation with Marc-François Lacan, October 5, 1990; and letter from Marc-François Lacan to E.R., October 3, 1986.

28. Conversation with Madeleine Lacan-Houlon, March 4, 1983.

2. Faces on the Ward

1. See *HPF* 1:269–435.

2. On dynamic psychiatry, see Henri F. Ellenberger, *The Discovery of the Unconscious: The History and Evolution of Dynamic Psychiatry* (New York: Basic; London: Allen Lane, 1970). On Janet and Bergson, see *HPF* 1:223–269.

3. Sigmund Freud, *Three Essays on the Theory of Sexuality* (1905), *SE* 7:125. For pansexualism, see *SE* 7:134.

4. On the question of the intellectual approach, see *HPF* 2:19–115; and *JL & Co.*, pp. 3–100.

5. J.L., *Revue neurologique* 2 (1926): 410–418.

6. See *HPF* 1, part 4.

7. Michel Collée and Olivier Husson, "Entretien avec Julien Rouart" (conversation with Julie Rouart), *Frénésie* (autumn 1986): 109.

8. Letter from H. Ellenberger to E.R., January 11, 1992.

9. Conversation with Paul Sivadon, January 24, 1990; and Paul Sivadon, interview in *Ornicar?*, no. 37 (1986): 143.

10. Paul Sivadon, "J'étais interne des asiles de la Seine, 1929–1934" (I was an intern in the mental hospitals of the department of the Seine from 1929 to 1934), *Actualités psychiatriques* 2 (1981).

11. Sigmund Freud and Joseph Breuer, *Studies on Hysteria* (1895), in *SE* 2.

12. For Edouard Toulouse and Georges Heuyer's careers, see *HPF* 1:206–210 and 344.

13. J.L., "Abasie chez une traumatisée de guerre," *Revue neurologique* 2 (1928): 233–237.

14. Text reprinted in *DPP*, 1975.

15. See *HPF* 1:66–73.

16. S. Freud, *Fragment of an Analysis of a Case of Hysteria* (1905), in *SE* 7:3.

17. H. Codet and R. Laforgue, "L'Influence de Charcot sur Freud," *Progrès médical* 22 (May 30, 1925). See *HPF* 1:75.

18. André Breton, *Oeuvres complètes* (Paris: Gallimard, "La Pléiade," 1988), 1:949. See also *HPF* 2:23 (*JL & Co.*, p. 7).

3. Psychiatry Teachers

1. Claude Lévi-Strauss, *Tristes Tropiques*, trans. John and Doreen Weightman (New York: Atheneum, 1974), pp. 19–20.

2. Jean Delay, "L'Oeuvre d'Henri Claude" (The work of Henri Claude), *L'Encéphale* 4 (1950): 373–412; Claude Quétel and Jacques Postel, *Nouvelle Histoire de la psychiatrie* (Toulouse: Privat, 1983); Henri Claude, "Les Psychoses paranoïdes," *L'Encéphale* (1925): 137–149; Paul Bercherie, *Les Fondements de la clinique* (The principles of clinical practice) (Paris: Navarin, 1980).

3. R. Laforgue and R. Allendy, preface to *La Psychanalyse et les névroses* (Paris: Payot, 1924).

4. Quoted in Silvia Elena Tendlarz, *Le Cas Aimée: Etude historique et structurale* (doctoral thesis, University of Paris VIII, June 1989).

5. Gaëtan Gatian de Clérambault, *Oeuvres psychiatriques* (Paris: Frénésie-édition, 1988); Tendlarz, *Le Cas Aimée*; *HPF* 2:121–127 (*JL & Co.*, pp. 105–112); Elisabeth Renard, *Le Docteur G. G. de Clérambault: Sa Vie et son oeuvre (1872–1934)*, preface by Serge Tisseron (Paris: Delagrange, 1992); Danièle Arnoux, "La Rupture entre Lacan et de Clérambault," *Littoral* 37 (spring 1993).

6. Conversation with Paul Sivadon, January 24, 1990.

7. J.L., "Structures des psychoses paranoïaques," reprinted in *Ornicar?*, no. 44 (1988).

8. P. Sérieux and J. Capgras, *Les Folies raisonnantes* (Reasonable madness) (Paris: Alcan, 1909; rpt., Marseilles: Laffitte Reprints, 1982).

9. Jules de Gaultier, *Le Bovarysme* (Paris: Mercure de France, 1902). For the psychiatric sources of J.L.'s work, see Tendlarz, *Le Cas Aimée*.

10. J.L. "Structures des psychoses paranoïaques," p. 7.

11. Ibid., p. 10.

12. Conversation with Julien Rouart, January 1984; conversation with Renée Ey, September 30, 1983; H. Ellenberger, letter to E.R. See *HPF* 2:124 (*JL & Co.*, p. 109).

13. J.L. "Folies simultanées" (Simultaneous madnesses), *Annales médico-psychologiques* 1 (1931): 483–490.

14. J.L. "Ecrits inspirées: Schizographie" (Inspired writings: Schizography) *Annales médico-psychologiques* 2 (1931): 508–522, reprinted in *DPP*.

15. J.L., "Ecrits inspirées," pp. 379–380. On surrealism and psychoanalysis, see *HPF* 2:19–49 (*JL & Co.*, pp. 12–34).

16. Tendlarz, *Le Cas Aimée*, pp. 85–93.

17. Henri Delacroix, *Le Langage et la pensée* (Language and thought) (Paris: Alcan, 1930).

18. See Ferdinand de Saussure, *Course in General Linguistics*, trans. Wade Baskin (New York: McGraw-Hill, 1966).

PART II: CRAZY LADIES

4. The Story of Marguerite

1. *SASDLR* 1 (July 1930), reproduced in *SASDLR* (Paris: J.-M. Place, 1976).
2. See *HPF* 2, chap. 1 (*JL & Co.*, p. 110).
3. Dali, "L'Ane pourri."

4. Patrice Schmitt, "Dali et Lacan dans leurs rapports à la psychose paranoïaque" (Dali and Lacan and their attitudes to paranoid psychosis), *Cahiers Confrontation* (autumn 1980): 129–135.

5. Sarane Alexandrian, *Le Surréalisme et le rêve* (Surrealism and dreams) (Paris: Gallimard, 1976).

6. "De quelques mécanismes névrotiques dans la jalousie, le paranoïa et l'homosexualité," *RFP* 5 (1932): 391–401; newly translated as *Névrose, psychose, perversion* (Paris: PUF, 1973).

7. On the question of SPP translations at this period, see *HPF* 1:376–395. For the Schreber case (published in English as "Psycho-analytic Notes on an Autobiographical Account of a Case of Paranoia," in *SE* XII, 9–82), see *RFP* 5 (1932): 1.

8. See J.L., *DPP*, p. 258 n. 7.

9. J.L., *DPP*, p. 154.

10. *Le Journal,* April 19, 1931. See also Tendlarz, *Le Cas Aimée*; and Jean Allouch, *Marguerite; ou, L'Aimée de Lacan* (Paris: EPEL, 1990).

11. *Le Temps,* April 21, 1931.

12. Ibid.

13. On the myth of Atlantis, see P. Vidal-Naquet, "Athènes et l'Atlantide," in *Revue des études grecques* (Review of Greek studies) 27 (1964).

14. J.L., *DPP*, p. 156.

15. Ibid., p. 204.

16. By agreement with Didier Anzieu I refrained from reconstructing the story of Marguerite in *HPF* 2. It is now possible to do so, thanks to new sources and personal accounts: Allouch, *Marguerite*; Tendlarz, *Le Cas Aimée*; D. Anzieu, *Une Peau pour des pensées: Entretien avec G. Tarrab* (Your thoughts or your life: Conversation with G. Tarrab) (Paris: Clancier-Guénaud, 1986); and "Historique du cas Marguerite," *Littoral* (April 27–28, 1989).

17. Anzieu, *Une Peau*, p. 16.

18. J.L., *DPP*, p. 224.

19. Ibid., p. 159.

20. Anzieu, *Une Peau*, pp. 8–9.

21. Jean Allouch and Danièle Arnoux, "Historique du cas Marguerite: Suppléments, corrections, lectures," *Littoral* 37 (spring 1993).

22. J.L., *DPP*, p. 161.

23. Ibid., p. 162.

24. On the Daudet affair, see *HPF* 1:59–67.

25. J.L., *DPP*, pp. 295–296.

26. See *HPF* 1:340–342.

27. Reprinted in J.L., *DPP*, p. 182.

28. Ibid., p. 195.

29. Ibid.

30. Tendlarz, *Le Cas Aimée*, pp. 330–331.

31. J.L., *DPP*, p. 171.

5. *In Praise of Paranoia*

1. J.L., *DPP*, p. 178; and conversation with Françoise de Tarde-Bergeret, September 4, 1991. It should also be noted that in 1922 Jacques Rivière published a short story, dedicated to Proust, which was called *Aimée*. It is not impossible that Lacan knew this text.

2. Georges Politzer, *Critique of the Foundations of Psychology: The Psychology of Psychoanalysis*, trans. Maurice Apprey (Pittsburgh: Duquesne University Press, 1994); *HPF* 2:71–87 (*JL & Co.*, pp. 60–67).

3. Ramon Fernandez, *De la personnalité* (Paris: Au sans pareil, 1928).

4. J.L., *DPP*, pp. 42–43.

5. On Minkowski's career, see *HPF* 1:413–435.

6. Karl Jaspers, *Psychopathologie générale* (Paris: Alcan, 1928), first published in Berlin in 1913. See *General Psychopathology*, translated from the seventh German edition (1959) by J. Hoenig and Marian W. Hamilton (Manchester: Manchester University Press, 1962). See also François Leguil, "Lacan avec et contre Jaspers" (Lacan with and against Jaspers), *Ornicar?*, no. 48 (1989): 5–23; G. Lanteri-Laura. "La Notion de processus dans la pensée psycho-pathologique de K. Jaspers" (The notion of process in the psychopathological thought of K. Jaspers), *EP* 27, no. 4 (1962): 459–499; and idem, "Processus et psychogenèse dans l'oeuvre de Lacan" (Process and psychogenesis in Lacan's work), *EP* 2, no. 4 (1984): 975–990.

7. Leguil, "Lacan avec et contre Jaspers."

8. J.L., *DPP*, pp. 277–279.

9. Ibid., p. 253.

10. Ibid. p. 265.

11. See Bernard Ogilvie, *Lacan, le sujet* (Lacan, the subject) (Paris: PUF, 1987).

12. J.L., *DPP*, p. 266. Jean-Etienne-Dominique Esquirol (1772–1840) was a French physician and alienist, born in Toulouse.

13. This is how I described it in *HPF* 2:129 (*JL & Co.*, p. 114).

14. J.L., *DPP*, p. 280.

15. For the interpretation of the second topology, see the end of chap. 18.

16. J.L., *DPP*, p. 303.

17. Jean Allouch, *Marguerite; ou, L'Aimée de Lacan* (Paris: EPEL, 1990), p. 551.

6. Reading Spinoza

1. Baruch Spinoza, *The Ethics*, Book III, proposition 57, in *The Collected Works of Spinoza*, ed. and trans. E. Curley (Princeton: Princeton University Press, 1985); Robert Misrahi, "Spinoza en épigraphe de Lacan" (Spinoza as an epigraph to Lacan), *Littoral* 3–4 (February 1982). See also E.R., "Lacan et Spinoza: Essai d'interprétation" (Lacan and Spinoza: An attempt at interpretation), in *Spinoza au vingtième siècle*, ed. O. Bloch (Paris: PUF, 1992).

2. J.L., *DPP*, p. 337.

3. Bernard Ogilvie, *Lacan, le sujet* (Lacan, the subject) (Paris: PUF, 1987), p. 63.

4. J. Allouch, *Lettre pour lettre* (Toulouse: Erès, 1984), p. 186.

5. G. Lanteri-Laura and Martine Gros, *Essai sur la discordance dans la psychiatrie contemporaine* (Essay on the discordance in contemporary psychiatry) (Paris: EPEL: 1992).

6. *HPF* 1:131.

7. J.L., *DPP*, p. 342.

8. Quoted by Misrahi, "Spinoza en épigraphe de Lacan," p. 75.

9. J.L., *DPP*, p. 343.

10. Spinoza, *Ethics*. It should be noted that in the translation in the Pléiade edition (Paris, 1954), R. Caillois translates *affectus* by *sentiment* (feeling) and renders both *discrepat* and *differt* as *différer* (to differ or defer) (p. 465).

11. Conversations with Célia Bertin, January 20, 1989, and with Marc-François Lacan, October 5, 1990. On the trip to Morocco, see Judith Miller, *Visages de mon père* (Faces of my father) (Paris: Seuil, 1991); and an unpublished note written for E.R. by Baber Johansen.

12. "Olesia" is a diminutive form of "Alexandra."

13. See D. Desanti, *Drieu la Rochelle; ou, Le Séducteur mystifié* (Drieu la Rochelle; or, The seducer mystified) (Paris: Flammarion, 1978); and P. Drieu la Rochelle, *Journal, 1939–1945* (Paris: Gallimard, 1992), p. 96.

14. Conversation with Olesia Sienkiewicz, March 8, 1990.

15. Separate conversations with Olesia Sienkiewicz, March 8, 1990; Julien Rouart, January 1984; Paul Sivadon, January 24, 1990; and Renée Ey, September 30, 1983.

16. J.L., *E*, pp. 67 and 162.

17. See *Ornicar?*, no. 29 (1984).

18. Henri Ey, *L'Encéphale* 2 (1932): 851–856.

19. *L'Humanité*, February 10, 1933. See also A. Cohen-Solal, in collaboration with H. Nizan, *Paul Nizan, communiste impossible* (Paris: Grasset, 1980).

20. René Crevel, *Le Clavecin de Diderot* (Diderot's harpsichord) (Paris: Pauvert, 1966), pp. 163–164. See *HPF* 2:70 (*JL & Co.*, p. 55); and "Note en vue d'une psycho-dialectique," in *SASDLR* (Paris: J.-M. Place, 1976), pp. 48–52.

21. *Le Minotaure* 1 (1933; rpt. Paris: Skira, n.d.).

22. Michel Surya, *Georges Bataille, la mort à l'oeuvre* (Georges Bataille, death at work) (Paris: Librairie Séguier, 1987; rpt., Paris: Gallimard, 1992).

23. Philippe Robrieux, *Histoire intérieure du PCF* (Inner history of the French Communist Party), 4 vols. (Paris: Fayard, 1984); and conversation with Olesia Sienkiewicz, March 8, 1990. See also, despite its inaccuracies, B. Souvarine's prologue to the reprint of *La Critique sociale: Revue des idées et des livres* (Paris: La Différence, 1983).

24. *La Critique sociale*, pp. 120–121.

7. The Papin Sisters

1. J.L.'s text, which appeared first in *Le Minotaure*, is reproduced without alteration in *DPP*.

2. I have already dealt with the story of the Papin sisters, from a different point of view, in *HPF*:140–141 (*JL & Co.*, pp. 125–127). See Francis Dupré (Jean Allouch), *La Solution du passage à l'acte* (The acting-out solution) (Toulouse: Erès, 1984); Paulette Houdyer, *Le Diable dans la peau* (In love with the devil) (Paris: Julliard, 1966); Frédéric Pottecher, *Les Grands Procès de l'histoire* (Historic trials) (Paris: Fayard, 1981).

3. I disagree with M. Borch-Jacobsen, who in *Lacan: The Absolute Master*, trans. Douglas Brick (Stanford: Stanford University Press, 1991), pp. 21–27, attributes to Lacan an entirely Hegelian interpretation of the Aimée case, whereas, when he wrote his thesis, Lacan hadn't yet read a word of Hegel. Nor do I agree with Jean Allouch, according to whom Lacan's clinical theory changed between Aimée and the Papin sisters. The change consists simply in Lacan's inclusion of a Hegelian perspective.

PART III: MAN'S ESTATE

8. Private Life and Public Life

1. J.L., *Du discours psychanalytique* (University of Milan, May 12 1972, unpublished); *Scilicet* 6/7 (1975): 9.

2. See *HPF* 2:124–138 (*JL & Co.*, pp. 109–124).

3. For Rudolph Loewenstein, see *HPF* 1:343–362; Célia Bertin, *Marie Bonaparte: A Life* (New York: Harcourt Brace Jovanovich, 1982); rpt., New Haven: Yale University Press, 1987); Elisabeth Roudinesco, "Entretien avec Philippe Sollers," *L'Infini* (spring 1983).

4. I met Germaine Guex (d.) in Geneva in June 1982.

5. *RFP* 2, no. 1 (1923) and 4, no. 2 (1930–1931).

6. *HPF* 1:356–357; E.R., "Loewenstein," *Ornicar?*, no. 31 (1984).

7. Conversation with Catherine Millot, June 17, 1992.

8. Letter from J.L. to Olesia Sienkiewicz, August 26, 1933.

9. Letter from J.L. to Olesia Sienkiewicz, August 31, 1933.

10. J.L., *L'Encéphale* 11 (1933): 686–695.

11. Letter from J.L. to Olesia Sienkiewicz, October 24, 1933.

12. Separate conversations with Sibylle Lacan, May 3, 1990, Célia Bertin, February 4, 1990, and Marc-François Lacan, October 5, 1990; Jacques Mialaret, "Sylvain Blondin (1901–1975)," *Bulletin de l'Académie nationale de médecine* 159, no. 5 (session of May 6, 1975).

13. Conversation with Alicia Borinsky in October 1990.

14. Conversation with Paul Sivadon, January 24, 1990.

15. Claude Girard, "Histoire de la formation dans la SPP" (History of training in the SPP), *RIHP* 2 (1989).

16. Conversation with Georges Bernier. Bernier's real name was Georges Weinstein. He changed it to "Bernier" after the Second World War, when he returned from the United States.

17. J.L., "Interventions à la SPP" (Speeches delivered at the SPP), reprinted in *Ornicar?*, no. 31 (1984).

18. See chap. 9.

9. Fascism: The End of the Viennese Epic

1. On this matter, see *HPF* 2:165–178, with full bibliography (*JL & Co.*, pp. 151–164). See also "Psychanalyse et psychanalystes durant la Deuxième Guerre mondiale" (Psychoanalysis and psychoanalysts during the Second World War), *RIHP* 1 (1988); E.R., "Réponse à Alain de Mijolla à propos de l'affaire Laforgue" (Reply to Alain de Mijolla concerning the Laforgue affair), *Frénésie* 6 (autumn 1988); and G. Cocks, *La Psychothérapie sous le Troisième Reich* (Paris: Les Belles Lettres, 1987). Documents about the Laforgue affair are to be found in *Confrontation* 6 (autumn 1986); and *Psyche* (Frankfurt) 12 (December 1988).

2. Thomas Mann, "Freud and the Future" (May 9, 1936), in *Essays of Three Decades*, trans. H. T. Lowe-Porter (New York: Knopf, 1948), p. 412.

3. Richard Sterba, *Réminiscences d'un psychanalyste viennois* (Toulouse: Privat, 1986); Max Schur, *Freud: Living and Dying* (London: Hogarth and Institute of Psycho-Analysis; New York: International Universities Press, 1972).

4. Harald Leupold Löwenthal, "L'Emigration de la famille Freud en 1938," *RIHP* 2 (1989): 459–460.

5. Unpublished journal of Marie Bonaparte; Célia Bertin, *Marie Bonaparte: A Life* (New York: Harcourt Brace Jovanovich, 1982; rpt., New Haven: Yale University Press, 1987), p. 202; *HPF* 2:148 (*JL & Co.*, p. 134).

6. Opening and closing speeches by Ernest Jones, "Bulletin of the IPA," *IJP* (1939): 116–127; "The New General Institute for Psychological Research and Psycho-Therapy, of which the Psycho-Analytical Society is a separate department, was founded in May 1936," *IJP* (1939): 123.

7. David Steel, "L'Amitié entre Sigmund Freud et Yvette Guilbert," *NRF* 352 (May 1, 1982): 84–92.

8. Quoted in Bertin, *Marie Bonaparte*, p. 245.

9. Letter from R. Loewenstein to Jean Miel, September 12, 1967, Collections of the Manuscript Division, Library of Congress, Washington. See Bluma Swerdloff and Ellen Rowntree, "The Education of an Analyst: Selection from an Interview with Rudolph Loewenstein, M.D.," Library of Congress. See also the draft of a letter from R.L. to Henri Sauget, December 4, 1966, Library of Congress, communicated by Nadine Mespoulhès in connection with an article in preparation on Adrien Borel.

10. The Philosophy School: Alexandre Koyré and Others

1. Conversation with Pierre Verret, December 14, 1989, quoted in *Littoral* 27/28 (April 1989): 197–198.

2. Ibid.; and letter from J.L. to Pierre Verret, November 13, 1933, quoted in *Littoral* 27/28 (April 1989): 199.

3. Jean Audard, "Du caractère matérialiste de la psychanalyse," reprinted in *Littoral* 27/28 (April 1989): 197–198. See *HPF* 2:67 (*JL & Co.*, p. 51).

4. Alexandre Koyré, *De la mystique à la science* (From mysticism to science), in *Cours, conférences, documents, 1922–1962* (Lectures, papers, and documents, 1922–1962), ed. Pietro Redondi (Paris: EHESS, 1986), p. 3.

5. *Cahiers de l'Herne* (special issue on Henry Corbin) 39 (1981). See Etienne Gilson, *La Philosophie et la théologie* (Paris: Fayard, 1960).

6. A. Koyré, *Etudes d'histoire de la pensée scientifique* (Studies in the history of scientific thought) (Paris: Gallimard, Tel, 1973), p. 11.

7. Published in English as *Galileo Studies*, trans. John Mepham (Atlantic Highlands, N.J.: Humanities Press, 1978).

8. A. Koyré, "Entretiens sur Descartes" (Talks on Descartes), in *Introduction à la lecture de Platon* (Introduction to the reading of Plato) (Paris: Gallimard, 1962).

9. On this point, see Christian Jambet, "Y a-t-il une philosophie française?" (Is there such a thing as French philosophy?), *Annales de philosophie* (Beirut: Université Saint-Joseph, 1989).

10. Edmund Husserl, *The Crisis of the European Sciences and Transcendental Phenomenology*, trans. David Carr (Evanston, Ill.: Northwestern University Press, 1970), p. 299.

11. Michel Foucault, "La Vie, l'expérience et la science," *Revue de métaphysique et de morale* 1 (1985). 3–14.

12. See François Dosse, *New History in France: The Triumph of the Annales*, trans. Peter V. Conroy, Jr. (Urbana: University of Illinois Press, 1994); Jacques Revel, "L'Histoire sociale dans les *Annales*," *Lendemains* 24 (1981); André Burguière, "La Notion de 'mentalité' chez Marc Bloch et Lucien Febvre: Deux conceptions, deux filiations," *Revue de synthèse* 111–112 (July–December 1983); Bronislaw Geremek, "Marc Bloch, historien et résistant," *Annales ESC* 5 (September–October 1986): 1091–1105.

13. Lucien Febvre, *Pour une histoire à part entière* (For a complete history) (Paris: EHESS, 1962), p. 844.

14. See Burguière, "La Notion de 'mentalité,'" p. 38.

15. Jean-Paul Sartre, *Critique de la raison dialectique* (Paris: Gallimard, 1985), p. 844. This work was translated as *Critique of Dialectical Reason*, trans. Alan Sheridan (New York: Verso, 1990); however, the quotation cited in the text does not appear in the translation.

16. Vincent Descombes, *Modern French Philosophy* (Cambridge: Cambridge University Press, 1980). See also *HPF* 2:149–156 (*JL & Co.*, pp. 134–142); and Jean Wahl, *Les Malheur de la conscience chez Hegel* (E, p.587).

17. Koyré, *De la mystique à la science*, p. 24.

18. Boris Souvarine, *La Critique sociale: Revue des idées et des livres* (Paris: La Différence, 1983), p. 123.

19. See *HPF* 2 (*JL & Co.*), part 1, chap. 1.

20. Georges Bataille, "Figure humaine" (Human face) and "Le Bas matérialisme de la gnose" (The base materialism of gnosis), in *Documents* (Paris: Mercure de France, 1968). See Raymond Queneau, "Premières Confrontations avec Hegel," *Critique* 195–196 (August–September 1963): 694–700.

21. *La Critique sociale*, p. 6.

22. *Cahiers de l'Herne*, p. 6.

23. *Bifur* 8 (n.d.).

24. Georges Bataille and Raymond Queneau, "Les Fondements de la dialectique hégélienne," in *La Critique sociale*, pp. 209–214.

25. A. Koyré, "Rapport sur l'état des études hégéliennes en France" (1931), "Note sur la langue et la terminologie hégéliennes" (1931), and "Hegel à Iéna" (1934), in *Etudes d'histoire de la pensée philosophique* (Paris: Gallimard, 1971). See also Redondi, *Cours, conférences, documents*, p. 42; G. W. F. Hegel, *The Phenomenology of Spirit* (1807), trans. A. V. Miller (Oxford: Clarendon, 1977); and idem, *The Jena System, 1804–5: Logic and Metaphysics*, trans. John W. Burbidge and George di Giovanni (Kingston: McGill-Queen's University Press, 1986).

26. Koyré, "Hegel à Iéna," p. 189.

27. *Cahiers de l'Herne*, p. 44.

28. *Transcendance de l'ego* appeared in volume 7 of *Recherches philosophiques* and was published in book form by the Parisian firm of Vrin in 1965. It has been translated into English as *The Transcendency of the Ego: An Existentialist Theory of Consciousness* (New York: Noonday, 1957; rpt., New York: Octagon Books, 1972).

29. J.L., *S. VIII*. This seminar is being translated, under the title *Transference*, by Bruce Fink (New York: Norton, forthcoming).

30. Georges Bataille, *Oeuvres complètes* (Paris: Gallimard, 1970), 6:416; and Dominique Auffret, *Alexandre Kojève, la philosophie, l'Etat, la fin de l'Histoire* (A.K., philosophy, the State, and the end of History) (Paris: Grasset, 1990).

31. Auffret, *Alexandre Kojève*, p. 45.

32. Ibid., pp. 46–49.

33. Ibid., p. 90.

34. Gilles Lapouge, interview with A. Kojève, *La Quinzaine littéraire* (July 1968); Michel Surya, *Georges Bataille, la mort à l'oeuvre* (Georges Bataille, death at work) (Paris: Librairie Séguier, 1987; rpt., Paris: Gallimard, 1992), pp. 197 and 231, respectively.

35. Auffret, *Alexandre Kojève*, p. 154.

36. Ibid., p. 238.

37. Lapouge, interview with A. Kojève.

38. Denis Hollier, *The College of Sociology*, trans. Betsy Wing (Minneapolis: University of Minnesota Press, 1988), p. 86; see pp. 85–93.

39. Pierre Macherey, "Lacan avec Kojève, philosophie et psychanalyse," in Bibliothèque du Collège International de Philosophie, ed., *Lacan avec les philosophes* (Paris: Albin Michel, 1991), pp. 315–321.

40. Jean-Luc Pinard-Legry, "Kojève, lecteur de Hegel" (Kojève as a reader of Hegel), *Raison présente* 68 (1980); Descombes, *Le Même et l'autre*; Auffret, *Alexandre Kojève*; and Pierre Macherey's unpublished lectures on the introduction of Hegelianism into France. See A. Kojève, *Introduction à la "Phénoménologie de l'esprit"* (Paris: Gallimard, 1947); and idem, *Introduction à la lecture de Hegel* (Paris: Gallimard, 1947), trans. and abridged as *Introduction to the Reading of Hegel*, trans. James F. Nichols (Ithaca: Cornell University Press, 1980).

41. See *HPF* 2:153–155 (*JL & Co.*, pp. 139–141).

42. On E. Minkowski, see *HPF* 1:413–431.

43. *Recherches philosophiques* 5 (1935–1936): 425.

44. Ibid., p. 430. Lacan performed the same act of self-hagiography in 1935, in his review of Henri Ey's book *Hallucinations et délires* (Hallucinations and delusions) in *Evolution psychiatrique* 1 (1935): 87–91.

45. Letter from J.L. to Henri Ey, May 4, 1935, H.E., communicated by Patricia Clervoy.

46. Unpublished handwritten document by A. Kojève, communicated by D. Auffret.

47. See Auffret, *Alexandre Kojève*, p. 447; and A. Kojève, "Genèse de la conscience de soi" (Genesis of self-awareness) (unpublished manuscript).

48. Here again Mikkel Borch-Jacobsen is mistaken when he says Lacan's main source on the subject of the cogito was Sartre's "La Transcendance de l'ego." That article was published in *Recherches philosophiques* after Lacan had started considering the same idea. If Lacan's and Sartre's terminology were the same, that is because they were both influenced by Husserl and Heidegger. Lacan read Sartre's article much later on. J. Allouch, in *Lettre pour lettre* (Toulouse: Erès, 1984), and Philippe Julien, in *Jacques Lacan's Return to Freud*, trans. D. B. Simiu (New York: New York University Press, 1994), both play down the importance of Kojève's teaching to J.L.'s Hegelianism. Alain Juranville, in *Lacan et la philosophie* (Paris: PUF, 1984), doesn't address the question.

11. Marienbad

1. See *HPF* 1:158–159; Elisabeth Young-Bruehl, *Anna Freud: A Biography* (New York: Summit, 1988); and Phyllis Grosskurth, *Melanie Klein: Her World and Her Work* (New York: Knopf, 1986).

2. Grosskurth, *Melanie Klein*, p. 197.

3. Ibid., p. 195.

4. S. Freud, *Two Case Histories: Analysis of a Phobia in a Five-year-old Boy ("Little Hans")* (1909), in *SE* 10:3; Hermine von Hug-Hellmuth, *Journal psychoanalytique d'une petite fille* (Psychoanalytical journal of a little girl) (Paris: Denoël, 1975; rpt., 1987); *Essais psychanalytiques*, ed. and trans. by Dominique Soubrenie (Paris: Payot, 1991); Pamela Tytell, *The French Psychoanalytic Culture: French Psychoanalysts and Their Relationship to the Literary Text*, 3 vols. (Ph.D. diss., Columbia University, 1979).

5. Hanna Segal, *Klein* (London: Fontana Modern Masters, 1979).

6. Grosskurth, *Melanie Klein*; Melanie Klein, *The Psycho-Analysis of Children*, trans. Alix Strachey (London: Hogarth, 1932). See vol. 2 of *The Writings of Melanie Klein* (London: Hogarth, 1975).

7. Segal, *Klein*, p. 41.

8. Melanie Klein uses the word *fantasy* in the sense of unconscious fantasy.

9. On ego psychology, see *HPF* 2:181ff. (*JL & Co.*, pp. 167ff.).

10. On the history of the idea of the "mirror stage," see *HPF* 2:143–149 (*JL & Co.*, pp. 129–134).

11. J.L., *E*, p. 67.

12. See Henri Wallon, *Les Origines du caractère chez l'enfant* (The origins of character in children) (Paris: Boivin, 1934), pp. 190–207. See also Bernard Ogilvie, *Lacan, le sujet* (Lacan, the subject) (Paris: PUF, 1987), pp. 96–119.

13. J.L., "Vues paléobiologiques et biopsychiques," *Revue française de psychanalyse* 3 (1938): 551 (reprinted as "L'Angoisse et le corps morcelé," *Ornicar?*, no. 31 [1984]: 11).

14. For this question as treated by René Laforgue, see *HPF* 1:289–297.

15. P. Grosskurth, *Melanie Klein* pp. 133ff.

16. J.L., *E*, pp. 184–185.

17. J.L., "La Direction de la cure et les principes de son pouvoir," *La Psychanalyse* 6 (1961): 163. Translated as "The Direction of the Treatment and the Principles of Its Power," in *EAS*, p. 239.

18, Unpublished notes by Françoise Dolto, June 16, 1936, F.D.

19. E. Young-Bruehl, *Anna Freud*, p. 468.

20. J.L., "La Psychiatrie anglaise et la guerre," *Evolution psychiatrique* 1 (1947): 293–312.

21. Unpublished journal of Guillaume de Tarde, June 9, 1936, communicated by Françoise de Tarde-Bergeret.

22. J.L., *E*, p. 73.

PART IV: FAMILY HISTORIES

12. Georges Bataille and Co.

1. Michel Leiris, *Journal, 1922–1989*, annotated by Jean Jamin (Paris: Gallimard, 1992). See Michel Surya, *Georges Bataille, la mort à l'oeuvre* (Georges Bataille, death at work) (Paris: Librairie Séguier, 1987; rpt., Paris: Gallimard, 1992), pp. 109 and 127, respectively.

2. *HPF* 1:343–362.

3. Surya, *Georges Bataille*, pp. 474 and 622.

4. Ibid., pp. 105 and 122.

5. Autobiographical note, *Oeuvres complètes* (Paris: Gallimard, 1970), 7:45.

6. Madeleine Chapsal, *Envoyez la petite musique* (Bring on the band) (Paris: Grasset, 1984). See Surya, *Georges Bataille*, pp. 109, 127.

7. Théodore Fraenkel, *Carnets, 1916–1918* (Paris: Editions des Cendres, 1990), p. 7; *HPF* 1; Marguerite Bonnet, *André Breton et la naissance de l'aventure* (André Breton and the birth of the adventure) (Paris: Corti, 1975).

8. Conversation with Michel Fraenkel, November 21, 1991.

9. Fraenkel, *Carnets*, p. 65. See Max Nordau, *Degeneracy*, 2 vols. (Berlin, 1893–1893).

10. Conversation with Michel Fraenkel.

11. Ibid.

12. Laurence Bataille, *L'Ombilic du rêve* (The dream's navel) (Paris: Seuil, 1987), p. 67.

13. Separate conversations with Laurence Bataille (d.), Michel Fraenkel, and Michel Surya.

14. M. Surya, *Georges Bataille*, pp. 158 and 185.

15. André Bazin, *Jean Renoir* (Paris: Champ libre, 1971), pp. 210–211.

16. Célia Bertin, *Jean Renoir: A Life in Pictures*, trans. Mireille and Leonard Muellner (Baltimore: John Hopkins University Press, 1991), p. 73.

17. Bataille, *Oeuvres complètes* 3:60, 3:433–434, 2:130.

18. Ibid., 3:61.

19, Ibid., 3:60.

20. M. Leiris, "L'Impossible 'Documents,' " *Critique* 195–196 (August–September 1963).

21. Bertin, *Jean Renoir*, p. 111.

22. René Gilson, *Jacques Prévert: Des Mots et merveilles* (Jacques Prévert: Words and wonders) (Paris: Belfond, 1990).

23. Jean Renoir, *My Life and My Films*, trans. Norman Penny (New York: Atheneum, 1974), p. 113.

24. Bernard Chardère, "Jacques Prévert et le groupe Octobre," *Premier Plan* 14 (November 1960).

25. Jean Renoir, "Entretiens et propos" (Interviews and statements), *Les Cahiers du cinéma*, 156. For Henriette Dufour, see later in this chapter.

26. Bataille, *Oeuvres complètes* 3:403.

27. Ibid.

28. Georges Bataille gives an account of the incident in *Oeuvres complètes* 5:514: "Notes on *Le coupable* [The culprit]," October 21, 1939.

29. Bataille, *L'Ombilic du rêve*, p. 55. The article that gave the book its title appeared in *Etudes freudiennes*, no. 23 (1984).

30. Ibid., p. 57.

31. André Masson, *Correspondance, 1916–1942: Les Années surréalistes*, introduced and annotated by Françoise Levaillant (Paris: La Manufacture, 1990).

32. Leiris, *Journal*. Pierre Assouline doesn't mention this detail in *An Artful Life: A Biography of Daniel-Henry Kahnweiler*, trans. Charles Ruas (New York: Weidenfeld, 1990). Louise Godon was born January 22, 1902, and married Leiris on February 2, 1926. Lucie and Daniel were married on July 2, 1919.

33. Bataille, *Oeuvres complètes* 3:395.

34. Leiris, *A propos de Georges Bataille* (Paris: Editions Fourbis, 1988), p. 239.

35. Undated letters from Boris Souvarine to Olesia Sienkiewicz. See also above, p. 60.

36. Renoir, "Entretiens," p. 156.

37. See Guy de Maupassant, "A Country Excursion," in *Boule de suif and Other Stories*, trans. and ed. Ernest Boyd (Freeport, N.Y.: Books for Libraries Press, 1971), p. 197.

38. Bazin, *Jean Renoir*, p. 47.

39. *Les Cahiers du cinéma* 8 (January 1952): 45.

40. *Acéphale* 1 (June 24, 1936), reprinted by Jean-Michel Place in Paris in 1980.

41. Ibid.

42. HPF 2:116–156 (*JL & Co.*, pp. 101–142).

43. *Acéphale* 2–3 (January 1937).

44. See Pierre Boudot, *Nietzsche et l'au-delà de la liberté* (Nietzsche and beyond of liberty) (Paris: Aubier-Montaigne, 1970); Dominique Bourel and Jacques Le Rider, *Nietzsche et les Juifs* (Nietzsche and the Jews) (Paris: Cerf, 1991); and Geneviève Bianquis, *Nietzsche en France* (Paris: Alcan, 1928).

45. Bonnet, *André Breton*, p. 52.

46. Charles Andler, *Nietzsche*, 3 vols. (Paris: Gallimard, 1958).

47. H.-F. Peters, *Nietzsche et sa soeur Elisabeth* (Paris: Mercure de France, 1978), p. 316.

48. Karl Jaspers, *Nietzsche: An Introduction to the Understanding of His Philosophical Activity*, trans. Charles F. Wallraff and Frederick J. Schmitz, 2d ed. (South Bend, Ind.: Regnery/Gateway, 1979). See also P. Hebber-Suffrin, *Le Zarathoustra de Nietzsche* (Paris: PUF, 1988).

49. P. Macherey, "Bataille et le renversement matérialiste" (Bataille and the materialist reversal), in *A quoi pense la littérature?* (What does literature think about?) (Paris: PUF, 1980), pp. 97–114.

50. Bataille, *Oeuvres complètes* 1:389.

51. HPF 2:19 37. (*JL & Co.*, pp. 3–21).

52. José Pierre, *Tracts surréalistes* (Paris: Le terrain vague, 1980), 1:298.

53. Surya, *Georges Bataille*, pp. 229 and 274.

54. Bataille, *Oeuvres complètes* 2:62–63.

55. Denis Hollier, *The College of Sociology*, trans. Betsy Wing (Minneapolis: University of Minnesota Press, 1988), pp. xii–xiii. See also Carolyn Dean, *The Self and Its Pleasures: Bataille, Lacan and the History of the Decentered Subject* (Ithaca, N.Y.: Cornell University Press, 1992).

56. Conversation with Sibylle Lacan, April 14, 1990.

57. Conversation with Thibaut Lacan, April 14, 1991.

58. Conversation with Sylvia Lacan in February 1984, with Laurence Bataille (d.) in March 1983, and with Jenny Aubry (d.).

59. Conversation with Thibaut Lacan.

60. Separate conversations with Célia Bertin and Frédéric François, November 14, 1991.

61. Conversation with Sibylle Lacan; and private conversation.

62. Boris Kochno, in the exhibition catalog *Balthus* (Paris: Centre Georges Pompidou, 1983), p. 328.

63. Masson, *Correspondance*, p. 430. The picture is reproduced in Judith Miller, *Visages de mon père* (Faces of my father) (Paris: Seuil, 1991).

13. Between Lucien Febvre and Edouard Pichon

1. *HPF* 2:156. (*JL and Co.*, p. 142). See "La Famille," in *Encyclopédie française* (Paris: Larousse, 1938), 8:40.3–16, and 42.1–8.

2. I refer to the text as F and quote from it as it appeared in the *Encyclopédie*. Lucien Febvre's memorandum is dated February 5, 1937. It was communicated to me by Peter Schöttler, who found it in Febvre's archives. It is printed in *Genèses* 13 (autumn 1993).

3. Lucien Febvre, memorandum, section 5. His italics. [*Translator's note: Nénette* is a rather Rabelaisian nickname—*néné* = tits—the equivalent of "chick" and perhaps referring to a female "junior." The head of administration was Pierre Tisson, with whom Febvre didn't get along.]

4. Conversation with H. Gratiot-Alphandéry, January 11, 1990.

5. Jocrisse—a credulous simpleton—is a stock character in early French theater and in Molière's *Sganarelle*.

6. M. Klein, "Early Stages of the Oedipus Conflict" (1928), *International Journal of Psycho-Analysis* 7, reprinted in vol. 1 of *The Writings of Melanie Klein* (London: Hogarth, 1975). Published in French translation in *RPF* in 1930.

7. Jakob von Uexküll is cited in *DPP* but not in F.

8. Bernard Ogilvie, *Lacan, le sujet* (Lacan, the subject) (Paris: PUF, 1987), p. 61. Lacan *was* aware of what he was doing: he cites Comte and Bonald in his bibliography.

9. Thomas Mann, "Freud and the Future" (May 6, 1936), in *Essays of Three Decades*, trans. H. T. Lowe-Porter (New York: Knopf, 1948), p. 412.

10. J.L., F, section A, 8:40.6.

11. Ibid., 8:40.8.

12. Ibid., 8:40.15. See Henri Bergson, *The Two Sources of Morality and Religion*, trans. R. Ashley Audra and Claudesley Brereton, with the assistance of W. Horsfall Carter (New York: Holt, [1935]).

13. Ibid., 8:40.16.

14. Jacques Le Rider, *Modernity and Crises of Identity: Culture and Society: Fin-de-siècle Vienna*, trans. Rosemary Morris (New York: Continuum, 1993).

15. Edouard Pichon, "La Famille devant M. Lacan," reproduced in *Cahiers Confrontation* 3 (spring 1980).

16. Letter from Edouard Pichon to Henri Ey, July 21, 1938, H.E.

17. Pichon, "La Famille devant M. Lacan."

18. Ibid., pp. 134–135. The bloodless revolution of the fourth of September 1870 led to the proclamation of France's Third Republic, which lasted until 1940.

PART V: WAR AND PEACE

14. Marseilles, Vichy, Paris

1. Marie Bonaparte, unpublished journal.

2. Epilogue to *HPF* 1. On Freud's death, see Max Schur, *Freud: Living and Dying* (London: Hogarth and Institute of Psycho-Analysis, 1972; New York: International Universities Press); and Peter Gay, *Freud: A Life for Our Time* (London: Dent, 1988).

3. *L'Oeuvre*, September 28, 1939. See *Nervure* 1, no. 3 (February 1990). Documentation by Chantal Talagrand.

4. Alain de Mijolla, "La Psychanalyse et les psychanalystes entre 1939 et 1945," *RIHP* 1 (1900): 168–178. See also *HPF* 2:166–178 (*JL & Co.*, pp. 152–164).

5. R. Allendy, *Le Journal d'un médecin malade* (Paris: Denoël, 1944). See also *HPF* 1:370 ff.

6. Célia Bertin, *Marie Bonaparte: A Life* (New York: Harcourt Brace Jovanovich, 1982; rpt., New Haven: Yale University Press, 1987).

7. *HPF* 1:430; E.R., "Laforgue ou la collaboration manquée: Paris/Berlin, 1939–1942," *Cahiers Confrontation* 3 (spring 1980).

8. See *HPF* 2; Mijolla, "La Psychanalyse et les psychanalystes."

9. See Mijolla, "La Psychanalyse et les psychanalystes," p. 170.

10. Conversation with Georges Bernier, October 2, 1991.

11. Letter from J.L. to Sylvain Blondin, October 24, 1939, Thibaut Lacan archives.

12. Letter from J.L. to Sylvain Blondin, May 29, 1940, Thibaut Lacan archives.

13. Jacques Mialaret, "Sylvain Blondin, éloge" (In praise of Sylvain Blondin), *Bulletin de l'Académie nationale de médecine*, vol. 159–5, session of May 6, 1975.

14. Michel Surya, *Georges Bataille, la mort à l'oeuvre* (Georges Bataille, death at work) (Paris, Librairie Séguier, 1987; rpt., Paris: Gallimard, 1992), pp. 288, 344.

15. Ibid., pp. 301, 364.

16. Judith Miller, *Visages de mon père* (Faces of my father) (Paris: Seuil, 1991), p. 54.

17. Célia Bertin, *Jean Renoir*, (Paris: Perrin, 1986), p. 229.

18. Conversation with Sylvia Lacan, February 1984; and with Georges Bernier, October 2, 1991.

19. *HPF* 2:161. (*JL & Co.*, p. 147).

20. Conversation with Catherine Millot, December 18, 1989.

21. Conversation with Daniel Bordigoni, July 20, 1989.

22. François Tosquelles, *Psychiatries* 21 (May–June 1975), quoted in Jean Allouch, *Marguerite; ou, L'Aimée de Lacan* (Paris: EPEL, 1990), p. 523. On Saint-Alban and institutional psychotherapy, see *HPF* 2:203–204 (*JL & Co.*, p. 190).

23. Conversation with Georges Bernier.

24. Julien Green, *Le Langage et son double* (Language and its double) (Paris: Seuil, Points, 1987), p. 181.

25. Conversation with Georges Bernier.

26. Conversation with Nadia Pastré, September 18, 1991. See also M. Surya, *La Vie intellectuelle à l'époque de Vichy et sous l'Occupation, 1940–1944* (Marseilles: CDRP, 1987).

27. Conversation with Nadia Pastré; and with Flavie Alvarez de Toledo, September 12, 1991.

28. Conversation with Georges Bernier; and Simone de Beauvoir, *The Prime of Life*, trans. Peter Green (New York: Paragon House, 1992), pp. 401 and 412.

29. Conversation with Sybille Lacan, September 16, 1991.

30. Conversation with Célia Bertin. For Laforgue and the question of his "collaboration" with the Nazis, see note 7 above and *HPF* 2:167 ff. (*JL & Co.*, p. 153 ff.).

31. Conversation with Sibylle Lacan; with Thibaut Lacan, April 14, 1991; and with Marc-François Lacan, October 5, 1990. See also Sibylle Lacan, *Un Père puzzle* (Paris: Gallimard, 1994).

32. Conversation with Georges Bernier.

33. Conversation with Françoise Choay, October 22, 1991.

34. Conversation with Sibylle Lacan.

35. Conversation with Bruno Roger, June 8, 1991. *Disparu*, "disappeared," is also a euphemism for "dead."

36. Sybille Narbatte, *Le "Réseau allemand" des Cahiers du Sud* (The "German network" of the *Cahiers du Sud*), proceedings of the colloquium on Franco-German cultural relations, Paris, December 6, 7, and 8, 1990, 2:511; Jacques Grandjonc and Theresia Grundtner, eds., *Zones d'ombre 1933–1944* (Dark Areas 1933–1944) (Aix-en-Provence: Alinéa, 1990); two letters from J.L. to Jean Ballard, *RIHP* 1 (1988): 179.

37. Conversation with Georges Bernier.

38. André Masson, *Correspondance, 1916–1942: Les Années surréalistes*, introduced and annotated by Françoise Levaillant (Paris: La Manufacture, 1990), p. 475. Masson left on April 1, 1941, Breton on March 25.

39. Private conversation, September 14, 1991.

40. Surya, *Georges Bataille*, pp. 350 and 425.

41. Conversation with Claude Lévi-Strauss, November 13, 1990.

42. Jacques Decour, *Comme je vous en donne l'exemple* (As I myself demonstrate), texts introduced by Aragon (Paris: Editions Sociales, 1945); conversation with Sibylle Lacan.

43. G. W. F. Hegel, *The Phenomenology of Spirit* (1807), trans. A. V. Miller (Oxford: Clarendon, 1977). See also Jacques d'Hondt, "Le Destin français de l'oeuvre," *Magazine littéraire* 293 (November 1991): 32.

44. Beauvoir, *The Prime of Life*, pp. 442–443.

45. M. Leiris, *Haut mal* (Paris: Gallimard, 1943).

46. Surya, *Georges Bataille*, pp. 315 and 317 and pp. 379 and 382.

47. See Herbert Lottman, *The Left Bank: Writers, Artists and, from the Popular Front to the Cold War* (San Francisco: Halo, 1991); Deirdre Bair, *Simone de Beauvoir: A Biography* (New York: Summit, 1990).

48. *Les Lettres françaises* (clandestine) 12 (December 1943).

49. Beauvoir, *The Prime of Life*, pp. 444–445.

50. Jean-Paul Sartre, *Situation I* (Paris: Gallimard, 1947).

51. Ibid., p. 174.

52. Georges Bataille, *Oeuvres complètes* (Paris: Gallimard, 1970), 6:90.

53. Pablo Picasso, *Documents iconographiques* (Geneva: Pierre Cailler, 1954).

54. Bair, *Simone de Beauvoir*, p. 293.

55. Conversation with Zanie Campan, December 4, 1991.

56. S. de Beauvoir, *The Second Sex*, trans. and ed. H. M. Parshley (New York: Knopf, 1975), p. 269; *HPF* 2:517 (*JL & Co.*, pp. 511–512).

57. Françoise Gilot, *Life with Picasso* (New York: McGraw-Hill, 1964); Arianna Stassinopoulos-Huffington, *Picasso Creator and Destroyer* (New York: Simon and Schuster, 1988), p. 300.

58. Conversation with Georges Bernier.

15. Thoughts on Human Freedom

1. He says so himself in his correspondence with his brother-in-law; see the May 29, 1940, letter, quoted above.

2. J.L., "La Psychiatrie anglaise et la guerre," *Evolution psychiatrique* 1 (1947): 293–312.

3. J.L., "Le Temps logique et l'assertion de certitude anticipée: Un nouveau sophisme," *Cahiers d'art* (1940–1944), reproduced in *E*, pp. 197–213, with many modifications ("Logical Time and the Assertion of Anticipated Certainty," trans. Bruce Fink and Marc Silver, *Newsletter of the Freudian Field* 2 [1988]: 4–22); "Propos sur la causalité psychique," in *Les Problèmes de la*

psychogenèse des névroses (Paris: Desclée De Brouwer, 1950), reproduced, with very little alteration, in *E*, pp. 151–193. See also "Le Nombre 13 et la forme logique de la suspicion" (The number thirteen and the logical form of suspicion), *Ornicar?*, no. 36 (1986): 7–20.

4. Sigmund Freud, *Group Psychology and the Analysis of the Ego* (1921), in *SE* 18:67.

5. Michel Plon, "Au-delà et en deçà de la suggestion," (Beyond and shy of suggestion), *Frénésie* 8 (autumn 1989): 96.

6. Myriam Revault d'Allonnes, "De la panique comme principe du lien social" (Panic as principle of the social bond), *Les Temps modernes*, no. 527 (June 1990): 39–55.

7. J.L., "Propos sur la causalité psychiatrique," in *E*, p. 168.

8. Ibid., p. 193.

9. Notes by J.L. on sophisms, February 27, 1935, J.-A.M.; conversation with Françoise Choay, October 22, 1991;; Erik Porge, *Se compter trois, le temps logique chez Lacan* (Counting oneself as three: Logical time in Lacan) (Toulouse: Erès, 1989).

10. J.L., "Le Temps logique," p. 32 ("Logical Time," p. 6).

11. E.R., "Sartre lecteur de Freud" (Sartre as a reader of Freud), *Témoins de Sartre* (Witnesses to Sartre), *TM* (special issue) 1 (1990).

12. J.L., "Le Temps logique," p. 42. In *E*, p. 213, the phrase "indétermination existentielle" has been replaced by "détermination essentielle," which removes the 1945 reference to Sartre, existentialism, and phenomenology. See "Logical Time," p. 19.

13. Georges Canguilhem, *Vie et mort de Jean Cavaillès* (Life and death of Jean Cavaillès), Les Carnets de Baudasser (Ville-franche: Pierre Laleur, 1976), p. 39.

16. *Double Life*

1. Conversations with Célia Bertin, February 4, 1990; and with Thibaut Lacan, April 14, 1991.

2. Conversation with Frédéric François, November 14, 1991.

3. Conversation with Sibylle Lacan, November 30, 1989.

4. Conversation with Bruno Roger, June 8, 1991.

5. Conversation with Thibaut Lacan.

6. Ibid.

7. Conversation with Marc-François Lacan, October 5, 1990.

8. Ibid.

9. Judith Miller, *Visages de mon père* (Faces of my father) (Paris: Seuil, 1991), p. 27.

10. Conversations with Marc-François Lacan, October 5, 1990; and with Madeleine Houlon, April 22 and May 21, 1991.

11. Letter from J.L. to Ferdinand Alquié, December 17, 1948.

12. Conversation with Marc-François Lacan, December 1, 1991.

13. Conversation with Madeleine Houlon, May 21, 1991.

14. Conversation with Marc-François Lacan, December 1, 1991.

15. Catalog of the Musée Courbet, Ornans, 1991; Peter Webb, *The Erotic Arts* (New York: Farrar, Straus, and Giroux: 1975); *HPF* 2:305 (*JL & Co.*, p. 294). The picture was put on display at the Musée d'Orsay in 1995, to the accompaniment of much publicity.

16. Madeleine Chapsal, *Envoyez la petite musique* (Bring on the band) (Paris: Grasset, 1984).

17. Miller, *Visages de mon père*, p. 34.

18. Ibid., p. 152.

19. Conversation with Thibaut Lacan.

20. Conversation with Célia Bertin.

21. Conversation with Cyril Roger-Lacan, July 3, 1991.

22. Conversation with Sibylle Lacan, September 10, 1991.

23. See exhibition catalog *Balthus* (Paris: Centre Georges Pompidou, 1983), p. 324.

24. Conversation with Laurence Bataille (d.), March 1983; letter from J.L. to D. W. Winnicott, *Ornicar?*, no. 33 (summer 1985): 10 (in *Television: A Challenge to the Psychoanalytic Establishment*, trans. Denis Hollier, Rosalind Krauss, and Annette Michelson [New York: Norton, 1990], pp. 75–77); *HPF* 2:305–306 (*JL & Co.*, p. 295).

25. *HPF* 2:135–136 (*JL & Co.*, p. 121).

26. Conversation with Sven Follin, January 11, 1990; Jacques Chazaud, "Vestiges du passage à Ville-Evrard d'une aliénée devenue illustre" (Traces left at Ville-Evrard by a madwoman who later became famous), *EP* 55, 3 (1990): 633. See *Littoral* 37 (April 1993).

27. Marie-Magdeleine Chatel, "Faute de ravage, une folie de la publication" (Publishing mania as a surrogate for violence), *Littoral* 37 (April 1993).

28. Conversation with Annie Anzieu, October 15, 1992.

29. Letter from Didier Anzieu to E.R., October 14, 1986.

30. Jean Allouch, *Marguerite; ou, L'Aimée de Lacan* (Paris: EPEL, 1990), p. 552.

31. Conversation with Christine Anzieu, February 4, 1993.

17. An Unsatisfactory Encounter with Melanie Klein

1. Letter from James Strachey to Edward Glover, April 28, 1940. See Riccardo Steiner, "La Politique de l'émigration des psychanalystes" (The psychoanalysts' emigration policy), *RIHP* 1 (1988): 302; and Phyllis Grosskurth, *Melanie Klein: Her World and Her Work* (London: Hodder and Stoughton, 1986), p. 257.

2. D. W. Winnicott, *The Spontaneous Gesture: Selected Letters by D. W. Winnicott*, ed. F. Robert Rodman (Cambridge: Harvard University Press, 1987), p. 73.

3. *HPF* 2:187 (*JL & Co.*, p. 173).

4. Letter from Melanie Klein to S. Scott, January 28, 1948; Grosskurth, *Melanie Klein*, p. 377.

5. Letter from J.L. to Henri Ey, undated, Renée Ey archives.

6. J.L., "L'Agressivité en psychanalyse," *RFP* 3 (1948), reproduced in *E*, pp. 101–124, with a change in the first sentence; and as "Aggressivity in psychoanalysis," in *EAS*, pp. 8–29.

7. J.L., "Le Stade du miroir comme formateur de la fonction du Je, telle qu'elle nous est révélée dans l'expérience psychanalytique," *RFP* 4 (1949): 449–455, reproduced in *E*, pp. 93–100 ("The Mirror Stage as Formative of the Function of the I as Revealed in Psychoanalytic Experience," in *EAS*, pp. 1–7), with several changes: e.g., the adverb *radicalement* is replaced by *directement* (which belongs to every philosophy of the cogito) (p. 93 ["The Mirror Stage," p. 1]).

8. *HPF*, vol. 2 (*JL & Co.*); Grosskurth, *Melanie Klein*, pp. 376 ff; and Henri Flournoy, "Le Congrès international de Zurich," *RFP* 14-1 (1950): 129–137.

9. Letter from J.-B. Boulanger to E.R., June 18, 1992.

10. Grosskurth, *Melanie Klein*, pp. 371 and 391–392. See also Melanie Klein's correspondence with Daniel Lagache (letters of September 6, 1957; October 2, 1957; March 17, 1958; April 28, 1958; November 7, 1958; March 27, 1959), W.G.; and letter from Boulanger to E.R.

PART VI: ELEMENTS OF A SYSTEM OF THOUGHT

18. Theory of Treatment: Kinship Structures

1. On the split of 1953, see *HPF* 2:236–265 (*JL & Co.*, pp. 223–253).

2. Letter, dated March 15, 1953, published in "La Scission de 1953" (The split of 1953), *Ornicar?* (supplement), no. 7 (1976): 72.

3. On the third generation, see *HPF* 2:288–304 (*JL & Co.*, pp. 277–294).

4. For J.L.'s lecture "Psychanalyse dialectique?" see the listings for 1951, 1952, and 1953 in the general bibliography. See also administrative committee meeting of March 2, 1953, *Analytica* 7 (Paris: Navarin, 1978), p. 10; Juliette Favez-Boutonier, *Documents et débats*, May 11, 1975, p. 60; *HPF* 2:244 (*JL & Co.*, p. 231).

5. On Lacan's practice during the fifties, see *HPF* 2:245–247 (*JL & Co.*, pp. 232–234).

6. Letter from J.L. to M. Balint, August 6, 1953, André Haynal archives. See also M.-C. Beck, "Correspondances," *Bloc-notes de la psychanalyse* (Note-pad of psychoanalysis) 10 (1991): 171.

7. For the different versions of the "Rome Discourse," see "Fonction et champ de la parole et du language en psychanalyse," *La Psychanalyse* 1 (1956): 81–166, reprinted in *Ecrits*, pp. 229–322 ("Function and Field of Speech and Language in Psychoanalysis," in *EAS*, pp. 30–113).

8. *HPF* 2:272 (*JL & Co.*, p. 260).

9. Letter from J.L. to Marc-François Lacan, Easter 1953, M.-F.L.

10. On the subject of psychoanalysis and the church, see *HPF* 2:206–218 (*JL & Co.*, pp. 192–205).

11. Letter from J.L. to Marc-François Lacan, September 1953, M.-F.L.

12. *HPF* 2:273 (*JL & Co.*, p. 261).

13. Claude Lévi-Strauss, *The Elementary Structures of Kinship*, trans. J. H. Bell, J. R. von Sturmer, and R. Needham (London: Eyre and Spottiswood, 1949; rpt., New York: Beacon, 1969). Saussure's *Cours de linguistique générale* was translated by Wade Baskin as *Course in General Linguistics* and published in New York by the Philosophical Library in 1959.

14. See Bertrand Pulman, "Les Anthropologues face à la psychanalyse: Premières réactions" (Anthropologists and psychoanalysis: First reactions), *RIHP* 4 (1991); "Aux origines du débat ethnologie/psychanalyse: W. H. R. Rivers (1864–1922)," *L'Homme* 100 (1986); "C. G. Seligman (1873–1940)," *Gradhiva* 6 (1989).

15. See George W. Stocking, "L'Anthropologie et la science de l'irrationnel: La rencontre de Malinowski avec la psychanalyse freudienne" (Anthropology and the science of the irrational: Malinowski and Freudian psychology), *RIHP* 4 (1991); and Bronislaw Malinowski, *Journal d'ethnographe* (An ethnographer's diary) (Paris: Seuil, 1985).

16. Bronislaw Malinowski, *Sex and Repression in Savage Society* (1926; reprint, Chicago: University of Chicago, 1985); Ernest Jones, *Essays in Applied Psychoanalysis*, 2 vols. (London: Hogarth; New York: International Universities Press, 1964); Geza Roheim, *Psychoanalysis and Anthropology: Culture, Personality and the Unconscious* (New York: International Universities Press, 1950).

17. Jean Jamin, "L'Anthropologie et ses acteurs," in *Les Enjeux philosophiques des années cinquante* (The philosophical stakes of the fifties) (Paris: Centre Georges-Pompidou, 1989); Maurice Merleau-Ponty, "De Mauss à Claude Lévi-Strauss," in *Eloge de la philosophie* (Paris: Gallimard, Folio, 1960).

18. Lévi-Strauss, *Elementary Structures*, p. 24.

19. Claude Lévi-Strauss, "The Place of Anthropology in the Social Sciences and Problems Raised in Teaching It," in *Structural Anthropology*, trans. Claire Jacobson and Brooke G. Schoepf (New York: Basic, 1963), pp. 346–381.

20. Conversation with Claude Lévi-Strauss, January 13, 1990.

21. Didier Eribon and Claude Lévi-Strauss, *Conversations with Claude Levi-Strauss*, trans. Paula Wissing (New York: University of Chicago Press, 1991), p. 73.

22. Claude Lévi-Strauss, "De quelques rencontres" (Some encounters), *L'Arc* (special issue on Merleau-Ponty), reprinted in *L'Arc* (Paris: Duponchelle, 1990), p. 43.

23. Conversation with Jacques Sédat, February 6, 1992.

24. On Rudolf Hess, conversation with Madeleine Delay, October 22, 1992. See Denis

Hollier, preface to Denis Hollier, ed., *Le Collège de sociologie* (Paris: Gallimard, Idées, 1975; rpt., Paris: Gallimard, 1995).

25. Eribon and Lévi-Strauss, *Conversations with Claude Levi-Strauss*, p. 73–74. Lévi-Strauss mentions Lacan by name only once, in *Introduction to the Work of Marcel Mauss*, trans. Barbara Freeman (London and Boston: Routledge and Kegan Paul, 1987). Merleau-Ponty mentions it only three times, in *Les Relations avec autrui chez l'enfant* (Children's relations with others) (Paris: CEDES, 1975). See also *Le Visible et l'invisible* (Paris: Gallimard, 1964) (*The Visible and the Invisible*, trans. A. Lingis [Evanston Ill.: Northwestern University Press, 1969]); and *Merleau-Ponty à la Sorbonne, résumés des cours, 1949–1952* (Dijon: Cynara, 1988), pp. 50, 95–96, 109–117, 319, 321.

26. Claude Lévi-Strauss, "Le Sorcier et sa magie," in *Anthropologie structurale*, p. 202 ("The Sorcerer and His Magic," in *Structural Anthropology*, p. 183).

27. Ibid., p. xxxii. See also Robert Georgin, *De Lévi-Strauss à Lacan*, Les Cahiers Cistre (Lausanne: L'Age d'homme, 1983).

28. J.L., "Sur Les Rapports entre la mythologie et le rituel" (On the connections between mythology and ritual), *Bulletin de la Société française de philosophie* 3 (1956): 114.

29. Comment by Lacan on the lecture on symbolic function that Lévi-Strauss gave at the Hôpital Sainte-Anne on November 30, 1954, in J.L., *S. II*, pp. 46–48 (*Seminar II: The Ego in Freud's Theory and in the Technique of Psychoanalysis: 1954–1955*, trans. Sylvana Tomaselli [New York: Norton, 1988], pp. 33–35).

30. *HPF* 2: 267 (*JL & Co.*, p. 255, where the the phrase *relève orthodoxe*" is translated as "orthodox sublation"; *relève* is French for the German *Aufhebung* [= *sublation*] used by Hegel as having the opposite meanings of "distraction" and "preservation"); and E.R., *Généalogies* (Paris: Fayard, 1994).

31. J.L., "Le Mythe individuel du névrosé," *Ornicar?*, nos. 17–18 (1979): 289–307; "Le Symbolique, l'imaginaire et le réel," unpublished lecture; "La Chose freudienne; ou, Le Sens d'un retour à Freud," *EP* 1 (1956): 225–252, reproduced in *E*, 401–436, with a considerable number of changes, and translated as "The Freudian Thing; or, The Meaning of the Return to Freud in Psychoanalysis," in *EAS*, pp. 114–145.

32. Sigmund Freud, "Notes upon a Case of Obsessional Neurosis (the 'Rat Man')" (1909), in *SE* 10. See Patrick Mahony, *Freud and the Rat Man* (New Haven: Yale University Press, 1986).

33. J.L., "Mythe individuel du névrosé," pp. 305–306.

34. J.L., "Sur Les Rapports entre la mythologie et le rituel."

35. Dan Sperber, "Le Structuralisme en anthropologie," in *What Is Structuralism: An Interdisciplinary Perspective: Linguistics, Mathematics, Literature, Folk-Lore, Anthropology, Psychology* (Minneapolis: University of Minnesota, 1980); Mahony, *Freud and the Rat Man*, p. 70; Eribon and Lévi-Strauss, *The View from Afar*, p. 105.

36. Freud, *SE* 10:210.

37. J.L., *EAS*, p. 100. On the many discussions arising out of J.L.'s Rome paper, see *HFP* 2:275–280 (*JL & Co.*, p. 263), in particular the contributions of Didier Anzieu, Serge Leclaire, and Wladimir Granoff.

19. A Resounding Tribute to Martin Heidegger

1. Hugo Ott, *Martin Heidegger: A Political Life*, trans. Allan Blunden (New York: Basic, 1993), p. 190; Victor Farias, *Heidegger and Nazism* (Philadelphia: Temple University Press, 1989).

2. Quoted in Ott, *Martin Heidegger*, p. 338. See also Karl Löwith, *Ma Vie en Allemagne avant et après 1933* (My life in Germany before and after 1933) (Paris: Hachette, 1988).

3. Quoted in Ott, *Martin Heidegger*, p. 338.

4. Jean-Paul Sartre, "A More Precise Characterization of Existentialism," in Michel Contat and Michel Rybalka, eds., *The Writings of Jean-Paul Sartre*, trans. Richard C. McCleery (Evanston, Ill.: Northwestern University Press, 1974), 2:156.

5. Issues of *Les Temps modernes* published from November 1946 to July 1947; Alexandre Koyré, "L'Evolution philosophique de Heidegger," *Critique* 1 (June 1946) and 2 (July 1946). See G. Friedmann, "Heidegger et la crise de l'idée de progrès entre les deux guerres" (Heidegger and the crisis in the idea of progress between the two wars), in *Eventail de l'histoire vivante* (Panorama of living history) vol. 1, *Hommage à Lucien Febvre* (Paris: Armand Colin, 1953); Martin Heidegger, "Le Discours du Rectorat: L'Université allemande envers et contre tout, elle-même" and "Le Rectorat, faits et réflexions," *Le Débat* (October 27, 1983); "Martin Heidegger," *Les Cahiers de l'Herne* 45 (1983); *Magazine littéraire* (special issue on Heidegger) 235 (November 1986).

6. See Friedmann, "Heidegger et la crise."

7. Joseph Rovan, "Mon Témoignage sur Heidegger," *Le Monde*, December 8, 1987. See Jacques Havet, *Nécrologie de Jean Beaufret*, yearbook of the Alumni Association of the ENS (Paris: ENS, 1984), pp. 82–94.8.

8. See Jean-Michel Palmier, "Heidegger et le national-socialisme," *Les Cahiers de l'Herne* 45 (1983): 351.

9. Jean Beaufret, *Dialogue avec Heidegger*, 4 vols. (Paris: Minuit, 1977–1985).

10. Martin Heidegger, "Letters on Humanism," in *Basic Writings*, ed. David Farell Krell (New York: Harper and Row). See also Mouchir Aoun, "Approches critiques de la *Lettre sur l'humanisme* de Heidegger," in *Annales de philosophie* (Beirut: St. Joseph University, 1989).

11. Ott, *Martin Heidegger*, p. 366.

12. Private conversation, December 21, 1989.

13. Conversations with Kostas Axelos, May 1985; and with Françoise Gaillard, March 26, 1992.

14. For the different versions of the "Rome Discourse," see chap. 18, n. 7, above.

15. Marie-Claude Lambotte, "Entretien avec Jean Beaufret" (Conversation with J.B.), *Spirales* 3 (April 1981).

16. Martin Heidegger, "Logos," trans. J.L., *La Psychanalyse* 1 (1956): 59–79.

17. See Jean-Paul Aron, *Les Modernes* (Paris: Gallimard, 1984); Beaufret, *Dialogue avec Heidegger*, 4:75–88; Lucien Goldmann, letter in *Le Monde*, January 25, 1988.

18. Unfortunately I haven't been able to consult the Jean Beaufret archives, lodged with the IMEC. But it is unlikely that he collaborated in the translation of "Logos," as Judith Miller asserts in *Visages de mon père* (Faces of my father) (Paris: Seuil, 1991), p. 86. As Beaufret himself says, at Guitrancourt he worked on the translation of the Cerisy lecture. On the trip to Chartres, see HPF 2:309–310 (*JL & Co.*, pp. 298–299).

19. Lacan's translation was the first to appear in France. André Préau, in his own later version, makes no mention of Lacan's and even seems to have known nothing about it. See Martin Heidegger, *Essais et conférences* (Essays and lectures) (Paris: Gallimard, Tel, 1958). It should also be noted that Nicholas Rand, who has written two consecutive commentaries on "Logos," doesn't mention Lacan's translation either: see *Cahiers Confrontation* 8 (1982) and *Le Cryptage et la vie des oeuvres* (Paris: Aubier, 1989). Moreover, not until the second version of his commentary on "Logos"—i.e., after Victor Farias's book had been published—does Nicholas Rand point out that Heidegger's text shows traces of his involvement with Nazism. See E.R., "Vibrant Hommage de Jacques Lacan à Martin Heidegger" (A resounding tribute by J.L. to M.H.), in Bibliothèque du Collège International de Philosophie, ed., *Lacan avec les philosophes* (Paris: Albin Michel, 1991).

20. Jean Bollack and Heinz Wismann, *Héraclite; ou, La Séparation* (Paris: Minuit, 1979). See

also Jean Bollack, "Heidegger l'incontournable" (Heidegger the inevitable), *Actes de la recherche en sciences sociales* 5–6 (1975); and idem, "Réflexions sur les interprétations du logos héraclitéen," in *La Naissance de la raison en Grèce* (The Birth of Reason in Greece), Actes du Congrès de Nice, May 1987. I am indebted to Jean Bollack for the information he provided about Lacan's translation of "Logos" during our conversation of April 16, 1992.

21. André Préau was to translate this term as *nonocculation*, in Heidegger, *Essais et conférences*, p. 254, and Jean Beaufret used the phrase *ouvert sans retrait*, in *Dialogue avec Heidegger*, 4:78.

22. It was Bertrand Ogilvie who pointed out this omission to me. Stoian Stoianoff subsequently drew my attention to the difference between the two versions: *Festschrift für Hans Jantzen* (Berlin: Geb. Mann, 1951); and *Vorträge und Aufsätze* (Pfullingen: Gunther Neske, 1954).

23. J.L., *S. VIII*.

24. J.L., "Liminaire" (Introduction), *La Psychanalyse* 1 (1956): vi.

25. J.L., "L'Instance de la lettre dans l'inconscient; ou, La Raison depuis Freud," *La Psychanalyse* 3 (1958): 47–81, reproduced in *E*, pp. 493–528, with some modifications. See "The Agency of the Letter in the Unconscious or Reason since Freud," in *EAS*, pp. 146–178.

26. Ibid., p. 528 ("The Agency of the Letter," p. 175).

27. Lacan's eagerness can be seen in the postcard written to Judith on February 29, 1956. Lacan's translation of "Logos" had just been published. He wrote: "We should have seen Martin Heidegger today but missed him because of the bad weather. To console myself I've been reading him all day and explaining him to your mother" (*Visages de mon père*, p. 88).

28. Anecdote related publicly by Maurice de Gandillac, March 18, 1988; letter from Jean Wahl, March 26, 1958, IMEC.

29. Quoted by G. Granel and S. Weber, in Bibliothèque du Collège International de Philosophie, *Lacan avec les philosophes*, pp. 52 and 224.

30. Conversation with Catherine Millot, May 1990.

20. Intersecting Fates: Jacques Lacan and Françoise Dolto

1. See F.D., *Correspondance, 1913–1938*, annotated by Colette Percheminier (Paris: Hatier, 1991).

2. Ibid., p. 106. Letter from Anastase Demmler, March 29, 1921.

3. Ibid., p. 125. Letter from Suzanne Marette (later Marette-Demmier), September 20, 1922.

4. Trans. note: In the French, the author uses the phrase *psychanalyse d'enfant* to denote the theory and *psychanalyse d'enfants* (*enfants* in the plural) to refer to practice.

5. F.D., *Enfances* (Childhoods) (Paris: Seuil, Point-Actuels, 1986).

6. F.D., *Correspondance*, p. 51.

7. Ibid., p. 57.

8. Ibid., pp. 44, 53, 64.

9. Ibid., p. 215.

10. The analysis with Laforgue lasted from February 17, 1934, to March 12, 1937. The dates F.D. gave me for *HPF* 2 were wrong.

11. Letter of June 15, 1938, F.D., *Correspondance*, pp. 560–574.

12. Ibid., p. 571.

13. In *Enfances* F.D. makes no reference to her family's Maurassian attitudes. She mentions neither racism nor anti-Semitism, though she deals quite forthrightly with relational difficulties.

14. I had an opportunity to ask her the question.

15. F.D., *Psychanalyse et pédiatrie* (Paris: Seuil, 1971).

16. Manuscript notes by Edouard Pichon on F.D.'s thesis and exchange of letters, both in F.D.

17. On the SPP vocabulary committee, see *HPF* 1:376–395. Edouard Pichon, *Développement psychique de l'enfant et de l'adolescent* (Paris: Masson, 1938). *Aimance* is a punning combination of the French words for "magnet" and "loving."

18. F.D. and E.R., "Des Jalons pour une histoire: Entretien" (Staking out a story: A conversation), in *Quelques Pas sur le chemin de Françoise Dolto* (Steps toward Françoise Dolto) (Paris: Seuil, 1988), p. 12.

19. Ibid.

20. At the time my 1988 interview with F.D. took place I didn't have access to archives enabling me to check the reliability of her memory. In fact, like Bonaparte's, her diaries do not refer to the 1936 meeting.

21. E.R. and Philippe Sollers, "Entretien sur l'histoire de la psychanalyse en France" (Conversation about the history of psychoanalysis in France), *L'Infini* 2 (spring 1983).

22. Claude Halmos, "La Planète Dolto," in *L'Enfant et la psychanalyse* (Paris: CFRP, Esquisses psychanalytiques, 1993).

23. Jean-Chrysostome, born February 20, 1943, later "Carlos."

24. See *Quelques Pas*. F.D. thinks it was great respect rather than true friendship.

25. Personal reminiscences.

26. *HPF* 2:277–278 (*JL & Co.*, pp. 265–266); and F.D., *Au jeu du désir* (Paris: Seuil, 1981), pp. 133–194.

27. *La Psychanalyse* 1 (1956): 226 and 250.

28. Ibid., p. 224.

29. At a colloquium at Royaumont in May 1986.

30. Letters from J.L. to F.D. Archives, F.D.

31. Conversation with Catherine Dolto-Tolitch, March 3, 1993.

21. The Symposium and the Storm

1. For the story of the third generation of French psychoanalysts and the negotiations between the SFP and the IPA, see *HPF* 2:288–376 (*JL & Co.*, pp. 277–369). On Daniel Lagache, see ibid., 2:218–236 (205–222).

2. Conversation with F.D., reported in ibid., 2:329 (319).

3. Among the standard rules some are written and concerned with technique, and some are "oral" or "implicit" and concerned with ethics. It is by virtue of an "oral" rule that homosexuals are excluded from all training activities in the IPA.

4. *HPF* 2:331 (*JL & Co.*, p. 321). The committee carried out two series of interrogations, one between May 15 and the end of June 1961 and another in January 1963 (when a a fifth member—Solms—joined the original committee). I have already given detailed accounts of these inquiries in *HPF* 2.

5. Phyllis Grosskurth, *Melanie Klein: Her World and Her Work* (London: Hodder and Stoughton, 1986).

6. I met Ilse Hellman in London in 1982: she hadn't changed her opinion.

7. Pierre Turquet's two reports have remained secret to this day. We know the gist of the first from the letters exchanged by Granoff, Leclaire, Turquet, Lacan, and Perrier and that of the second from Granoff's and Perrier's notes. In both sets of notes it is emphasized that Lacan's expulsion is permanent and irrevocable. Lacan was to describe this act as a "Major Excommunication," alluding to the *herem* against Spinoza. See *L'Excommunication, Ornicar?*

(supplementary issue), no. 8 (1977): 41–45. For the Edinburgh "Recommendations" and the Stockholm "Directive," see pp. 19, 81, 82; and *HPF* 2 (*JL & Co.*).

8. They grouped together to propose the motion known as that of the "motion passers": J. Laplanche, J. L. Lang, J. B. Pontalis, D. Widlöcher, R. Pujol, V. Smirnoff, J. C. Lavie.

9. On the procedure of the *passe*, see *HPF* 2:450–468 (*JL & Co.*, pp. 443–461).

10. J.L., "Variantes de la cure type," reproduced in *E*, 323–362, with considerable modifications. On the debate with Maurice Bouvet, see *HPF* 2:280–285 (*JL & Co.*, pp. 268–274).

11. See E.R., "L'Amérique freudienne," *Magazine littéraire* 271 (November 1989).

12. J.L., "Situation de la psychanalyse de la psychanalyse et formation du psychanalyste en 1956," *Etudes philosophiques* (special issue) 4 (1956): 567–584, reproduced in *E*, 459–491, with few changes.

13. Ibid., in *E*, p. 483.

14. J.L., "La Direction de la cure et les principes de son pouvoir," *La Psychanalyse* 6 (1961): 149–206, reproduced in *E*, 585–645, without much change.

15. Ibid., in *E*, p. 601 (*EAS*, 226–280).

16. On the fantasy of the stealing of ideas and of plagiarism in the history of psychoanalysis, see *HPF* 1:102–103; and Michel Schneider, *Blessures de mémoire* (Memory's wounds) (Paris: Gallimard, 1981).

17. These are the terms used in an undated letter to Serge Leclaire at the same period. In "Situation de la psychanalyse" Lacan wrote that no obstacle should be placed in the way of the avowal of desire.

18. Lacan used Henri Estienne's 1578 version of the *Symposium*, of which he owned a first-edition copy. It was sold at public auction on October 5, 1991; see G. Loudmer's catalog of the sale, p. 14. See *The Collected Dialogues of Plato, Including the Letters*, ed. E. Hamilton and H. Cairns (New York: Pantheon, 1961).

19. See Jean-Louis Heurion, *L'Agalma: La Référence platonicienne dans le discours de Lacan*, presented as a thesis to the EHESS, under the direction of Heinz Wismann, Paris, 1989 (Paris: Point Hors-Ligne, 1993).

20. J.L., "Problèmes cruciaux pour la psychanalyse," S. XII, March 1965.

21. Jean Hyppolite, "Commentaire parlé sur la Verneinung de Freud," in J.L., *E*, pp. 879–887 (*Seminar I: Freud's Papers on Technique*, trans. John Forrester [New York: Norton, 1988], 52–61); J.L., "Introduction au commentaire de Jean Hyppolite sur la *Verneinung* de Freud" and "Réponse au commentaire de Jean Hyppolite sur la *Verneinung* de Freud," seminar of February 10, 1954, *La Psychanalyse* 1 (1956): 17–28 and 41–49, reprinted in *Ecrits* (Paris: Seuil, 1966), pp. 369–380 and 381–400; and S. I. See also Pierre Macherey, "Le Leurre hégélien" (The Hegelian trap), *Bloc-notes de la psychanalyse* 5 (1985).

22. *L'Inconscient*, proceedings of the colloquium held at Bonneval (Paris: Desclée De Brouwer, 1966). On events at the colloquium itself and the debate between Laplanche and Lacan and on the writing of Merleau-Ponty's text, see *HPF* 2:317–328 (*JL & Co.*, pp. 307–317).

23. Letter from J.L. to Wladimir Granoff, July 27, 1961, W.G.

24. Letters from Marie Bonaparte to Anna Freud, June 20, 1961, and to the IPA council, July 14, 1961, Library of Congress, Washington, D.C.

25. On the question of having been "negotiated," see *S. XI*, p. 10 (*Seminar XI: The Four Fundamental Concepts of Psychoanalysis* [New York: Norton, 1978], p. 4).

26. Letter from Jean Laplanche to J.L., S.L.; conversation with Daniel Widlöcher, reported in *HPF* 2:366–367 (*JL & Co.*, pp. 357–358).

27. On the way J.L. defended his pupils, in particular, Christian Simatos, see W.G. and *HPF* 2:353 (*JL & Co.*, p. 342).

28. Letters from S.L. to J.L., June 24, 1963, transmitted to W.G., S.L. and W.G.; from J.L. to

S.L., June 24, 1963, S.L.; and from J.L. to Paula Heimann, June 27, 1963, not sent, S.La. These three letters are quoted in *HPF* 2:356 (*JL & Co.*, p. 347).

29. *HPF* 2:359 (*JL & Co.*, p. 350).

30. On Hesnard, see E.R., "A propos d'une lettre de A. Hesnard," *Les Carnets de psychanalyse* 2 (winter 1991–1992): 159–162.

31. Françoise Dolto, in *La Croix*, September 12, 1981.

22. Structure and the Name-of-the-Father

1. Madeleine Chapsal's interviews have been collected as *Envoyez la petite musique* (Bring on the band) (Paris: Grasset, 1984).

2. Conversation with Madeleine Chapsal, November 21, 1991.

3. Madeleine Chapsal, *La Chair de la robe* (The flesh beneath the gown) (Paris: Fayard, 1989).

4. Chapsal, *Envoyez la petite musique*, p. 36.

5. Conversation with Madeleine Chapsal.

6. Letters from J.L. to Madeleine Chapsal, December 28, 1956, and January 18, 1957.

7. Chapsal, *Envoyez la petite musique*, p. 37.

8. "Clefs pour la psychanalyse," was reprinted in *L'Ane* 48 (October–December 1991), omitting mention of Madeleine Chapsal's name.

9. Sigmund Freud, "A Difficulty in the Path of Psycho-Analysis," in *S.E.* 17:137.

10. Chapsal, *Envoyez la petite musique*, p. 41.

11. *HPF* 2:105–108 (*JL & Co.*, pp. 89–93).

12. See E.R., *Généalogies* (Paris: Fayard, 1994).

13. Carl Gustav Jung, *Modern Man in Search of a Soul*, trans. W. S. Dell and Cary F. Raynes (New York: Harcourt Brace Jovanovich, 1933).

14. Conversation with Roland Cahen, November 21, 1989.

15. Only the first volume of Jones's biography (in English) had appeared at this time. It ends with the break between Jung and Freud. See Ernest Jones, *The Life and Work of Sigmund Freud*, 3 vols. (London: Hogarth, 1953–1957). The biography is also published in a single-volume abridgement by Lionel Trilling and Steven Marcus (London: Hogarth; New York: Basic, 1961).

16. J.L., "La Chose freudienne; ou, Le Sens d'un retour à Freud," *EP* 1 (1956): 225–252, reproduced in *E,* 401–436, with a considerable number of changes and translated as "The Freudian Thing; or, The Meaning of the Return to Freud in Psychoanalysis," in *EAS*, pp. 114–145; the citation is on p. 116. See also *S. III*, pp. 83 and 266 (*The Psychoses*, trans. Russell Grigg [New York: Norton, 1993]; the pagination corresponds to that in the French edition).

17. On the fact that no historian of Freudianism substantiates the phrase about the plague, see Pamela Tytell, *The French Psychoanalytic Culture: French Psychoanalysts and Their Relationship to the Literary Text*, 3 vols. (Ph.D. diss., Columbia University, 1979).

18. See Richard Sterba, *Réminiscences d'un psychanalyste viennois* (Toulouse: Privat, 1986); and "Vienne et la psychanalyse," *Austriaca* 21 (November 1985), texts collected by Jacques Le Rider, University of Haute-Normandie.

19. *SE* 22:80.

20. J.L. frequently returns to the "Wo es war": see *S. I*, p. 257 (*Freud's Papers on Technique: 1953–1954*, trans. John Forrester [New York: Norton, 1988], pp. 231–232), and *S. VII*, S. XIV, S. XVII, sessions of January 11 and March 15, 1967, as well the debate with Angelo Hesnard, November 6, 1956, published as "Réflexions sur le *Wo es war, soll Ich werden*, de S. Freud," *La Psychanalyse* 3 (1957): 323–324. See *HPF* 1:380; and Sigmund Freud, *New Introductory Lectures on Psycho-Analysis*, in *SE* 22:80.

21. M. Merleau-Ponty, *In Praise of Philosophy*, trans., with a preface, by John Wild and James M. Edie (Evanston, Ill.: Northwestern University Press, 1963), pp. 54–55.

22. *El* came out in 1953.

23. J.L., *S. I*, pp. 271–299 (*Seminar I: Freud's Papers on Technique*, trans. John Forrester [New York: Norton, 1988], pp. 247–272).

24. J.L., *S. II*, pp. 207–224, 225–240, 275–300 (*The Ego in Freud's Theory and in the Technique of Psychoanalysis: 1954–1955*, trans. Sylvana Tomaselli, with notes by John Forrester [New York: Norton, 1988], pp. 175–190, 191–205, 235–273); and *S. IX*, session of January 10, 1962.

25. J.L., *S. III*, p. 248 (*The Psychoses*, p. 248). "L'Instance de la lettre dans l'inconscient; ou, La Raison depuis Freud," appeared in *La Psychanalyse* 3 (1958): 47–81, and was reproduced in *E*, pp. 493–528. See "The Agency of the Letter in the Unconscious or Reason since Freud" in *EAS*, pp. 146–178. See also *S. IX*, session of December 6, 1961.

26. J.L., "Subversion du sujet et dialectique du désir dans l'inconscient freudien," in *E*, p. 819 (*EAS*, p. 316). See *S. IX*, session of December 6, 1961.

27. The papers presented at the Royaumont colloquium were published in *La Psychanalyse* 6 (1961). Lacan's contribution, written on Easter 1960, was reproduced in *E*, pp. 647–684, under the title "Remarque sur le rapport de Daniel Lagache: 'Psychanalyse et structure de la personnalité.'" See Daniel Lagache, "Structure de la personnalité," in *Oeuvres complètes*, vol. 4 (Paris: PUF, 1982). For the other important texts in this second, structuralist revision, see "Position de l'inconscient," in *E*, pp. 829–850 ("Position of the Unconscious," trans. Bruce Fink, in Bruce Fink, Richard Feldstein, and Maire Jaanus, eds., *Reading Seminar XI: Lacan's Four Fundamental Concepts of Psychoanalysis* [Albany: SUNY Press, 1995], pp. 259–282); "La Métaphore du sujet," in *E*, pp. 889–892 ("Metaphor of the Subject," trans. Bruce Fink, *Newsletters of the Freudian Field* 5 [1991]: 10–15); and "Séminaire sur les noms-du-père," November 20, 1963 (unpublished in French; in English, "Introduction to the Names-of-the-Father Seminar," in *Television: A Challenge to the Psychoanalytic Establishment*, trans. Denis Hollier, Rosalind Krauss, and Annette Michelson [New York: Norton, 1990], pp. 81–95).

28. Edgar Allan Poe, "The Purloined Letter" (1845), in *The Tell-Tale Heart and Other Writings* (New York: Bantam, 1982). Derrida commented on Lacan's treatment of this theme. The subject is deal with at length in *HPF* 2 (*JL & Co.*).

29. On the history of the term *Spaltung*, see *HPF* 1:115–133.

30. Roman Jakobson, *Essais de linguistique générale* (Paris: Minuit, 1963). See idem, *Selected Writings* (The Hague: Mouton, 1962), vol. 1.

31. J.L., *E*, pp. 517 and 800 (*EAS*, pp. 166 and 298). On Lacan's linking of Saussure and Pichon, see *HPF* 2:317–319 (*JL & Co.*, pp. 307–309). See Françoise Gadet, *Saussure and Contemporary Culture*, trans. Gregory Elliott (London: Hutchinson Radius, 1989).

32. Anika Lemaire, *Jacques Lacan* (Brussels: Mardaga, 1977), trans. D. Macey (London: Routledge and Kegan Paul, 1977), p. xiii. See "Radiophonie," *Scilicet* 2/3 (1970): 55–99.

33. The first mention of *points de capiton* occurs in *S. III*, pp. 293–306 (*The Psychoses*, pp. 293–306).

34. J.L., *E*, p. 799 (*EAS*, p. 297).

35. Roman Jakobson and Jean-José Marchand, "Entretiens," *Archives du vingtième siècle* (February 10, 1972; January 2, 1973; September 14, 1974), presented on *La Sept* TV channel, October 7, 1990. See "Jakobson," *L'Arc* 60 (1975); *Poétique* 7 (1971); Roman Jakobson, *Russie, folie, poésie* (Russia, madness, poetry) (Paris: Seuil, 1986); and Roman Jakobson and Krystyna Pomorska, *Dialogues* (Cambridge, Mass.: MIT Press, 1983). See also "Entretien avec Robert Georgin," *Les Cahiers Cistre* (Lausanne: L'Age d'homme, 1978); François Dosse, *Histoire du structuralisme* (Paris: La Découverte, 1991), 1:76–83; Dominique Desanti, *Les Clefs d'Elsa* (Keys to Elsa/Elsa's keys) (Paris: Ramsay, 1983).

36. Xavier Dauthic, "La Filiation de Husserl," and Léon Robel, "Les Années de forma-

tion," in *Les Cahiers Cistre* (Lausanne: L'Age d'homme, 1978). See Elmar Holenstein, *Jakobson* (Paris: Seghers, 1975).

37. See Tzvetan Todorov, *Théorie de la littérature: Texts by the Russian Formalists* (Paris: Seuil, 1966); and *Action poétique* 63 (1975).

38. See S. Tretiakov, *Dans le front gauche de l'art*, texts introduced by Henri Deluy (Paris: Maspero, 1977). *Action poétique* 48 (1971).

39. Roman Jakobson, "Structuralisme et téléologie," *L'Arc* 60 (1975).

40. Nikolai Trubetskoi, *Principles of Phonology*, trans. Christiane A. M. Baltaxe (Berkeley: University of California Press, 1969); "Thèses du cercle de Prague," *Change* 4 (1969); Roman Jakobson, "Formalisme russe, structuralisme tchèque," *Change* 3 (1969): 59–60.

41. In *HPF* 1, relying on evidence from Olivier Flournoy, I said that Jakobson revealed to Raymond de Saussure the importance of his father's work. But Claude Lévi-Strauss, Mireille Cifali, and Henri Vermorel have modified this interpretation. See H. Vermorel, "Notice inédite de Raymond de Saussure, avec citation de deux lettres de Claude Lévi-Strauss," and Mireille Cifali, "Présentation d'une lettre de Raymond de Saussure à Bally," *Bloc-notes de la psychanalyse* 5 (1985): 147. See also Roman Jakobson, "Three Aspects of Language and Two Types of Aphasic Disturbance," in Jakobson and Morris Halle, *Fundamentals of Language* (The Hague: Mouton, 1956).

42. "Entretien avec Robert Georgin," p. 17.

43. Didier Eribon and Claude Lévi-Strauss, *Conversations with Claude Lévi-Strauss*, trans. J. Neugroschel and P. Ross (Harmondsworth: Penguin, 1987), p. 41.

44. J.L., S. XIV, session of February 10, 1967.

45. "Entretien avec Robert Georgin," p. 17.

46. Conversation with Robert Georgin, March 3, 1992.

47. Théodore Flournoy, *Des Indes à la planète Mars* (From the Indies to the planet Mars) (Paris: Seuil, 1983). On Saussure and the anagrams, see Gadet, *Saussure*; and Jean Starobinski, *Words upon Words: The Anagrams of Ferdinand de Saussure*, trans. Olivia Emmet (New Haven: Yale University Press, 1979).

48. *HPF* 2:190–202 (*JL & Co.*, pp. 176–189).

49. Conversation with Hélène Gratiot-Alphandéry, January 11, 1990.

50. René Zazzo, "Nécrologie de A. Léontiev," *L'Année psychologique* 82 (1982): 541.

51. See A. Massuco Costa, *La Psychologie soviétique* (Paris: Payot, 1977).

52. Separate conversations with Maurice de Gandillac and Ivan Svagelski, June 10, 1992.

53. Letter from Jean Lacouture to E.R., November 4, 1985.

54. Eribon and Lévi-Strauss, *The View from Afar*, p. 57; and letter from Claude Lévi-Strauss to E.R., January 20, 1992.

55. Conversation with Françoise Giroud, January 31, 1992; Françoise Giroud, *Leçons particulières* (Private lessons) (Paris: Fayard, 1991), p. 132.

56. The law of January 3, 1972, on descent, now obviates such problems.

57. Letter from Edmonde Charles-Roux to E.R., January 8, 1992.

58. The funeral took place on October 19. Conversations with Madeleine Houlon in March 1983; with Marc-François Lacan on May 3, 1990; and with Sibylle Lacan on June 4, 1990.

59. J.L., *S. VIII*, p. 329. The sentence quoted here was corrected in *Le Transfert dans tous ses errata* (Paris: EPEL, 1991), p. 121.

60. Chapsal, *Envoyez la petite musique*, p. 75.

61. J.L., *S. III* (*The Psychoses*).

62. Ibid., p. 361.

63. Freud-Laforgue correspondence, presented by André Bourguignon, *NRP* 15 (spring 1977). See André Bourguignon and A. Manus, "Hallucination, déni de la réalité et scotomi-

sation," *Annales médico-psychologiques* 138 (February 2, 1980); Sigmund Freud, "Negation" (1925), in *SE* 19:235.

64. J. Damourette and E. Pichon, "Sur la signification psychologique de la négation en français," reproduced in *Bloc-notes de la psychanalyse* 5 (1985).

65. See M. Merleau-Ponty, *The Phenomenology of Perception* (1945), trans. Colin Smith (London: Routledge and Kegan Paul, 1962); *HPF* 1:314–320, 376–395; *HPF* 2:310–312 (*JL & Co.*, p. 299–302); J.L., "Introduction au commentaire de Jean Hyppolite sur la *Verneinung* de Freud" and "Réponse au commentaire de Jean Hyppolite sur la *Verneinung* de Freud," seminar of February 10, 1954, *La Psychanalyse* 1 (1956): 17–28 and 41–49, reprinted in *Ecrits* (Paris: Seuil, 1966), pp. 369–380 and 381–400. See also *S. I*, pp. 53–73 (*Seminar I*, 42–61); and *S. III*, pp. 21–361 (*The Psychoses*, pp. 21–361).

66. See André Green, "L'Objet (a) de Lacan, sa logique et la théorie freudienne," paper delivered on December 21, 1965, during *S. XIII*, reproduced in *Cahiers pour l'analyse*, vol. 3 (Paris: Seuil, 1966).

67. *S. I*, pp. 137–182 (*Seminar I*, pp. 118–159).

68. Hermann Nunberg, *Principles of Psychoanalysis*, trans. Madlyn and Sidney Kahr, with a foreword by Sigmund Freud (New York: International Universities Press, 1953).

69. J.L., *S. I*, p. 161 (*Seminar I*, p. 141). It was in relation to this that Lacan used the diagram of the "inverted bouquet."

70. J.L., *S. III*, p. 329 (*The Psychoses*, p. 329).

71. J.L., *S. IX*, session of December 6, 1961, transcribed by Michel Roussan. The allusion is to a famous example of incoherence in Molière.

72. D.-P. Schreber, *Memoirs of My Nervous Illness*, trans. and ed. Ida Macalpine and Richard A. Hunter, introduced by Samuel M. Weber (Cambridge: Harvard University Press, 1988); Octave Mannoni, "Schreber als Schreiber," in *Clefs pour l'imaginaire* (Clues to the imaginary order) (Paris: Seuil, 1969); A. Tabouret-Keller, "Une Etude: La Remarquable Famille Schreber," *Scilicet* 4 (1973); *Schreber inédit*, texts introduced by H. Israéls and J. Quackelbeen (Paris: Seuil, 1986); Maud Mannoni, *Education impossible* (Paris: Seuil, 1973); Sigmund Freud, "Psycho-Analytical Notes on an Autobiographical Account of a Case of Paranoia" (1911), *SE* 12:3; *Correspondance Freud/Ferenczi* (Paris: Calmann-Lévy, 1992), p. 249.

73. *HPF* 1:127–128.

74. *The Correspondence of Sigmund Freud and Sandor Ferenczi*, vol. 1, *1908–1924*, ed. Eva Brabant, Ernest Falzeder, and Patrizia Giampieri Deutsch, trans. Peter T. Hoffer (Cambridge: Harvard University Press, Belknap, 1993), letter 171, written October 6, 1910; *The Freud/Jung Letters: The Correspondence between Sigmund Freud and C. G. Jung*, trans. Ralph Manheim and R. F. C. Hull (Cambridge: Harvard University Press, 1988), letter 70F, p. 121. See Henri F. Ellenberger, *The Discovery of the Unconscious The History and Evolution of Dynamic Psychiatry* (New York: Basic; London: Allen Lane, 1970). See also Chawki Azouri, *J'ai réussi là où le paranoïaque échoue* (I have succeeded where the paranoid patient fails) (Paris: Denoël, 1991). Azouri thinks Freud doesn't speak of Schreber's father because by thus concealing the paternal element he sets himself up as the father of his own work. Hence the idea that the theory saying that paranoia lies at the root of homosexuality is a resistance to the problem of the father. A very interesting hypothesis, but one that I don't entirely share.

75. See *Le Cas Schreber*, a collective work (Paris: PUF, 1979), in particular the article by Ida Macalpine and Richard Hunter (1953). See also Ellenberger, *A la découverte de l'inconscient*, p. 450; and Peter Gay, *Freud: A Life for Our Time* (London: Dent, 1988).

76. The chronology of J.L.'s interpretation of the Schreber case is as follows: *S. I*, p. 185 (*Seminar I*, p. 163); *S. II*, pp. 275–288 (*Seminar II: The Ego in Freud's Theory and in the Technique of Psychoanalysis: 1954–1955*, trans. Sylvana Tomaselli [New York: Norton, 1988], pp. 235–247); and *S. III*, pp. 11–24 and 349–363 (*The Psychoses*, pp. 11–24 and 349–363). See "D'une ques-

tion préliminaire à tout traitement possible de la psychose," *La Psychanalyse* 4 (1958): 1–50, reproduced in *E*, pp. 531–583 with many changes ("On a Question Preliminary to Any Possible Treatment of Psychosis," in *EAS*, pp. 179–225). Schreber's *Mémoirs* were published serially in French in *Cahiers pour l'analyse*, and Lacan provided an introduction in 1966 that was reproduced in *Ornicar?*, no. 38 (1986).

PART VII: THE POWER AND THE GLORY

23. Dialogue with Louis Althusser

1. On the history of *Laienanalyse*, see *RIHP* 3 (1990).
2. Georges Canguilhem."Qu'est-ce que la psychologie?" (What is psychology?), in *Etudes d'histoire et de philosophie des sciences* (Paris:Vrin, 1968).
3. Michel Foucault, *Folie et déraison: Histoire de la folie à l'âge classique* (Paris: Gallimard, 1972); Didier Eribon, *Michel Foucault*, trans. Betsy Wing (Cambridge: Harvard University Press, 1991). Foucault's *Folie et déraison* is published in English as *Madness and Civilization:A History of Insanity in the Age of Reason*, trans. Richard Howard (New York:Vintage, 1988).
4. Michel Foucault, "Entretien avec Madeleine Chapsal," *La Quinzaine littéraire* 15 (May 15, 1966).
5. Note 14 of Louis Althusser, *Revue de l'enseignement philosophique* 5, 13th year (July 1963).
6.Yann Moulier-Boutang, *Louis Althusser: Une Biographie* (Paris: Grasset, 1992), p. 363; and conversation with Yann Moulier-Boutang, November 6, 1991.
7. Louis Althusser, *The Future Lasts Forever:A Memoir*, ed. Olivier Corpet andYann Moulier Boutang, trans. Richard Veasey (New York: The New Press, 1993), p. 122; and conversation with Louis Althusser (d.), January 18, 1985.
8. Quoted in Moulier-Boutang, *Louis Althusser*, p. 375.
9. On this subject, see Michel de Certeau, *The Mystic Fable*, trans. Michael B. Smith (Chicago: University of Chicago Press, 1992).
10. Althusser, *The Future Lasts Forever*, p. 171.
11. Ibid., p. 124.
12. Raymond Klibansky, Erwin Panofsky, and Fritz Saxl, *Saturn and Melancholy: Studies in the History of Natural Philosophy, Religion, and Art* (London: Nelson, 1964).
13. Althusser, *The Future Lasts Forever*, p. 134.
14. Letter from J.L. to Louis Althusser, November 21, 1963, IMEC. See also *Magazine littéraire* 304 (November 1992).
15. Letter from J.L. to Louis Althusser, December 1, 1963, IMEC.The article was published in *La Pensée* and reproduced in *For Marx*, trans. Ben Brewster (New York:Vintage, 1970).
16. Letter from Louis Althusser to J.L., November 26, 1963, IMEC.
17. This evening can be reconstructed on the basis of Althusser's letter of December 4, 1963, IMEC. In the interview I had with Louis Althusser before he died, he mistakenly dated his first meeting with Lacan as having taken place at a lunch in July 1963. This error is repeated in *The Future Lasts Forever*, pp. 186–187.The diaries deposited with the IMEC and the letter of November 21, 1963, show that the meeting was in fact a dinner and that it took place on December 3, 1963, as is also indicated by Althusser's letter of December 4, 1963. See *HPF* 2:387 (*JL & Co.*, p. 379).
18.As he later explained in a letter written July 11, 1966, IMEC, urging Lacan to read *Capital*.
19. Althusser, *The Future Lasts Forever*.
20. Letter from L. Althusser to J.L., December 4, 1963, IMEC.
21. See *L'Excommunication, Ornicar?* (supplementary issue), no. 8 (1977): 87; and *HPF* 2:363 (*JL & Co.*, p. 354).

22. On Lacan's interpretation of Spinoza's excommunication, see *HPF* 2:368–381 (*JL & Co.*, pp. 359–369).

23. The text of this talk was published in *Ecrits*, pp. 851–854, and was translated into English by Bruce Fink as "On Freud's '*Trieb*' and the Psychoanalyst's Desire," in *Reading Seminars I and II: Lacan's Return to Freud* (Albany: SUNY Press, 1996), pp. 417–421.

24. I described this episode in *HPF* 2:398 (*JL & Co.*, p. 390). See also J.L., *E*, pp. 851–854 ("On Freud's '*Trieb*' and the Psychoanalyst's Desire," trans. Bruce Fink, in *Reading Seminars I and II: Lacan's Return to Freud* [Albany: SUNY Press, 1996], pp. 417–421). I gained further information from conversations with Paul Ricoeur, March 7, 1985, and Jean-Paul Ricoeur, July 12, 1985. In a letter of August 20, 1991, Charles Reagan, biographer of Paul Ricoeur, told me that Ricoeur didn't keep any letters from or photographs of Lacan.

25. Conversation with Maurice de Gandillac, November 10, 1989.

26. On this period, see *HPF* 2:381–393 (*JL & Co.*, pp. 373–385). My sources are conversations with Jacques Rancière, March 1, 1985, and Etienne Balibar, February 7, 1985, as well as Etienne Balibar's lecture notes.

27. Louis Althusser, unpublished lecture, IMEC.

28. "Freud et Lacan," reproduced in *Positions* (Paris: Editions sociales, 1973), p. 13, and reprinted in Louis Althusser, *Writing on Psychoanalysis: Freud and Lacan*, ed. Olivier Corpet and François Matheron, trans. with a preface by Jeffrey Mehlman (New York: Columbia University Press, 1996), pp. 33–34, 35.

29. Letter from J.L. to Louis Althusser, July 6, 1964, IMEC.

30. At Châteauroux.

31. Jacques-Alain Miller, *Entretien avec François Ansermet sur le Séminaire* (Paris: Navarin, 1985), p. 21.

32. See Althusser's notes on Jacques-Alain Miller's papers delivered on January 21 and 28 and February 4, 1964, IMEC; and Etienne Balibar's lecture notes. Balibar mentioned the 1932 thesis and the concept of foreclosure just before J.-A. Miller did. See note by L. Althusser, December 17, 1963, IMEC.

33. J.L., *S. XI*, p. 31 (*Seminar XI: The Four Fundamental Concepts of Psychoanalysis* [New York: Norton, 1978], p. 29).

34. Letter from J.L. to L. Althusser, February 22, 1964, IMEC.

35. Louis Althusser and Etienne Balibar, *Reading Capital*, ed. Olivier Corpet and Yann Moulier Boutang, trans. Richard Veasey (New York: The New Press, 1993), and Althusser, *For Marx*. See Donald Martel, *L'Anthropologie d'Althusser* (Ottawa: Editions de l'Université d'Ottawa, 1984).

36. Althusser, *The Future Lasts Forever*, p. 209.

37. Jenny Aubry, personal reminiscences.

38. *Le Débat* 50 (May–August 1988).

39. Lucien Sebag, *Marxisme et structuralisme* (Paris: Payot, 1964).

40. Althusser, *The Future Lasts Forever*, pp. 188–189. confirmed through conversations with Hélène Gratiot-Alphandéry, January 11, 1990, and Marie-Claire Bloom, January 6, 1985. Althusser had told me the same thing in 1985; see *HPF* 2:292–293 (*JL & Co.*, pp. 281–282).

41. Louis Althusser, letter to René Diatkine, July 18, 1966, IMEC, reproduced in *Ecrits sur la psychanalyse* (Paris: Stock/IMEC, 1993). [It was really the theory that was worth the rest.]

24. "I hereby found . . ." : Kant with Sade

1. "Founding Act," trans. Jeffrey Mehlman, in *Television: A Challenge to the Psychoanalytic Establishment*, trans. Denis Hollier, Rosalind Krauss, and Annette Michelson (New York: Norton, 1990), p. 97. The founding document was first published in the 1965 yearbook of the

EFP. The story of the tape recorder is told by René Major, "Depuis Lacan" (Since Lacan), *Césure* (bulletin of the CP) 1 (1991): 178; and by Dominique Bonnet, "Ces Grands Médecins," liaison bulletin of the SNPP and the AFPEP, in *Dire et agir* (Speaking and acting; liaison bulletin of the SNPP and the AFPEP) 45 (December 1986). I shall not deal here with the history of the EFP or the third split, which led to the founding of the OPLF, which has already been dealt with in *HPF* 2:425–482 (*JL & Co.*, pp. 417–477).

2. See *HPF* 2:440 (*JL & Co.*, p. 433).

3. Texts published in the first yearbook of the EFP, 1965.

4. EFP circular of September 19, 1964. Drafts in S.L. show that the text was written by Lacan.

5. Conversation with François Wahl, November 19, 1991.

6. J.L., *S. VII* (*The Ethics of Psychoanalysis*, trans. Dennis Porter [New York: Norton, 1992]). See E.R., "Lacan et Spinoza, essai d'interprétation," contribution to the colloquium *Spinoza au vingtième siècle*, under the direction of Olivier Bloch (Paris: PUF, 1992).

7. J.L., *S. XI*, pp. 237–248 (*Seminar XI: The Four Fundamental Concepts of Psychoanalysis* [New York: Norton, 1978], pp. 263–276).

8. J.L., "Kant avec Sade," *Critique* 191 (1963): 291–313, reproduced in *E*, pp. 765–790, with important changes ("Kant with Sade," trans. James Swenson, *October* 51 [1989]).

9. *E* omits the reference to *L'Histoire de la folie*. On the impact on the history of French literature of the arguments put forth in Max Horkheimer and Theodor Adorno, *The Dialectic of Enlightenment* (New York: Seabury, 1944), see Jean-Pierre Salgas, "Métamorphoses de Lazare, écrire après Auschwitz," *Art Press* 173 (October 1992).

10. Emmanuel Kant, *The Critique of Practical Reason*, trans. T. K. Abbott, in *Kant's Critique of Practical Reason and Other Works on the Theory of Ethics* (New York: Longmans, Green, 1952).

11. See André Tosel, *Kant révolutionnaire, droit et politique* (Paris: PUF, 1988), p. 18; and Hans Dieter Gondek, *Angst Einbildungskraft Sprache, Kant, Freud, Lacan* (Munich: Boer Verlag, 1990).

12. See Hannah Arendt, *Eichmann in Jerusalem: A Report on the Banality of Evil* (New York: Penguin, 1977).

13. Marcelle Marini, *Jacques Lacan: The French Context*, trans. Anne Tomiche (New Brunswick, N.J.: Rutgers University Press, 1992), was the first to notice the analogy between Lacan's thinking and that of Arendt. See Philippe Julien, "Trois Réponses à la folie des passions," *Littoral* 27–28 (April 1989); and Myriam Revault D'Allonnes, "*Amor mundi*, la persévérance du politique," in *Ontologie et politique* (Paris: Tierce, 1989).

14. J.L., "Kant avec Sade." In the 1966 version, Lacan adds "in vain" after "freedom to desire" and replaces "the only one for which one dies" by "the freedom to die" (*E*, p. 783). Thus, two years after the founding of the EFP, he stressed his pessimism as to the possibility of real freedom for the subject.

15. Ibid., in *E*, p. 785.

16. On this question, see Myriam Revault D'Allonnes, *D'une mort à l'autre* (Paris: Seuil, 1989).

17. Louis de Saint-Just, *Oeuvres complètes* (Paris: Editions Gérard Lebovici, 1984), p. 979.

18. See Amos Funkenstein, "Interprétations théologiques de l'Holocauste: Un bilan," in *L'Allemagne nazie et le génocide juif* (Paris: Gallimard-Seuil, 1985).

19. J.L., *S. XI*, p. 246 (*Seminar XI*, pp. 274–275). "Kant with Sade" has been popularized in U.S. university circles by Slavoj Zizek, who is close to the ECF. His rather strange interpretation likens Lacan's Sade to a figure typical of Stalinian totalitarianism, who may be symmetrically compared with "the libidinal subject of neoliberal society." This turns Lacan into an ideologue of "postmodernity." See Slavoj Zizek, "Sur Le Pouvoir politique et les mécanismes idéologiques," *Ornicar?*, no. 34 (1985): 41–60. See also idem, *The Sublime Object of Ideology* (London: Verso, 1989).

20. On the history of the groups and the reviews, see the statistics and tables in *HPF* 2 (*JL & Co.*).

21. Serge Leclaire, among others, in *Etat des lieux de la psychanalyse* (Paris: Albin Michel, 1991).

22. On François Perrier's resignation from the directorate of the EFP, see *HPF* 2:450–468 (*JL & Co.*, pp. 443–461).

23. Draft of letter from François Perrier to J.L., January 12, 1965, J.S.

24. Letter from J.L. to François Perrier, January 12, 1965. J.S.

25. *The* Ecrits*: Portrait of an Editor*

1. See *HPF* 2:414–425 (*JL & Co.*, pp. 407–417).

2. Jacques Derrida, "Pour l'amour de Lacan," in Bibliothèque du Collège International de Philosophie, ed., *Lacan avec les philosophes* (Paris: Albin Michel, 1991), pp. 406–407.

3. Conversation with François Wahl, September 8, 1992.

4. Jean Allouch, *Marguerite; ou, L'Aimée de Lacan* (Paris: EPEL, 1990), p. 43. Jenny Aubry found herself in the same situation and got Lacan to have passages from his thesis typed out and put into a book that she kept in her library.

5. Conversation with François Wahl, March 9, 1990. See A. Porot, *Manuel alphabétique de psychiatrie* (1951; rpt., Paris: PUF, 1975).

6. Conversation with François Wahl.

7. Ibid.

8. Ibid.

9. Ibid.

10. Conversation with François Wahl, November 19, 1992.

11. Umberto Eco, in *L'Ane* 50 (April–June 1992): 13. See idem, *The Open Book*, trans. Anna Cancogni (Cambridge: Harvard University Press, 1989); and idem, *A Theory of Semiotics* (Bloomington: Indiana University Press, 1976).

12. Eco, in *L'Ane*, p. 14.

13. U. Eco, preface to *La struttura assente: Introduzione all ricerca semiologica* (Milan: Bompiani, 1968), the Italian edition of *A Theory of Semiotics*, not included in the French or English editions.

14. Conversation with Paul Flamand, December 4, 1989.

15. Ibid.

16. See chapter 23.

17. Conversations with François Wahl, March 9, 1990, November 19, 1991, and September 10, 1992. See *HPF* 2:421 (*JL & Co.*, p. 413).

18. *HPF* 2:413 (*JL & Co.*, p. 405).

19. Ibid.

20. Paper by J.-A. Miller, in J.L., S. XII, session of February 24, 1965.

21. The text published in *Les Cahiers pour l'analyse* 1/2 (1966): 37–49, under the title "La Suture (Eléments de la logique du signifiant)," was very different from the paper given on February 24, 1965.

22. Gottlob Frege, *The Foundations of Arithmetic: A Logico-Mathematical Enquiry into the Concept of Number*, trans. J. L. Austin (Oxford: Blackwell; New York: Philosophical Library, 1953).

23. The marriage took place at Guitrancourt on November 12, 1966.

24. Georges Bataille's name occurs in *E* on p. 583.

25. The table was published in *Les Cahiers pour l'analyse* 1/2 (1966): 167–175.

26. In J.L., *E*, p. 894.

27. See André Robinet's review in *Les Nouvelles littéraires*, February 9, 1967; Lucien Sève's in *La Nouvelle Critique*, March 1967; François Chatelet's in *Le Nouvel Observateur*, January 11 and 17, 1967; Louis Beirnaert's in *Etudes*, March 1967; and Jean-François Revel's in *L'Express*, December 18–25, 1986.

28. Didier Anzieu, *La Quinzaine littéraire*, November 15, 1966.

29. Contract for *Scilicet*, March 11, 1968.

30. The five texts were "Le Séminaire sur *La Lettre volée*" ("The Seminar on 'The Purloined Letter' "), "Le Stade du miroir" ("The Mirror Stage"), "Fonction et champ de la parole et du language en psychanalyse" ("Function and Field of Speech and Language in Psychoanalysis"), "La Chose freudienne" ("The Freudian Thing"), and "L'Instance de la lettre" ("The Agency of the Letter in the Unconscious").

31. Letter from J.L. to Bruno Flamand, January 12, 1970. See letters from Bruno Flamand to J.L., January 9, 1970, and January 19, 1970.

32. Letter from Bruno Flamand to J.L., February 13, 1970.

33. Note by François Wahl, February 21, 1970, and letter from J.L. to Bruno Flamand, February 24, 1970, as reported by Wahl in conversation, March 3, 1990.

34. As reported by François Wahl in conversation, March 3, 1990.

35. J.L., lecture in Milan, May 12, 1972, in *Lacan in Italia* (Milan: La Salamandra, 1978), p. 42; S. XIX, session of June 14, 1972. Allouch, *Marguerite*, contains all the references in *DPP*, pp. 511–516. See Didier Anzieu, *L'Auto-analyse de Freud*, 2 vols. (Paris: PUF, 1975).

36. Letter from J.L. to Jacques Postel, March 3, 1972.

37. See *L'Arc* 58 (1974).

38. J.L., *DPP*, contract of March 19, 1975.

39. Introduction to the reprint of *DPP*, internal document of March 27, 1975. See also François Wahl, preface to Alain Badiou, *Conditions* (Paris: Seuil, 1992).

40. Instead of Gaëtan Gatian de Clérambault.

26. Revolution: Jean-Paul Sartre and Jacques Lacan, Alternate Contemporaries

1. Didier Eribon conducted the unpublished interview just after Lacan's death, in September 1981. The interview Foucault gave to the *Corriere della sera* was translated in *L'Ane* 37 (January–March 1989).

2. Jean-Paul Sartre, *The Freud Scenario*, trans. Quintin Hoare (Chicago: University of Chicago Press, 1985).

3. Bernard Pingaud, in introduction to number of *L'Arc* on Lacan, reprinted by Duponchelle in 1990, on pp. 3–4.

4. Ibid., pp. 87–96.

5. J.L., interview with Gilles Lapouge for *Figaro littéraire* 9 (December 1966).

6. See Jean-François Sirinelli, *Manifestes et pétitions au vingtième siècle* (Paris: Fayard, 1990), p. 231.

7. HPF 2:551—583 (*JL & Co.*, pp. 547–580).

8. The history of the GP is still to be written. On the relationship between Sartre and Benny Lévy, see the contradictory accounts of Annie Cohen-Solal, *Sartre* (Paris: Gallimard, 1985), and Deirdre Bair, *Simone de Beauvoir: A Biography* (New York: Summit, 1990). See also Simone de Beauvoir, *Adieux: A Farewell to Sartre*, trans. Patrick O'Brian (New York: Pantheon, 1984); and Hervé Hamon and Patrick Rotman, *Génération*, 2 vols. (Paris: Seuil, 1987 and 1988). On Lacan and Maoism, the only book of interest is Bernard Sichère, *Le Moment lacanien* (Paris: Grasset, 1983). See also Philippe Soulez, "L'Action de la formule: Une Contribution à la lecture de la quatrième question de 'Radiophonie,' " *Littoral* 36 (October 1992); Ernest Gellner, *Reason and Culture: A Sociological and Philosophical Study of the Role of*

Rationality and Rationalism (Cambridge, Mass.: Basil Blackwell, 1992); and Sherry Turkle, *Psychoanalytic Politics: Freud's French Revolution* (New York: Basic, 1978).

9. Conversation with Irène Diamantis, October 5, 1992. This story is told with many inaccuracies by Samuel Lepastier, in "La Rencontre entre psychanalystes et étudiants à la faculté de médecine de Paris en Mai 1968," *RIHP* 5 (1992): 404–405.

10. Session of May 15, 1968. See *HPF* 2:461 (*JL & Co.*, p. 455).

11. Conversation with Irène Diamantis.

12. Françoise Giroud, "Quand l'autre était dieu," reproduced in *RIHP* 5 (1992).

13. J.L., "Radiophonie"; see also S. XIX, session of June 14, 1972, unpublished, and *S. XX* (*Encore*, trans. Bruce Fink [New York: Norton, 1997]).

14. Letters from Serge Leclaire to Jacques-Alain Miller, July 9, 1969; and from Serge Leclaire to Michel Foucault, reproduced in *HPF* 2:557 (*JL & Co.*, p. 552).

15. Conversation with François Wahl, November 19, 1991.

16. The word *meute* (pack) was used by J.L. to Sollers to designate his young guard at the ENS. See *HPF* 2:731 n. 116 (*JL & Co.*, p. 747 n. 116).

17. Hamon and Rotman, *Génération*, 2:182.

18. The phrase "l'analyste ne s'autorise que de lui-même" is in the second version of the "Proposition du 9 octobre 1967 sur le psychanalyste de l'Ecole"; see *Scilicet* 1 (1968).

19. Marie-Pierre de Cossé-Brissac, "Lacan ou 'l'heur' de la vie," in *Connaissez-vous Lacan?*, a collective work (Paris: Seuil, 1992), p. 18. See *HPF* 2:456ff. (*JL & Co.*, pp. 449–450). 1

20. The split occurred on January 25–26, 1969. The OPLF (Quatrième Groupe), was founded on March 17.

21. Michel Foucault, "Qu'est-ce qu'un auteur?" (What is an Author?), reprinted in *Littoral* 9 (June 1983). See also, in the same number, Jean Allouch, "Les Trois Petits Points du retour à" (The three dots of the return to). J.L. comments on Foucault's "Qu'est-ce qu'un auteur?" before the Société française de philosophie, February 22, 1969, appeared in *Bulletin de la Société française de philosophie* 3 (1969): 104, and were reprinted in *Littoral* 9 (1983): 31–32.

22. This theme was to be developed further in *The Archeology of Knowledge*, trans. A. M. Sheridan Smith (New York: Pantheon, 1972), which Foucault was finishing at this time. On the place of Foucault in the history of the psychiatric and psychoanalytic movement, see Maurice Pinguet, "Les Années d'apprentissage," *Le Débat* 41 (September–November 1986).

23. Foucault, "Qu'est-ce qu'un auteur?," p. 31; and Jean Allouch, "Freud; ou, Quand l'inconscient s'affole" (Freud; or, When the unconscious panics), *Littoral* 19–20 (April 1986).

24. Foucault, "Qu'est-ce qu'un auteur?," p. 28.

25. Ibid., p. 32. See also François Dosse, *Histoire du structuralisme* (Paris: La Découverte, 1991), 2:159–161.

26. I was one of the linguistics students at the Sorbonne who "went out onto the streets" in May 1968 to defend "structures."

27. See *HPF* 2:542–543 (*JL & Co.*, pp. 538–539).

28. J.L., *S. XVII*, p. 239. See *HPF* 2:557–583 (*JL & Co.*, pp. 552–580).

29. The expression *père-sévère* was Lacan's own; cf. "Petit Discours aux psychiatres," presented before the Cercle psychiatrique H. Ey–Sainte-Anne on November 10, 1967.

30. In this connection, see the accounts of Roland Castro and Jean-Michel Ribettes, reproduced in *HPF* 2:431, 432 (*JL & Co.*, pp. 423. 425).

31. Pierre Goldman, *Dim Memories of a Polish Jew Born in France*, trans. Joan Pinkham (New York: Viking, 1977), p. 57.

32. Conversation with Moustapha Safouan, February 7, 1985.

33. *HPF* 2:558 (*JL & Co.*, p. 553).

34. Alain Badiou had compared this logic to a metaphysics; see "Marque et manque: A

propos du zéro," *Cahiers pour l'analyse* 10 (1969). See also *L'Etre et l'événement* (Paris: Seuil, 1988).

35. *HPF* 2:563–566 (*JL & Co.*, pp. 559–562). See Ludwig Wittgenstein, *Tractatus Logico-Philosophicus*, German with English translation by C. K. Ogden and F. P. Ramsey, with an introduction by B. Russell (London: Routledge and Kegan Paul, 1922).

36. Notes by Didier Eribon for a text on intellectuals and politics, *Nouvel Observateur* November 16–22, 1995; conversation with Gilles Deleuze.

37. Maria Antonietta Macciocchi, unpublished journal.

PART VIII: IN SEARCH OF THE ABSOLUTE

27. Oriental Yearnings and a Series of Bereavements

1. François Cheng, "Entretien avec Judith Miller," *L'Ane* 48 (December 1991): 48.

2. Lao-tzu, *Tao te ching*, trans. D. C. Lau (London: Penguin Classics, 1964). See K.T. Houang and Pierre Leiris, *Lao-Tseu, La Voie et sa vertu* (Paris: Seuil, 1949).

3. Cheng, "Entretien," p. 54.

4. Unpublished journal of M. A. Macciocchi.

5. There is a portrait of Laurent Lacan in Judith Miller, *Visages de mon père* (Faces of my father) (Paris: Seuil, 1991), p. 14. See the genealogy in this volume.

6. Unpublished journal of M. A. Macciocchi.

7. Ibid.

8. Ibid.

9. *TQ* 59 (1974): 7. See Philippe Sollers, *Women*, trans. Barbara Bray (New York: Columbia University Press, 1970), pp. 77–79.

10. *TQ* 59 (1974); The trip to China began on May 20 1974. See M. A. Macciocchi, *De la Chine* (Paris: Seuil, 1971).

11. Quoted in Dominique Auffret, *Alexandre Kojève, la philosophie, l'Etat, la fin de l'Histoire* (A.K., philosophy, the State, and the end of History) (Paris: Grasset, 1990), p. 341.

12. See J.-A. Miller's brilliant account of this question in "Lacan et la chose japonaise," *Analytica* (1988). See J.L., "Avis aux lecteurs japonais" (Notice to Japanese readers), January 2, 1972, *Lettre mensuelle de l'ECF* (ECF monthly newsletter) (September 1981); idem, S. XVIII, session of May 12, 1971; and idem, "Lituraterre," *Littérature* 3 (October 1971).

13. Letter from J.L. to Maurice Kruk, April 26, 1971; and written account by Maurice Kruk, both in the Thibaut Lacan archive.

14. Ibid.

15. Inventory of the estate, S.La.; and Guy Loudmer, catalog of June 27–28, 1991.

16. Conversation with Thibaut Lacan, March 23, 1991. Pierre Lacan, born December 16, 1969, died December 19, 1969.

17. Conversations with Bruno Roger, June 8, 1991; and with Sibylle Lacan, April 14, 1990.

18. Conversation with Catherine Millot, June 17, 1992.

19. Conversation with Sibylle Lacan.

20. Letter from J.L. to Paul Flamand, June 14, 1973.

21. Conversation with Cyril Roger-Lacan, July 3, 1991.

22. Conversation with Fabrice Roger-Lacan, September 11, 1991.

23. Ibid.

28. Mathemes and Borromean Knots

1. J.L., "Of Structure as an Inmixing of an Otherness Prerequisite to any Subject Whatever,"

contribution, with discussion, to a symposium at Johns Hopkins University, October 18–21, 1966, reprinted in R. Macksey and E. Donato, eds., *The Structuralist Controversy: The Languages of Criticism and the Sciences of Man*, 2d ed. (Baltimore: Johns Hopkins University Press, 1982).

2. We shouldn't forget that the Berlin scholar Wilhelm Fliess and the writer Otto Weininger had also tried to construct a mathematics of human sexuality. See Jacques Le Rider, *Le Cas Otto Weininger: Racines de l'antisémitisme et de l'antiféminisme* (Paris: PUF, 1982); and Frank Sulloway, *Freud: Biologist of the Mind* (New York: Basic, 1979).

3. J.L., S. XIX.

4. On the matheme, see *HPF* 2:556–567 (*JL & Co.*, pp. 553–564). On the taking over of the psychoanalysis department at Paris VIII, see pp. 557–583 (pp. 554–580).

5. A. Lalande, *Vocabulaire technique et critique de la philosophie* (Paris: PUF, 1976).

6. Letter from Paul Flamand to J.L., February 25, 1974. Lacan signed the contract for the program on February 19, 1974. The film was shown on TV on two successive Saturdays (March 9 and 16, 1974), at 11 P.M., as part of a series called "Un Certain Regard."

7. Contract for Connexions du champ freudien, January 28, 1975; letter from François Wahl to Paul Flamand, December 20, 1974.

8. Gérard Miller, *Les Pousse-au-jouir du maréchal Pétain* (Paris: Seuil, 1975).

9. Ibid., p. 9.

10. Circular from J.-A. Miller and Jean Clavreul, September 1974. See *HPF* 2:576 (*JL & Co.*, p. 573).

11. J.-A. Miller, "Théorie de Lalangue," *Ornicar?*, no. 1 (January 1975).

12. See *HPF* 2:577 (*JL & Co.*, p. 574).

13. Conversation with G. Th. Guilbaud, reported in *HPF* 2:564–565 (*JL & Co.*, pp. 560–561); *Abords topologiques*, Littoral 5/6 (June 1982); F. Tingry, *Recherches logiques et linguistiques pour la psychanalyse: Nom propre et topologie des surfaces* (doctoral thesis, UER de sciences humaines cliniques, Paris VII, 1983).

14. Conversation with Michel Thomé, June 8, 1990.

15. *HPF* 2:567 (*JL & Co.*, p. 563).

16. Topology is present in S. XVIII (1970–1971) to S. XXVI (1978–1979).

17. Michel Thomé and Christian Léger, in Pierre Soury, *Chaînes et noeuds*, edited and published in three volumes by Michel Thomé and Christian Léger in 1988.

18. Ibid, vol. 3, doc. 30.

19. Conversation with Michel Thomé.

20. Soury, *Chaînes et noeuds*, vol. 3, doc. 46.

21. Accounts by Dolorès Jaulin and Christine Thibault, in ibid., vol. 2, docs. 230 and 232.

22. *HPF* 2:511–530 (*JL & Co.*, pp. 506–526).

23. Letter from J.L. to Michel Thomé, December 18, 1973, Michel Thomé archives. See Carlos Castaneda, *L'Herbe du diable et la petite fumée* (Paris: Soleil noir, 1972).

24. Conversation with Michel Thomé.

25. Reported by Bernard Jaulin, June 14, 1977. See Soury, *Chaînes et noeuds*, vol. 2, docs. 236 and 104.

26. Letter from J.L. to Pierre Soury, February 9, 1976, Michel Thomé archives.

27. Letter from J.L. to Pierre Soury, February 25, 1977.

28. As argued by the mathematician Emile Artin in *The Collected Papers* (Reading, Mass.: Addison-Wesley, 1965). See also Martin Gardner, *Fractal Nosic, Hypercards and More: Mathematical Recreations from Scientific American Magazine* (New York: Freeman, 1992).

29. Jean-Toussaint Desanti, *Les Idéalités mathématiques* (Paris: Seuil, 1968).

30. Conversation with J.-T. Desanti, February 5, 1990.

31. Conversations with Jean-Michel Vappereau, May 7 and December 5, 1991; letter from J.-M. Vappereau to E.R., November 1992.

32. Ibid.

33. J.-M. Vappereau, "Début de la lecture de Jacques Lacan," *Cahiers de lecture freudiennes* (Lysimaque) 5 (October 1984): 25–44; idem, "D'un calcul dans les champs d'existence du noeud," *Ornicar?*, no. 28 (January 1984): 133–143; idem, *Essaim, fascicule de résultats no. 1* (Paris: Point Hors-Ligne, 1985); *Etoffe, Topologie en extension* (Paris) 2 (1988).

34. J.L., S. XIX, sessions of March 3 and 8, 1972. On this, see vol. 2 of Joël Dor's excellent *Introduction à la lecture de Lacan* (Paris: Denoël, 1992); and Pierre Lavalle, "Les Négotiations et les univers du discours," in Bibliothèque du Collège International de Philosophie, ed., *Lacan avec les philosophes* (Paris: Albin Michel, 1991).

35. J.L., S. XX, pp. 61–82.

36. See J.L., "Hommage fait à Marguerite Duras du *Ravissement de Lol V. Stein*," *Cahiers Renaud-Barrault* 52 (1965): 7–15.

37. J.L., S. II, pp. 177–204 (*The Ego in Freud's Theory and in the Technique of Psychoanalysis: 1954–1955*, trans. Sylvana Tomaselli, with notes by John Forrester [New York: Norton, 1988], pp. 146–171); S. XVII, pp. 117–135; and S. XXII, session of February 11, 1975, *Ornicar?*, no. 4 (October 1975): 94. See Sigmund Freud, *The Interpretation of Dreams* (1905), in vols. 4 and 5 of *SE*. See also Perry Meisel and Walter Kendrick, eds., *Bloomsbury/Freud: The Letters of James and Alix Strachey, 1924–1925* (New York: Basic, 1985).

38. Gallimard had published these three works in French: *Ulysse*, trans. Valéry Larbaud (1937); *Stephen le héros*, trans. L. Savitzky (1948); and *Finnegans Wake*, trans. A. du Bouchet, introduced by Michel Butor (1962).

39. "Entretien avec Jacques Aubert," *L'Ane* 6 (autumn 1982): 6.

40. Jean Paris, *Joyce par lui-même* (Paris: Seuil, 1967). See also *TQ* 30 (summer 1967). On *Finnegans Wake*, see *Change* 1 (1968); *L'Arc* (special issue on Joyce) 36 (1968); and *Change* 11 (May 1972), which includes Jean Paris's article "L'Agonie du signe."

41. Conversation with Jean Paris, December 1, 1992.

42. The text reproduced in the proceedings of the symposium under the title "Joyce, le symptôme II" (Lille: CNRS Publications, 1979) is not that delivered by J.L. on the day in question but a version written three years later. The text actually delivered is known in the form of a transcription made by Jacques-Alain Miller on the basis of notes by Eric Laurent and entitled "Joyce, le symptôme I," that appeared in Jacques Aubert, ed., *Joyce avec Lacan* (Paris: Navarin, 1987).

43. J.L., "Joyce, le symptôme I," pp. 22–23.

44. Ibid., p. 22.

45. Catherine Millot, *La Vocation de l'écrivain* (Paris: Gallimard, 1991).

46. J.L., S. XXIII, session of December 16, 1975, *Ornicar?*, no. 7 (June–July 1976): 3; and conversation with Michel Thomé, November 14, 1992.

47. J.L., S. XXIII, session of February 10, 1976 (see *Ornicar?*, no. 8 [winter 1976–1977]); and ibid., session of February 17, 1976. See also Eric Laurent, "Jouissance le symptôme," *L'Ane* 6 (autumn 1982): 8.

48. Paris, *Joyce par lui-même*, p. 173.

49. J.L., S. XXIII, session of February 10, 1976, *Ornicar?*, no. 8 (winter 1976–1977): 6.

50. Proceedings of the colloquium, reproduced in Aubert, *Joyce avec Lacan*.

51. On the first trip to the United States, see J.L., S. XIII, session of March 23, 1966.

52. The main texts of J.L. translated into English at that period were "Fetishism: The Symbolic, the Imaginary and the Real," in *Perversions: Psychodynamics and Therapy*, trans. Nimède Safouan (New York: Random House, 1956; rpt., ed. S. Lorand and M. Balint, London: Ortolan, 1965), pp. 265–276; "The Mirror-Phase as Formative of the Function of the I," trans. Jean Roussel, *New Left Review* 51 (1968): 71–77; "The Function of Language in Psychoanalysis," trans. Anthony Wilden, in Anthony Wilden, ed., *The Language of the Self*

(Baltimore: Johns Hopkins University Press, 1968); "The Insistence of the Letter in the Unconscious," trans. Jean Miel, in Jacques Ehrmann, ed., *Structuralism* (New York: Doubleday, Anchor, 1970), pp. 101–137; "Of Structure as an Inmixing of Otherness Prerequisite to Any Subject Whatever" and "Intervention sur in l'exposé 'Of Structure as an Inmixing of Otherness Prerequisite to Any Subject Whatever,' " in Macksey and Donato, *The Structuralist Controversy*; "Seminar on 'The Purloined Letter,' " trans. Jeffrey Mehlman, *French Freud Structural Studies in Psychoanalysis, Yale French Studies* 48 (1972): 39–72.

53. Stuart Schneiderman, *The Death of an Intellectual Hero* (Cambridge: Harvard University Press, 1983), p. 164. Catherine Clément's version of the same legend, without the story of the boat, appears in *Vies et légendes de Jacques Lacan* (Paris: Grasset, 1981), p. 30. I started to reha-bilitate the truth in 1968, thanks to evidence from Sylvia Lacan and Laurence Bataille.

54. *Scilicet* 6/7 (1976): 9. Further details derived from conversation with Pamela Tytell, November 13, 1992.

55. *Scilicet* 6/7 (1976): 20.

56. Paul Newman, "Lettre d'Amérique," *Ornicar?*, no. 7 (June–July 1976): 103.

57. Conversation with Pamela Tytell.

58. Conversation with Serge Doubrosky, November 24, 1992.

59. Conversation with Pamela Tytell.

60. I was present at this scene.

61. Sherry Turkle, *Psychoanalytic Politics: Freud's French Revolution* (New York: Basic, 1978), p. 238. See *Scilicet* 6/7 (1976), for a shortened transcription.

62. This passage does not occur in the *Scilicet* transcription; Robert Georgin reproduced it in *Jakobson*, Les Cahiers Cistre (Lausanne: L'Age d'homme, 1978), p. 129.

63. I was often told this story by Mitsou Ronat, who had transcribed Noam Chomsky's version of it. Sherry Turkle doesn't mention it in *Psychoanalytic Politics* but does speak of another dialogue between the two men; see p. 244.

64. Turkle, *Psychoanalytic Politics*, pp. 222–223; and conversation with Pamela Tytell.

65. The correspondence between J.L. and Pierre Soury (and the others) began December 18, 1973, and ended March 2, 1979.

66. Denis Hollier, *La Figure du fond* (The pattern in the carpet) (Paris: Galilée, 1992), p. 104.

67. François Rouan, "Entretien avec Bernard Noël," *La Quinzaine littéraire*, June 15, 1970. See also Hubert Damisch, "La Peinture est un vrai trois," in *Catalogue du Musée national d'Art moderne* (Paris: Centre Georges-Pompidou, 1983).

68. Hollier, *La Figure du fond*, p. 55; and Edward Fry, in *Catalogue du Musée national d'Art moderne* (Paris: Centre Georges-Pompidou, 1983), p. 87.

69. Conversation with François Rouan, February 17, 1992; François Rouan, "Voyage autour d'un trou" (Journey around a hole) (a lecture), *Actes* (review of the ECF), November 19, 1991, p. 136.

70. J.L., *S. XX*, p. 105 (*Encore*, trans. Bruce Fink [New York: Norton, 1997], p. 105).

71. Conversation with François Rouan.

72. Ibid.

73. Ibid.

74. Reproduced in *Catalogue du Musée national*. After this, Lacan produced only some very brief letters and some drawings.

75. *HPF* 2: 636–641 (*JL & Co.*, pp. 634–39). I won't repeat here the history of the disso-lution of the EFP.

76. Letter from J.L. to E.R., March 4, 1977, published in *HPF* 2:638 (*JL & Co.*, p. 636).

77. Soury, *Chaînes et noeuds*, vol. 3, docs. 55 and 57.

78. Ibid., docs. 59 and 61. Information also drawn from conversation with Michel Thomé.

79. Soury, *Chaînes et noeuds*, vol. 3, doc. C, p. 2.

29. Psychoanalysis Reduced to Zero

1. On the congress at Deauville, see *HPF* 2:639–641 (*JL & Co.*, pp. 637–639).

2. On the Confrontation experiment, see ibid., pp. 583–618 (pp. 580–615).

3. On F. Guattari and G. Deleuze's *Anti-Oedipus*, trans. R. Hurley, M. Seem, and H. Lane (New York: Viking, 1977), see *HPF* 2:635 (*JL & Co.*, p. 633).

4. François Roustang, *Un Destin si funeste* (Paris: Minuit, 1976).

5. Cornélius Castoriadis, "Le Psychanalyse, projet et élucidation: 'Destin' de l'analyse et responsabilité des analystes," *Topique* 19 (April 1977): 73, 74.

6. Ibid., pp. 28–29.

7. The following books contain accounts of treatments with Lacan: François Weyergans, *Le Pitre* (The clown) (Paris: Gallimard, 1973), the only such text published while Lacan was still alive; Stuart Schneiderman, *The Death of an Intellectual Hero* (Cambridge: Harvard University Press, 1983); Pierre Rey, *Une Saison chez Lacan* (Paris: Laffont, 1989); Jean-Guy Godin, *Jacques Lacan, 5 rue de Lille* (Paris: Seuil, 1990); and François Giroud, *Leçons particulières* (Paris: Fayard, 1990). See also the accounts I have published in *HPF* 2, of Didier Anzieu, Octave Mannoni, Anne-Lise Stern, Francis Hofstein, Antoinette Fouque, Danièle Arnoux, Gérard Pommier, Jean-Michel Ribettes, Roland Castro, Colette Soler, and Rosine Lefort. See also Jean Allouch, *132 bons mots avec Jacques Lacan* (Toulouse: Erès, 1988).

8. Schneiderman, *Death of an Intellectual Hero*, pp. 133–34.

9. Conversation with Pierre Rey, January 22, 1992.

10. Rey, *Une Saison*, p. 32.

11. Ibid., pp. 132, 113.

12. Godin, *Jacques Lacan, 5 rue de Lille*, pp. 155, 109.

13. Giroud, *Leçons particulières*, pp. 124, 128.

14. Conversation with Françoise Giroud, January 31, 1992.

15. On this subject, see the various accounts published in the *Revue de l'Ecole de la cause freudienne* 20 (February 1992).

16. Conversation with Houda Aumont, September 30, 1992.

17. Conversation with Claude Halmos, May 13, 1993.

18. I made this suggestion in *Action poétique* 82–83 (1980).

19. Conversations with Thibaut Lacan, September 8, 1991; with Sibylle Lacan, September 3, 1991; and with Cyril Roger-Lacan, July 3, 1991.

30. Tomb for a Pharaoh

1. Catherine David, *Le Nouvel Observateur*, October 12, 1981.

2. I do not here relate the story of the dissolution of the EFP. I dealt with in detail in *HPF* 2:648–677 (*JL & Co.*, pp. 647–677). But that episode is the background to this chapter.

3. Conversation with Jenny Aubry, February 10, 1990. Aubry has often told me the story of this lunch. The diagnosis of facial paralysis was confirmed to me by one of Lacan's doctors (there were several of them), who wished to remain anonymous. The regressive vascular incident in the brain was noted in August 1980.

4. Conversation with Pamela Tytell, November 13, 1992.

5. Jenny Aubry, "Memorandum," unpublished manuscript.

6. See *Almanach de la dissolution* (Paris: Navarin, 1986), p. 11.

7. The letter was published in *Le Monde*, January 9, 1980, and reproduced in *Ornicar?*, nos. 20/21 (1980).

8. The recordings of the 1980 seminars were given to me by Patrick Valas.

9. The text of Althusser's contribution to the meeting at the PLM–Saint-Jacques Hotel is to be found in IMEC. For J.L.'s last texts, see the bibliography.

10. Conversations with Solange Faladé, February 13, 1986; and with Jacques-Alain Miller, May 11, 1985. The two accounts were published in *HPF* 2:654 (*JL & Co.*, p. 653). Solange Faladé's theory has always been confirmed by Laurence Bataille (conversation of May 15, 1985). On the changes in J.L.'s writing and signature, see Jacqueline Pinon, "Présentation d'écriture," based on documents supplied by E.R., *La Graphologie* 2, no. 202 (April 1991): 13–28.

11. In 1985 I asked Jacques-Alain Miller to let me see the original text—in vain.

12. Agreement of February 1, 1980, archives concerning the estate, S.La.

13. Conversation with Catherine Millot, November 10, 1992.

14. Claude Dorgeuille, *La Seconde Mort de Jacques Lacan* (The second death of Jacques Lacan) (Paris: Actualité freudienne, 1981), p. 26.

15. Handwritten account by Octave Mannoni dated September 27, 1986, J.A.

16. Typed account by Maude Mannoni dated March 8, 1982, J.A.

17. Letters from Louis Mérienne to Thibaut Lacan, April 22, 1982; from Marcel Czermak to Thibaut Lacan, March 9, 1982, both in J.A.

18. Mercel Czermak to Thibaut Lacan.

19. Typed account by Jean Clavreul, March 3, 1982. J.A.

20. Account by Jean-Louis Gault, *Revue de l'Ecole de la cause freudienne*, 20 (February 1992): 125.

21. J.L.'s will, S.La.

22. See Dorgeuille, *La Seconde Mort*, pp. 28–29.

23. Conversation with Jacques-Alain Miller, February 14, 1981; *Almanach de la dissolution*, p. 75.

24. I discuss all these events at length in *HPF* 2:648–679 (*JL & Co.*, pp. 590–677). The statutes of the ECF, ratified by the Préfecture de Paris on January 19, 1981, are reproduced in *La Seconde Mort*, and in the *Revue de l'Ecole de la cause freudienne* 20 (February 1992): 85–86. They are initialed by J.L., who is named as president.

25. See *Revue de l'Ecole de la cause freudienne*, p. 86; and J.-A. Miller, "Acier l'ouvert," *L'Ane* 42 (April–June 1990): 21.

26. Pierre Legendre, "Administrer la psychanalyse," *Pouvoirs* 11 (1981): 205–218.

27. Conversation with Thibaut Lacan, April 14, 1991.

28. See *HPF* 2:679 (*JL & Co.*, p. 679).

29. The death certificate indicates that Lacan was living at 74, rue d'Assas.

30. Conversations with Sibylle Lacan, September 3, 1991; and with Marc-François Lacan, January 3, 1993.

31. The funeral preparations made in this case are now general practice. Information supplied by the Institut français de thanatopraxie, founded in 1963. Whatever explanations are given about the circumstances of Lacan's death, the paradox remains.

32. For a review of press reaction to Lacan's death, see *HPF* 2:680–682 (*JL & Co.*, pp. 680–82).

33. Conversation with Marc-François Lacan.

34. Maria Antonietta Macciocchi, unpublished journal.

PART IX: LEGACIES

31. History of the Seminar

1. *HPF* 2:568–573 (*JL & Co.*, pp. 564–69).

2. On J.L.'s seminars, see bibliography.

3. Jacques Nassif's thesis was eventually published: see *Freud l'inconscient* (Paris: Galilée, 1977).

4. Letter to J.L. from François Wahl, April 21, 1970.

5. HPF 2:570 (JL & Co., p. 567).

6. Contract of October 19, 1972, canceled.

7. Letter from J.L. to Paul Flamand, November 6, 1972.

8. Contract for S. XIII, November 29, 1972, S.La. See also J.-A. Miller, *Entretien sur le Séminaire avec François Ansermet* (Paris: Navarin, 1985).

9. Conversation with J.-A. Miller, October 27, 1985; HPF 2:568 (JL & Co., pp. 564–65).

10. Conversation with François Wahl, November 19, 1991.

11. See Robert Linhart, *L'Etabli* (Paris: Minuit, 1978).

12. In his dedication to Jenny Aubry; see HPF 2:571 (JL & Co., p. 567).

13. Letters from J.L. to Paul Flamand, February 13, 1973; and from Paul Flamand to J.L., February 14, 1973.

14. Afterword by J.L., S. XI, pp. 252–254; the afterword is not included in the present English translation.

15. Note by J.-A. Miller, in J.L., S. XI, p. 249 (*The Four Fundamental Concepts of Psychoanalysis*, trans. Alan Sheridan [New York: Norton, 1978], p. xi).

16. Conversation with François Wahl, November 19, 1991.

17. Letter from J.-A. Miller to François Wahl, May 6, 1982.

18. Letter from J.L. to Paul Flamand, December 6, 1977.

19. Draft letter of February 14, 1980. I haven't found J.L.'s reply.

20. Contract for S. III, October 23, 1980, S.La.

21. Letter from François Wahl to E.R., May 25, 1992.

22. Legal document, August 28, 1987, S.La.

23. Michel Lapeyre, "Constitution d'un index du *Séminaire* de Jacques Lacan: Observations et avertissements," *Pas tant* (June 1982–July 1983). For the controversy surrounding the index, see HPF 2:690 (JL & Co., p. 690).

24. The reissued text appeared as *Les Complexes familiaux* (Paris: Navarin, 1984).

25. *Libération*, December 14–15, 1885.

26. Letter from Laurence Bataille to Colette Soler, November 25, 1982. See also E.R., HPF 2:693 (JL & Co., p. 693). Laurence Bataille let me see her letters of resignation, together with the replies, before she died.

27. Written testimony by François Wahl, July 27, 1985.

28. *Le Discours psychanalytique* 1 (October 1981).

29. Letters from François Wahl to Contardo Calligaris, September 29, 1981; and to J.-A. Miller, September 30, 1981.

30. Miller, *Entretien sur le Séminaire*, pp. 14 and 17.

31. Conversation with François Wahl, November 19, 1991.

32. In J.L., S. VII, p. 377 (*The Ethics of Psychoanalysis*, trans. Dennis Porter [New York: Norton, 1992], p. 326). In the spring of 1984 J.-A. Miller had published nineteen pages of a draft of S. VII corrected by J.L. He had found them in a cardboard box; see *Ornicar?*, no. 28 (spring 1984): 7–18.

33. Conversation with Pierre Vidal-Naquet, November 4, 1992. I was able to get a copy of the corrections he made on his own copy. See also Annick Bouillaguet, "Remarques sur l'usage du grec prêté à Jacques Lacan par les éditeurs de son septième séminaire: L'Ethique de la psychanalyse," *Psychiatries* 79, 4 (1987).

34. Unpublished letters and documents by Gabriel Bergounioux, October 1 and November 1, 1985, and June 15, 1987. By the same author, see "Comment la sémantique se fit un nom" (How semantics made a name for itself), *Ornicar?*, no. 42 (autumn 1987–1988).

35. Letters from J.-A. Miller to John Forrester, September 26, 1985; from John Forrester to J.-A. Miller, February 2, 1986; and from John Forrester to E.R., February 11, 1993. For English translations of Books I and II of the Seminar, see *Freud's Papers on Technique: 1953–1954*, trans. John Forrester (New York: Norton, 1988), and *The Ego in Freud's Theory and in the Technique of Psychoanalysis: 1954–1955*, trans. Sylvana Tomaselli, with notes by John Forrester (New York: Norton, 1988). It should be noted that the reprinting of *Radiophonie*, from *S. XVII*, has been prevented because of J.-A. Miller's refusal to put Robert Georgin's name on the cover (conversation with Robert Georgin, January 26, 1992).

36. The petition appeared in *Le Monde*, January 14, 1991.

37. Catherine Clément, in *Magazine littéraire* 288 (May 1991): 99.

38. E.R., "Lacan retranché," *Libération*, March 7, 1991; right of reply exercised by Claude Cherki, March 21, 1991. I followed Cherki's criticism with a reply pointing out that J.L. left no instructions.

39. *Le Transfert dans tous ses errata*, collective work (Paris: EPEL, 1991), in which see especially Danièle Arnoux, "A qui la faute?" (Whose fault?). See also Catherine Millot, "Lacan au jugé," *L'Infini* 34 (summer 1991).

40. The interview was tape-recorded on September 22, 1992. The version published here was read over and corrected by Claude Cherki. I asked him, in a letter dated October 17, to point out the passage in the afterword to *S. XI* on the basis of which he attributed such pronouncements to Lacan (I enclosed a copy of the afterword); I have never received an answer to my question. Dominique de Liège, of EPEL, has confirmed to me that she didn't send Claude Cherki a copy of *Le Transfert dans tous ses errata*.

32. Freudian France: The State of Play

1. See appendices for the current membership of the various psychoanalytic groups. See also Serge Leclaire and APUI, *Etat des lieux de la psychanalyse* (The like of the land in psychoanalysis) (Paris: Albin Michel, 1991).

2. *Bulletin de l'Inter-Associatif de psychanalyse* (Paris: Albin Michel, 1991).

3. François Leguil, "L'Ecole en famille nombreuse" (School for members of large families), *L'Ane* 51 (July–September 1992): 35. See also a letter from Roberto Harari to E.R., February 9, 1992. A further source of information was a conversation with Isidoro Vegh, on February 16, 1990. On the history of psychoanalysis in Argentina, see *Freud en Buenos Aires 1910–1939*, collective work edited by Hugo Vezzetti (Buenos Aires: Punto Sur, 1989); A. Cucurullo, H. Faimberg, and Leonardo Wender, "La Psychanalyse en Argentine," in *Histoire de la psychanalyse*, collective work edited by Roland Jaccard, vol. 2 (Paris: Hachette, 1982); and Oscar Masotta, "Sur la fondation de l'EF de Buenos Aires," *Ornicar?*, nos. 20/21 (1980).

4. Serge Leclaire, interview, *Libération*, January 17, 1990. The founding document of the APUI, entitled "Association pour une instance ordinale des psychanalystes" and signed by Jacques Sédat, Serge Leclaire, Lucien Israël, Philippe Girard, and Danièle Lévy, was published by *Le Monde* on December 15, 1989. It prompted numerous polemical reactions: *Le Monde*, January 23, 1990; J.-A. Miller, "Le Paradoxe du psychanalyste," *Le Monde*, February 22, 1990; Jean Clavreul, "Mais si! Les psychanalystes aiment l'ordre," *Libération*, January 26, 1990; other reactions in *Libération*, January 22, 1990; and André Green, "Instance tierce ou rapport du tiercé," *Le Monde*, February 10, 1990.

5. *Libération*, January 21, 1991.

6. On Armando Verdiglione, see *HPF* 2:547–550 (*JL & Co.*, pp. 543–46).

7. Conversation with Muriel Drazien, June 15, 1991.

8. E.R., "Repli individuel et malaise collectif," *Magazine littéraire* 264 (April 1989).

9. See Bibliothèque du Collège International de Philosophie, ed., *Lacan avec les philosophes* (Paris: Albin Michel, 1991).

10. Parts of the controversy were printed at the end of Bibliothèque du Collège International de Philosophie, *Lacan avec les philosophes*.

11. Jean-Claude Milner, *Les Noms indistincts* (Paris: Seuil, 1983); Christian Jambet, *La Grande Résurrection d'Alamûth* (Lagrasse: Verdier, 1990). See E.R., "Entretien avec Christian Jambet," *Les Lettres francaises* (November 1990). Another work worth noting is Bertrand Ogilvie's excellent *Lacan, le sujet* (Lacan, the subject) (Paris: PUF, 1987). See also Alain Juranville, *Lacan et la philosophie* (Paris: PUF, 1984); and A. Kremer-Marietti, *Lacan et la rhétorique de l'inconscient* (Paris: Aubier-Montaigne, 1978). On Anika Lemaire's *Jacques Lacan* (London: Routledge and Kegan Paul, 1977), see *HPF* 2:325–326 (*JL & Co.*, pp. 315–316). For the most violent criticism of Lacan, see François George, *L'Effet 'Yau de Poêle* (Paris: Hachette, 1979); and François Roustang, *Lacan, De L'Equivoque à l'impasse* (Paris: Minuit, 1986). Note also Luc Ferry and Alain Renaut, *French Philosophy of the Sixties: An Essay on Antihumanism*, trans. M. Cattani (Amherst: University of Massachusetts Press, 1990), where Lacan's doctrine, like those of Derrida and Foucault, is interpreted as Nietzschean-Heideggerean antihumanism: i.e., in the authors' opinion, an antidemocratic philosophy hostile to reason and the Enlightenment—in short, obscurantist.

12. Conversation with François Leguil, November 20, 1992.

13. *Lacan*, a collective work edited by Gérard Miller (Paris: Bordas, 1986); Judith Miller, *Visages de mon père* (Faces of my father) (Paris: Seuil, 1991).

14. *Lacan*, p. 6.

15. *Connaissez-vous Lacan?*, a collective work (Paris: Seuil, 1992). The contributions of Françoise Giroud and Marie-Pierre de Cossé-Brissac do not adopt the generally hagiographical tone. "L'Implacable Accoucheur de l'être" is from the contribution "L'Effet Jacques Lacan," by Colette Soler; "sauvé Freud du désastre de l'oubli, de la trahison" is from "Lacan et l'avenir de Freud," by Serge Cottet.

16. See *Programme de psychanalyse, 1990–1991* (Paris: Analytica, 1991).

17. *Le Courrier de l'ECF*, September 1992. On the treatment technique in the ECF, see the astonishing account by Helena Schulz-Keil, "A Trip to Lacania," *Hystoria, Lacan Study Notes* 6–9 (1988).

18. Gérard Pommier, *La Névrose infantile de la psychanalyse* (Paris: Point Hors-Ligne, 1989), pp. 59–60; Jean Clavreul, *Le Désir et la loi* (Paris: Denoël, 1987), p. 49.

19. J.-A. Miller, "Acier l'ouvert," (dated December 9 and 11, 1989), *La Lettre mensuelle* 85 (January 1990): 4. See also the testimony of Judith Miller, Serge Cottet, and Eric Laurent, in *L'Ane* 42 (April–June 1990).

20. Conversations with Catherine Millot, June 17, 1992, and November 10, 1992.

21. Catherine Millot, "Du symptôme de l'Ecole de la cause freudienne," *L'Infini* 29 (spring 1990): 29–30.

22. See, for example, Sol Aparicio, "La Forclusion, préhistoire d'un concept," *Ornicar?*, no. 28 (spring 1984); Joël Dor, *Introduction à la lecture de Lacan* (Paris: Denoël, 1992), pp. 123–127; and Juan David Nasio, *L'Enseignement de sept concepts cruciaux de la psychanalyse* (Paris: Rivages, 1989). Nasio is the only one who finds a concept of foreclosure in Freud. See also, by way of contrast, Claude Rabant, "Déni et forclusion, thème conceptual," in *Inventer le réel* (Paris: Denoël, 1992), which separates Freud's concepts from those of Lacan. See also Marie-Claude Lambotte, *Le Discours mélancolique* (Paris: Anthropos, 1993). In the article on "Forclusion" in the *Grand Dictionnaire de la psychologie* (Paris: Larousse, 1991), Pascale Degrange (a member of the Association freudienne) identifies *Verwerfung* as a Freudian concept, translated by Lacan (p. 310). On the genesis of this amalgam, which to a certain extent goes back to the EFP's attempt to produce a dictionary of concepts, under the direction of Charles Melman, see

HPF 2:472 (*JL & Co.*, p. 466). See also the project for *Livre compagnon de Lacan* (Lacan Companion), EFP archives.

23. Conversation with the bookseller Thierry Garnier, February 1993.

24. See Jean Laplanche, André Bourguignon, Pierre Cotet, and François Robert, *Traduire Freud* (Translating Freud) (Paris: PUF, 1988); and E.R., "Freud à vos souhaits," *Libération*, April 14, 1988.

. . . .

General Bibliography of the Works
of Jacques Lacan

Books, Articles, Papers, etc. (1926–1978)

1926   with Th. Alajouanine and P. Delafontaine: "Fixité du regard avec hypertonie, pré-
        dominant dans le sens vertical avec conservation des mouvements automatico-
        réflexes; aspect spécial du syndrome de Parinaud par hypertonie associé à un syn-
        drome extrapyramidal avec troubles pseudo-bulbaires," *Revue neurologique* 2
        (1926): 410–418.

1928   with M. Trénel: "Abasie chez une traumatisée de guerre," *Revue neurologique* 2
        (1928): 233–237.

        with J. Lévy-Valensi and M. Meignant: "Roman policier: Du délire type halluci-
        natoire chronique au délire d'imagination," *Revue neurologique* 1 (1928): 738–739;
        Annales médico-psychologiques 1 (1928): 233–237; *L'Encéphale* 5 (1928): 550–551.

1929   with L. Marchand and A, Courtois: "Syndrome comitio-parkinsonien encéphali-
        tique," *Revue neurologique* 1 (1928): 128; *Annales médico-psychologiques* 2 (1929): 185;
        L'Encéphale 7 (1929): 672.

        with G. Heuyer: "Paralysie générale avec syndrome d'automatisme mental,"
        L'Encéphale 9 (1929): 802–803.
        with R. Torgowla: "Paralysie générale prolongée," *L'Encéphale* 1 (1930): 83–85.

1930   with A. Courtois: "Psychose hallucinatoire encéphalitique," *Annales médico-psycho-
        logiques* 1 (1930): 284–285; *L'Encéphale* 4 (1930): 331.

        with P. Schiff and Mme Schiff-Werthheimer: "Troubles mentaux homodromes
        chez deux frères hérédosyphilitiques," *L'Encéphale* 1 (1931): 151–154.
        "Crises toniques combinées de protrusion de la langue et du trismus se produisant
        pendant le sommeil chez une parkinsonienne post-encéphalitique: Amputation de
        la langue consécutive," *L'Encéphale* 2 (1931): 145–146; *Annales médico-psychologiques*
        2 (1930): 420.

1931 "Structures des psychoses paranoïaques," *Semaine des hôpitaux de Paris*, July 7, 1931, pp. 437–445; *Ornicar?*, no. 44 (spring 1988): 5–18.

with H. Claude and P. Migault: "Folies simultanées," *Annales médico-psychologiques* 1 (1931): 483–490.
"Ecrits inspirés: schizographie," *Annales médico-psychologiques* 2 (1931): 508–522; reprinted in *De la psychose paranoïaque dans ses rapports avec la personnalité*, 2d ed. (1932; rpt., Paris, Seuil, 1975), pp. 365–382.
with J. Lévy-Valensi and P. Migault: "Troubles du language écrit chez une para noïaque présentant des éléments délirants du type paranoïde (schizographie)," summarized in *Annales médico-psychologiques* 2 (1931): 407–408; summarized (as "Délire et écrits à type paranoïde chez une malade à présentation paranoïaque") in *L'Encéphale*.
with H. Ey: "Parkinsonisme et syndromes démentiels (protrusion de la langue dans un des cas)," *Annales médico-psychologiques* 2 (1931): 418–428.

1932 with H. Claude and P. Migault: "Spasme de torsion et troubles mentaux post-encéphalitiques," *Annales médico-psychologiques* 1 (1932): 546–551.

Translation of Sigmund Freud, "Some Neurotic Mechanisms in Jealousy, Paranoia and Homosexuality" (1922), *Revue française de psychanalyse*, no. 3 (1932): 391–401.
De la psychose paranoïaque dans ses rapports avec la personnalité, doctoral thesis, Faculté de médecine de Paris; published under same title by Le François, Paris, in 1932; reprinted in 1975 by Seuil; reprinted in 1980 as part of the series Points.

1933 "Hiatus Irrationalis" (poem), *Le phare de Neuilly* (1933) (review of Lise Deharme); *Magazine littéraire* 11 (1977): 121.

With H. Claude and G. Heuyer: "Un cas de démence précocissime," *Annales médico-psychologiques* 1 (1933): 620–624.
With G. Heuyer: "Un cas de perversion infantile par encéphalite épidémique pré-coce diagnostiquée par un syndrome moteur fruste," *Annales médico-psychologiques* 2 (1933): 221–223.
With G. Heuyer: "Alcoolisme subaigu à pouls normal ou ralenti: Coexistence du syndrome d'automatisme mental," *Annales médico-psychologiques* 2 (1933): 531–546.
"Le problème du style et la conception psychiatrique des formes paranoïaques de l'expérience," *Le Minotaure* 1 (1933): 68–69; reproduced in Seuil's 1975 reprint of *De la psychose paranoïaque dans ses rapports avec la personnalité* (Paris: le François, 1932), pp. 383–388.
"Motifs du crime paranoïaque: Le crime des soeurs Papin," *Le Minotaure* 3/4 (1933): 25–28; *Obliques* 2 (1972): 100–103; reproduced in Seuil's 1975 reprint of *De la psychose paranoïaque dans ses rapports avec la personnalité* (Paris: Le François, 1932), pp. 389–398.
"Exposé général de nos travaux scientifiques," reproduced in Seuil's 1975 reprint of *De la psychose paranoïaque dans ses rapports avec la personnalité* (Paris: Le François, 1932), pp. 399–406.
Report on eighty-fourth assembly of the Société suisse de psychiatrie, held at Nyons-Prangins, *L'Encéphale* 11 (1933): 686–695.
Comment on report by J. Piaget, "La psychanalyse et le développement intel-lectuel," presented at the Eighth Conference of Psychanalystes de langue française, December 19, 1933; published in *Revue française de psychanalyse*, no. 1 (1934): 34;

reprinted (as "Valeur représentative du crime paranoïaque") in *Ornicar?*, no. 31 (1984): 8.

1934   Comment on Ch. Odier, "Conflits instinctuels et bisexualité," *Revue française de psychanalyse*, no. 4 (1935): 683; reprinted (as "Psychanalyse et perversion") in *Ornicar?*, no. 31 (1984): 8.

Comment on M. Friedmann, "Quelques réflexions sur le suicide," *Revue française de psychanalyse*, no. 4 (1935): 686; reprinted (as "Le suicide") in *Ornicar?*, no. 31 (1984): 9.

1935   Comment on P. Schiff, "Psychanalyse d'un crime incompréhensible," *Revue française de psychanalyse*, no. 4 (1935): 690–691; *Ornicar?*, no. 31 (1984): 9–10.

Review of H. Ey, *Hallucinations et délires*, *Evolution psychiatrique* 1 (1935): 87–91.
Review of E. Minkowski, *Le temps vécu: Etudes phénoménologiques et psychologiques*, *Recherches philosophiques* 5 (1935–1936): 424–431.
Comment on O. Codet, "A propos de trois cas d'anoréxie mentale," *Revue française de psychanalyse*, no. 1 (1936): 127; reprinted (as "L'anorexie mentale") in *Ornicar?*, no. 31 (1984): 10.

1936   "Le stade du miroir: Théorie d'un moment structural et génétique de la constitution de la réalité, conçu en relation avec l'expérience et la doctrine psychanalytique," contribution to the Fourteenth International Congress of the IPA, Marienbad, August 2–8, 1936 (not handed in for publication); indexed as "The Looking-glass-phase" in the *International Journal of Psychoanalysis* 1 (1937): 78; and MS notes by F. Dolto, June 16, 1936.

"Au-delà du principe de réalité" *Evolution psychiatrique* (special issue) 3 (1936): 67–86; reproduced in *Ecrits* (Paris: Seuil, 1966), pp. 73–92.
Comment on P. Mâle, "La formation du caractère chez l'enfant (la part de la structure et celle des événements)," *Evolution psychiatrique* 1 (1936): 57–58.
Comment on H. Kopp, "Les troubles de la parole dans leur rapport avec les troubles de la motricité," *Evolution psychiatrique* 2 (1936): 108–110.
Comment on J. Rouart, "Du rôle de l'onirisme dans les psychoses de type paranoïaque et maniaque-dépressif," *Evolution psychiatrique* 4 (1936): 87–89.

1937   Comment on M. Bonaparte, "Vues paléobiologiques et biopsychiques," *Revue française de psychanalyse*, no. 3 (1938): 551; reprinted (as "L'angoisse et le corps morcelé") in *Ornicar?*, no. 31 (1984): 10–11.

Comment on D. Lagache, "Deuil et mélancolie," *Revue française de psychanalyse*, no. 3 (1938): 564–565; reprinted (as "Fixation maternelle et narcissisme") in *Ornicar?*, no. 31 (1984): 11.

1938   Comment on R. Loewenstein, "L'origine du masochisme et la théorie des pulsions," presented at the Tenth Conference of Psychanalystes de langue française, February 21–22, 1938; published in *Revue française de psychanalyse*, no. 4 (1938): 750–752; reprinted (as "L'instinct de mort") in *Ornicar?*, no. 31 (1984): 12–13.

"La famille," in *Encyclopédie française* (Paris: Larousse, 1938), 8:40.3–16 and 42.1–8; reprinted as *Les complexes familiaux dans la formation de l'individu* (Paris: Navarin, 1984), without subheadings or bibliography.

"De l'impulsion au complexe," summary of a comment, *Revue française de psych-analyse*, no. 1 (1939): 137–141; *Ornicar?*, no. 31 (1984): 14–19.
Comment on H. Ey, "Les problèmes physiopathologiques de l'activité hallucina-toire" (January 11, 1938), *Evolution psychiatrique* 2 (1938): 75–76.

1939   Comment on H. Baruk, "Des facteurs moraux en psychiatrie: La personnalité morale chez les aliénés," *Evolution psychiatrique* 2 (1939): 32–33.

1945   "Le temps logique et l'assertion de certitude anticipée: Un nouveau sophisme," *Cahiers d'art* (1940–1944): 32–42; reproduced in *Ecrits* (Paris: Seuil, 1966), pp. 197–213; translated by Bruce Fink and Marc Silver as "Logical Time and the Assertion of Anticipated Certainty," *Newsletter of the Freudian Field* 2 (1988): 4–22.

Lecture delivered at the ENS in the rue d'Ulm as part of a series organized by Georges Gusdorf in November. Unpublished.

1946   "Le nombre treize et la forme logique de la suspicion," *Cahiers d'art* (1945–1946): 389–393; *Ornicar?*, no. 36 (1986): 7–20; *Bulletin de l'Association freudienne* 16 (1986): 3–12.

"Propos sur la causalité psychique," *Journées psychiatriques de Bonneval*, September 28, 1946; published in *Le problème de la psychogenèse des névroses et des psychoses* (with L. Bonnafé, H. Ey, S. Follin, and J. Rouart) (Paris: Desclée De Brouwer, 1950), pp. 123–165 (with closing address, pp. 215–216); reproduced in *Ecrits* (Paris: Seuil, 1966), pp. 151–194 (without closing address).
Comment on A. Borel, "Le symptôme mental: Valeur et signification" (January 1946), *Evolution psychiatrique* 1 (1947): 117–122.
Comment on G. Ferdière, "Intérêt psychologique et psychopathologique des comptines et formulettes de l'enfance" (May 1946), *Evolution psychiatrique* 3 (1947): 61–62.

1947   "La psychiatrie anglaise pendant la guerre," *Evolution psychiatrique* 1 (1947): 293–312; *Bulletin de l'Association freudienne* 22 (1987): 9–16; reprinted in *La Querelle des diagnostics* (Paris: Navarin, 1986), pp. 15–42.

Answers to questions on "La psychiatrie anglaise pendant la guerre," *Evolution psy-chiatrique* 1 (1947): 317–318.
Comment on L. Bonnafé, "Le personnage du psychiatre (étude méthodologique)" (March 25, 1947), *Evolution psychiatrique* 3 (1948): 52–55.
"Problèmes psychosomatiques en chirurgie," *Annuaire de l'Académie de chirurgie de Paris* 73 (1947): 370–373.

1948   Comment on F. Pasche, "La délinquance névrotique," *Revue française de psych-analyse*, no. 2 (1949): 315; reprinted (as "Délinquance et passage à l'acte") in *Ornicar?*, no. 31 (1984): 19.

Comment on J. Leuba, "Mère phallique et mère castratrice," *Revue française de psy-chanalyse*, no. 3 (1949): 317.
Comment on J. R. Cuel, "Place nosographique de certaines démences préséniles (types Pick et Alzheimer)" (June 25, 1948), *Evolution psychiatrique* 2 (1948): 72.
Comment on H. Hécaen, "La notion de schéma corporel et ses applications en psychiatrie," *Evolution psychiatrique* 2 (1948): 119–122.

"L'agressivité en psychanalyse," presented at the Eleventh Conference of Psychanalystes de langue française, Brussels, May 1948; published in *Revue française de psychanalyse*, no. 3 (1948): 367–388; reproduced in *Ecrits* (Paris: Seuil, 1966), pp. 101–124; translated by Alan Sheridan as "Aggressivity in Psychoanalysis," in *Ecrits: A Selection* (New York: Norton, 1977), pp. 8–29.

"Essai sur les réactions psychiques de l'hypertendu," Congrès français de chirurgie, October 4–9, 1948, *Actes du Congrès*, pp. 171–176;

Comment on Ziwar, "Psychanalyse des principaux syndromes psychosomatiques," *Revue française de psychanalyse*, no. 2 (1949): 318.

Comment on S. A. Shentoub, "Remarques méthodologiques sur la socio-analyse," *Revue française de psychanalyse*, no. 2 (1949): 319.

1949   "Règlement et doctrine de la Commission de l'enseignement de la Société psychanalytique de Paris," *Revue française de psychanalyse*, no. 3 (1949): 426–435; reprinted in *La Scission de 1953*, supplement to *Ornicar?*, no. 7 (1976): 29–36.

"Les conseillers et les conseillères d'enfants agréés par la Société psychanalytique de Paris," *Revue française de psychanalyse*, no. 3 (1949): 436–441.

Comment on R. Held, "Le problème de la thérapeutique en médecine psychosomatique," *Revue française de psychanalyse*, no. 3 (1949): 446.

"Le stade du miroir comme formateur de la fonction du Je, telle qu'elle nous est révélée dans l'expérience psychanalytique," presented at the Sixteenth International Psychoanalytical Congress, Zurich, July 17, 1949; published in *Revue française de psychanalyse*, no. 4 (1949): 449–455; reproduced in *Ecrits* (Paris: Seuil, 1966), pp. 93–100; translated by Alan Sheridan as "The Mirror Stage as Formative of the Function of the I as Revealed in Psychoanalytic Experience," in *Ecrits: A Selection* (New York: Norton, 1977), pp. 1–7.

Comment on F. Dolto, "A propos de la poupée-fleur," *Revue française de psychanalyse*, no. 4 (1949): 566; reprinted (as "La poupée-fleur de F. Dolto") in *Ornicar?*, no. 31 (1984): 21–22.

Comment on J. Fretet in collaboration with R. Lyet, "La relation hallucinatoire," *Evolution psychiatrique* 2 (1949): 151–152.

Comment on J. Rouart, "Délire hallucinatoire chez une sourde-muette," *Evolution psychiatrique* 2 (1949): 236–238.

Comment on M. Bonaparte, "Psyché dans la nature ou les limites de la psychogenèse," *Revue française de psychanalyse*, no. 4 (1949): 570; reprinted (as "Le vivant et son *Umwelt*") in *Ornicar?*, no. 31 (1984): 22.

Comment on M. Bouvet, "Incidences thérapeutiques de la prise de conscience de l'envie du pénis dans des cas de névrose obsessionnelle féminine," *Revue française de psychanalyse*, no. 4 (1949): 571–572; reprinted (as "La mère phallique") in *Ornicar?*, no. 31 (1984): 22.

1950   With M. Cenac: "Introduction théorique aux fonctions de la psychanalyse en criminologie," presented at the Thirteenth Conference of Psychanalystes de langue française, May 29, 1950; published in *Revue française de psychanalyse*, no. 1 (1951): 5–29; reproduced in *Ecrits* (Paris: Seuil, 1966), pp. 125–149.

Lacan's response to contributions to the Thirteenth Conference, *Revue française de psychanalyse*, no. 1 (1951): 5–29; reprinted (as "Psychanalyse et criminologie") in *Ornicar?*, no. 31 (1984): 23–27.

Speech to the Congrès mondial de psychiatrie, Paris, September 18–27, 1950, published in *Actes du Congrès mondial de psychiatrie* (Paris: Hermann et Cie, 1952); reprinted in *Ornicar?*, no. 30 (1984): 7–10.

1951   "Intervention on transference," presented at the Fourteenth Conference of Psychanalystes de langue française, 1951; published in *Revue française de psychanalyse*, no. 1/2 (1952): 154–163; reproduced in *Ecrits* (Paris: Seuil, 1966), pp. 215–226; translated by Jacqueline Rose as "Intervention on Transference," in Juliet Mitchell and Jacqueline Rose, eds., *Feminine Sexuality: Jacques Lacan and the Ecole freudienne* (New York: Norton, 1982), pp. 61–73.

"Some reflections on the ego," presented to the British Psycho-Analytical Society, May 2, 1951; published in *International Journal of Psychoanalysis* 34 (1953): 11–17; reprinted in *Le Coq Héron* 78 (1980): 3–13.
Comment on G. Amado, "Ethique et psychologie d'un groupe d'adolescents inadaptés," *Evolution psychiatrique* 1 (1951): 28–29.
Comment on P. Fouquet, "Réflexions cliniques et thérapeutiques sur l'alcoolisme," *Evolution psychiatrique* 2 (1951): 260–261.
Comment on A. Berge, "Psychothérapie analytique et psychanalytique," *Evolution psychiatrique* 3 (1951): 382.
Comment on S. Lebovici, "A propos du traumatisme sexuel chez la femme" (June 19, 1951), *Evolution psychiatrique* 3 (1951): 403–404.
Comment on F. Pasche, "Cent cinquante biographies de tuberculeux pulmonaires," *Evolution psychiatrique* 4 (1951): 554–556.
"Psychanalyse dialectique?" first lecture to the SPP, December 1951. Unpublished. Announced in *IJP* 35, III.

1952   Comment on J. Dreyfus-Moreau, "Etude structurale de deux cas de névrose concentrationnaire," *Evolution psychiatrique* 2 (1952): 217–218.

Comment on M. Benassy, "Sur la théorie des instincts," and M. Bouvet, "Le Moi dan la névrose obsessionnelle, relations d'objets et mécanismes de défense," presented at the Fifteenth Conference of Psychanalystes de langue française, Paris, 1952. Unpublished. See *Revue française de psychanalyse*, no. 1 (1953): 212.
"Psychanalyse dialectique?," second lecture to the SPP, June 1952. Unpublished.

1953   Statutes proposed for the Institut de psychanalyse, January 1953, published in *La Scission de 1953*, supplement to *Ornicar?*, no. 7 (1976): 57–63.

Comment on J. Aubry, "Les formes graves de la carence de soins maternels" (January 23, 1953), *Evolution psychiatrique* 1 (1953): 31.
"Psychanalyse dialectique?, third lecture to the SPP, February 1953. Unpublished.
With R. Lévy and H. Danon-Boileau: "Considérations psychosomatiques sur l'hypertension artérielle," *Evolution psychiatrique* 3 (1953): 397–409; reprinted in *Ornicar?*, no. 43 (1987): 5–16.
"Le mythe individuel du névrosé; ou, Poésie et Vérité dans la névrose," presented at the Collège philosophique, Centre de documentation universitaire, 1953; transcribed by Michel Roussan; text established by Jacques-Alain Miller, *Ornicar?*, no. 17/18 (1979): 289–307; translated by Martha Evans as "The Individual Myth of the Neurotic," *Psychoanalytic Quarterly* 48 (1979).
"Le Symbolique, l'Imaginaire et le Réel," *Bulletin de l'Association freudienne* 1 (1982): 4–13.

"Fonction et champ de la parole et du langage en psychanalyse," presented at the Congress of Romance Language Psychoanalysts, Rome, September 26–27, 1953; published in *La Psychanalyse* 1 (1956): 81–166; reproduced in *Ecrits* (Paris: Seuil, 1966), pp. 229–322; translated by Alan Sheridan as "The Function and Field of Speech and Language in Psychoanalysis," *Ecrits: A Selection* (New York: Norton, 1977), pp. 30–113.

"Discours et réponse aux interventions," presented at the congress in Rome, September 26–27, 1953; published in *La Psychanalyse* 1 (1956): 202–211 and 242–255.

1954   "Introduction au commentaire de Jean Hyppolite sur la *Verneinung* de Freud" and "Réponse au commentaire de Jean Hyppolite sur la *Verneinung* de Freud," seminar of February 10, 1954, *La Psychanalyse* 1 (1956): 17–28 and 41–49; reproduced in *Ecrits* (Paris: Seuil, 1966), pp. 369–380 and 381–399.

1955   Comment on J. Favez-Boutonier, "Psychanalyse et philosophie," presented to the Société française de philosophie, January 25, 1955; summarized in *Bulletin de la Société française de philosophie* 1 (1955): 37–41; reprinted in *Rencontres psychanalytiques d'Aix-en-Provence* (Paris: Belles Lettres, 1985).

"Variantes de la cure type," *Encyclopédie médico-chirurgicale (EMC)*, *Psychiatrie*, 3.2.1955, no. 37812-C-10; omitted from *EMC* in 1960; reproduced in *Ecrits* (Paris: Seuil, 1966), pp. 323–362.

"Le séminaire sur *La lettre volée*" (April 26, 1955), *La Psychanalyse* 2 (1957): 1–44; reproduced in *Ecrits* (Paris: Seuil, 1966), pp. 9–61. See also *Le Séminaire*, vol. 2, *1954–1955* (Paris: Seuil, 1978), pp. 225–240; translated by Jeffrey Mehlman as "Seminar on 'The Purloined Letter,' " *Yale French Studies* 48 (1974), reprinted in John Muller and William Richardson, eds., *The Purloined Poe* (Baltimore, Md.: Johns Hopkins University Press, 1988).

"La chose freudienne; ou, Sens du retour à Freud en psychanalyse," repeat of a lecture delivered at the neuropsychiatric clinic in Vienna, November 7, 1955, *Evolution psychiatrique* 1 (1956): 225–252; reproduced in *Ecrits* (Paris: Seuil, 1966), pp. 401–436; translated by Alan Sheridan as "The Freudian Thing: or, The Meaning of the Return to Freud in Psychoanalysis," *Ecrits: A Selection* (New York: Norton, 1977), pp. 114–145.

Contribution to conference on mental anorexia, November 28, 1955. Unpublished. Indexed in *La Psychanalyse* 1 (1956): 290.

1956   Translation of M. Heidegger, "Logos," *La Psychanalyse* 1 (1956): 59–79 (last part of text not translated).

With W. Granoff: "Fetishism: The Symbolic, the Imaginary and the Real," in S. Lorand and M. Balint, eds., *Perversions: Psychodynamics and Therapy* (New York: Random House, 1956); 2d ed., (London: Ortolan, 1965), pp. 265–276.

Comment on C. Lévi-Strauss: "Sur les rapports entre la mythologie et le rituel," presented to the Société française de philosophie, May 21, 1956; published in *Bulletin de la Société française de philosophie* 3 (1956): 113–119.

"Situation de la psychanalyse et formation du psychanalyste en 1956," *Etudes philosophiques* (special issue) 4 (1956): 567–584; reproduced in *Ecrits* (Paris: Seuil, 1966), pp. 459–491.

Comment on A. Hesnard, "Réflexions sur le *Wo Es war, soll Ich werden*, de S. Freud" (1956), *La Psychanalyse* 3 (1957): 323–324.

1957   Comment on D. Lagache, "Fascination de la conscience par le moi," *La Psychanalyse* 3 (1957): 329.

Comment on G. Favez, "Le rendez-vous avec le psychanalyste" (1957), *La Psychanalyse* 4 (1958): 308–313.

"La psychanalyse et son enseignement," presented to the Société française de philosophie, February 23, 1957; published in *Bulletin de la Société française de philosophie* 2 (1957): 65–101; reproduced in *Ecrits* (Paris: Seuil, 1966), pp. 437–458; reprinted (as "Dialogue avec les philosophes français") in *Ornicar?*, no. 32 (1985): 7–22.

Comment on J. Favez-Boutonier, "Abandon et névrose," presented to the Société française de psychanalyse, May 7, 1957; published in *La Psychanalyse* 4 (1958): 318–320.

"L'instance de la lettre dans l'inconscient; ou, La raison depuis Freud," presented to the Philosophy group of the Fédération des étudiants ès lettres, Sorbonne-Paris, May 9, 1957; published in *La Psychanalyse* 3 (1958): 47–81; reproduced in *Ecrits* (Paris: Seuil, 1966), pp. 493–528; translated by Alan Sheridan as "The Agency of the Letter in the Unconscious or Reason since Freud," *Ecrits: A Selection* (New York: Norton, 1977), pp. 146–178.

Comment on P. Matussek, "La psychothérapie des schizophrènes," *La Psychanalyse* 4 (1958): 332.

Interview with Madeleine Chapsal, "Clefs pour la psychanalyse," *L'Express*, May 31, 1957; reprinted in M. Chapsal, *Envoyez la petite musique* (Paris: Grasset, 1984), pp. 38–66; reprinted in *L'Ane* 48 (1991), without mention of M. Chapsal.

"D'une question préliminaire à tout traitement possible de la psychose" (December 1957–January 1958), *La Psychanalyse* 4 (1958): 1–50; reproduced in *Ecrits* (Paris: Seuil, 1966), pp. 531–583; translated by Alan Sheridan as "On a Question Preliminary to Any Possible Treatment of Psychosis," *Ecrits: A Selection* (New York: Norton, 1977), pp. 179–225.

1958   "Jeunesse de Gide ou la lettre et le désir," *Critique* 131 (1958): 291–315; reproduced in *Ecrits* (Paris: Seuil, 1966), pp. 739–764.

"Die Bedeutung des Phallus" (The signification of the Phallus), presented at the Max Planck Institute, Munich, May 9, 1958; reproduced in *Ecrits* (Paris: Seuil, 1966), pp. 685–695; translated by Alan Sheridan as "The Signification of the Phallus," *Ecrits: A Selection* (New York: Norton, 1977), pp. 281–291.

"La direction de la cure et les principes de son pouvoir," presented at the International Conference of Psychoanalysts, Royaumont, July 10–13, 1958; published in *La Psychanalyse* 6 (1961): 149–206; reproduced in *Ecrits* (Paris: Seuil, 1966), pp. 585–645; translated by Alan Sheridan as "The Direction of the Treatment and the Principles of Its Power," *Ecrits: A Selection* (New York: Norton, 1977), pp. 226–280.

Comment on report by Daniel Lagache, "Psychanalyse et structure de la personnalité," presented at the International Conference of Psychoanalysts, Royaumont, July 10–13, 1958; published in *La Psychanalyse* 6 (1961): 111–147; reproduced in *Ecrits* (Paris: Seuil, 1966), pp. 647–684.

Contribution to Fourth International Congress on Psychotherapy, Barcelona, October 1958; published (as "La psychanalyse vraie et la fausse") in *L'Ane* 51 (July–September 1992).

Comment on S. Leclaire, "L'obsessionel et son désir" (November 25, 1958), *Evolution psychiatrique* 3 (1959): 409–411.

1959   "A la mémoire d'Ernest Jones: Sur sa théorie du symbolisme" (January–March 1959), *La Psychanalyse* 5 (1959): 1–20; reproduced in *Ecrits* (Paris: Seuil, 1966), pp. 697–717.

1960   "Ethique de la psychanalyse: La psychanalyse est-elle constituante pour une éthique qui serait celle que notre temps nécessite?," presented to the university faculties of Saint-Louis, Brussels, (March 9–10, 1960); published in *Quarto*, Belgian supplement to *La Lettre mensuelle de l'Ecole de la cause freudienne*, 6 (1982): 5–24.

Comment on C. Perelman, "L'idée de rationalité et la règle de justice," presented to the Société française de philosophie, April 23, 1961; published in *Bulletin de la Société française de philosophie* 1 (1961): 29–33; reproduced (as "La métaphore du Sujet") in *Ecrits* (Paris: Seuil, 1966), pp. 889–92; translated by Bruce Fink as "The Subject as Metaphor," *Newsletter of the Freudian Field* 5 (1989): 10–15.

"Propos directifs pour un congrès sur la sexualité féminine," presented at the international conference on psychoanalysis, municipal university of Amsterdam, September 5–9, 1960; published in *La Psychanalyse* 7 (1964): 3–14; reproduced in *Ecrits* (Paris: Seuil, 1966), pp. 725–736; translated by Jacqueline Rose as "Guiding Remarks for a Congress on Feminine Sexuality," in Juliet Mitchell and Jacqueline Rose, eds., *Feminine Sexuality: Jacques Lacan and the École freudienne* (New York: Norton, 1982), pp. 86–98.

"Subversion du sujet et dialectique du désir dans l'inconscient freudien," presented at "Les colloques philosophiques internationaux," Royaumont, September 19–23, 1960); reproduced in *Ecrits* (Paris: Seuil, 1966), pp. 793–827; translated by Alan Sheridan as "The Subversion of the Subject and the Dialectic of Desire in the Freudian Unconscious," *Ecrits: A Selection* (New York: Norton, 1977), pp. 292–325.

"Position de l'inconscient," congress at Bonneval, October 31–November 2, 1960); summarized in *L'Inconscient* (Paris: Desclée De Brouwer, 1966), pp. 159–170; reproduced in *Ecrits* (Paris: Seuil, 1966), pp. 829–850; translated by Bruce Fink as "Position of the Unconscious," in Bruce Fink, Richard Feldstein, and Maire Jaanus, eds., *Reading Seminar XI: Lacan's Four Fundamental Concepts of Psychoanalysis* (Albany: SUNY Press, 1995), pp. 259–282.

1961   "Merleau-Ponty," *Les Temps modernes* 184/185 (1961): 245–254.

Contribution to the Journées provinciales, October, SFP; recorded by Wladimir Granoff.

1962   "Kant avec Sade," *Critique* 191 (1963): 291–313; reproduced in *Ecrits* (Paris: Seuil, 1966), pp. 765–790 (without introductory note); translated by James Swenson as "Kant with Sade," *October* 51 (1989).

Contribution to Journées provinciales, March, SFP. Unpublished.
Lecture to EP, "De ce que j'enseigne," January 23, 1963; transcribed by Michel Roussan.

1963   Lecture on "Les noms du père" (title of 1963–1964 seminar, interrupted by the second split, November 20, 1963); notes by Françoise Dolto, Nicole Guillet, Jean Oury; transcribed by Laborde; reproduced in *L'Excommunication: La Communauté psychanalytique en France, Ornicar?* (special supplement), no. 8 (1977); translated by Jeffrey Mehlman as "Introduction to the Names-of-the-Father Seminar," *October* 40 (1987); reprinted in *Television: A Challenge to the Psychoanalytic Establishment*, trans. Denis Hollier, Rosalind Krauss, and Annette Michelson (New York: Norton, 1990), pp. 81–95.

1964　"Du '*Trieb*' de Freud et du désir du psychanalyste," Colloque "Technique et casuistique," University of Rome, January 7–12, 1964; published in *Archivio di filosofia, tecnica e casistica* (Padua: Cedam, 1964), pp. 51–53 and 55–60; reproduced in *Ecrits* (Paris: Seuil, 1966), pp. 851–854; translated by Bruce Fink as "On Freud's '*Trieb*' and the Psychoanalyst's Desire," in Bruce Fink, Richard Feldstein, and Maire Jaanus, eds., *Reading Seminars I and II: Lacan's Return to Freud* (Albany: SUNY Press, 1996), pp. 417–421.

Comment on P. Ricoeur, "Technique et non-technique dans l'interprétation," Colloque "Technique et casuistique," University of Rome, January 7–12, 1964; published in *Archivio di filosofia, tecnica e casistica* (Padua: Cedam, 1964), p. 44.
Comment on A. de Waelhens, "Notes pour une épistémologie de la santé mentale," Colloque "Technique et casuistique," University of Rome, January 7–12, 1964; published in *Archivio di filosofia, tecnica e casistica* (Padua: Cedam, 1964), pp. 87–88.
Comment on Filiasi Carcano, "Morale tradizionale et società contemporanea," Colloque "Technique et casuistique," University of Rome, January 7–12, 1964; published in *Archivio di filosofia, tecnica e casistica* (Padua: Cedam, 1964), p. 106.
Comment R. Marlé, "Casuistique et morales modernes de situation," Colloque "Technique et casuistique," University of Rome, January 7–12, 1964; published in *Archivio di filosofia, tecnica e casistica* (Padua: Cedam, 1964), p. 117.
Founding document of the Ecole freudienne de Paris, June 21, 1964; supplementary note; foreword; "Functioning and administration"; first and subsequent yearbooks of the Ecole freudienne de Paris; note on some doctrinal elements, September 19, 1964; circular on the Ecole freudienne de Paris, unsigned: draft texts in Lacan's handwriting, drawn up in collaboration with Serge Leclaire, in S.La.
"Le Sujet," lecture delivered at the ENS, rue d'Ulm; notes by Etienne Balibar, December 11, 1964, Etienne Balibar archives.

1965　"Hommage fait à Marguerite Duras du *Ravissement de Lol V. Stein*," *Cahiers Renaud-Barrault* 52 (1965): 7–15; and *Ornicar?*, no. 34 (1965): 7–13.

"La science et la vérité," *Cahiers pour l'analyse* 3 (1966): 7–30; reproduced in *Ecrits* (Paris: Seuil, 1966), pp. 855–877; translated by Bruce Fink as "Science and Truth," *Newsletter of the Freudian Field* 3 (1989): 4–29.

1966　"Réponse à des étudiants en philosophie" (February 9, 1966), *Cahiers pour l'analyse* 3 (1966): 5–13.

Six lectures delivered at American universities on "Le désir et la demande" (February–March 1966). Unpublished.
"Of Structure as an Inmixing of an Otherness Prerequisite to Any Subject Whatever," contribution, with discussion, to a symposium at Johns Hopkins University, October 18–21, 1966; published in *The Structuralist Controversy* (Baltimore: Johns Hopkins University Press, 1970), pp. 186–201.
Contribution to Collège de médecine discussion "La place de la psychanalyse dans la médecine," with G. Raimbault, J. Aubry, P. Royer, and H. P. Klotz), *Cahiers du Collège de médecine* 12 (1966): 761–774; reprinted (as "Psychanalyse et médecine")

in *Lettres de l'Ecole freudienne* 1 (1967): 34–61; reprinted in *Bloc-notes de la psych-analyse* (Geneva) 7 (1987).

Ecrits (Paris: Seuil, 1966). A collection of thirty-four titles, including articles, papers, etc., already mentioned, plus previously unpublished texts ("Ouverture de ce recueil"; "Présentation de la suite"; "Parenthèse des parenthèses"; "De nos antécé-dents"; "Du sujet enfin en question"; "D'un dessein"; "D'un syllabaire après-coup"; and "La métaphore du Sujet" [in the second edition]); and a glossary of major concepts and an annotated table of graphics (in the second edition), by Jacques-Alain Miller. Editorial work performed by François Wahl.

Introduction to translation by P. Duquenne and N. Sels of D. P. Schreber, *Mémoires d'un névropathe* (Paris: Seuil, 1975), not reproduced in the book itself; published in *Cahiers pour l'analyse* 5 (1966): 69–72; reprinted in *Ornicar?*, no. 38 (1986): 5–9. *Les Lettres françaises*, November 26, 1966.

Interview with Gilles Lapouge, "Un psychanalyste s'explique. Auteur mystérieux et prestigieux: Jacques Lacan veut que la psychanalyse redevienne la peste," *Le Figaro littéraire*, December 1, 1966.

"Petit discours à l'ORTF" (December 2, 1966), *Recherches* 3/4 (1976): 5–9.

Interview for the Radio-Télévision Belge (December 14, 1966), *Quarto* 7 (1982): 7–11.

Interview with Gilles Lapouge, "Sartre contre Lacan: Bataille absurde," *Le Figaro lit-téraire*, December 22, 1966.

Interview with François Wahl, broadcast February 8, 1967; published in *Bulletin de l'Association freudienne* 3 (1986): 6–7.

1967   Proposal of October 9, 1967, on the psychoanalyst of the Ecole, first version, *Analytica* 8 (1978): 3–26.

Proposal of October 9, 1967, on the psychoanalyst of the Ecole, second version, *Scilicet* 1 (1968): 14–30.

Closing address of the Journées sur les psychoses chez l'enfant, Paris, October 22, 1967; published in *Recherches* (special issue) (December); reprinted in *Enfance aliénée* 2 (1968): 143–152; reprinted in *Enfance aliénée* (Paris: UGE, 10/18, 1972), pp. 295–306; reissued as *Enfance aliénée, l'enfant, la psychose et l'institution* (Paris: Denoël, 1984), pp. 255–267.

"Petit discours aux psychiatres" (November 10, 1967), Cercle psychiatrique H. Ey–Sainte-Anne.

Interview for *Fiera letteraria*, 1967, pp. 11–18.

Speech to the Ecole freudienne de Paris, December 6, 1967; published in *Scilicet* 2/3 (1970): 9–24.

"La méprise du Sujet supposé savoir," presented at the Institut français in Naples, December 14, 1967; published in *Scilicet* 1 (1968): 31–41.

"Une procédure pour la passe" (October 9, 1967); published in *Ornicar?*, no. 37 (1986): 7–12.

"De Rome 53 à Rome 67: La psychanalyse. Raison d'un échec," University of Rome, December 15, 1967, *Scilicet* 1 (1968): 42–50.

"De la psychanalyse dans ses rapports avec la réalité," presented at the Institut français, Milan, December 18, 1967; published in *Scilicet* 1 (1968): 51–60.

1968   "Introduction de *Scilicet* au titre de la revue de l'Ecole freudienne de Paris," *Scilicet* 1 (1968): 3–13.

"Jacques Lacan commente la naissance de Scilicet," interview with R. Higgins, *Le Monde*, March 16, 1968.

Contribution to "Psychanalyse et psychothérapie," the congress of the Ecole freudienne de Paris, Strasbourg, October 12, 1968; published in *Lettres de l'Ecole freudienne* 6 (1969): 42–48.

Comment on P. Benoit, "Thérapeutique—Psychanalyse—Objet," presented at the congress of the Ecole freudienne de Paris, Strasbourg, October 12, 1968; published in *Lettres de l'Ecole freudienne* 6 (1969): 39.

Comment on M. Ritter, "Du désir d'être psychanalyste, ses effets au niveau de la pratique psychothérapique de l'élève analyste," presented at the congress of the Ecole freudienne de Paris, Strasbourg, October 12, 1968; published in *Lettres de l'Ecole freudienne* 6 (1969): 92–94.

Comment on J. Nassif, "Sur le discours psychanalytique," presented at the congress of the Ecole freudienne de Paris, Strasbourg, October 12, 1968; published in *Lettres de l'Ecole freudienne* 7 (1970): 40–43.

Comment on M. de Certeau, "Ce que Freud fait de l'histoire," note on "Une névrose démoniaque au dix-septième siècle," presented at the congress of the Ecole freudienne de Paris, Strasbourg, October 12, 1968; published in *Lettres de l'Ecole freudienne* 7 (1970): 84.

Comment on J. Rudrauf, "Essai de dégagement du concept psychanalytique de psychothérapie," presented at the congress of the Ecole freudienne de Paris, Strasbourg, October 12, 1968; published in *Lettres de l'Ecole freudienne* 7 (1970): 136–137.

Comment on J. Oury, "Stratégie de sauvetage de Freud," presented at the congress of the Ecole freudienne de Paris, Strasbourg, October 12, 1968; published in *Lettres de l'Ecole freudienne* 7 (1970): 146 and 151.

"En guise de conclusion," closing address to the congress of the Ecole freudienne de Paris, Strasbourg, October 12, 1968; published in *Lettres de l'Ecole freudienne* 7 (1970): 157–166.

1969   Address to admissions jury of the EFP, delivered to the assembly before the vote, January 25, 1969; published in *Scilicet* 2/3 (1970): 49–51.

Comment on M. Foucault, "Qu'est-ce qu'un auteur?" presented to the Société française de philosophie, February 22. 1969; published in *Bulletin de la Société française de philosophie* 3 (1969): 104; reprinted in *Littoral* 9 (1983): 31–32.

Text by J. Lacan given to J. Aubry. November 10, 1969; published in *Enfance abandonnée: La carence de soins maternels* (Paris: Scarabée, A.-M. Métailié, 1983); reprinted (as "Deux notes sur l'enfant") in *Ornicar?*, no. 37 (1986): 13–14.

Answer to request for biographical and bibliographical information, in D. Hameline and H. Lesage, eds., *Anthologie des psychologues français contemporains* (Paris: PUF, 1969), pp. 322–323.

"Le discours de l'universitaire," first impromptu of Vincennes, delivered December 3, 1969; the first of four lectures to be presented in the 1969–1970 seminar; published with the second (as "Analyticon") in *Magazine littéraire* 121 (1977): 21–24.

Presentation of the publication of the *Ecrits* (December 14, 1969), *Ecrits I* (Paris: Seuil, Points, 1970).

"Préface" (Christmas 1969), in Anika Lemaire, *Jacques Lacan*, 2d ed. (Brussels: P. Mardaga, 1970).

1970   "Des unités de valeur," second impromptu of Vincennes, (March 14, 1970); the second of four lectures to be delivered in the 1969–1970 seminar; published with the first (as "Analyticon") in *Magazine littéraire* 121 (1977): 21–24. See *L'Envers de la psychanalyse*, in *S. XVII*. The last two lectures were not delivered.

Comment on Ph. Rappard, "De la conception grecque de l'éducation et de l'enseignement de la psychanalyse," presented at "L'enseignement de la psychanalyse," the congress of the Ecole freudienne de Paris, April 17–19, 1970; published in *Lettres de l'Ecole freudienne* 8 (1971): 8–10.

Comment on papers by M. Montrelay and F. Baudry, "Sur l'enseignement de la psychanalyse à Vincennes," presented at the congress of the Ecole freudienne de Paris, April 17–19, 1970; published in *Lettres de l'Ecole freudienne* 8 (1971): 187.

Comment on Ch. Melman, "Propos à prétention roborative avant le Congrès," presented at the congress of the Ecole freudienne de Paris, April 17–19, 1970; published in *Lettres de l'Ecole freudienne* 8 (1971): 199 and 203–204.

Closing address to congress of the Ecole freudienne de Paris, (April 19, 1970); published in *Lettres de l'Ecole freudienne* 8 (1971): 205–217; reprinted in *Scilicet* 2/3 (1978): 391–399.

"Radiophonie," directed by Robert Georgin, broadcast on June 5, 10, 19, and 26, 1970, by RTB, and on June 7, 1970, by ORTF; *Scilicet* 2/3 (1970): 55–99; first version read by J.L. during the April 8, 1970 seminar; typescript of original version, Robert Georgin archives. See *S. XVII*.

Introduction (September 1970), *Scilicet* 2/3 (1970): 5–6.

Commentary, dated October 1, 1970, on his December 6, 1967, talk to the EFP; published in *Scilicet* 2/3 (1970): 24–29.

Comments delivered before Dr. G. Daumezon, *Bulletin de l'Association freudienne*, January 1987.

1971   Comment on Ch. Bardet-Giraudon, "Du roman conçu comme le discours même de l'homme qui écrit," presented at "La technique psychanalytique," congress of the Ecole freudienne de Paris, Aix-en-Province, (May 20–23, 1971); published in *Lettres de l'Ecole freudienne* 9 (1972): 20–30.

Comment on P. Lemoine, "A propos du désir du médecin," presented at "La technique psychanalytique," congress of the Ecole freudienne de Paris, Aix-en-Province, (May 20–23, 1971); published in *Lettres de l'Ecole freudienne* 9 (1972): 69, 74–78.

Comment on J. Guey, "Contribution à l'étude du sens du symptôme épileptique," presented at "La technique psychanalytique," congress of the Ecole freudienne de Paris, Aix-en-Province, (May 20–23, 1971); published in *Lettres de l'Ecole freudienne* 9 (1972): 151–155.

Comment on S. Ginestet-Delbreil, "La psychanalyse est du côté de la vérité," presented at "La technique psychanalytique," congress of the Ecole freudienne de Paris, Aix-en-Province, (May 20–23, 1971); published in *Lettres de l'Ecole freudienne* 9 (1972): 166.

Comment on A. Didier-Weill and M. Silvestre, "A l'écoute de l'écoute," presented at "La technique psychanalytique," congress of the Ecole freudienne de Paris, Aix-en-Province, (May 20–23, 1971); published in *Lettres de l'Ecole freudienne* 9 (1972): 176–182.

Comment on P. Mathis, "Remarque sur la fonction de l'argent dans la technique analytique," presented at "La technique psychanalytique," congress of the Ecole freudienne de Paris, Aix-en-Province, (May 20–23, 1971); published in *Lettres de l'Ecole freudienne* 9 (1972): 195–196, 202–205.

Comment on S. Zlatine, "Technique de l'intervention: Incidence de l'automatisme de répétition de l'analyste," presented at "La technique psychanalytique," congress of the Ecole freudienne de Paris, Aix-en-Province, (May 20–23, 1971); published in *Lettres de l'Ecole freudienne* 9 (1972): 245–255, 260.

Comment on C. Conté and L. Beirnaert, "De l'analyse des résistances au temps de l'analyse," presented at "La technique psychanalytique," congress of the Ecole freudienne de Paris, Aix-en-Province, (May 20–23, 1971); published in *Lettres de l'Ecole freudienne* 9 (1972): 334–336.

Comment on J. Rudrauf, "De la règle fondamentale," presented at "La technique psychanalytique," congress of the Ecole freudienne de Paris, Aix-en-Province, (May 20–23, 1971); published in *Lettres de l'Ecole freudienne* 9 (1972): 374.

Comment on S. Leclaire, "L'objet a dans la cure," presented at "La technique psychanalytique," congress of the Ecole freudienne de Paris, Aix-en-Province, (May 20–23, 1971); published in *Lettres de l'Ecole freudienne* 9 (1972): 445–450.

Comment on P. Delaunay, "Le moment spéculaire dans la cure, moment de rupture," presented at "La technique psychanalytique," congress of the Ecole freudienne de Paris, Aix-en-Province, (May 20–23, 1971); reproduced in *Ecrits II* (Paris: Seuil, Points), 1971; reprinted in *Lettres de l'Ecole freudienne* 9 (1972): 471–473.

Closing address to the congress at Aix-en-Provence, (May 20–23, 1971); published in *Lettres de l'Ecole freudienne* 9 (1972): 507–513.

Opinion of Jacques Lacan on D. Desanti, "Un métier de chien," *Le Monde*, November 19, 1971.

"Lituraterre," *Littérature* 3 (1971): 3–10; reprinted in *Ornicar?*, no. 41 (1984): 5–13. See *S. XVIII*, session of May 12, 1971.

1972   "Avis aux lecteurs japonais," preface to Japanese translation of the *Ecrits*; published in *La Lettre de l'Ecole de la cause freudienne* 3 (1981): 2–3.

"L'Etourdit" (July 14, 1972), *Scilicet* 4 (1973): 5–52.

Opening address to the Journées de l'Ecole freudienne de Paris, September 29–30 and October 1, 1972; published in *Lettres de l'Ecole freudienne* 11 (1972): 2–3.

Comment on C. Conté, "Sur le mode de présence des pulsions partielles dans la cure," presented at the Journées de l'Ecole freudienne de Paris, September 29–30 and October 1, 1972; published in *Lettres de l'Ecole freudienne* 11 (1972): 22–24.

Comment on M. Safouan, "La fonction du père réel," presented at the Journées de l'Ecole freudienne de Paris, (September 29–30 and October 1, 1972); published in *Lettres de l'Ecole freudienne* 11 (1972): 140–141.

Comment on J. Allouch, "Articulation entre la position médicale et celle de l'analyste," presented at the Journées de l'Ecole freudienne de Paris, (September 29–30 and October 1, 1972); published in *Lettres de l'Ecole freudienne* 11 (1972): 230.

Contribution to round table organized by J. Clavreul, at the Journées de l'Ecole freudienne de Paris, (September 29–30 and October 1, 1972); published in *Lettres de l'Ecole freudienne* 11 (1972): 215.

"Propos en guise de conclusion aux *Journées de l'Ecole freudienne de Paris*" (October 1, 1972), *Lettres de l'Ecole freudienne* 11 (1972): 215.

"Du discours psychanalytique," presented at the Institute of Psychology in the Faculty of Medicine, University of Milan, (May 12, 1972); published in *Lacan in Italia, 1953–1978* (Milan: La Salamandra, 1978); reprinted in *Bulletin de Association freudienne* 10 (1984): 3–15.

"La mort est du domaine de la foi," presented at the Main Rotunda of the University of Louvain, October 13, 1972; published in *Quarto*, Belgian supplement to *La Lettre mensuelle de l'Ecole de la cause freudienne* 3 (1981): 5–20; broadcast during *Océaniques*, FR3, televised November 11, 1988 (film distributed by MK7).

"Jacques Lacan à l'Ecole belge de psychanalyse," presented during an extraordinary session of the Ecole belge de psychanalyse, (October 14, 1972); published in *Quarto*, Belgian supplement to *La Lettre mensuelle de l'Ecole de la cause freudienne* 5 (1981): 4–22.

1973   "La psychanalyse dans sa référence au rapport sexuel," presented at the Museum of Science and Technology, Scuola Freudiana, Milan, (February 3, 1973); published in *Bulletin de l'Association freudienne* 17 (1986): 3–13.

Contribution to meeting organized by the Scuola Freudiana, Milan, (February 4, 1973); published in *Bulletin de l'Association freudienne* 18 (1986): 3–13.

Interview with B. Poirot-Delpech: "Propos élucidés," *Le Monde*, April 5, 1973.

"Note italienne" (1973), *Ornicar?*, no. 25 (1982): 7–10; published (as "Lettre adressée à trois psychanalystes italiens" and dated April 1974) in *Spirales* 9 (1981): 60; reprinted in *La Lettre mensuelle de l'école de la cause freudienne* 9 (1982): 2.

Contribution on hysteria, presented at the Journées d'études of the Alliance française, July 1973. Unpublished.

Statement by Lacan on France-Culture about the Twenty-eighth International Psychoanalytical Congress, Paris, July 1973; published in *Le Coq Héron* 46/47 (1974): 3–8.

Introduction to German edition of the *Ecrits* (Freiburg: Walter, 1980) (October 7, 1973); reprinted in *Scilicet* 5 (1975): 11–17.

Contribution to working session of "L'Ecole freudienne en Italie," congress of the Ecole freudienne de Paris, La Grande-Motte, (November 1–4, 1973); published in *Lettres de l'Ecole freudienne* 15 (1975): 235–244.

Comment on introductory papers by J. Clavreul and J. Oury, presented at the congress of the Ecole freudienne de Paris, La Grande-Motte, (November 1–4, 1973); published in *Lettres de l'Ecole freudienne* 15 (1975): 16–19.

Comment on introductory paper by S. Leclaire, presented at the congress of the Ecole freudienne de Paris, La Grande-Motte, (November 1–4, 1973); published in *Lettres de l'Ecole freudienne* 15 (1975): 26–28.

Contribution to the congress of the Ecole freudienne de Paris, La Grande-Motte, November 1–4, 1973; published in *Lettres de l'Ecole freudienne* 15 (1975): 69–80.

Contribution to debate on "La formation des analystes," at the congress of the Ecole freudienne de Paris, La Grande-Motte, (November 1–4, 1973); published in l'Ecole freudienne 15 (1975): 132–139.

Contribution to working session on "La passe," at the congress of the Ecole freudienne de Paris, La Grande-Motte, (November 1–4, 1973); published in *Lettres de l'Ecole freudienne* 15 (1975): 185–193; reprinted (as "Sur l'expérience de la passe") in *Ornicar?*, no. 12/13 (1977): 117–123.

Contribution to working session on "Le Dictionnaire," presented by Ch. Melman, at the congress of the Ecole freudienne de Paris, La Grande-Motte, (November 1–4, 1973); published in *Lettres de l'Ecole freudienne* 15 (1975): 206–210.

1974   *Télévision*, interview with Jacques-Alain Miller, filmed by Benoît Jacquot, transmitted by the ORTF, March 9 and 16, 1974; text published (as "*Télévision*") (Paris: Seuil, 1974); cassette produced by Vision-Seuil, 1990; translated by Denis Hollier, Rosalind Krauss, and Annette Michelson as *Television: A Challenge to the Psychoanalytic Establishment* (New York: Norton, 1990), pp. 3–46.

"L'Eveil du printemps," preface to Frank Wedekind's play; published in *L'Eveil du printemps* (Paris: Gallimard, 1974).

"La logique et l'amour," clinical approach to nervous and mental diseases, Rome, March 21, 1974. Unpublished.

Contribution, Scuola Freudiana, Milan, March 30, 1974. Unpublished.

Letter to three Italian psychoanalysts (April 1974); published (as "Lettre adressée à trois psychanalystes italiens") in *Spirales* 9 (1981): 60; reprinted in *La Lettre mensuelle de l'Ecole de la cause freudienne* 9 (1982): 2; also published (as "Note italienne" and dated 1973) in *Ornicar?*, no. 25 (1982): 7–10.

Contribution to a meeting under the auspices of La Cause freudienne, Milan, June 1, 1974. Unpublished.

Press conference, Seventh Congress of the Ecole freudienne de Paris, Rome, (October 31–November 3, 1974); published in *Lettres de l'Ecole freudienne* 16 (1975): 6–26.

Opening address, Seventh Congress of the Ecole freudienne de Paris, Rome, (October 31–November 3, 1974); published in *Lettres de l'Ecole freudienne* 16 (1975): 27–28.

Third contribution to the Seventh Congress of the Ecole freudienne de Paris, Rome, (October 31–November 3, 1974); published in *Lettres de l'Ecole freudienne* 16 (1975): 177–203.

Closing address, Seventh Congress of the Ecole freudienne de Paris, Rome, (October 31–November 3, 1974); published in *Lettres de l'Ecole freudienne* 16 (1975): 360–361.

1975   "Peut-être à Vincennes?" proposal by Lacan (January 1975), *Ornicar?*, no. 1 (1975): 3–5.

Reply by Lacan to a question, Strasbourg, January 26, 1975; published in *Lettres de l'Ecole freudienne* 17 (1976): 221–223.

Opening address to the Journées de l'Ecole freudienne de Paris, (April 12–13, 1975); published in *Lettres de l'Ecole freudienne* 18 (1976): 1–3.

Lacan's reply to M. Ritter, at the Journées de l'Ecole freudienne de Paris, (April 12–13, 1975); published in *Lettres de l'Ecole freudienne* 18 (1976): 8–12.

Contribution to "Les concepts fondamentaux et la cure," working session at the Journées de l'Ecole freudienne de Paris, (April 12–13, 1975); published in *Lettres de l'Ecole freudienne* 18 (1976): 35–37.

Contribution to "La forclusion," working session at the Journées de l'Ecole freudienne de Paris, (April 12–13, 1975); published in *Lettres de l'Ecole freudienne* 18 (1976): 89.

Contribution to "L'éthique de la psychanalyse," working session at the Journées de l'Ecole freudienne de Paris, (April 12–13, 1975); published in *Lettres de l'Ecole freudienne* 18 (1976): 154.

Contribution to "Du plus un," working session at the Journées de l'Ecole freudienne de Paris, (April 12–13, 1975); published in *Lettres de l'Ecole freudienne* 18 (1976): 220–245.

Contribution to "Du plus un et de la mathématique," working session at the Journées de l'Ecole freudienne de Paris, (April 12–13, 1975); published in *Lettres de l'Ecole freudienne* 18 (1976): 246–257.

Closing address to the Journées de l'Ecole freudienne de Paris, (April 12–13, 1975); published in *Lettres de l'Ecole freudienne* 18 (1976): 258.

"Introduction à cette publication," presentation of RSI (Real, Symbolic, Imaginary), *Ornicar?*, no. 2 (1975): 88.

"Joyce, le symptôme," *Actes du cinquième symposium James Joyce* (Paris: Editions du CNRS, 1979); reprinted in *L'Ane* 6 (1982): 3–5; reprinted (as "Joyce, le symptôme II") in *Joyce avec Lacan*, ed. Jacques Aubert (Paris: Navarin, 1987), pp. 31–36.

"Joyce le symptôme I," opening of international symposium on James Joyce, June 16, 1975; text established by Jacques-Alain Miller on the basis of notes taken by Eric Laurent, published in *Joyce avec Lacan*, ed. Jacques Aubert (Paris: Navarin, 1987), pp. 21–29.

Lecture in Geneva on "Le symptôme," (October 4, 1975); published in *Bloc-notes de la psychanalyse* 5 (1985): 5–23; translated by Russell Grigg as "Geneva Lecture on the Symptom," *Analysis* 1 (1989): 7–26.

Lecture at the auditorium of the School of International Affairs, Columbia University, December 1, 1975; published in *Scilicet* 6/7 (1975): 53–63; unpublished transcription by Pamela Tytell.

Lecture at the Massachusetts Institute of Technology, (December 2, 1975); published in *Scilicet* 6/7 (1975): 53–63; unpublished transcription by Thérèse Parisot; reproduced in Sherry Turkle, *Psychoanalytic Politics: Freud's French Revolution* (New York: Basic, 1978; London: Burnett, in association with André Deutsch, 1979); reproduced in Robert Georgin, *Jakobson*, Les Cahiers Cistre, no. 5 (Lausanne: L'Age d'homme, 1978), p. 129.

Opening address, Journées d'études de l'Ecole freudienne de Paris, June 14–15, 1975); published in *Lettres de l'Ecole freudienne* 24 (1978): 7.

Comment on A. Albert, "Le plaisir et la règle fondamentale," Journées d'études de l'Ecole freudienne de Paris, (June 14–15, 1975); published in *Lettres de l'Ecole freudienne* 24 (1978): 22–24.

Closing address, Journées d'études de l'Ecole freudienne de Paris, (June 14–15, 1975); published in *Lettres de l'Ecole freudienne* 24 (1978): 247–250.

"Freud à jamais," interview with Emilio Granzotto, Rome. Unpublished.

Lectures and interviews at North American universities, Yale University, Kanzer Seminar, November 24, 1975; published in *Scilicet* 6/7 (1975): 7–37.

Lecture, Law School Auditorium, Yale University, (November 25, 1975; published in *Scilicet* 6/7 (1975): 38–41.

"Freud y el psicoanalisis," interview, *Biblioteca Salvat* (Barcelona) 28 (1975): 10–19.

1976   Contribution to Champ freudien lectures, (March 9, 1976); published in *Analytica*, supplement to *Ornicar?*, no. 9 (1977).

Closing address to the congress of the Ecole freudienne de Paris, Strasbourg, (March 21–24, 1976); published in *Lettres de l'Ecole freudienne* 19 (1976): 555–559.

"Faire mouche" (on Benoît Jacquot's film *L'Assassin musicien*), *Le Nouvel Observateur*, March 29, 1976.

Preface (May 17, 1976) to the English edition of S. XI, *The Four Fundamental Concepts of Psychoanalysis*, trans. Alan Sheridan (London: Hogarth/Institute of Psycho-Analysis, 1977; New York: Norton, 1978; reprint, London: Penguin, 1979), pp. vii–ix; reprinted as "Les quatre concepts fondamentaux de la psychanalyse" *Ornicar?*, nos. 12/13 (1977): 124–126.

Introductory note to presentation of the 1953 split; published in *La Scission de 1953*, supplement to *Ornicar?*, no. 7 (1976): 3.

Comment on M. Ritter, "A propos de l'angoisse dans la cure," presented at the

Journées de l'Ecole freudienne de Paris, (October 31–November 2, 1976); published in *Lettres de l'Ecole freudienne* 21 (1977): 89.

Comment on J. Petitot, "Quantification et opérateur de Hilbert," presented at the Journées de l'Ecole freudienne de Paris, (October 31–November 2, 1976); published in *Lettres de l'Ecole freudienne* 21 (1977): 129.

Reply by Lacan to questions on knots and the unconscious, at the Journées de l'Ecole freudienne de Paris, (October 31–November 2, 1976); published in *Lettres de l'Ecole freudienne* 21 (1977): 471–475.

Closing address, Journées de l'Ecole freudienne de Paris, October 31–November 2, 1976; published in *Lettres de l'Ecole freudienne* 21 (1977): 506–509.

1977   "Ouverture de la Section clinique," *Ornicar?*, no. 9 (1977): 7–14.

"Propos sur l'hystérie," Brussels, (February 26, 1977); published in *Quarto*, Belgian supplement to *La Lettre mensuelle de l'Ecole de la cause freudienne* 2 (1981): 5–10.

"C'est à la lecture de Freud," preface to Robert Georgin, *Lacan*, Les Cahiers Cistre (Lausanne: L'Age d'homme), 1977.

Closing address, Journées d'études de l'Ecole freudienne de Paris, (September 23–25, 1977); published in *Lettres de l'Ecole freudienne* 22 (1978): 499–501.

"Une pratique de bavardage," November 15, 1977, session of S. XXV, established by Jacques-Alain Miller, *Ornicar?*, no. 19 (1979).

1978   Comments on M. Safouan, "La proposition d'octobre 1967 dix ans après," presented at "L'expérience de la passe," conference of the Ecole freudienne de Paris, Deauville, (January 7–8, 1978); published in *Lettres de l'Ecole freudienne* 23 (1978): 19–21.

Contribution to the twenty-third centenary of Aristotle celebrated at UNESCO, (June 1, 1978). Unpublished.

Comment on J. Guey, "Passe à l'analyse infinie," presented at "L'expérience de la passe," conference of the Ecole freudienne de Paris, Deauville, (January 7–8, 1978); published in *Lettres de l'Ecole freudienne* 23 (1978): 94.

Closing address to "L'expérience de la passe," conference of the Ecole freudienne de Paris, Deauville, (January 7–8, 1978); published in *Lettres de l'Ecole freudienne* 23 (1978): 180–181.

Closing address to Ninth Congress of the Ecole freudienne de Paris, Paris, (July 6–9, 1978); published in *Lettres de l'Ecole freudienne* 25 (1979): 219–220.

"Objets et représentations," Deniker department, Hôpital Sainte-Anne, (November 10, 1978). Unpublished.

"Lacan pour Vincennes" (October 22, 1978), *Ornicar?*, no. 17/18 (1979): 278.

Text for catalog of François Rouan exhibit, Musée Cantini, Marseilles, 1978; reprinted, on the occasion of the François Rouan exhibit, October 27, 1983–January 1, 1984, in *Catalogue du Musée national d'Art moderne* (Paris: Centre Georges-Pompidou, 1983), pp. 88–94.

UNREALIZED PROJECTS

"Morale de la psychanalyse," announced in *NRF* 1, no. 4 (1935).

"Essai de logique collective," announced in "Le temps logique et l'assertion de certitude anticipée: Un nouveau sophisme," *Cahiers d'art* (1940–1944): 32–42

"Le cas Rudolph Hess," announced in *Critique* (1947).

The Seminar (1951–1979)

What follows is a nonexhaustive list of notes, shorthand versions, and transcriptions of the twenty-six seminars, spanning the years 1953 through 1963, when the seminar took place at the Hôpital Sainte-Anne; 1964 to 1969, when it took place at the Ecole normale supérieure; and 1969 to 1980, when it was held at the Faculté de droit du Panthéon. From 1964 to 1980 the seminar took the form of lectures delivered by Lacan as lecturer under the auspices of the Ecole pratique des hautes études.

BEFORE THE SEMINAR ITSELF: SEMINAR − 1: *L'Homme aux loups (The Wolf Man); Seminar 0: L'Homme aux rats (The Rat Man)*

1953–1954   Jacques Lacan's manuscript notes
                    Notes by members of the audience

BOOK I: LES ÉCRITS TECHNIQUES DE FREUD

1953–1954   Shorthand version: J.L.'s version
                    Text established by Jacques-Alain Miller (J.-A.M.) (Paris: Seuil, 1975)
                    Freud's Papers on Technique: 1953–1954, trans. John Forrester (New York: Norton, 1988)

BOOK II: LE MOI DANS LA THÉORIE DE FREUD ET DANS LA TECHNIQUE PSYCHANALYTIQUE

1954–1955   J.L. version
                    Text established by J.-A.M. (Paris: Seuil, 1977)
                    Corrections: Gabriel Bergounioux (G.B.)
                    The Ego in Freud's Theory and in the Technique of Psychoanalysis: 1954–1955, trans. Sylvana Tomaselli, with notes by John Forrester (New York: Norton, 1988)

BOOK III: STRUCTURES FREUDIENNES DANS LES PSYCHOSES

1955–1956   J.L. version
                    Notes by Jean Laplanche (J.La.)
                    Text established (as *Les Psychoses*) by J.-A.M. (Paris: Seuil, 1981)
                    Corrections: G.B.; Marcel Czermak, *Le Discours psychanalytique* 2 (June 1983)
                    The Psychoses, trans. Russell Grigg (New York: Norton, 1993)

BOOK IV: LA RELATION D'OBJET ET LES STRUCTURES FREUDIENNES

1956–1957   J.L. version
                    Notes by J.La.
                    Notes by Paul Lemoine (P.L.)
                    Summary by Jean-Bertrand Pontalis (J.-B.P.), *Bulletin de psychologie* 10, nos. 7, 10, 12, 14 (1956–1957); no. 11 (1957–1958)
                    La Relation d'objet, text established by J.-A.M. (Paris: Seuil, 1994)

BOOK V: LES FORMATIONS DE L'INCONSCIENT

1957–1958—J.L. VERSION

Notes by P.L.

Summary by J.-B.P., *Bulletin de psychologie* 11, nos. 4, 5 (1957–1958); 12, nos. 2, 3, 4 (1958–1959)

Notes by P.L.

The session of March 5, 1958, was published in *Magazine littéraire* 313 (September 1993), with text established by J-.A.M.

BOOK VI: LE DÉSIR ET SON INTERPRÉTATION

1958–1959

J.L. version

Notes by J.La.

Summary by J.-B.P., *Bulletin de psychologie* 13, nos. 5, 6 (1959–1960)

Incomplete recording

The final three sessions were translated by James Hulbert as "Desire and the Interpretation of Desire in *Hamlet*," *Yale French Studies* 55/56 (1977): 11–52

BOOK VII: L'ÉTHIQUE DE LA PSYCHANALYSE

1959–1960

J.L. version

Notes by J.La.

Transcription: Moustapha Safouan

Recording

MS version: Jean Oury (J.O.)

Laborde version

Text established by J.-A.M. (Paris: Seuil, 1986)

Corrections: G.B.; Annick Bouillaguet, "Remarques sur l'usage du grec prêté à Jacques Lacan," *Psychiatries* 79 (1984): 4

Pierre Vidal-Naquet: corrections of chapter on Antigone; two letters to Jacques-Alain Miller

Account with interpolations of seminar on ethics, notes by J.L., *Ornicar?*, no. 28 (1984): 7–18

The Ethics of Psychoanalysis, trans. Dennis Porter (New York: Norton, 1992)

BOOK VIII: LE TRANSFERT DANS SA DISPARITÉ SUBJECTIVE, SA PRÉTENDUE SITUATION, SES EXCURSIONS TECHNIQUES

1960–1961

J.L. version

Notes by J.La.

Notes by P.L.

Recording: J.O.

Shorthand version: Laborde

Stenotyped version: Madame Brivette

Transcription: *Stécriture* (1983–1985), with corrections, notes, and critical apparatus

Text established (as *Le transfert*) by J.-A.M. (Paris: Seuil, 1991)

Le transfert dans tous ses états (Paris: EPEL, 1991), with corrections based on
the Seuil edition
Transference, trans. Bruce Fink (New York: Norton, forthcoming)

BOOK IX: L'IDENTIFICATION

1961–1962   J.L. version
Shorthand version: Monique Chollet (M.C.)
Stenotyped version
Notes by Claude Conté, P.L., Irène Roubleff, J.La.
Transcription: Michel Roussan, with corrections, notes, critical appara-
tus, and index

BOOK X: L'ANGOISSE

1962–1963   J.L. version
recording: Solange Faladé (S.F.)

LES NOMS DU PÈRE (SINGLE SESSION)

November 20, 1963   Laborde version
Notes by Monique Guillet
Notes by Françoise Dolto
Manuscript version: J.O.
"Introduction to the Names-of-the-Father Seminar," trans.
Jeffrey Mehlman, *October*
40 (1987); reprinted in *Television: A Challenge to the*
Psychoanalytic Establishment, trans. Denis Hollier, Rosalind
Krauss, and Annette Michelson (New York: Norton, 1990),
pp. 81–95

BOOK XI: LES QUATRE CONCEPTS FONDAMENTAUX DE LA PSYCHANALYSE

1964   J.L. version
recording: S.F.
stenotyped EFP version (from recording): Madame Pierakos
Text established by J.-A.M. (Paris: Seuil, 1973)
reprint of text established by J.-A.M., with postface by J.L. (Paris: Seuil, Points, 1990)
Summary: EPHE yearbook
Notes by Louis Althusser on four sessions (May 27 and June 3, 10, and 17), IMEC
The Four Fundamental Concepts of Psychoanalysis, trans. Alan Sheridan (London:
Hogarth/Institute of Psycho-Analysis, 1977; New York: Norton, 1978; reprint,
London: Penguin, 1979)

BOOK XII: PROBLÈMES CRUCIAUX DE LA PSYCHANALYSE (ORIGINALLY, "LES POSITIONS SUBJECTIVES DE L'EXISTENCE ET DE L'ÊTRE")

1964–1965   Recording, EFP stenotyped version: S.F.
J.L. version
Laborde version

Notes by Jenny Aubry (J.A.)
Summary: EPHE yearbook

BOOK XIII: L'OBJET DE LA PSYCHANALYSE

1965–1966   Recording, EFP stenotyped version: S.F.
J.L. version
Laborde version
EPHE summary

BOOK XIV: LA LOGIQUE DU FANTASME

1965–1966   Recording
EFP stenotyped version: S.F.
J.L. version
Laborde version
Patrice Fava (P.F.) version
Notes by J.A.
Summary: EPHE yearbook
Account by Jacques Nassif, in *Lettres de l'Ecole freudienne* 1 (1967): 11–17;
2 (1967): 7–23; 3 (1967): 3–33

BOOK XV: L'ACTE PSYCHANALYTIQUE

1967–1968   Recording
EFP stenotyped version: S.F.
J.L. version
Laborde version
P.F. version
Notes by J.A.
Summary: EPHE yearbook
Account by Jacques Nassif, in *Lettres de l'Ecole freudienne* 4 (1967): 3–23

BOOK XVI: D'UN AUTRE À L'AUTRE

1968–1969   Recording: Patrick Valas (P.V.)
EFP stenotyped version and recording: S.F.
J.L. version
Laborde version
P.F. version
Notes by J.A.
Transcription: Jacques Nassif
M.C. version
Notes by members of the audience
Summary: EPHE yearbook
Extracts from session of February 26, 1969, in *Littoral* 9 (1983)

BOOK XVII: L'ENVERS DE LA PSYCHANALYSE

1969–1970   Recording: P.V.
Stenotyped version

Laborde version
Version by Patrick Guyomard (P.G.) and Lucien Kokh
M.C. version.
Session of December 3, 1969, published as "Premier impromptu de Vincennes," *Magazine littéraire* 121 (February 1977)
Session of April 8, 1970 (first version of "*Radiophonie*")
Text established by J.-A.M. (Paris: Seuil, 1991)

BOOK XVIII: D'UN DISCOURS QUI NE SERAIT PAS DU SEMBLANT

1970–1971   Recording: P.V.
Stenotyped version
M.C. version
P.G. version
Session of May 12, 1971, published as "Lituraterre" in *Littérature* 3 (1971): 3–10; reprinted in *Ornicar?*, no. 41 (1984): 5–13

BOOK XIX: . . . OU PIRE (LE SAVOIR DU PSYCHANALYSTE)

1971–1972   Two series of alternate papers, some delivered at the Hôpital Sainte-Anne and some at the Faculty of Law.
Recording: P.V.
Stenotyped version
M.C. version
P.G. version
Summary: EPHE yearbook

BOOK XX: ENCORE

1972–1973   Recording: P.V.
Stenotyped version
M.C. version
Text established by J.-A.M. (Paris: Seuil, 1975)
The Seminar of Jacques Lacan, ed. Jacques-Alain Miller (New York: Cambridge University Press, 1988)
Encore, trans. Bruce Fink (New York: Norton, 1997)

BOOK XXI: LES NON–DUPES–ERRENT

1973–1974   Recording: P.V.
Stenotyped version
M.C. version
P.G. version

BOOK XXII: RSI

1974–1975   Recording: P.V.
Stenotyped version
M.C. version
P.G. version
Text established by J.-A.M., *Ornicar?*, nos. 2, 3, 4, 5 (1975)

BOOK XXIII:LE SINTHOME

1975–1976   Recording: P.V.
                Stenotyped version
                M.C. version
                P.G. version
                Text established by J.-A.M., *Ornicar?*, nos. 6, 7, 8, 9, 10, 11 (1976–1977)
                Transcription: team from *Littoral*

BOOK XXIV: L'INSU QUE SAIT DE L'UNE BÉVUE S'AILE À MOURIR (L'INSUCCÈS
    DE L'UNBEWUSSTE)

1976–1977   Recording: P.V.
                Stenotyped version
                M.C. version
                P.G. version
                Text established by J.-A.M., Ornicar?, nos. 12/13, 14, 15, 16, 17/18
                (1977–1979)

BOOK XXV: LE MOMENT DE CONCLURE

1977–1978   Recording: P.V.
                Stenotyped version
                M.C. version
                P.G. version
                Text of one session, November 15, 1977, established by J.-A.M., pub-
            lished as "Une pratique de bavardage," *Ornicar?*, no. 19 (1979)

BOOK XXVI: LA TOPOLOGIE ET LE TEMPS (THE "SILENT" SEMINAR)

1978–1979   Recording: P.V.
                Stenotyped version

Typed or Printed Texts Bearing Lacan's Name or Signature (1980–1981)

Letter of dissolution (January 5, 1980), read at The Seminar of January 8, 1980; recorded by
    Patrick Valas (P.V.); published in Le Monde, January 9, 1980, and in *Ornicar?*, nos.
    20/21 (1980): 9–10; reprinted in the yearbook and statutory texts for 1982 (ECF).
"L'autre manque" (January 15, 1980), read at The Seminar; recorded by P.V.; published in *Le
    Monde*, January 26, 1980, and in *Ornicar?*, nos. 20/21 (1980): 11–12; reprinted in the
    yearbook and statutory texts for 1982 (ECF).
Letter to *Le Monde* (January 24, 1980), published in *Le Monde*, January 26, 1980, and in
    Ornicar?, nos. 20/21 (1980): 13; reprinted in the yearbook and statutory texts for
    1982 (ECF).
"Delenda est" (March 10, 1980), *Le Monde*, March 17, 1980; *Delenda* (Temporary Bulletin of
    the Cause freudienne) 1 (1980): 1.
"Décollage" (March 11, 1980), read at The Seminar; recorded by P.V.; published in *Ornicar?*,
    nos. 20/21 (1980): 14–16; reprinted in the yearbook and statutory texts for 1982
    (ECF).
Speech delivered by Lacan at the Hotel PLM–Saint-Jacques, published in *Le Matin*, March 18,
    1980.

"Monsieur A" (March 18, 1980), read at the seminar; recorded by P.V.; published in *Ornicar?*,
    nos. 20/21 (1980): 17–20; reprinted in the yearbook and statutory texts for 1982 (ECF).
Letter to members of the EFP (March 24, 1980: "Lacan's" list for the election of the commit-
    tee at the general meeting of April 27, 1980), distributed within the EFP.
"Lumière" (May 15, 1980), read at The Seminar; recorded P.V.; published in *Delenda*
    (Temporary Bulletin of the Cause freudienne) 4 (1980): 1–4; reprinted in *Ornicar?*,
    nos. 22/23 (1981): 7–10.
"Le malentendu" (June 10, 1980), read at The Seminar; recorded by P.V.; published in *Courrier
    de la Cause freudienne* 1 (July 1980); reprinted in *Ornicar?*, nos. 22/23 (1981): 11–14.
Letter to the members of the EFP, distributed within the EFP.
Presentation of the last Seminar (June 10, 1980), to introduce the first number of the *Courrier
    de la Cause freudienne* (June 29, 1980), published in *Courrier de la Cause freudienne* 1
    (July 1980).
The Caracas Seminar (on Lacan's teaching and psychoanalysis in Latin America), Caracas
    (July 12–15, 1980), published in *L'Ane* 1 (1981): 30–31.
Invitation to international meeting in Paris, February 1982, extended at the Caracas meet-
    ing; published in *Courrier de la Cause freudienne* 2 (September 1980).
Letter (for the *Cause freudienne*): "Il y a du refoulé, toujours, c'est irréductible . . ." (October
    23, 1980); published in *Courrier de la Cause freudienne* 3 (October 1980); reprinted
    in the yearbook and statutory texts for 1982 (ECF).
Letter to members of the SCI (December 4, 1980), *Courrier de la Cause freudienne* (December
    1980).
Letter: "Voilà un mois que j'ai coupé avec tout, ma pratique exceptée . . ." (first letter to the
    forum, January 26, 1981); published in *Actes du Forum de l'Ecole de la Cause freudi-
    enne* (March 28/29, 1981); and in *Courrier de la Cause freudienne* (January 1981);
    reprinted in the yearbook and statutory texts for 1982 (ECF).
Letter: "Mon fort est de savoir ce que attendre signifie . . ." (second letter to the forum, March
    11, 1981); published in *Actes du Forum de l'Ecole de la Cause freudienne* (March 28/29,
    1981); and in *Courrier de la Cause freudienne* (January 1981); reprinted in the year-
    book and statutory texts for 1982 (ECF).
Note: The texts published in the yearbook for 1982 were omitted from subsequent year-
books.

Titles and Subheadings in the 1938 Article on the Family

The title of the original manuscript (1938) was *Situation de la réalité familiale*. For his 1984 reissue of the article in book form, Jacques-Alain Miller used the title *Les Complexes familiaux
dans la formation de l'individu*, the subtitle *Essai d'analyse d'une fonction en psychologie*, the sub-
heads "Le complexe, facteur concret de la psychologie familiale" and "Les complexes familiaux en pathologie."
The titles and subtitles used in the *Encyclopédie française* edition of 1938 were:
Section A: La Famille
Introduction: L'institution familiale, structure culturelle de la famille
        humaine
        Hérédité psychologique
        Parenté biologique
    La famille primitive: Une institution
Chapter 1. Le complexe, facteur concret de la psychologie familiale
        Définition générale du complexe
        Le complexe et l'instinct

Sublimation de la réalité
>Originalité de l'identification oedipienne
>L'imago du père

Le complexe et la relativité sociologique
>Matriarcat et patriarcat
>L'homme moderne et la famille conjugale
>Role de la formacion familiale
>Déclin de l'imago paternelle

Névroses de transfert
>L'hystérie
>La névrose obsessionnelle
>Incidence intellectuelle des causes familiales

Névroses de caractère
>La névrose d'autopunition
>Introversion de la personnalité et schizonoïa
>Dysharmonie du couple parental
>>Prévalence du complexe de sevrage
>Inversion de la sexualité
>Prevalence du principe mâle

Correspondence

The following is a nonexhaustive inventory.

Louis Aragon: one letter (September 15, 1967); 1 visiting card. Source: Fonds Elsa Triolet-Aragon; CNRS.

Fernand Alquié: six letters (1928–1956), including an important one in 1956 on Descartes. Source: Bibliothèque municipale de Carcassonne, 60817-AL QMS 34.

Louis Althusser: eight letters (1963–1969). Source: IMEC; two letters published in *Magazine littéraire*, no. 304 (November 1992), and in Louis Althusser, *Ecrits sur la psychanalyse* (Paris: Stock, 1993).

Jenny Aubry: three letters (1953–1978). Source: J.A.; one letter published by Jacques-Alain Miller in *La Scission de 1953*, supplement to *Ornicar?*, no. 7 (1976).

Xavier Audouard: five letters (1963–1969), on the split and the crisis of the "passe." Source: X.A.

Jean Ballard: two letters (1941–1952). Source: *RIHP* 1 (1988): 179.

Michaël Balint: three letters (1953), including a very long one on the split and Rome (August 6, 1953), and one (July 14, 1953) published in *La Scission de 1953*, supplement to *Ornicar?*, no. 7 (1976). Source: André Haynal.

Georges Bataille: one postcard. Source: Bibliothèque nationale.

François Baudry: one letter (October 16, 1974). Source: François Baudry.

Georges Bernier: six letters (1934–1949). Source: Georges Bernier.

Sylvain Blondin: two letters (1939 and 1940), on the collapse of France. Source: Thibaut Lacan.

Madeleine Chapsal: seventeen amorous letters with poems (1955–1974). Source: Madeleine Chapsal.

Irène Diamantis: one letter (July 13, 1969). Source: Irène Diamantis.

Françoise Dolto: thirteen letters (1960–1979). Source: F.D.

Jean-Luc Donnet: one letter (March 17, 1969). Source: Jean-Luc Donnet; published in *HPF* 2:589–590 (*JL & Co.*, pp. 586–587).

Georges Dumézil: one letter (March 4, 1969). Source: Didier Eribon.

Henri Ey: ten letters (1935–1977). Source: R.E.

Michel Foucault: one letter (March 8, 1968). Source: Published in Michel Foucault, *Une histoire de la vérité* (Paris: Syros, 1985).

Claude Frioux: one letter, on the creation of a department of psychoanalysis at Paris VIII (November 10, 1974). Source: J.-A.M.; published in *HPF* 2:578 (*JL & Co.*, p. 574).

Wladimir Granoff: nine letters (1953–1963), including one of seven pages (July 24, 1961); the longest and most political of these help to explain the second split. Source: W.G.; quoted in *HPF* 2:288–368 (*JL & Co.*, pp. 277–359).

Heinz Hartmann: one letter (June 21, 1953). Source: *La Scission de 1953*, supplement to *Ornicar?*, no. 7 (1976).

Paula Heimann: one letter in English, not sent (June 27, 1963). Source: S.L.; quoted in *HPF* 2: 356–357 (*JL & Co.*, pp. 346–347).

Lucien Israël: one letter, just a few words, in shaky writing (January 20, 1981). Source: S.La.

Maurice Kruk: two letters (April 16, 1971). Source: Thibaut Lacan.

Marc-François Lacan: three letters (1953–1962), including one about meeting the pope (June 17, 1953). Source: M.-F.L.

Sibylle Lacan: eighteen letters (1959–1973). Source: S.La.

Daniel Lagache: one letter (June 26, 1958). Source: W.G.

Serge Leclaire: seventeen letters in all: sixteen very long letters, indispensable for understanding the second split, cited in *HPF* 2:288–368 (*JL & Co.*, pp. 277–359), source: S.L.; one letter (November 10, 1963), published in *L'Excommunication: La Communauté psychanalytique en France, Ornicar?* (special supplement), no. 8 (1977).

Michel Leiris: four letters (1935–1976). Source: Fonds Jacques Doucet.

Rudolph Loewenstein: one letter (July 14, 1953). Source: *La Scission de 1953*, supplement to *Ornicar?*, no. 7 (1976).

Maria Antonietta Macchiocchi: one letter (June 23, 1972). Source: Maria Antonietta Macchiocchi.

Maud Mannoni: six letters (1970–1976). Source: Maud Mannoni.

Sacha Nacht: one letter (January 16, 1953). Source: Marc Nacht.

Jenny Pdosse: two letters (1960 and 1966). Source: Jenny Pdosse.

François Perrier: five letters (1964–1969). Source: J.S.

Niccolo Perrotti: one letter (July 14, 1953). Source: *La Scission de 1953*, supplement to *Ornicar?*, no. 7 (1976).

Michel Plon: two letters, including one on games theory (May 17, 1976). Source: Michel Plon.

Jacques Postel: one letter, on the republication of the thesis (March 23, 1972). Source: Jacques Postel.

Robert Pujol: two letters (1963). Source: Robert Pujol.

Elisabeth Roudinesco: one letter, on the suicide of Juliette Labin (March 14, 1977). Source: E.R.

Ramon Sarro: one letter (October 26, 1972). Source: *Freudiana* (Barcelona) 4, 5 (1992); and *L'Ane* 51 (July–September 1992).

Jacques Sédat: one letter (October 10, 1977). Source: J.S.

Tomás Segovia: several letters on the Spanish translation of the *Ecrits*. Source: Thomàs Segovia.

Olesia Sienkiewicz: five very fine love letters (1933–1934). Source: Olesia Sienkiewicz.

Pierre Soury and Michel Thomé: fifty-three letters (1973–1979). Source: Michel Thomé.

Guillaume de Tarde: one postcard (April 1, 1951). Source: Françoise de Tarde-Bergeret.

Pamela Tytell: five letters (1975–1976). Source: Pamela Tytell.

Alphonse de Waelhens: five letters (1954–1959). Source: Institut supérieur de philosophie de l'université de Louvain.

François Wahl, Paul Flamand, and Bruno Flamand, at Seuil: seventeen letters (1968–1978).

Jean Wahl: one letter (March 26, 1958). Source: IMEC.

Donald W. Winnicott: one letter (August 5, 1960). Source: *Ornicar?*, no. 33 (1984): 7–10.

Letter to members of the SPP assembly. Source: *La Scission de 1953*, supplement to *Ornicar?*, no. 7 (1976).

Addressee unknown: one letter, just a few words, in shaky writing (January 28, 1981). Source: S.La.

Administrative letter (October 27, 1965). Source: Judith Miller, *Visages de mon père* (Paris: Seuil, 1991).

Head physician, Franciscan hospital, Pau: one letter (June 24, 1940). Source: Judith Miller, *Visages de mon père* (Paris: Seuil, 1991).

"Pour Vincennes": two circular letters (October 18, 1974, and September 20, 1976). Source: J.A.-M.

TYPED LETTERS WITH J.L.'S SIGNATURE

François Wahl: one letter (July 7, 1980).

Préfecture de police: one three-page letter, initialed, with note certifying accuracy (February 21, 1980); registration of *La Cause freudienne*. Source: J.A.

Real estate agents of the EFP: one letter (December 18, 1980). Source: J.A.

Members of the EFP: one letter (June 16, 1980). Source: J.A.

Translations

Note: This list was accurate as of 1993. Up-to-date information about English-language translations is to be found in the Notes on the main text.

ECRITS

Italy   Einaudi, 1974

Japan   Kobundo, 1972

Spain and Latin America   Siglo XXI (Mexico), 1971 (translated by Tomás Segovia)

ECRITS (Selection)

Brazil   Perspectiva, 1976, eight titles:

          "Ouverture de ce recueil"
          "Le séminaire sur 'La Lettre voleé' "
          "De nos antécédents"

"Le stade du miroir comme formateur de la fonction du Je"
"Du sujet enfin en question"
"Fonction et champ de la parole et du langage en psych-
analyse"
"La chose freudienne"
"L'instance de la lettre dans l'inconscient"

Denmark Rhodos, 1973, eight titles:

"Au dela du 'Principe de réalité' "
"Le stade du miroir comme formateur de la fonction du Je"
"Le séminaire sur 'La Lettre volée' "
"L'instance de la lettre dans l'inconscient"
"D'une question préliminaire à tout traitement possible de la
psychose"
"Subversion du sujet et dialectique du désir dans l'inconscient
freudien"
"La signification du phallus"
"La métaphore du sujet"

Germany

Quadriga (2 volumes), 1986; rpt. 1991
Suhrkamp (paperback; 1 volume), 1975
Walter (3 volumes), 1973, rpt. 1978; 1975; 1980, seventeen titles:

"Le séminaire sur 'La Lettre volée' "
"Le stade du miroir comme formateur de la fonction de Je"
"Fonction et champ de la parole et du langage en psych-
analyse"
"La direction de la cure et les principes de son pouvoir"
"L'instance de la lettre dans l'inconscient"
"La métaphore du sujet"
"D'une question préliminaire à tout traitement possible de la
psychose"
"La signification du phallus"
"Kant avec Sade"
"Subversion du sujet et dialectique du désir dans l'inconscient
freudien"
"Position de l'inconscient"
"La science et la vérité"
"De nos antécédents"
"Le temps logique et l'assertion de certitude anticipée"
"Introduction au commentaire de Jean Hyppolite sur la
'Verneinung' de Freud"
"Réponse au commentaire de Jean Hyppolite sur la
'Verneinung' de Freud"
"Propos directifs pour un Congrès sur la sexualité féminine"

also:

"La famille" (1938)
"Maurice Merleau-Ponty" (1961)

Norway

Gyldendal Norsk, 1985, seven titles:

"Intervention sur le transfert"
"Fonction et champ de la parole et du langage en psych-
analyse"
"Variantes de la cure type"
"La chose freudienne"
"La direction de la cure et les principes de son pouvoir"
"Du '*Trieb*' de Freud et de désir du psychanalyste"
"Position de l'inconscient"

Serbia

Prosveta, 1983, seven titles:

"Le stade du miroir comme formateur de la fonction du Je"
"Fonction et champ de la parole et du langage en psych
analyse"
"La chose freudienne"
"L'instance de la lettre dans l'inconscient"
"La direction de la cure et les principes de son pouvoir"
"La signification du phallus"
"Subversion du sujet et dialectique du désir dans l'inconscient
freudien"

Sweden

Natur och Kultur, 1989, three titles:

"Le stade du miroir comme formateur de la fonction du Je"
"Fonction et champ de la parole et du langage en psych-
analyse"
"L'instance de la lettre dans l'inconscient"

also:

"Le mythe individuel du névrosé" (text established by
Jacques-Alain Miller, *Ornicar?*, nos. 17/18 [1979])

"Jacques Lacan," by Jacques-Alain Miller, *Encyclopaedia Universalis* (1979); reprinted
in *Ornicar?*, no. 24 (1981)

United States/Great Britain

Norton and Tavistock, 1977, English rpt. 1980, 1982, nine titles:

"Le stade du miroir comme formateur de la fonction du Je"
"L'agressivité en psychanalyse"
"Fonction et champ de la parole et du langage en psychanalyse"
"La chose freudienne"
"L'instance de la lettre dans l'inconscient"
"D'une question préliminaire à tout traitement possible de la
psychose"
"La signification du phallus"
"La direction de la cure et les principes de son pouvoir"
"Subversion de sujet et dialectique de désir dans l'inconscient
freudien"

TÉLÉVISION

Germany

Quadriga, 1988

Holland
>Psychanalytische Perspektieven (Université de Grand), 1990

Israel
>Et Vasefer, 1992

Italy
>Einaudi, 1982

Japan
>Soldo Sha, 1992

Spain and Latin America
>Anagrama, 1977

United States and Great Britain
>Norton, 1990

DE LA PSYCHOSE PARANOÏAQUE DANS SE RAPPORTS AVEC LA PERSONNALITÉ

Brazil
>Forense, 1987

Italy
>Einaudi, 1980

Japan
>Asahi Shuppan Sha, 1987

Spain and Latin America
>Siglo XXI (Mexico), 1976

LE SÉMINAIRE I: LES ECRITS TECHNIQUES DE FREUD

Brazil
>Zahar, 1979

Germany
>Walter, 1978
>Quadriga, 1990

Great Britain
>Cambridge University Press, 1988

Italy
>Einaudi, 1978

Japan
>Iwanami Shoten, 1991

Portugal
>Don Quixote, 1986

Spain and Latin America

Paidos, 1981

United States
Norton, 1988

LE SÉMINAIRE II: LE MOI DANS LA THÉORIE DE FREUD ET DANS LA TECHNIQUE DE LA PSYCHANALYSE

Brazil
Zahar, 1985

Germany
Walter, 1980
Quadriga, 1991

Great Britain
Cambridge University Press, 1988

Italy
Einaudi, 1991

Spain and Latin America
Paidos, 1983

United States
Norton, 1988, rpt. 1991

LE SÉMINAIRE III: LES PSYCHOSES

Brazil
Zahar, 1985

Italy
Einaudi, 1985

Germany
Quadriga, forthcoming

Japan
Iwanami Shoten, 1987 (vol. 1), 1991 (vol. 2)

Spain and Latin America
Paidos, 1984

United States
Norton, 1993

LE SÉMINAIRE VII: L'ETHIQUE DE LA PSYCHANALYSE

Brazil
Zahar, 1988

Germany
Quadriga, forthcoming

Slovenia
> Delavska Enotnost, 1988

Spain and Latin America
> Paidos, 1988

United States
> Norton, 1992

LE SÉMINAIRE XI: LES QUATRE CONCEPTS FONDAMENTAUX DE LA PSYCHANALYSE

Brazil
> Zahar, 1979

Catalonia
> Edicions 62, 1990

Germany
> Quadriga, 1987
> Walter, 1978, rpt. 1980

Great Britain
> Hogarth Press, 1977
> Chatto and Windus/Penguin (paperback), 1979, rpt. 1986, 1987

Greece
> Kedros, 1983

Italy
> Einaudi, 1979

Serbo-Croatia
> Naprijed, 1986

Slovenia
> Cankarjeva Zalomba, 1980

Spain and Latin America
> Paidos, 1986

United States
> Norton, 1978, paperback rpt. 1981

LE SÉMINAIRE XVII: L'ENVERS DE LA PSYCHANALYSE

Brazil
> Zahar, 1992

Germany
> Quadriga, forthcoming

Spain and Latin America
> Paidos, 1992

LE SÉMINAIRE XX: ENCORE

Brazil
>   Zahar, 1982

Germany
>   Quadriga, 1986, rpt. 1991

Italy
>   Einaudi, 1983

Slovenia
>   Problemi, 1986

Spain and Latin America
>   Paidos, 1981

United States
>   Norton, 1997

Bibliographical Sources

Bousseyroux, Michel, Pierre Bruno, Marie-Jean Sauret, and Eric Laurent. "Index Séminaire III: Les Psychoses" (concepts, notions, proper nouns). Ed. Michel Lapeyre. *Pas tant* 8/10 (June 1982–July 1983).

——. "Index Séminaire XX: Encore." Ed. Michel Lapeyre. *Pas tant* 8/10 (June 1982–July 1983).

Clark, Michael. *Jacques Lacan: An Annotated Bibliography*. 2 vols. New York: Garland, 1988.

De Frutos Salvador, Angel. *Los Ecristos de Jacques Lacan. Variantes textuales*. Madrid/Mexico: Siglo XXI, 1994.

De Wolf, Michel. "Essai de bibliographie complète." *Magazine littéraire* 121 (February 1977).

Dor, Joel. *Bibliographie des travaux de Jacques Lacan*. Paris: Interéditions, 1983.

——. *Nouvelle bibliographie des travaux de Jacques Lacan*. Thesaurus Lacan, vol. 2. Paris: EPEL, 1994.

Ecole lacanienne de psychanalyse. *Le Transfert dans tous ses états*. Paris: EPEL, 1991.

Heinrichs, Hans Jürgen. "Bibliographie der Schriften von Jacques Lacan." *Psyche* 34 (1980).

Marini, Marcelle. *Lacan*. Paris: Belfond, 1986 (*Jacques Lacan: The French Context* [New Brunswick, N.J.: Rutgers University Press, 1992]).

Muller, John, and William Richardson. *Lacan and Language: A Reader's Guide to Ecrits*. New York: International Universities Press, 1982.

Taillandier, Gérôme. "Chronique des Séminaires," *Littoral* 13 (June 1984); 18 (January 1986); 22 (April 1987); 23/24 (October 1987); 26.

——. "Le Phallus: Une Note historique." *Esquisses psychanalytiques* 9 (spring 1988).

Wilden, Anthony. "Jacques Lacan: A Partial Bibliography." *Yale French Studies* 36–37 (1966).

Index